STATE AND LOCAL
GOVERNMENT
AND
PUBLIC-PRIVATE
PARTNERSHIPS

State and Local Government and Public-Private Partnerships ⸺

A POLICY ISSUES HANDBOOK

William G. Colman

GREENWOOD PRESS
New York • Westport, Connecticut • London

Library of Congress Cataloging-in-Publication Data

Colman, William G.
   State and local government and public-private partnerships : a
policy-issues handbook / William G. Colman.
    p.   cm.
  Bibliography: p.
  Includes index.
   ISBN 0–313–26206–3 (lib. bdg. : alk. paper)
   1. State-local relations—United States.   2. Intergovernmental
fiscal relations—United States.   3. Privatization—United States.
I. Title.
JS348.C65   1989
353.9'293—dc19   88–24627

British Library Cataloguing in Publication Data is available.

Library of Congress Catalog Card Number: 88–24627
ISBN: 0–313–26206–3

First published in 1989

Greenwood Press, Inc.
88 Post Road West, Westport, Connecticut   06881

Printed in the United States of America

The paper used in this book complies with the
Permanent Paper Standard issued by the National
Information Standards Organization (Z39.48–1984).

10 9 8 7 6 5 4 3 2 1

Contents

Illustrations

FIGURES

TABLES

APPENDICES

Preface

The purpose of this book is to analyze the present legal, structural, financial, and political underpinnings of those policy and functional areas of domestic government that seem to be the most critical nationally. Generally, state and local governments already bear, or are assuming, primary legal, policy, and financial responsibility for these areas, in which the highest degrees of institutional capacity, commitment, competence, and integrity are essential. A further purpose is to describe the current and emerging agenda of state and local governments and of the increasing number of private profit and nonprofit segments that are taking on ever-widening responsibilities for leadership and performance in state and local affairs.

On occasion, attention will be drawn to major changes in structure, resources, and commitment of the three levels of government and associated private performers in these crucial areas since the mid-seventies. In qualitative analysis the two or more sides of the major issues will be presented, along with analyses of how state-local governments have responded in the past or might respond in the future, given emerging trends.

So that readers may be aware of the vantage point from which these issues are viewed by the author, let me say that few if any of them are susceptible to certain or easy resolution. I personally believe in a very strong state and local role in the American federal system, complemented where appropriate in terms of economic efficiency and of fiscal and social equity or balances thereof by nonprofit and profit sectors of the national economy. These personal beliefs are drawn from, and leavened by, various periods of professional administration in various capacities in federal and state government and in local politically elected and appointive office.

I am indebted to many associates and friends in government and academia for ideas and suggestions shared with me over many years. For the book itself,

I am grateful for the accommodative help of the librarians at the Office of State Services in the headquarters of the various associations of state government, the Urban Institute, and the Advisory Commission on Intergovernmental Relations (ACIR). Special thanks go to Joan Casey for indexing and for other editorial assistance. Additionally, professional staff members of the International City Management Association (ICMA), the National Governors' Association, (NGA) and other organizations of state and local government have provided many pieces of useful data and other materials. Reports of the Committee for Economic Development (CED) have been very helpful in reporting on the private-sector role in domestic governance and on public-private partnerships in states and localities. For quantitative data I have relied primarily upon the Bureau of the Census of the U.S. Department of Commerce, the Bureau of Labor Statistics of the Department of Labor, the ACIR, and surveys conducted by the ICMA and other organizations of state and local government. For examples connected with issues being examined, frequent use has been made of the writings of Neal Peirce, the first, and in 1988 still the only, nationally syndicated columnist devoting exclusive attention to the affairs of state and local governments. Also drawn upon frequently have been the policy reports of the ACIR because of its primary attention to state and local government issues, frequently involving relationships with the national government, and because of its legal status as a bipartisan national body, a majority of the members of which are elected officials of state and local government. Additional sources for this book and references for practitioners and scholars are presented in the bibliographical essay.

STATE AND LOCAL
GOVERNMENT
AND
PUBLIC-PRIVATE
PARTNERSHIPS

Introduction: American Federalism, the Private Sector, and the Public Service

The latter half of the twentieth century in America has been characterized by continual stress and strain, both societally and governmentally. The foci of this stress have also shifted constantly. This dynamic state of affairs has been reflective both of global conditions and of internal forces. The strongest of these forces worldwide has been the quickening pace of scientific and technological advance, which has made the economies of the industrialized and developing nations more volatile while raising the expectations of the underdeveloped countries and heightening economic, social, and political tensions. This same drive to improve human amenities has manifested itself in the United States among low-income and minority groups.

A NEW DOMESTIC GOVERNMENT ENVIRONMENT IN THE UNITED STATES

The instruments of domestic government at national, state, and local levels all face formidable problems over the foreseeable future. The national government continues to seek ways to deal with macroeconomic trends, cyclical changes, budget deficits, social insurance (with its associated health issues and the impacts of lengthening life spans), and interstate commerce regulation. Technological progress and environmental constraints make the regulatory process more difficult.

Much of the literature in the fields of public administration, public finance, and public policy, for a long while and for understandable reasons, has tended to focus on national government affairs. However, the state and local sectors of our governmental system will continue to bear the brunt of coping with many of the yet-unforeseen problems and issues of domestic governance, at least for an extended period of years. This book examines the state and local government scene in two regards: (1) how best to organize, finance, and deliver the myriad of state and local public services; and (2) how best to confront at America's grass roots several of the major public policy dilemmas likely to dominate to a considerable degree the domestic side of our governmental system over the next decade.

The center of gravity in domestic governance in the United States is shifting significantly away from Washington to state capitols, county courthouses, and city halls. Due to public fiscal resource scarcity, this focus is likely to prevail during the foreseeable future. Certain economic and political imperatives must be met:

- The reduction in scope and intensity of federal domestic programs results in new demands for state and local action.
- Greatly changed and continually changing world and national economies, both in terms of structure and viability, affect domestic governance in the United States and require appropriate adjustments.
- Continued eruption of new problems calling for public policy concern or action more frequently than not falls primarily upon state or local governments.
- If domestic government is to remain manageable and responsive to the economy as a whole, a constant evaluation, pruning, and sharpening of priorities is imperative so that talent and fiscal resources will be available and deployed most effectively to meet new, inevitable, but now unforeseen needs.
- The labor market, health industry, various state, local, and community institutions, and public opinion must develop ways to adjust to an aging population and to meet issues of intergenerational equity.
- An urban underclass problem persists despite two decades of federal-state-local and civic-business-labor attention. The need increases for state and local experimentation with health, correctional, and employment measures and with educational reforms directed toward improving academic standards and toward reinstating some kind of value consciousness in the classroom.
- There are conflicting and concurrent forces of economic growth and decline that shift to and fro among regions and within states to be taken into account.
- There is a new, expanding private-sector role in financing public infrastructure and in delivering public services, heretofore the nearly exclusive domain of state and local government officials and public employees.
- Growing ownership and other financial participation by state-local governments in private undertakings, especially at the local level, consequently blurs intergovernmental and public-private accountability.
- The increasing complexity of U.S. regulatory and legal systems results in a need for intergovernmental, procedural, and equity reforms.

THE FEDERALISM DIMENSION

The question of the relation of the States to the Federal Government is the cardinal question of our constitutional system. It is a question which cannot be settled by the opinion of one generation, because it is a question of growth and every successive stage of our political and economic development gives it a new aspect, makes it a new question.[1]

In this oft-quoted statement Woodrow Wilson noted the continual change in the federal system. A broad look at the evolution of American federalism over the past two hundred years and a closer look at the post–1975 period quickly verify the applicability of Wilson's 1917 comment to the contemporary scene.[2]

Earlier Periods

The need for ultimate national constitutional supremacy and the role of the Supreme Court in achieving it became crystal clear in some early decisions of the Court (*Marbury v. Madison,* 1803, and *McCullough v. Maryland,* 1819). Federal-state responsibilities and the role of government in U.S. society changed relatively little for a quarter century until the slavery issue began to approach a flash point. The issue of national supremacy was again tested, but this time on the battlefield instead of in the courthouse. The role of the national government began to expand in the regulatory area in the period following the Civil War. The first quarter of the new century was marked by little expansion in the peacetime national role and by judicial constraints upon the exercise by the states of police powers in the interests of public health and safety.

Real ferment again ensued with the advent of the New Deal in 1933, with vast expansion in national government domestic concerns, laws, and programs— in grants-in-aid to states and in the regulatory area pursuant to the interstate commerce clause. In the same period judicial restraint was lifted, and state and national police powers were unleashed and expanded. The period of the fifties to the mid-seventies was marked by still further expansion in the role of the national government, partially in response to new and urgent problems and partially as a result of the apathy of state governments in responding to local government needs arising from postwar urbanization. As a consequence, local government was brought into what had been dual federalism, making the new relationship tripartite—national, state, and local—with many federal programs aiding and regulating local governments directly, bypassing state governments in the process.[3]

During this same period, many new institutional arrangements were made for the study, monitoring, and coordination of federal-state-local relations: for example, the Commission on Intergovernmental Relations (the Kestnbaum Commission, 1954–55); the Advisory Commission on Intergovernmental Relations (1959); intergovernmental relations posts in the White House, in many executive agencies, and in subcommittees in both houses of the Congress; and similar organizational arrangements in most states and in many larger cities and counties. In brief, the forty-year period 1935–75 was characterized by (1) growth in federal aid programs; (2) growth of federal regulation, both that which accompanied federal aid and that undertaken for the purpose of regulation per se; and (3) new organizational arrangements at all three levels of government to handle the new complexities in federalism.

1978–88: A Decade of Intergovernmental Change

The continued expansion in national government vis-à-vis state and local governments began to slow in the mid-seventies, marked by the "anti-Washington" stance of the incoming Carter administration. During the early part of this pendulum swing, economic deregulation (airlines, railways, trucking) was enacted. There was a move also toward more centralized control within the federal executive branch over agency issuance of new regulations. Federal aid as a percentage of state-local government expenditures peaked around 1978 and began a steady decline.

Three important structural and fiscal changes occurred in intergovernmental relations in the ensuing years: (1) substantial reductions in federal taxes, constraining federal budgetary growth in general and federal aid in particular, with federal aid as a percentage of state and local government outlays decreasing from a fiscal year 1978 high of 26.5 percent to 18.1 percent in 1988 and an estimated 17.1 percent for 1989[4] (a decline intensified between 1985 and 1989 by the cessation of federal revenue sharing assistance to local governments). The drastically changing fiscal roles of the federal and state-local sectors of the national economy are reflected by governmental revenue *from all sources* as percentages of the GNP. In 1966, the respective percentages were 15.4 and 9.1; 1976, 13.8 and 11.6; and 1986, 13.7 and 12.5;[5] (2) consolidation of many compartmentalized federal "categorical" aid programs into broader block grants, with simultaneous cutbacks in accompanying aid "strings;" (3) a greatly enlarged role for state governments and substantially increased roles for the combined state-local sector.[6] This last aspect was recognized and encouraged by the incoming Bush Administration.

Although the wisdom of these changes is, and will continue to be, heatedly debated by federalism scholars, federal, state, and local officials, and many competing interest groups, it is a near certainty that the changes are not passing phenomena. They have been reflective of a number of economic, political, and social realities. (1) Conditions of international economic competition are increasingly fierce, so that U.S. management, labor, and governments are being pressed into higher efficiencies. (2) Consequent stringencies in public revenue availability in the face of taxpayer resistance to higher taxes and newly emerging problems confront all three levels, necessitating new public expenditures. (3) A more materialistic outlook by the post-Vietnam generations of Americans leads to a more laissez-faire approach to societal issues than ever before.

A recentralization of domestic governmental activities back to Washington will be hindered greatly by the increased fiscal, administrative, and personnel capacities of state-local governments and by new machinery created by state and local laws now in place, each tailored to individual situations. Forceful and consistent action and surgical skill carried out by a succession of Congresses would be required to reassemble anything approaching the mid-seventies vintage of federal aid and regulatory programs and to reinstate the Washington micro-management mode of that time. Any move in this direction by a future administration and Congress will be resisted strongly by state and local officials and their bureaucracies, and there will be a host of private-sector parties in new and strengthening relationships with these levels of government.

Washington conceivably could buy its way back into a dominant role in domestic governance, but neither the fiscal capability nor the economic justification for such an action appears likely over the foreseeable future. (Some observers fear that as a possible consequence of this fiscal impotence, a future Congress might attempt to regain a micromanagement role through regulatory measures, such as recategorizing block grants and reinstituting the many regulatory strings that formerly accompanied them.)

THE PRIVATE-SECTOR DIMENSION

Over the 1978–88 period the nature and scope of the profit sector role in the formulation and execution of state and local policies and programs expanded significantly. Nonprofit organizations also expanded their participatory influence in those functional areas in which they had long been active, and they entered new ones. The principal change, however, was the growing injection of private funds into public activities and public money into private ventures. Other kinds of public-private relationship changes occurred as well.

Shift from Tax-based to User-based Financing

A rapid expansion of "user-based financing" (UBF) has occurred, with user fees (and segregated taxes, as on motor and aviation fuel) sufficient in amount not only to recover capital costs but also to provide operation and maintenance costs, either wholly or in part. In more and more jurisdictions, full or partial user-based financing of capital and operating costs has been spreading into more facility categories, such as libraries, schools, museums, and a wide variety of recreational facilities such as swimming pools and golf courses. Private capital also has become significant in some public elementary and secondary schools, not only in physical facility improvements but also in subject matter areas (for example, "adopt a school" programs, computer purchases, and business education courses).

Private Financing of Public Infrastructure

A steadily increasing flow of private funds directly into the provision of public physical facilities (out-of-pocket, in contrast to investment in public revenue bonds) also has occurred. This evolved as a result of (1) declining public funds and increasing financial needs for the construction, replacement, or rehabilitation of roads, bridges, sewage treatment plants, schools, libraries, and other public buildings and (2) stronger state and local restrictions upon new private development for environmental and other "growth management" reasons (for example, the conditioning of development permits upon the availability of adequate public facilities). In turn, a frequent cause for decline in public revenues has been the adoption of tax and expenditure limitations (TELs) by public initiatives in some states (for example, propositions 13 and 2½ in California and Massachusetts) and by legislative action in others. A third major causative factor has been the increasingly frequent conclusion by state and local governments that a privately financed and operated facility would be more economical than one under public operation, or that such a mode would be more acceptable to the general public.

State-Local Government Participation in Private Ventures

Large-scale public-private financial relationships as a part of city government economic development date back to the federal urban renewal programs of the fifties. As a part of central-city revitalization efforts, the relationships expanded to encompass tax abatements and governmentally provided infrastructure to accommodate new or immigrating businesses, which began to evolve in the late seventies and early eighties into "enterprise zones." These later modes often involved state as well as local governments as financial and technical partners.

A longer and possibly ultimate step, the acquiring of equity positions in private projects serving no public purpose other than a contribution to economic development, private employment, and the state or local tax base (for example, retail shopping centers, luxury hotels, and office buildings), is now being taken by a wide range of state, local, and special-district governments. These governmental involvements hold considerable fiscal hope in an era of constraint; they also raise problems of antitrust violations and conflict of interest. The expansion of public entrepreneurship, like user fees and other use of private enterprise in the public interest, was spurred by the adoption of fiscal limitations and made easier by public dissatisfaction with governmental efficiency evidenced in public political choices over the 1975–85 decade.

Question of Private Delivery of State-Local Public Services

"Privatization"is a misleading shorthand term for shifting a public service to private auspices for delivery to consumers/taxpayers. In the early and mid-eighties this phenomenon was associated closely with, and attributed to, the policies and philosophy of the Reagan administration. Actually, state and local governments for years had been relying on private contractors to deliver an appreciable, but not large, portion of public services, especially in the construction of state highways and local roads and streets and in the performance of specialized or seasonal functions such as snow plowing in areas where snows were uncommon. However, by 1970 it was becoming evident in some cities that particular services, such as refuse collection, were costing considerably more when performed by municipal employees rather than by private contractors.

Consequently, throughout the seventies an increasing number of local governments began experimenting with private instead of public employee service delivery. Part of the motivation for these experiments was fiscal savings through improved productivity; during a period of relatively high strength of public employee unions, the possibility of contracting out a portion of a service gave the local government considerable leverage in collective bargaining with employees engaged in delivering the service.

By 1980 local experimentation and actual shifts to private delivery were beginning to arouse the interest of state governments, with much attention given to correctional services. Also, public managers were looking at a range of modes that included the contracting option but went far beyond it. These changes were confirmed and examined in a 1982 survey by the International City Management Association (ICMA). (A followup ICMA survey in 1987 of more limited scope showed the trend toward alternative arrangements continuing, but not markedly expanding except in dealing with the rapidly emerging problem of the homeless, where contracting and use of volunteers were being used widely.)[7] In addition to contracting for delivery of a service, either with neighboring units of government or with one or more private providers, the other modes increasingly used by local governments included franchise agreements, vouchers, use of volunteers, neighborhood self-help groups, and homeowners' associations, and "load shedding." Here the government gets out of the picture, and the service is obtained in the marketplace, with or without public regulation or public incentives, such as tax abatements for the installation of smoke alarms and tax credits to organizations or persons providing uncompensated services.

SOCIOECONOMIC DISARRAY AND THE URBAN UNDERCLASS

As the United States moves toward the next century, some social factors assume new urgency. The most serious of these—because it not only weakens the nation's social fabric but poses an equal threat to economic vitality—is that of the "urban underclass." It is multidimensional, involving abuse of health, alienated social behavior, educational failure, and essentially permanent unemployment, with monetary needs often met either through illegal activity or welfare-type assistance or some combination of the two. It has become increasingly apparent that this is as much a behavioral problem as an economic or income problem, despite the fact that most members of the underclass have low incomes.[8] The prevailing characteristics, in addition to low income, include lack of education, labor market experience, literacy, residence mobility options, and stable family relationships.[9]

State and local governments are on the firing line of public responsibility (in the governmental sense) in this area, because the many health, educational, job-training, and other services essential for dealing with the many facets of the problem are delivered at the state-local level. This delivery system includes state and local public agencies, with private social agencies often bearing a large share of the cost and delivery responsibility. But if disadvantaged urban youth are to live personally rewarding and societally responsible lives, education and jobs are the inseparable and indispensable elements. The first is a predominantly public regulatory and service function and the second a predominantly private function, because over four-fifths of the jobs in the labor force are in the non-governmental sector.

To begin to mitigate the condition that has prevailed and worsened despite mammoth public and substantial private expenditure of money and effort, the combined and cooperative endeavor of the private and public segments of localities and states will be absolutely essential. Mobilization of these combined resources in dealing with the underclass problem will require, as in the past, effective public-private partnership undertakings. These civic and business partnerships with state and local governments have a long and positive history in the United States and have assumed increased importance in the wake of the economic and fiscal squeeze affecting regional, state, and local economies. They constitute a major resource in addressing the variety of socioeconomic challenges that will be confronting urban communities across the country in the difficult years ahead.

REGULATORY/LEGAL SYSTEMS: ECONOMIC COSTS AND EQUITY DILEMMAS

Widespread and increasing concern abounds among many segments of public opinion regarding the economic and equity effects of the twin explosions of regulation and litigation over the past two decades. Much of the legal basis for new regulatory activity has rested in acts of Congress in environmental, health, and occupational and product safety fields. However, much of the executive responsibility has been left to the states and through and by them to local governments. This has especially been the case in the environmental area. It is up to the states to develop, legislate, and administer plans and programs to achieve federally imposed standards and goals in air and water pollution. It is also up to the states to experiment with and to develop the most cost-effective and equitable means of dealing with sediment control and runoff, solid and hazardous wastes, and other environmental protection areas in which federal legislation is not definitive.

Growing from the increased volatility of world and national economies, the national regulatory framework for financial institutions and for corporation finance and governance has fallen into disarray. State legislatures have struggled to fill part of the policy vacuum in reaction to critical problems arising in these areas. Although most signs point toward the ultimate national preemption of regulatory authority in such fields as banking, corporate takeovers, and security market practices, state governments in the meantime will have to cope as best they can with these issues, furnishing highly useful experience and information in the process.

In contrast to the various regulatory areas in which authority is shared between national and state governments, the responsibility for the growing complexity of civil legal systems and procedures and possible improvements in them lies primarily with the states, although some of their activities and outputs are susceptible to federal judicial review of national constitutional aspects. The rising tide of litigation, especially in tort liability and limits thereon, and the extension of legal standing to more and more litigants are, and will continue to be, faced principally by state legislatures and courts, with the possible exception of national standards on certain types of tort liability awards. Here the states face a serious challenge; it is up to them to formulate effective and equitable modifications to their own laws that can in turn provide a basis for action by states generally. Thus they not only can but must move quickly in their traditional role as political laboratories for the nation.

THE PUBLIC ADMINISTRATION DIMENSION

These issues and trends clearly indicate that public administration as a profession and people engaged in it as a career face startling new environments in the years ahead. Around the world the pace of technological and other changes has made it increasingly questionable to forecast the future by projecting the present. However, the combination of technical change, resource scarcity, and seemingly satisfactory experiences with greatly increased private-sector involvement in public programs and in the delivery of public services makes highly improbable a return to the half-century trend of steadily expanding governmental services delivered by a growing corps of government administrators and employees. Public administration is in the midst of substantial and wrenching change, as are individuals in, or training to enter, this profession.

In 1986 a committee made up of twenty-five members of the National Academy of Public Administration (NAPA) was asked by the academy's Board of Trustees to examine the public administration field, consult with the academy membership of around 325, and report to the board on what appeared to be the most important and urgent issues and problems likely to confront the profession over the ensuing ten to fifteen years and on what seemed to be the most appropriate role for the academy to play in those governance areas. In the process of its deliberations the committee polled the NAPA membership on several questions, including the identification of the most crucial issues confronting public administration in the years ahead. The five issues identified by the respondents were (1) state of the public service; (2) public-private-sector relationships; (3) problems of fiscal constraint, discipline, and resource scarcity; (4) intergovernmental relations; and (5) the need for new management structures and processes appropriate to a changed public policy environment.[10]

In its report to the NAPA Board of Trustees the committee noted the dramatic changes that had been taking place in the public administration field since 1960, from an emphasis on administrative management and central staff activities such as personnel, budgeting, and organization/management systems to policy analysis and program design and evaluation—in other words, a shift from central to functional management. The committee observed that the effect of post–1960 changes had been to increase greatly the role of state and local government in domestic governance and in service delivery, with the states once again functioning as the nation's political laboratories. Also noted was an increased private- and nonprofit-sector role in service delivery; the growing role of noncareer appointees in public program administration; and the convergence of professional skills required in business and public administration.

Beginning in the late seventies, an increasing concern about the state of the public service began to appear in public administration literature. Part of this appeared to be based upon the anti-Washington rhetoric characterizing the 1976 and 1980 national political campaigns. However, the focus of most of the discussion then and subsequently was upon the federal civil service. In 1987 a national commission, headed by former Federal Reserve Chairman Paul Volcker and financed from nongovernmental sources, was established to examine the problem in a comprehensive fashion. It is the belief of many state and local officials and of observers of the state-local scene such as Neal Peirce that the morale of state-local professional personnel is, with exceptions here and there, quite good. This is not surprising, because the environment in those governments is one of searching out new ways to meet public problems; in the national government the emphasis is upon a series of holding and retrenchment actions. In 1988 the ICMA annual survey of professional managers in local government, with 1,508 responding, showed that on a scale of 1 to 5 on level of satisfaction with their job and profession, 90 percent were highly or moderately satisfied; 10 percent (4 and 5) were not.[11]

In 1985, no doubt in recognition of the increased role of state and local governments in the domestic scene, the Ford Foundation established a program of Innovation Awards in State and Local Governments. Cases included in the 1987 and 1988 awards illustrate the range of problems and opportunities for improved governance in states and localities.

- The Georgia penal system was faced with severe overcrowding; the Department of Corrections developed a continuum of options to incarceration, targeting young offenders. Prison sentences decreased 10 percent, and $165 million in victim restitution and two million hours of work resulted from the substitution of supervised community work for incarceration.

- Illinois adopted the first statewide approach to the teenage pregnancy problem. Parents Too Soon, among other aspects, involved adolescent males, an omission noted earlier by a congressional committee regarding then-existing state programs.

- A communitywide public-private Domestic Abuse Prevention program was developed in Duluth.

- A public-private partnership effort in St. Louis established a Homeless Services Network that arranged shelter for all homeless people in the city in 1986. (the mayor attributed a large part of the success of the program to its "privatization").[12]

- A State of Missouri Parents as Teachers program operated through local school districts and supported parents in the first stages of child education.

- A New York City work program of probationers in small businesses was administered by a nonprofit organization under sponsorship of the city department of probation.

- A San Diego Single Room Occupancy (SRO) hotel rehabilitation and preservation program.

- A Vermont statewide Library Automation project.

- A Kentucky Parent and Childhood Education program to curb the intergenerational illiteracy cycle in rural areas.[13]

1986 award recipients included (1) State of Arizona groundwater management code; (2) New York City case management for at-risk children; (3) Illinois minority adoption program; (4) Leslie, Michigan, family learning center; (5) Saint Paul block nurse program; and (6) Illinois quality-incentive program in long-term health care.[14]

Information on innovations in state and local government and in the development of fruitful business-government and other collaborative civic undertakings is disseminated through the "Big Seven" organizations and their research subsidiary, the Academy for State and Local Government.[15] Another initiative, notable because of the centrality of the issue, was begun in 1986 in Memphis and Shelby County to combat inner-city poverty.[16]

As will be evident throughout this book, whatever else the internal organization and management problems of a particular state or local government may be, state and local professional managers face many problems in the years ahead— some frustrating, but nevertheless challenging in nearly all respects. As they face these formidable tasks, state and local political leadership and public managers alike will be considering ways in which these institutions of state and local government need to be re-formed and reinvigorated to cope with the new environments. In this undertaking the admonition of John Gardner is most pertinent: "It is not [just] a question of excellence. A society that has reached the heights of excellence may already be caught in the rigidities that will bring it down. An institution may hold itself to the highest standards and yet already be doomed to the complacency that foreshadows decline."[17]

Elmer Staats, in referring to the famous words of John F. Kennedy ("Ask not what your country can do for you—ask rather what you can do for your country''), said: "This is the challenge of the public service. In one way or another it has always been so, and I suppose always will be. Public service is more than an occupational category. It is the discovery, as Harold Laski put it long ago, that people serve themselves only as they serve others."[18] A key question arising from time to time in the examination of policy issues confronting state and local government and public-private partnerships is the extent to which the concept of the public service expressed by Laski and Staats is in the process of being broadened beyond the boundaries of government.

NOTES

1. Wilson, W., *Constitutional Government in the United States* (New York: Columbia University Press, 1917), 173.

2. Hawkins, R., ed., *American Federalism: A New Partnership for the Republic* (San Francisco: Institute for Contemporary Studies, 1982) (a collection of papers on federalism from varying points of view).

3. Walker, D., *Toward a Functioning Federalism* (Cambridge, Mass.: Winthrop Publishers, 1981), 19–99; and Elazar, D., *American Federalism: A View from the States,* 3rd ed. (New York: Harper & Row, 1984).

4. U.S. Advisory Commission on Intergovernmental Relations (ACIR), *Significant Features of Fiscal Federalism, 1988, Edition.* Report M–155 II. July, 1988, Table 8.

5. Shannon, J., "Federalism's Fiscal Fable," *Intergovernmental Perspective,* Summer, 1988, 22–23.

6. Nathan, R., and Derthick, M., "Reagan's Legacy: A New Liberalism among the States," *New York Times,* December 18, 1987, op-ed.

7. Valente, C., and Manchester, L., *Rethinking Local Services: Examining Alternative Delivery Approaches,* Management Information Service, Special Report no. 12 (Washington, D.C.: International City Management Association (ICMA), March 1984); and ICMA, "Patterns in the Use of Alternative Service Delivery Approaches," (preliminary results of 1987 survey) *The Municipal Year Book 1979.* (Washington, D.C.: ICMA April, 1989). See also: Touche Ross, *Privatization in America* (survey). (Washington, D.C.: Touche Ross, 1987); National Commission for Employment Policy, *Privatization and Public Employees* (case studies). (Washington, D.C.: May, 1988).

8. Ricketts, E. R., and Sawhill, I. V., *Defining and Measuring the Underclass* (Washington, D.C.: Urban Institute Press, December 1986).

9. National Research Council Committee on National Urban Policy, "The Urban Underclass," in *Critical Issues for National Urban Policy* (Washington, D.C.: National Academy Press, 1982), 33–53.

10. National Academy of Public Administration, *Report of the Academy Committee on the Future to the Board of Trustees* (Washington, D.C.: National Academy of Public Administration, October 31, 1986).

11. *ICMA Newsletter* 68, no. 22 (November 21, 1988): 2.

12. Peirce, N., "America's Best Homeless Program," *Nation's Cities Weekly,* January 18, 1988, 4.

13. *Innovations in State and Local Government, 1987* and *1988* editions. (Boston, Mass.: Harvard Business School Press, 1987), 4–13 and 3–12, respectively.

14. Ibid., 1987 ed., 16.

15. *Innovations: Ideas for Local Government* (Washington, D.C.: ICMA, in cooperation with the Council of State Governments and the Academy for State and Local Government, 1987). The "Big Seven" comprise, in addition to ICMA and CSG, the National Governors' Association (NGA), National Association of Counties (NACO), National League of Cities (NLC), National Conference of State Legislatures (NCSL), and the U.S. Conference of Mayors (USCM).

16. *Free the Children: Breaking the Cycle of Poverty* (Memphis: Shelby County Government, October 1987).

17. Gardner, J., *Renewing: The Leader's Creative Task,* Leadership Papers 10 (Washington, D.C.: Leadership Studies Program, Independent Sector, 1988), 3.

18. Staats, E., "Public Service and the Public Interest," *Public Administration Review*, March–April 1988, 605.

Chapter 1 ─────────────────────────

Overview of Legal, Organizational, and Financial Structures of American State and Local Governments

In this chapter the place of state and local governments in the federal system will be examined. Legal, organizational, and financial structures of state and local governments, including state-local relationships, are reviewed, and the chapter concludes with a brief summary of the major issues of local government structure and finance likely to confront both of these governmental levels in the nineties.

THE LEGAL POSITION OF STATES IN THE FEDERAL SYSTEM

Two provisions of the U.S. Constitution establish the basic roles of the national and state governments in the American federal system, with three other provisions giving additional guidance.

Article VI, section 2, provides: "This Constitution, and the laws of the United States which shall be made in pursuance thereof; and all treaties made, or which shall be made, under the authority of the United States, shall be the supreme law of the land; and the judges in every State shall be bound thereby, any thing in the Constitution or laws of any State to the contrary notwithstanding."

In the absence of any other provisions to the contrary, one would assume that the national government is supreme in every respect and could enact laws governing any subject, thereby overriding any state laws on the matter. However, as a part of the ratification process, the U.S. Constitution acquired ten amendments, called the Bill of Rights. The Tenth Amendment provides: "The powers not delegated to the United States by the Constitution, nor prohibited by it to the States, are reserved to the States respectively, or to the people."

James Madison, in *The Federalist*, said:

The powers delegated by the proposed Constitution to the federal government are few and defined. Those which are to remain in the State governments are numerous and indefinite. The former will be exercised principally on external objects, as war, peace, negotiation and foreign commerce; with which last the power of taxation will, for the most part, be connected.

The powers reserved to the several States will extend to all the objects which, in the ordinary course of affairs, concern the lives, liberties, and properties of the people and the internal order, improvement, and prosperity of the State.[1]

Aside from defense and foreign affairs, the provisions for domestic governance contained in the Constitution as part of the powers of the Congress include (1) post offices and post roads; (2) patents; (3) currency; (4) punishment of counterfeiting; and (5) naturalization. In addition, a key power is delegated to the federal Congress—"to regulate commerce with foreign nations, and among the several States, and with the Indian tribes." This is the "interstate commerce clause," from which stemmed a considerable part of subsequent federal legislation on economic and commercial matters. It also is an important substantive constraint upon the states because as the country developed, much of its commerce assumed an interstate character, and states were restrained from interfering with its flow.

In addition to the commerce and supremacy clauses, two other parts of the Constitution dilute the restrictive language of the Tenth Amendment. The Bill of Rights and the Fourteenth and Fifteenth amendments contain equal protection, due process, and other individual and civil rights provisions. Second, the first of the eighteen powers conferred upon the Congress is "to lay and collect taxes, duties, imposts and excises, to pay the debts and provide for the common defense and general welfare of the United States." This is the "general welfare" clause, which is the base of most federal grants-in-aid to state and local governments, including the various rules and requirements accompanying the individual grants.

The judicial potency of the Tenth Amendment as a bar to federal intrusion into state jurisdiction in domestic government has waxed and waned since the adoption of the Constitution. In recent years it had a rebirth in 1976, when the Supreme Court held that state and local government employees performing "traditional" functions of those levels could not be brought under the federal Fair Labor Standards Act because they were performing noninterstate duties and thereby were sheltered from federal intrusion by the Tenth Amendment.[2] Nine years later, by a five-to-four vote of the Court, the 1976 decision was reversed, with the minority seeming to promise an early return to the question.[3]

Presently, subject to the substantive interstate commerce and general welfare clauses and to the civil rights and other process clauses of the Constitution, the states have wide latitude in taking and holding new ground in innumerable areas of domestic government and in providing most of the ground rules under which people's day-to-day lives are conducted. These include the following:

Most of the criminal justice system excluding federal crimes, and nearly all the area of civil litigation

The financing and governance of public K–12 and higher education

The regulation of the practice of medicine, law, and countless other professions and trades

Much of the regulation of public health and safety under the state "police power"

Regulation of land use and other forms of urban and rural development, usually through delegation to local units of government

Establishing and maintaining election machinery, including the drawing of election district lines, for both state and federal elections

Determination of the structure and functions of local government, as well as its financing by taxes and other means

CENTRALITY OF STATES AND LOCALITIES IN DOMESTIC GOVERNANCE

The state-local sector of the national economy and of the domestic portion of our governmental system is large and growing. Four major aspects of this sector are (1) services performed; (2) employees engaged; (3) dollar outlays for public services; and (4) regulatory functions conducted.

Services, Employees, and Outlays

• In 1986 state and local government employees comprised about 12.9 percent or one-eighth of the total U.S. labor force (compared to a federal employee composition of 3.1 percent).[4]

• Expenditures of these governments from own revenue sources comprised 11.3 percent of gross national product (GNP) in 1987 (compared to 23.7 percent for all federal expenditures, including defense and interest on the national debt).[5]

• State and local "own source general revenue" (excluding federal aid to state-local governments, and insurance trust, utility, and liquor store revenue) totaled $571.2 billion in fiscal year 1987 (compared with $664.5 billion at the federal level).[6]

• For 1987, domestic public expenditure, for current purposes excluding national defense and international relations ($319.1 billion) and interest on the national debt ($146.2 billion) on the federal side and debt interest of $41.8 billion on the state-local side, totaled $1,237.1 billion. Such state-local outlays amounted to $650.6 billion, compared to $586.5 billion by the federal government, of which $282.2 billion was for Social Security.[7]

• Of the fourteen largest direct expenditures for domestic public services (those of $10 billion or more) as recorded by the Census Bureau for 1987, the state-local sector was dominant in education ($226.7 billion to $32.0 billion); highways ($52.2 billion to $13.5 billion); hospitals ($40.1 billion to $8.0 billion); police protection ($24.7 billion to $4.2 billion); corrections ($16.6 billion to $.8 billion) (early 1987 prison population was 44,000 federal and 501, state);[8] sanitation/sewage ($21.3 billion to none); parks/recreation ($11.0 billion to $1.6 billion); tax collection and other financial administration ($12.8 billion to $5.8 billion); fire protection ($10.9 billion to none) and judicial/legal ($10.1 billion to $2.3 billion). The federal government was dominant in postal services ($32.2 billion to none); natural resources ($85.0 billion to $9.7 billion, due in considerable part to agricultural price supports, a measure for economic stabilization); and veterans' services ($17.1 billion to $0.1 billion). Shared functions were welfare ($74.1 billion federal and $82.5 billion state-local) health, $12.3 billion and $16.9 billion, community development/housing ($20.2 billion federal and $11.8 billion state-local).[9]

Tables detailing these orders of magnitude are presented later in this chapter.

Regulatory Functions and State Constitutions

In contrast to the service role, the regulatory roles of the respective federal and state-local sectors are more evenly matched, with the federal side exclusive or dominant, pursuant to the U.S. Constitution, in regulating and facilitating the flow of interstate commerce, and the states' "police power" regulation in health and safety leading or dominant in many other aspects, especially in the fields of criminal and civil justice, health, land use control, and occupational licensing. In environmental regulation, overall policy and minimum standards are established federally, with the enforcement and administrative aspects mostly left to the states.

It is important to note that in environmental and other regulatory areas, the substantial federal role often was preceded by state regulation (for example, California in air pollution, Maryland in hospital cost controls). Also, except for product manufacturing standards, individual state standards can and often do exceed federal requirements. The same situation applies to individual rights, where some state constitutions afford protection going beyond the Bill of Rights or the Fourteenth Amendment. This has been the case in education finance, where several state constitutions in their equal protection clauses establish equality of educational opportunity as a fundamental right, while the Supreme Court has found in the negative. Similar contrasting findings have occurred in free speech, permissible searches, and the implementation of the *Miranda* rule.[10]

A few other points about state constitutions are relevant here. In general, the states have a relatively free hand in drafting and amending their constitutions, constrained only by (*a*) the provisions of the U.S. Constitution as discussed earlier and (*b*) the willingness of the state's voters to approve the constitution as a whole and amendments to it as they arise. For example, the Model State Constitution published by the National Municipal League (renamed the National Civic League in 1987) provides under Powers of the State: "Section 2.01. Powers of Government. The enumeration in this constitution of specified powers and functions shall be construed neither as a grant nor as a limitation of the powers of state government but the state government shall have all of the powers not denied by this constitution or by or under the Constitution of the United States."[11]

Conventional wisdom on constitution (and local government charter) drafting has long held that only fundamental principles should be included in the document, with the implementation of the principles left to the legislative body to enact through statute or local ordinance. This drafting principle is easier to preach than to practice. Some of the earlier state constitutions have managed to avoid through the years the accumulation of "statutory clutter" (Vermont, 1793, currently 6,600 words, and New Hampshire, 1784, 9,200 words), as have some more recent ones (Alaska, 1956, 13,000 words, and North Carolina, 1970, 11,000 words).[12] One of the contributing factors to greater length is the tendency of many state constitutions to contain separate articles on the major substantive and functional areas of state policy-making, such as education, corrections, health, welfare, the chartering of corporations, and, more recently, environmental protection.

LOCAL GOVERNMENT STRUCTURE

Counties, cities, towns, townships, and school and other special districts comprise the structural framework of local governments in the United States. These governments provide the bulk of public services rendered to the people, and it is with these governmental units that people are most acquainted. Although local governments deliver most of the public services, local taxpayers may not be meeting all, most, or any of the costs of a particular service; it may be paid for by the citizens who use it, such as a city parking garage, or wholly or partially by the state government, such as a state park or hospital for the mentally ill. Most frequently, the money for the service comes from a mixture of sources. Regardless of financing or the federal or state requirements that go along with it, political accountability rests primarily with the delivering agent—the local government or one of its franchisees or contractors.

With some important qualifications, it can be said that local government has only the powers and responsibilities that are prescribed or delegated by the state; they are the political subdivisions and the legal creatures of the state. Sometimes local government officials are able to perform well in spite of sins of omission or commission by the parent state government; sometimes they are inspired or required by the parent state to improve their responsiveness and productivity. Always they are greatly influenced by the actions or inactions of the state governor and legislature. The efficiency, equity, and general quality of their performance is affected crucially by the state in four respects: (1) the organizational structure provided or allowed; (2) the functions and duties with which they are charged or which they are permitted to carry on; (3) the extent to which territorial adjustments to population growth or decline are permitted; and (4) the revenue sources authorized for their use.

Types and Numbers of Units of Local Government

Local governments are of two overall types: (1) units of general local government and (2) all other units, comprising school districts and a wide variety of other special-purpose districts, authorities, and other entities.

Units of general government carry on a range of functions and comprise municipalities (cities and villages); counties; and towns or townships. Munici-palities, usually but not always meaning cities, are found in all states; a municipal government is defined by the Census Bureau as a political subdivision in which a municipal corporation has been established to provide general local government for a specific population concentration in a defined area.

Counties exist in a great majority of states; the exceptions are Connecticut, Rhode Island, the District of Columbia, and limited portions of other states where certain county areas lack a distinct county government. In Louisiana, counties are known as "parishes," and in Alaska "borough" governments re-semble county governments elsewhere.

Township governments exist in twenty states and are distinguished from mu-nicipalities in that they serve inhabitants of areas defined without regard to population concentrations. The township category includes "towns" in the six New England states, New York, and Wisconsin and some "plantations" in Maine and "locations" in New Hampshire, as well as governments called "town-ships" in other areas. "Unorganized townships" are not counted in the census; these are used for geographical survey and land location purposes in a number of states and do not have a government or governing body.

Special-purpose governments, in contrast to cities, counties, and some town-ships, perform usually but one function, or on occasion one or more additional but closely related functions, such as a water and sewer district. The most important of the special-purpose local governments is the school district; these are two types—independent and dependent. The latter category comprises those school systems that are regular agencies of general-purpose governments and are not a political subdivision in any sense of the word. The other special districts, the most numerous local government form, numbering nearly 30,000, have, like school districts, been established for a particular functional purpose, such as water supply and sewage disposal.

Table 1.1 summarizes the number and population size of the areas served by the three types of general local government and the numbers of school and special districts in 1977, 1982, and 1987. Special districts are the most rapidly growing local unit types; this was the case in 1962 and for each succeeding five-year period. The number of school districts dropped dramatically in the post–World War II period, but the rate of decrease has tapered sharply downward in more recent periods. Special districts comprised 35 percent of all local units in 1987, compared to 20 percent in 1962.

The number of the various types of local governments varies considerably among regions and states. Three major factors influence the numbers in each state: (a) history: once a pattern is formed, changing it is extremely difficult; both residents and officials of the unit, along with its employees, strongly resist change; (b) population settlement patterns: the more separate concentrations of population there are, the greater will be the number of municipalities needed; and (c) powers granted to county governments: since most states are divided into county areas, each with a government, the more restricted the powers of

Table 1.1
Units of Local Government in the United States, 1977, 1982, and 1987

Type	Number of Units			1987 Population Size[a]		Below
	1987	1982	1977	50 K+	10-50 K	10 K
County	3,042	3,041	3,042	785	1,559	698
Municipal	19,205	19,076	18,862	468	1,865	16,867*
Township	16,691	16,734	16,822	107	939	15,645
School Dist.[b]	14,741	14,851	15,174	NA	NA	NA
Special Dist.	29,487	28,588	25,962	NA	NA	NA

Source: Bureau of the Census, *1987 Census of Governments, Government Units in 1987*, GC87–1 (P), November 1987, 1–7, and associated census data.

[a] NA = data not available.
* Includes five existing but inactive units.
[b] (1) Enrollment data in table 5.7.

county government are, the more municipalities or townships will be needed; conversely, where the county is the "chosen instrument" of local government, with broad powers available, fewer incorporated municipalities are usually found. These factors explain in considerable part the kinds of variations found in the 1987 census of governments.[13]

County governments number 100 or more in seven states, with Texas having 254. The smallest county in the country was Loving County in Texas, with 100 inhabitants in 1987; the largest was Los Angeles County, with more than 8.5 million. States with the smallest number of counties were Delaware, 3; Hawaii, 4; Rhode Island, 5; New Hampshire, 10; Alaska, 12; and Vermont, 14. Other states with over 100 counties were Georgia, 159; Kentucky, 120; Missouri, 114; and Kansas, Illinois, and North Carolina with 105, 102, and 100, respectively.[14]

Municipalities were most numerous in Illinois with 1,279; Texas, 1,156; Pennsylvania, 1,022; Iowa, 955; Ohio, 940; and Missouri, 930. At the other extreme were Hawaii, 1; Rhode Island, 8; and New Hampshire, 13. Illinois also led the list for special districts with 2,782, followed closely by California, 2,732; Texas, 1,891; and Pennsylvania, 1,802. Those with the fewest such districts were Alaska and Hawaii, 14 each; Louisiana, 24; Rhode Island, 83; and Vermont, 95.

Township governments, in contrast to counties and municipalities, are multiregional and not nationwide in use, being found only in the New England, Middle Atlantic, and North Central regions. However, in these areas nearly a fifth of the nation's population (over 50 million) is served by township governments. These governments range widely in operational scope. By general state law in New England, New Jersey, and Pennsylvania, and to some degree in Michigan, Minnesota, New York, and Wisconsin, township (or town) governments are vested with relatively broad powers. Also, where they include closely settled territory, they perform functions commonly associated with municipal governments. Frequently reported township-owned and operated services are libraries, sewerage, landfills, and water supply.

In certain of the New England states, the town governments are commonly responsible for local schools as well as for other governmental functions. By contrast, many township governments in the North Central states perform only a very limited range of services for predominantly rural areas.

Special-district governments are independent, limited-purpose governmental units (other than school district governments) that exist as separate entities with substantial administrative and fiscal independence from general-purpose local governments. These 29,487 districts counted in 1987 had grown by over 1,400 during the preceding five years, continuing an upward trend of several decades to create new governmental units needed to meet additional government service and resource requirements. Although they are found in all states and even in the District of Columbia, their general use is concentrated in a dozen or so states, accounting for about two-thirds of their use.

Of the more than 29,000 districts, 93 percent were performing a single function in 1987, with natural resources (6,473), fire protection (5,063), housing and community development (3,460), and water supply (3,056) the most frequent single functions. More than 5,600 of these governments are concerned with water supply either as the sole function or as one of a combination of functions, often with sewerage. Since both water and sewage travel downhill, stream basin topography often dictates the use of special districts with multicounty or parts-of-county boundaries rather than a coordinated melange of city and county governments. Special districts naturally exist more frequently in urbanized or urbanizing areas. In states that tend to make wide use of these districts, the number in metropolitan areas is especially marked.

School district governments. The 1987 census count excluded about 1,500 ''dependent'' districts that functioned as integral parts of city, county, or township governments. As in the other types of local government, state laws for their organization and operation vary widely. About 4,000 districts serve areas that are coterminous with some other government, usually a county, city, or township. California, Illinois, and Texas each had more than 1,000 school districts, accounting for nearly a third of the nation's total; (twenty-five states had 1,000 or more in 1942). In five states (Alaska, Hawaii, Maryland, North Carolina, and Virginia) and the District of Columbia there are no independent school districts for budget and taxing purposes, although elected boards of education govern some of them and all public schools are administered by systems that are agencies of the county or city government or of the state (Alaska, Hawaii, and sparsely populated areas of Maine).

County subordinate taxing areas, although not local units of government, are authorized by law in many states so that specific improvements or special services within a defined area can be provided through a financial and administrative mechanism without the need to resort to an independent special district. Often this device enables the delivery of urban services such as water and sewer facilities, fire protection, and streets or street lighting, with the additional costs being met by an additional tax on the assessed value of property in the area reflected in the annual property tax bill from the county government.

Neighborhood subunits of government and citizen associations, although not counted in the census, are important parts of or adjuncts to local units of government in many urban areas. Some cities, such as Indianapolis, Washington, D.C., St. Paul, New York, and Boston, have at one time or another over the past two decades established either formal subunits of the city government or "neighborhood city halls," or combinations of the two forms. For example, a number of cities and urban counties have decentralized certain health and human service operations into community-area multiservice centers to provide "one-stop shopping" for services.

Effective manifestations of neighborhood and community governance are found in a number of urban areas in addition to those already mentioned, including Portland, Oregon, Sacramento, and Dayton. ACIR for a number of years has proposed that states enact legislation to authorize the formation of subunits of government at the initiative either of the city or county governing body or by the petition of neighborhood citizens. (An extract from the ACIR-proposed draft legislation is carried in appendix 1.A.)

Legally established neighborhood organizations of the kind described here or less formal neighborhood citizen associations comprise an important adjunct to local government in a majority of urban areas, rising to urge or oppose local government actions affecting them. They are a large and growing part of the local government political scene, and many function as a regular part of the local legislative process, usually on a consultative or advisory basis, but with considerable influence.[15]

Homeowner, cooperative, and condominium associations also play an important adjunct role in local government in many urban areas. In their simplest forms these nonprofit corporations, comprising owners of homes, apartments, or condominiums in a development or subdivision, carry on a combined watchdog, governance, and service function and may on occasion supplement or replace municipal services. In some respects they constitute "private governments."[16] In 1973 the Community Associations Institute was formed as a service and backstopping organization for these associations, which number in the thousands.[17] Various aspects of these associations and their boards are discussed in chapters 3 and 4 as they pertain to the delivery of public services, civic betterment, and community revitalization and other economic development efforts.

Organizations for metropolitan and other substate regional planning and coordination were created for widely varying purposes in the sixties and thereafter, initially at the instigation and mandate of the federal government for purposes of interlocal review and comment on federal grant-in-aid applications, but later by state governments to facilitate intercounty and other regional planning and coordination on a statewide basis.

David Walker has identified seventeen forms of interlocal cooperation in metropolitan areas, ranging from informal consultation among elected officials of the counties and municipalities in the area to an elected metropolitan government, forming an intermediate, general-purpose layer between local and state governments.[18] Only in Toronto, Ontario, has a full-fledged metropolitan government been established in North America. It is approached in one sense in Portland, Oregon, which has an elected, multipurpose body to finance and coordinate the delivery of a variety of services to the metropolitan area. It is approached in another sense in the Twin Cities of Minneapolis and St. Paul, where a state-appointed metropolitan council exercises a group of general-purpose coordinative powers over the local governments in the area.

In many metropolitan areas the substate regional entities often took the form of "councils of governments" (COGs), made up of one or more elected officials from each unit of local government in the area. These organizations served and continue to serve many useful purposes: (1) interchange of information on common problems; (2) a forum for conflict resolution; (3) a mechanism for cooperative endeavors of a multilateral nature, such as consolidated procurement; and (4) collecting and disseminating information to the public on areawide issues and problems. These metropolitan and substate organizations are backstopped by the National Association of Regional Councils (NARC), which issues publications and provides technical assistance to member organizations. As of early 1988 there were 525 councils of governments, of which 35 served metropolitan areas of 1 million population or over, 123 served areas of 300,000 to 1 million, and 367 served smaller metropolitan and other substate regional areas.[19]

Metropolitan areas are defined and classified by the Office of Management and Budget (OMB) in the Executive Office of the President. These areas are formally designated as "metropolitan statistical areas" (MSAs). Such areas either have a city or urbanized area of 50,000 population or over and a total area population of 100,000 or more. The area must include a central city and a central county, with other adjoining county areas included if they meet certain economic, demographic, and commuting criteria. MSAs are "stand-alone" metropolitan areas and are not part of larger populated areas. "Primary metropolitan statistical areas" (PMSAs) have 1 million or more population and may be surrounded by or adjoin "stand-alone" MSAs. "Consolidated metropolitan statistical areas" (CMSAs) are areas within which two or more PMSAs have been designated. (For example, the Dallas–Fort Worth CMSA has two PMSAs, each of which contains one central city and two or more counties.) As of May 1988 the OMB was formally identifying 262 MSAs, 71 PMSAs, and 20 CMSAs.[20]

Forms of Municipal and County Government

Separation of legislative/policy and managerial functions has been a continuing and often controversial issue in municipal government for most of this century. It became an increasingly important consideration in county government after

1946 when urban populations began to grow and to spread to suburban areas. Additionally, corrupt behavior of city officials in the early 1900s sparked a nationwide municipal reform movement, a part of which was the need for well-qualified professional management at the top of city government, coupled with merit-based rather than patronage selection of city employees.

Societal complexity brought an increasing number of functions and responsibilities to local governments, especially in heavily urbanized areas, creating a perceived need for (a) concentrated political accountability and (b) policy and managerial capability over a wide range of issues and activities. Especially in urban county government these needs encouraged in some areas a separation of legislative/policy-making and executive functions parallel to those provided in the U.S. Constitution and all of the state constitutions—an executive branch headed by a president or governor and a legislative body with only general control, through appointment confirmation and general legislative oversight processes, of executive departments. But in such a legislative-executive separation the need for a career-type professional administrator as second in command to the elected executive was recognized.

Municipal and township governments in the United States tend to follow two major forms. (1) The mayor-council form occurs in two types. The "strong-mayor" type consists of a multimember council elected by district, at large, or a combination of the two, and a mayor elected at large, who enjoys veto power over council-enacted legislation, subject to override, and who is responsible for carrying out the laws enacted by the council. Under the "weak-mayor" type, the mayor is either elected by the council and serves as a presiding officer or becomes mayor by virtue of receiving the largest number of votes in the councilmanic election. The mayor's duties under this form are largely ceremonial. This role is compatible with the council-manager form.

(2) Under the council-manager form, a manager is appointed by, and is responsible to, the council and serves as the chief administrative officer of the jurisdiction, overseeing personnel and financial administration and developing policy alternatives for council consideration. The manager is responsible for execution of policies and programs adopted by the council.

Two other forms of municipal government exist, one in declining usage and the other peculiar to the New England region. Under the commission form, responsibility for both administration and policy is vested in the multimember commission, with administration and oversight of the municipal departments divided among the commission members, each commissioner supervising one or more departments. Under the town meeting form, all voters meet as necessary to set policy and choose selectmen to carry out the adopted policies.

In county government there are three major forms. (1) The traditional commission form corresponds in general to the commission form of city government on the policy-making side. However, much of the functional administration is divided among independently elected officials, often specified in state constitutions (a sheriff for law enforcement, a treasurer for finance, an assessor, a collector of revenue, a prosecuting attorney, and so on). (2) The county administrator form corresponds to the council-manager form of city government. (3) The elected county executive form has a clear separation of legislative and executive functions, as in the strong-mayor type of mayor-council form of city government, with the executive serving as political and policy leader as well as representing the county government in relationships with neighboring jurisdictions and the state government. As in similar types of city government, a professionally qualified and career-type administrator often serves under the executive as the day-to-day manager of the county government's executive branch.

Two major issues are associated with the organizational form and the method of electing members of the governing bodies of local government. Proponents of the council-manager plan argue that it provides a more effectively managed and a less politicized atmosphere for the local government. Defenders of the strong-mayor, elected-executive forms contend that for more populous cities and counties, a clear legislative-executive separation is in the interests of policy leadership and managerial responsiveness to the citizenry. Political accountability is focused upon both branches and measured by the perceived efficacy of policy leadership and managerial effectiveness on the part of the executive and of policy-decision judgment on the part of the legislative body.

For many years the National Municipal League and other supporters of the council-manager plan argued strongly for at-large election of all governing body members in order that each member be required to take a jurisdiction-wide rather than a parochial, district-oriented view of policy issues. On the other side, it was argued that each area was entitled to a representative who understood its special needs and would help protect it from being overrun by an unsympathetic majority. At-large advocates often agreed that districts for residential qualification were desirable in order to meet the "needs familiarity" test and to assure geographic balance on the governing body.

In more recent years the issue of at-large versus district elections has been rendered moot in many jurisdictions having sizeable racial minority populations. Courts have held in a number of instances that exclusively at-large elections tend to discriminate against racial minorities. Consequently, an increasing number of city and urban county governments have been moving toward either district-based representation or a combination of at-large and district seats.

The National Civic League and the International City Management Association strongly support the council-manager concept of city and county government organization. The National League of Cities, with member cities of each form and comprising both mayors and council members, endorses both of the municipal forms. The U.S. Conference of Mayors, with mayor membership of cities of 30,000 and over, tends strongly toward the mayor-council form but supports also the concept of a professional chief administrative officer in charge of general management of the city government.

Issues of Local Government Formation and Boundary Change

State standards and policies governing the formation and incorporation of new units of local government—especially municipalities and special districts—and the municipal annexation of unincorporated territory have been crucial and contentious since the turn of the century. Many of the nation's cities acquired the bulk of their existing land areas through annexation; however, beginning in the early 1900s, some states, by statute or constitution, brought annexation of territory by larger cities to a virtual halt and kept it there, especially in the Northeast.

For example, in the 1980–86 period cities in New York and New Jersey annexed territory containing 200 people in each state, and in Pennsylvania the statewide total was 100. During the same period, Portland, Oregon, annexed nearly 50,000 people in 181 actions, Houston over 50,000 in 30 actions, Charlotte over 26,000 in 22, and Fresno 36,000 in 305. In 1986 alone a quarter-million persons and 750 square miles were added to cities across the country. In population added, the leading states were Texas, Oregon, North Carolina, California, Georgia, and Tennessee. There were 249 new incorporations in the 1980–86 period, less than half the 508 formations in the equivalent part of the seventies.[21]

Annexation and incorporation must be considered together; it is one thing for a city to annex unincorporated territory but quite another for one city to annex another, with such mergers extremely rare. After 1900, as large cities began to come under attack for corruption and other reasons, public opinion and state legislative attitudes about annexation changed drastically. People living on the urban fringe started to resist annexation as they contemplated city taxes and were concerned about the growing immigrant populations of the cities and the potential changes in political dominance. Then, as today, people wanted to move to less crowded surroundings and acquire a house on a nice lot. They saw incorporation as highly preferable to annexation. They could show that a little city of their own would be more economical than the big city.

Concurrently, pressures for redistricting the legislative bodies began to increase. Many legislatures at that time were apportioned on a strict population basis. Calls for change in this basis were aimed at reducing the voting power of big-city delegations, and constitutions were amended accordingly. Rural domination of state legislatures ensued and continued until the late sixties when the U.S. Supreme Court mandated a one-man, one-vote apportionment basis, citing the equal protection clause of the Fourteenth Amendment.

During the long period of rural domination, annexation laws were tightened and incorporation laws were liberalized. These developments set the pattern for population settlement and local government structure in the nation's metropolitan areas; the pattern was solidified in the wake of school integration decisions of the courts in the mid-fifties as millions of white residents deserted central cities for suburbia. In recent years racial integration has increased substantially in most metropolitan areas as higher-income black families have migrated to the suburbs. Income rather than race has become the major segregating factor in population distribution in many but not all metropolitan areas. Furthermore, modifications to income segregation are increasing in many suburban areas acquiring populations heterogeneous in both economic and ethnic characteristics.

Major readjustment of existing county and city boundaries in most states and metropolitan areas is beyond the pale of political feasibility. Also, in light of complexities of public facility ownership and bonded indebtedness, both legal and equity principles argue against such attempts. However, the major issue of incorporation remains, because metropolitan and other urbanized areas continue to grow. One school of thought holds that strict standards of fiscal viability, political accountability, and socioeconomic integration should be enacted by state legislatures to govern annexation, special-district formation, incorporation, and other boundary adjustments. This was presented in a 1969 report of the ACIR on *Urban America and the Federal System*, in which several criteria for a viable and equitable urban unit of general local government were enunciated. These included the following:

1. Providing a high degree of political unity to match the area's economic unity
2. Supplying efficiently a wide range of public services and a variety of community facilities
3. Providing on an equitable basis via taxation, user charges, and borrowing for at least a large part of its financial needs without predominant reliance upon state or federal assistance
4. Being clearly accountable to the people it serves, taxes, and regulates
5. Establishing reasonable priorities among the competing needs of various public programs
6. Adapting public policies to the diverse conditions of various parts of the area
7. Anticipating emerging problems and modifying governmental programs accordingly
8. Stimulating enlightened civic interest and participation in public affairs
9. Serving as a socially cohesive force, helping to promote intergroup harmony and reconciliation

The report went on to propose state legislation to "discourage the helter-skelter proliferation of small, non-viable units of local government" through the establishment of strict standards for new incorporations within metropolitan areas, the creation of local government boundary commissions at either the state or local level, and the withholding of state aid from "non-viable" units of local government.[22] Before and following the report, several states legislated the creation of state and/or local boundary review bodies, including Minnesota, Michigan, Oregon, California, and Washington, among others.

In general, the pace of new local unit formation slowed significantly in areas where strict formation standards began to apply. However, another view held that the choice of citizens as to how they wish to form and organize their local governments should be subject to minimal interference from overlying units of government. This parallels the economic and governmental theories of "public choice": people should be free to "vote with their feet" in selecting where and how to live, but should have a very high degree of self-determination as to local government structure and formation. If people living in an unincorporated area near an already existing city wish to form their own municipal unit rather than joining the city or continuing to get their public services from the county government, they should not be deterred in the attempt.

Although long apparent, the desirability of distinguishing between (a) providing for the delivery of a public service and (b) delivering the service began to be stressed with increasing frequency as the need for cost-effective local budgets appeared in the 1978–87 period. The pattern of small governments with limited or practically no service-delivery responsibility and the cost-effectiveness of such arrangements was demonstrated years ago in Los Angeles County, where many municipalities contracted with the county to deliver all or most of their services—most dramatically illustrated by the city of Lakewood with 100,000 population obtaining all of its services in that manner.[23] From the standpoint of budgetary economy, the advantages of contracting are overwhelming in many situations. (Contracting with other governments and the private sector for service delivery, along with the use of additional delivery alternatives, is explored in depth in chapter 3.) Also, it has been demonstrated that where government is the deliverer, the concerns of employee unions and other delivery-oriented issues tend to distract the governing body from the interests of citizen consumers.[24]

From a service-delivery standpoint, incorporation is fully warranted under a number of situations: (a) where a suitable range of urban services is not available and will not be made available by the overlying county through such measures as subordinate taxing areas; (b) where the overlying county does not have adequate planning and zoning regulations in effect so as to provide economic, aesthetic, and other protection to community residents and their properties and where it is not possible through county and adjoining city action to provide such protection; and (c) where the adjoining city does not have in place, or the capacity and willingness to immediately put into place, the necessary new or expanded public facilities to accommodate the potential annexees. This third condition often arises when an adjacent area without urban facilities or services desires to be annexed to a city but is refused admission because of the additional city costs to be incurred.

However great the economic and fiscal advantages of specialized or non- or limited-delivery local units may be—and they are substantial—the question of equity remains, and it has two major dimensions: service-delivery results and fiscal resource allocation results. Because of its economic efficiencies, the small-unit approach is equitable to all of its residents and is not injurious to its neighbors in terms of delivery results. This may or may not be the case in resource allocation.[25] This is especially a problem if the group wishing to incorporate has currently or prospectively at its disposal for property taxation a valuable commercial or industrial facility that employs people from many parts of the metropolitan area; the inequity is exacerbated greatly if the group succeeds in incorporation and then proceeds through the zoning process to exclude housing of a type needed or desired by the facility employees. Essentially, a relatively few people, occupying a high tax base, would have carved out an enclave within which residential taxes would be low or nonexistent and where only higher-income people could afford to live due to exclusionary zoning (such as two-acre lot requirements). (Certain of these kinds of zoning-motivated incorporation were found unconstitutional in a St. Louis County case in 1971.)[26]

The potential abuses of low population requirements and other liberal incorporation standards can be avoided while accommodating citizen demand for a small, noncongested community by permitting incorporation of limited-purpose municipalities. The function of the unit would be to provide and pay for whatever level and quality of services the residents desired; land use and certain other regulatory functions such as building codes would be carried out by the overlying county or township. This arrangement is prevalent in a considerable number of states where the "urban county" form exists. Limited-purpose municipalities within them provide whatever kind of service delivery, pricing, and taxing the residents prefer, while minimizing the fiscal equity problems arising from "zoning in" desirable revenue-producing activities and "zoning out" all housing and other public facilities needed by people working in and desiring to live in the community.

Special-district formation has been an issue of considerable controversy for several decades but more among local government officials and scholars of government than among citizens generally. The controversy usually is more localized and narrowly focused than arguments about the twin issues of incorporation and annexation because in most cases the question of whether a proposed district is needed revolves around a single service or two or more closely related services. The state and national organizations of general local governments and most public administration scholars and research organizations such as the ACIR took a generally negative position toward the formation of special districts, holding that they often are duplicative, fragment the local tax base, and as a rule "clutter up" the local government scene.

However, when such districts are examined on a category-by-category or case-by-case basis, many are found to be justified when measured against criteria of economy, effectiveness, and taxpayer choice and accountability. Some are not warranted at the outset when so measured but prove their worth subsequently. Many others are formed because of the inability or the unwillingness of general local government to render the desired service or to render it with the desired range of choice as to level and intensity. Often special districts can provide service more efficiently because of areal flexibility and their ability to finance capital expansion on a revenue bond basis. They are conducive to efficient consumption by providing a mechanism through which a diversity of taxpayer and consumer preferences can be met.[27]

Occasionally the function of a special district may be absorbed by the general local government, or the purpose of the district's establishment may have been achieved, but the district continues to exist on paper. This is confusing to citizens and causes difficulties in governmental reporting. Both critics and defenders of the special-district type of local government concur in the desirability of state legislation to "sunset" nonfunctioning districts. Also, most observers agree that with the increase in user-based financing through revenue bonds and service charges, the efficacy of the special-authority/district device is enhanced in a growing number of situations.

In general, district formation seems warranted when (1) the general-purpose city or county is unable or unwilling to provide the desired service, either directly or via the creation of a special taxing area; (2) the service area is dictated by topographical or other physical or technical factors that cause its boundaries to extend beyond one or more counties or to cover only parts of two or more such units; (3) the level and intensity of service available from the general-purpose government is less flexible than could be provided effectively by a public or private deliverer (for example, solid waste collection); and (4) a commingling of public and private funds is necessary in financing the facility or service, or independent borrowing in the bond market with dedicated revenues is required and the general government is without the necessary legal flexibility for the operation.[28]

From another point of view, the greater opportunities for civic and political participation by citizens of governmental units of smaller population often are undervalued by analysts of governmental structure and finance. James Michener presented this view most eloquently at a meeting of state legislators in Philadelphia in the early sixties by pointing out the lessened likelihood of the individual citizen feeling a personal attachment to, and interest in, a local government or school district as these units became consolidated into larger ones. Given the low voter participation of the electorate in most elections and the apparent public disdain and disinterest toward government, this factor of participation opportunity needs to be given careful consideration in local government reorganizations.[29]

DISCRETIONARY POWERS OF LOCAL GOVERNMENTS

As in the case with structure, the powers of local government come from the state through specific delegation, devolution, or other legal transfer. Also, the ways by which, and the degree to which, this power delegation or transfer occurs vary greatly from state to state. Data on the extent of delegation and changes in delegation are available primarily from the *Municipal Yearbook,* the biennial *Book of the States* of the Council of State Governments (CSG), and, on a less regular basis, the ACIR. Each *Municipal Yearbook* contains a section on major state actions taken during the preceding year or two that affect local governments, with special note of changes in state-local sharing of power and responsibility. Each edition of the *Book of the States* carries a description of constitutional amendments adopted in the preceding biennium, a major portion often applying to local government powers. Each edition also has a section on interstate and state-local relations.

Constitutional Devolution of Powers to Local Government

Although each state constitution contains provisions on local government, not all of them grant discretionary authority to local governments or to their legal voters. As of 1980 no powers were granted by the state constitution to any type of local government in Alabama, Arkansas, Delaware, Indiana, Kentucky, Mississippi, North Carolina, Vermont, and Virginia. However, relatively broad discretionary powers can be granted by statute in these and other states.[30]

Constitutional approaches to the powers of local units vacillated considerably from the end of the Revolutionary War to 1955; state concerns with local-unit efficiency and the prevention of corruption waxed and waned in individual states over this period. Initially, several states dealt with local powers grudgingly and in highly specific terms. Then concern arose about the evils of "special laws," and some states curbed the ability of the legislature to pass such laws, relying instead on general grants of power from the state to the local units. In 1921 the National Municipal League proposed a constitutional provision that divided state and local powers in specific terms in the constitution, with the legislature forbidden to change the local powers.

Under this "state within a state" approach it was necessary to amend the constitution in order to make any changes in the division of powers. Finally, in 1953 the American Municipal Association (now the National League of Cities) employed Dean Jefferson B. Fordham to draft new language that might be more flexible for both the state and the local governments. With two exceptions— civil law governing civil relations and the definition and punishment of a felony— the new language essentially delegated to municipal governments all powers capable of delegation, subject to state preemption by general act of the legislature. After 1953 all states except Oregon amending their constitutions in this subject area followed the Fordham approach. With the exception of Alaska, Montana, and Pennsylvania, which adopted the Fordham provision in toto, some powers additional to the civil relations and felony exceptions were also reserved to the state.

A precedent known as Dillon's Rule was another legal complication in the delegation of state power to local governments. It was promulgated by Judge John F. Dillon in 1868 and was later upheld by the U.S. Supreme Court in 1903 and 1923.[31] This rule held that any delegation by the state had to be explicit and had to be interpreted strictly. The effect of this rule has been mitigated substantially under the Fordham devolution of powers approach, wherein local units are free to act unless preempted by state legislative action.

At this point it is desirable to qualify the generalization that local governments have no inherent power and are creatures of the state in every sense of the word. State courts display from time to time a "strong localist orientation" when interpreting constitutional provisions on education finance and other subjects. They sometimes explicitly take into account the "values" associated with local control and discretion, thus by implication creating a state constitutional value to such discretion. However, the courts have not attempted to define these values in legal terms, so that a judicial commitment to the ideal of local self-government, although present, cannot be dissected into specific legal parts.[32]

Determining Factors in State Devolution

The 1981 ACIR report on *Measuring Local Discretionary Authority* lists the following factors that influence strongly the precise state allocation of powers to local units:[33]

1. The political culture of the state and its tradition of strong or weak counties, cities, and townships, both in general and in relation to one another.
2. The length of the state legislative session; if it is infrequent (every two years) and short (sixty days), it is unable to exercise much detailed control over local affairs.
3. The number of local units; if it is small, the legislature can dabble more easily.
4. The complexity and length of the state constitution and the ease of the amendment process.
5. The political strength of organizations of local officials and public service unions (in practically every state there is a state municipal league and, outside of New England, a state association of counties; in most larger cities and many urban county governments there is at least one public employee organization).

Advantages of Devolution

According to proponents, the advantages of a broad state grant of discretionary authority to local units of government include the following:

1. Local experimentation to solve problems and provide public services more expeditiously is encouraged.
2. Citizen interest in local affairs is stimulated because citizens then possess the authority to initiate discretionary functions and other activities.
3. Education of residents in civic affairs is promoted because major decisions are made at the local level.
4. The most expeditious solution of public problems is promoted since local citizens know the conditions best.
5. A major burden is removed from the state legislature, allowing it to concentrate on statewide issues and problems. In other words, local discretionary authority is a substitute for special legislation and also may be viewed as local initiative replacing dependence upon the legislature for permission to initiate action.

6. Citizen alienation from government that may result from decisions being made by state bureaucrats who are insensitive to the views of local residents may be reduced.

This list, taken from the 1981 ACIR report,[34] would find general support from both state executive officials and organizations of local governments and their officials. Depending on the state, some individual state legislators and some chairpersons of local government committees in the legislature favor a tighter rein on local governments. Also, in "special legislation" states, where bills affecting a particular county or city must clear the legislative delegation from that area, the legislators often favor less rather than more devolution.

But the apathy and sometimes hostility that in former years characterized the attitudes of state legislators toward local governments are in the process of change. In 1986 a task force of the National Conference of State Legislatures (NCSL) adopted a landmark report on state-local relations, beginning with the following recommendation.

Legislators should place a higher priority on state-local issues than has been done in the past. The time has come for states to change their attitudes toward local governments—to stop considering them as just another special interest group and to start treating them as partners in our federal system of providing services for citizens.[35]

General and Special Legislative Handling of Local Affairs

At one of the stages in evolving suitable state legislative and constitutional approaches to delegation of powers necessary for local self-government, a strong aversion to "special legislation" developed. There was concern about how legislative charters were granted to particular local units and about possible corrupting aspects of this procedure; the answer at the time was to place prohibitions in the constitution of "special legislation"—legislation directed toward a single local government.

However, it soon became apparent that for numerous specific powers or functions, it was neither possible nor reasonable to convey the same type or degree of power to a large city as to a crossroads village. Consequently, the constitutional prohibitions were modified, either by amendment or interpretation, to permit legislation to apply only to one or more classes of cities or towns/townships. Then the number of classifications began to multiply.

The study and survey conducted by Professor Joseph Zimmerman in providing the basis for the 1981 ACIR report on local discretionary authority found that nearly all of the fifty state constitutions were still prohibiting special legislation, with the exceptions of Colorado, Connecticut, Delaware, Florida, Idaho, Maine, North Carolina, South Dakota, and Vermont. Yet in practice most of the states are able, through the classification process or through outright special legislation, to deal with specific metropolitan areas and individual local governments.

In Maryland, for example, as in several other Southern and border states, a clear differentiation exists between ''local laws'' and general legislation of state-wide application. If a majority of the legislative delegation of each house from a particular county agrees on a bill that applies to and affects only its own county, the bill is automatically passed by each house of the legislature and signed by the governor, as a combination of legislative courtesy and political pragmatism. Of course, if such legislation is found legally flawed, it is either withdrawn or vetoed by the governor. Realistically, in much of the state constitutional language about special legislation, there is profuse differentiation with little difference.

Differential Power Devolution to Cities and Counties

Not surprisingly, the ACIR survey of local discretionary authority found that counties had been granted significantly fewer powers than cities by the state constitution and statutes, especially in regard to ability to alter the structure of government; exceptions to these findings were in Alaska, Oregon, and North Carolina, where cities and counties enjoyed comparable authority. Although not delineated in the survey, in a considerable number of states substantial discrimination is exercised between modernized or ''charter'' counties—usually in urban areas—and the general run of counties. Here the modernized counties are granted as much discretionary authority as cities, and often more, because of their greater areal scope, which is very important in dealing with urban functions.

Degrees and Kinds of Devolution

The ACIR staff constructed indices of residual state control, running from 1 (greatest degree of freedom from state control and consequent highest extent of devolution) to 5, based upon the detailed Zimmerman survey of state and local officials in each state. Separate indices were prepared for (1) structure, (2) functional areas, (3) finance, and (4) personnel, with a composite index merging the four on a weighted basis. The ACIR report cautioned against overreliance on differences in individual rankings but emphasized the composition of each end of the spectrum. Table 1.2 shows the top eight and bottom eight states in four aspects of discretionary authority: combined index for cities, counties, and other general units; cities only; counties only; and the relative fiscal dominance or passivity of the state in revenue burden sharing with the local units.

The full listing of states and the ratings given in the ACIR report are carried in appendix 1.B. In interpreting table 1.2 and appendix 1.B, the data currency factor must be kept in mind, despite the fact that changes in the scope and degree of discretionary authority devolved have occurred at a very slow pace. But change they do, as shown in the following extracts from the sections on changes affecting local government of the *Municipal Yearbook*:

More pluses than minuses were recorded—from a local government point of view—during the period mid–1982 to mid–1983 in the area of intergovernmental relations. In

Table 1.2

High- and Low-ranking States in Degree of Local Discretionary Authority Delegated or Devolved

(A) Combined Index	(B) Cities Only	(C) Counties Only	State Fiscal Domi- nance[a]
Eight Highest (In alphabetical order)			
Alaska	Connecticut	Alaska	2
Connectucut	Maryland	Arkansas	2
Maine	Maine	Delaware	1
Maryland	Michigan	Louisiana	2
North Carolina	Missouri	North Carolina	2
Oregon	North Carolina	Oregon	2
Pennsylvania	Oregon	Pennsylvania	1
Virginia	Texas	South Carolina	1
Eight Lowest			
Idaho	Idaho	Colorado	3
Iowa	Nevada	Idaho	2
Massachusetts	New Mexico	Massachusetts	1
Mississippi	New York	Missouri	2
Nevada	Rhode Island	Nebraska	3
New Mexico	South Dakota	Ohio	1
South Dakota	Vermont	Texas	1
West Virginia	West Virginia	Vermont	2

Source: ACIR, *Measuring Discretionary Authority*, Report M–131, November 1981, table 20, p. 59.

* Applies to states in column A. 1 = dominant. 2 = strong. 3 = modest to weak.

general, states accorded more power to local governments or relinquished strictures that had been applied formerly. States also introduced actions designed to increase their cooperation with local governments or to assist them in their operations. . . . The state supreme court in Wyoming upheld the extraterritorial power of cities to enforce ordinances outside their boundaries. . . . In Connecticut, the state commissioner of environmental quality will now be allowed to delegate to a municipality enforcement authority for certain environmental quality programs, including solid waste, air and tidal wetlands programs.[36]

Local governments were given the tools and flexibility to carry out their functions by their various state governments in 1985, continuing on a track identified last year. State actions—except in one area—physical planning—enhanced the ability of cities and counties to serve their citizens and to set their own agendas. . . . During 1984–85, three states increased home rule or expanded local government powers. . . . But as usual, there were areas where states preempted local decision making. For example, firearms regulation was taken away from local governments in at least three states.[37]

Decentralizing and devolutionary trends, coupled with uncertain economic and fiscal conditions . . . posed major challenges to state and local policy makers during the past year [1985–86]. . . . For example, new local government reorganization procedures were adopted in Georgia; in Maine, state financial support for regional commissions and councils of government was more than doubled. New laws were enacted in New Hampshire and Massachusetts to provide county home rule, and South Dakota counties were given authority to adopt the manager form of government. The South Dakota legislature also expanded the joint powers act to allow local governments to enter into agreements for any purpose other than taxation. . . . Major studies of local government functions and organization were launched in at least four states: Florida, New Jersey, Virginia and Washington.[38]

In 1987 liberalizing actions were taken to diversify local revenue sources; conversely, state control was increased in some states over local land use decisions that impeded public facility siting and use of mobile homes.[39]

Similarly, the *Book of the States, 1986–87 Edition,* reported the following changes:

1. A Colorado constitutional amendment allowing 5 percent of the registered voters to place a home-rule charter on the ballot

2. North Dakota's statute allowing county commissioners to authorize drafting of a home-rule charter

3. Alaska provisions in 1985 allowing certain classes of local government to adopt a home-rule charter

4. Court decisions in New Hampshire and New York striking down local vetoes of hazardous waste treatment and electric generating sites

5. Illinois legislation in 1984 allowing municipalities to sign cooperative agreements with any governmental or nonprofit community service unit for expenditures covering senior centers, transportation, and social services[40]

FINANCE: STATE TAXING, SPENDING, AND BORROWING LIMITS

State-Local Expenditures as Factors in Regional and State Economies

Table 1.3 relates state-local expenditures to personal income. State-by-state data appear in Appendix 1.C. It should be emphasized that the federal percentages shown in the table pertain only to the federal portion of the state-local expenditures—that is, the federal aid part of the state-local outlays. They include none of the other direct federal payments in the regions and states, such as defense contracts, federal payrolls, Social Security payments, and other outlays.

The highest states for total state-local expenditures were California, $76.1 billion; New York, $64.3 billion; Texas, $36.8 billion; Illinois, $27.2 billion; Pennsylvania, $26.0 billion; and Michigan, $25.4 billion. The lowest were Vermont, $1.4 billion; South Dakota, $1.6 billion; Delaware, $1.78 billion; North Dakota, $1.84 billion; and Idaho, $1.98 billion.

For percentage of state personal income, the highest were Alaska, 53.2 percent; Wyoming, 33.7; District of Columbia, 25.9; and New Mexico and Montana,

Table 1.3

Summary by Region of Federal, State, and Local Shares of State-Local Direct Expenditures and Their Proportion of State Personal Income, 1986

(Amounts in billions of dollars)

Region	Amount	% of P.I.	Percentage Financed By Fed.	State	Local
U. S.	$604.5	18.3%	19%	46%	35%
New England	32.8	16.3	20	53	27
Mideast	127.8	19.2	20	41	40
Great Lakes	101.1	17.8	19	46	35
Plains	42.6	18.3	18	46	36
Southeast	119.3	17.6	20	47	33
Southwest	56.5	17.8	15	43	42
Mountain	19.1	20.7	20	42	38
Far West*	97.3	18.3	18	50	31
Alaska	5.0	53.2	10	69	22
Hawaii	2.9	19.7	19	64	18

Source: ACIR, *Significant Features of Fiscal Federalism, 1988 Edition*. Report M–155–II. 1988, tables 47.1 and 48. (For state detail see Appendix 1.C.)

   * Excludes Alaska and Hawaii.

25.2. The lowest were New Hampshire, 13.9 percent; Connecticut, 14.4; Missouri, 14.6; Virginia, 15.4; and Florida, 15.9.

For state percentage of state-local direct general expenditures, the highest were Alaska, 69 percent; Hawaii, 64; New Mexico, 62; and Delaware and North Dakota, 58. The lowest were New York, 36 percent; New Hampshire and Colorado, 38 each; and Texas, 39. The variations in this category reflect widely varying state policies on state-local tax and other revenue sharing with local governments as well as other fiscal relations that do not appear in these expenditure data.

State-Local Sharing of Fiscal Responsibilities

The four major areas of state-local direct expenditures (funds spent directly by state and local governments) are public education, welfare, health and hospitals, and highways. In all four of these areas there are blocks of federal money— over one-half in the case of welfare. The federal government also expends large amounts directly in the welfare field on supplemental security income (federal payments directly to needy aged, blind, or disabled persons). In relation to total government outlays, the federal role is large in welfare, moderate in highways, and relatively small both in health and hospitals and in public education. Tables 1.4 and 1.5 show by region the federal, state, and local shares of state-local disbursements for welfare and highways and for health/hospitals and public education, respectively. State-by-state detail in these four expenditure areas is shown in appendices 1.D and 1.E.

Table 1.4
**Federal, State, and Local Shares of State-Local Spending for Welfare and
Highway Services and Facilities, Fiscal Year 1986**

(Amounts in billions of dollars)

Region	Welfare				Highways			
	Amt.	Fed.	St.	Loc.	Amt.	Fed.	St.	Loc.
U. S .	$74.6*	57%	36%	7%	$49.4*	29%	45%	26%
New England	5.2	50	47	3	2.4	27	44	29
Mideast	19.6	59	27	14	9.1	27	41	32
Gr. Lakes	15.2	51	42	7	7.9	27	48	25
Plains	5.0	54	34	12	5.0	27	43	30
Southeast	11.0	70	28	3	11.1	31	50	19
Southwest	4.0	57	36	7	5.9	25	46	29
Mountain	1.6	63	32	6	2.2	35	41	24
Far West**	12.4	52	44	4	5.2	34	37	29
Alaska	.3	39	56	6	.5	22	68	10
Hawaii	.3	58	40	1	.1	29	36	35

Source: ACIR, *Significant Features of Fiscal Federalism, 1988 Edition*, Report M–155–II, 1988,
tables 51 and 53.

* Does not include expenditures financed directly by the federal government ($25.8 billion
and $568 million for welfare and highways, respectively, in FY 1986).
** Excludes Alaska and Hawaii.

The federal share of welfare spending varies among regions. The Southwest
region shows a federal share identical with the U.S. average of 57 percent;
variations in the federal share in other regions range from 13 above in the
Southeast to 7 below for New England.

Welfare is predominantly a federal-state program and responsibility in most
states; however, it imposes a substantial load on local governments in several
states and a very heavy one in a few. As shown in appendix 1.D, states where
local governments bore more than a 20 percent share were Arizona, 31 percent;
Minnesota, 23 percent; New Hampshire, 22 percent; and New York, 21 percent.
States bearing 50 percent or more were Washington, 59 percent; Alaska, 56
percent; Massachusetts, 52 percent; and Maryland and Illinois, 50 percent each.
Low states were North Carolina, 14 percent; Arkansas and South Carolina, 15
percent; New York, 17 percent; and Idaho and Mississippi, 19 percent each.

For highways, the Mountain and Far West states enjoyed the highest federal
shares (35 and 34 percent against the national average of 29 percent). Otherwise,
regional averages varied little. For health and hospitals, the federal share varied
little among regions but greatly among states due to the impact that a single
large federally aided project could have on a single year's data from a small
state.

Educational expenditure data in table 1.5 and appendix 1.E are for 1985–86.
Aggregate national data for 1986–87 are summarized at this point.

Table 1.5

Federal, State, and Local Shares of State-Local Spending for Health/Hospitals and K–12 Public Education Facilities and Services, Fiscal Year 1986

(Amounts in billions of dollars)

Region	Health/Hospitals				K-12 Education*			
	Amt.	Fed.	St.	Loc.	Amt.	Fed.	St.	Loc.
U. S.	$53.6*	7%	48%	45%	$151.3*	6%	50%	44%
New England	2.6	9	73	18	8.2	5	40	55
Mideast	10.0	6	57	37	31.8	5	43	52
Gr. Lakes	8.4	7	49	44	26.1	5	42	53
Plains	3.8	7	45	48	10.5	6	44	50
Southeast	14.1	8	40	52	30.0	9	55	36
Southwest	4.6	8	41	50	15.9	8	51	41
Mountain	1.5	14	44	43	5.4	5	46	49
Far West **	8.2	6	46	48	23.4	7	67	26
Alaska	.1	4	70	26	.8	5	78	17
Hawaii	.2	9	88	3	.6	9	91	Neg

Source: ACIR, *Significant Features, 1988 Edition*, Report M–155–II, tables 55 and 57.

* Does not include health/hospital direct federal spending ($15,093 million in FY 1986).
** Excludes Alaska and Hawaii for health/hospitals; includes them for education.
Neg. = negligible (about $200,000).

Total direct governmental expenditures for education services (not including libraries) in 1986–87 were $240.7 billion, outranked only by Social Security payments ($282.2 billion) and national defense ($319.1 billion). Of the $240.7 billion, $32.0 billion was expended by the federal government and $226.7 billion by state-local governments. Of the latter sum, $60.2 billion went to higher education (state colleges and universities and state-local community colleges), with $50.7 billion spent by state governments, $7.6 billion by local community college or school districts, $1.5 billion by county governments, and $420 million by city governments. Libraries accounted for $3.6 billion nationally ($425 million federal, $3.3 billion state-local), with states spending $.6 billion, cities, $1.6 billion, counties, $.8 billion, special districts, $.4 billion and townships, $.2 billion. Within the overall education services category, nationally in 1987, the major portion, $156.8 billion, or nearly two-thirds, went for elementary and secondary (K–12) education.[41]

As of 1986, federal aid to K–12 education, totaling $15.13 billion was concentrated largely on students from disadvantaged homes (state personal income or reflections of that measure therefore being a factor in state allocations), with Mississippi receiving a 16 percent federal share and the Southeast region 9 percent in contrast to the national average of 6.5 percent. Except for South Dakota and New Mexico, all of the double-digit states for the federal component were in the Southeast region. The local share was highest in New Hampshire, 90 percent, followed by Nebraska, 67 percent, and Oregon, 66 percent. The highest state shares were: Hawaii, 91 percent; Alaska, 78 percent; and Washington, 76 percent and New Mexico, 75 percent.

Subsequent estimates by the National Education Association for school year 1986–87 tracked quite closely with the prior years. In comparative state and local proportions of nonfederal school revenue, the respective proportions for the two periods were 53.3 and 43.8 percent. States with highest state shares were Hawaii, 99.8 percent; New Mexico, 86.6 percent; Alaska, 81.5 percent; Alabama, 79.4 percent; Washington, 78.6 percent; and Kentucky, 78.0 percent. States with highest local shares were New Hampshire, 90.2 percent; Nebraska, 67.2 percent; Oregon, 66.6 percent; South Dakota, 62.4 percent; Missouri, 62.6 percent; Virginia, 60.6 percent; and Wisconsin, 60.4 percent.[42]

State Restrictions on Local Government Taxes and Spending

From the mid-seventies onward, public caution and often downright hostility toward increased taxing and spending by all levels of government became increasingly pronounced, especially at the state-local level. That this change in public opinion came about is not surprising; the preceding two decades had witnessed record expansions in public policy initiatives. Federally, the expansions began in the later Eisenhower years and lasted through the Nixon-Ford administrations, concentrated in the Great Society programs enacted during the Johnson period. In state and local governments, population increases, the flight to the suburbs spurred by a wide range of housing, transportation, and education incentives, and the need to meet the state-local matching requirements of the many new federal programs all combined to necessitate sizeable tax increases. For many years during the 1958–78 period, annual state-local spending increases outpaced annual GNP growth.

Consequently, in the early seventies public initiatives to place caps on local and state increases in expenditures and taxation began to be adopted, often by popular constitutional initiative rather than state legislative action. The rising tide of public demand for tighter fiscal control gained nationwide attention with the adoption of Proposition 13 in California as an amendment to the state constitution. Massachusetts, with its Proposition 2½, and several other states caught the "Prop–13" fever, with the result that by the late eighties nearly all states had fiscal control measures in place, directed primarily at local units, but with several applicable to the state government as well.

The principal types of limitations on local tax and expenditure powers now in effect in many states are as follows. The definitions used are those of the ACIR in its annual report on *Significant Features of Fiscal Federalism.*[43]

Overall property tax rate limit (OPTRL) refers to the maximum rate that may be applied against the assessed value of property without a vote of the local electorate. The rate is usually expressed as millionths per dollar of assessed

Table 1.6
Summary of State Restrictions on Local Government Tax and Expenditure Powers, 1985

Restriction Type	No. States Imposing	Date of Imposition Pre-1970	1970-77	Post-1977
PTRL - O$^1_2$	12	7	2	3
PTRL - S	31	24	5	2
PTLL	22	2	8	12
GRL	6	0	4	2
GEL	6	0	4	2
AIL	7	0	1	6
TIPT	14	1	7	6

Source: ACIR, *Significant Features of Fiscal Federalism, 1987 Edition*, Report M–151, June 1987, table 78, pp. 116–117, derived in turn from surveys of state revenue departments, October 1985.

Key: 1 = overall PTRL; 2 = specific PTRL.

value. The overall limit refers to the aggregate tax rate of all local governments— municipal, county, school districts, and special districts (if applicable).

Specific property tax rate limit (SPTRL) refers to limits on individual types of local governments (that is, separate limits for cities, counties, and so on) or limits on narrowly defined services (excluding debt).

Property tax levy limit (PTLL) refers to the maximum number of dollars of revenue that a jurisdiction can raise from the property tax. This is typically enacted as an allowed annual percentage increase in the total dollars raised in the jurisdiction from the property tax levy.

General revenue limit (GRL) refers to the total dollar amount of revenue from both property and nonproperty tax sources that a local government is allowed to collect during a fiscal year.

General expenditure limit (GEL) refers to the maximum number of dollars that a jurisdiction can either appropriate or spend during a fiscal year. Usually this is legislated as an allowed annual percentage increase in operating expenses.

Assessment increase limits (AIL) protect taxpayers from escalating tax bills caused by appreciating property values. Such limits on assessment increases force local governments to increase tax rates for needed additional revenue rather than rely on the automatic revenue windfall caused by rising property values— often induced by inflation.

Full disclosure or truth-in-property taxation (TIPT) refers to a procedure to promote public discussion and political accountability through advertised public hearings.

Table 1.6 summarizes limitations in place in late 1985; state-by-state detail is shown in appendix 1.F.

Limitations on the number of dollars of property taxes collected, in contrast to rate limitations, came into vogue subsequent to 1977; these limitations are impossible to evade by rate shuffling and catch automatic increases due to population or economic growth, inflation-induced or other increases in property values, or other upward external causes of growth in the assessable base. A levy limitation drives the local government to (a) nonproperty taxes, which usually require state legislative approval, or (b) user charges or other nontax revenue sources.

The state-by-state table in appendix 1.F shows that only five states were without any of the listed restrictions on local government revenue and expenditures; interestingly, four were in New England—Maine, New Hampshire, Vermont, and Connecticut.

State Limitations on Local Government Borrowing

State and local government long-term (more than one year) debt includes "general-obligation" (GO) bonds, guaranteed by the taxing power of the governments, as well as nonguaranteed or "revenue" indebtedness that pledges only some nontax source—for example, rents, charges, or tolls related to the bond purpose—as credit. In recent years nonguaranteed debt has grown dramatically, especially mortgage revenue, pollution control, and industrial revenue bonds. Most state constitutions, statutes, or both place certain restrictions on issuance of local GO debt, usually expressed in maximum debt outstanding as a percentage of the local property tax base.

For the fiscal year 1986–87, state and local governments combined had $718.7 billion of debt outstanding, with $131.8 billion issued that year and $82.1 billion retired. Of the amount outstanding, $201.5 billion was GO debt and the remainder revenue debt. Local governments had $453.0 billion outstanding, including $134.7 of GO debt.[44]

In limiting GO debt to a percentage of the local assessable property tax base, state restrictions define that base in three principal ways: (1) market value (if the local or state-imposed assessment rule is 50 percent of market, the market value of the local assessable base would be the assessed value of the base times two); (2) locally established assessed value, or the state-assessed value if the utility or other property is assessed by the state; (3) state-equalized assessed value (many states provide for equalization of local assessments by a state agency or board in order to minimize inequities arising from contrasting conservativeness or liberality of the local assessor).

In addition to a percentage of property base type of limitation, several states require local voter approval of the issuance of guaranteed (GO) debt; in some cases, instead of voter approval, an extraordinary majority of the local governing board must approve the issuance. In 1986, referenda requirements included the following: California—two-thirds voter approval for all cities, counties, and school districts; Delaware—approval of extraordinary majority of governing body; Idaho counties—debt incurred in a year cannot exceed revenue for year without two-thirds voter approval; Missouri counties and cities—debt can exceed percentage limit by up to 5 to 10 percent by two-thirds voter approval; New York—three-fifths voter approval required for school district debt; Tennessee—three-fourths referendum majority required for industrial building bonds; Virginia counties—referendum approval required for all GO bonds.[45]

For a long time, particularly before 1977, the conventional policy thinking of many students of government and public administration and many local government officials held that there should be no state-imposed restrictions on local tax rates, expenditure amounts, or issuances of debt. If the governing body spent, borrowed, or taxed too much, its members would be turned out of office at the next election. This belief was supported over a considerable period by the ACIR and organizations of local government. Pro and con arguments on this issue are presented in chapter 2 as part of the challenge of governance in an era of resource scarcity and the question of whether or not fiscal parameters to representative democracy are desirable.

State Financial Mandates upon Local Governments

While state governments are assisting local governments financially with one hand, they often are mandating local governments to make financial outlays with the other—costs that the local government probably would not incur were it not ordered to do so by the state. As state and local growth in population and economic activity occurs, new needs arise in health, law enforcement, and other functions. As a result, state legislation is enacted to ensure that new public functions are carried out and appropriate responsibilities exercised at the local level. By this means the state moves toward usually desirable economic and social goals.

Often, however, other mandates reflect the political inability of the state legislatures to resist pressures of local interest groups—churches, fire and police personnel, teachers, charitable organizations, and others. Resulting laws are passed ordering local governments across the state to increase pay and pensions, decrease working hours, remove real estate owned by various nonprofit organizations from the tax rolls, or to take other actions that increase the budget of the local government. The ACIR has classified these mandates into five groups:

1. "Rules of the game" mandates that relate to the organization and procedures of local government, holding of elections, and the enforcement of the state criminal code within the local unit's boundaries

2. "Spillover" mandates that deal with new programs or enrichment of government programs in health, environment, and other fields, where statewide uniformity of treatment is required from equity or legal standpoints

3. "Interlocal equity" mandates that require localities to act or refrain from acting in order to avoid injury to or conflict with neighboring jurisdictions, as in environmental standards or tax assessment procedures

4. "Loss of local tax base" mandates where the state removes property from the local tax base, such as exemption of property of veterans' organizations from the property tax and food or medicine from the local sales tax

5. "Personnel benefit" mandates where the state enriches local government salary or wage levels, working conditions, or pension benefits for selected groups of employees of local units.[46]

Regardless of their merits of purpose, these kinds of mandates, especially the last two, constitute interference in areas that are otherwise designated as pre-rogatives of local governments, either in state constitutions or statutes. In the same ACIR report that classified the mandates, 1976 survey results found the most expenditure mandates to exist in New York (60 out of 77 possibilities), California (52), Minnesota (51), and Wisconsin (50). The fewest were imposed in West Virginia (8) and Alabama (11), along with several other Southern and border states. Responding to pressures from state and national organizations of local government, ACIR, and others, states began to examine their mandate procedures and to adopt remedial legislation. Many adopted legislative proce-dures requiring a fiscal note be attached to any bill with mandating provisions, such note to indicate the extent of increased cost the bill would impose on local units of government. Some other states began to adopt statutes or constitutional amendments that required the state to reimburse the local units for all or part of costs attributable to certain types of mandates. By 1988, a General Accounting Office (GAO) study found that one-third of the states had adopted a reimburse-ment requirement.[47]

The 1984–85 *Book of the States* reported the approval in 1984 by voters in two states of constitutional amendments related to state mandates and associated costs to local governments. New Hampshire voters ratified an amendment re-quiring state reimbursement of mandated costs, and New Mexico approved an amendment stipulating either reimbursement or the provision of a new revenue source to cover the cost of the mandated service.[48]

The 1986 report of the Task Force on State-Local Relations of the National Conference of State Legislatures stated in regard to mandates: "State govern-ments impose many costly requirements on local governments. In view of the harsh new fiscal environment faced by state and local governments, the Task Force recommends that states review their mandates on local governments . . . [and] consider relaxing or eliminating those requirements and in some cases assuming the cost of complying with them."[49]

State Financial Aid to Local Governments

Even at the height of federal aid to local governments (the 1977–79 period under most measures, centering on 1978 as the peak), state aid to these units far exceeded federal aid. This was true on an aggregated basis for each state, but for individual cities or counties, the federal aid often exceeded state aid. For the general-purpose units of government, the significance of state aid is under-played in most states because of the large amounts of state money going to elementary and secondary education. While such aid does not show up in city, county, or township budgets, it affects greatly the perception of the individual citizen of his or her total local tax burden.

Although the magnitudes of state aid to local governments increased greatly over the 1974–85 period, the dominance of education aid showed little change. The percentage of state aid for major local purposes in 1974 was as follows: state-local revenue sharing and other general support, 10.5 percent; education, 59.0 percent; public welfare, 15.3 percent; highways, 7.0 percent; and "other," 7.5 percent. By 1984 general support had dropped to 9.9 percent; education had grown to 62.3 percent; welfare was down to 11.0 percent; highways were down to 5.2 percent; and "other" was up to 10.0 percent.[50]

However, when local government general revenue as a whole is examined, the role of state aid is striking. For the nation as a whole in 1986–87, it comprised the largest single segment, 29.1 percent of total revenue, compared to 24.8 percent for property taxes, 4.2 percent for federal aid. (Of the federal portion, more than one-eighth was general revenue sharing, which ceased in 1987.)[51]

FINANCE: REVENUE SOURCES AND PUBLIC ATTITUDES

Due to the wide variety of taxes, charges, and other sources of revenue used by state and local governments, it is necessary at the outset of this review to state the definition of each of these sources. Since most of the revenue data used here will be taken directly from Census Bureau reports or from other reports based on census data, the definitions used are those of the Census Bureau unless otherwise noted.[52]

Revenue Source Definitions

Tax and other monies coming into governments or other public entities constitute "revenue," in contrast to "income" as used in personal budgeting and corporate finance. Governmental revenue as reported by the census is subdivided as follows.

Revenue includes all amounts of money received by a government from external sources—net of refunds and other correcting transactions—other than from issuance of debt, liquidation of investments, and as agency and private trust transactions. Revenue excludes noncash transactions such as in-kind commodities or services. Revenue is divided into four major categories: (1) general revenue; (2) utility; (3) liquor store; and (4) insurance trust.

General revenue comprises all government revenue except utility, liquor store, and insurance trust revenue. General revenue is divided into two categories: (1) intergovernmental revenue and (2) general revenue from own sources.

Intergovernmental revenue comprises amounts received from other governments as fiscal aid in the form of general support and shared revenues, grants-in-aid for specific functions or purposes, and specific services for the paying government (for example, care of prisoners or contract research) or in lieu of taxes. Its principal categories are federal aid to state and/or local governments, state aid to local governments, and at the local level, interlocal grants or contracts.

Own source revenue is raised internally by the governmental unit through its own actions—imposition of taxes, fees, charges, fines, and so on. It comprises three major categories: (1) tax revenue, (2) current charges, and (3) miscellaneous general revenue.

Tax revenues are compulsory contributions exacted by a government for public purposes, except employee and employer assessments for retirement and social insurance purposes (insurance trust revenue). Tax revenue is general revenue and comprises amounts received, including interest and penalties but excluding protested amounts and refunds, from all taxes imposed by a government. It excludes "tax shares," such as the local share of a state amusement tax. Such a share is intergovernmental revenue, not own source tax revenue. For purposes of this chapter, taxes are divided into four major groups: (1) property, (2) sales, (3) income, and (4) miscellaneous taxes.

Property taxes are imposed on owners of property and calculated on the basis of its value. They include taxes related to property as a whole, real property, personal property, tangible property, and intangible property and may be imposed at a single rate or at classified rates or on selected property such as motor vehicles or certain intangibles.

Sales taxes include "licenses" at more than nominal rates, based on volume or value of transfers of goods or services and upon gross receipts or gross income. They comprise two major categories, general and selective.

Income taxes include individual income taxes measured by net income and taxes distinctively imposed on special types of income such as interest and dividends; and corporate income taxes on net income of corporations and unincorporated businesses.

Miscellaneous taxes include license taxes (motor vehicle registration, corporations, occupations, hunting and fishing, and so on); severance; death and gift; documentary and stock transfer; and "other taxes."

Current charges, the second major category of own source general revenue, are amounts received from the public for performance of specific services benefiting the person charged (such as parking fees, swimming pool use, college and school tuition charges, laboratory fees, school lunch sales, and park and museum admissions).

Miscellaneous general revenue, the last of the three own source revenue categories, includes (1) interest earnings, (2) special assessments, (3) sale of government property, and (4) "other general revenue."

Utility revenue comprises four major types: water, electricity, gas, and transit and any other revenue from sale of utility commodities and services to the public and to other governments, but not to the parent government.

Figure 1.1
State and Local Government Revenue by Major Financial Sector and Source, 1986–87

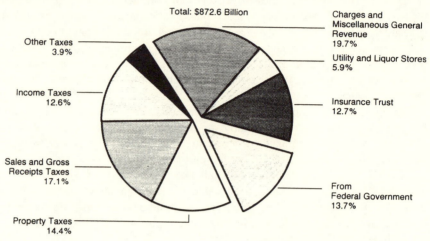

Total: $872.6 Billion

Charges and Miscellaneous General Revenue 19.7%

Utility and Liquor Stores 5.9%

Insurance Trust 12.7%

From Federal Government 13.7%

Property Taxes 14.4%

Sales and Gross Receipts Taxes 17.1%

Income Taxes 12.6%

Other Taxes 3.9%

Source: Bureau of the Census, *Government Finances in 1986–87*, November 1988, xix.

Liquor store revenue is from government liquor store operations.

Insurance trust revenue, the fourth of the major revenue categories, includes employer, employee, and other contributions to employee retirement, workers' compensation, and other insurance trust systems. Figure 1.1 portrays the combined use of major revenue sources by state and local governments.

Contrasting Revenue Sources of State and Local Governments

Two long-stated and increasingly incorrect allegations of scholars and state and local officials are that most federal revenue comes from the personal income tax and thereby the federal government has preempted the income tax for its purposes, and therefore it is only fair that the federal government share this source by rebating to states and localities a portion of personal income taxes collected from their areas (federal revenue sharing).

The first generalization probably should be the case, but is not because of the way the federal budget is set up. Federal government revenues from individual income taxes in Fiscal Year 1987 were $392.6 billion; Social Security tax revenues were $275.9 billion.[53] Given 1986 federal tax reform legislation reducing the nominal maximum income tax rate to 28 percent and the increase in Social Security taxes effective for 1988, it is doubtful that individual income taxes will long remain the leading source of federal revenues. (This illustrates one of the arguments advanced for separating insurance trust fund income and outgo from the federal budget and consequent readings of the annual deficit.)

The growing use of the personal income tax by state and local governments

Table 1.7
Use of General Revenue Sources by State and Local Governments, Combined and Separately, Fiscal Year 1987

(Billions of Dollars)

	State-Local Amount	State Amount	%	Local Amount	%
General Revenue	$686.2[a]	$419.5	100.0	$410.3	100.0
Federal Aid	115.0	95.5	22.8	19.5[b]	4.8
State Aid	---	---	---	136.8[b]	33.3
Tax Revenue	405.1	246.9	58.9	158.2	38.6
Property	121.2	4.6	1.0	116.6	28.4
Sales/Gross Receipts	144.3	119.8	28.6	24.5	6.0
Individual Income	83.7	76.0	18.1	7.7	1.9
Corporate Income	22.7	20.7	4.9	1.9	.5
Other Taxes	33.3	25.8	6.2	7.5	1.8
User Charges and Misc. General Revenue	166.0	77.1[c]	18.4	95.8	23.3

Source: Bureau of the Census, *Government Finances in 1986–87*. November 1988, table 2, p. 2.

[a] Pass-through of federal aid from state to local units and state aid to local governments causes separate totals of general revenue to exceed the combined total.
[b] Federal aid consists only of direct aid to local units; state aid includes some federal funds initially received by the state and passed on to local units.

underscores the inaccuracy of the second generalization. Of course, states are free to tax anything except customs duties and the flow of interstate commerce, and their use of that power is illustrated by the data presented in table 1.7. Two other generalizations about tax use are still correct, but one is getting chancy for the future. First, state governments tend to leave the property tax largely or exclusively to their local governments for use. Second, the property tax is the major source of own source revenue for local governments, but this is also getting to be a close call, especially in some of the more populous jurisdictions.

The table highlights (1) the importance to local governments of combined federal and state aid—38.1 percent of total local general revenue; (2) that the proportion of local general revenue to be raised from taxes and that coming from external aid is approximately equal; and (3) within the tax group, the relative continued dominance of the property tax as a tax source, as compared to income, sales, and other taxes, but likewise, the importance of user charges and the mix of "other taxes"—about 25 percent—as an important hunting ground for local governments in search of new revenue sources, especially in light of the apparent mood of state legislatures to be more inclined to authorize nonproperty sources of revenue for local government use than heretofore. Not shown in the table is $41.5 billion in net proceeds from state lottery operations in 23 states and the District of Columbia.[54] This is a rapidly growing revenue source for state gov-

Table 1.8

Percentage Distributions of Tax Revenue by Major Source, by Level and Type of Government, for 1957, 1977, and 1987

	Property Taxes			Sales Taxes			Income Taxes		
	1957	1977	1987	1957	1977	1987	1957	1977	1987
All Governments	13.0	14.9	12.8	20.9	20.0	20.4	60.4	59.6	61.7
Federal	0.0	0.0	0.0	15.9	9.5	9.0	81.3	86.8	88.3
State-Local	44.6	35.5	29.9	32.9	34.5	35.6	9.5	21.8	26.3
State	3.3	2.2	1.9	58.1	51.8	49.0	17.5	34.3	39.2
Local	86.7	80.5	73.7	7.2	11.1	15.5	1.3	5.0	6.1
City	72.7	60.0	49.1	15.8	22.3	28.2	3.1	11.9	14.6
County	93.7	81.2	73.5	2.8	12.4	18.8	0.0	2.4	2.7
School Districts	98.6	97.5	97.5	.1	.9	.9	.2	.7	.8
Townships	93.6	91.7	92.3	2.1	3.4	.2	.4	1.8	2.2
Special Dists.	100.0	91.2	72.4	0.0	7.6	24.0	0.0	0.0	0.0

Source: ACIR, *Significant Features of Fiscal Federalism 1987*, June 1987, table 32.3, pp. 44–45. Data computed by ACIR staff, based on Bureau of the Census, *Government Finances*, for 1957 and 1977. 1987 data: *Government Finances in 1986–87*, 1988, table 6, p. 7.

ernments, with four additional states beginning lotteries in FY 1988 and the total number of state and District of Columbia lotteries reaching 32 following the November 1988 elections.

Table 1.7 underscores the very light use of the property tax by state governments and the approaching parity between sales and income taxes as a state revenue source (28.6 and 23.0 percent, respectively). An examination of appendix 1.G shows (1), as of FY 1986, a considerable variation in state policy regarding local use of sales and individual income taxes and (2) regional and state differences in the extent of local use of the property tax. In 1986, seven states were not taxing earned or unearned income—Alaska, South Dakota, Florida, Texas, Wyoming, Nevada, and Washington. Connecticut, New Hampshire, and Tennessee were not taxing earned income (wages and salaries).

State and local tax policies as to sources of tax revenue changed greatly over the nearly three-decade period 1957–87. These changes are shown in table 1.8. They included the following:

1. At the state level, a drop in an already negligible use of the property tax, a moderate decline in the sales tax portion, and a more than doubled use of the combined corporate and individual income tax, which rose from 17.5 percent of all state tax revenue in 1957 to 39.2 percent in 1987.
2. At the city level, a drop in property tax dominance from 72.7 percent in 1957 to 49.1 percent in 1987 and increased income tax use from 3.1 to 14.6 percent.
3. Counties followed a similar but less marked trend: property tax reliance dropped from 93.7 to 73.5 percent. Replacing most of the drop was increased use of the sales tax, from 2.8 percent in 1957 to 18.8 percent in 1987.

The table does not include the "other taxes" category for the three selected

Table 1.9
Percentage Distribution by Region of Local Government General Revenue
Sources, Fiscal Year 1986

(Amounts in millions of dollars)

Region	Gen. Rev. Amount	Fed. Aid	State Aid	Local Taxes	User Charges	Other Rev.
U. S.	$380,662.6	5.4%	33.3%	38.1%	13.2%	10.0%
New England	16,731.0	7.6	30.5	49.1	8.6	4.3
Mideast	87,324.2	6.3	30.9	45.6	9.5	7.6
Great Lakes	61,948.8	5.5	32.6	41.3	12.7	8.0
Plains	25,762.6	4.9	30.8	36.2	15.0	13.1
Southeast	70,761.6	5.4	32.8	32.1	18.0	11.8
Southwest	36,560.9	4.5	29.5	37.7	13.7	14.6
Mountain	11,785.5	4.7	28.7	39.5	12.6	14.5
Far West*	67,131.4	4.2	42.3	29.8	14.0	9.7
Alaska	2,065.4	3.2	41.0	26.2	12.8	16.8
Hawaii	681.2	17.1	7.1	59.5	8.9	7.4

Source: ACIR, *Significant Features of Fiscal Federalism, 1988 Edition* M-155-II, table 65, derived
in turn from tapes of Governments Division, Bureau of the Census.

* Excludes Alaska and Hawaii.

years. From the same data sources and in the same year order as the table, the
percentages were as follows: all governments, 5.7, 5.6, 5.3; federal, 2.7, 3.7,
2.7; state-local, 13.0, 8.2, 8.6; state, 21.1, 11.7, 11.2; and local, 4.8, 3.4, 4.5.
There was moderate (4 to 8 percent) proportionate use in 1986 of the "other
taxes" category by the general units of local government and from 0 to 2 percent
for the special types. Also not shown on table 1.8 or any of the preceding tables
is a breakdown of revenue sources for special districts. For the 1985–86 period,
they were as follows in billions of dollars: total revenue, $44.7, made up largely
of $32.7 in general revenue and utility revenue of $11.6; external revenue, $9.4,
of which $4.9 was federal, $1.8 state, and $2.7 local; and own source revenue,
$23.3, of which $12.1 came from user charges, $4.8 from taxes, and $6.4 from
miscellaneous general revenue—mostly special assessments and interest earnings.[55]

Local Government Revenue Sources

Table 1.9 shows a percentage distribution by region of the principal sources
of general revenue of local government as among federal aid, state aid, locally
imposed taxes, user charges, and miscellaneous sources.

In the Southeast region in FY 1986, total taxes represented 32.1 percent of
local general revenue, with the property tax representing 22.1 percent in contrast
to user charges at 18.0 percent. Alabama used property taxes to the least extent
of any state; they accounted for only 9.5 percent of general revenue (compared

to sales tax at 9.7 percent, other taxes at 5.8 percent, and user charges at 22.8 percent).

State-by-state detail of this summary information is carried in appendix 1.G along with a breakdown of the proportionate yields from the various types of locally imposed taxes.[56] That appendix shows the five states in which state aid comprises the highest proportion of local general revenue: New Mexico, 49.2 percent; California, 44.3 percent; Delaware, 43.4 percent; West Virginia, 42.8 percent; and Wisconsin, 41.7 percent. The lowest states were Hawaii, 7.1 percent (a special case because of its unique state-local relationship); New Hampshire, 12.5 percent; and Nebraska, 19.4 percent.

Of the $126.8 billion of state aid to local governments in 1986, $29.5 billion went to counties, $24.6 billion to municipalities, $2.9 billion to townships, $68.0 billion to school districts, and $1.8 billion to special districts.[57] The extent to which the state accords revenue sharing or general support assistance to local governments is a major aspect of state aid as a revenue source for local units. A census breakdown by function of state intergovernmental payments to local governments in 1986, including federal aid to governments channeled through the state, not earmarked for particular local governments, shows the amounts in billions and relative percentages in descending order to be education, $81.9 and 62 percent; public welfare, $16.3 and 12.3; general support, $13.4 and 10.2; highways, $6.5 and 4.9; health, $4.6 and 3.5; transit subsidies, $1.7 and 1.3; corrections, $.9 and .7; sewerage, $.78 and .5; community development and housing, about $.7 and .5; police, $.4 and .3; and "other," $4.9 and 3.7. General support comprised about 10 percent of the total, but was third on the priority list—well behind education, but closely behind welfare, and far ahead of highways, health, and the other functional categories. The high states in amounts of general support ($1 billion or more each) were California, $1.856; New York, $1.134; New Jersey, $1.060; and Wisconsin, $1.050.[58]

Public Attitudes on Taxes

In 1972 the ACIR, using the Gallup organization under contract, began polling the general public on attitudes toward taxes. Table 1.10 shows some changing opinions. (The drop in unpopularity of the federal income tax—from 38 to 33 percent between 1985 and the summer of 1988—might be attributable, at least in part, to 1986 tax reform legislation.) The comparable 1987 figure was 30 percent.

OTHER ISSUES OF STATE-LOCAL STRUCTURE AND FINANCE

Issues of (1) use of special districts, (2) freedom to incorporate new municipalities, (3) state devolution of powers to local units of government, and (4) state mandating of local government expenditures have been discussed in this

Table 1.10
Answer to Question: Which Do You Think Is the Worst Tax, That Is, the Least Fair? (Percentage of U.S. Public)

	1972	1975	1978	1981	1985	1988
Federal Income Tax	19%	28%	30%	36%	38%	33%
Local Property Tax	45	29	32	33	24	28
State Sales Tax	13	23	18	14	16	18
State Income Tax	13	11	11	9	10	10
Don't Know	11	10	10	9	10	11

Source: ACIR, *Changing Public Attitudes on Governments and Taxes 1988*, S–17, September 1988, table 6, p. 4.

chapter, along with references to contrasting views. Other issues inherent in the state and local financial information presented in the foregoing sections will be dealt with in subsequent chapters. Questions as to the targeting of state financial aid to distressed communities, the use of equalizing formulas in such aid, and the relative priorities of the functions for which the aid is given will be examined in the next chapter, which deals with governance in an era of resource scarcity, as well as the issue of which of the two levels of government should assume primary responsibility for certain major functions. The question of whether public services should be financed from the general tax base or from charges levied upon the users of the service is reviewed in considerable detail in chapter 3. The question of how schools are best financed and the extent to which financial aid to school districts should be earmarked for disadvantaged pupils, wherever they are, or should be targeted to districts with the lowest fiscal capacity will be reviewed in chapter 5 in connection with the problems of the urban underclass and rural poverty.

However, a significant and controversial question associated with the preceding section of this chapter is most appropriately examined at this point—the extent to which state and local tax systems are fair and efficient and the kinds of changes that might be considered. This question comprises several component issues and relates to each of the three major taxes used by state and local government.

Non use or Limited Use of Income Taxes by Some States

The traditional approach by most states to the adoption of a personal income tax has been "never, until we have to." Although the state income tax is perceived as fair by most of the American public in the ACIR and other polls, residents of those states without an income tax feel very strongly the other way. A top federal bracket of 50 percent prior to 1986, the consistently unfavorable view of the public toward the federal tax, and the relatively high rates in some states created a hard-nosed anti–income tax attitude among residents in states without one. Indeed, one of the factors considered by retirees in moving to

Florida has been not only the climate, but the absence of a state income or death tax in that state.

Furthermore, most of the states without a significant income tax are able to do without one because of other circumstances that reduce the need for the additional revenue. Alaska formerly had an income tax but has not used it for several years because of the North Slope oil bonanza. The use of severance taxes on oil has served also as a substitute in Texas and Wyoming. Florida and Nevada are able to export to visitors a part of their tax burden via sales and casino taxes respectively. The states of Washington and South Dakota do not have satisfactory substitutes; in each case proposals for a state income tax have been voted down in referenda or in political campaigns with one candidate supporting—and losing.

States having high income tax rates yielded to pressures emanating from federal tax reform legislation and took action to reduce rates, broaden bases, and reduce the number of brackets.[59] Brackets and top rates for 1987 appear in Appendix 1.H. In 1986 the highest rate was 13.5 percent in New York, with other high rates in West Virginia and Iowa (13 percent). However, subsequent to the 1986 federal tax reform legislation, the high-bracket states nearly without exception lowered their top rate to single digits and also followed the federal lead by cutting the number of brackets by one-half or more.

Regressivity of the Sales Tax

This problem has been mitigated in a number of states by the exclusion of food and medicine from the taxable sales. In 1987 Florida, in search of desperately needed revenue, expanded the sales tax to cover a wide range of professional and other services. Most states have both an income and a sales tax, and where that is the case, the sales tax can be defended on the basis of balance. As of early 1988 only five states were without a sales tax—New Hampshire, Delaware, Montana, Oregon, and Alaska. New Hampshire had a 5 percent tax on interest and dividends; Delaware's top income tax rate was 8.8 percent; and Alaska had been able to forgo both a sales and an income tax due to oil resources. Oregon and Montana both had relatively high income taxes (top rates of 9 and 11 percent, respectively).

Property Tax Reform

This has long been an important and controversial issue in state and local elections. Most of the controversy arises from the assessment process. The NCSL's State-Local Relations Task Force in its 1986 report stated that the property tax "has a valid role to play in a balanced state-local tax system." The report went on to urge, however, that assessment systems be improved, that the poor be shielded from excessive property tax burdens, and that "truth-in-taxation" measures be enacted to "improve public understanding of why property tax payments may be increasing."[60] Major efforts to improve assessment systems have centered on state takeover of the entire assessment process, state assessment of utility property, appointment instead of election of assessors, statewide equalization of property tax assessments, and strengthening professional qualifications of assessors through examinations, licensing, and other means. Effective 1986 property tax rates—tax payment divided by market value—averaged 1.16 percent nationwide, with high states (2.0 percent and over) being Rhode Island, New Jersey, New York, Nebraska, and Michigan, and low states (.51 percent and below) being Louisiana, Alabama, and Hawaii.[61]

Overall Issue of State Capability

With the beginning of the New Deal and the active steps taken by the federal government to deal with economic and social issues, scholars and members of Congress alike began to predict the disappearance of the states as effective partners in the federal system. Luther Gulick is quoted as saying in 1933, "I do not predict that the states will go, but affirm that they have already gone."[62]

Although Gulick apparently was jesting, the attitude of many was that the states no longer mattered now that Washington was taking over the tough problems. The disaffection of local officials in urban areas grew to a high pitch following World War II when the suburbs were forming and the legislatures continued under rural domination due to the apportionment of seats according to counties or other areas rather than population. Laws in many Southern and border states that segregated the races became national issues. School desegregation decisions in the fifties and legislative reapportionment decisions and civil rights legislation in the sixties wrought great changes, not only in the South but in every state. But it took two decades for state governments as a whole to gain recognition as increasingly effective and powerful actors on the domestic scene.

In a 1985 report on *The Question of State Government Capability,* the ACIR found: "While progress has been uneven among the states and among indicators of improved state-local relations, ... overall, states are now more appreciative of local, and particularly urban problems than they have been in the past." In a formal recommendation the commission stated, without dissent, the following:

The Commission concludes that the states are pivotal actors in our federal system. The Commission, moreover, finds that the kinds of responses that the states—both individually and sometimes collectively—provide to the challenges facing them will determine the future resilience, effectiveness and political balance of our federal system. Finally, the Commission believes that governors and state legislatures must recognize the necessity for state leadership if future public policy challenges are to be successfully surmounted.[63]

On the other hand, although agreeing that some improvement in state-local relations had taken place, local government officials in a number of states continued to view the State House as alien territory. Some civic and community organization activists contended that both state and local governments were falling short on competence, performance, and sensitivity to the needs of poor people. "While they have received much more money and power . . . , state and local governments have not commensurately increased their capacity, perfor-mance, and accountability . . . have not exercised sound planning and adminis-trative skills, and have been insensitive to . . . low income neighborhoods. . . . The quality of local and state government personnel and administration, while substantially improving, has failed to keep up with new responsibilities [they] have assumed under block grants and federal decentralization."[64] In the ensuing chapters the particular ways that states have been meeting—or failing to meet— the difficult tasks they have been facing and will face in increasing numbers and intensity into and through the nineties will be examined closely, and an attempt will be made to assess their assets and shortcomings in a way that will be helpful as they and their associated local governments and their private-sector partners chart their future courses.

NOTES

1. Madison, J., "No. 45," *The Federalist Papers* (New York: Mentor Books. The New American Library of World Literature, 1961) 292–293.

2. U.S. Supreme Court, *National League of Cities v. Usery,* U.S. 833, 96 S Ct. 2465, 45 L. Ed. 2nd 245 (1976).

3. U.S. Supreme Court, *Garcia v. San Antonio Metropolitan Transit Authority,* 105 S Ct. 1005 (1985).

4. Bureau of the Census, unpublished data from March 1987 *Current Population Survey,* P–60, no. 156 Spring 1988, table LJ3.

5. U.S. Advisory Commission on Intergovernmental Relations (ACIR), *Significant Features of Fiscal Federalism, 1988 Edition,* Report M–155-I, December 1987, 2.

6. Bureau of the Census, *Government Finances in 1986–87,* GF86 No. 5, November 1988, table 2, p. 2.

7. Ibid.

8. U.S. Department of Justice, Bureau of Justice Statistics, *Correctional Populations in the United States, December 1986, 1988,* table 5.6.

9. Bureau of the Census, *Government Finances in 1985–86,* 2.

10. Mosk, S., "The Emerging Agenda in State Constitutional Law," *Intergovern-mental Perspective* (Spring 1987): 19–22. See also: ACIR, *State Constitutional Law: Cases and Materials,* M–159, October 1988.

11. National Municipal League, *Model State Constitution, 6th ed.* (New York: National Civic League, 1963), 3.

12. Council of State Governments (CSG), *Book of the States,* 1986–87 edition, vol. 26 (Lexington, Ky.: CSG, 1986), 14.

13. Bureau of the Census, *1987 Census of Governments, Governmental Organization,* Preliminary Report. GC 87–1 (P), November 1987, 1–7.

14. Bureau of the Census, *County Population Estimates, July 1, 1987,* Series P–26, no. 87-A, September, 1988.

15. See Hallman, H., *Neighborhoods: Their Place in Urban Life* (Newbury Park, Calif.: Sage, 1984); idem, "Defining Neighborhood," *National Civic Review,* October

1984, 428–429; Rieger, F., "Neighborhoods and Community Control: Effects of West German Consolidation," *National Civic Review*, October 1984, 446–450; Nauman, J., and Koehler, C., "Sacramento County/Community Councils: A New Partnership on Planning," *National Civic Review*, September–October 1983, 416–422; and Epstein, P., "How Citizen Participation Spruces Up Performance," *National Civic Review*, March/April 1987, 147–151 (examples in Portland, Oregon, Washington, D.C., Dayton, and New York).

16. Rosenberry, K., "Condominium and Homeowner Associations: Should They Be Treated like Mini-Governments?" *Zoning and Planning Report*, October 1985, 153–158.

17. Community Associations Institute, *Publications Catalog, 1988–89* (Alexandria, Va.: Community Associations Institute, October 1988).

18. Walker, D., "Snow White and the 17 Dwarfs: From Metro Cooperation to Governance," *National Civic Review*, January–February 1987, 14–28.

19. National Association of Regional Councils, *Directory of Regional Councils, 1987–88* (Washington, D.C.: National Association of Regional Councils, February 1987).

20. Office of Management and Budget (OMB), *Metropolitan Statistical Areas, 1986*, updated in Bureau of the Census press release, July 24, 1987, and by telephone with OMB, May 1988.

21. Miller, J., "Municipal Annexation and Boundary Change," *Municipal Year Book, 1988* (Washington, D.C.: International City Management Association, 1988), 59–67.

22. ACIR, *Urban America and the Federal System*, Report M–47, 1969, 82–87.

23. ACIR, *Governmental Structure, Organization, and Planning in Metropolitan Areas*, Report A–5, 1961, 25.

24. Downs, A., *Urban Problems and Prospects*, 2nd ed. (Chicago: Rand McNally, 1976), 227–242.

25. For contrasting views, see Merget, A., and Berger, R., "Equity as a Decision Rule in Local Services," in Rich, R., ed., *Analyzing Urban-Service Distributions* (Lexington, Mass.: Lexington Books, 1982), 21–44; and Ostrom, E., "Size and Performance in a Federal System," *Publius*, 6 (Spring 1976) 33–73.

26. *Park View Heights Corporation, et al. v. City of Black Jack, et al.*, Complaint, United States District Court for the Eastern District of Missouri, Eastern Division, January 7, 1971. Subsequently, *U.S. v. City of Black Jack*, 508 F2d 1179 (8th Cir. 1974), *cert. denied*, 4 ss U.S. 1042 (1975). Later, initial plaintiffs sought injunctive relief, and on August 28, 1979, the Eighth Circuit Court of Appeals held that the City of Black Jack must provide affirmative housing opportunities to overcome the discriminatory impact of its violation of the Fair Housing Act, as found in the earlier litigation. *Park View Heights Corp. v. City of Black Jack*, 8th Cir., no. 78–1660.

27. Downing, P., and DiLorenzo, T., "User Charges and Special Districts," in Aronson, J. R., and Schwartz, E., eds. *Management Policies in Local Government Finance*, 3rd ed. (Washington, D.C., ICMA, 1987), 277–284.

28. For contrasting views, see ACIR, *The Problem of Special Districts in American Government*, Report A–22, May 1964, and *Urban America and the Federal System*, 87; Colman, W., *Cities, Suburbs, and States* (New York: Free Press, 1975), 291; and Hawkins, R., *Self Government by District* (Stanford, Calif.: Hoover Institution Press, 1976).

29. On low voter turnout, see Miller, W., et al., *American National Election Study, 1984: Pre- and Post-Election Survey File* (Ann Arbor, Mich.: Inter-University Consortium for Political and Social Research, 1986), summarized in *National Civic Review*, (May–June, 1987) 193.

30. Except where otherwise indicated, data on the extent of power delegation in this chapter are drawn from ACIR, *Measuring Local Discretionary Authority,* Report M–131, November 1981. This report was prepared by Zimmerman, J. F., and the ACIR staff.

31. *City of Clinton v. Cedar Rapids and Missouri Railroad Company,* 24 Iowa 455 at 461 (1868); *Atkins v. Kansas,* 191 U.S. 207 at 220–21 (1903); and *City of Trenton v. New Jersey,* 262 U.S. 182 (1923).

32. Briffault, R., "State-Local Relations and Constitutional Law," *Intergovernmental Perspective,* Summer–Fall 1987, 10–17.

33. ACIR, *Measuring Local Discretionary Authority,* 12–13.

34. Ibid., 18.

35. National Conference of State Legislatures (NCSL), *Recommendations of the Task Force on State-Local Relations* (Denver, Colo.: National Conference on State Legislatures, August 5, 1986), 2.

36. Kouba, D., "Significant State Actions Affecting Local Governments," *Municipal Yearbook, 1984,* January 1984, 87–88.

37. Muzychenko, J., "Significant State Actions Affecting Local Governments," *Municipal Yearbook, 1986,* 57.

38. Roberts, J., "Significant State Actions Affecting Local Governments," *Municipal Yearbook, 1987,* 54–55.

39. Katsuyama, B., "State Actions Affecting . . . ," *Municipal Yearbook, 1988,* 86–99.

40. Zimmerman, J., "Developments in State-Local Relations, 1984–85," *Book of the States, 1986–87 Edition,* 433–437.

41. Bureau of the Census, *Government Finances in 1986–87,* tables 1, 2, 5, 10, pp. 1, 2, 6, 10, for national intergovernmental data. ACIR, *Significant Features, 1988 Edition* M–155 II for state by state data.

42. National Education Association, *Estimates of School Statistics, 1987–88* (Washington, D.C.: National Education Association, April 1988), 7.

43. ACIR, *Significant Features of Fiscal Federalism, 1987 Edition,* table 64, pp. 116–117.

44. Bureau of the Census, *Government Finances in 1986–87,* table 13, p. 16.

45. ACIR, *Significant Features of Fiscal Federalism, 1987 Edition,* table 80, pp. 118–125.

46. ACIR, *The Question of State Government Capability,* Report A–98, January 1985, 296–302. See also Lovell, C., Kneisel, R., Neiman, M., Rose, A., and Tobin, C., *Federal and State Mandating on Local Governments: An Exploration of Issues and Impacts,* Final Report to the National Science Foundation (Riverside: Graduate School of Administration, University of California, Riverside, June 20, 1979).

47. General Accounting Office (GAO), *Legislative Mandates: State Experiences Offer Insights for Federal Action* (GAO-HRA–88–75) September 1988.

48. Zimmerman, J., "Developments in State-Local Relations in 1984–85," *Book of the States, 1986–87 Edition,* 433.

49. NCSL, *Report of State Recommendations of the Task Force on State-Local Relations,* August 5, 1986, 8.

50. Kane, V., "State Aid to Local Governments," *Book of the States, 1986–87 Edition,* 438–452.

51. Bureau of the Census, *Government Finances in 1986–87,* tables 5 and 6, pp. 6 and 7.

52. Ibid., app. A, pp. 113–123.

53. Ibid., table 2, p. 2.

54. Bureau of the Census, *State Government Finances in 1987,* GF87, no. 3, table 35, p. 55, and *Government Finances in 1985–86,* p. ix.

55. Bureau of the Census, *Government Finances, 1985–86* table 29, p. 46.

56. ACIR, *Significant Features of Fiscal Federalism, 1988 Edition.* M–155 II. table 65, p. 70.

57. Bureau of the Census, *Government Finances in 1985–86* table 29, p. 46.

58. Bureau of the Census, *State Government Finances in 1986,* table 14, p. 31.

59. Gold, S., "The State Government Response to Federal Income Tax Reform: Indications from the States that Completed Their Work Early," *National Tax Journal,* September 1987, 431–444.

60. NCSL, *Recommendations of the Task Force on State-Local Relations,* 70.

61. ACIR, *Significant Features of Fiscal Federalism, 1988 Edition.* M–155 I, p. 70.

62. ACIR, *Question of State Government Capability,* 1.

63. Ibid., 400–401.

64. Eisenberg, P., "Governance and the Excluded," *National Civic Review,* September–October 1987, 374–382.

Chapter 2 ——————————————————————

Domestic Governance in an Era of Resource Scarcity

The seventies and eighties were tumultuous times for state and local governments. In succession occurred a continued rapid expansion of the role of government in American society; a period of tax revolt, recession, partial recovery, inflation, and more recession; and recovery and steady economic growth accompanied by increasingly worrisome fiscal and economic dilemmas. Cutting across the period was a sharp rise, then an inexorable decline in federal aid to state and local governments (fiscal years 1970–88), as shown in figure 2.1. Most state and local governments, and indeed most central cities, met these times with striking resiliency and during the later period were building up their fiscal reserves. This indicated a more conservative course, due at least in part to lessons learned from the excesses of the seventies.[1]

As testing and trying as the past two decades have been for state-local legislators and executives, the nineties will offer no respite from painful decisions—most of which will involve the cutting of service and other expenditure cloth to fit the resource pattern. Major problems and problem areas that developed in the late eighties will demand resolute action, while others just beginning to surface will need to be met head-on. Finally, due to the rapid pace of change, presently unknown and unforeseen issues will have arisen and will acquire center stage by century's end.

In this chapter, an overview of the major present and projected revenue-expenditure gaps will be followed by an examination of the means by which financial responsibilities among national, state, and local areas of government might be realigned or sorted out. Subsequently, the following issues and problems will be explored: (1) whether or not fiscal parameters for representative democracy have become necessary; (2) five key issues of economic and fiscal equity; (3) fiscal policy and management issues; and (4) the process of evaluating existing programs and implementing cutback management.

Figure 2.1
The Rise and Decline of Federal Aid, 1958–88 (As a Percentage of State-Local Outlays)

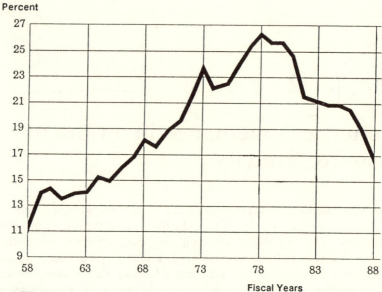

Source: ACIR Staff.

OVERVIEW OF STATE-LOCAL FISCAL NEEDS AND RESOURCES IN THE NINETIES

First, it is necessary to state the underlying economic and fiscal assumptions concerning the national economy so that the reader may make appropriate judgments about the efficacy of particular alternative policy approaches. A continued constrained federal role is assumed. In the event that (*a*) a federal value-added tax were enacted, (*b*) the federal deficit were reduced greatly, and (*c*) the public through its representatives in Congress expressed a desire and willingness for the initiation of national health insurance, federalization of welfare and Medicaid costs, and multiplication of the federal financial role in public education by a factor of three or four, the resulting agenda for state and local governments would be vastly different from the one to be examined here. It would be dominated by considerations of how best to deploy the considerable state-local resources and the extent to which the respective tax burdens upon their citizens could be lightened. Under any circumstances, the performance of the U.S. economy will determine to a significant but not conclusive extent the range of fiscal problems and potential alternative approaches thereto.

National Economic and Fiscal Assumptions

More than likely, the national economy over the next few years will be characterized by

- Modest to slow economic growth, interspersed with recessions and real or feared flare-ups of inflation;
- a slow movement of the nation's trade balance away from a state of peril toward uneasy stability;
- gradual disinvestment in, and diversification of, the nation's agricultural economy; a continued but slowed shift from manufacturing to services, with some areas of manufacturing resurgence, including the emergence of new materials and processes; and a continued shift from labor- to capital-intensive investment;
- a quickening pace of technological change;
- a continued increase in health costs arising from an aging population and advances in medical technology;
- incremental progress on chronic unemployment and welfare reform;
- a slowed growth rate in public expenditure, braked by international imperatives at the national level and intense competition among needs claimants at the state-local level, with further commingling of public and private spending for public purposes;
- a painful financial shakeout in national financial institutions; and
- a continuation of relatively high real interest rates.

As a frame of reference for these guesses, the January 1988 economic projections through 1993 by the U.S. Congressional Budget Office were as follows: real GNP growth, 2.6–7 percent; GNP deflator, 4.1 percent; unemployment, 6.2–5.8 percent; and ten-year interest rate on Treasury notes, 9.5 percent, declining to 7.4 percent.[2]

Major New or Intensified Fiscal Needs

The late eighties found the states and their local governments struggling to keep their expenditures within available tax and other revenues. Table 2.1 shows real (adjusted for inflation) budget increases and decreases for state and federal governments during the 1979–89 decade. These data were drawn from a survey of the National Association of State Budget Officers and illustrate the extent to which the slowdown in state spending paralleled the behavior of the national economy, while the net federal increase was nearly double that of the states.

In chapter 1 fiscal expenditure data were presented for the public service functions for which state-local governments combined were expending the largest amounts. The leading functions for combined general expenditure (excluding water, gas, electric, and transit utility expenditures) in descending order were

Table 2.1
Comparisons of State and Federal Real Annual Budget Changes for Selected Years, 1979–89

Year	State	Federal
1979	1.5%	1.9%
1982	-1.1	1.5
1984	3.3	2.3
1986	3.7	3.0
1987	2.6	.9
1988*	2.3	2.8
1989*	1.4	1.3
1979–87 Average	1.6	3.0

Source: National Governors' Association—National Association of State Budget Officers, *Fiscal Survey of the States*, March 1988, table 1, p. 3.

* Estimated.

(1) K–12 education; (2) welfare; (3) higher education; (4) highways; (5) hospitals; (6) police protection; (7) health services; (8) corrections; (9) sewerage; and (10) housing and community development. With the addition of public higher education and corrections for state government and fire protection for local governments, the resulting thirteen functions would accommodate the priorities of both state and local governments if each were listed separately (except that local governments would not be very much concerned with higher education, and state governments would be concerned only with fire prevention and not at all with fire fighting except for forest fires).[3] State aid, as noted earlier, is concentrated in the functions of joint concern: K–12, health, welfare, highways, and community development.

As of early 1988, spending priorities expressed by governors were concentrated in education (thirty-one states); economic development (twenty-two); and human resource programs (15): Alabama (infant mortality); Arizona and Delaware (children and pregnant women); Florida, Hawaii, and Idaho (prenatal care); Illinois, Iowa, Kentucky, Maine, and Missouri (welfare reform); Massachusetts (health insurance, homeless, day care); New York (AIDS, Medicaid eligibility expansion); and Tennessee and Virginia (indigent health care). Six states were emphasizing environmental programs (Connecticut, Delaware, New York, Pennsylvania, Rhode Island, and Vermont).[4]

The expenditure areas selected for closer examination in the course of this book are the following:

• Economic adjustment assistance, arising from continuing structural change in agriculture and associated industries, as well as manufacturing

- Health needs, arising from (1) an aging population and consequent long-term care needs of the very old (those over eighty); (2) new medical technology; (3) size of the uninsured population, especially the portion comprising the "working poor" and the lower part of the middle-income class; and (4) Medicaid and other health components of the urban underclass problem, including AIDS and intravenous (IV) drug use
- Public physical infrastructure needs, arising from (1) replacement and retirement in stagnant or declining areas and (2) new and shifting populations in growth areas
- Housing for low-income families and shelter, in institutions or otherwise, of the growing homeless population
- Inner city schools, a fiscal and social disaster area.
- Crime drugs, and corrections—an area of increasingly critical problems with few effective mitigants in sight
- Public welfare—along with the state-local share of the federal Medicaid program, the expenditure category ranking consistently as second to education
- Day care—an expenditure area cutting across all income classes as the proportion of women of child-bearing age in the labor force continues to increase and as day-care availability, or its lack, becomes an increasingly important component of welfare reform and the movement of persons from public assistance rolls into the labor force

These areas ignore partially, but not entirely, those functional areas not supported from the general tax base. The physical infrastructure area is huge fiscally and monumental managerially; some of its components, such as hazardous waste disposal, depend on a large share of "responsible party" financing, which depends in turn on the vagaries of insurance coverage and regulation and tort liability—both areas nearly exclusively under state regulation. The physical infrastructure category and its financing will be covered in chapter 4, as will day-care services for working women, economic adjustment assistance, and low/moderate-income housing and shelter of the homeless. The health, early childhood and K–12 education, and welfare components of the urban underclass and rural poverty problem will be addressed in chapter 5, and the insurance/tort liability issue in chapter 6.

Fiscal Resource Problems and Opportunities

"Fiscal resources" is a broad term; it is not synonymous with "fiscal revenues." To the extent that nongovernmental assets and processes are employed to secure a public objective, a public resource has been drawn upon, but money has not flowed into or out of a government treasury. The role of the private profit and nonprofit sectors in the achievement of public objectives is dealt with in various contexts in this book; it is increasingly evident at many stages of public policy formulation and execution.

"Fiscal revenues" are monies that come into public treasuries from taxes, fees, charges, aid from other levels of government, interest on idle cash balances, and a variety of public finance processes, including lottery revenues. For present purposes, tax revenue—mandatory levies upon the public for support of governmental activities or achievement of public objectives—can be considered in two categories. (1) "Earmarked taxes" are dedicated to a given purpose; when a motorist pays a gasoline tax at the pump, the payor knows that the tax being paid is for the construction and upkeep of the roads of the particular state or locality. (2) "General taxes," such as those on income, sales, and property, go into the general fund of the levying government or agency, and the payor identifies the amount paid with the unit of government imposing the tax—federal, state, local, or other—which may be characterized in the taxpayer's mind as "our public servants in Richmond," "those politicians in Washington," or "those [expletive deleted] bureaucrats at city hall."

Taxpayer resistance always has been a major problem in securing adequate general tax revenue. That resistance sharpened in the late seventies and, though perhaps abated somewhat, is likely to continue through the indefinite future, fluctuating with public opinion of governments and their perceived responsiveness, efficiency, fairness, and integrity. The degree of resistance also varies with the type of tax, as demonstrated by the ACIR opinion polls, and with the reasons for liking or disliking a particular tax. Those reasons constitute significant elements in public policy decisions as to which tax source is selected for an attempted increase or reduction. The lesser resistance to public service financing through earmarked taxes tied to a particular service or through user charges imposed for a service is one of the factors accounting for increased use of those revenue sources in recent years.

Fear of deterrence to business and industry location causes state and local governments to analyze carefully the impact of a particular tax or other revenue measure upon the future location decisions by private enterprises that might consider moving into or leaving the state or locality. Threats to leave usually, but not always, have been associated with a selective tax of some kind, imposed on a particular product or activity (a stock transfer tax arouses brokerage firms, and a sales tax on professional services angers lawyers, architects, and others).

Moving from problems associated with taxes to those involved in other revenue sources, one of the major issues for both state and local governments throughout the eighties was the decreased relative flows of intergovernmental aid. Federal aid had been decreasing in absolute amount in several functional areas and in real dollars in practically all areas. State aid increased in absolute amount from year to year through most of the seventies and well through the eighties, but when adjusted both for inflation and for the gaps left in local functions formerly directly aided by the federal government, it has declined in a number of states.

Opportunities for "revenue enhancement" necessary to meet the new or intensified problems discussed in this chapter exist in considerable breadth and depth but will not come easily. Two favorable factors are inherent in the existing state-local revenue systems. First, most states—not all—have strong revenue systems in place, comprised of broad-based sales and income taxes and an array of earmarked and other selective taxes. It would be surprising if there were more than two or three states that were not utilizing both sales and income taxes by the mid-nineties. Only five states are without a sales tax and a similar handful without an income tax; fiscal pressures, especially in education, will hasten the inevitable in such states as Texas, Washington, Oregon, Delaware, and the few others, forcing them to equip themselves with both the horse and carriage of broad-based taxation. Also, despite the Florida setback through overreach, extension of the sales tax base to cover selected services may occur in a number of states.

Second, at the local level, the use of nonproperty taxes has been increasing, and there are several indications that state legislatures are going to be more lenient in this respect, as recommended in the state-local relations report of the National Conference of State Legislatures. Lotteries, racing, and off-track betting will contribute additional revenues, but at a lesser rate of increase than in the seventies and eighties.

Several state-local nontax alternatives are available in summoning the additional fiscal resources needed in the years ahead. Possibilities of (a) reducing demand through influencing consumer behavior, (b) use of nonservice approaches in the fulfillment of public obligations, and (c) expenditure savings via improved and new devices in administrative and financial management are reviewed in a later section. Additionally, expanded use of user-based financing and use of private contracting and other alternative modes of public service delivery, including divestment to the private sector with or without continued public regulation, all offer significant opportunities to state and local policymakers and administrators. These are examined in chapter 3.

SORTING OUT NATIONAL AND STATE-LOCAL RESPONSIBILITIES

It is necessary at this point to consider the criteria under which prior, present, and future operating and fiscal responsibilities of the three areas of government in the federal system have been or will be assumed or assigned. Federal aid to state and local governments is a sizeable block of money, and although in 1987 it comprised only about 17 percent of those governments' revenues, it might be reduced further in some areas and increased in others, depending upon the extent to which national interests are at stake in each case. Local governments depend upon taxes for less than one-third of their total revenues, with state aid comprising another third and a combination of user charges, federal aid, and miscellaneous nontax revenues making up the final third. Here again, the flow and composition of state aid must, as in the past, be based to a large extent on the nature of the function and the extent to which its aspects are localized or spill over into statewide concerns.

In this section intergovernmental responsibility criteria will be examined as follows: (a) criteria for federal involvement; (b) additional criteria relating to federal aid (criteria for federal regulatory involvement and national preemption of state regulatory powers will be examined in chapter 6); and (*c*) criteria for state allocation of functional responsibilities between the state government and its instrumentalities on the one hand and the local and other substate levels of government on the other, and at the substate level among types of local government (for example, substate regional organizations of local governments; a general local government—city, county, or township; or special multicounty or other local districts or authorities).

Criteria for National Government Involvement

In its report to the Congress in 1955, the Commission on Intergovernmental Relations (the Kestnbaum Commission) included in its recommendations criteria for future federal involvement in areas previously handled solely by state and local governments. Subsequently, the Advisory Commission on Intergovernmental Relations (ACIR) pursued its legal mandate to give continuing attention to federal-state-local relationships, including recommendations to national and state-local governments as to improved allocation of responsibilities. Two of its reports dealt specifically with state-local criteria for allocations of functional responsibilities and for federal involvement.

In 1984–85 a Committee on Federalism and National Purpose (known as Evans-Robb after its cochairpersons, Senator Daniel Evans of Washington and former governor Charles Robb of Virginia) was established, with one of its purposes being the formulation of criteria for a better separation of responsibilities among the three levels of government; it reported in December 1985. The Congressional Budget Office (CBO) also had given considerable study to federalism criteria, including both general criteria and those pertaining especially to the nation's physical infrastructure.

In its 1955 report the Kestnbaum Commission recommended the following as criteria necessary to justify national action:

1. When the national government is the only agency that can summon the resources needed for an activity (for example, national defense or economic stabilization)
2. When the activity cannot be handled within the geographic and jurisdictional limits of smaller governmental units, including those that could be created by interstate compact
3. When the activity requires a nationwide uniformity of policy that cannot be achieved by interstate action (for example, immigration and naturalization or national currency)
4. When a state through action or inaction does injury to the people of other States (for example, river pollution)
5. When states fail to respect or to protect basic political and civil rights that apply throughout the United States[5]

The Congressional Budget Office (CBO) in its report on the role of the federal government in a federal system proposed the following three criteria for federal involvement:

1. "Spillovers" or external effects; that is, costs or benefits from particular activities that cross jurisdictional borders
2. Benefits from centralized coordination; that is, efficiency or other gains from centralized planning and coordination of services
3. Poor distribution of resources; that is, inequities or hardships that are unusually severe for certain groups or regions in the country[6]

In its 1981 report on an agenda for American federalism the ACIR made the following comment on the extent to which the criterion of national interest had been disregarded in federal programs:

Federal grant-in-aid programs have never reflected any consistent or coherent interpretation of national needs. At present, the federal government's assistance or regulatory activities reach to even the most traditionally local fields. Individual programs have been created largely on a hit or miss basis, chiefly reflecting the entrepreneurial activities of policy makers and organized interests. [Also,] limited national objectives have proven difficult to specify in politically meaningful terms.[7]

Regarding another criterion for the division of labor among levels of government—political accountability—the ACIR noted that the record might suggest "a decline in popular control through state and local governments as well as rising levels of political alienation, an increasing atomization of national political processes, and a growing overload of national decisionmaking institutions."[8]

In its 1986 report the Evans-Robb Committee suggested three bases for distinguishing between responsibilities of national and of state-local governments: (a) the policy function—setting goals and standards; (b) the financial function—funding the program and deciding how much to provide; and (c) the administrative function—delivering the service and deciding on the delivery system. The committee concluded that the national government should have responsibility when (a) nationwide uniformity of policy, finance, or administration is important or (b) it is necessary to raise revenues from the nation as a whole and distribute them to various parts of the country. The committee concluded further that states and localities should have responsibility when (a) diversity of policy, finance, or administration is important—when solutions should be tailored to different regions or localities—or (b) experimentation by officials responsible to local electorates is key to meeting the public need for the program.[9]

The following list is an amalgam of the criteria that have been proposed over the past thirty-plus years, with the antecedent of each, including a modification or two indicated by fiscal and administrative considerations.

1. The "fiscal magnitude" criterion: when the national government is the only agency that can summon the resources needed for the activity (for example, defense; maintenance of economic stability) (Kestnbaum). This criterion might be modified to read, after the parenthetical examples, "and where the activity is not susceptible to user-

based financing through fees, assessments, and other charges attributable to the activity imposed upon users." This modifier is of relevance to various public services but is especially pertinent to the financing of physical infrastructure.

2. The "multistate" criterion: when the activity cannot be handled within the geographic and jurisdictional limits of smaller governmental units or of a unit that could be created by compact (for example, regulation of radio and television) (Kestnbaum).

3. The "uniformity" criterion: when the activity requires a nationwide uniformity of policy that cannot be achieved by interstate action. Sometimes there must be an undeviating standard and hence an exclusively national policy (for example, immigration, air navigation system) (Kestnbaum, Evans-Robb, and others).

4. The "negative spillover" criterion: when a state through action or inaction does injury to the people of another state (for example, state barriers to the flow of interstate commerce) or when spillovers or external effects (especially negative ones) cross jurisdictional borders (CBO and Kestnbaum).

5. The "efficiency/effectiveness/coordination" criterion: when there are marked benefits in efficiency or other gains from centralized planning and coordination of services (for example, imposition of nationwide child-support informational exchange and collection procedures) (CBO).

6. The "resource distribution/severe incidence" criterion: when there is a poor distribution of resources or where the problem or inequities are unusually severe for certain groups or regions in the country (energy and weatherproofing problems affect poor families unusually severely) (CBO).

7. The "geographic equity" criterion: for example, the Ohio River states and the acid rain issue. This criterion becomes relevant when national action becomes necessary under other criteria and the incidence of interstate fiscal responsibility becomes an issue (Evans-Robb).

8. The "civil rights" criterion: when states fail to respect or to protect basic political and civil rights that apply throughout the United States (strengthened through subsequent court decisions and by the post–1955 array of civil rights legislation and the application of the U.S. Bill of Rights to state personal, property, and other rights issues) (Kestnbaum).

9. The "mandated expenditure" criterion: an additional criterion, the sharing of the cost of expensive facilities, services, or other expenditures necessitated by federal regulatory requirements (for example, wastewater plants and hazardous waste cleanups).

The nine criteria for federal involvement might be summarized as follows: (1) fiscal magnitude and nonsusceptibility to user-based financing; (2) multistate issue and not susceptible to interstate compact handling; (3) uniformity; (4) negative spillover; (5) efficiency, effectiveness, and coordination; (6) severe incidence to region or group; (7) geographic equity; (8) civil rights; and (9) federally mandated state-local expenditure to meet a regulatory requirement.

Criteria for Distinguishing State and Local Responsibilities

The Evans-Robb Committee proposed that where state constitutions do not mandate action specifically at the state or local level, states, rather than localities, should have responsibility when (1) local government boundaries create barriers to effectively raising revenues and delivering services or (2) resources and responsibilities must be distributed among localities and there is no overwhelming reason for the federal government to decide how they should be distributed.[10] These proposals were prefaced by a high emphasis upon whether or not, in an earlier day, a provision was placed in a state constitution directing that a given level or type of government carry out a function. Constitutional amending processes could be initiated in cases where later developments indicated a needed change.

The important substantive issue of resource redistribution pervades the state-local responsibility question for a number of functions carrying a high positive or negative spillover. Spillover is the basis for a high state share in the financing of public elementary and secondary education. Others argue that state acceptance of too much fiscal responsibility for a function causes overcentralization and a blurring of political accountability. These issues are explored subsequently in connection with state aid to education and state revenue sharing with local units.

Considerations in addition to the Evans-Robb criteria arise when localities cannot agree on the site of an undesirable facility such as a prison; when a state of small geographical area may find it more economical to deliver a service such as regional landfills; or when local experimentation in the delivery of an activity such as "workfare" requirements for welfare recipients may produce new and more effective approaches.

In regard to the assumption by local units or the assignment by the state to them of functional responsibilities, the ACIR in its 1974 report suggested four broad criteria—economic efficiency, fiscal equity, political accountability, and administrative effectiveness. For purposes of economic efficiency, functions should be assigned to jurisdictions (1) large enough to realize economies of scale, but not so large as to incur contrasting diseconomies; (2) willing to provide alternative service offerings at a price range and service level acceptable to the local citizenry; and (3) willing to adopt pricing policies for their functions when appropriate—in other words, to employ user-charge financing rather than using the general tax base.

For equity purposes, functions should go to units that (1) are large enough to encompass the costs and benefits of a function or that are willing to compensate other units for providing the functional services; (2) have adequate fiscal capacity to finance their public service responsibilities in a manner insuring interpersonal and interjurisdictional fiscal equalization; and (3) are able to absorb the financial risks involved.

To achieve political accountability, a unit responsible for a function should (1) be controllable by, accessible to, and accountable to its residents and (2) maximize the conditions and opportunities for active and productive citizen participation.

Conditions for administrative effectiveness include (1) a functional responsibility range sufficiently broad for competing interests to be considered and

balanced; (2) geographic adequacy for effective performance; (3) formal determination of goals and means of achieving them and periodic reassessment of
goals in the light of performance standards; (4) willingness to pursue measures
of intergovernmental cooperation; and (5) adequate legal authority and management capability to perform the function.[11]

These criteria, proposed by the ACIR in the mid-seventies, are formidable
and often cannot be followed completely, because a choice frequently arises
between having a service delivered or doing without. This is especially the case
where citizens desire a range of choices of type and quality of a service. Often
the unit of general government is unable or unwilling to provide such a choice,
necessitating a special district, neighborhood unit, or nongovernmental organization performing under contract. Sometimes the best solution is the general
government unit even though not all of the criteria can be met, or some other
arrangement that provides more flexibility to service users.

The most difficult and controversial criterion in the cluster proposed by the
ACIR is the assurance of personal and interjurisdictional equity in service delivery. To reach any such goal often would necessitate a wide range of economic
heterogeneity in the unit's population, and the critics of the criterion sometimes
claim that fiscal equity would be transformed into a redistributive function at
the local level.

Arrangements for State-Local Consultation and Cooperation

In its 1986 report on state-local relations the NCSL task force stated: "A
specific organization dedicated to state-local issues is needed because the pro-
found changes in this area require ongoing study." The report went on to suggest
that such an organization could perform four important functions: "Provide a
forum for discussion of long-range state-local issues . . . ; conduct research on
local developments and new state policies; promote experimentation in intergovernmental processes . . . ; and develop suggested solutions to state-local problems."[12]

As of mid–1987 twenty-five states had an advisory body of local officials, a
legislative commission, or a body structured along the lines of the ACIR (three,
four, and eighteen, respectively).[13] The last category typically has members
representing each major type of local government along with executive and
legislative branch officials of the state government. The task force emphasized
that the organization should be created by statute, not by executive order, thereby
assuring a legislative role; that it should be either part of the legislature or an
independent entity, not part of the executive branch; that it should have an
adequate budget ($200,000 annually was stated as a minimum) and a qualified
staff of at least four persons; and finally, that local governments should participate
in financing the organization.

FISCAL CONSTRAINTS: PARAMETERS FOR REPRESENTATIVE DEMOCRACY?

As shown in appendix 1.F, forty-five of the fifty states have placed in their state constitutions or statutes specific restrictions upon the exercise of tax and expenditure powers by the state government itself and/or local governments. As of October 1985, eighteen of the forty-five had placed limits on the state government itself—eight by constitutional provision and ten by state statute. Six states—four of them in 1978 or later—had placed general revenue limits on local governments (Maryland, Minnesota, Mississippi, Missouri, Nebraska, and Washington). Six states, two in 1978 or later, had imposed a general expenditure limit—usually a maximum permissible percentage increase over the preceding year (Arizona, California, Colorado, Kansas, Minnesota, and New Jersey). (Of the foregoing, Minnesota was limiting both general revenues and expenditures.)

Thirty-four other states (excluding the eleven just mentioned and the five without any limitations) had imposed one or more types of limitations on local property taxes (some of the eleven states imposing revenue or expenditure limits also had imposed property tax limits). Countless individual units of local government over the country—many prior to the late seventies and a great many more subsequently—have incorporated similar restraints into their local charters, which at the local level correspond to state constitutional provisions; in most cases charters can only be adopted or amended by a vote of local residents.

Given the prevalence of stringent legal fiscal constraints that state and local governments have imposed upon themselves, it is well to consider several issues at this point: (1) the impact upon, and the relationship to, new structural fiscal constraints at the national level, which began to be advanced in the early eighties; (2) the impact that the constraints have had upon the effectiveness and equity with which state-local fiscal policies and practices have adjusted to public opinion; (3) the reasoning that led to the wave of state-adopted constraints; and (4) some alternative criteria for considering the adoption of new constraints and the modification or repeal of existing ones.

Contrasting Constraints at State-Local and National Levels

In mid–1987 the ACIR published a controversial report, criticized by some on both substantive and methodological grounds, containing the results of surveys and studies directed toward ascertaining results of particular measures of fiscal discipline employed by state governments and the possible relevancy of such experience to the framing of appropriate measures for consideration at the national level. The surveys examined the nature and extent of nine fiscal discipline tools being used in the states. The particular restraints and the numbers of states using them, as of 1984, were (a) balanced budget requirement (49; only Vermont without); (b) gubernatorial line-item veto (43; Maine, New Hampshire, Rhode Island, Vermont, Indiana, North Carolina, and Nevada without); (c) constitutional debt restrictions (30); (*d*) tax and spending limits (18); (*e*) extraordinary majority required to enact or increase a tax (7); (*f*) indexation of state income tax to inflation (10); (*g*) fiscal impact note review of legislative bills (41); (*h*) program evaluation and sunset procedure (29); and (*i*) requirement for "rainy day" fund (24).[14] Appendix 2.A shows the state-by-state breakdown of the use of the nine measures. (Due to extensive activity in the states concerning these measures and a considerable lag between survey and publication dates, incidence numbers in the table should be interpreted broadly.)

An explanation of the last four of the listed measures is necessary, because their relevance to reduced taxing and spending may not be apparent at first glance. Indexation of the state income tax prevents the state government from reaping an "inflation dividend" for which the legislature is not required to accept formal responsibility. As is the case with parts of the federal income tax code, gross income each year is deflated by the consumer price index (CPI) or other appropriate measure of inflation.

Under a "fiscal note" procedure, any bill reaching the floor must bear a note prepared by the legislative fiscal office as to the cost to the state budget for the forthcoming and future years in the event the bill were enacted. In many states the note procedure has been broadened to identify any evident or hidden costs to local governments. At the federal level, at the behest of the ACIR and organizations of state and local government, the Congress adopted a procedure whereby the CBO prepares a similar note as to any new costs that would accrue to state-local governments if the bill were enacted.[15]

Beginning in the mid-seventies, state governments, in the interests of effective fiscal and administrative management, began to enact "sunset" legislation, setting a recurring expiration date for state regulatory and other programs. Normally a sunset law requires an evaluation of the activity as to whether or not its goals have been met and whether it should be continued in its existing form, modified, or allowed to expire, such evaluation to be completed well in advance of the expiration date. By this means, programs of low priority or those that had been created by thin legislative majorities would come under scrutiny and would die unless reenacted; the procedure also facilitates the "retuning" of activities in the light of new circumstances to assure optimum effectiveness.

Constitutional or statutory provisions to set aside stabilization, contingency, or "rainy day" funds were enacted as a result of the painful experiences of state governments in times when the national economy became especially volatile. Naturally the mandatory maintenance of such funds reduces the amount of funds available for other purposes. Critics of such requirements claim that the state government is placed in a position of not only having to have a balanced budget, but to run a surplus most of the time, thus adding a deflationary factor to the state's economy.

The ACIR found that in a cross-state comparison for 1984 "more restrictive fiscal discipline measures were associated statistically with lower levels of per capita state government spending, a greater avoidance of deficits, and a tendency toward lower levels of per capita tax levies.'' The report concluded that ''contrary to the assertions of some critics of fiscal restraints, such devices may play a significant role both in reducing the size of state budget deficits and in holding down the rate of growth of state spending. This effect may be directly 'caused' by the fiscal limitations or it may be an indirect result of the establishment of a political consensus—reflected in the implementation of fiscal limits by a state—favoring disciplined fiscal behavior.''[16]

No constitutional restraint is placed upon the spending power of the national government, so long as the necessary authorizing legislation and subsequent appropriations are enacted. In the late eighties debate raged over constitutional amendments (1) to require a balanced budget; (2) to require an extraordinary majority in each house of the Congress to enact an unbalanced set of appropriations; or (3) to authorize a presidential line-item veto, subject to a specific override by a two-thirds, three-fifths, or simple majority. It was argued that federal deficits had become so chronic that a systemic problem existed and required constitutional remedy. Others argued that the problem was a political aberration and would be resolved as voters replaced high-spending officials or voted to raise taxes.[17]

Observed Impacts of Post–1977 Tax-Expenditure Limitations

Deep concern among many groups of citizens and state and local officials swept across the country following the adoption in California of Proposition 13. Predictions of fiscal chaos, elimination of programs assisting low-income people, closing schools, shortening the school year, or otherwise harming public education, and other dire consequences were widespread. In the ensuing years a number of studies were conducted as to the root causes and observable effects of Proposition 13, Proposition 2½ in Massachusetts, and similar fiscal austerity measures adopted in their wake. It is desirable to note a cross-section of these studies before proceeding to examine the pros, cons, and future alternative courses of public policy in this area.

Using a variety of survey results and data contained in other studies, John Citrin and Donald Green concluded that ''the history of the tax revolt in California provides a clear example of a political feedback loop: dissatisfaction with high property taxes stimulated protest (input) that led to reform (output), and this in turn assuaged discontent by more closely aligning opinion and policy.''[18] Citrin and Green found that one group—elderly homeowners buying their residences prior to mid–1975—gained disproportionately from Proposition 13 because their assessments were rolled back to levels of the 1975–76 tax year, with future annual increases from that base limited to 2 percent.

During the period 1978–82, changes in real per capita operating expenses for major local functions increased for police (8.9 percent) and decreased for fire (−2.0 percent), public schools (−4.2 percent), parks and recreation (−9.7 percent), and streets and roads (−16.5 percent). These increases and decreases followed rather precisely the preference ranking of services in California public opinion polls. The authors concluded by observing that "the passage of Proposition 13 transformed the culture of policy-making in California. Austerity and self-reliance became the new symbols of legitimacy. . . . the prevailing hostility to new taxes means that only sustained economic growth in the private sector can provide the wherewithal for government to expand."[19]

Using census, NCSL, ACIR, state budget officer, and other surveys and studies, Daphne Kenyon and Karen Benker found individual passage or failure among the numerous constitutional and other initiatives before states in the years following Proposition 13 to be "irrelevant in most cases because they succeed in bringing their message to lawmakers merely by being serious contenders for adoption. Their message is that government growth should not exceed state economic growth." They concluded further that the most important result of the tax revolt was the sharp alteration in nearly all state spending policies; they pointed out that between 1974 and 1978 average constant-dollar spending grew 1.5 percent annually, but between 1978 and 1983 it fell by .1 percent annually.[20]

The Rand Corporation, citing three of its studies done in 1981–82 covering ten cities in three states (California, Kansas, and New Jersey), reported that tax-limiting laws had reduced state and local taxes for residents in eight of the ten cities studied, with all income groups benefiting, but with lower-income tax-payers realizing a slightly larger reduction than others. It also found a reduction in average tax burdens as a percentage of income from 19 to 18 percent for New Jersey cities studied and from 18 to 16 percent for California cities, but an increase from 12 to 16 percent in Kansas (attributed by the researchers to loopholes in the Kansas law).[21] The report further noted that in all the ten cities except Montclair and Newark, both in New Jersey, overall tax burdens shifted slightly in a progressive direction.

Elaine Sharp and David Elkins studied the impact of a stringent addition to the Missouri state constitution (the Hancock amendment of 1979–80) that required local voter approval of any new or increased revenue source involving a fee. (State law already required voter approval for most new taxes.) Their analysis of subsequent spending patterns in the seven largest Missouri cities found no tendency for state bailout of potential revenue losses; a vigorous and sometimes successful search for nonfee revenue sources such as those carried in the "miscellaneous revenue" category used by the Census Bureau (for example, fines and forfeitures and investment income); in St. Louis and Kansas City an increased use of nonguaranteed debt; and in all of the cities pressure for further revenue diversification.[22]

David Lowery found that aside from dampening effects upon revenue yield, the tax revolt had had positive, if unintended, consequences for the equity of state-local revenue systems: "If one views greater elasticity and progressivity as important criteria and as desirable attributes of a sound fiscal system . . . , then the answer is clear. State and state-local tax systems were somewhat better after the tax revolt than they had been before."[23]

Comparisons of revenue and expenditure data for California's twenty-five largest cities (cities over 100,000 population in 1982, excluding Los Angeles and the city-county of San Francisco) were made by Alan Saltzstein for the fiscal years 1978–79 and 1981–82. The comparisons showed an aggregate increase in spending over the period, exceeding the increase in the CPI (50 percent against 36 percent); eleven of the cities finding cutback management necessary (spending increases less than those in the CPI); and significant aggregate changes in spending priorities—more for police and less for parks and recreation, overall, but in some cities increased priority for public works in contrast to police and fire.

Saltzstein observed that contrary to expectations, the typical large California city continued to grow in the post-Proposition 13 period, but with considerable changes in priorities. He concluded that underestimated in previous analyses had been "the ability of cities to insulate themselves from environmental shocks. Few city services are mandated by state law. . . . cities also have the revenue flexibility to increase fee income to compensate for the loss of property tax revenue. Legislative approval was not needed to institute such fees, as it was in school districts."[24]

The Center for Public Policy and Administration at California State University, Long Beach, examined 105 cities in Los Angeles and Orange counties and found six patterns of response to the need for expenditure reduction. These were (1) volunteer work and other direct citizen involvement; (2) corporate-charitable assistance, such as executive loans; (3) increased management efficiencies; (4) joint venturing and resource development, bringing community organizations into the service delivery system; (5) selling services via user charges rather than providing them from tax-base sources; and (6) contracting out service delivery wherever indicated.[25]

In considering the root causes of the "tax revolt" of the 1977–86 period, public perceptions of overtaxation and unfairness of particular taxes have been mentioned. Lance deHaven-Smith explored the extent to which ideology was a component of public disaffection with state and local taxing and spending policies, using Florida's proposed Amendment 1, which was placed on the November 1984 ballot by voter initiative (and later removed through court action), as the basis of a public opinion survey of a proportionate stratified sample of voters in Palm Beach County. Of the sample, 47 percent planned to vote against the amendment, while 42 percent were for it.

Findings from the Florida survey tended to controvert two conceptions from other analyses: (1) that popular support for fiscal limitations is rooted in a single set of widely shared beliefs and (2) that voters are satisfied with the overall level of government services but support fiscal limitations as a means of increasing efficiency and reducing corruption. The findings of the survey showed that support for Amendment 1 was based on diverse reasons and that antigovernment ideology was only one of several components of support. Second, the findings showed support of cuts in some services, but with a variance between the ideologically oriented and other groups. The ideological portion, in contrast to self-interest orientation, was markedly higher among supporters than among opponents of the fiscal limitation amendment (36 to 35 percent among supporters and 18 to 52 percent among opponents). Among all respondents, 24 percent fell into the ideological category versus 43 percent interest-oriented and 33 percent having no issue content. Of the undecided category, the divisions among ideological, interest-oriented, and no-issue content were 5, 27, and 68 percent, respectively.[26] A somewhat different set of findings emerged from a survey of voter opinion in Massachusetts, where the pro-limitation vote was directed toward lower taxes and increased efficiency rather than the substitution of other revenues for the property tax.[27]

Client Group Pleas and Taxpayer Resistance

As a member, and for a year the presiding officer, of the board of education of an urban county (Montgomery, Maryland) and subsequently as a member of the county governing body, this writer gained the impression that local and state budget laws and procedures had been stacked, probably not intentionally, to favor the spending side of budget decisions as opposed to fiscal frugality. The economic self-interests of those favoring and opposing particular expenditures have been explained by Anthony Rufulo:

Special interest groups have a strong incentive to get programs passed that favor themselves while taxpayers at large do not have an equally strong incentive to fight such programs. The benefit to the special interest groups can be large for each of a small number of members; they have a strong incentive to lobby. But a very large number of taxpayers will be splitting the bill, and so the tax savings to any of them for opposing the program are small. On net, then, projects sponsored by special interests have an unduly high probability of being enacted.[28]

Organizations of local government officials, and many public finance, political science, and public administration scholars and practitioners have long held that fiscal provisions in state constitutions and local charters should deal only with the processes of executive budgeting and legislative appropriation, without any quantitative prescriptions or limitations. It is argued that spending levels are matters of policy and consequently should be left to the political process whereby voters would elect, eject, or reject those representatives disregarding the fiscal policy preferences of a majority of the voters. In one of its early reports the ACIR recommended "the lifting of constitutional limitations on local powers to raise property tax revenue," observing that "such limitations are inimical to local self-government and should be lifted."[29]

Calls by state-local officialdom, employee groups, and concerned citizens to preserve self-government and the theory of representative democracy were not sufficient to stem the tax revolt tide that was rising in the 1975–84 decade. Repeated predictions of fiscal chaos, wholesale slashing of services, and closing of schools were to no avail. The various observed positive and negative impacts of the tax revolt enactments have been reviewed; the conceptual case for the incorporation of fiscal parameters within the representative democracy theory now needs to be considered.

The phenomena of increased specialization and professionalization of public service delivery, growing unionization, and the increasing impact of judicial decisions on fiscal policy are said to have blurred and all but obliterated the fine line of budgetary accountability that is supposed to run from the citizen to the elected executive and legislative officials and back to the citizen. The citizen, theoretically, dissects the innumerable fiscal actions taken and renders an informed verdict at the next election.

Before the tax revolt, the budget-hearing and decision-making procedures of most local governments apparently were tilted toward the spending side, given the rapid growth of special-interest groups and single-issue politics. Any single group interested in an item in the budget—music teachers, for example—could show up in force at the proper time in the budget hearing and make its views forcefully known. The group would then show up at the time when votes were taken on budget items and observe carefully and unmistakably the vote of each governing board member on the single item in which they were interested. They were then in a position to reward their friends and punish their enemies at election time. But for the general run of taxpayers who were favorable to economy in government, the task of deciphering scores of votes in order to identify particular board members with fiscal "responsibility" or "irresponsibility," as the case might be, was nearly impossible, even if the citizen attended all of the sessions and read all of the minutes.

These arguments seemed compelling to many, especially at the national level, in contrast to state and local governments. There the combination of (*a*) campaign financing through political action committees (PACs) of the special-interest groups, (*b*) the absence of any constitutional or other process restraints, and (*c*) the opportunity of siphoning off countless barrels of spending from the sea of deficit arithmetic made fiscal prudence or lack thereof absolutely impossible to associate with an individual member of Congress. However, it is one thing to concede the validity of the point that without external constraints public spending at the state and local level tends to get out of hand, and quite another to devise constraints that are sufficiently firm to balance the spending and saving pressures in the budgetary process, yet flexible enough to permit effective governance.

Possible Constraint Criteria

Several major considerations enter into the placement and framing of fiscal limitations upon the state itself and upon local units of government.

Constitutional (and local charter) or statutory (and local ordinance) provisions. One of the basic tenets of state constitution drafting mentioned earlier was to confine provisions to basic principles and to leave process of implementation to the legislative body. In its 1962 report the ACIR, after stating the conventional arguments against state restrictions on local taxing powers of the kind listed in appendix 1.F, recognized that some or many states would prefer to retain or adopt such limitations and suggested that if they did, the limitations should be placed in statutes rather than in the constitution. In addition to the drafting principle, the report cited the position of the National Municipal League: "Ideally, a constitution should be silent on the subject of taxation and finance, thus permitting the legislature and the governor freedom to develop fiscal policies for the State to meet the requirements of their time."[30]

Moving from an earlier ideal to the recent and present reality, many states continue to prefer the incorporation of fiscal limitations in their constitutions. Proposition 13 and many of its successors have been in that form. There are two major ways to amend a state constitution: in 1984–85 seventeen states allowed amendment by constitutional initiative petition, and all states continued to provide for initiation of amendments by the legislature. Additionally, all states provide for a constitutional convention, either to consider certain amendments or to revise the constitution as a whole, although nine states do not have these explicit provisions in their constitutions.[31]

Two principal objections to the constitutional initiative and referendum are (1) inflexibility and (2) single-issue orientation. Once a specific measure is written into a constitution or charter, it can be removed or modified only by resubmission to the electorate. Often an amendment by initiative is drawn narrowly, with a single objective in mind, with no attention to the necessity of appropriate meshing with other parts of the constitution or with collateral laws already on the books. The legislative process usually ensures language that carries essential amendments to other legislation and, while assuring the attainment of the new policy objective, incorporates and integrates it into the existing constitutional and statutory framework.

As Joseph Zimmerman and others have emphasized, there is a middle ground—the "indirect initiative." Under this procedure, the petitioned proposition is first referred to the state legislature upon the certification of the necessary number of signatures. Should the legislature fail to act on the proposal within a time period ranging from forty days in Michigan to adjournment of the legislature in Maine, the proposition automatically is placed on the ballot. Other states authorizing the indirect initiative are Massachusetts, Nevada, and Washington. In Massachusetts, Ohio, and Utah, if the legislature fails to approve the petitioned proposal, additional signatures must be collected before it finally goes on the ballot. The failure of the Massachusetts legislature to place a substitute proposal on the ballot forced the voters to choose between the status quo and Proposition 2½ in November 1980.[32]

A strong argument for placing fiscal limitation amendments in the constitution or charter is that if they are based on statute or ordinance, they are subject to annual tinkering, watering-down, or repeal by the state legislature or local governing body. Also, if the legislative body, more subject to pressure from the

spending than from the saving side, refuses to cut back, then a charter or constitutional initiative is the only recourse of the "silent majority," assuming that
those favoring a cutback are a real rather than a claimed majority. However,
placement in a constitution or charter carries with it a prerequisite for equity and
flexibility for adjustment within specified parameters.

Object and method of limitation. Limitations may be upon taxing powers or
expenditures, and if on taxing powers, usually on the property tax. If the limitation is on the property tax, it should be in terms of the value of taxable property
equalized to full market value, in order to eliminate the influence of interjurisdictional differences in the ratio of assessed value to market value. If the limitation
is on expenditures rather than taxes, a frequent base is the extent of permitted
annual increase over a base year, or the preceding year, with the extent sometimes
in terms of a stated percentage in excess of or less than the increase in the
consumer price index. A periodic adjustment for population growth is sometimes
included.

Required appraisal of impact. It is desirable that the constitutional or statutory
provision imposing the limitation require the examination by the legislature, at
one or more specified intervals, of the impact of the limitation with appropriate
reporting to the public. This is especially useful for newly imposed limitations
or for limitations of a type not in use in other states or localities.

ECONOMIC AND FISCAL EQUITY ISSUES IN STATE-LOCAL FINANCE

As would be expected in fifty different state-local financial systems, the ground
rules for which are set by the respective states, a great many issues of fairness
arise: as to type of tax—sales, income, property; as between taxes and other
methods of raising revenue; and about particular features of particular taxes,
most especially income and property taxes. Also, there are numerous equity
questions regarding state expenditure policy, particularly state aid to local governments, school aid being the most important, and about the extent to which
state governments should endeavor to equalize fiscal needs and resources among
local jurisdictions.

Five equity areas will be examined: (1) intergenerational equity in state-local
tax, spending, employee pension, and other resource allocation policies; (2)
intergovernmental equity in property taxation, both in assessment practices and
in state-mandated exclusions from the local property tax base; (3) central-city
suburban relationships, including their demographic, economic, and fiscal dimensions; (4) the closely related and more general issues of state aid to distressed
communities and state measures for interlocal fiscal equalization; and (5) intergovernmental and other equities involved in interstate and interlocal competition
for revenue resources. (Similar competition in service delivery is explored in
detail in connection with alternative public service delivery modes in chapter
3.)

Intergenerational Equity in State-Local Policies

In terms of substantive depth, fiscal magnitude, emotional intensity, and political difficulty, intergenerational equity certainly will be one of the most serious domestic policy questions confronting governments, state-local as well as national, during the rest of the century. In brief, it is concerned with the respective impact of public policies upon the active labor force, on the one hand, and the retired and the rest of the population sixty-five and over, on the other. Ever since the enactment of the Social Security Act of 1935, public policy leadership at all three levels of domestic governance has tended to legislate an increasingly wide range of economic and other preferences to assist the elderly population. With advances in medical technology and consequent lengthening life spans, the proportion of elderly in the population has increased greatly, with resulting growth in political influence. The American Association of Retired Persons (AARP), between 27 and 28 million strong and far outnumbering the labor movement numbers in its heyday, and other organizations of the elderly have learned the "litmus test" approach to political campaigns and have begun to apply it with increasing intensity.[33]

Some of the principal dimensions of this equity issue are the following:

- The elderly make up a growing proportion of the population.
- The number of retirees in relation to the active labor force also is rising; in terms of retirement costs, more and more retirees are being supported by fewer and fewer contributors to pension plans. This is further sensitized by the increasing proportion of the work force represented by minorities, in contrast to a predominantly white retiree population.
- Retirees enjoy a considerable number of tax preferences, such as exclusion of some or all of state and/or local government pension benefits from taxable income (of forty-three states with an income tax, one-half do not tax the pension benefits of state employees);[34] many of states do not tax any of the Social Security benefit, although one-half of the benefit is considered as income for federal tax purposes.
- Persons sixty-five and over are mandated half-fare travel on federally aided mass transit systems, regardless of income.
- Many state and local housing finance agencies subsidize elderly-occupied housing, regardless of income.
- A significant portion of elderly medical costs, regardless of income, is supported federally from nonpremium sources for the Medicare program (that is, from general revenues of the Treasury).
- Senior citizens enjoy a wide variety of discounts at retail counters, in airline fares, and for a wide range of other consumer products and services.
- Many states and localities have mandated property tax exemptions, credits, and other preferences for the elderly, with no reference to income, and similar preferences not based on need have been incorporated into the federal tax code (for example, the $125,000 exclusion from capital gains calculation in the sale of a residence).

• Many services provided to the elderly by nonprofit organizations are subsidized in varying degrees by state and/or local governments.

Many of these preferences are extended regardless of income. Rationalizing preferences to the elderly and handicapped over and above those extended to others in the same income class is not difficult. More difficult to rationalize has been the extension of preferences to those with no demonstrable economic need. Many or most of those categories of economic and fiscal preferences were enacted in earlier years when a substantial proportion of the poor were elderly. This appears to be no longer the case, but the elderly nearly always are in a tenuous situation physically and emotionally, and nursing home costs can absorb a small fortune.

The economic status of the elderly. In relation to the rest of the population, the economic situation of those sixty-five and over improved markedly during the high-inflation period of the late seventies and early eighties, when the compounding effect of full cost-of-living adjustments (COLAs) raised the consumption resources of Social Security annuitants, federal civil service and military retirees, and retirees under the many other public and private pension plans that provided for partial or full COLAs. Most of those retirees enjoyed net gains from inflation because the consumer price index tended to overstate out-of-pocket consumption costs for retired people, especially those covered by Medicare.[35]

Prior to the early eighties poverty was perceived to be much more pervasive among the elderly than in the working-age population. That such is not now the case is shown by table 2.2. Even under official poverty rate definitions (the number with cash incomes below the poverty line as a percentage of the total population), rates for elderly persons were lower than for the general population of all ages (12.4 and 13.6 percent) and much lower than for children (20.5 percent).

For all persons in the prime earning group (ages 25–64), the official 1986 poverty rate was 9.8 percent, compared to 12.4 percent for elderly persons. However, with noncash benefits taken into account, the comparative rates for the prime and elderly groups were 7.0 and 3.0 percent when using the market value measure of the noncash benefits and 8.6 and 8.0 percent when using the recipient value measure. From a public policy standpoint, the most disturbing contrasts are found in the comparative rates for elderly persons and children (12.4 and 20.5 percent under the official definition, 3.0 and 13.8 percent by market value, and 8.0 and 17.7 percent by recipient value).

Since the late seventies debate has raged over the federal definition of poverty, which includes only cash income received. The Department of Health and Human Services on one side and the Congressional Budget Office on the other, each supported by a wide range of officials and scholars, have produced many treatises on this question. Researchers in the poverty and income fields developed three principal methods of treating noncash transfers, such as Medicare and housing assistance. The Census Bureau, in determining which of the many kinds of

Table 2.2

Persons, Families, and Unrelated Individuals below Poverty Level, by Official Definition and Alternative Values of Noncash Transfers, 1986 (In Millions)

Category	Total Pop.	Official Definition		Noncash Transfers* Mkt. Val.		Recip. Val.	
		No.	%	No.	%	No.	%
Persons	238.55	32.37	13.6	21.37	9.0	27.59	11.6
Under 18	62.95	12.88	20.5	8.69	13.8	11.13	17.7
Age 18-24	26.46	4.13	15.6	3.30	12.5	3.78	14.3
Age 25-64	121.17	11.89	9.8	8.53	7.0	10.45	8.6
Age 65 +	27.98	3.48	12.4	.85	3.0	2.24	8.0
In Families	205.46	24.75	12.0	16.26	7.9	21.00	10.2
Fem Hs. Ch.**	12.76	6.94	54.4	4.28	33.5	5.89	46.1
Unrel. Indivs.	31.68	6.85	21.6	4.42	13.9	5.85	18.5
Males	14.48	2.54	17.5	1.98	13.7	2.36	16.3
Age 65 +	2.10	.41	19.7	.08	3.7	.29	13.8
Females	17.20	4.31	25.1	2.44	14.2	3.49	20.3
Age 65 +	7.09	1.90	26.8	.41	5.8	1.20	16.9
Below 65	10.11	2.41	23.9	2.03	20.0	2.29	22.6

Source: Bureau of the Census, *Estimates of Poverty Including the Value of Noncash Benefits, 1986*, Technical Paper 57, July 1987, and associated selected unpublished data.

* Includes Medicaid, food stamps, etc.
** Female householder with children, no husband present.

noncash transfers should be counted if the poverty measure were expanded from cash income only, decided that based on data availability and reliability, only four categories should be counted. These appear to make up a large portion of all noncash transfers: food stamps, school lunches, housing assistance, and medical care provided through Medicaid, Medicare, and private insurance.[36]

The three methods of calculating the value of the in-kind transfers are (1) market value, which is an estimate of what the good or service would cost if bought in the private market (for example, if food stamps received purchased $50 worth of groceries, $50 is added to income; for a one-week stay in a hospital, with the patient paying $100 and the federal Medicare program reimbursing the hospital for the remaining $700, $700 is added to income received); (2) the recipient/cash equivalent value, which is an estimate of how much cash individuals would have to be given in place of the noncash benefit to make them feel equally well off (this is usually less than the market value because of differences in individual priorities of consumption); and (3) the budget-share method which assumes that the value of an in-kind benefit cannot exceed the amount the families with cash incomes near the poverty level would spend on that specific item. This resembles in some respects the consumer "market basket" approach in calculating the consumer price index (CPI). Of the three methods of noncash benefit valuation, the market value is highest, the recipient cash value the lowest, and the budget share in between. If the budget-share approach were used in table 2.2, the percentage of elderly falling below the poverty line would have been about halfway between the market value and recipient value rates.

In addition to the issue of including noncash benefits in defining poverty and determining their valuation has been the question of the extent to which assets or "wealth" should be counted in assessing the adequacy of economic resources in meeting consumption needs. Problems of data availability have restricted this question to theoretical debate. Other issues associated with the measurement of poverty include (1) great variations in living costs among regions and between metropolitan and nonmetropolitan areas; (2) whether or not a separate cost-of-living index for the retired population is warranted; and (3) adjustment of poverty thresholds based on pretax income to account for varying tax burdens.

In summary, it would appear that on balance, the economic status of the elderly will continue to improve throughout the nineties. The principal factor operating against that assumption is the possibility that the rate of increase in life expectancy at higher age levels will be at a pace far beyond the gradual edging-up of expectancy over the past half century. On the other side is the sharply increased incidence of pension protection in addition to Social Security for persons reaching seventy-five during the coming decade, plus the likelihood of spreading the risks of nursing home costs during the same period as current probes in that area come to fruition.

In commenting on the alarming increase in poverty among children, Americans for Generational Equity (AGE) stated that "throughout American history, each new generation has grown up to be richer than the one that went before" and observed that such is no longer the case.[37] U.S. Senator Patrick Moynihan observed that the United States has become "the first society in history in which a person is more likely to be poor if young rather than old."[38] However, groups representing the aged, such as the American Association of Retired Persons, argue strongly that the elderly are not unduly favored.[39]

The AARP has pointed out that a great many of the elderly are women and often physically frail. It disputes the alleged finding of "the rich elderly." It points to its support of increased funding for children's programs and for many other community and social causes benefiting groups in which the elderly have few if any eligible members and disputes the categorization of the organized elderly groups as being "cradle robbers" and a "self-interested army." "The Association . . . rejects the concept of an age war. The concept of generational conflict—created by the false notion that funding support for social insurance programs is having a detrimental effect on the economic prospects of younger Americans—could hamper serious efforts to meet the economic and social needs of all age groups."

On the state-local property tax front, the AARP argues that "states should provide substantial property tax relief to elderly homeowners and renters of low- and moderate-income." On income taxes, "states should provide at least as favorable income tax treatment of older persons as is presently provided under the Internal Revenue Code . . . and should not subject Social Security cash benefits to income tax liability; federal taxation of Social Security benefits was part of a Congressional package to help finance the Social Security System, with the resulting revenues returned to the program fund.''[40]

Consumption needs and pension benefits. Replacement ratios often are used in analyses of public and private retirement systems to relate postretirement consumption requirements to preretirement consumption outlays. Some argue that in some plans these ratios tend to be fixed at a higher level than necessary for consumption, in contrast to income maintenance. In a study of replacement ratio requirements in 1983–84, Michael Dexter found the following:

- A wide variation by income group in the proportion of final pay required to maintain preretirement consumption levels in the postretirement period; only a modest (.5 to 1.2) "factor multiplier" (factor times years of service produces percentage of final pay to be provided in pension benefit) was required to maintain preretirement consumption levels in public or corporate plans fully integrated with Social Security.

- An even wider variation among income groups of savings rates and outlays for gifts and contributions than previously estimated in pension policy analyses.

- Substantially lower tax burdens than previously estimated for given levels of income for preretirement, as compared to postretirement, age groups; this decreased estimate was attributable primarily to the state-local tax system exemptions and pension preferences in a number of states.

- A substantial downward change in key consumption component percentages of expenditure from preretirement to postretirement.

- A lowered degree of relevance and reliability of the replacement ratio concept if subsequent benefit amounts are inflation-adjusted to prices rather than to active worker compensation levels.[41]

In addition to a greater gross (but not usually net) outlay by retired persons for medical care and a drop to negligible outlays for education, a further major item of differentiation between preretirement and postretirement pointed out in the Dexter study was for gifts and contributions. Using studies by the Bureau of Labor Statistics (BLS) Consumer Expenditure Survey as a base for comparing average budget shares of a marginal dollar of new expenditure, the study found that where only 6.5 percent of the average budget share went to gifts and contributions in the preretirement age group, a full 31 percent of the marginal expenditure dollar was devoted to this purpose in the postretirement group. This was most striking in the higher-income group; at lower income levels the economic pressure on the necessity items was naturally higher.[42]

Given the changing economic status of the elderly, an examination of state-local tax preferences for that group clearly is in order. Since a considerable number of state income taxes use "adjusted gross income" on the federal return as a starting point, four elderly preferences in the federal tax code should be noted: (1) increased standard deduction for elderly, nonitemizing taxpayers; (2) elderly income credit; (3) the exclusion of at least one-half of Social Security benefits from gross income; and (4) the $125,000 exclusion from profit derived from sale of a home.

It should be noted also that federal legislation in 1983 to effect changes in the Social Security system (subjecting one-half of benefits to taxation for those persons in higher-income brackets) and subsequent tax reform legislation in 1986 injected a substantial measure of means-testing into what had been blanket tax breaks for the elderly, regardless of income. Eliminating the prior additional exemption to all elderly persons and substituting an increase in the standard deduction for nonitemizers effectively removed well-to-do elderly taxpayers from the preference. Similarly, the elderly income credit phases out as income increases. However, more than half the states continued the earlier and more liberal federal preferences for their own income tax purposes. A state-by-state breakdown of income exclusions and exemptions appears in appendix 2.B.

Most states provide substantial preferences in property taxes for elderly homeowners through a "circuit breaker" or "homestead exemption" program. A few states allow this preference—a shield for lower-income homeowners and renters from the so-called regressive features of property taxation—to all taxpayers, but most restrict it to the elderly. A few have no income ceiling for the exemption or circuit breaker. A final property tax preference worth noting is that of a freeze on increased assessments or rates upon residential property owned by the elderly as of a certain date; this proviso was a part of Proposition 13 in California.

Attempts to means-test preferences for the elderly would understandably encounter strong opposition. As Philip Longman noted, means-testing of entitlements in emphasizing the diversity of the elderly population would erode the political solidarity of the constituency.[43]

State-Local Equities in Property Assessment and Taxation

Closely related to the intergenerational issues in taxation just discussed is the intergovernmental issue of state mandating of local property tax exemptions. In the revenue field a long-standing, serious, and often inequitable state mandate has been the exclusion from assessment and subsequent taxation of various types and ownerships of real, and sometimes personal, property. On occasion, the exclusion is based on use, regardless of ownership. Every five years the Census of Governments shows the state-by-state distribution of the net assessed value of real estate—residential, commercial, industrial, utility, and other—and of personal property—automobiles, factory equipment, inventories, and many other items. The 1982 census presented the following information on values of property excluded from taxation.[44]

- 1981 values of locally assessed property approximated $2.7 trillion, a net increase of 151 percent over the net assessed value in 1976.

- 1981 values assigned to excluded property by twenty-three states and the District of Columbia totalled $259.6 billion. This was 9.3 percent of the national total of locally assessed value; this meant that other property tax payers had to pick up the $259.6 billion shortfall if it were assumed that no property should be excluded, which of course would be erroneous.

- Of the $2.7 trillion of locally assessed property, all but $272 billion was real property. Many of the states had abandoned the assessment of all personal property; remaining state-assessed property included railroads and other utilities, requiring individual expertise for satisfactory appraisal.

- Of the $259.6 billion mandated to be excluded from the local tax base, 49.2 percent was governmentally owned property (federal, state, and local); 8.7 percent was owned by private educational institutions, 5.8 percent by religious organizations, and 5.7 percent by charitable organizations. Nearly a third, 30.5 percent, fell into the "other" or "unallocable" category. This last category probably is the one most deserving of careful review by state legislatures.

The average effective property tax rate for the United States as a whole was 1.16 percent in 1986 (the effective rate being the total dollar amount of property tax paid on a piece of property in a given year divided by the market value of that property).[45]

Property excluded or removed from the tax base falls into several major classifications. (1) The most widespread is property used for purposes acknowledged to be publicly beneficial—churches, hospitals, and educational institutions; use and ownership together usually are required for total exemption. (2) Some states exempt particular classes of property, such as utilities, subjecting them instead to a form of special property or other tax. (3) Individual states exempt specified new industrial plants, usually for up to ten years, to attract industry to locate in the state. (4) Specific legislative action exempts particular property in individual jurisdictions. (5) Many states provide incentives for activities such as pollution control and energy conservation via property tax exemption.

Under the 1.16 percent average effective rate, the annual "loss" to local governments from exclusions from the tax base is about $3 billion. Careful screening of exempt property, especially in the miscellaneous category, could yield some additional revenue for hard-pressed communities. Each new enactment warrants careful review. For example, in 1986, New Jersey and New York ranked first and fourth in the country (Oregon and Michigan being second and third) in the severity of their effective property tax rates—2.33 and 2.22 percent, respectively. The New York legislature in its 1987 session enacted new partial property tax exemptions benefiting 197,000 veterans; this resulted in an annual saving for the veterans of $18.3 million in county, town, and city taxes, an average of nearly $100 per veteran. The new exemption removed $1.6 billion from the tax rolls of general local governments (but did not affect school districts), shifting the action's burden to nonexempt property owners.[46] One of the reasons for the action was that some Korea and many Vietnam veterans had received national benefits totaling less than those of World War II veterans. This kind of action, while logical within the context of the veteran population, was hardly defensible on intergovernmental and fiscal grounds. Stated another way, the issue is whether or not states can afford to endeavor to correct gaps in national redistribution policies, and if so, whether it should be done at the expense of local governments that often have little voice in such decisions.

Central-City—Suburban Disparities

Various studies, beginning in the late sixties, examined socioeconomic and fiscal disparities between the nation's larger central cities and their suburbs. The disparities were marked in economic, racial, and fiscal terms throughout much of the seventies and into the eighties.[47] By the mid-eighties they had begun to lessen somewhat in racial and economic terms due to minority middle-income movement to the suburbs and gentrification of central-city neighborhoods, with some of the in-migrants coming from the suburbs. Anecdotal evidence began to appear in the mid-eighties indicating that some of the earlier distressed central cities of the Northeast were experiencing economic improvement.[48]

However, as will be examined at length in chapter 5, a substantial number of census tracts in many of the major central cities have become "underclass areas," where economic and social problems are overwhelming. Despite the movement of blacks and other minorities of middle income to the suburbs, many central cities at the end of the eighties were characterized by continuing population loss, concentration of poor and minority populations, shifting of employment opportunities for less skilled workers to employment centers outside the city, and marked disparities in income and per capita public expenditures in comparison with suburban areas.

Socioeconomic indicators of central-city distress include changes in (1) total population; (2) minority proportion of population; (3) real personal income; (4) patterns of journeys to work; and (5) the proportions of the various categories of employment (manufacturing, retail and wholesale trade, and selected services) found respectively in the central city and the suburbs. Censuses of population occur every ten years interspersed with interim surveys; the business census occurs every five years, the past three being in 1977, 1982, and 1987, and results are published approximately two years subsequently.

Table 2.3 shows central-city and metropolitan-area population data for 1970, 1980, and 1986 for the fifteen largest cities as of mid–1986. The proportionate gains and losses do not necessarily indicate real change because the areal composition of either the city (through annexation or detachment) or of the metropolitan area (through the addition of one or more suburban counties) may have changed. However, both population and the proportionate share of area population make up one of the several indicators that assist in distinguishing among growing, stable, stagnant, and declining central-city economies.

Also of significance is the extent of population loss over a period of years. Of the sixty cities with estimated populations of 250,000 and over, seventeen

Table 2.3

Central-City Population as Percentage of Metropolitan-Area Population, 1970, 1980, and 1986, for Fifteen Largest Cities in 1986

City	City Population			Metro Area Population			City Percent		
	1970	1980	1986	1970	1980	1986	'70	'80	'86
New York	7,896	7,072	7,263	9,077	8,275	8,473	87	85	86
Los Angeles	2,812	2,969	3,259	7,042	7,477	8,296	40	40	39
Chicago	3,369	3,005	3,010	6,093	6,060	6,188	55	50	49
Houston	1,234	1,611	1,729	1,891	2,735	3,231	65	59	54
Philadelphia	1,950	1,688	1,643	4,824	4,717	4,826	40	36	34
Detroit	1,514	1,203	1,086	4,554	4,488	4,335	33	27	25
San Diego	697	876	1,015	1,358	1,862	2,201	51	47	46
Dallas	844	905	1,004	1,556	1,957	2,401	54	46	42
San Antonio	654	810	914	888	1,072	1,276	74	76	72
Phoenix	584	790	894	967	1,509	1,900	60	52	47
Baltimore	906	787	753	2,089	2,199	2,280	43	36	33
San Francisco	716	679	749	1,482	1,489	1,588	48	46	47
Indianapolis	737	701	720	1,111	1,167	1,213	66	60	59
San Jose	460	629	712	1,065	1,295	1,402	43	49	51
Memphis	624	646	653	834	913	960	75	71	68

Source: Bureau of the Census, *Provisional Estimates for Metro. Areas*, P–26, no. 86A, 1970, 1980, and *Ranking of Cities by 1986 Population*, CB 87–165, rev., November 11, 1987.

lost population during the six-year period 1980–86, five losing approximately 5 percent or more: Detroit (9.7), Buffalo (9.4), Pittsburgh (8.7), Cleveland (6.6), and Milwaukee (5.0). Of the same class of cities (250,000 and over), those experiencing substantial declines in real total income in the 1970–80 period were Hartford and Detroit (21.8); Newark and Cleveland (21); St. Louis (20.7); Buffalo (19.3); Philadelphia (12.0); Louisville (11.2); New York (10.6); and Baltimore (10.3).[49]

On a national aggregated basis for 1970–80, changes in nominal income by type of households showed that within metropolitan areas, income for all households rose by 99.9 percent for metro areas as a whole, by 92.2 percent in central cities, and by 100.4 percent in suburbia. Respective central-city suburban increases for specific types of households were as follows: white family households, 99.1 and 107.1 percent; black family households, 100.0 and 132.8 percent; white nonfamily households, 128.8 and 141.6 percent; and black nonfamily households, 113.6 and 173.1 percent. Only in the South, for white, male-headed households, did the central-city increase approach parity with suburbia (115.8 and 117.7 percent).[50]

Table 2.4 shows, for metropolitan areas with a work force of 500,000 or more, the proportions of city residents working inside the city and proportions of suburban residents working inside the city for 1970 and 1980. By 1970 the role of suburbia as "bedroom communities" for the central city had changed markedly. The proportion of the labor force residing in the suburbs but working in the city was decreasing. Increasingly workers were working at growing job centers in suburbia itself; some were commuting to work in newly formed suburbs farther out—"exurbia." A significant difference is noted, however, between the older cities of the Northeast and those of the South and West. By no means is this attributable solely to expanding or stagnating economies; in those states where cities are relatively unrestricted in annexing unincorporated areas, thus keeping the city boundaries ahead of population spread, most of the metropolitan-area population and jobs remained within city boundaries, as in Houston and other cities in Texas, Arizona, Oregon, and North Carolina and other Southern states.

Table 2.5 shows central-city industrial employment as a percentage of those categories of employment in the metropolitan area. Tables 2.4 and 2.5 are critical in socioeconomic terms. As commuting flows into the city lessen, and as new job creation occurs primarily in suburbia, a formidable transportation barrier faces central-city residents seeking work.

Although Roy Bahl and Philip Dearborn [as referenced in the first paragraph of this chapter] found the relative fiscal position of cities to be better in the mid–1980s than before, educational needs and poor inner-city school conditions indicate much larger fiscal needs in the future. If these needs are met from state aid, the relative city-suburban position can remain stabilized, but if local taxes must be raised to meet the problem of declining schools, the interlocal fiscal disparities may begin to widen again.

State Aid to Distressed Localities: Fiscal/Economic Issues

As shown in tables 1.4 and 1.5, the local government proportions of the four major expenditure categories in the state-local sector—public K–12 schools, welfare, highways, and health/hospitals—were 44, 7, 26, and 45 percent respectively. There was a wide range among the individual states (appendices 1.D and 1.E). It was found also that state financial aid comprised the largest single segment of local government revenue from all sources. However, general state aid—unrestricted as to purpose, or "revenue sharing"—as a proportion of total state assistance dropped from 10.5 percent in 1974 to 9.9 percent in 1984, with education a dominating 62.3 percent of all state aid in the latter year.

To get at the fiscal equity issues involved in state aid, it is necessary to examine the factors that determine the intrastate distribution of aid among the local governments and local areas as it relates both to local government budgets and to local economies. There are two key policy issues. (1) What are the most appropriate indicators of local fiscal capacity? (2) To what extent can or should state programs be targeted toward, or carry the most substantial relief for, communities under the greatest fiscal and/or economic stress? Such considerations are likely to be even more important and controversial in future state policy and in state-local relations than heretofore. They were more prominent in the eighties than earlier because of the greater recessionary impact upon some sectors of the

Table 2.4

Places of Residence and Work in MSAs with Work Force of 500,000 or More, 1970 and 1980 (In Percents)

Area	1970 City Residents Wkg. City	Wkg. OCC	Suburban Res Wkg. City	Wkg. OCC	1980 City Resdts. Wkg. City	Wkg. OCC	Sub. Rsdts. Wkg. City	Wkg. OCC
Anaheim CA	45.9	48.2	18.9	76.3	40.9	48.8	16.1	74.7
Atlanta	68.8	15.4	39.2	55.4	65.0	23.7	26.9	65.6
Baltimore	67.0	22.8	28.9	65.6	66.6	21.1	26.9	65.6
Boston	68.4	17.8	22.9	70.2	66.0	22.2	20.8	71.3
Chicago	74.0	16.7	24.4	70.0	71.4	16.8	20.2	71.2
Cincinnati	67.3	25.2	34.9	60.8	68.0	23.6	32.0	61.8
Cleveland	66.4	22.8	39.4	56.0	63.2	26.7	31.3	62.3
Dallas-Ft. W.	79.6	12.3	44.7	50.7	74.7	15.5	38.8	52.7
Detroit	59.6	31.5	22.1	73.1	57.1	29.9	15.0	74.2
Houston	82.2	9.2	42.9	51.7	77.5	8.2	43.8	43.0

Kan.Cy.MO	68.9	19.4	37.3	56.1	68.1	22.9	31.4	60.0
LosAngeles–Long Beach	66.8	25.5	28.4	65.1	63.7	26.2	22.2	65.1
Miami	51.0	39.0	28.3	63.7	56.8	29.9	31.4	53.0
Milwaukee	69.6	22.9	33.5	62.0	67.0	24.9	30.1	62.4
Minneapolis–St.Paul	74.7	19.2	41.0	55.1	69.6	22.6	28.9	63.6
New York	82.0	7.1	64.0	24.4	82.9	5.5	19.6	71.2
Newark	50.9	39.8	11.6	81.7	43.9	26.8	7.6	63.1
Philadelphia	75.6	13.1	19.1	83.6	78.1	13.1	15.7	76.5
Pittsburgh	74.5	20.7	22.3	72.8	78.7	21.3	25.3	74.7
St. Louis	70.5	19.5	27.0	66.4	75.6	24.4	23.0	69.3
San Diego	78.1	15.3	31.6	62.3	79.3	20.7	31.4	61.7
San Fran–cisco	75.5	14.1	26.2	67.2	72.7	15.7	23.0	66.5
Seattle	81.1	13.5	42.6	52.6	78.6	14.6	36.2	56.7
Washington	65.7	17.1	30.3	63.3	69.6	16.5	28.0	64.1

Source: Bureau of the Census, *U.S. Census of Population, 1970: Detailed Population Characteristics, U.S. Summary,* 1677–1678; *U.S. Census of Population, 1980: Detailed Population Characteristics,* PC80–1–D, State Reports.

OCC = outside central city.

Table 2.5
Central-City Population and Industrial Employment as Percentages of MSA Population and Industrial Employment, 1972–82

Metro Area	CC Population			Manufacturing			Retail Trade			Wholesale Trade			Selected Services		
	'70	'80	'86	'72	'77	'82	'72	'77	'82	'72	'77	'82	'72	'77	'82
New York	87	85	86	80	77	74	77	73	71	82	77	74	86	84	82
Los Angeles	40	40	39	36	38	38	47	41	39	47	42	41	57	49	49
Chicago	55	50	49	47	41	37	45	38	32	52	44	35	64	58	51
Houston	65	59	54	66	70	66	72	72	68	88	88	84	81	79	80
Philadelphia	40	36	34	41	35	31	37	32	28	73	40	34	70	41	35
Detroit	33	27	25	33	27	25	27	19	15	44	32	24	46	32	24
San Antonio	74	76	72	82	81	84	83	83	82	82	81	92	89	90	88
San Francisco	48	46	47	24	22	26	41	26	26	52	32	27	58	47	41
San Diego	51	47	46	70	57	69	53	51	49	70	70	68	72	69	69
Atlanta	29	20	16	37	31	28	48	33	26	55	40	27	68	54	40
Phoenix	60	52	47	73	69	62	60	56	54	83	77	74	73	69	65
Denver	47	35	31	51	40	33	45	38	33	76	64	59	67	58	52
Baltimore	43	36	33	50	44	39	43	33	30	63	50	42	56	49	40
St. Louis	26	19	17	38	37	32	27	21	18	47	40	33	48	36	25
Buffalo	42	35	34	35	33	33	35	29	24	52	40	39	55	47	40
Cleveland	36	30	29	49	46	41	36	29	24	55	45	41	60	50	41

Source: Bureau of the Census, *Census of Manufactures: Geographic Area Series,* MC–72, MC 77–A, 82–A; *Census of Retail Trade: Geographic Area Series,* RC–72, RC–77, and RC–82; *Census of Wholesale Trade: Geographic Area Series,* WC–72, WC–77, and WC–82; *Census of Service Industries: Geographic Area Series,* SC–72, SC–77 and SC–82; *1970 and 1980 Census of Population* and News Release CB87–165 (rev.), population of cities of 100,000 and over, 1987.

economy than others, with pockets of distress coexisting with economic health elsewhere in a given state.

For intergovernmental aid allocation from federal to state governments, population was the dominant measure of need from the beginning of grant programs in the late 1800s until the late 1940s, when for some programs, per capita income became an additional allocating factor, as well as a matching factor. From state to local governments, population always was the primary allocating factor, but with assessable property becoming an additional consideration, first in school aid and later, in some states, for revenue sharing. Personal income had become an allocating factor in six states by 1982.[51]

By the fifties states were getting into noneducational aid for particular services, and toward the end of the eighties these aided categories were covering most of the local service spectrum when viewed nationwide among all the states. Allocation factors for categorical aid normally include one or more specific aspects of the service—numbers or proportions of the aid targets, such as crippled children, low-income families, or deteriorated housing units.

In the financially dominant area of elementary and secondary education, many state school aid formulas are tied to special pupil categories in addition to pupil population, assessable property value, and other general allocating factors. Compensatory education is weighted heavily in many states, along with special education for the physically handicapped, gifted children, and those needing bilingual, vocational, or other forms of education that impose incremental additional costs on the school district.

Measuring fiscal capacity has been a subject of considerable difficulty and controversy for public finance scholars, legislators, and interest-group members since the fifties, when the per capita income factor began to cause arguments within the Congress and among the states. Agricultural states tended to benefit from the factor because wealth rather than income was an important factor in farming, with many farmers "living poor and dying rich," and because rural living costs were considerably lower than in urban areas.

In 1960 members of the ACIR directed that a study be made of alternative measures of fiscal capacity. The resulting study by Alice Rivlin and the late Selma Mushkin produced a possible measure based on a "representative tax system" (RTS).[52] Simply stated, a national aggregate of state-local taxes was broken down into its principal components, and proportionate shares of the total base were calculated. (At that time, the property tax comprised about 45 percent, far more than in later years.) Those proportionate bases, along with the average national effective rate for each tax, were then applied to each state against its own potential base, and total potential yields were computed and averaged. An index of relative tax capacity resulted, which showed the potential for each state if its different bases were utilized proportionately to the national average. Relative tax effort could then be derived for any state by comparing its actual collections with its capacity, and in turn with the national average.

In the ensuing years public officials and finance scholars devoted considerable attention to the issue. RTS was refined and improved by various researchers, and new alternatives were developed both to per capita income (PCI) and to RTS, including representative revenue system (RRS), gross state product (GSP), total taxable resources (TTR), export-adjusted personal income (EAI), export-ability, and others.[53] As of 1986 all of these except EAI were being calculated regularly by government agencies.[54] EAI figures had been constructed for U.S. cities by Helen Ladd and colleagues.[55]

These measures of state fiscal capacity are very important in federal-state fiscal relations and of considerable concern to local governments; they form a backdrop to consideration of the most appropriate measure for local fiscal capacity for appropriate use by states in the distribution of financial aid to local governments. ACIR produced a study by Allen Manvel in the early seventies on the application of RTS to local areas.[56] Later, the practicality of the EAI, the income-adjusted alternative, was demonstrated by an index for seventy-eight major U.S. cities in a 1986 report for the Department of Housing and Urban Development (HUD). (Illustrative indices per unit of service responsibility were Atlanta, 1.20; Boston, 1.17; Denver, 1.09; Oakland, .99; San Antonio, .73; and Detroit, .64.)

This approach by Ladd and colleagues defined fiscal capacity of a local government as the amount of its revenue that a unit can raise from broad-based taxes at a given tax burden on its residents; this measure varies with (a) resident income and (b) the ability of the unit to export part of its tax burdens to non-residents, as through an earnings tax.[57] (In addition to earnings taxes, user charges applied to residents and nonresidents alike, as for parking garages and meters, also represent exportation to the extent of nonresident use and assume increased importance in defining exportability as the proportion of unit revenues derived from charges instead of taxes continues to increase.)

Measuring economic need or distress is difficult in any case and is very controversial when the measures are to be used in allocating money among competing recipients. Whereas the measurement of fiscal capacity applies to governmental units, to the geographical boundaries of the county, township, or municipality, and to its resident population, the measurement of economic distress is applied more easily to larger economic or geographic areas—a county, trading area, or metropolitan area. If the measure is to be used for fund allocation to local units, it needs to be disaggregated to the unit involved. This becomes difficult in the case of smaller municipalities, because much of the local economic data generated through the U.S. Census and Labor Statistics bureaus typically cover only the counties and the larger city areas.

Commonly used measures of economic health include, among others, changes in population or per capita income over time intervals, rates for unemployment, percentage of population receiving aid to families with dependent children (AFDC) or other welfare payments, percentage of housing units subsidized for low-income purposes, incidence of felony arrests for the population, commercial and residential vacancy rates, and percentage of residents whose incomes fall below the poverty line.

An important element of state financial relief of local economic or fiscal conditions is the extent to which the state delivers directly or finances all or practically all of a given service or function (for example, courts, corrections, the nontuition part of community colleges, the "general assistance" category of public welfare, the nonfederal portion of AFDC and Medicaid, and property tax assessment). If the proportion financed or performed by the state is high, commensurately less burden is placed on local revenue sources. Second, to the extent that categorical aid carries a high state share (as for K–12 public education, in a dozen or more states where the state share exceeds two-thirds), there is less burden to be relieved in the units with low fiscal capacity. Finally, to the extent that state categorical or general state aid programs incorporate allocation factors based on the fiscal capacity and economic health measures discussed earlier, the poorer units are relieved, and the more affluent are assessed. This is the basic process and policy issue of equalization.

Should aid allocation go beyond population or some other "equal share" factor and incorporate considerations of relative wealth or poverty? Does equity equate with equality? It does not so equate in the private for-profit sector and the many other fields in which competitive effort is involved; it does at the polling place, in church, and in many other places, and equal protection of the laws is guaranteed under the U.S. Constitution. In many public as well as most private organizations, personnel compensation depends to varying degrees on productivity and other personal abilities and traits.

Should local units of government and their budgets be assured of a level playing field regardless of the cost-consciousness of their managements? The answer in many cases ranges from "no" to "yes, to a certain extent." Often the basic policy question is the extent; that is determined by the makeup of state aid formulas.[58] One body of opinion is unsympathetic to any kind of fiscal redistribution; others believe that any redistribution should occur at the national, not at the state, metropolitan, or local level; still others support fiscal equalization as a social and economic goal wherever there are wide economic or fiscal disparities.

The perceived need for interlocal equalization arises from the following situation: individuals in different taxing jurisdictions but at the same income level, paying the same amount in taxes, could receive widely disparate public services. There are two possible causes for this "horizontal inequity" where those of equal incomes have access to unequal levels of public services: (1) divergent per capita incomes of individual residents and (2) geographically divergent abilities of governments to export tax burdens.

The divergency of per capita incomes is especially controversial in education finance—for example, in the issue of wealthy people living in areas with ample tax bases and consequently paying a relatively small percentage of income for broad public services. On the second point, the matter of public choice comes in; if a jurisdiction provides a level of public service too low for one's satisfaction, one does not settle there, or if already living there, one can move to a better-performing jurisdiction. However, economic inefficiency arises when the location decisions of households and firms are distorted by noneconomic considerations—for example, when they move solely to minimize tax liability for a given level of public service.[59] These conflicting policy goals are reflected in four types of arrangements in public education finance:

1. A foundation plan, whereby the state government provides a guaranteed minimum level of per pupil support.

2. District power equalizing which provides that a given local tax rate should yield a certain level of education funding, and the legislature mandates a local imposition of that rate; if at that rate the yield falls short of the specified dollar level, the state makes up the difference.

3. Full state funding, whereunder the state assumes all responsibility for school finance; an issue remains as to whether wealthy jurisdictions could supplement the state level and restore their superiority in quality (assuming that dollars translate into quality, a debatable proposition when high levels are reached).

4. A voucher program, whereby education vouchers are given for each school-age child and the parents can utilize them at any public or private school. This would represent a maximum degree of consumer choice.[60]

The equalization issue does not arise as sharply when state programs designed to aid economically blighted areas are discussed. In this case market forces have often worked their will, and particular industries or firms on which the community and its residents have depended for employment, economic stability, and a share of its public revenues have had to go out of business or move elsewhere to better marketing areas.

In 1979 the Department of Housing and Urban Development requested that the ACIR and the National Academy of Public Administration examine the role of state government in shaping community conditions, with a focus on state aid to distressed communities. Over a four-year period, 1980–83, this state activity was studied, using as indicators state programs or policies believed to be helpful to distressed communities; a fourth and final report was issued in November 1985.

The program indicators fell into five policy areas; the first three—housing, economic development, and community development—comprised programs that helped communities meet specific needs related to their distress. In the other two areas—state-local fiscal relations and enhancing local self-help capabilities—the programs were aimed at relieving local governments of part of their financial burdens or provided them with the authority to respond to their own concerns. The final report comprised three sets of materials: (1) a narrative volume presenting survey results and the findings and recommendations of the commission; (2) a program catalog describing 776 state programs benefiting distressed communities; and (3) eighteen pieces of draft state legislation covering the twenty program indicator areas.[61]

It is one thing for a state to maintain any or all of these programs for general applicability across the state; it is quite another to target the state financial assistance involved to the communities in most distress. In the tabulation of state activity, targeting required the use of unemployment or other criteria of distress or blight. To be counted for any of the program indicators, a state had to meet the "targeting" definition for that area or program. For example, for a community to be "distressed," it had to be in the bottom 25 percent of all jurisdictions of the same class throughout the state; a state aid program for housing, economic development, and community development had to give explicit priority to distressed people, places, or firms and be at least 50 percent funded by the state.

However, the stringency of several of the definitions left something to be desired; for most programs, a quantitative measure, such as the lowest 25 percent, might well be required in future tabulations of the extent of targeting. (If targeting definitions are too mushy in policy-making and program formulation, the old adage attributed to Benjamin Franklin comes into play: A benefit to all becomes a benefit to none.)

The report found a continuing increase in state aid to local communities over the duration of the project. Some programs that were loosely defined, such as welfare (state "help" with non-federal share and a "substantial" contribution to local K–12 public education) showed, not surprisingly, universal state participation. Program areas with more discriminating criteria showed more limited state participation. These involved housing rehabilitation grants and loans (9 states); customized job training (12); industrial development bonds for local projects (11); and state reimbursement for local costs of complying with certain state mandates(12).

Interstate and Interlocal Economic and Fiscal Competition

At the outset it is necessary to identify and classify the components of intergovernmental competition in the broad sense. One way to classify these is by objective, type of competition employed, and jurisdictions involved. The major objectives usually are one or more of the following:

- Economic development, often by incentives for business creation, location, or relocation (for example, encouraging entrepreneurship through facilitating access to venture capital; incentives for a newly forming business to locate in the jurisdiction, or for an existing business to move from another location into the jurisdiction; and incentives to businesses already in the jurisdiction that are considering closing down or moving away to remain in the jurisdiction)

- Income-base enhancement by incentives to highly educated and/or high-income individuals to locate in the jurisdiction

- Expenditure load-shedding by excluding undesirable businesses and classes of individuals that require greater service outlays than are likely to be returned in revenues

- Enhancement of quality of life (for example, by service improvements, law enforcement, or environmental regulation)

Principal types or vehicles of competition include the following:

- Tax competition via liberalization, such as property tax abatements and income tax credits for new investment or job creation, and/or via constraint (for example, no income tax or a low, flat-rate tax; no or low estate or inheritance tax)
- Tax competition through collusion with adjoining jurisdictions (the public equivalent to private price fixing)
- Expenditure competition via infrastructure, good schools, other public facility or service amenities, or service quality and public choice, enabling consumers and taxpayers to get the level of service they desire at prices they are willing to pay
- Regulatory competition via relaxation to attract or retain businesses with a favorable tax-base/service-demand ratio or via regulatory constriction in land use regulation or governmental boundary actions in incorporation or annexation to enhance both quality of life and favorable public tax-expenditure ratios
- Regulatory collusion between or among neighboring jurisdictions to thwart retaliatory relocation by businesses or individuals

Governmental areas and types that are involved in economic and fiscal competition are expanding toward the universal on international, interstate, and interlocal levels. Most but not all of the competition is horizontal; in national-state and state-local levels of concurrent jurisdiction, especially in the regulatory area, vertical competition may arise in standard setting or enforcement.

The principal interests and concerns expressed about intergovernmental competition have tended to center on economic efficiency and fiscal equity. The efficiency and equity aspects of (a) service delivery and user-based financing and (b) environmental and other regulatory systems are examined in chapters 3 and 6, respectively. Here, primary attention will be directed to tax and fiscal aspects of competition.

Economic and fiscal competition among states and between and among localities for the purpose of attracting business and industry of the type that adds valuable property to the tax base but does not require many public services has been extant for all of the post–World War II period. The use of tax-exempt industrial development bonds was a key weapon in this endeavor, but was curbed in several important respects by federal tax reform legislation in 1986. Property tax abatements for newly locating businesses also played a key role. The principal equity questions were (1) the use of property tax exemptions or abatements to entice business location; (2) credits against state and/or local income taxes for new investment and job creation; and (3) provision of public infrastructure especially tailored to a new or relocating enterprise.

As in the case of other subtractions from the property tax base of a locality, other local taxpayers or service users must make up the lost revenue. Always present is the question of the relative importance of state and local taxes in locational decisions and the question of the equity and effectiveness of particular forms of tax breaks extended. It should be noted here that the general issue of fiscal competition among governments, which formerly was criticized in many quarters as being uneconomic and inequitable, is receiving new examination in the light of resource scarcities.

In a 1963 report the ACIR found as follows regarding the use of industrial development bonds to attract business and industry: "We conclude that the industrial development bond tends to impair tax equities, competitive business relationships and conventional financing institutions out of proportion to its contribution to economic development and employment. It is therefore a device which the Commission does not endorse or recommend." U.S. Senator Edmund Muskie of Maine, a member of the commission, dissented as follows: "I do not concur. . . . [States and their local governments] should be encouraged—not discouraged—to attack problems of economic stagnation and underemployment . . . ; providing opportunity and incentive for industry and employment, through a free enterprise economy is a proper and legitimate concern of local government which does not materially differ from the provision of water, sewage disposal, [and] roads. . . . "[62]

Nearly a quarter century later, John Shannon, executive director of the ACIR through the mid-eighties, in addressing the issue of interjurisdictional economic and fiscal competition, noted several new developments that warranted a "hard new look at this tough old issue." He listed the following factors:

- Interjurisdictional tax competition is now winning over some supporters in academia— a place that had traditionally been quite hostile to notions of tax competition and tax concessions—who argue that such competition restrains the growth of government and promotes greater efficiency in the public sector.
- The growing vulnerability of domestic manufacturers to international competition quickens the search for low-cost locations within the United States.
- The rise of "fend for yourself" federalism naturally intensifies interjurisdictional tax competition.
- The intensification of such competition is bound to raise a major equity issue—not all states and localities enter this competitive arena on anything that even closely resembles equal terms.

Shannon went on to observe that

a state with anemic resources such as Alabama cannot be expected to compete on equal terms with its robust neighbor, Florida. . . . a poverty plagued Newark cannot compete effectively with a neighboring Westchester County, New York. . . . the national government will have to even out the competitive playing field—at least that part located in the interstate [commerce] arena. . . . It is not in the long range interest of those who favor the maintenance of a competitive environment to let the winners win too much and the losers lose too much.[63]

Susan Stephenson and Roger Hewett pointed out that "the problem encountered by a state attempting to raise tax revenues is that state economies are open. If a state . . . [raises] tax rates, it may find that its tax base shrinks as residents shift their economic activities elsewhere." They go on to explain that tax revenue decisions by a given state inevitably depend at least in part on the tax policies of other states, and that if two adjoining states are in need of a tax increase, they may act collusively, but if such bilateral action puts the two of them out of step with the interstate regional situation, they may find themselves at a competitive disadvantage unless their other regional neighbors decide to follow suit.[64]

On economic efficiency, the public choice and procompetition theory holds that, as in the private sector, more competition means better service with lower prices (taxes). Henry Aaron, James Buchanan, William Niskanen, and many others have argued that local governments, when taking into account the response of prospective residents, will provide more and better public services than if migration were not possible. Sjoquist contended that the greater the number of separate governments in metropolitan areas, the less likely that the per capita expenditures of the central city, as well as the other jurisdictions, would rise.[65]

Retail sales, especially in metropolitan areas, have been found to be quite sensitive to interlocal differentials in sales taxes. Anecdotal evidence abounds of auto trips across local and state lines for reasons of sales tax differentials (Massachusetts and New Hampshire; Virginia, District of Columbia, and Maryland). John Mikesell and William Fox in separate studies found statistically significant differences in this regard, the former using cross-sectional data on 173 metropolitan areas and the latter using 3 metropolitan areas in Tennessee close to state borders with Georgia, Virginia, and Kentucky. Fox also found that state income taxes had little effect on retail establishment location decisions.[66]

James and Leslie Papke concluded (within the 1986 context of deductibility for federal income tax purposes of state and local business taxes as well as general sales taxes) that in general, "lower state-local business taxes . . . will not repel business and most likely will encourage it." They observed also, "There is . . . an expanding body of empirical studies employing state-of-the-art statistical techniques and computational technology that indicate that state and local taxes do influence the geographical pattern of business location."[67]

On the fiscal equity side of the competition question, it is difficult to ascertain serious equity impacts upon classes of individuals arising from interstate tax and expenditure competition. Some of the strategies adopted may bear unfavorable results for the treasury of a particular state and thereby impact upon that state's taxpayers as a group. At the local government level, aggressive tax and other incentive actions, especially by well-heeled suburban jurisdictions, may hasten the migration of employers from central cities to lower-rent suburban areas. While this kind of intrametropolitan competition may be beneficial in terms of cost and quality of public services, it can have serious implications for central-city employment. This underscores the need, in those states having one or more central cities that are moving into serious economic difficulty, for the state government to examine its own economic development incentive and state aid policies as they apply to interlocal competitive situations.

Cost-effectiveness of Business Location Incentives

The array of economic, fiscal, expenditure, and other incentives, in addition to credits, abatements, and other tax preferences, that are used by state and local governments to attract and retain business and industry is astounding. For example, a directory compiled in 1986 by the National Association of State Development Agencies shows the major categories of incentives and the number and identity of states in which the state government or its units offer the particular incentive. The major nontax categories include customized industrial training (41); direct state loans (26); locally issued industrial development revenue bonds (IDRBs) (45); state-issued IDRBs (25); IDRB guarantees (9); loan guarantees (15); privately sponsored development credit corporations (11); state grants (14); and state-funded or state-chartered equity/venture capital corporations (8).[68] Nationwide, the cost in revenue forgone of the multitude of tax incentives plus the published and hidden amount of direct outlays and indirect subsidies involved in these nontax incentives undoubtedly runs into many billions of dollars.

However, relatively few, if any, truly comprehensive and penetrating analyses of the totality and composition of this universe have been undertaken that address the cost-benefit issue. The key question in ascertaining the benefit of an incentive is "what would have happened if it had not been offered and used?" Obviously, answers must be tentative in many cases. But given the magnitudes involved, it would appear that careful studies to establish the relative effectiveness of particular incentives is a crucial matter for state-local consideration in an extended period of fiscal austerity.

FISCAL AND ADMINISTRATIVE POLICY AND MANAGEMENT ISSUES

Delivering state and local public services in an efficient, effective, and equitable manner, while being politically responsive to often-clashing community-wide, neighborhood, and other substate regional objectives and public opinion, will be an even more crucial challenge to state and local officials in the nineties than previously, because of the scarcity of resources and the prospects of slower economic growth than in the prior two decades. In the days when the economic growth pie was enlarging continually, slippage, inefficiency, and downright wasting of money was tolerated. To tolerate it under present and forthcoming circumstances, when the economic growth pie is slow, stagnant, or declining, is unacceptable public policy. Despite the substantial progress made during the eighties, to maintain the rigor of cutback management in the face of new and increasing expenditure needs in some areas will be difficult, and to proceed even further in increasing the scope and yield of revenue sources and simultaneously reducing and eliminating marginal, and low-priority programs will be trying indeed for elected officials and professional public managers.

Nonetheless, as is being demonstrated and documented in these pages, more resources can be had, and expenditures can be further reduced. In the concluding section of this chapter on domestic governance in the face of resource scarcity, a checklist of possible changes in fiscal policy and administrative management will be presented for consideration. All are difficult, and most have significant disadvantages as well as advantages. All on the policy side are controversial, both in terms of desirability and implementation. Each one, however, enjoys wide support—as well as objections—from public policy analysts, and each has been adopted and is in place in a number of state and/or local governments. Additional explanation and references will be provided for those not discussed earlier. The first set of options deals with increased revenues in terms of source, yield, or both. Similarly, options for fiscal economies in program or administrative expenditure and more prudent management practices will be noted. Most of these require state legislative action, and appendix 2.C lists titles of substantive sections of draft legislation developed by the ACIR to illustrate the kinds of subsidiary policy choices that are involved.

Expanded Revenue Sources and Yields

Already mentioned has been the desirability of state authorization, for use by general-purpose local governments, of revenue sources additional to the property tax. Some cogent criteria for considering a new tax were set forth in a 1987 book on *Management Policies in Local Government Finance*. In summarized form, these were as follows:

1. Fairness. A tax should reflect the ability to pay of those who bear its burden, or the tax burden should be matched by benefits received.
2. Certainty. The rules of taxation should be clearly stated and evenly applied.
3. Convenience. The tax should be convenient to pay, with due dates that can coincide with the income stream of taxpayers.
4. Efficiency. Fair administration should be feasible and efficient, with administration/collection costs a minor fraction of the revenue obtained.
5. Productivity. The tax should produce sufficient, stable revenue.
6. Neutrality. Unless overwhelmingly socially desirable, a tax should not distort the way the state or community would otherwise use its resources.[69]

Expansion in user-based financing moves all or part of the financing of a given function from the general tax base to the users of the service being delivered. As analyzed in detail in chapter 3, this shift, if handled properly, can render the financing of particular functions more equitable and free up a commensurate part of the general tax base for other purposes.

Extension of state sales tax to selected services can render this tax less regressive in its overall incidence. Some states have done this to a limited extent (Hawaii, New Mexico, and South Dakota as of 1987); a comprehensive extension was enacted in Florida in early 1987 to professional services provided by lawyers, accountants, and consultants and to personal services, such as for dry cleaning, health clubs, landscaping, and auto repairs, but with medical services remaining exempt from the sales tax. It was also applied to services supplied in Florida by out-of-state suppliers. The expanded tax base was scheduled to produce an additional $700 million annually in new revenue under the state 5 percent sales tax.[70] Violent opposition, especially to its application to out-of-state advertising firms, caused repeal of the tax.

Reappraisal of exclusions and exemptions from the local property tax base, with those applying to individuals being repealed or restricted to middle- or lower-income levels if appropriate, can enhance both revenue yield and tax equity. Also, local governments should be authorized to negotiate with owners of excluded or exempt property to establish payment for services rendered directly to the property. As any services are shifted to user-based financing, the resulting charges to users can be applied likewise to organizations owning or operating tax-exempt properties. Better state and local appraisal and record keeping on these properties could create the context in which citizens or legislators would demand that tax-exempt groups start to pay a share of the ever-rising costs of taxes and government services.[71]

Instituting and regionalizing lotteries can bring new or expanded revenues to state governments; lotteries were generating over $10 billion in 1987, with two-thirds of the U.S. population living in lottery states. Among the then nonlottery states, Idaho, Indiana, Virginia, Minnesota, and Kentucky adopted lotteries in 1987 and 1988.[72] Of the lottery states, the ones with the largest estimated annual yields in 1987 were California, New York, Pennsylvania, and Illinois.[73] In the New England and mid-Atlantic states, interstate groupings had been formed or were under consideration to enable larger prizes, reduce administrative costs, and gain increased yields.

Indexation of state and local income taxes, whereby the income base is adjusted for inflation, can increase political accountability. At the beginning of 1987, eight of the forty states with a broad-based income tax were indexing (Arizona, California, Colorado, Iowa, Maine, Minnesota, Montana, and Wisconsin); South Carolina earlier had repealed its indexing plan.[74]

Broadening of state and local income tax bases and reducing marginal rates can be a revenue-neutral change to spur investment and improve the equity of the tax among income classes. In 1987, 18 states increased the standard deduction, 17 raised the personal exemption, 13 adopted a new bracket structure, and 12 lowered tax rates.[75]

State legislative action for "full disclosure" and a "constant-yield" basis for the local property tax, along the lines of Florida's property tax disclosure law, can be instituted. The constant yield is the rate that will produce no more money than was generated in the preceding year from the property tax, unless the governing body acts specifically to increase the constant-yield rate after advertised public hearings on the question.[76]

Means-testing state-local tax credits and other preferences in state and local laws that expend or forgo revenue is increasingly desirable in an era of resource scarcity. Legislating a preference usually has the effect of increasing the tax burden of all other taxpayers to make up for the reductions granted through the preference. Called "tax expenditures" at the national level and in a number of states, these preferences constitute as much of a drain on the state or local treasury as would direct outlays, and they need to be viewed with the same degree of criticality and objectivity as existing or proposed expenditures for grants of public funds to the favored organizations or individuals. Those preferences not contained in the federal tax code might be especially targeted, such as property tax "circuit breaker" laws that carry no income ceiling and laws that exclude all Social Security benefits from taxable income (in contrast to federal taxation of one-half for those above certain income levels). As of 1985 twenty-four states by exemption or credit were failing to tax federal military and civil service retirement benefits, at a total loss of state-local income tax revenue of over $400 million per year for the preference to civil service retirees alone. (Data were not available for military retirees, but the costs for them probably were in the same order of magnitude.) Some of the larger state revenue losses, in millions of dollars, for the federal civil service preference were New York ($125), Michigan ($39), Minnesota ($36), and Illinois ($30).[77]

It may be questionable public policy for well-to-do retirees and others to receive tax breaks that must be financed by younger generations with substantially lower average incomes. This is not to say that the initial enactment of the preferences was ill-advised. In many states it was quite the opposite. Many of the credits directed to individuals were passed in the early postwar years when (1) most elderly retirees were at the lower end of the income scale; (2) homeownership was being encouraged, especially for returning veterans; and (3) competing claims for the state-local dollar were much less intense than now. In an environment of resource scarcity, all tax preferences require a new look, especially in those areas where economic conditions leading to the original enactments no longer prevail. Among state budgetary tools, the review of "tax expenditures" is largely neglected.[78]

Reform of property tax assessment structure and procedures can enhance equity and efficiency and thereby improve public confidence in what is perceived as the most unfair of all the tax types. Major steps in assessment reform are (*a*) assumption of the assessment function by the state (as in Maryland and Montana), or utility and industrial property assessment by the state (as in Wisconsin); (*b*) locally appointed, state-certified assessors; (*c*) state standards, rules, and professional certification of assessors; (*d*) assessment-ratio analyses and state equalization of assessment on full market value basis; (*e*) countrywide assessing areas; and (*f*) state publication of studies and interlocal comparisons where assessment is done locally.[79] In twenty-eight states as of late 1987, localities elected their asssessors; thirteen provided for appointment; and in ten states, both local election and appointment prevailed.[80]

State authorization of local income or sales taxes provides local governments with a broad-based nonproperty tax and thereby affords revenue diversification at the local level as recommended by the NCSL Task Force on State-Local Relations in 1986. As of 1987 eleven states authorized certain types or classes of local governments to impose an income tax of a specified maximum rate, usually "piggybacked" onto the state income tax, with the state collecting both the state and local portion and returning the latter. The total number of local governments authorized to impose income taxes was 3,545, of which 2,782 were in Pennsylvania, where cities, boroughs, townships, and school districts were all permitted to use the tax. Excluding Pennsylvania, 763 local units in the United States were using a local income tax, usually the larger units (for example, 10 cities in Alabama, 24 counties in Maryland, 2 cities—New York and Yonkers—in New York, 2 cities in Missouri, and 25 counties in Kentucky). Most of the rates used were at the 1 or 2 percent level, with Detroit taxing residents at 3 percent and nonresidents at 1.5.[81]

In 1987, 6,892 local units were using a local sales tax, with this use permitted in twenty-nine states. The most units were in Illinois with 1,375 (1,271 cities, 102 counties, and 2 transit districts); California had 445 units (380 cities, 58 counties, and 7 transit districts). Pennsylvania, which uses the income tax widely at the local level, does not permit local sales taxes. Like the income tax, the local sales tax usually is piggybacked onto the state tax.[82]

State-Local Functional or Financial Shifts

Functional transfers, state or county service delivery under contract, and state technical assistance offer another set of options that can improve economic efficiency and afford significant fiscal economies in many instances.

Shift of high spillover functions from local to state level enhances financial equity because the benefit of the service being rendered is by no means confined to the geographic boundary of the local unit. Such shifts have been stimulated by local financial stringency. Municipal institutions of higher education and local court and correction systems are major examples where shift to the state system is both equitably desirable and economically attractive to local units.[83]

Transfer of selected functions from small cities to counties and similar transfers from small to larger units can provide economies of scale and consequent fiscal savings to both governments. The volume and nature of functional transfers over the decade of the mid-seventies to the mid-eighties is described in chapter 3.

Expansion of state technical assistance and contract service to small local governments often can afford better-quality service at lower cost to the local unit. ''Resident trooper'' arrangements by state police agencies to sparsely populated counties, local participation in state procurement of high-volume items, and technical help in designing local road and bridge improvements are examples of the wide array of savings in this category.

Full state funding of the nonfederal share of Medicaid, AFDC, and food stamp administration has been adopted entirely or partially in many states on fiscal and equity grounds. On the other hand, some states leave most financial responsibility for ''general assistance'' (for example, unemployed single people) to local governments because of the perceived need to have local involvement in eligibility decisions. Under such state-supervised, locally financed and administered welfare systems, there are strong arguments, based on population mobility and other grounds, for the state to assume at least half the general assistance cost.[84]

However, attention to welfare reform and to the movement of recipients to private-sector employment after appropriate job-search, counseling, training, and other assistance places this question in a new context. Local government public services, nonprofit organizations, and local private employers have to be carefully harnessed together to make such efforts successful. If local governments have a financial stake in lowering welfare costs, the motivation of local officials and taxpayers toward a change in welfare emphasis from one of income maintenance to one of preparation for work may be enhanced.

State Assistance and Supervision in Local Fiscal Management

In their relationships with local governments, states play a combined role of supervision and assistance. The supervisory role has been summarized as being directed toward the purposes of (1) fostering local fiscal control; (2) ensuring financial solvency; (3) promoting efficient and effective management of resources by local governments; and (4) overseeing local performance of programs managed or financed by the state.[85] Of particular relevance here are two of the major types of state supervision over local fiscal management—standards for accounting and reporting, and state monitoring and supervision in the case of local financial crises.

Sound, accurate, and uniform accounting, auditing, and financial reporting is essential, both for purposes of state monitoring of local fiscal management and for comparability among jurisdictions. It is necessary also for prudent and accountable management at the local level. In a report issued in 1973, the ACIR urged states to ''require that financial statements be prepared in conformity with generally accepted government accounting principles and that they obtain the opinion of an independent auditor with respect to the financial statement or if an unqualified opinion cannot be expressed, the reasons, and any findings as to violations of state or local laws.'' The commission found that as a consequence of inadequate accounting and reporting, ''some cities have drifted into financial emergencies.''[86] Draft state legislation developed by the ACIR on the subject carries the following substantive sections: methods of accounting; audits required—contents, submission, and penalties for failure to reply; and a local government accounting (oversight) commission.[87]

Watching local government financial conditions and intervening with supervision and assistance also is a crucial role for the state government. This step was essential in both New York State (New York City) and Ohio (Cleveland) in the seventies. In a 1985 report updating the one of 1973, the ACIR found that fiscal management conditions in large cities had improved markedly and that both the fiscal and economic bases of these cities were much more stable.[88]

Local Government Actions to Improve Their Financial Position

Like charity, most of the needs and opportunities for improving and strengthening state-local financial management begin at home, in city and county governments. From the late forties until the mid-seventies, the tone and temper of local officials and managers was program initiation, program growth, and an ever-expanding staff. The starting point for a budget was the prior one, with the only real question being the size of increment that could be financed from economic growth and increased state and federal aid without having to raise the property tax rate.

Fiscal blood pressure began to rise, and with the decline in federal aid, the budget mind-set changed from incremental budgeting to decremental budgeting— rather than how to meet new needs, budgeting became "the grim business of which needs not to meet."[89] There are several individual areas of local fiscal management that public managers agree must receive continual attention. Collectively, the opportunities are quite high for savings that can be plowed back into the budget and lessen appreciably the extent of necessary cutbacks in program outlays.

Maintaining a watchful eye on the government's credit position is essential to maintaining or improving the rating of the securities it must market to provide for capital replacement as needed. Self-rating provides a perspective as to how rating agencies and bond purchasers may view the government in comparison with other governments. Positive factors (balanced budgets, diversity and steady growth in revenue bases, liquidity, a steady personnel situation, and an even debt schedule) need to be inventoried. Negative ones (deficits for more than one fiscal year, carrying over of short-term debt, increases in lower-income population, taxes and debt close to the legal limit, unrest in the government's work force, and previous incidents of financial gimmickry) need to be recognized and assiduously addressed.[90]

Moderating consumer behavior so as to reduce demand for new services is a preventive strategy. If nonservice alternatives to a new public program can be found to satisfy an expressed need and public acquiescence obtained, resources that would have been applied can be redeployed elsewhere.[91] This approach is particularly appropriate at the neighborhood level and is examined further in chapter 3 as an alternative service delivery mode and as a basis for forming public-private partnerships.

Insurance savings through risk management become increasingly important as state-local exposure to tort liability and other risks increases. These are manifested by (*a*) the increasing cost and even unavailability of insurance in the commercial market; (*b*) the growing number of damage claims against governments and the spectacular increase in award amounts; (*c*) court decisions and legislative actions moderating immunity of public officials; and (*d*) the expansion of direct state and local provision of professional services in health and related fields.

Through careful risk analysis, high-deductible, self-insurance approaches, and interlocal and state-local insurance pooling, risks and premiums can be kept manageable. The ICMA helped form the Public Risk and Insurance Management Association (PRIMA) in 1978 to act as an information clearinghouse for states, cities, counties, and other governmental units and public agencies.[92]

Assuring prudent pension system benefits, funding, and management is another fiscal imperative, especially for local governments. Because of the smaller size of most local government systems, actuarial soundness is harder to achieve and maintain than in large systems where the risk is spread much more widely. One of the major elements of fiscal mismanagement in state-local governments in the sixties and seventies was the reckless abandon with which governing bodies enriched public employee pension benefits without appropriate and adequate financial arrangements, including actuarial reappraisals to keep abreast of changing demographics.

As public employee unions grew stronger, many state and local executives in bargaining persuaded unions to agree to moderate immediate wage and salary demands in return for enrichment of future pension benefits. Concurrently, the explosion in medical technology, with drastic reductions in heart attacks, communicable diseases, and other former health risks was lengthening the human life span, and earlier actuarial estimtes of future benefit costs were being outmoded. During the 1975–84 period, inflation was wreaking havoc in those jurisdictions whose pension plans provided for automatic benefit adjustments, but at the same time, inflation was enriching pension funds.

All of these developments dictated widespread change in pension system policy and management. Several types of state and local actions became necessary to meet the deficits and manage windfalls. These included (*a*) periodic reporting of system condition; (*b*) system consolidation and integration; and (*c*) funding of benefit-enrichment actions as they occurred. The 1987 National Governors' Association (NGA) policy statement on public pension plans urged states to take corrective action along several lines:

- Use of appropriate methods of reporting and disclosure
- Regular independent financial audits conducted by an auditor not employed by the retirement system

- Regular actuarial evaluations, using accepted and current assumptions
- Adequate funding of benefit costs.
- Establishment of guidelines on fiduciary responsibilities (prudence, ethics, conflict of interest)
- Encouragement, where feasible, of plan consolidation
- Encouragement, where feasible, of portability of membership[93]

Neal Peirce, an astute observer of state and local government affairs over a long period, reported that in addition to the inflation windfall, "states started to clean up their act. They broadened their portfolios, hired savvy pension managers, [and] threw out archaic investment rules such as bans on buying stocks." He then asked, "Will the [pension] funds' gains unravel as soon as the stock market begins its inevitable downward cycle?" A case in point was Philadelphia, which yearly was having to pay out half its property tax collections to fund a pension system with a $1.5 billion unfunded liability arising from politically expedient decisions of earlier years, resulting in a benefit structure providing up to 95 percent of final salary upon retirement.[94]

Failing to crack down on local government corruption threatens the credibility of the governments involved and erodes the image of public servants in general, both elected and appointed. The nature of the competitive bidding process and the decision-making power of government officials is especially prone to collusion, bribery, and other white-collar crimes. Prosecutions and convictions through the federal judicial system of elected and appointed officials in many counties in the South and elsewhere, and the string of disclosures in New York City, heightened public awareness of the corruption problem in the mid-eighties. The procurement function by its nature is one of the most afflicted. Where states offer local governments the opportunity to join cooperative purchasing endeavors, some of the possibilities of collusion are removed. An inquiry by a state legislative commission in New York found that the existence of a state contract price for a commodity in which the local government was able to participate forced local vendors to meet or beat that price to retain their business.[95]

State Government Measures to Strengthen Fiscal Management

Short-term, expedient actions were outlined by Gerald Miller in 1983 that states could take to deal with the fiscal squeeze confronting them. These elements in a budget-reducing strategy included (*a*) general reductions, consisting of across-the-board percentage reductions; unpaid furloughs; hiring limitations; layoffs; union concessions; travel restrictions; procurement restrictions; and tighter space standards; (*b*) selective reductions, consisting of selected operating cuts, reduction of capital expenditures, and elimination of duplicative services; and (*c*) timing/accounting changes, consisting of moving expenditures to the next fiscal year and moving expenditures to special funds or entities.[96]

State legislative appropriation of federal aid funds enhances fiscal and political accountability, preventing legislators and executives from viewing aid as a ''free lunch.'' In 1976 the ACIR recommended that state legislatures include all federal aid in appropriation bills; prohibit spending of federal funds over the amount appropriated by the legislature; and set specific spending priorities by establishing subprogram allocations. The primary justification cited by ACIR and others for this procedure was to restore and maintain the political accountability of the legislature and governor in the appropriation and expenditure of all funds under control of, or in trust with, the state government and to prevent buck-passing between state and federal authorities.[97]

EVALUATING STATE-LOCAL PROGRAMS AND SETTING NEW PRIORITIES

Probably the most crucial element, yet the one most often lacking in setting new priorities for state and local governments in the nineties, is provision for, and a consistent and courageous conduct of, program evaluation. Despite widespread agreement among legislators, executives, and the general public on the urgent necessity of this activity, observance in the breach was the rule in preceding decades, and only in very recent years has the evaluation activity been forced onto a more rigorous basis by the fiscal necessities confronting state and local government. (Competent program evaluation continues at the national level by the General Accounting Office, although most of its outstanding work goes unheeded by the Congress, especially on any calls for elimination of marginal activities.)

Merely to list some of the basic weaknesses in most governmental evaluation activities is to underscore the importance of the need for new rigor in the process.

- Evaluation has not taken place at all in many programs; despite the adoption of sunset procedures by twenty-nine states,[98] much of the effort has been concentrated on regulatory rather than service activities.

- Evaluation often does not begin until the program is approaching the end of its authorized period (or the time specified for a review). Planning for and beginning the evaluation process need to proceed concurrently with program planning and the initiation of program operations. Evaluation machinery should be in place at the outset, rather than being jerry-built as program termination threatens.

- Evaluation too often is left to the same unit or subunit that is managing program operations, which leads obviously to self-serving treatment, despite the facade of an agency unit contract with an ''independent'' outside group to conduct the review.

- Evaluation activity too rarely makes cost-benefit assessments of results between and among programs. All too often, evaluation of a particular program is carried out within the narrow objective of ascertaining whether or not substantial (or appreciable) benefits are being realized, without relating such benefits to costs or even considering the issue of whether some other existing program or the adoption of a completely new approach might achieve more benefits at less cost. (A not unusual experience in serving on program evaluation panels is to hear findings of limited accomplishments dismissed with the comment that some other programs are accomplishing even less, and that it would be unfair to terminate or reduce the program being evaluated in the absence of more critical looks at "some really bad ones".)[99]

The Program Evaluation Process

At state and local levels of public management, as well as in the national government, the program evaluation process is closely tied to, and in many cases is an extension of, the audit process, a traditional and crucial segment of overall financial management in both private and public sectors. This connection was articulated clearly by the U.S. comptroller general in 1972 in defining "performance audits," one element of which encompassed a specific function—analysis of the results of government programs—added to the comptroller general's responsibilities under the Legislative Reorganization Act of 1970.[100] Performance audits were described as having three elements.

The first of these, "financial matters and compliance with," is to determine (a) whether financial operations are properly conducted, (b) whether the financial reports of an audited entity are presented fairly, and (c) whether the entity has complied with applicable laws and regulations. The second, "economy and efficiency," determines whether the entity is managing or utilizing its resources in an economical and efficient manner and the causes of any undesirable practices, including inadequacies in management information systems, administrative procedures, or organizational structure. The third, "program results," determines whether the desired results or benefits are being achieved, whether the objectives established by the legislature or other authorizing body are being met, and whether the agency has considered alternatives that might yield desired results at a lower cost.[101]

A 1982 report by the Urban Institute to the U.S. Department of Housing and Urban Development set forth a number of factors relevant to the assessment of local government fiscal management. These were (1) integrity of the financial management system, including such elements as accurate reports of financial condition under generally accepted accounting principles (GAAP), prevention of unauthorized expenditures, consistent following of procedures, and accurate reporting of cost and performance; (2) quality of management and its standards of quality and efficiency; and (3) program effectiveness, rated through measurable or ascertainable action-effect relationships.[102]

The authorizing legislation for the activity or program is the base against which program results are measured. On occasion, the question of whether or not the program itself should be terminated and the achievement of the objectives envisioned originally left to the market or otherwise divested from governmental responsibility is considered. Such situations often occur when a performance audit finds a complete lack of program success and a recommendation that one or more alternative approaches to the objectives be considered.

Many searching and painful questions need to be explored if the evaluation is to serve its purpose. These include such criteria for targeting programs for initial inquiry as the following: (1) What are the time-honored functions of the organization that have not undergone close scrutiny in recent years? (2) What programs serve a relatively small or isolated clientele? (3) What programs provide services available from other private or public organizations? (4) What programs have consistently fallen below their goals and expectations?[103]

Once a program has been targeted, various substantive questions peculiar to the activity area will require review. For a program involving the delivery of a social or other service to the public, for example, the following factors would be pertinent: (1) degree to which the program has achieved its stated purposes; (2) the degree of unintended positive or negative side effects; (3) whether or not the service is delivered in the quantity and scope necessary to meet the needs of the client population—for example, the percentage of those legally eligible who are being served; (4) speed of responsiveness; (5) degree of courtesy and dignity conveyed to clients; (6) accessibility of the service; (7) views and "grading" of the service by users; and (8) cost factors and their relation to benefits.[104]

The effort to institute in state governments a periodic program evaluation process through a sunset process, or automatic termination if not reauthorized, had met with only limited success by 1980. Nevertheless, a survey by the Council of State Governments found that interest in the approach remained high among state legislators and others, with 69 percent of the 1,000 respondents believing that program performance evaluation should be given high priority in state government.[105]

Many of the states tended to focus the enabling legislation upon the regulatory agencies in order to keep the scope and volume of required evaluations manageable, thereby overlooking the agencies and programs incurring significant expenditures. Second, relatively few agencies or programs were terminated. Critics argue that the premise of automatic termination is unreasonable and unnecessary, and that the likelihood of ensuing controversy may cause legislatures to give rubber-stamp approval for continuing outdated legislation. It may very well be that the automatic termination concept is too rigid to be practical.

Prior to the tax revolt the usual reaction to an evaluation recommendation for terminating a program that had made little or no progress toward its stated mission was to "reshuffle and transfer [the nonperforming programs] from one bureau to another, or put a new person in charge to improve operations." In a long-term period of resource scarcity, it probably will be increasingly necessary to terminate programs. "If these programs are in fact cut loose and the needs which they serve are shown to be essential, new programs will emerge over time to meet these needs and these will be carried out in a more effective manner than the previous ones."[106]

The Budgetary Process

State and local governments typically operate under two budgets—a capital budget to provide for additions or improvements to the government's physical infrastructure, and an annual or biennial operating budget. Often a substantial part of the operating budget is the cost of servicing previously incurred debt, annual servicing consisting of interest and retirement of part of the principal. Also in the operating budget are requirements for maintenance of the physical infrastructure as well as its operation. (Major replacement, rehabilitation, and reconstruction needs associated with the infrastructure usually are financed at least in part from borrowing and consequently are carried in the capital budget.) It is through the operating budget process that priorities for initiating, continuing, increasing, reducing, or eliminating programs are established. In a state or large local government many causes, objectives, and claims compete for fiscal resources, and when resources are growing less rapidly than program needs, either expenses must be cut or taxes or other revenues increased.

State and local government budgets rest on four major bases that largely determine the relative comfort or austerity and the policy direction of the budget. These are (1) socioeconomic—income, education, and associated characteristics of the state or local jurisdiction; (2) legal—pertaining principally to those fiscal constraints in the constitution, charter, laws, or ordinances of the kind discussed earlier and those specifying the principal phases of the budget cycle and the time intervals required; (3) financial—prevailing and forecasted economic and fiscal conditions and costs or savings anticipated for the forthcoming fiscal period arising from recommended expansions or retrenchment measures; and (4) policy/political—the state or local tradition on the role of government in society and the prevailing public support or hostility regarding the governmental entity.

Richard Lindholm, David Arnold, and Richard Herbert in 1975 and Paul Solano and Marvin Brams in 1987 outlined the principal phases and procedural steps in the cycle of the typical local government operating budget.[107] They are essentially the same for state government, except that in some states the budget is prepared and carried out on a biennial rather than an annual basis. Three broad phases are involved in the budget cycle: preparation, adoption, and implementation. The results of program evaluations completed during the preceding year comprise an important input during the preparation phase.

The preparation phase is lengthy, beginning soon after the adoption of the previous budget. As soon as tax rates and other actions associated with adoption are completed, planning begins on budget guidelines for preparation of the next year's budget. The guidelines are based on preliminary policy and political assessments: (1) financial status of the jurisdiction; (2) economic conditions and trends in the state or locality and its surrounding areas; (3) major program changes and/or new initiatives; (4) labor relations; and (5) estimation of likely wage and price levels.

Preparation of expenditure estimates begins within the various organizational units of the entity after receipt of budgetary guidelines. For jurisdictions on a July–June fiscal year, this step often is well under way in late fall.

The review of expenditure estimates takes place at the upper levels of the executive or management side of the governmental entity. At this stage, pressures from internal departments and external interest groups begin to gather strength.

Estimating revenues is a separate process, but is carried on more or less concurrently with the preparation of expenditure estimates. Own source revenue, including enterprise fund and other miscellaneous revenue, usually can be predicted with greater certainty than intergovernmental aid because the latter depends considerably upon policy/political decisions at federal and/or state levels.

Budgetary forecasting, running into multiyear periods, is the next essential step, after expenditure and revenue estimates have been prepared, reviewed, and revised.

Preparing the budget document includes making drafts of a budget message and the accompanying revenue and expenditure estimates; in larger units of government these are usually broken down by agency, function, and other categories, fortified by a wide array of charts and other exhibits.

Reviewing and adopting the budget occurs on the governing body or legislative side and is the crux of the priority-setting and fiscal decision-making process. The governor, mayor, county executive, or city or county administrator presents the budget, and immediately thereafter an often-lengthy public hearing process ensues. It is at this stage that the tilt of the process toward the spending side discussed earlier may become apparent. Major actors at the hearing stage include agency or department heads and their entourage of substantive experts; employee representatives; officials of affected interest groups (for example, the local chamber of commerce, the League of Women Voters, parent-teacher associations if the school budget or anything affecting schools is involved, taxpayer associations, and neighborhood citizen associations).

After a period of many days or weeks, the legislative body completes its voting on individual segments of the budget and adopts the revised budget, which becomes the basis of fiscal management for the forthcoming year and allocates available resources to the various programs. At the local level, subsequent to adoption of the budget and at some date prior to the beginning of the new fiscal year, the governing body sets the property tax rate and the rates or fee levels for any other tax or revenue sources that are necessary to sustain the adopted budget.

During the ensuing fiscal year, the final stage of the budget cycle, budget implementation or execution, occurs, involving the monitoring of spending rates, the collection of revenues, the periodic allocation of appropriations, and the submission of required accounting and other fiscal reports to the governing body and to the general public. In volatile or difficult fiscal periods revisions to the budget may have to be considered.

Priority Setting and Cutback Management

At the two priority-setting stages in the budget cycle—decisions on the executive side as to the program areas in which to seek substantial increases or decreases and decisions on the legislative side on the final composition of the budget—a number of options for budgetary economies always exist, and this number expanded substantially from the mid-seventies to the late eighties. For state or local governments that are in an economic and/or population growth situation, the choices may be difficult and savings in many areas necessary in order to make room for greatly expanded outlays for infrastructure and other purposes.

The situation in stable or declining economies obviously is much more painful. Here multiyear plans and programs for reducing public expenditure are necessary, and a combination of fiscal ingenuity and political courage is a priceless quality in both the legislative and executive arenas. Whether affluent or austere, all, or practically all, state and local governments will be engaged during the nineties with what is called "cutback management" and its efficiency and equity implications.

Early in the tax revolt period, Charles Levine analyzed the cutback management process, defining the term as "managing organizational change toward lower levels of resource consumption and organizational activity" and identifying four aspects of resource scarcity that make retrenchment management especially difficult. (1) Acceptance of change in austerity circumstances is much harder to accomplish than in an expansionary period because rewards for acceptance of change are unavailable. (2) Many employee protection and preference devices (tenure, veterans' and affirmative-action preferences, and collective bargaining agreements) deter or prevent the targeting of cuts, thereby forcing wasteful, mindless, and—for taxpayers—terribly inequitable resorts to across-the-board cuts. (3) Reductions in force, no matter how fairly carried out, inevitably lower employee morale and deter productivity increases that might help offset the effects of cuts. (4) The enjoyment, pride, and esprit de corps in working in the organization is eroded when it is in the process of being reduced or dismembered.[108]

A basic decision confronting government or private managers and governing boards is whether to make selective or organizationwide percentage cuts when faced with the necessity of budget reduction. Unless the necessity for reduction is of a one-year or other predictably short duration and/or of a magnitude sufficiently modest or negligible, the targeted approach is the more equitable for taxpayers or stockholders and in the institutional best interests of the organization or public entity. Selective cuts are more difficult, substantively and politically, and not just because employee morale and other interests must be respected. Selective cuts depend upon (1) objective and sustainable evaluations of the relative contributions being made by component units of the organization and

(2) in the case of governments, the equity among populations being served by the respective units.

Additional considerations, questions, and problems in cutback management include the following:

- The easiest cuts, both in public and private sectors, are in staff rather than line categories, since these services exist to facilitate the work of the line departments and have no public constituency; while easy, cuts in staff support yield relatively small savings.

- The most dependent parts of the population—the poor, minorities, and the handicapped—are the most expensive to serve in certain functional fields, such as education; consequently, cuts based on per capita costs or number of population served are highly inequitable. This is not to say that social services should be held less accountable than other functions for efficient operations, only that the measures of effectiveness and efficiency need to take into account in a quantitative way the inherently higher per capita costs.

- Under long-term conditions of fiscal stress, state and local governments may need to consider changes in traditional principles of personnel management and of labor-management relations, with engagement of certain categories of employees on a contract, project, term, or other basis that permits greater flexibility in the work force. Permanence of tenure and involuntary separation solely on the basis of seniority may not be compatible with some of the fiscal realities facing these governments in the nineties.[109]

NOTES

1. Bahl, R., "Urban Government Finance and Federal Income Tax Reform," *National Tax Journal* 40, no. 1 (March 1987): 1–18 (Presidential Address, 79th Annual Conference, National Tax Association–Tax Institute of America (NTA–TIA), Hartford, Connecticut, November 1986). See also Dearborn, P., "Fiscal Conditions in Large American Cities, 1971–1984" (Paper prepared for the National Research Council Committee on National Urban Policy, August 1986); and Peterson, G., "Urban Policy and the Cyclical Behavior of the Cities," in Peterson, G., and Lewis, C., eds., *Reagan and the Cities* (Washington, D.C.: Urban Institute, 1986), 11–35.

2. U.S. Congressional Budget Office (CBO), *The Economic and Budget Outlook: Fiscal Years 1989–1993*, A Report to the Senate and House Committees on the Budget, February 1988, pt. 1, p. xxi.

3. Bureau of the Census, *Government Finances, in 1984–85*, table 29, p. 46.

4. National Governors' Association (NGA)–National Association of State Budget Officers (NASBO), *Fiscal Survey of the States, March 1988* (Washington, D.C.: National Association of State Budget Officers, March 1988), 5.

5. Commission on Intergovernmental Relations (Kestnbaum Commission), *A Report to the President for Transmittal to the Congress*, June 1955, 62–64.

6. CBO, *The Federal Government in a Federal System: Current Intergovernmental Programs and Options for Change*, August 1983, xiv–xviii.

7. U.S. Advisory Commission on Intergovernmental Relations (ACIR), *An Agenda for Federalism: Restoring Confidence and Competence*, Report A–86, June 1981, 94.

8. Ibid., 95.

9. Committee on Federalism and National Purpose (Evans-Robb), *To Form a More*

Perfect Union (Washington, D.C.: National Conference on Social Welfare, December 1985), 6–7, 9–10.

10. Ibid., 8.

11. ACIR, *Governmental Functions and Processes, Local and Areawide*, Report A–45, February 1974, 99.

12. National Conference of State Legislatures (NCSL), *Recommendations of the Task Force on State-Local Relations*, August 5, 1986, 3–4.

13. Tetelman, M., "State-Local Panels: An Overview," *Intergovernmental Perspective*, Summer/Fall 1987, 26–29.

14. ACIR, *Fiscal Discipline in the Federal System: National Reform and the Experience of the States*, Report A–107, July 1987, table 2, 38; 45–46. For critical review of the report, see: review of Gold, S., "Fiscal Discipline in the Federal System: National Reform and the Experience of the States." *Public Budgeting & Finance*, Summer 1988, 112–114.

15. P.L. 97–108.

16. ACIR, *Fiscal Discipline*, 45–46.

17. Ornstein, N., "The Politics of the Deficit," in Cagan, P., ed., *Essays in Contemporary Economic Problems: The Economy in Deficit* (Washington, D.C.: American Enterprise Institute, 1985), 311–333.

18. Citrin, J., and Green, D. P., "Policy and Opinion in California after Proposition 13," *National Tax Journal* 38, no. 1 (March 1985): 15.

19. Ibid., 32.

20. Kenyon, D., and Benker, K., "Fiscal Discipline: Lessons from the State Experience," *National Tax Journal* 37, no. 3 (September 1984): 433–446.

21. "Tax-Limiting Laws: Revolution or Business as Usual?" *Rand Research Review*, Spring 1982, 1–3. The Rand Corporation reports cited were *Fiscal Restraint in Local Government: A Summary of Research Findings*, R–2645-FF/RC, April 1982; *How Fiscal Restraint Affects Spending and Services in Cities*, R–2644-FF/RC, January 1982; and *Fiscal Restraints and the Burden of Local and State Taxes*, R–2646-FF/RC, August 1981.

22. Sharp, E., and Elkins, D., "The Impact of Fiscal Limitation: A Tale of Seven Cities," *Public Administration Review*, September–October 1987, 385–392.

23. Lowery, D., "After the Tax Revolt: Some Positive, If Unintended, Consequences," *Social Science Quarterly* 67 (December 1986): 736–750.

24. Saltzstein, A., "The Effects of Proposition 13 on City Spending: Services and User Fees in Large Cities, 1978–1982" (Paper presented at the Annual Conference of the American Society for Public Administration, Denver, April 1984) (Fullerton: Department of Political Science, California State University, Fullerton, 1984), 8, 11.

25. Barber, D., "Alternative Revenue Raising: A Post–Prop. 13 Retrospective," *National Civic Review*, December 1984, 549–555.

26. deHaven-Smith, L., "Ideology and the Tax Revolt," *Public Opinion Quarterly* 49, no. 3 (Fall 1985): 300–309.

27. Ladd, H., and Wilson, J. B., "Why Voters Support Tax Limitations: Evidence from Massachusetts' Proposition 2 ½," *National Tax Journal* 35, no. 2 (June 1982): 121–148. See also Kirlin, J., *The Political Economy of Fiscal Limits* (Lexington, Mass.: Lexington Books, 1982); Levy, F., "On Understanding Proposition 13," *Public Interest* 56, no. 66 (Summer, 1979): 89, and Abrams, B. and Dougan, W., "The Effects of Constitutional Restraints on Governmental Spending," *Public Choice* (49) 1986, 101–116.

28. Rufulo, A., "Upward Biases in Government Spending," *Business Review* (Federal Reserve Bank of Philadelphia), November/December 1978.

29. ACIR, *State Constitutional and Statutory Restrictions on Local Taxing Powers,* Report A–14, October 1962, 6.

30. National Municipal League, *Salient Issues of Constitutional Revision,* (New York: National Municipal League, 1961), 136.

31. Council of State Governments, *Book of the States, 1986–87 Edition,* 4.

32. Tvedt, S., "Enough Is Enough: Proposition 2½ in Massachusetts," *National Civic Review,* November 1981, 527–533.

33. Collins, G., "As Nation Grays, A Mighty Advocate Flexes Its Muscles," *New York Times,* April 2, 1987.

34. *Governing: States and Localities* 1 no. 3 (December 1987): "State Pensions Set Off Debate over Equity," 16.

35. U.S. General Accounting Office, *A CPI for Retirees Is Not Needed Now But Could Be in the Future,* 1982.

36. CBO, *Reducing Poverty among Children*, Appendix A, "Measuring Poverty," May 1985, 149–173. See also Garfinkel, I., ed., *Income-Tested Transfer Programs: The Case For and Against* (New York: Academic Press, 1982), 12–14; Bureau of the Census, *Alternative Methods for Valuing Selected In-Kind Transfer Benefits and Measuring Their Effect on Poverty,* Technical Paper 50, March 1982, 28–31, 38–44, 58–69, 127–134; and Danziger, Sheldon, and Gottschalk, P., "The Measurement of Poverty: Implications for Antipoverty Policy," Discussion Paper no. 709–82 (Madison, Wis.: Institute for Research on Poverty, 1982).

37. Americans for Generational Equity, *The Challenge of an Aging Society: Planning for the Baby Boom Generation's Retirement,* Statistical Abstract—Staff Draft (Washington, D.C.: Americans for Generational Equity, January 13, 1987), 24. See also *Generational Journal* 1, no. 1 (April 1988). New journal on generational issues.

38. Moynihan, D., *Family and Nation* (New York: Harcourt Brace Jovanovich, 1986), 112.

39. Kaplan, S., "The New Generation Gap: The Politics of Generational Justice," *Common Cause Magazine,* March–April 1987, 13–15.

40. American Association of Retired Persons (AARP), "Investing in America's Families: The Common Bond of Generations" (Statement to House Select Committee on the Aging, May 14, 1986). See also AARP, *Summary of the 1987 National Legislative Policy,* (state tax policy) (Washington, D.C.: American Association of Retired Persons, 1987), 86–90.

41. Dexter, M., *Replacement Ratios: A Major Issue in Employee Pension Systems* (Washington, D.C.: National Committee on Public Employee Pension Systems, March 15, 1984), 55.

42. Ibid., 32.

43. Longman, P., *Born to Pay: The New Politics of Aging in America* (Boston: Houghton Mifflin, 1987), 175–176.

44. Bureau of the Census *1982 Census of Governments,* vol. 2, GC82 (2), *Taxable Property Values and Assessment-Sales Ratios,* February 1984, xlvi–li.

45. ACIR, *Significant Features of Fiscal Federalism, 1988,* M-155-II, table 30, p. 70.

46. "Tax Exemptions Benefit Veterans," *New York Times,* September 27, 1987, sec. 2, p. 55.

47. Manson, D., and Schnare, A., "Changes in the City/Suburban Income Gap,

1970–84,'' Urban Institute Project 3376, November 1985. See also Stanley, D., *Cities in Trouble,* National Urban Policy Roundtable (Columbus, Ohio: Academy for Contemporary Problems; replaced by Washington, D.C.: Academy for State and Local Government, December 1976).

48. Voisin, E., "New Jersey Cities Freshen Image to Reflect New Economic Reality,'' *City and State,* November 1987, 35 (Jersey City, Trenton, Camden, and Paterson). See also Johnson, D., "The View from Poorest U.S. Suburb,'' *New York Times,* April 30, 1987. Lublin, J., "Suburban Population Ages, Causing Conflict and Radical Changes,'' *Wall Street Journal,* November 1, 1984, 1 (Falls Church, Virginia, and Babylon, New York); Schmidt, W., "Riding a Boom, Downtowns Are No Longer Downtrodden,'' *New York Times,* October 11, 1987. (Chicago, Cleveland, Boston, New York, San Francisco, Los Angeles, St. Louis, and Indianapolis); and Narvaez, A., "In Newark, Demand for Property is Booming,'' *New York Times,* September 27, 1987, 45.

49. ACIR, *Fiscal Disparities: Central Cities and Suburbs, 1981,* M–138, August 1984, table 13, pp. 34–35.

50. Manson and Schnare, "Changes in the City/Suburban Income Gap,'' tables III–16 and III–19, pp. 58, 61.

51. ACIR, *The States and Distressed Communities, Final Report* A–101, December 1985, 152.

52. ACIR, *Relative Measures of State and Local Fiscal Capacity and Tax Effort,* M–16, October 1962.

53. U.S. Department of Commerce, Bureau of Economic Analysis, *Experimental Estimates of Gross State Product by Industry,* Staff Paper 42, May 1985. See also Sawicky, M., "The Total Taxable Resources Definition of State Revenue-raising Ability,'' and Carnevale, J., "Experimental Estimates of Total Taxable Resources,'' in U.S. Department of the Treasury, Office of State and Local Finance, *Federal-State-Local Fiscal Relations,* Technical Appendix, September 1985; Aten, R., "Gross State Product: A Measure of Fiscal Capacity,'' in Reeves, C., ed., *Measuring Fiscal Capacity* (Cambridge, Mass.: Lincoln Institute of Land Policy, 1986); Barro, S., "Improved Measures of State Fiscal Capacity: Short-Term Changes in the PCI and RTS Indices,'' *Federal-State-Local Fiscal Relations,* Technical Appendix; and Morgan, W., and Mutti, J., "The Exportation of State and Local Taxes in a Multilateral Framework: The Case of Business Type Taxes,'' *National Tax Journal* 38, no. 2 (June 1985): 191–208.

54. ACIR, *Measuring State Fiscal Capacity: Alternative Methods and Their Uses,* M–150, September 1986.

55. Ibid., Appendix E: Ladd, H., and Yinger, J., "Measuring the Fiscal Capacity of U.S. Cities.''

56. ACIR, *Measuring the Fiscal Capacity and Effort of State and Local Areas,* M–58, March 1971.

57. Ladd, H., Yinger, J., et al., "The Changing Economic and Fiscal Conditions of Cities.'' (Report to the Department of Housing and Urban Development, 1986). See also Bradbury, K., and Ladd, H., "Changes in the Revenue-raising Capacity of U.S. Cities, 1970–1982,'' *New England Economic Review,* March/April 1985, 20–37.

58. Bradbury, K., et al., "State Aid to Offset Fiscal Disparities across Communities,'' *National Tax Journal* 38, no. 2 (June 1984): 151–170. For contrasting views, see Peterson, P., *City Limits* (Chicago: University of Chicago Press, 1981); and Peterson, P., Rabe, B., and Wong, K., *When Federalism Works* (Washington, D.C.: Brookings

Institution, 1986). Also see Hilley, J., "The Distributive Impact of Education Finance Reform," *National Tax Journal* 36, no. 4 (December 1983): 503–509.

59. ACIR, *Measuring State Fiscal Capacity: Alternative Methods,* 30–37.

60. ACIR, *Distressed Communities,* 153–166.

61. Ibid., 218–219. The three preceding reports were *The States and Distressed Communities: The 1981 Annual Report,* M–133 (U.S. Department of Housing and Urban Development, HUD–615-CPD), June 1982; *The States and Distressed Communities: The 1982 Annual Report,* M–136 (HUD–643-CPD), October 1983; *The States and Distressed Communities: State Programs to Aid Distressed Communities. Catalog of State Programs, 1983.* M–140 (February 1985).

62. ACIR, *Industrial Development Bond Financing,* Report A–18, June 1963, 15.

63. Shannon, J., "Interstate Tax Competition—The Need for a New Look," *National Tax Journal* 39, no. 3 (September 1986): 339–340. See also McGuire, T., "Interstate Tax Differentials, Tax Competition, and Tax Policy," *National Tax Journal* 39, no. 3 (September 1986): 367–373. For further contrasting views, see Epple, D., and Zelenitz, A., "The Implications of Competition among Jurisdictions: Does Tiebout Need Politics?" *Journal of Political Economics* 89 (December 1981): 1197–1217; Hawkins, R., *American Federalism: A New Partnership for the Republic* (San Francisco: Institute for Contemporary Studies, 1981); Ferris, J., "The Public Spending and Employment Effects of Local Service Contracting," *National Tax Journal,* (June 1988). 209–217; Hovey, H., "Curbing Interstate Tax Competition," *State Policy Reports* 5 (May 13, 1987): 4–9; and Niskanen, W., Jr., *Bureaucracy and Representative Government* (Chicago: Aldine-Atherton, 1971).

64. Stephenson, S., and Hewett, R., "Strategies for States in Fiscal Competition," *National Tax Journal* 38, no. 2 (June 1985): 219–226.

65. Sjoquist, D., "The Effect of the Number of Local Governments on Central City Expenditures," *National Tax Journal* 35, no. 1 (March 1982): 79–87; Aaron, H., "Local Public Expenditures and the Migration Effect," *Western Economic Journal,* December 1969, 385–390; and Buchanan, J., "Principles of Urban Fiscal Strategy," *Public Choice,* Fall 1971, 1–16.

66. Fox, W., "Tax Structure and the Location of Economic Activity along State Borders," *National Tax Journal* 39, no. 4 (December 1986): 387–401. See also: Mikesell, J., "Central Cities and Sales Tax Rate Differentials: The Border City Problem," *National Tax Journal,* June, 1970, 206–214.

67. Papke, J., and Papke, L., "Measuring Differential State-Local Tax Liabilities and Their Implications for Business Investment Locations," *National Tax Journal* 39, no. 3 (September 1986): 357–366.

68. National Association of State Development Agencies, *Directory of Incentives for Business Investment and Development in the United States: A State-by-State Guide,* 2nd ed. (Washington, D.C.: Urban Institute Press, 1986), 11–14, 683–687.

69. Raphaelson, A., "The Property Tax," in Aronson, J. R., and Schwartz, E., *Management Policies in Local Government Finance,* 3rd ed. (Washington, D.C.: International City Management Association, 1987), 201. See also: ACIR, *Local Revenue Diversification: Local Income Taxes,* Report SR–10. August 1988.

70. Benker, K., *Fiscal Survey of the States, September, 1987* (Washington, D.C.: National Governors' Association–National Association of State Budget Officers, September 1987), 17.

71. Florestano, P., "Revenue-raising Limitations on Local Government: A Focus on

Alternative Responses," *Public Administration Review* 41: (Special Issue, January 1981): 122–124, 125, 126–130.

72. NGA-NASBO, *Fiscal Survey of the States, March, 1988*, 69–70.

73. Bureau of the Census, *State Government Finances in 1987*. GF87 No. 3, table 35. (1988) 55.

74. ACIR, *Significant Features of Fiscal Federalism, 1987 Edition*, M–151 II. June 1987, 70–73.

75. NGA-NASBO, *Fiscal Survey, 1988* 14; ACIR, *Significant Features, 1988 Edition*. M155-I. table 14, pp. 22–25.

76. Florestano, "Revenue-Raising Limitations," 123, 129.

77. U.S. Department of the Treasury, Office of State and Local Finance, *Federal-State-Local Fiscal Relations*, September 1985, table X.5, p. 333.

78. Benker, K., "Tax Expenditure Reporting: Closing the Loophole in State Budget Oversight," *National Tax Journal* 39, no. 4 (December 1986): 403–417.

79. ACIR, *The Role of the State in Strengthening the Property Tax*, Report A–17, June 1963, 14. See also Petersen, J., Stallings, C. W., and Spain, C., *State Roles in Local Government Financial Management: A Comparative Analysis* (Washington, D.C.: Government Finance Research Center, June 1979), 50–53, for discussion of difficulties in achieving changes in assessment systems.

80. Clatanoff, R., *Patterns of Property Tax Administration in the United States*, Research and Information Series no. 5 (Chicago: International Association of Assessing Officers, 1986), 96–97.

81. ACIR, *Significant Features of Fiscal Federalism, 1988* 46.

82. Ibid., 57.

83. See Levine, C., Rubin, I., Wolohojian, G., "Resource Scarcity and the Reform Model: The Management of Retrenchment in Cincinnati and Oakland," *Public Administration Review*, November/December 1981, 619–628; Florestano, "Revenue-raising Limitations," 127.

84. NCSL, *Recommendations of the Task Force on State-Local Relations*, 10: "As part of the 'sorting-out' process, states should move in the direction of assuming major poverty-related costs from local governments."

85. Petersen, Stallings, and Spain, *State Roles in Local Government*, 5.

86. ACIR, *City Financial Emergencies: The Intergovernmental Dimension*, Report A–42, July 1973, 68. See also Petersen, Stallings, and Spain, *State Roles in Local Government*, 28–33; and Holder, W., "Financial Accounting, Reporting, and Auditing," in Aronson and Schwartz, *Management Policies in Local Government Finance*, 158–175.

87. ACIR, "4.101. State Regulation of Local Accounting, Auditing, and Financial Emergencies," (draft state legislation), 1979.

88. ACIR, *Bankruptcies, Defaults, and Other Local Government Financial Emergencies*, Report no. A–99, March 1985.

89. McCaffery, J., "Revenue Budgeting: Dade County Tries a Decremental Approach," *Public Administration Review*. Special Issue, (January 1981): 179–189.

90. Wall, M., *Evaluating Your City's Credit Position*, ICMA, Management Information Service Report 12, no. 6, June 1980.

91. ICMA, *Rediscovering Governance Tools: New Applications for Urban Neighborhoods*, Management Information Service Report 12, no. 8, August 1980. See also

Horton, R., "Expenditures, Services, and Public Management," *Public Administration Review* 47, no. 5 (September/October 1987): 378–384.

92. *Risk Management Today: A How-to Guide for Local Government* (Washington, D.C.: ICMA, in cooperation with the Public Risk and Insurance Management Association, 1985). (Sections include risk administration; risk finance; special areas of risk; and risk control in the workplace.)

93. National Governors' Association, *NGA Policy Positions, 1986–87*, January 1987, sec. A–7.

94. Peirce, N., "Pension Systems Wise Up, Get Lucky," *Public Administration Times,* June 1, 1987, 2.

95. New York State Legislative Commission on Expenditure Review, *Local Government Use of State Contracts,* October 1979, 21–22.

96. Miller, G., remarks in symposium on "The Triple Deficit Crisis: Federal, State, and Local," *National Tax Journal* 36, no. 3 (September 1983): 383–393.

97. ACIR, *The States and Intergovernmental Aids,* A–59, February 1977, 79–83, "4.114, State Budgeting and Appropriation of Federal Monies Received by the State," (draft state legislation) 1979.

98. ACIR, *Fiscal Discipline,* 38.

99. Some of the opening comments in this section are drawn from Colman, W., *The Neglected Agenda of State and Local Government,* The Martin L. Faust Lecture Series in Public Administration (Columbia: Institute of Public Administration, University of Missouri-Columbia, 1979), 30–31. See also: Harlow, K. and Windsor, D., "Integration of Cost-Benefit and Financial Analysis in Project Evaluation," *Public Administration Review* (September–October 1988) 918–928.

100. Mosher, F., *The GAO: The Quest for Accountability in American Government* (Boulder: Westview Press, 1979), 169–203, gives a review of the entry of the GAO into the program evaluation area.

101. U.S. General Accounting Office, Comptroller General of the United States, *Standards for Audit of Governmental Organizations, Programs, Activities, and Functions* (Washington, D.C.: Government Printing Office, 1972), 2.

102. Hayes, F., Grossman, D., Mechling, J., Thomas, J., and Rosenbloom, S., "Linkages: Improving Financial Management in Local Government" (Prepared for the U.S. Department of Housing and Urban Development, 1982), 161–169. See also: Becker, C., ed., *Performance Evaluation: An Essential Management Tool* (Washington, D.C.: ICMA, 1988).

103. McTighe, J., "Management Strategies to Deal with Shrinking Resources," *Public Administration Review,* January/February 1979, 86–90.

104. Hatry, H., Bloer, L., Fisk, D., and Kimmel, W., *Program Analysis for State and Local Governments* (Washington, D.C.: Urban Institute, 1976), 38.

105. Council of State Governments, *Sunset: Expectation and Experience,* 1981; summarized in *National Civic Review,* December 1981, 612–615.

106. McTighe, "Management Strategies," 88–89.

107. Lindholm, R., Arnold, D., and Herbert, R., "The Budgetary Process," in Aronson, J. R., and Schwartz, E., eds., *Management Policies in Local Government Finance* (Washington, D.C.: International City Management Association, 1975), 68–87, and Solano, P., and Brams, M., "Budgeting" in the 1987 3rd edition, 143–152.

108. Levine, C., "Cutback Management in an Era of Scarcity: Hard Questions for Hard Times," *Intergovernmental Personnel Notes* (U.S. Office of Personnel Manage-

ment), January/February 1979, 11–14. In the same issue of the publication, see also Graves, C., "Contingency Planning: Effective Government with Fewer Resources" (San Diego County, California), 15–16, and Freedman, E., "A Poorman's Guide to Restricting Local Government Taxes" (Rochester, New York), 17–19.

109. Merget, A., "Coping with the Budget Crunch: Municipal Financial Trends," *Urban Data Service Reports* 12, no. 12 (ICMA, December 1980): 9.

Chapter 3 —————————————————————————

Forging New and Effective Public-Private Partnerships

The new and emerging common interests of state and local governments and the private sector were summarized as follows in a Committee for Economic Development (CED) report in 1982:

America's urban communities possess the resources of an advanced and affluent society: highly educated and skilled individuals, productive social and economic institutions, sophisticated technology, physical infrastructure, transportation and communications networks and access to capital. Developing this potential will require cooperation.

Local governments will need to define their role and manage their operations in new ways. They will require active assistance and appropriate legal, financial, and administrative tools from their state governments. To make full use of the private sector's potential, local governments will need to adopt an entrepreneurial approach that anticipates needs, seeks out opportunities, and encourages an effective coalition of public and private efforts.

The private sector, in turn, needs to determine what it realistically can contribute. If it sets its goals too high, its performance will fail to match expectations. . . . However, if the local private sector is unwilling to make a sufficient commitment of money and effort, its community will lose position to those that respond more energetically.[1]

The seventies and eighties witnessed an expansion and intensification of public-private-sector relationships at both state and local levels. Spurred by national business organizations such as the Committee for Economic Development and the Business Roundtable, corporation boards and chief executive officers began to devote increased attention and resources to the exercise of "corporate social responsibility," with particular stress on business participation in and assistance to local government and community betterment. The urgency for strengthened public-private-sector collaboration was heightened by the decreasing federal role in assisting state-local activities, beginning in 1978 and accentuated by the Reagan administration.

In this chapter several forms and manifestations of public-private-sector relationships will be examined:

- Growing convergence of public and private sectors in domestic governance
- Shifts in public financing from predominant reliance upon general tax bases to user fees and developer exactions
- Increased commingling of public and private funds for public purposes, including private financing of public infrastructure and public participation in private ventures on an equity basis
- Private delivery of more public services
- A wide variety of public-private "general partnerships" for civic betterment and economic development

GROWING CONVERGENCE OF PRIVATE AND PUBLIC SECTORS IN DOMESTIC GOVERNANCE

Public-private collaboration to achieve one or more public purposes, either as a primary goal or as an ancillary benefit, is of long standing, both locally and nationally. By the late eighties these activities were intensifying at an accelerating rate, encompassing the following spectrum: (1) private-sector advice to state and local governments—a long-standing traditional function, especially for incoming administrations; (2) a shifting of public revenue sources from general to special tax bases and from tax-based to user-based financing; (3) public revenue bond financing of private nonprofit and profit facilities and projects; (4) formation of quasi-public and private nonprofit economic development corporations; (5) private performance of public functions under contract or franchise; and (6) public divestiture of specific functions to the private marketplace, with or without continued public regulation. In analyzing the five newer activities for policy efficacy, fiscal equity, and administrative effectiveness, it is necessary first to classify, define, and describe them.

Classification of Economic Sectors and Public Functions

For present purposes, the "private sector" encompasses both profit and non-profit organizations and individuals acting in a private, nongovernmental capacity, including volunteer work in the pursuit of civic or other public goals. The "public sector" includes governing boards, agencies, and other instrumentalities of federal, state, or local governments, such as cities, counties, and school and other special districts; the term also encompasses corporations, authorities, or other entities established under state or local law as "municipal corporations" that exercise governmental authority.

Governmental (public) powers and activities generally comprise two major areas—regulation and service delivery. Here we will deal with regulation only to the extent that it pertains to quality, cost, and other aspects of services to the public under franchise or other arrangements between government and private deliverers of the service. Other aspects of public regulation of private activity will be covered in chapter 6.

Conceptual and Definitional Bases

The CED in its 1982 report suggested the following distinction and characterization of the two constituent sectors of the national economy as they pertain to the state/local scene.

The public sector, or government, is . . . a political institution. It sets the boundaries for, alters, or may specifically state the goals of the community, which includes the private sector. The organizations and individuals who make up the private sector, in turn, are not just economic units; they are also participants in that political process. The public sector [also] . . . is a principal component of the urban economy. Local governments, in conjunction with state and federal agencies and an array of public institutions, are sizable employers, purchasers of goods and services, providers of basic economic services, and generators of income through federal and state grants and payrolls.

The private sector is far from the homogeneous grouping of businesses imagined in the conventional perception. In addition to profit-making firms, it is comprised of a rich mosaic of nonprofit organizations such as hospitals, schools, museums, labor unions, community development and venture-capital organizations, cooperatives, and other self-help groups. . . . [Those] organizations that do not attempt to generate a profit are variously defined as the nonprofit, independent, voluntary and third sector. . . .   The activities of the private sector have clear public consequences, and the individuals and organizations of the private sector, as members of the community, have an interest in, and a responsibility for, public concerns.[2]

Characteristics of Public and Private Organizations

In a 1975–76 comprehensive survey of public administration literature comparing public and private organizations, Robert Backoff, Charles Levine, and Hal Rainey found some areas of agreement, but no overall conclusions emerged as to major similarities and differences between the two types. There was consensus, however, on a number of points that are relevant to this discussion. (1) Free market-derived revenue, in contrast to appropriated revenue, tends, on the public-sector side, to result in higher operational and resource allocation efficiencies. (2) The mandatory and monopolistic nature of many government activities restricts flexibility in consumer and taxpayer choices. (3) Public administrators have less autonomy and flexibility if there is a diffusion of authority between and among legislators and executives. (4) Greater caution and rigidity hamper organizational performance in the public sector.

The authors concluded that based on the literature, ''there are indications of a number of important differences between public and private organizations which cannot be ignored in considerations of management, research, training and practice.'' Comparisons are even more difficult due to considerable expansion in (1) the forms and functions of state and local public, quasi-public, and quasi-private corporations and authorities delivering public services and (2) the increased commingling of public and private funds and responsibilities in financing public infrastructure and delivering local public services. It becomes next to impossible to define a ''typical government agency,'' particularly in local government.[3]

Barry Bozeman has concluded that organizations can no longer be tidily characterized as public or private and that ''public'' does not necessarily mean governmental. He argues that all organizations, not just governmental ones, but private and nonprofit concerns also, are in effect public organizations, since all are subject to varying degrees of political authority. Conversely, Ronald Moe has argued that ''public and private sectors have distinctive characters . . . premised on legal principles, not economic or social science theories. . . . the public sector is being . . . altered and ultimately harmed by the deliberate blurring of these characteristics. This . . . constitutes a challenge not only to the practice of public administration but to the theoretical basis of the discipline.''[4]

FINANCING PUBLIC SERVICES: SHIFTS FROM GENERAL TAX BASE TO USER FEES AND DEVELOPER EXACTIONS

The role of user-based taxes, fees, and charges in financing state and local services began growing in the fifties and expanded at a greatly quickened pace from the mid-seventies on. The 1977–87 decade was marked by (1) an increasing number of tax-expenditure limitations placed on state and local governments; (2) growing gaps between public service demand and revenue availability; and (3) a corresponding tightening of revenue-expenditure balancing brought about by inflation, recession, and federal aid cutbacks. Additionally, the decade saw an increasingly evident public support of user-based financing (UBF), in preference to general taxation, in the financing of public services.[5]

Local and state governments have moved aggressively, in response to fiscal need and political opportunity, to achieve higher revenue yields by increasing rate or fee levels in the more traditional user-financed functions and by extending the concept to additional functions. As this occurs, numerous issues and problems arise for elected officials and public administrators. There is no answer to, and indeed no way to discuss informatively, the overall question of the goodness or badness and fairness or unfairness of user-based financing (UBF). Rather, the UBF role must be appraised in the context of such considerations as (a) the varying types of services; (b) the kinds of benefits flowing from them; (c) the equities of financing alternatives, including that of using service charges where appropriate to avoid larger reductions in service levels necessitated by a budget squeeze; and (*d*) the economies and diseconomies of various fiscal and administrative procedures.

Definitions for User-based Financing

Special care is needed in defining revenue types and categories because adequate analysis requires some reshuffling of existing Bureau of the Census categories of revenue sources. It is necessary also to define UBF broadly in scope, but precisely in content, so that it represents a package of discrete components that can be aggregated or disaggregated in various ways, depending on the issue under consideration. The only data that allow such a packaging are those generated in the annual reports on *Government Finances* issued annually by the Governments Division of the Bureau of the Census. For present purposes, the following will apply:

User-based Financing (UBF) consists of four components:

1. User-based taxes and licenses. State-local taxes on motor fuel and fees for motor vehicle registration, and for issuance or renewal of operator licenses.

2. Service fees and charges. All items relevant to state and local governments appearing under the census category of "current charges" and subclasses thereunder. Additionally, "service fees and charges" includes water system and transit system revenues carried by the census as components of "utility revenues." (Gas and electric power revenues are not included here because of their sporadic occurrence in the nation as a whole.)

3. Special assessments. Compulsory contributions collected from property owners benefited by public improvements such as paving, water/sewer lines, and the like. Special assessments comprise one of the components of "miscellaneous general revenue" in the census tables.

4. Lottery Revenues. These come from voluntary participation by players; revenues often are earmarked for special purposes.

Own Source General Revenue is total state and local government revenue minus federal and state aid; this definition goes beyond census classifications to include not only the rest of general revenue, but water and transit system revenues as well.

Development Exactions embrace a wide range of contributions, both voluntary "donations" and mandatory "impact fees," and both cash and in-kind transfers made by developers to local and state governments to help cover physical infrastructure costs associated with new developments. Although related closely to special assessments, this category of UBF is not quantified in any of the tables.

Charges and Fees are technically separable, but are used interchangeably in this section. Tabular data presented here are arranged so that readers can draw their own conclusions as to whether the definitional framework is too broad, and if so, they can narrow it appropriately for their own calculations and comparisons.

Table 3.1

User-based Financing Related to Other Own Source Revenue of State and Local Governments for 1975–76 and 1985–86

| | 1975-76 | | | | | | 1985-86 | | | | | | | |
| | St&Loc | | State | | Local | | St&Loc | | State | | Local | | All Cities | |
Category	Amount	Per-cent	Amount	Per-cent	Amount	Per-cent	Amount	Per-cent	Amount	Per-cent	Amount	Per-cent	Amount	Per-cent
Own Source Rev.[a]	207,589	100.0	108,376	100.0	99,209	100.0	546,021	100.0	295,839	100.0	250,182	100.0	95,713	100.0
User Based Financ.	50,607	24.4	25,666	23.7	24,936	25.1	128,318	23.5	58,227	19.7	70,091	28.0	30,298	31.6
User Based Taxes & Licenses[b]	13,404	6.5	13,016	12.0	388	.4	23,342	4.3	22,461	7.6	881	.3	359	.4
Service Fees & Charges	37,203	17.9	12,650	11.7	24,548	24.7	104,976	19.2	35,766	12.1	69,210	27.7	29,939	31.3
Current Charges	29,320	14.1	11,652	10.8	17,668	17.8	80,400	14.7	29,987	10.1	50,413	20.2	18,072	18.9
Water Revenues	4,463	2.1	—	Neg.	4,458	4.5	13,250	2.4	59	Neg.	13,201	5.3	9,203	9.6
Transit Revenues	1,566	.8	—	—	1,566	1.6	4,453	.8	878	.3	3,575	1.4	1,578	1.6
Spec. Assessments	879	.4	23	Neg.	856	.9	2,163	.4	142	Neg.	2,021	.8	1,086	1.1
Lottery Revenues[c]	975	.5	975	.9	—	—	4,700	.9	4,700	1.6	—	—	—	—

Taxes^d	143,408	69.1	76,240	70.3	67,189	67.7	349,709	64.0	205,593	69.5	144,116	57.6	50,514	52.8
Property	57,001	27.5	2,118	2.0	54,884	55.3	111,711	20.5	4,355	1.5	107,356	42.9	25,061	26.2
Indiv. Income	24,575	11.8	21,448	19.8	3,127	3.2	74,417	13.6	67,469	22.8	6,948	2.8	5,486	5.7
General Sales	32,045	15.4	27,333	25.2	4,711	4.7	90,710	16.6	74,821	25.3	15,889	6.3	9,034	9.4
Other Taxes^e	29,787	14.3	25,341	23.4	4,447	4.5	72,871	13.3	58,948	19.9	13,923	5.6	10,933	11.4
Other Gen. Revenue	13,574	6.5	6,470	6.0	7,104	7.2	67,994	12.5	32,019	10.8	35,975	14.4	14,901	15.6
Interest Earnings	6,973	3.3	3,387	3.1	3,587	3.6	35,850	6.5	17,745	6.0	18,105	7.2	7,336	7.7
Other Gen. Revenue	6,601	3.2	3,083	2.9	3,517	3.6	32,144	5.9	14,274	4.8	17,870	7.2	7,565	7.9

Source: Bureau of the Census, *Governmental Finances, 1975–76*, tables 4 and 11; *Government Finances in 1985–86*, tables 6 and 27; *City Government Finances in 1975–76* and *1985–86*, table 1.

[a] Own source general revenue as used in census reports, plus water, transit, and lottery revenue; except for water and transit revenue, it does not include any of census "Other than General Revenue" categories: gas and electric utilities, liquor store, and insurance trust revenue (Social Security, unemployment compensation, employee retirement, and other trust revenues).

[b] Taxes on motor fuels and auto registration and fees for drivers' licenses.

[c] Lottery revenue as reported in *Governmental Finances*, from unpublished data in 1975–76 and p. xiv for 1985–86.

[d] Excluding motor fuel taxes.

[e] Major yields, 1975–76 and 1985–86, respectively, in billions of dollars: Corporation income, 7.3 and 20.0; selective sales and gross receipts, 22.5 and 44.3; estate/inheritance/gift, 1.5 and 2.5. Percentages do not always add exactly to 100 due to rounding.

133

Figure 3.1
**Major Components of Own Source General Revenue of Local Governments:
Taxes, User-based Financing (UBF), and Miscellaneous General Revenue (MGR),
1985–86 (Amounts in Billions)**

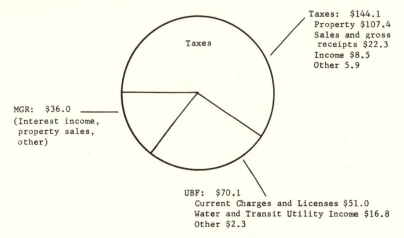

Taxes

Taxes: $144.1
Property $107.4
Sales and gross
  receipts $22.3
Income $8.5
Other 5.9

MGR: $36.0
(Interest income,
 property sales,
 other)

UBF: $70.1
Current Charges and Licenses $51.0
Water and Transit Utility Income $16.8
Other $2.3

Source: Bureau of the Census, *Government Finances in 1985–86*, November 1987, tables 6, 12,
        pp. 7, 16.

UBF as a Proportion of Own Source Revenue (OSR)

As shown in table 3.1, UBF in 1975–76 totaled $50.6 billion out of combined
state and local OSR of $207.6 billion, or 24.4 percent; for state OSR, UBF
represented 23.7 percent, and for local government it represented 25.1 percent.
In 1985–86 the percentage of OSR represented by user-based financing decreased
slightly to 23.5 percent for state and local governments combined, with the state
percentage at 19.7 percent, down from a decade earlier, but with the local
proportion increasing to 28.0 percent and with all cities standing at 31.6 percent.

The picture presented by the table is striking when viewed against the historical
background of local government finance, where for a long time the property tax
dominated the revenue side. For local governments in 1985–86, property tax
revenue comprised 42.9 percent of OSR, while for all cities, UBF outdistanced
property tax revenue 31.6 to 26.2 percent. Figure 3.1 shows the relative shares
of OSR produced by UBF, the major broad-based taxes, and other taxes and
other categories of OSR.

In addition to general expansion, UBF spread from larger to smaller jurisdictions and from a few traditional fields such as water/sewer utilities, school
lunches, and municipal parking lots and garages to many new areas, including
fire protection, solid waste collection and treatment, emergency rescue services,
libraries, and recreation. "Developer exactions" have comprised an especially
rapidly growing revenue source and are examined later in this section.

Table 3.2
Preferences for Local Revenue Sources, 1987

	1	2	3	4	5	6
Total Public	9%	20%	9%	33%	17%	12%
Household income:						
Under $15 K	10	18	5	28	20	19
$15-24.9 K	8	21	10	31	20	10
$25+ K	9	22	12	39	12	6
$40+ K	11	20	16	38	10	5
White	9	20	10	35	16	10
Nonwhite	6	20	6	23	23	22
Under Age 35	9	23	8	34	15	11
Age 35-44	7	19	12	35	18	9
Age 45-65	10	19	11	33	15	12
Over Age 65	11	16	4	31	23	15
Northeast	10	16	7	30	19	18
North-Central	12	22	11	33	14	8
South	8	20	10	36	16	10
West	6	23	8	33	17	13

Source: ACIR, *Changing Public Attitudes on Governments and Taxes, 1987*, Report S–16, tables 16, 17–19, September 1987, pp. 29–32.

1 = Income tax. 2 = Sales tax. 3 = Property tax. 4 = User charges. 5 = No revenue increase. 6 = Don't know.

High Political Acceptability

Polls conducted for the Advisory Commission on Intergovernmental Relations (ACIR) by the Gallup organization and surveys by other organizations over the 1977–87 decade showed a rising acceptability, and indeed a preference, for user fees over taxes as local revenue sources. In 1987, in response to the question: "If your local government decided to raise a small amount of additional revenue to help meet costs and improve services, which ones of these would you prefer?" (with four alternatives—local sales, income, or property taxes, or "charges for specific services"), 33 percent opted for charges, 20 percent for the sales tax, 9 percent each for income and property taxes, and 12 percent for the "don't know" category. Seventeen percent declined to concede any need for an increase. A more general question in the 1988 poll as to the best way to meet needs for "public works services," user fees and charges received a 35 percent response; dedicated taxes, 37 percent; general taxes, 12 percent; don't spend more, 7 percent; and don't know/other, 9 percent. Table 3.2 shows preferences for income, racial, age, and regional groupings.

Prior surveys showed a like preference for user charges (for example, 1981, 55 percent; 1986, 49 percent). In most years prior to 1987 the question was more tersely put (1986: Suppose your local government must raise more revenue . . .). Table 3.2 indicates that for all groups, user charges received a more favorable response than any of the other three sources. The perceived regressivity of charges carried some weight with lower-income and minority respondents. Dislike of the property tax and leeway in consumer choice provided by fees/charges (contrasted to no choice when the service is financed from the general tax base) may have helped account for the high comparative level of acceptability afforded to UBF.

Basic Economic Concepts

"The economic case for the expansion and rationalization of pricing in the urban public sector rests essentially on the contribution it can make to allocative efficiency." So wrote Selma Mushkin in 1972.[6] The concept is fundamental and relevant to those public services, functions, and subfunctions where the benefits flowing from the rendered service are divisible—precisely or approximately— as between individuals or firms on the one hand and the community on the other. To arrive at and administer the resulting pricing system is a local government administrative cost, and the net benefit in terms of resource allocation efficiency must significantly exceed such cost to make any particular shift to UBF economically worthwhile, although fiscal needs or equity might in themselves warrant the shift. In general, however, to go to a UBF system for a given service depends on the presence of two features—benefit separability or divisibility and chargeability.

In general, divisibility of the service into individual and community benefit portions encompasses a range of goods from private (benefit primarily individual) and mixed (private good endowed with a public purpose, such as urban water supply) to public (no way of excluding any consumer from benefiting, such as an air pollution monitoring system or a mosquito control program). Price mechanisms range from a charge or fee fully or largely supporting a service to a combination of a fee or charge and a public subsidy supported from the general tax base.

Table 3.3 shows the extent to which expenditures for the major urban service classifications used by the census were being met by UBF in large cities in 1985– 86. Not shown in the table, but drawn from the same data set is the fact that total UBF revenue for the larger cities, as a proportion of own source general revenue (OSGR) calculated in the same manner as for other governments in table 3.1, comprised 29.5 percent, compared with 31.6 percent for all cities. Large-city tax revenue was 65.9 percent of OSGR, with the property tax segment at 27.6 percent, compared to 26.2 percent for all cities.[7]

Following are three categories of economic and fiscal advantages often cited for UBF. Two derive from efficiency aspects of resource allocation; the other relates to improved equity between users and nonusers and to income and other variables.

Table 3.3

Aggregate User-based Revenue by Function as a Percentage of Functional Spending for Cities 300,000 and Over, 1985–86

(In Millions of Dollars)

Function	UB Revenue	Total Expend	% UB
Highways	$688.4	$2,559.1	26.9
Hospitals	938.8	2,904.9	32.3
Sewerage	1,832.7	2,859.9	64.1
Other Sanitation	343.7	1,786.5	19.2
Utilities	8,959.0	11,993.7	74.7
Housing & Comm. Dev.	625.8	3,213.4	19.5
Airports	1,207.5	1,383.2	87.3
Water Transport	295.7	294.4	100.4
Parkng Facilities	217.2	233.0	93.2
Parks-Recreation	391.9	2,074.1	18.9
Higher Education	97.3	410.1	23.7

Source: Bureau of the Census, *City Government Finances in 1985–86*, GF86, no. 4, 1987, table 7, pp. 94–95.

(1) Charges plus vehicle registration fees, motor fuel taxes. (2) If $861.7 million state aid for highways, nearly entirely derived from motor fuel taxes and licenses, were included, UB percentage would be 60.6. (3) Includes $1,535.6 of capital outlay. (4) Water, transit, electric power, and gas.

- Measuring and regulating demand. UBF affords a tangible way for citizens to register a preferred intensity of a service and in this manner can serve as a valuable planning tool for local government. UBF can prevent wastage that would occur if the service were free (water), and it can level out demand through peak-period charges.

- Preventing or minimizing the shifting of part of social costs of private activity to the community. UBF may often be a more efficient and equitable mechanism than regulation to achieve a particular socioeconomic objective (for example, charges for extra police to handle rush-hour traffic at a plant entrance).

- Equity improvements. Improved balances can be obtained between (1) users and non-users of a predominantly private good (for example, parking, enrichment courses in adult education); (2) residents and nonresidents of a service-providing jurisdiction; and (3) tax-exempt and taxpaying organizations, institutions, and property.

Political Considerations

In addition to the question of representative versus direct democracy, which in the latter case has the citizen voting on issues such as tax and spending levels, there are two further questions involved when a shift is made from tax financing to UBF. One is the extent to which the political constituency loses breadth and diversity as more services are placed into more protected or more vulnerable arenas of competition in the resource allocation process. A second question deals with the benefits and losses accruing to low-income residents when service financing is shifted wholly or partially to a UBF basis.

The first question is the extent to which UBF results in service "unbundling." An important economic and political aspect of UBF is that it opens up taxpayer choices about service use and intensity. As cited by George Peterson, the extreme case of service-revenue unbundling occurs in Ohio, where almost all revenue increases have to be approved by voters and are tied to designated expenditure purposes, resulting in public voting on separate levies for mental health, hospitals, education, and other services.[8] Such a separation of functions and their respective financial sources into insulated compartments in local or state budgeting negates the principle of a broad heterogeneous constituency in which resource claims are assessed comprehensively and competitively. A model like the Ohio one requires that such an assessment take place part by part and rarely as a whole.

However, UBF need not appreciably fragment the comprehensiveness or cohesion of general local government. Not only are there alternatives, but many services are of the mixed category, so that it is both practical and equitable to finance only a part of the respective expenditure from fees or charges. This leaves the public portion (plus, in some cases, a further portion to allow a less than full charge against low-income groups) to be covered by a budgetary subsidy. In other words, in mixed services the public part is financed by subsidy from the general tax base, and if it is necessary to partially shield disadvantaged consumers from part of the private financing, an additional "hardship" subsidy is paid, also from general tax funds. Consequently, although concerned with smaller numbers, the arena of competition is not really narrowed; the competition is about the subsidy size relative to other services.

Equity Considerations

For services that are divisible (public versus private proportion) and administratively chargeable, UBF can result in substantially improved economic and fiscal equity. If such a service is being financed from general taxation, the group receiving the private good is being subsidized by the general public; this inequity is ameliorated by a shift to UBF. Second, user fees can encourage conservation, so that careful users are rewarded and the extravagant pay more. Third, of greater importance, a shift to charges for use of facilities costly to build and maintain (such as museums, libraries, and community colleges) can produce revenue from use by nonresidents of the jurisdiction. Fourth, user charges can be imposed upon tax-exempt organizations, provided they are assessed in a nondiscriminatory manner. If the jurisdiction is a state capital or university town, providing services such as water, sewers, and solid waste collection from general revenues can be costly and inequitable to local taxpayers. Likewise, if the jurisdiction has an active tax abatement to attract industry, the cost of the program in terms of revenue loss can be considerably reduced if user charge functions are factored out of the tax base beforehand.

Regressive or other unfavorable impacts upon lower-income individuals are cited frequently as major arguments against imposition of user charges for household-type services such as water, sewers, and solid waste collection and for recreational and cultural facilities and activities. It is argued that the household services, though individual in benefit, are necessary for safe and sanitary living and that any charge is bound to require a higher proportion of a poor person's income than of a middle or higher income. Recreational facilities in low-income neighborhoods generally exercise a stabilizing influence on social behavior. A second equity argument holds that a shift in revenue source away from general taxation can crowd the social service portion of the public budget into a more vulnerable competitive position. These are serious arguments and require careful examination.

Mushkin and others have pointed out that in many local governments the economic incidence of user charges is less regressive than the property tax being displaced (rent being a high-proportion budget item of a low-income family). Further, less intensive use of libraries and museums by low-income residents means that the introduction of user charges reduces the subsidy previously enjoyed by higher-income users partially paid by the low-income group. This improvement in equity is especially marked if low-income persons are given a reduced charge to use these facilities, with the discount being covered by a transfer from the general fund.

Finally, there are specific and simple methods of shielding low-income people from user charges on services with a significant health, welfare, or community stabilization element (such as low- or no-cost tickets or passes to low-income residents). In any event, protection of the disadvantaged ought not to be an excuse for subsidizing the well-to-do.[9] This point has relevance also in metropolitan-run transit or other user-financed services, where it is sometimes argued that fares or other charges should be lower and subsidies higher in those jurisdictions having larger proportions of low-income residents. A more equitable answer is the subsidization of low-income passengers by discounted passes or other means.

Concern about the budgetary shortchanging of the social services is based on two related points. First, a majority of the functions and services that meet the two UBF criteria (divisibility and chargeability) lie outside the social service field. This leaves police, fire, and social services competing against one another within a small arena, with little doubt as to which of the three suffers from having the least political clout.

Second, as George Peterson has pointed out, for many years a majority of Americans have consistently rated welfare-related services as a primary area of potential budgetary savings (like foreign aid at the national level). These services have typically been the only group for which across-the-board cutbacks have commanded support from a majority of voters.[10]

The feared political vulnerability of the social services in an increasingly UBF-oriented state and local budget framework may be mitigated by additional factors, however. Many functions are mixed, necessitating a combination of charges and subsidies and requiring competition among all of the subsidy claimants. Also, several parts of the social services category are themselves susceptible to means-tested user charges (as the school-lunch program has been for a long time). These include public health clinics, emergency ambulance services, and certain other hospital services, all of which could produce some additional revenues.[11]

Finally, earmarking of revenues from charges, although a tempting corollary to UBF on the part of budget officers, is by no means necessary. Except for utility and other business-type functions requiring enterprise fund accounting, service revenues can go either directly into the general fund or eventually into the fund after passing through a service fund for accounting and subsidy calculation purposes. (Activities financed entirely or primarily through a combination of revenue bonds and user fees are often under pressure from bond-rating agencies, especially if the local government is not in good fiscal health, because the rating agencies like to see revenues insulated from the "exigencies" of state and local budgeting.) Revenues from additional service fields can loosen the fiscal squeeze upon public budgets and thus ease somewhat the position of all resource claimants, including the social services.

Fiscal and Administrative Alternatives in UBF Implementation

With the steady increase of UBF, both for capital repair and replacement and for operating revenues, state and local governments and their citizens and legislative bodies need to examine alternative ways in which these shifts can best be accommodated in fiscal policy, equity, and administrative terms.

Additional Fiscal Policy Considerations. The issues of fund earmarking and service pricing need consideration. Fund earmarking usually occurs when tax or charge revenue from service users is segregated in a fund reserved exclusively or primarily for financing the function's operating expenditures and debt service on its bond obligations. This earmarking is associated usually with utility, transportation, and other user-financed services; services characterized by more of a mix of private and public benefit should not be earmarked, so that the competitive arena for resource claims is kept as inclusive as possible. But some contend that for physical infrastructure, the condition may be so serious and the temptation to delay needed maintenance so strong that the conventional objections to earmarking should be set aside until maintenance and construction priorities come into better balance.[12] (Often this imbalance is attributable to the greater visibility and political credit attendant upon opening a new facility than upon completing its periodic overhaul.)

Pricing is often difficult; the price should reflect the full cost of that part of the service to be of private benefit. Often such a price or charge will have three components—quantity, capacity, and location. These three elements were described in a report by Public Technology, Inc.,[13] a nonprofit organization maintained collectively by the "Big Seven" state-local organizations (Council of State Governments, International City Management Association, National Association of Counties, National Conference of State Legislatures, National Governors' Association, National League of Cities, and U.S. Conference of Mayors):

- The quantity component reflects the short-run cost of current output, generally done with a single charge, varying with the quantity of the service consumed. Where peak loads occur daily, as in traffic or power consumption, the rate per unit would rise during peaks, so as to reflect the short-run costs at the time of consumption.

- The capacity component covers the difference between the quantity charge and the full costs of production at designed capacity level. (This is per capita cost of facility construction or expansion amortized over facility life.)

- The location component reflects the long-run delivery cost to residents of different location and density classifications.

The end product of an ideal user charge system is a combination of charge components that adds up to higher costs for higher demanders of the service and higher costs for residents who live in areas more expensive to serve. Because they reflect the cost of serving people, the charges provide residents and officials with information on the desirability of increasing the supply. Developers and prospective new residents can decide whether the value to them of developing a new area is greater than the cost of providing the public service. They also can observe the quantity demand during peak times at the higher peak price. If the revenues exceed the cost of expansion, it is worthwhile to expand the facility.

Obviously, the development of a user-charge structure and the internal composition of it will vary according to type of service and other factors, such as allocation of costs of water supply and wastewater treatment capacity expansion between old and new urban developments, assuming that the expansion is occasioned entirely by growth rather than quality standards.

Development exactions are related closely to the expansion factors just mentioned, but also have significant equity and legal aspects. The exactions issue also is related to voluntary participation by the private sector in the financing of public infrastructure, especially in those cases where the absence of an adequate road, school, or other facility is holding up local approval of a large-scale urban development—commercial, industrial, or residential.

Subsequent to passage of Proposition 13 in California, development exactions became a major source of local government revenue in that state. After World War II local governments in many if not most urbanizing states began to impose development-related fees and infrastructure requirements—water and sewer hookup charges, building permit fees, and required provision of streets and storm drains within the new subdivision. Subsequently, required donations of open space began to be tied into cluster and other types of residential subdivision zoning regulations.

In 1968 the ACIR proposed that states consider mandating the private dedication of park and school sites as a part of new development.[14] Next, in Florida, California, and elsewhere, additional impact fees and requirements came into use under the rationale that the new subdivision would house children who would need school facilities, and that increased traffic would require widened arterial roads in the "general vicinity." Any new or expanded public facility in the jurisdiction that could be identified as necessitated by the marginal increases in demand created by the proposed new development then became the object of some kind of fee.

In California local governments turned also to the state's Environmental Quality Act, which gave localities the power to "mitigate" environmental harm arising from new developments. Mitigation began to take various forms; localities began to impose new requirements on developers (called "CEQA exactions" after the act). In return for a developer's "donation" of various infrastructure components, projects could be expedited and approved; absence of a donation might cause the governing body to drag its feet. Developers began giving to localities such items as school buildings, recreation centers, and freeway interchanges to the point that developer exactions reached nearly half the total public capital formation in the state in normal development years.[15]

Not surprisingly, a large amount of litigation arose in states that were imposing impact fees or exactions. The crux of the controversy, still continuing, is the basic concept of user charges—separation of functions into private and community components. Legal questions as to whether the "donations" are gifts, charges, or taxes have had obvious financial ramifications in state, local, and federal tax liabilities. Development exactions, if adequately documented and equitably administered, can produce a fairer division of the tax burden between residents and "newcomers" because impact fees or in-kind equivalents permit accounting for a substantial part of the "real cost" of new urban growth. However, it is less clear in this area where equity lies, and the exactions comprise the most controversial of all the UBF categories discussed here.

Other Administrative and Legal Considerations

Three additional aspects of user-charge administration must be noted: (1) the structure within which the user-financed function is carried out, ranging from full integration within an executive-branch departmental structure or placement in an independent special district or authority with earmarked funds, to divestiture to the marketplace; (2) the extent to which administrative cost can be a deterrent to initiating UBF; and (3) very importantly, administrative procedures to shield low-income users from full charges for mixed-benefit services without any stigma or embarrassment.

Structure. Advantages of integration within a departmental structure include more effective coordination with the rest of the state or local government; less compartmentalization in the government's operating budget; and as a probable corollary, less use of separate, earmarked funds. On the other side is cited the tendency in some governmental bodies to raid maintenance funds for more attractive political undertakings, such as cutting a ribbon or laying a cornerstone.

Another possibility is creation of a subordinate taxing area; this device enables servicing of an area smaller than the entire city or county while staying within an integrated framework, yet accommodating differing service levels, as between densely and sparsely populated areas. If the service area is not confined to a single state or local government jurisdiction, and especially if it includes parts, rather than the whole, of the territories of several jurisdictions, a multijurisd-ictional functional district or authority may be required. (The New York Port Authority, covering parts of New York and New Jersey, and the Washington Suburban Sanitary Commission, delivering water and sewer utilities to major parts of two Maryland counties adjacent to Washington, D.C., are examples of bistate and bilocal functional authorities.)

The degree of independence of the district or authority from controls by local governments in the areas being served depends largely on the function and its geography, financing, and politics. A major advantage of the independent au-thority, especially in a time of resource scarcity, is the higher degree of ''res-oluteness'' in administering a user-charge function and of resisting the political temptations of setting a rate too low to cover costs. However, such an authority's budget, accompanied by data on the rates required to sustain it, should be subject to review by the general government(s) concerned.

Administrative Costs, which vary widely among functions, arise from (1) collecting consumption data on the service or product; (2) calculating delivery costs at the estimated consumption volume; and (3) collecting the user charge. Obviously a parking meter is less costly than a toll booth attendant; a water meter is all that is needed to measure volume and provides the data for automated calculating and billing for water and sewerage; monitoring toxic waste discharge from an industrial establishment is very costly. The spread of computerized record keeping and billing has greatly reduced administrative costs in many of those local government functional services susceptible to UBF.

Free or Discounted Service to Low-Income Users. There are three musts here: the system must be equitable, efficient, and unobtrusive. Shielding of low-income users by long-established procedures has met the three requirements fully; as noted earlier, sliding payment scales have been used in social service areas such as mental health and day-care centers. With the increased use of computers, it is quite feasible to extend UBF to libraries, public health clinics, and alcohol/drug treatment facilities, as well as to the entire park and recreation area. Each book checked out, inoculation given, or other service provided is put into the computer, with periodic billings sent out, and payment delinquencies producing a reminder on the occasion of the next contact. But does such a system meet the test of unobtrusiveness and protection of privacy?

The availability of a reduced rate or exemption must be publicized generally and posted in government facilities, with users advised in such publicity of one or more telephone numbers from which an application or certification form can be requested for mailing. The form attests to income level and is signed by the individual and returned by mail or in person at a library or other local government neighborhood office. It can be checked in the local tax or other office if desired, or entered directly into the agency or central computer system, and a bar-coded card can be mailed to the applicant; this assures that service, admission, or other use of a covered facility or service can be accessed in a normal way, with discounts or "no charge" automatically calculated, the user billed by mail, and payment made by mail (or in person at a branch office if the user prefers). Procedures approximating these are simple, anonymous, and equitable and have been in steadily increasing use by local government agencies.

State Authorization and Assistance for Local Application of User-based Financing

The state government has two roles regarding the introduction of UBF by local governments: legislative authorization and technical assistance. In a 1985 report the ACIR recommended that states take certain actions on local fees and charges.[16] Draft state legislation to implement the recommendation included (1) statutory authority to impose fees and charges under certain criteria and procedures, including separability, chargeability, equity among classes of citizens and taxpayers, and feasibility " . . . through income certification and other means, of [mitigating] in unobtrusive ways . . . part or all of the impact upon low income users of those services found to have a significant element of socio-economic stabilization or other public benefits"; (2) authorizing and directing an appropriate state agency to serve as a clearinghouse on user-charge information by publishing and disseminating data on current charges in various other local jurisdictions in the state and elsewhere; and (3) assisting local governments in the development of new areas for user-charge utilization.[17]

Summary Observations

Several key points emerge from the examination of UBF:

- UBF is a major factor in local government fiscal policy in an era of fiscal restraint and enjoys a high degree of political support.
- Public acceptability will erode if revenue yields are pursued in ways that are perceived as fiscally unwarranted or economically inequitable among or within user groups.
- A major challenge confronts both state and local legislators and administrators in grasping the opportunities of fiscal yield and economic equity offered by UBF, while making sure to protect the financial and structural integrity of general local government and to appropriately shield low-income users of those public services having a high social and public benefit.

COMMINGLING PRIVATE AND PUBLIC FUNDS FOR PUBLIC PURPOSES

In the post–Civil War years a number of states engaged in extensive speculative activity directed toward getting railroads built within or across their borders. Many of these ventures failed, with consequent losses to bondholders and state governments. In the resulting backlash new state constitutions were written, and others were amended to prohibit any use of public funds or credit in connection with private undertakings. Some of these provisions were so tightly written and interpreted by the courts that further amendments were needed in the 1950s to permit state-local participation in federal urban renewal and other programs and subsequently to permit issuance of industrial development bonds for the purpose of attracting business and industry to state or local areas.

In 1968 the ACIR published a draft constitutional amendment for consideration by the states whose constitutions still contained restrictive language. The draft, republished in 1984, was patterned on an amendment adopted in 1967 by New York State and provided that "notwithstanding any other provision of this constitution, the state, its political subdivisions, and any public corporation may, as provided by law, where a public purpose will be served, grant or lend its funds to any individual, association, or private corporation for purposes of participating or assisting in economic or community development."[18]

Controversy has continued on many individual state and local projects as to what is a public purpose. The same kind of question arises when private interests wish to contribute to public enterprises; in both cases—public money into private activity and private into public—concern is voiced about the commingling of funds. Will private financing of public infrastructure corrupt the government into giving special future favors to the contributor, or will government, in putting money into a private activity, risk a conflict of interest with the partner company in a future regulatory or other context? Nevertheless, the commingling continues to grow as public-private relationships expand into new areas.

Private Financing of Public Infrastructure

In a 1986 report to the president and Congress the National Council on Public Works Improvement (NCPWI) noted several factors that draw greater public attention to increasing the private-sector role in financing public infrastructure:

• Decline (except for transportation) in federal aid for capital investment in public works

• Deterrence of state and local governments through state or locally imposed tax and expenditure limitations from fully compensating for federal cuts

- Rapid growth in some areas and aging facilities in others, causing increased need for expanded or renovated facilities
- Wider political acceptance of user fees in financing public facilities[19]

As noted earlier, developer exactions, either in the form of "impact fees" or of coerced donations to local governments as part of the development approval process, have been constituting a major source of public revenue in a growing number of states and localities. Here the other side of the exaction coin appears—truly voluntary private sharing in the costs of new or replaced infrastructure necessary to accommodate new development. Another major source of private capital for infrastructure also will be reviewed—private construction of a facility and lease-back to a state or local government.

Donations of Infrastructure by Developers. Where the availability of adequate infrastructure capacity—roads, schools, recreation, and so on—is a legal condition under state law (as in Florida, effective 1991) or local ordinance (as in Montgomery County, Maryland) for new development, developers may find it in their financial interest to finance, wholly or in part, the missing piece or pieces of infrastructure needed for their project to qualify for build-out ahead of the time by which the budgeting process would bring the needed pieces on line. This kind of private financial participation tends somewhat toward the California "bargaining" situation, but with an important difference—the facilities required are established considerably in advance of the approval process for the subdivision or other development; the necessity of the particular improvement is specified in the local government capital improvement program, and if it does not come on-line soon enough to fit the developer's build-out plans, it may be delayed, but its earlier approval stands.

A very fine line indeed is required to distinguish genuinely voluntary financial participation from an exaction of the California type where a local government moves a developer application along at a glacial pace, if at all, until a donation of a library, interchange, or whatever turns out to be sufficient for the application to move at normal speed. It has been pointed out that in California a substantial number of donations represent negotiated agreements between private and public parties.[20] The comparative volume of general-obligation debt issued by California local governments over a five-year period before and following the adoption of Proposition 13 underlines the fiscal dilemma facing local governments and developers during the period: in millions of dollars, the total yearly issuances were, for 1976, 117 issues for $489; 1977, 105 for $377; 1979, 58 for $243; and 1980, 20 for $76.[21]

An important fiscal equity distinction between impact fees on the one hand and "bargained donations" on the other is that courts have generally required the impact fee to have a direct relationship to a specific project. California city-county 1986 survey respondents reflected strong concern about the bargaining relationship and advised substitution of a legal-formula approach for bargaining.[22] A direct fee-project relationship was legislated in 1987. A series of U.S. Supreme

Court decisions in that same year tended to place a greater burden on the local government side, as examined in chapter 6.

Municipal Leasing. John Peterson pointed to two strong imperatives that, in a time of resource scarcity, drive state and local government officials to look favorably toward various kinds of leasing arrangements whereby private capital is provided for the construction of a facility that will then be leased back to the governmental unit: (1) legal expediency, where there are strict limitations in force on the amount of state or local debt that can be outstanding—particularly compelling where the facility is for a function not susceptible to user-based financing, wherein revenue bonds rather than general-obligation debt could be used; and (2) potential savings that might accrue from such factors as lower construction costs arising from the private use of nonunion labor and wider choice in procurement of building materials.[23]

Peterson further listed advantages and disadvantages of leasing a facility privately built, in contrast to public financing of the construction where title resides in the governmental unit from the outset. Advantages included the following:

- Usually a lease obligation is not included as long-term debt in calculation of a government's debt limitation, nor is it generally subject to voter approval.
- Costs and delays in bond sales—legal fees, prospectus preparation, and possibly a referendum—are usually avoided.
- Leasing is often a suitable means for financing capital assets too expensive to fund on a one-shot basis out of current revenue but with lives too short to warrant bond financing (for example, major equipment).
- For equipment, technological change makes ownership imprudent; sophisticated types often require a continuing vendor relation.

Disadvantages included the following:

- Financing costs are higher due to builder's risk that the lease might be broken.
- The governmental unit may be sued for violating the spirit of a constitutional or statutory bond limitation.[24]

In contrast to a general lease outside the tax-exempt framework, a lease-purchase arrangement for a facility that can only be used for a public purpose, such as a state university library, has several advantages and has enjoyed wide use. The Government Finance Officers Association estimated an annual volume of $5 billion for the 1979–85 period.[25] Its popularity is enhanced by the fact that lease income is guaranteed by the local government and is tax exempt to the institutional holder of the debt. Since the debt is structured like a revenue bond, it usually falls outside state debt limitations, and title to the facility passes to the governmental unit when the debt is retired. In the larger transactions the lessor frequently is a financial institution or group of institutions, which buys the lease from the original owner/builder/financier. The institution or group then becomes the lessor and receives lease payments as the return of interest and principal on the debt.

Financial Entrepreneurism in State and Local Governments

Throughout the fifties and sixties larger local governments were involving themselves financially in federal housing, urban renewal, and model-cities programs aimed at revitalization of central business districts and of poor neighborhoods.[26] With some exceptions, such as New York, Pennsylvania, and Michigan, state governments did not begin to put substantial state funds and credit into the financing of housing and local economic development activities until the seventies. Large-scale financial involvements began with state housing finance assistance, which by 1983 was under way in forty-seven states. Although this assistance was large in scale, state risks were usually modest. Tax-exempt revenue bonds were issued, with principal and interest payments often supplied by private mortgage lenders, augmented by rental assistance programs of the federal Department of Housing and Urban Development.

Subsequently, states began to permit creation of, and to financially assist, a wide variety of "community-based organizations," such as community development corporations and neighborhood improvement associations. Finally, in the early eighties states began to establish state agencies to stimulate venture-capital formation and to assist these enterprises in financial and other ways.

More or less concurrently, local governments began to participate on an equity basis (that is, profit and loss sharing) in large-scale private urban development and redevelopment projects. These governmental ventures—state and local—involve both substantial opportunity and risk. Most of these economic development projects are carried out by public-private partnerships, often in legal form as public, private profit, or nonprofit corporations and often with a commingling of public and private funds.

These activities comprise a wide variety of for-profit ventures by local and sometimes by state governments. They have been aimed at the dual objectives of community betterment and increased public revenues in the form of project profits, with the latter substituting for the more politically onerous alternatives of taxes or user charges and fees. Equity participation in private business ventures can be profitable for the taxpayers, unless, of course, the private partner fails and the public investment is lost, in which case the jurisdiction's financial position is worsened, with unfavorable future consequences to its citizen "shareholders."

The types of entrepreneurial activities examined here are (1) land assembly or disposition; (2) financing of sports and other facilities; and (3) other equity participation in private ventures.

Land assembly has long been an indispensable tool for state and local economic development and other public purposes. The original economic basis for land assembly was the formation of a "critical mass" of land that was sufficient for the purpose of one or more viable enterprises and that would, after appropriate private development, provide an enlarged property tax base, the added increment of which would return at least the initial investment of the governmental unit in its assembly.

In the sixties and subsequently, local governments began to assemble land for noneconomic development purposes, such as ensuring that the future development of strategically located parcels of land would be compatible with the jurisdiction's comprehensive plan or land use plan. Such parcels, if developed in the "wrong way," could cause adjoining land to be utilized in uneconomic or other ways detrimental to the public interest.

An additional major objective of land assembly began to emerge in the mid- to late seventies, like developer exactions, in response to tax and expenditure limitations or other budget restraints. The new objective was to utilize yet another source of revenue through the joint redevelopment with private enterprise of available land, under which the local unit would participate on an equity basis.

Commercial sports facilities serve not only as a source of revenue to the financing local unit (city or urban county) but also as an assist to economic development and a contribution to the unit's "image" and "civic pride." On the whole, the major public-financed sports facilities (major-league baseball, hockey, football, and basketball) have had a break-even outcome on a cash basis, with the economic development and image contributions as extras. Typically, after ascertaining that a stadium or other facility, if built, will bring in a big-league franchise, the city or county issues revenue bonds for its construction. Consequent lease payments plus very substantial proportions or fixed amounts of scoreboard advertising, concessions, television rights, and other aspects are structured so as to be adequate or more to cover interest and principal payments on the revenue bonds. The structure of the franchise and lease agreements varies from case to case, often but not always augmented by a percentage of the gate above a designated attendance threshold.

The usual financial arrangements were given a special touch by the 1987 session of the Maryland General Assembly, which authorized revenue bonds to be issued by a public authority to be created in the Baltimore area. Not one but two stadiums will be built in the inner city, with the bonds guaranteed by the state. The guarantee depended on obtaining a second big-league franchise and on the formation of a "sports lottery" to be conducted by the authority, hopefully not too competitive with the already-existing state lottery. The proceeds from the new lottery, together with the attendance admissions, television concessions, and so on, were presumed sufficient to cover principal and interest on the revenue bonds and to yield a modest profit.

Equity participation in other commercial ventures, including shopping malls, such as the one in Fairfield, California,[27] central business district redevelopment in Norfolk, Virginia,[28] and major office buildings in which the local government is a participant,[29] is becoming more frequent. From the viewpoint of state and local governments, the attractiveness of these kinds of ventures is obvious, with the degree of attraction correlating directly with the criticality of the local budget situation. On the other hand, equity ventures undertaken in periods of local economic growth may become at risk during cyclical or other downturns.

Two more serious doubts arise on matters of principle. First, if carried to extremes, these commercial activities sponsored or financed in part by local governments can cause citizen/taxpayer backlash if deals go sour or if government competition with private business is perceived; the backlash could be harmful to other public-private partnerships for civic or economic development. Second, as in the case of a shopping mall or other business in which healthy competition exists, the governmental unit, as part owner of a particular enterprise, may be in a position of conflict of interest when executing regulatory functions under the state police power that may affect enterprises competing with the one with which the unit is a partner. For instance, if one of the competitors applies for a rezoning of some kind and is turned down, especially if on a technicality not well understood by the average citizen, serious doubts could arise as to the integrity of the local government governing body and the officials involved in the business transactions and in the zoning decision.

EXPLORING OPTIONAL METHODS OF STATE-LOCAL SERVICE DELIVERY

It is clear that many people want less government, but in the 1970s people also decided that they wanted more decisions made in the public interest, decisions concerning civil rights, children's rights, women, [and] the purposes to which science and technology should be put. People have come to expect a lot more decisions from government, but that doesn't necessarily mean that government has to deliver more services. It is possible to think of ways we could have more governance with less government.[30]

The relative role of government in the national economy and in society generally has been a central issue of public policy since American independence and, as in any modern capitalist society, will continue to be debated in economic, political, and other terms. As applied to state and local government, the delivery agents of most public services, the issue assumes a subsequent dimension: following a decision that assuring the public availability on equitable terms of a particular service is a governmental concern and responsibility, how, under what conditions, and by what method(s) shall it be delivered to the consumer/taxpayer?[31]

Until the sixties the traditional method of delivering a public service had been, or at least had been perceived by most public administrators and the general public to be, through a governmental agency, financed out of general tax revenues, delivering or making available a service uniformly accessible without charge via public administration professionals accountable to elected officials accountable in turn to the voters. This had been the conventional theory of representative democracy and of public administration in the United States.

As already noted on the fiscal side, the public, either via its legislatures or through initiative and referendum processes, has from time to time determined that some fiscal and other parameters needed to be imposed upon the representative model. There were exceptions to the theory on the administrative side as well; in the War on Poverty, for example, state and local governments began to be bypassed, with nonprofit organizations called "community action agencies" delivering the federally assisted services to the poor.

By the early to mid-seventies the issues of (1) what an appropriate governmental responsibility was, and (2) if it was a public one, the appropriate level, agency, and delivery method were beginning to overlap. Because of the complex relationship between the two, a shorthand term, "privatization," was adopted and inappropriately applied by many to embrace both issues. For several of the alternative delivery methods that will be examined here, the service itself remains a governmental responsibility—programwise and moneywise—but may be delivered by a profit or nonprofit firm, wholly or in part. Across the spectrum, none of the alternatives except divestiture to the free market fit the concept of shifting all responsibility from the public to the private sector in a manner comparable to the divestiture of steel and other state-owned enterprises in Britain and France and the sale of Conrail by the U.S. government.

Some point out that the first decision—public or private responsibility—is a broad one of public policy in which ideology properly plays an important role, while the second—how best to carry out a governmental function—is a fiscal/administrative one and properly beyond ideology. Alan Campbell observed that

the proper role of government in relation to [assuring the availability of services] is a policy issue that must be determined by the political process. Once policy decisions have been made, however, effective and efficient delivery of services is a management, not an ideological issue. The issue should not be confused by the careless use of the word "privatization."[32]

However logical the ideological/management differentiation may be in theory, it blurs in practice because of perceptions of relative efficiency and equity factors. On efficiency, Campbell further notes, with some support from opposite philosophical quarters, that

although some very efficient government jurisdictions can be found in the United States, such efficiency on average is an exception. The public sector does not possess those built-in incentives for efficiency that characterize successful business practices. In short, there is no "bottom line." Finding an adequate substitute for that bottom line still eludes both practitioners and students of public management.[33]

Anthony Rufulo draws a similar comparison, but one related specifically to labor costs and productivity:

Competitive pressures give firms in the private sector a strong incentive to keep costs down. But these pressures are not as strong in the public sector, since government usually has a monopoly on the services it provides and doesn't have to compete for sales. . . . And government budgets are so complex that most citizens don't know how much they're being charged in taxes for any of the myriad services they have to buy. Thus they are not in a position to find out whether any of these services could be provided at a lower cost.[34]

The case for reexamination of the traditional role of government in arranging for and delivering public services has been clearly and forcefully articulated by Ted Kolderie: "[The governmental] role need not be as owner and operator. . . . The essential role is . . . a policy role: to see what needs to be done, to insure that it is done and provide public financing if required. Government is essentially an arranger of things; at times, it is a buyer." He also points out the need for "a new theory of accountability, to replace the outworn notions that bureaucracies are adequately responsible to policy through management, and that policy makers are adequately responsive to citizens through elections. This traditional theory does not serve effectively in bringing down costs and improving performance."[35]

Public Service Availability and Financing

Local government (and occasionally state government) in most instances has the following policy options concerning the initiation, continuance, or divestment of any potential or existing service or facility. The government may decide that availability to the public under free market pricing, government financing or subsidy, or other conditions should be assured by public law or other action, or it can decide that such availability should be left to the private market (for example, a decision to get into, stay out of, or get out of providing for one or more municipal golf courses open to the general public). If it decides to stay out of, or divest the service/facility to, the market, it can elect to do so with or without public regulation of the cost, quality, or other aspects of the service.

If the local or other government decides that the availability of the service/ facility is to be a public concern, then it must decide two major questions—how to pay for it and how to deliver it. The response to these two questions in the policy analysis and decision process was much simpler in the earlier years of public finance and administration. If it was to be a public matter it would be financed by taxes and delivered by public employees, period.

More recently, however, many state and local governing bodies have been adding new options to the financing decision. Not new is the practice of benefit assessments; if the service/facility confers a special benefit to particular property owners, such as a water or sewer line, a benefit assessment probably will be imposed on a front-foot or other basis. If the service/facility, such as roads and highways, is used primarily or exclusively by a particular occupational or other grouping of the population, such as motor vehicle owners/drivers, it probably will be financed through a segregated or earmarked tax, as on motor fuels, or a user charge, such as an auto registration fee and driver's license price, or a combination of these, with financing perhaps supplemented on occasion from the general tax base.

Also, it has become a major option to appraise those services that tend to be used on a selective basis—much by some people and little or none by others—such as a municipal swimming pool. The financing method probably will primarily be admission charges, with perhaps supplementary financing from the general fund to subsidize use by low-income or other disadvantaged users.

A Spectrum of Alternative Service Delivery Modes

The range of service delivery alternatives is quite broad; its consideration may fall into at least four major situational contexts: (1) when the jurisdiction's budget is up for general policy review, such as by an incoming administration, with a view to identifying parts or items for future in-depth study; (2) when one or more services are up for periodic or other systematic analysis; (3) when evolving revenue-expenditure relationships dictate a rigorous review of services being rendered; (4) when it has been decided that a problem or condition has grown to the point that a new service should be arranged for by the jurisdiction, and a determination needs to be made as to how it is to be financed and delivered.

Before an analysis of several major alternatives in state and local public service delivery, as applied to the principal line functions and services—mostly local, some state—some further definitional and qualifying notes are in order.

- Some definitions are applied here that differ from most of the service delivery literature: "provide for" and "arrange for" will be used interchangeably and in lieu of "provide," and "arrangers" will be used in lieu of "providers" because of the similarity of meaning between provide and deliver (in other contexts in public or private management, "provide" and "deliver" are synonymous—medical care providers means physicians and hospitals). Likewise, "deliver" and "delivery" will be used instead of "produce," "producer," or "product."

- In the earlier (pre–"Japan, Inc.") days the smug complacency of corporate management and union leadership in the private sector was mirrored in the public sector, both being reflective of the attitudes and preferences of American society; but economic and fiscal chickens came home to roost, with restoration of competitiveness, "more bang for the buck," and "doing more with less" becoming the new priorities for the nineties.

- There is a need for longer-range trend data, both quantitative and qualitative, on results from application of alternative methods and the processes by which governmental units have implemented the chosen method.[36]

- Although fiscal pressure has stimulated elected officials and public managers to consider private-sector and other alternative avenues of service delivery, from an ideal management standpoint the optimal objective of highest performance at least cost is expected to prevail, regardless of revenue circumstances.[37]

Considered here are the principal delivery alternatives now in use by local governments in the United States, along with a brief definition and the service

Table 3.4

Extent of Exclusive Use of Local Government Employees for Delivery of Line Services by County and City Governments, 1982

```
===============================================================
Top Ten Services Delivered        Eleven Services Delivered
    Most Exclusively                  Least Exclusively

    Service            %            Service                %
---------------------------------------------------------------
Traffic/Parking Enf.   90   Vehicle Towing/Storage          7
Meter Maint./Collec.   88   Day  Care  Facility Oper.       7
Street/Pkg. Lot Clng.  84   Drug/Alcohol Trtmnt. Progs.    10
Code Enforcmnt./Insp.  82   Operating Cult./Arts Progs.    11
Snow Plowing/Sanding   79   Op. Men.Hlth/Retard Progs.     13

Park Maint./Landscpg.  76   Hospital Oper. & Management    18
Police-Fire Communic   75   Elderly Programs               19
Parking Lot/Garage Op. 75   Paratransit Syst O&M           19
Crime Prev./Police          Museum  Operation              21
      Patrol           74   Bus Syst. Oper. & Maint.       26
Auditor'm/Conv. Ctr.Op.70   Public Health Programs         26
---------------------------------------------------------------
```

Source: Valente, C. F., and Manchester, L. D., *Rethinking Local Services: Examining Alternative Delivery Approaches* (Washington, D.C.: International City Management Association, 1984), xv.

field or fields in which each is most prevalent. In most cases the definitions follow those used by the International City Management Association (ICMA) in its surveys of local government delivery modes[38] or by the ACIR in its occasional surveys, beginning in the early sixties, of interlocal contracts and other arrangements between or among governmental units for service delivery.[39] In general, the order of listing runs from the highest degree of local government control (delivery exclusively by local government employees) to complete divestiture of a service to the private sector, with no subsequent governmental regulation of its cost or quality.

Delivery by government employees is the "traditional" mode described earlier. In 1982 ICMA surveyed a total of something over 3,000 city and county governments, centered around a key question as to which of nine delivery methods was being used for each of forty-plus functions. The methods embraced all of those discussed here with the exception of divestiture. The response percentage rate ran in the high forties. A full summary of the responses by function and method is shown in appendix 3.A; table 3.4 shows the functions falling at each end of the public-private spectrum by extent of exclusive use of respondent local governments' employees.

As one would expect, a regulatory or enforcement function, such as traffic police or code enforcement, would be expected to be most frequently performed exclusively by government employees; in the survey 90 percent of the responding units reported that this was the case. The rapidity with which the percentage of respondents reporting exclusive use drops into the low eighties and seventies was striking; police patrol in a substantial proportion of cases no longer was being carried out solely, or practically so, by sworn officers or other persons on the government payroll.

Delivery by another unit of government embraces two basic types. An "intergovernmental service contract" is an arrangement between two governmental units in which one pays the other for the delivery of a particular service to the inhabitants within the jurisdiction of the paying government. A "joint service agreement" is an agreement between two or more governments for the joint planning, financing, and delivery of a service to the inhabitants of all jurisdictions participating in the agreement.

The services most frequently covered by contracts and service agreements as reported in the 1983 ACIR survey, with 2,069 cities and counties responding, the number reporting in parentheses, were, for contracts, jails/detention homes (327); sewage disposal (267); animal control (218); tax assessing (210); solid waste disposal (209); water supply (201); and police/fire communications (186). For joint service agreements, with 2,039 responding, the leaders were libraries (195); police/fire communications (193); fire prevention/suppression (165); sewage disposal (160); jails/detention homes (149); and solid waste disposal (147).[40]

Purchase of service contracting with private firms involves a binding agreement in which the local government pays a profit or nonprofit organization to provide a specific level and quality of service. Citizens, through taxes or user fees, pay the local government, which in turn pays the contractor. This mode is used most frequently for public works and transportation, health and human services, housekeeping services, and some public safety services.

Franchise agreements are agreements in which a local government grants one or more private organizations authority to provide a public service within a geographic area. The citizen pays the deliverer directly for the service. The local government may or may not regulate level, quality, or price charged for the service. It is used most frequently for residential and commercial solid waste collection, public utility functions, airport operations, vehicle towing, and ambulance/emergency medical services.

Subsidy arrangements are financial or in-kind contributions to private organizations or individuals that are used to allow a service to be delivered at a lower price, to enhance its quality, or to increase the level of service, thereby allowing it to be delivered despite its unmarketable character otherwise. Subsidies have been used most often in the health and social services area, with the deliverer usually being a nonprofit organization.

Vouchers represent a market approach, in which citizens/consumers are given a coupon with a monetary value usable toward the purchase of a local service; the recipient is free to choose a supply source from which to buy the service. Vouchers have been used for services such as paratransit, day care, and child welfare.

Volunteer personnel work without pay, but may receive reimbursement for out-of-pocket expenditures. All or part of a service may be staffed entirely with volunteers, and they have been used frequently in recreation, public safety, and human service functions. They can be used in nearly all nonmanagerial or non-regulatory capacities.

Self-help is a mode under which neighborhoods and individual citizens can be encouraged and utilized by local governments to assist in producing the services they use and consequently to reduce the amount of government activity required. This approach has been used in neighborhood watch patrols, day care, elderly and cultural programs, and alley, street, and small-park maintenance.

Regulatory and tax incentives can be used by state or local governments to encourage the private sector to provide a public service or to reduce the demand for a service. Regulatory incentives can be used to encourage the formation of commuter bus and paratransit services, for example. Tax incentives have been used to encourage homeowner associations to take care of their own trash collection and street maintenance.

Divestiture of or "shedding" a service means removing it wholly or partially from any kind of governmental responsibility. A local government may decide that it no longer needs, or no longer can afford to maintain, public golf courses. This becomes exclusively a "private good," is left to the free market, and comprises complete divestiture. A local government having a citizenry of high per capita income may decide to divest its city or county hospital, but pass a local law requiring some or all private or nonprofit hospitals to accept Medicare and Medicaid patients and a designated portion of "charity" patients. Or it may decide to sell its sewage treatment plant, with continued applicability of state and local laws regarding effluent quality and a provision that sewage treatment bills be based on water consumption. Such arrangements comprise "divestiture with regulation."

Scope and Trends in Alternative Service Delivery Methods

ICMA, Harry Hatry, and ACIR, among others, monitored the evolution of "contracting out" and other alternative methods of local service delivery for a number of years, beginning in the early to mid-seventies. Keon Chi[41] and other scholars[42] have examined the use of private-sector channels in services delivered by state governments. Survey and anecdotal reports from those and other sources are drawn upon here with illustrative examples.

In addition to "line" services, there is, of course, a substantial number of "support" or "housekeeping" services that might be expected to fall mostly into the "traditional" mode of delivery. That is generally but not completely the case. A 1981 survey was conducted by the National Institute of Governmental Purchasing, addressing municipalities of 25,000 and over and counties of 50,000 and over, with 233 and 143 responses, respectively.[43] It showed practically exclusive "own government" delivery of such policy-related functions as planning, budget, personnel, purchasing, and the enforcement service of tax collection; it also showed 80 percent or over private-sector participation in technical repair and maintenance functions such as office and computer equipment and in building construction and vehicle repair.

The institute survey showed also, however, 42.9 percent private-firm participation in janitorial service for cities and 42 percent for counties, and 18.1 and 13.3 percent respectively for grounds maintenance. An institute official observed informally in mid–1987 that subsequent to 1981, the trend toward contracting and other non-public-employee delivery methods had accelerated greatly and that the direction of the trend showed no signs of abating, as the "competitiveness" theme from the private sector was being picked up by more and more state and local governments.

Trends in Delivery Mode Selection by Local Governments

Trend data on changes in service delivery choice, although not yet adequate, were becoming more comprehensive and conclusive in certain respects by the late eighties. In addition to the impressions conveyed by the Institute of Governmental Purchasing, three sets of survey data had become available by 1988: the ACIR 1976–83 survey; the ICMA 1982–83 survey published in 1984; and the Touche Ross survey, cosponsored by ICMA and the Privatization Council, conducted in mid–1987 and published later that year. Some of the 1982 findings have already been summarized, and the remainder are covered later in this chapter. The ACIR and Touche Ross results are summarized here.

In the ACIR survey data were obtained on transfers of service responsibility for local functions and services over the period 1976–83; they showed some shift to private-sector modes of delivery, but not at the rate of change estimated in the literature during that period. A summary of the ACIR data is presented in table 3.5.

In the table transferred functions are listed in the order of the proportion of total transfers that went to the private sector. Some relationships can be noted between the seven- to eight-year trend covered by the transfers and the ICMA "snapshot" afforded in its 1982 survey, even though the categories used in the two surveys are not exactly the same. Of the ten services showing the most preference for private-sector handling in contrast to transfers to other units of government, only mass transit/paratransit provide a stark match—high in the proportion of private-sector transfer preference and among the ten delivered least exclusively by own government in the ICMA survey. However, a direct correlation is seen in several others.

For combined percentages of respondents using profit and nonprofit contracting and franchising for individual services, shown in appendix 3.A, utilization percentages for other services in the top ten transfer preference categories were refuse collection, 50 percent and 63 percent for residential and commercial refuse versus 49 and 29 percent for "own government" delivery (that is, 49 percent of the respondents reported exclusive reliance on their respective units for delivery of residential refuse collection, with 50 percent choosing a private-sector

Table 3.5

Major Transfers of Line Services from Cities and Counties to Other Public Units or to Profit and Nonprofit Organizations, 1976–83

Service	Total Trfrs.	From Cit.	From Cntys.	To (1)	To (2)	To (3)	(4)
Refuse Collection	139	124	15	24	105	0	75.5
Emer. Med./Ambulnce	54	38	16	22	18	15	61.1
Park Oper. & Maint.	27	22	5	12	12	3	55.5
Str./Br. MaintConst.	31	21	10	14	17	0	54.8
Recreation Facil.	39	29	10	18	7	14	53.8
Trfic. Sig. Inst/Main.	32	29	3	16	15	1	50.0
Solid Waste Disposal	119	99	19	63	50	6	47.1
Mass Transit/ParaTr.	58	50	8	36	9	13	37.9
Animal Control	72	62	10	45	9	18	37.5
Sewage Disposal	55	49	6	44	8	3	20.0

Source: ACIR, *Intergovernmental Service Arrangements for Delivering Local Public Services: Update 1983*, Report A–103, October 1985, 118–121.

Transferred to (1) another governmental unit; (2) a profit organization; (3) a nonprofit organization. (4) Percentage of total transfers that went from public to private sector.

mode—an essentially even split of hotly contested territory). For solid waste disposal, 35 percent used private-sector contracting, 31 percent used other governmental units, and 38 percent own government exclusively with own government a less than 50 percent exclusive deliverer. For street maintenance (65 percent), traffic signal installation and maintenance (54 percent), park operation and maintenance (76 percent), and animal control (63 percent), the local government was the majority deliverer, but each of these services during the period covered by the transfer data was being transferred to private-sector handling in substantial degrees.

Reasons given by respondents in the ACIR survey for shifts in delivery responsibility or mode were dominated by three principal themes: cost economy, better availability of qualified personnel, and adequacy of equipment and facilities. Frequently, a governmental unit may find that to continue to provide a service itself, it needs to invest in additional facilities or equipment and/or hire more people; consequently it may begin a shift by contracting out the overflow, or alternatively it may contract out all or most of the service and retrench accordingly.

In the Touche Ross survey data were gathered by means of a questionnaire survey conducted in July 1987. The queries were sent to city managers or county executives of all cities of more than 5,000 and all counties of more than 25,000. Nineteen percent returned completed questionnaires.

In contrast to the ICMA 1982–83 survey that covered both delivery modes and functions, the Touche Ross survey dealt with only one mode—contracting out—but for that mode covered qualitative factors, such as perceived advantages, contracting results, and perceived impediments to the mode. The survey covered also the "privatization" of facilities and the sale of assets. The principal findings on contracting for services were the following:

- Nearly all respondents had contracted out one or more services.

- Perceived advantages of contracting out were cost savings (mentioned by 74 percent of respondents); "solving labor problems" (50 percent); "sharing of risk" (34 percent); and "higher quality service" (33 percent).

- Impediments to contracting out were perceived as loss of control (51 percent); union or employee resistance (47 percent); politics (42 percent); and lack of belief in benefits (38 percent).

- Services most frequently contracted out in the last five years were solid waste (59 percent); vehicle towing and storage (45 percent); and building and grounds maintenance and service (43 percent).

- Cost saving was the principal reason for contracting out in the case of a great majority of the services; lack of staff was the major reason in the case of certain administrative services and airport management.

- Cost savings of 40 percent or more were reported by 10 percent of respondents; 30 to 39 percent by 6 percent; 20 to 29 percent by 24 percent; 10 to 18 percent by 40 percent; and a loss by 2 percent.[44]

Trends in Mode Selection among State Governments and Abroad

State government consideration of alternative service delivery modes seems to have begun to intensify a few years subsequent to local government experimentation.[45] Surveys conducted by the National Governors' Association in 1980 and 1982 showed that most contracts were limited to capital construction and professional services. A survey by the Council of State Governments of general administrative services showed that a majority of states were contracting for some of their legal, medical, and other professional services.

However, for line functions, the first break away from the traditional mode came in correctional services and facilities. It became apparent, prior to the 1986 enactment of tax reform legislation, that due to tax and other financial factors, private construction and lease-back arrangements were advantageous to both state and local governments and to private firms. Policy decisions on correctional facilities became increasingly difficult due to (1) decrees from both state and federal courts directed toward inmate rights and overcrowding, (2) increasing public resistance to most correctional facility site location decisions by state executive officials, and (3) federal cutbacks and other financial constraints.

Consequently, nearly any arrangement that promised fiscal savings, faster construction, and some kind of a buffer between governors/state legislators and the general public in the intractable correctional services area was instantly attractive to policymakers. This occurred in Tennessee, Pennsylvania, and California, with Connecticut, Indiana, Oklahoma, and Maryland considering taking such action. The early eighties also saw contracting out or other private-sector involvement in the following areas:

- Mental health services/facilities in Arizona and Kentucky and the delivery of social services in Massachusetts
- Water or wastewater treatment facilities in Colorado and Utah
- Toxic waste cleanup in New Jersey
- Juvenile facilities in Florida, Massachusetts, Michigan, Oklahoma, Pennsylvania, Rhode Island, Texas, and Washington and jails in New Mexico and Texas

European countries and Japan also were taking steps at national, intermediate, and local levels to initiate alternative delivery modes. George Wynne noted several developments in Europe as of 1986.[46]

In Germany the national Chamber of Industry and Commerce established a Privatization Exchange to enable a matching of private capabilities with public agency needs. However, the strong German economy, with lessened fiscal pressures upon local governments, caused interest in such matching to subside, with the result that offerings from private firms greatly outstripped state and local agency requests for bids. The German League of Cities, however, found in a 1986 survey that forty-eight types of public services had been contracted out at one time or another by municipalities; responding cities reported positively on their contracting experiences and indicated that displacement of city employees had been limited.

In Japan public and private sectors had been commingled to a much greater extent than in other capitalist countries; local public law enterprises, with minority shareholder participation by banks, insurance companies, and others having naturally close ties to governmental agencies, were carrying out a wide range of public, commercial, and other quasi-private activities.

In Britain, the Thatcher government had encouraged contracting and other use of the private sector by local governments. In France stock in denationalized state enterprises was highly oversubscribed.[47] In Denmark the Falck corporation for several decades had operated a combination of towing, road-service, ambulance, and fire-fighting services, patronized by both private- and public-sector firms and agencies and individual customers. In 1982 more than half the Danish cities were relying on it for fire fighting.[48]

Some General Factors in Considering Alternative Modes

Several major considerations confront public officials in deciding whether or not to move from the traditional "own government" responsibility for delivering a particular service. These comprise general considerations applicable to any service or mode and specific criteria applicable to a particular mode or service.

The general considerations include the following, not in any particular order; any one may be crucial in a given situation:

• Strength of evidence supporting views that the existing traditional mode is overly costly, cumbersome, or of unsatisfactory quality, or that the delivery method is inequitable among classes of users or is otherwise so flawed as to be impervious to restoration to a state of optimal efficiency (that is, "unless it's broke, don't try to fix it")

• Strength of evidence that one or more alternative modes have sufficient stability and strength to assure continuity of service over an extended time period

• Degree of confidence that among the potential alternative mode(s) there are other or competing suppliers, so that a private monopoly will not replace a public one

• Assurance that legal and moral obligations of the governmental unit to public employees currently delivering the service will be met and that the cost of meeting them is included in all comparative financial estimates

• Degree to which experience in other jurisdictions over a substantial time period has demonstrated the workability of one or more of the alternative modes under consideration

• Degree to which personnel and procedures are adequate for rigorous monitoring and evaluation of delivery performance under the new mode selected

Carl Valente and Lydia Manchester listed the following steps that should follow a policy decision to institute a new service or a management decision to appraise an already existing service that is not already being evaluated on a systematic basis:

• Determining the necessary service level
• Determining who should pay for the service and how
• Identifying who can deliver the service
• Determining the most suitable service delivery mode or approach
• Planning the implementation of that approach
• Evaluating the service and the performance of the deliverer on a regular basis[49]

Criteria Applicable to Specific Modes and/or Services

Purchase of Service Contracting. In 1974 Lyle Fitch, who had served as city administrator of New York City, identified major features of contracting that should be considered in applying it to a particular service.[50] The following factors favored contracting:

• Competition, not only between private and public delivery, but equally important, between or among private organizations
• Economies of scale

- Escape from the rigidities of personnel, budget, and other central management controls of government agencies
- Greater freedom to discontinue contractors or services that prove to be less effective (for example, sometimes it is easier to cancel a contract than to fire a department head)
- Use of incentive devices such as bonuses for superior performance

Disadvantages included the following:

- Danger of becoming locked into a relationship with a single firm
- Extralegal activities (that is, corruption) practiced by contractors, elected and politically appointed officials, civil servants, or others in the processes of contract awarding and monitoring
- Difficulty of drawing contracts that cannot be quantified or otherwise defined in such a way that cost comparisons remain feasible and that performance incentives remain applicable
- Necessity of close monitoring of contract performance, thereby requiring the recruitment or retention of high-paid expertise
- Difficulty of compelling a deficient contractor to perform
- Frequent necessity of displacing public personnel, with consequent equity issues and union confrontation

Also raised by public employee unions, such as the American Federation of State, County, and Municipal Employees (AFSCME), as an important danger in the contracting process is the tendency of some firms to enter a very low bid (''lowballing'') on the theory that once the firm is into a relationship, losses from the initial bid can be recouped at successive renewal stages; an attempt to thwart this strategy by negotiating a longer-term contract at the outset raises the potential damage that would occur from ''deficient performance.''[51]

These pros and cons point up some ''musts'' for the governmental unit: avoiding ''sole sourcing'' on any contracts except in some extremely scarce professional and technical sources; forming and using a rigorous contract-negotiating and monitoring capability; for some services, such as refuse collection and street maintenance, retaining an in-house capability as a yardstick against which to measure cost and performance; and the maintenance of active and continuing competition among potential and current private suppliers.

Of all the major services, refuse collection apparently represents an area of great opportunity for cost savings and performance improvement, often fueled by intracity or intracounty competition between private contractor and local government crews. Of the services listed in table 3.5, refuse collection showed the greatest private-sector tilt during the 1976–83 period. Several other important factors influence its susceptibility to competition:

- Performance quality and output factors are measurable to a high degree (for example, cost per ton; numbers and types of service complaints).

- There is greater susceptibility to productivity improvement; the nature of the work tempts idling on the job.
- It is more heavily unionized than most services, resulting in higher costs won in collective bargaining agreements, while many contractor personnel are nonunion, at least at the outset (this factor raises several legal and equity considerations discussed later in this section).
- Where in-house capability is retained, outside competition often brings down costs and causes work-rule modification, with government crews winning back contracts (in Phoenix in the early eighties, competitive bidding for five contracts gave city crews three areas and private contractors the other two).[52]

E. S. Savas has noted several additional reasons for using competitive "dual-track" systems wherever feasible:

- Contracts are useful in handling newly annexed territory or territory being otherwise added to the service area, avoiding investment in new equipment while waiting for comparative results or when there is a large increase in work volume.
- This provides a feasible way to test out contracting before a complete shift.
- The service is less vulnerable to job actions by either contractor or government personnel.
- The government retains a cadre of expertise, facilitating the change back to a government work force if contracting does not work out.[53]

The size of the service area—geographic or population—may be a crucial factor in large jurisdictions for such services as refuse collection. Breaking down jurisdiction or urban district boundaries into two or more service districts, with separate bidding competition for each, may often produce an increased number of bidders, because not as large a crew or firm is needed to handle the volume. This was the case in Montgomery County, Maryland, where in the early seventies population growth created a condition where only one firm was able to bid because of equipment and personnel requirements, and that firm became a monopoly supplier. In order to generate competition, the county government broke down the single urban district into nine smaller districts, with lively bidding in each district and a substantial drop in costs.

In 1976 a study was undertaken under the auspices of the Columbia University Graduate School of Business of refuse collection costs in a sample of 314 cities ranging in size from 2,500 to over 700,000 and covering three delivery modes: (1) own government unit, using municipal employees; (2) collection by a private firm under contract or franchise with the city; and (3) collection by a private firm in direct relation to customers, and sometimes in competition with other firms, and with some residents taking care of their own refuse in order to save pickup costs. Of the 314 cities, 101 were delivering directly, 92 were contracting for citywide collection service, and 121 were letting the private sector and residents handle it on a catch-as-catch-can basis. Respective municipal, private contract, and unregulated private collection costs for cities under 10,000 varied little on a per ton basis between municipal and contract workers: $16.58, $15.75, and $26.35. For cities 50,000 and over the results were strikingly different: $19.65, $13.26, and $30.05.[54]

A 1984 study by Ecodata, Inc., for the U.S. Department of Housing and Urban Development comparing municipal and contract delivery of eight services showed the following comparative unit costs for contract and own government, respectively: street cleaning, $9.93 and $14.17; janitorial services, $3.74 and $6.49; refuse collection, $21.16 and $29.97; payroll preparation, $6.13 and $5.93; traffic signal maintenance, $1,303.38 and $2,039.44; asphalt overlay construction, $42.85 and $83.99; turf management, $57.92 and $81.09; and street tree maintenance, $37.08 and $50.80. The relative cost saving of contract over municipal delivery was highest for asphalt overlay construction and lowest for payroll preparation, where contractor cost was 3.4 percent higher than for municipal delivery.[55]

Franchising. The principal differences between franchising and contracting are the following: (1) the user pays the deliverer, thereby removing all or most financial transactions from the public revenue-expenditure stream; (2) delivering firms may be protected against competition within the service area, depending upon whether the franchise is exclusive or nonexclusive; and (3) the government regulates price and quality of service via the franchise (as in an electric or gas utility) instead of through contract terms and specifications. Franchising also approaches divestiture of a service; indeed it is nearly synonymous with "divestiture with regulation." Nonexclusionary franchises resemble a license because deliverers can compete against one another, as in most private services. In the ICMA survey refuse collection again emerged as a significant mode (15 to 20 percent using franchises); other services using it were street lighting (14 percent); meter reading (10 percent); recreation facility operation/maintenance (9 percent); and vehicle towing (7 percent).

Subsidies. Subsidies may be used in two principal ways. (1) Under a system of user-based financing, services are delivered at discounted prices to low-income users, with the delivering agency or contractor reimbursed out of general funds for the cost of the discounts. (2) Subsidies may also be used to enable a delivering organization to "remain whole" while delivering a needed but uneconomic service at the market-clearing level. ICMA survey respondents showed moderate use of subsidies in cultural/arts programs (18 percent), museum operation (17 percent), paratransit (14 percent), and emergency medical/ambulance service (8 percent).

Decisions on subsidies usually are based on less precise and objective data than for contracting and franchises. For this reason, they can be used in lieu of contracts, where tight specifications and output measurement are prerequisites. However, the ICMA data show contracts with nonprofit organizations being used more frequently than subsidies in nearly all the human services. Respective percentages for contracts (nonprofit organizations) and subsidies for these services were day care, 37 and 15; child welfare, 24 and 8; elderly, 29 and 13; public and elderly housing, 18 and 5; drug/alcohol treatment, 41 and 13; and mental health, 40 and 15.

Lester Salamon found similarly high use in the early eighties of the nonprofit sector in delivering human services. For national, state, and local governments combined, the respective percentage uses of nonprofit organizations, for-profit businesses, and government itself in service delivery were 42, 19, and 39 for human services as a whole. By individual services, the percentages were social services, 56, 4, and 40; employment and training, 48, 8, and 43; housing and community development, 5, 7, and 88; health, 44, 23, and 33; and arts and culture, 51, negligible, and 49.[56]

To the extent that the reported contracts cover anything approaching full cost of facility/program operations, a basic fiscal equity question needs to be noted. Too often, for a service that is especially needed and used largely but not entirely by low-income persons, the whole rather than a substantial share is borne by public funds, instead of by user-based financing with free or discounted service provided on a means-tested basis.

Volunteer Personnel and Self-Help. Although comprising separate delivery modes, use of volunteers by government agencies and reliance upon neighborhood and other self-help activities frequently overlap. This is because nearly all volunteer work by individuals is "self-help" in a community sense, and nearly all organization-conducted self-help activities rely heavily on volunteer personnel. The principal differentiating factor noted in the ICMA survey was that self-help involves much activity at private initiative, without government involvement or supervision, while volunteers, as counted in the survey, work in a local government agency or program.

However, the civic and conceptual linkage is both close and critical. Self-help and volunteer work, together with civic organizations and other public-private partnerships (discussed later), all constitute a vital element in American democracy. Yet government and citizenry in many communities, and especially in large cities, have become disconnected and interalienated. While the physical distance between the local citizen's home and the local government can be measured in blocks or a very few miles, the psychological separation often is in light-years. The same is often true of citizen perspectives of state capitals and of Washington, D.C.

George Fredrickson, in calling for a return to "civism" in public administration, noted that "the single greatest conceptual and theoretical problem we face [in domestic governance] is the reconstruction of the sense of community. . . . Without a strong sense of community, public administrators will continue to constitute a threat [in the minds of the citizens] and a scapegoat for elected officials."[57] Stuart Butler harshly singles out professionals and professional standards as culprits: "Local institutions and associations are generally the avenue of first preference when the citizen needs help. Yet these institutions have been elbowed out of the way by the professionalized, federalized and detached organizations that owe their creation and continued existence to the liberal view of a national community. . . . professionals should be on tap, not on top."[58]

In addition to the service delivery role played by many self-help and other nonprofit organizations, many of them also help finance or otherwise arrange for the availability and accessibility of services. Incentives under the Federal Tax Code and the income tax laws of many states encourage citizen participation in these activities and thereby reduce significantly the scope of governmental responsibility on the financial side.[59]

The ICMA survey excludes three categories of work from the volunteer mode of local government service delivery. (1) Although serving public purposes in many ways, persons working for charitable and other community betterment organizations are not included in the delivery mode unless they are part of a local government volunteer program. (2) Interns and others receiving modest stipends in a government agency are not included; only those unpaid, other than expenses, are included. (3) Coerced unpaid work, as in court-ordered community- or victim-restitution programs, is not included.

Vouchers. Of all the alternative delivery modes short of divestiture, vouchers offer the widest range of supplier choice to the consumer of a service, and the opportunity of choosing is another of the cornerstones of democratic government. Valente and Manchester note two major potential advantages of vouchers:

First, whereas a single government agency will provide one or a few variations of service, alternative suppliers will offer a larger variety. This comes closer than government to satisfying individual tastes and preferences of consumers. Second, choice operates as a quality control and efficiency regulator. A consumer who is unhappy with a service provided by a single governmental agency can only complain or move elsewhere. A consumer who has a choice of alternative suppliers can take his or her business elsewhere. Suppliers who fail to satisfy consumers will have an incentive to improve; if they don't, they may suffer financially, perhaps to the point of going out of business.[60]

The ICMA survey showed limited use of vouchers: elderly programs and paratransit operation/maintenance (3 percent); day-care facility operation, cultural/arts, and public health programs (2 percent each); and hospital operation, recreation, drug/alcohol treatment, mental health/retardation, and child welfare (1 percent each). Hatry notes some additional potential use for vouchers for homemaker services and foster or group homes.[61]

The social services cluster offers the major area of opportunity for application of the voucher mode, but it also presents some of the most heated opposition. "Client choice" in the use of direct or indirect public assistance has long been a difficult issue. It centers upon the ability of disadvantaged persons to make "informed choices" in the marketplace. Under the food stamp program (which Stuart Butler has termed our largest and most successful voucher program), recipients of the stamps can use them only for food, but they, not the government, determine the grocer and the menu. Likewise for housing vouchers, the recipients can use them only for shelter, but they, not the government, select the landlord; however, the landlord selected must be on a list of housing providers meeting governmental standards. Others argue that low-income people are often not in a position to make wise judgments about the housing market.[62] (The same might be said about many other individuals and savings/loan associations who venture unsuccessfully into real estate or stock market options.)

The argument about vouchers is part of a larger question. Some public services, especially in the human services area, are established and maintained primarily because they are needed by poor people. Yet in operation the counseling and other useful services are provided free of charge. To deal with this ''free rider'' problem, vouchers offer one, but not the only, method for shielding low-income persons from the cost of services having a considerable measure of community as well as personal benefit.

Divestiture. The term ''load-shedding'' also is used to identify this ultimate method of eliminating or minimizing the responsibility of state and local governments for a given public service. On occasion, it is logical and feasible for these governments to get out of or ''exit'' from responsibility for direct delivery of a service through franchising, vouchering, and other modes, but with continued ''public utility'' type of regulation. For certain areas of a jurisdiction, de facto complete divestiture can occur through responsibility assumption by one or more self-help associations; or a private utility serving a community might assume, for the duration of its franchise, responsibility for trimming trees near its lines, which in older communities takes in practically all of the public domain. In such cases the jurisdiction can discard the tree-trimming function. Hatry notes that in France the building inspection function has been assumed by the insurance industry within the home policy approval process.[63]

For quite a number of local governments, where there are both a strong civic tradition and strong nonprofit organizations, full divestiture of a significant range of services in the cultural/arts/recreational areas may be feasible, so long as there is continued access of low-income people to these facilities and services. A general grant or tax incentive from the local or state government to a coalition of nonprofit groups or their contributors, respectively, for this purpose would be a simple and fair arrangement; the grant or tax incentive would constitute a single remaining umbilical cord between the government and the service cluster.

Involvement or Noninvolvement in a New Function: The Day-care Example. Day-care services comprise one of the most rapidly expanding social services in the United States, and local governments in all urbanized and many rural areas are confronted with decisions on at least some limited aspects of this activity. Day-care service is an economic must for many younger families where it is necessary for the mother to be in the work force and a usual necessity where the mother is pursuing an independent career. The facets of state and local government concern with day care include the following:

- As an employer, (*a*) complying with an employer's legal responsibilities, if any, concerning the availability of day-care services for its employees and/or (*b*) arranging for day-care services for its employees as a fringe benefit in its compensation plan
- As a possible direct deliverer of services to its own employees or to low-income or other segments of the community
- As a subsidizer or other arranger of day-care services to community segments
- As a service deliverer or arranger in connection with the training of persons or groups planning to deliver day-care services
- As a regulator of day-care services delivered by the profit or nonprofit sectors or by individuals, with such regulation ranging from licensing, inspection, and other standards and supervision to routine registration of deliverers

Thus a wide range of choices faces the local government in its decision as to how broadly and deeply it wishes to be involved in the day-care area. Several of the alternative delivery modes are applicable to day care, with own government delivery seemingly the rare exception and a strong tendency to keep delivery in the private sector, supplemented by public subsidies, tax incentives, vouchers, or other arrangements to fulfill the public obligation to assure access to day-care services for mothers going off welfare into private employment, either as a general policy or as part of the process of welfare reform.

Personnel Management and Productivity Issues

Before a move from own government delivery of a given service to any of the alternative modes, attention must be given to various personnel issues, and for franchising or any other mode that involves protection of a private deliverer from competition, legal issues of an antitrust or related nature may arise. Regardless of the mode or the urgency of its adoption and implementation for fiscal or other reasons, these issues must be confronted and considered before final action is taken and fully or largely resolved in detail before the transition is completed. Otherwise, public credibility and support will erode, and the chances of eventual success of the move will be perilously lessened.

Shifting from own government delivery to any of the alternative modes carries two major personnel management dimensions—labor-cost comparisons and impact upon affected public employees.

Labor cost comparisons frequently stimulate or impel state or local agencies to shift, or to consider shifting, service delivery to another mode. Before making a decision, public managers should make sure that all the elements in labor-cost comparison have been identified and taken into account. Usually the two principal quantitative factors in these comparisons are comparative pay and benefit levels and comparative output per person or other appropriate measure of labor productivity.

In comparing pay in the public and private sectors, it is necessary to consider not only wage and salary levels, figures for which are relatively easy to come by, but total compensation. Often the quantification and compilation of data on total compensation is quite difficult. For example, in the fringe benefit area, pensions and health services are the most costly components. Obtaining for each of two workers with equal pay, age, years of service, and survivorship coverage the "life value" of each of the two workers' pension benefits will provide a proportionate value relationship per capita between the pension costs of the public agency service unit and those of the private firm personnel that would be engaged in the contract being bid. Any such comparison would be reliable for a particular firm but not for other firms. Likewise, health benefits can be costed out, as well as annual, sick, and personal leave allowances. All of these costs can be added up for the public work force, but must be calculated separately for each competing private firm.

Rufulo and others have pointed out basic differences in pay levels and productivity relationships in public and private sectors that may be present in the state or local government unit. Rufulo notes: "The net effect of civil service [tenure] and of tying municipal wages to private sector wage rates probably is to make the benefit that the public sector employee receives from any increase in productivity relatively low. Civil servants, therefore, are likely to have less of an economic incentive than their private sector counterparts to increase productivity."[64]

Much of the validity or lack thereof in Rufulo's observation depends on the kind of private-sector sample taken on wage rates. Some surveys, following the thrust of the Davis-Bacon Act applicable to federal contracts, may be limited to "prevailing rate" firms that might well represent a minority of firms and/or employees in the jurisdiction or metropolitan area and thus tilt the result toward the higher end of wage rates; surveys in smaller communities undertaken by the local government, if properly constructed statistically and related occupationally to the makeup of the municipal unit work force, should indicate fairly well the private-sector wage levels for comparable work.

However, a different problem arises in the relation of fringe benefit costs between large firms and small firms in any private-sector sample. By and large the benefit levels are higher in the larger firms; many small firms have low, if any, fringe benefits other than Social Security. Furthermore, in the smaller firms turnover is likely to be higher than in government employment, with a smaller proportion of the private employees "vesting," or qualifying for maximum pension or vacation benefits. Thus for many of the line services in local government, where the potential private deliverers are quite likely to be small, the public-sector benefits probably will be generous by comparison.

By the same token, if the public work force is organized and the competing private firm is not, some probability factors, mostly subjective, should be cranked into the comparative calculations. Employee pressure may well develop in the private firm, either to organize or to get pay and benefits more closely approximating those of their predecessors, with the result that when the contract is up for renewal, a dramatically new comparative cost picture will emerge.[65] (In contract terminology, such a case might be termed "unintentional lowballing" on the part of the contractor.)

Productivity data are highly relevant in cost comparisons, but it is important that they be differentiated and considered separately from compensation comparisons. They are less susceptible to political debate and are not as subject to change from the initial contract award to renewal as are pay and benefits, unless the government work force is persuaded, as a result of losing the contract the first time, to agree to drastic work-rule and other productivity-related changes.

Impacts of a mode shift upon public employees can be well identified, planned, negotiated, and implemented so as to achieve optimal equity for both employees and taxpayers; if they are implemented hastily, disastrous results can accrue. It is necessary at the outset to assess both economic impacts upon employees for reasons of cost and equity and political effects upon public support. One of the principal arguments for "dual tracking" a service is that shifts can be effected in stages, lessening employee impact and minimizing involuntary separation from the public service through a combination of intra- and interagency transfers and attrition. Quite often it is both necessary and desirable to include in contracts or franchises a provision for employee transfers to the new employer with employment guaranteed for a specified period. Likewise, it is always desirable to discuss possible alternative modes with employees before any public hearings or other formal steps are undertaken.

Special attention needs to be directed to minority and female employment. It has been pointed out that minority employees comprise a larger proportion of the public labor force than of the total labor force.[66] This disproportion remains, but to a slightly reduced degree, for state and local government employment, as shown in table 3.6. The data in the table are national in scope, and proportions vary considerably from one state-local jurisdiction to another. For example, in Phoenix minority representation in the city work force has been higher than in the city working population as a whole (reportedly 31 versus 16 percent in the mid-eighties), and it is claimed that for at least some contracts, minority representation in the contractor work forces were smaller than under the city government.[67]

Phoenix operates a "dual-track" system, and in another context the city public information officer stated that "contracting for municipal services is saving . . . taxpayers millions, but not in every case is it because the private sector works more cheaply. Much of the saving can be attributed to the vastly increased productivity generated internally whenever city work crews are placed in head to head competition against outside vendors." The city auditor reported that over a multiyear period ending in 1982, the city had put twenty-two service contracts out for bid, with private vendors winning twelve and city work forces ten. The city procedures require discussions with union leaders before advertising for bids.[68] The Phoenix practice of consulting with employee groups, or union leaders if employee groups are organized, warrants emulation in other jurisdictions, because it lessens employee tensions, minimizes or avoids potential em-

Table 3.6

**Total Labor Force and Government Employment by Race for Employed Persons
Age 15 and Over, 1986 (In Thousands)**

Employment Type & Race	Total With Earngs.	In Gov't	% of Total L.F.	State- Local Govt.	% of Total L.F.
All Races, Full & PT	126,414	18,764	14.8	15,035	11.9
Full Time; Year Round	74,332	12,466*	16.8	9,622*	12.9
White, Full & PT	109,779	15,288	13.9	12,426	11.3
Full Time; Year Round	64,762	10,220	15.8	7,998	12.3
Black, Full & P.T.	12,925	2,866	22.2	2,183	16.9
Full Time; Year Round	7,309	1,869	25.6	1,377	18.8
Hispanic, Full & P.T.	8,613	958	11.1	761	8.8
Full Time, Year Round	4,859	625	12.9	477	9.8

Source: Bureau of the Census, unpublished March 1987 Current Population Survey data, table LJ3,
"Class of Worker of Longest Job in 1986, Civilian Workers 15 Years Old and Over, by
Total Money Earnings in 1986, by Sex, Work Experience, and Race," P 60, no. 156,
Spring 1988.

Totals include "other races" not shown separately.
* Excludes many public school teachers.
Persons of Hispanic origin may be of any race.

ployee hardships, and maximizes benefits to taxpayers that a vigorous and fair
competition produces.

Antitrust and Other Legal Issues

For all of the alternative delivery modes discussed here except that by own
government, state constitutional and statutory provisions and state labor agency
standards and rules, as well as the local charter and ordinances thereunder, need
to be checked for permissibility of the contemplated alternative prior to its
consideration for adoption. Particular provisions that need to be checked include
(1) state immunity from antitrust violations (relevant to franchising and any other
arrangements that shelter private deliverers from competition) and the extent to
which that immunity has been explicitly passed on to local governments; (2)
obligations, rights, and benefits of public employees; and (3) limitations or
conditions contained in state authorizations to, or mandates upon, local governments relative to the particular service under consideration.

Another important legislative question arises regarding how to best secure
legal authorization for change if existing legislation is found insufficient or
prohibitory. One school of thought holds that the initiative for change must come
from outside government—for example, a number of potential private suppliers
coming forward and saying "we can do it better and cheaper," thereby giving

the local government a practical basis for asking for authorizing legislation to bring a principle to practice.[69]

This approach avoids confrontation with employee groups and others opposed to the general concept; such a confrontation might well be political in character and largely devoid of factual situations. Others contend that it is very difficult to generate enough interest among potential suppliers to persuade them to go public in a move that might be viewed as intrusive or greedy, and that the best course is to seek legislative authorization for the concept in broad and placatory language. This was done in the sixties and seventies to secure authority in all but one or two states for interlocal contracting and joint service agreements. Obviously, the approach to be taken must depend upon the perceived policy and political environment in the particular jurisdiction at a specific time.

Summary Comments on Alternative Service Delivery Methods

By expanding its policy options for public service financing and delivery from the traditional tax-based financing and own government delivery to a range of combinations of taxes, user charges and subsidies on the financing side and alternative modes on the delivery side, values of equity, efficiency, productivity, and consumer choice are served.

- By moving to user-based financing for appropriate services within necessary criteria and safeguards, equity among classes of taxpayers and service users is enhanced and efficiencies of resource allocation improved.
- By introducing cost comparisons and competition into service delivery, productivity can be improved markedly and service users given new options.
- Fiscal resource scarcity on the one hand and considerations of increased economy and equity for taxpayers and flexibility for service users on the other dictate careful consideration by governing bodies and public administrators of the kind of fiscal and delivery options presented here, with concurrent consideration of the potential pitfalls inherent in each alternative, including the traditional mode.

Major safeguards include the following:

- Avoiding private monopolies by assuring bidding competition
- Consultation with affected public employee leadership prior to any formal consideration of an alternative mode
- Maintenance wherever feasible of an in-house capability for competitive, comparative, fall-back, and other purposes
- Cautious entrance into new modes, including testing out and phasing in changes
- Maintenance in all cases of a rigorous and objective monitoring of performance for quality, cost, and other relevant factors

The crucially important management problem of selecting the most appropriate method for delivering public services has come to the forefront out of fiscal necessity, although many public managers have been probing the issue for several years. The coincidence of the subject with policy issues concerning the general role of government in American society has given the management issue heavy political and philosophical overtones. This discussion has focused on the management aspects.

GENERAL PARTNERSHIPS OF GOVERNMENT AND BUSINESS

Government and business have had a periodically changing community of interests since the founding of the Republic. Clipper ships furthered national political as well as economic interests abroad; the railroad barons helped settle the West and forge the beginnings of a truly national economy; and in each of the nation's war periods, close business-government relationships have been a must. The scope and intimacy of business involvement in the affairs of state governments for a long time depended significantly on the nature of the particular state economy and its physical resources and varied within states from one state administration to another. In local government, on the other hand, especially for the larger cities, the continuing community of private and public interests has been much more marked because the connection between political stability and predictability and local business progress and prosperity has been much more evident.

In the post–World War II period some states and cities, through a variety of financial and other incentives, began active campaigns to attract new businesses to their territories with a view to enhancing employment opportunities for their residents and enriching the tax base. In some jurisdictions, however, the public-private relationship was much broader and deeper, dating back to the early 1900s. In those places civic, in contrast to strictly business, leadership had begun to combat graft and corruption in City Hall and to establish organizations embracing labor, professional, business, and "informed and concerned citizenry" to study local governments and to recommend reforms. The National Municipal League, founded in 1894, gave leadership and support to many of the local civic organizations devoted to improving local government. In the forties and subsequently, many of the civic organizations began to broaden their interests and concerns to encompass not only the quality and integrity of local governments but also the efficacy of their policies.

Partnerships between government and nongovernment sectors during the fifties and sixties were stimulated greatly by programs of the federal government. These included (1) "slum clearance," later "urban renewal," legislation in 1949 and 1954; (2) economic development legislation to assist Appalachia and other depressed regions of the country; and (3) the Economic Opportunity Act of 1964 and its War on Poverty, built around local community action agencies, mandated to be structured so as to provide "maximum feasible participation of the poor." Although local business organizations were often represented in these local agencies, the driving force came from nonprofit social organizations and from private foundations.

Another set of organizations emerged from the urban riots of 1968, which erupted in the wake of the assassinations of Martin Luther King, Jr., and Robert F. Kennedy. Civic-business-labor organizations such as the Urban Coalition were formed at national and local levels, in addition to the National Alliance of Business, which centered much of its activity on providing job opportunities to the urban disadvantaged. All of these groups were striving toward the restoration of economic and social stability to depressed and alienated inner-city neighborhoods.

Major Bases for Civic and Economic Partnerships

It is not only logical but inevitable that in a democratic system governmentally and a capitalist, free enterprise system economically, the general goals and interests of public and private sectors be compatible and mutually supportive most of the time. For example, in the United States, at all levels of government, two goals strongly embraced by both sectors are steady economic growth and social stability. Occasionally, and on particular problems or issues, one would expect divergence and sometimes collision, especially over short time periods, and often concerning means rather than ends.

One would also expect, and historically this has been the case more often than not, that in times of economic stress, the short-term as well as long-term interests of both sectors would come closer together and would stimulate further cooperative or joint efforts toward economic stabilization, revitalization, and growth—nationally, regionally, and locally. During the 1977–87 decade, increasing emphasis was being placed by both the Carter and Reagan administrations upon the role of the private sector in public policy development and execution. This period saw the creation of new, and the expansion of existing, public-private partnerships in state and local governments.

This section deals with general civic and economic partnerships; chapter 4 examines specialized organizations, such as community development corporations and neighborhood improvement associations, formed in individual states or localities for purposes of economic revitalization. While there are other, more refined classifications of the several incentives for forming government-business general partnerships, it is sufficient here to distinguish between two broad bases—primarily civic and primarily economic. In general, the civic associations have multiple general goals of "community betterment," including many social and environmental objectives as well as economic growth and well-being, already identified as a common public-private goal at all levels of government. The civic goals usually are longer-term; the economic-driven associations may also be of long life, with longer-term objectives, but many are more sharply focused on particular economic aims or problems, often functionally oriented, such as housing or employment.

Some Civic Prerequisites. Regardless of whether a partnership or other public-private arrangement is civic- or economic-based, its chances of continuing success are augmented greatly if particular civic characteristics are present. The 1982 CED policy statement identifies the following:[70]

- A "positive civic culture" or a "tradition of civic activity" (that is, individuals and groups who are cooperative and trust one another), where mutual respect exists among the major component groups—business, labor, government, nonprofits, minorities, social institutions, and neighborhood associations
- A "realistic community vision" (that is, the community's view of itself, including ability to see beyond laws, plans, and other formal expressions to appraise and appreciate human feelings and motivations that go to make up the community's collective spirit) and a formulation of that vision and spirit in practical terms that gain public support, including major specifics of plan implementation (this characteristic will be recognized by many planners, administrators, and elected officials as a requisite condition also for any effective state or local planning process—strategic, comprehensive, land use, functional, or otherwise)
- One or more effective "building-block" civic organizations (an organization working toward overall community betterment, with a broad base of membership, including such elements as labor, business, neighborhood and homeowners' associations, taxpayers, and mixed income levels)
- A relationship among various groups and leaders that provides a means for intercommunication among single-purpose advocacy interests and for mediation of differences among organizations so that the general interest of all can be pursued with maximum effectiveness
- A tradition of nurturing and supporting "civic entrepreneurs"
- A relationship between local government and civic leadership that encourages continuity in public policy and civic goals and minimizes sudden changes in direction

Beginning about 1950, the National Municipal League (predecessor to the National Civic League) began an All-America City Award program. It provided recognition each year to some outstanding accomplishments of city governmental and civic leaderships in overcoming problems, instituting new and innovative programs of community improvement, or undertaking and putting in place long-range plans for a better city. Experience in the awards program and the conviction that a basic difference existed between communities that worked and those that did not led to the development in 1986 of a National Civic Index. The index formed the basis of the league's deliberations at its 1987 conference. It included eight different but interrelated aspects of community cohesion and spirit or the lack thereof:

- Citizen participation (How visible and active are local civic associations?)
- Leadership (Is government and civic leadership risk-taking and oriented to results?)
- Intergroup relations (Are there community programs to stimulate communication among diverse populations?)

- Civic education (Are schools teaching citizenship and civic responsibility, and are there opportunities for youth to participate in community activities?)
- Information sharing (How do citizens find balanced, accurate information about community issues and activities?)
- Capacity for cooperation and consensus building (Are there informal dispute resolution mechanisms short of the courtroom?)
- Strategic long-range planning (Is planning left entirely, or nearly so, to the local government?)
- Intercommunity cooperation (Does business do economic development, or the nonprofit sector provide services, on a regional basis?)[71]

Types of Civic Associations. Countless associations across the country bear the "civic" label. The larger, stronger, and more influential of the citywide or metropolitanwide civic associations fall into two principal groups, plus a third group, somewhat more specialized: (1) those that, although general in scope of interests, are "business-oriented"—principally led and financed by the business community and having a majority or predominance of business members; (2) those that are wholly civic in purpose and have a generalized base of formation and memberships that cuts across business, labor, academia, and other group and individual lines; and (3) those formed to improve the effectiveness of local and/or state government.

Business-Oriented Civic Associations

In its 1982 policy statement the CED characterizes these organizations as taking

a broad view of business interests as they relate to the economic strength, social harmony, environmental health and physical attractiveness of the community. They recognize not only that business stands to gain or lose by the fortunes of the community but also that as a principal and powerful component of the community, business can affect those fortunes through collective action. Their purpose is to be an effective participant in addressing the needs of the community, not to be an adversary of the non-business sector.[72]

The CED statement goes on to recommend to the business community nationwide that chief executive officers (CEOs) of corporations actively work with other community leaders and take steps such as jointly participating in forums, projects, and organizations, adapting their own goals and operations to take into account differences and changes among community groups and building coalitions with diverse groups to support the accomplishment of common objectives.

An example of a large and high-potential business-oriented civic organization identified in the CED report was the Greater Baltimore Committee formed in 1955 by one hundred large corporations in the area and pragmatically defining its purpose as "functioning as a citizen arm of the [local] government." In 1979 it merged with the Baltimore Metropolitan Chamber of Commerce and thereby changed from an elite group to one of several thousand members from small and medium-sized firms having interests and concerns quite different from those of the predecessor organization.

The CED recommendations were broadly replicated by several other national business organizations. The President's Task Force on Private Sector Initiatives (widely referred to as the Grace Commission) in one of its reports, entitled *Building Partnerships*, in late 1982 recommended that business firms as a whole over the ensuing four years double the level of cash contributions to nonprofit organizations engaged in public service; that they also double during that period the level of involvement in community service activities; that the then-current contributions and public involvement be reassessed to ensure that the most pressing human, social, and economic needs of their communities were being addressed effectively; and that they "commit themselves to active involvement in the development and enhancement of partnerships between the private and public sectors in their communities."[73]

In the same report the task force carried quotes from policy statements of organizations in addition to the CED. The Business Roundtable had called on the CEO of each of its member companies to "offer his personal and visible support for the principle of corporate involvement; urge his company to participate actively and provide the leadership force in helping communities solve problems; encourage volunteerism among all company employees; and strengthen . . . contributions and/or public affairs budgets as needed to support community service activities." The American Business Conference, Inc.—a business trade association representing the CEOs of one hundred of the country's medium-sized, high-growth companies—had set as its goal the encouragement of members to "maximize their community involvement." Following the national Business Roundtable format, similar roundtables existed in a dozen or more states in early 1988 (California, Massachusetts, Minnesota, New Jersey, Oregon, Pennsylvania, South Carolina, Washington, Wisconsin, and others). In general, their function is a blend of think tank, business lobby, economic development booster, and technical assistance provider, but focusing on long-term rather than short-term economic, fiscal, and related issues and problems.

Undoubtedly some of the national calls for increased community involvement by private business in 1981–82 were precipitated by national cutbacks in non-defense spending. (The U.S. Chamber of Commerce, in a statement similar to the three foregoing ones, cited a new era of greater self-reliance and less dependency on government). It should be emphasized, however, that many corporations and business organizations had been preaching greater community involvement for a decade or more (for example, the July 1971 CED policy report, *Social Responsibilities of Business Corporations*).

Broad-Based Civic Associations

In contrast to the business-oriented organizations, the broad, general-purpose associations tend to address social and political as well as economic issues and often, because of an academic constituency, undertake research and take positions on sensitive issues of local government organization and its strengths and weaknesses. The impetus for forming these broad-based civic organizations has come from varying sources. One cluster of organizations has come from the "good-government" movement and consequent formation of "bureaus of municipal research," with some subsequently dropping the "research" and evolving into "citizens' leagues" and other titles.

The more notable of this cluster were leagues and bureaus in New York, Philadelphia, Detroit, Minneapolis–St. Paul, Seattle, and St. Louis. The Citizens League in Minnesota, in particular, gathered strength over the years and became well known nationally. Its continuing activities in the Twin Cities area include (1) a research program, with a few major studies always under way; several of these have been the basis of Minnesota state legislation on the structure and financing of local government in the metropolitan area; (2) a biweekly newsletter, dealing with current problems and issues; (3) a public affairs program under which members of the league's study committees explain their work to city and county governments in the area and to the executive and legislative branches of the state government; and (4) other activities such as separate weekly community breakfasts in Minneapolis, St. Paul, and South Suburban areas; question-and-answer luncheons; and a public affairs directory at election time.

Government Research Associations

At the state level, and stemming also from the "good-government" movement, are statewide organizations in over thirty states; these, like their early municipal counterparts, are concerned with more economical and efficient state governments. They often are grouped generically as "taxpayer associations" and exercise influence with governors and state legislatures that is usually commensurate with the quality of data and objectivity of research. Some of the more influential at particular periods have been the state organizations in Texas, Pennsylvania, Connecticut, Massachusetts, Colorado, and Louisiana.

In the early thirties the Government Research Association (GRA) was formed, with membership prominently including the state and municipal research bureaus, plus university-based governmental research bureaus, functioning with varying degrees of independence from the academic discipline departments. These university bureaus often comprise a major component of the university's "community service" responsibility, which has traditionally been joined with teaching and research to constitute the tripartite mission of higher education institutions in the United States. (Despite its status as one of the three basic missions, community service has consistently ranked quite low in the academic reward system of most U.S. colleges and universities.)

In addition to the university- and municipal-based governmental research bureaus and the state "taxpayer leagues," many professional government administrators and researchers are members of the GRA. A close informational exchange relationship exists between the Tax Foundation, a national research organization in the taxation field, and the state taxpayer organizations. Support from private enterprise is substantial or dominant in the financial base of many of the state taxpayer organizations and for some of the civic associations, but support from general-purpose foundations is also very important for the latter group.

Other Examples of General Partnerships

General public-private partnerships in Pittsburgh and Portland, Oregon, offer further examples of differing roots, development, and maturity.[74] The first had its start in several of the "government reform" and taxpayer organizations and the second in neighborhood-based organizations; however, in each case they evolved into general citywide civic endeavors. The focus in Pittsburgh, beginning in the twenties with leadership from a municipal research bureau and the state economy league, was environmental (smoke abatement), physical, and institutional change; subsequently the partnership took on social and political change as a major role and finally emerged into comprehensive concern with social, governmental, and economic improvement.

The focus in Portland over a much shorter period beginning in the mid-seventies has been on neighborhood and citywide development, with continuing leadership coming from the government side and with private-sector leadership diffused and its participation selective. The partnership in Pittsburgh in the early period was led by the Mellon family's business and civic enterprises and by David Lawrence (mayor, 1945–61, later governor). In Portland, mayors Neil Goldschmitt (later federal secretary of transportation and then Oregon governor), William McCready, and Francis Ivancie and their colleague city commissioners provided the dominant leadership, but they continually courted and received assistance from various parts of the Portland business and neighborhood communities.

Evolution, Successes, and Failures of Public-Private Partnerships in the Civic Sector

Renee Berger has summarized the commonality of perceived need for public-private community partnerships from the respective standpoints of the for-profit and nonprofit parts of the private sector and the local government public sector. Business firms are concerned with (1) labor-force adequacy and consequently with the effectiveness of public education; (2) adequate public infrastructure, good housing, and stable neighborhoods to attract and hold their employees; and (3) community "quality of life." Nonprofits are also interested in housing, education, and social services, but are further concerned, as are business firms, with the most effective use of public resources and with the opportunity to contribute their unique talents toward community betterment. Local government wishes to minimize tax burdens, to explore alternative resource use in achieving community objectives, to stimulate improved public-private-sector relationships, and to avoid the emergence of a dependent population, instead providing opportunities for personal and civic growth.[75]

There is little argument about these common objectives. However, some raise points of caution that the partnership concept not be viewed as a cure-all and that more attention be given to evaluation of partnership accomplishments and especially to partnership failures and other potential negative consequences such as excessive corporate influence over nonprofit groups. Out of such evaluation could come criteria that would help guide public policy and private actions in the formative stages of a partnership.

Verne Johnson and Ted Kolderie caution that long-time partnerships can become sterile. They comment:

It was natural for such [a partnership] idea to emerge. For government, this promised technical assistance, political support, and often a way to undertake, or to continue programs and projects that taxpayers were unwilling to finance in a period of fiscal constraint. For business, after a long adversary relationship with government, the prospect of a cooperative "partnership" was particularly appealing.

The trouble is that partners must take each other as they are. So the private sector has accepted the public sector as it stands. The public/private partnership is a way to work with government, not to change it; to support it, not to challenge it.[76]

Stuart Langton points to other aspects for study and evaluation, including (1) the natural tendency to concentrate leadership in the community elite, neglecting the need for fresh viewpoints and a broader community perspective; and (2) the failure to involve citizens who may be significantly affected by the partnership effort, thus undermining the potential for substantial consensus, which is nearly always a requisite for ultimate success of a community effort. Berger echoed the first of these tendencies in a 1988 comment: "At the risk of touching a raw nerve, it must be said that most corporate community-involvement efforts have the same look today that they had 10 years ago. They work with the United Way, give to the local hospital, and give to the local university. This approach is aimed at picking winners."[78]

These points of caution underline the need for substantial research efforts supported from diverse quarters to plot the origins, progress, difficulties, and final products of the many categories of public-private partnerships. Such evaluations are the only sound basis for future policies; in the meantime, active experimentation on many fronts, including those discussed here, should continue.

NOTES

1. Committee for Economic Development (CED), *Public-Private Partnership: An Opportunity for Urban Communities* (New York: Committee for Economic Development, 1982), Appendix, 1.

2. Ibid., Appendix, 84–85.

3. Rainey, H. G., Backoff, R. W., and Levine, C. H., "Comparing Public and Private Organizations," *Public Administration Review*, March/April 1976, 233–244.

4. Bozeman, B., *All Organizations Are Public* (San Francisco: Jossey-Bass, 1987); Moe, R., " 'Law' versus 'Performance' as Objective Standard," *Public Administration Review*, March–April 1988, 674–676; idem, "Exploring the Limits of Privatization," *Public Administration Review*, November–December 1987, 453–478.

5. This section draws substantially from Colman, W., *A Quiet Revolution in Local Government Finance* (Washington, D.C.: National Academy of Public Administration, November 1983). See also U.S. Advisory Commission on Intergovernmental Relations (ACIR), *Local Revenue Diversification: User Charges*, SR–6, October 1987; ACIR, *Changing Public Attitudes on Governments and Taxes 1988*. Report S–17 (September 1988): 10; the following Rand Corporation reports: Pascal, A., ed., *Exploring Benefit-based Finance for Local Government Services: Must User Charges Harm the Disadvantaged?* Project N–2108-HHS, July 1984; Neels, K., and Caggiano, M., *The Entrepreneurial City: Innovations in Finance and Management for Saint Paul*, Project R–3123-SP/FF, October 1984; and Pascal, A., et al., *A Guide to Installing Equitable Beneficiary-Based Finance in Local Government*, Project R3124-HHS/SP/FF, EBBF, July 1984; Downing, P., and Frank F., "Recreational Impact Fees: Characteristics and Current Usage," *National Tax Journal* 36, no. 4 (December 1983): 477–490; and Singh, N., and Thomas, R., "User Charges as a Delegation Mechanism," *National Tax Journal* (39, 1) (March 1986): 109–113.

6. Mushkin, S. J., ed., *Public Prices for Public Products* (Washington, D.C.: Urban Institute, 1972), 11. See also: Windsor, D. and Harlow, K., "Integration of Cost-Benefit and Financial Analysis in Project Evaluation," *Public Administration Review*, September/October 1988, 918–928.

7. Bureau of the Census, *City Government Finances, 1985–86*, Table 7, 94–95.

8. Peterson, G. E., "The Allocative Efficiency and Equity Effects of a Shift to User Charges and Benefit-based Taxes," (unpublished) Urban Institute, January 1982.

9. Mikesell, J. R., *Fiscal Administration: Analyses and Applications for the Public Sector* (Homewood, IL.: Dorsey Press, 1982), 277. See also Rubin, I., "Municipal Enterprises: Exploring Budgetary and Political Implications," *Public Administration Review*, January-February 1988, 542–546.

10. Peterson, "Allocative Efficiency," 16.

11. Shields, P., "User Charges in Human Services: Overcoming Fiscal Decline," *New England Journal of Human Services*, reproduced with permission in Agranoff, R. (ed.) *Human Services on a Limited Budget* (Washington, D.C.: International City Management Association, 1983), 173–184.

12. Peterson, "Allocative Efficiency," 9–15.

13. Downing, P. B., "User Charges and Service Fees," *Information Bulletin* (Washington, D.C.: Public Technology, Inc.), 1980, 17–18.

14. ACIR, "5.206. Mandatory Dedication of Park and School Sites," (draft state legislation). (Washington, D.C.: 1975).

15. Misczynski, D. J., "California's Non-Plunge into Benefit Levydom" (Sacramento: State of California Office of Planning Research, January 22–23, 1982, Mimeographed).

16. ACIR, *The States and Distressed Communities: The Final Report*, Report A–101, November 1985, 205–206, 243–244.

17. ACIR, "3.205. State Assistance in User Charge Formulation and Administration," (draft state legislation) 1984.

18. ACIR, "6.107. Private Enterprise Involvement in Urban Affairs," (draft state legislation) 1975.

19. National Council on Public Works Improvement, *The Nation's Public Works: Defining the Issues*, September 1986, 27–29.

20. Kirlin, J. J., and Kirlin, A. M., "Public/Private Bargaining in Local Development," in *Public Choices—Private Resources: Financing California's Growth through Public-Private Bargaining* (Sacramento, CA: California Tax Foundation, 1982), ii–v, 23–26.

21. Ibid.

22. Cervero, R., "Paying for Off-Site Road Improvements through Fees, Assessments, and Negotiations: Lessons from California," *Public Administration Review*, January–February 1988, 534–541.

23. Peterson, J., et al., "Non-Debt Financing of Public Works Facilities," National Council on Public Works Improvement, October 1986, 42–43.

24. Ibid., 58–59.

25. Gillespie, J. W., Jr., "Tax Exempt Lease Purchase Financing," Morgan Stanley, *Government Lease Purchase Conference*, June 16, 1986, p. III–1.

26. This section draws significantly from Moore, B., ed., *The Entrepreneur in Local Government* (Washington, D.C.: International City Management Association, 1983).

27. Wilson, B. G., and Brown, D. D., "The Entrepreneurial Municipal Strategy," *Public Management*, April 1983, 10–12.

28. Wheeler, K. M., "Marketing and Entrepreneurship in Norfolk," in Moore, *Entrepreneur in Local Government*, 184–187.

29. Fisher, L. M., "Cities Turn into Entrepreneurs," *New York Times*, April 4, 1987, B–34–B–35.

30. Cleveland, H., interview quote in Fields, C. M., "Minnesota's Memorial to Hubert Humphrey: Not Just a Democratic Party Think Tank," *Chronicle of Higher Education*, October 28, 1981, 11. See also National Academy of Public Administration, *Third-Party Government and the Public Manager: The Changing Forms of Government Action*, (Washington, D.C.: National Academy of Public Administration, July 1987); Oakerson, R., "Local Public Economies: Provision, Production, and Governance," *Intergovernmental Perspective*, Summer–Fall 1987, 20–25; Darr, T., "Pondering Privatization May Be Good for Your Government," *Governing* 1, no. 2 (November 1987): 42–50; Miller, J., and Tufts, C., "Privatization Is a Means to 'More With Less,' " and Hatry, H., "Privatization Has Problems," *National Civic Review* March–April 1988, 100–111 and 112–117, respectively; and Moe, "Exploring the Limits of Privatization."

31. ACIR, *Performance of Urban Functions: Local and Areawide*, Report M–21, 1963; *A Handbook for Interlocal Agreements and Contracts*, Report M–29, 1967; and Fitch, L., "Increasing the Role of the Private Sector in Providing Public Services," in Hawley, D., and Rogers, D., eds., *Improving the Quality of Urban Management*, Sage Urban Affairs Annual Reviews, vol. 8 (Beverly Hills, Calif.: Sage Publications, 1974), 501–559. See also Fitch, L., "The Rocky Road to Privatization," Working Paper 87–1 (Berkeley: Institute of Governmental Studies, University of California, April 1987); and National Commission on Urban Problems (Douglas Commission), "Decentralization of

Municipal Services to Neighborhood City Halls,'' in *Building the American City* (Washington, D.C.: Government Printing Office, 1969), 350–354.

32. Campbell, A. K., ''Private Delivery of Public Services: Sorting Out the Policy and Management Issues,'' *PM Public Management*, December 1986, 5.

33. Ibid., 5.

34. Rufulo, A. M., ''Local Government Wages and Services: How Much Should Citizens Pay?'' *Business Review* (Federal Reserve Bank of Philadelphia), January/February 1977, 13–20.

35. Kolderie, T., ''Government in the Eighties: Shifting Roles and Responsibilities,'' *Transatlantic Perspectives*, no. 6 (January 1982): 7; idem, ''The Two Different Concepts in Privatization,'' *Public Administration Review*, July/August 1986, 285–291.

36. Hatry, H. P., *A Review of Private Approaches for Delivery of Public Services* (Washington, D.C.: Urban Institute Press, 1983), 9.

37. *ICMA Newsletter* survey, February 1986.

38. Valente, C., and Manchester, L., *Rethinking Local Services: Examining Alternative Delivery Approaches*, Management Information Service Special Report no. 12 (Washington, D.C.: International City Management Association, March 1984), 19–36.

39. ACIR, *Intergovernmental Service Arrangements for Delivering Local Public Services: Update 1983*, Report A–103, October 1985.

40. Ibid., 28, 34.

41. Chi, K. S., ''Privatization: A Public Option?'' *State Government News* (Council of State Governments), June 1985, 5–10.

42. De Hoog, R., *Contracting Out for Human Services* (Albany: State University of New York Press, 1984); and Schlesinger, M., et al., ''Competitive Bidding and State Purchase of Services: The Case of Mental Health Care in Massachusetts,'' *Journal of Policy Analysis and Management* 8, no. 2 (Winter 1986/87): 245–259.

43. National Institute of Governmental Purchasing, Inc., ''Fall 1981 Survey of County (50,000+) and Municipal (25,000+) Governments Regarding Contracts with Other Organizations for the Provision of Non-Professional Housekeeping Services,'' *Annual Procurement Survey, 1982* (Washington, D.C.: National Institute of Governmental Purchasing, Inc., 1982).

44. Touche Ross, *Privatization in America: An Opinion Survey of City and County Governments on Their Use of Privatization and Their Infrastructure Needs* (Washington, D.C.: Touche Ross, 1987), 5–14.

45. Chi, ''Privatization,'' 8–9.

46. Wynne, G. G., ''Privatization Initiatives around the World,'' *Public Management*, December 1986, 19–22. See also Brauchli, M., ''Finland Hopes to Boost Competitiveness with Program of Partial Privatization,'' *Wall Street Journal*, October 7, 1987, 31.

47. ''Capitalist Culture Takes Root in France,'' *Wall Street Journal*, May 11, 1987, 22. See also ''Can France's Great Sell-off Sell Chirac as President? The Popularity of Privatization Is His Key Political Asset,'' *Business Week*, May 25, 1987, 76.

48. Kolderie, T., *Many Providers, Many Producers: A New View of the Public Service Industry*, Publication no. HHH 82–4 (Minneapolis: Hubert H. Humphrey Institute of Public Affairs, University of Minnesota, April 1982), 33.

49. Valente and Manchester, *Rethinking Local Services*, xii.

50. Fitch, ''Increasing the Role,'' 551–552.

51. American Federation of State, County, and Municipal Employees, AFL-CIO

(AFSCME), "Beer Budgets—Champagne Costs," in *Passing the Bucks*, (Washington, D.C.: AFSCME, AFL-CIO 1984): 19–36.

52. Hatry, *Review of Private Approaches*, 22.

53. Savas, E. S., "Intracity Competition between Public and Private Service Delivery," *Public Administration Review*, January/February 1981, 46–52.

54. Stevens, B. J., and Savas, E. S., "The Cost of Residential Refuse Collection and the Effect of Service Arrangement," *Municipal Year Book, 1977*, table 4/4 (Washington, D.C.: International City Management Association, 1977), 200–205.

55. Stevens, B. J., ed., "Delivering Municipal Services Efficiently: A Comparison of Municipal and Private Service Delivery" (Prepared for the U.S. Department of Housing and Urban Development; New York: Ecodata, Inc., June 1984), 14.

56. Salamon, L., "The Non-Profit Sector in an Era of Retrenchment," *Journal of Public Policy* 6, no. 11 (1986): 7.

57. Frederickson, G., "The Recovery of Civism in Public Administration," *Public Administration Review*, January/February 1981, 501–508.

58. Butler, S., *Privatizing Federal Spending: A Strategy to Eliminate the Deficit* (New York: Universe Books, 1985), 105–106.

59. Ferris, J. M., "Coprovision: Citizen Time and Money Donations in Public Service Provision," *Public Administration Review*, July/August 1984, 324–333.

60. Valente and Manchester, *Rethinking Local Services*, 43.

61. Hatry, *Review of Private Approaches*, 43. See also Woodson, R. L., *A Summons to Life: Mediating Structures in the Prevention of Youth Crime* (Cambridge, Mass.: Ballinger Publishing Co., 1981).

62. Struyk, R. and Bendick, M., (Eds.), *Housing Vouchers for the Poor: Lessons from a National Experiment* (Washington, D.C.: Urban Institute Press, 1981).

63. Hatry, *Review of Private Approaches*, 70.

64. Rufulo, "Local Government Wages and Services," 17.

65. AFSCME, "Beer Budgets—Champagne Costs," 19.

66. Suggs, R. E., "Minorities and Privatization: Issues of Equity," *Focus* (Washington, D.C.: Joint Center for Political Studies) 13, no. 2 (February 1985): 3, 6, 14–15.

67. Dantico, M., "The Impact of Contracting Out on Minorities and Women," in *When Public Services Go Private* (Washington, D.C.: AFSCME, AFL-CIO, 1987), 25–29.

68. Hughes, M., "Contracting Services in Phoenix," *PM*, October 1982, 2–4. See also Dudek & Company, *Privatization and Public Employees: The Impact of City and County Contracting Out on Government Workers* (Washington, D.C.: National Commission for Employment Policy, May 1988).

69. Kolderie, T., *Many Providers, Many Producers*, 28–35.

70. CED, *Public-Private Partnerships*, 9.

71. Gates, C., "The National Civic Index: A New Approach to Community Problem Solving," *National Civic Review*, November–December 1987, 472–479; see also in the same issue, "National Civic Index Bibliography," 521–529.

72. Ibid., 12.

73. President's Task Force on Private Sector Initiatives, *Corporate Community Involvement* (New York: Distributed by Citizens Forum on Self-Government/National Municipal League, 1984), 7.

74. Fosler, R. S., and Berger, R., eds., *Public-Private Partnerships in American Cities*

(Lexington, Mass.: Lexington Books, 1982), 59–127, 201–241. See also Fosler, R. S., *The New Economic Role of American States* (New York: Oxford University Press, 1988).

75. Berger, R., "Building Community Partnerships: Vision, Cooperation, Leadership," *National Civic Review*, May 1983, 249–255.

76. Johnson, V., and Kolderie, T., "Public-Private Partnerships: Useful But Sterile," *National Civic Review*, November 1984, 503–511.

77. Langton, S., "Public-Private Partnerships: Hope or Hoax?" *National Civic Review*, May 1983, 256–261.

78. Berger, R., "U.S. Government-Business Cooperation (A Critique)," *National Civic Review*, January–February 1988, 39.

Chapter 4

Coping with Simultaneous Growth and Distress

Drastic changes in the world and in the United States have produced a national economic environment within which businesses and individuals alike will find it necessary to compete more fully and skillfully, work harder, and save more in order to maintain their traditional profitability and personal standards of living. Real wages began to decline in the late seventies under the ravages of inflation, and concurrently the U.S. economic position in the world began to worsen. The national economy shifted drastically away from the production of goods and into the provision of services—health, government, financial, and a variety of professional and semiprofessional services attributable to explosions of information and communications technology, medicine, and other fields. The increasing volatility of the national economy and the structural changes sweeping through it, including the reduced fiscal capacity of the national government, confront state and local governments with both stringent challenges and new opportunities in a changed environment, termed by Scott Fosler as "the new economic federalism."[1]

These governments must first recognize and continue adapting to basic world and national economic and demographic change, including an aging U.S. population and changing labor-force composition; the decline and gradual demise of the traditional family farm, especially those farms engaged in livestock and grain production; and the need for many states and localities to concern themselves with export as well as domestic trade. Second is the associated requirement for continual labor-force retraining, relocation, and other adjustments to the marketplace.

Additionally, the following dimensions of economic, social, and fiscal change need to be examined: (1) arranging for—not necessarily financing or delivering—those day-care, transportation, housing, and other services that are necessary to ensure, to the maximum extent possible, continuing employment opportunity for a labor force vastly different in makeup from that of prior generations of

Americans; (2) dealing with requirements for building, replacing, and retiring public physical infrastructure throughout urban and rural America; (3) coping, by state governments, with economic growth in some areas and severe distress in other areas of their respective territories; and (4) revitalizing neighborhoods and communities through local public-private partnerships.

Regarding the major public responsibilities for elementary, secondary, and higher education, attention in this chapter will be concentrated upon education for economic and social capabilities in the years ahead; general reform issues at both K–12 and higher-education levels also will be discussed. Special problems in education for urban underclass and other educationally disadvantaged children will be covered in chapter 5.

THE CHANGING U.S. ECONOMY AND ITS LABOR FORCE

Beginning in the mid-seventies and accelerating thereafter, three basic changes evidenced themselves prominently, although some had been under way prior to that time: (1) the context for the domestic economy was changing from national to international; (2) shifts were occurring within and among the manufacturing, agricultural, and service sectors; and (3) the composition of the nation's labor force was changing, with much greater change to come in the late eighties and the nineties.

Globalization of the Economy

Transportation and communication technology transferred the national economies of the industrial countries into parts of a world economy, and on the whole, the U.S. economy lost ground in this transformation process. Foreign trade as a growing proportion of gross domestic product (GDP) was a somewhat secondary part of total U.S. production until well into the seventies. However, by the eighties it had risen to one-quarter of real U.S. GNP from about one-sixth in 1970. About 1975 the U.S. trade balance began to decline sharply on the merchandise account side, and by 1980 both it and the current account balance were in steep decline.[2] In 1986 the U.S. trade deficit had reached $170 billion annually, or 4 percent of GNP. Foreign countries were not taking U.S. goods in return; they were said to be buying America instead.[3]

From the mid-seventies on, in terms of economic growth, the U.S. economy began mirroring the world economy. Between 1960 and 1985 the world economy grew 3.9 percent; the United States, with 3.1 percent, lagged behind. It lagged in 1979, 1980, and 1981; it bettered the world rate in 1982–85, but fell behind again in 1986–87.[4] Both corporate management and labor organizations reacted with alarm to the growth of imports from abroad and gave the impression that many jobs were being lost in the process.

However, it has been pointed out that foreign trade creates many jobs, and that for jobs lost through imports, others are gained through exports. Charles

Stone and Isabel Sawhill, in a study for the National Commission for Employment Policy in 1986, estimated that between 1972 and 1979 nearly a million more jobs were created by exports than were lost to imports. By contrast, between 1979 and 1984 trade contributed to declining employment across a broad range of industries employing nearly a quarter of the U.S. labor force. Nearly 2 million jobs were estimated to have been lost to imports, most of them in manufacturing and most of the rest in agriculture.[5]

By the late eighties the deteriorating U.S. position in the world economy was viewed by many if not most citizens as the nation's number one problem. However, wide differences of opinion existed among international economists and Western leaders in finance and trade as to the permanence of the U.S. disadvantaged condition. Nevertheless, there was, toward the end of the eighties, some consensus on a few steps that should be taken in certain areas of the national and world economies to remedy conditions seriously in need of correction:

- Management-labor cooperation to permit more flexible responses in the U.S. manufacturing sector—modification of middle-management turf consciousness and rigid union work rules
- Cessation of reliance on foreign savings to reduce the U.S. budget deficit
- Strong measures to improve productivity in the marketplace

Trade and other opportunities for state and larger local governments in a global economy began to appear in a general way by the early eighties, although a few coastal and border states were developing bilateral commercial partnerships at a much earlier time. State and large city and county delegations began to visit counterparts abroad to discuss product sales and other business opportunities— often the establishment by foreign firms of offices or factories in the state or locality, and increasingly, the sale of products or services in which the state or locality felt it excelled.

In July 1984 the National Governors' Association (NGA) adopted a policy statement emphasizing the role of state governments in international trade and listing the activities already under way in trade promotion by drawing upon the extensive knowledge of their respective business communities. These included the following:

- Providing marketing assistance for business by organizing trade missions and trade fairs, establishing overseas trade offices, hosting foreign delegations, and developing tourism programs
- Developing technical assistance programs in such fields as export education, marketing, investing, and advertising, and coordinating export finance programs of the private sector and state and federal governments
- Providing tax, financial, and training incentives to attract foreign investors

- Developing international trade promotion activities targeted to economically depressed and rural areas, parts, and small businesses
- Embarking on trade programs involving regional cooperation
- Promoting infrastructure development (for example, deep-water ports) as a basis for international trade[6]

The policy statement concluded by proposing state-federal partnership actions of the following kinds:

- Educating the public about the importance of world trade and foreign relations to our own economic well-being and security
- Delivering commercial services and counseling to individual firms entering international markets
- Identifying barriers to trade faced by American businesses and finding ways to eliminate them
- Providing the basis for technological innovation by promoting basic research and encouraging commercial application of research findings[7]

By late 1987 the activities of individual states overseas had reached the point that a NGA official remarked casually that the state governments had more staff assigned to Tokyo than to Washington, D.C. (an underlining for the eighties of both the globalization of the economy and of the reduced federal role in domestic governance). For example, the New York–New Jersey Port Authority created a trading company called XPORT, which gives technical assistance to private establishments in starting up or improving their export business. In 1985 the NGA reported that at least twenty states were involved in an industrial extension service of one kind or another as part of their economic development programs to attract or help expand enterprises in particular industries—a kind of state industrial policy.[8]

Despite the great and growing importance of foreign trade, the primary opportunities for most state and local governments lie at home. Many states and localities look overseas and to other parts of the country for business enterprises to locate within their respective jurisdictions. With occasional exceptions—as when a very large employer decides to move into or out of a medium- or small-sized jurisdiction—most of the increase in jobs and new businesses comes from firms already located in the jurisdiction. This fact underlies one imperative for economic development agencies and officials of state and local governments, if a public policy has been duly adopted that looks toward improving the economic base of the jurisdiction: to see to it that (1) existing businesses and community business leadership are provided with both the opportunity and the public policy climate for expansion and diversification, and (2) absolutely no dispensable governmental barriers stand in their way.

The Shift from Manufacturing and Agricultural Production to Provision of Services

The shift from goods to services brought misgivings to many U.S. economists and political leaders—the former because the intricate interrelationships among production, pricing, distribution, and supply and demand had for so many centuries been the foundation of commerce and of much of economic theory. Clichés about "taking in one another's washing" had long been associated with service and staff functions, and transportation and communications were viewed as auxiliaries to the major economic raison d'être of goods production. The "outsourcing" of supply and assembly operation to foreign countries was viewed with apprehension by many domestic corporate managers.

The shift of capital and labor out of agriculture proceeded slowly but inexorably from the late twenties onward, not only in the United States but in most industrialized and developing countries. However, governmental policies in the United States and elsewhere have been directed continuously toward slowing down the inevitable, rather than to any serious effort to adapt to basic economic change. Cultural values, combined with the active political strength of farm voters and others associated with agricultural industries, have permitted change at little more than glacial rates.

For a closer look at the service sector—which some detractors equate with fast-food outlets—the larger categories, in millions of employees in November 1986, were retail trade (16.4), education (9.1), government exclusive of education and health (8.8), health care (7.2), and finance, insurance, and real estate (4.9).[9] Some services have a large proportion of higher-paid employees, such as those in research and development, computer software, and similar establishments, while others, such as retail trade and restaurants, have a large proportion of lower-paid occupations. Coincident with the 1983–87 recovery period in the U.S. economy, considerable controversy arose regarding the effect the shift from manufacturing to services would have on the American middle class. Barry Bluestone and Bennet Harrison, in a study conducted for the Joint Economic Committee of the Congress, presented data on the proportion of low-, middle-, and high-income employees in new jobs created during two comparative periods, 1979–84 and 1973–79. The data showed that the proportion of net employment growth in low-income employment was 20 percent in the earlier period and nearly 60 percent in the later period. For middle-income employment, the proportion was 64 percent in the earlier period and 48 percent in 1979–84. For higher-income employment, the earlier proportion was 16 percent, but in the later period was a negative 5.5 percent.[10]

On the other hand, Patrick McMahon and John Tschetter, in a 1986 analysis, showed that high-earning occupations were employing a growing share of the work force, with the top third portion increasing from 25.2 percent in 1973 to 29 percent in 1982 and the bottom third decreasing from 40.6 to 38.5 percent. During the same period, however, the number of workers in the bottom third of the wage bracket range grew from 31.9 to 35.7 percent, the middle third dropped from 34.8 to 31.7 percent, and the top third decreased slightly from 33.3 to 32.6 percent.[11] In income terms, the Congressional Budget Office (CBO) found family incomes, properly adjusted, rising 20 percent from 1970 to 1986 instead of dropping 4 percent without adjustment.[12] (Difficulties in measuring income and poverty are examined in chapter 5.)

Apparently the high-tech and other high-paying services were employing a growing share of the workers, but more workers were working in the low-wage categories. This was the inevitable outcome of the large shift of employees away from auto and steel industries, where wage scales had gotten farther and farther ahead of manufacturing wages in general. A large part of the workers laid off from autos and steel as capacity was reduced undoubtedly took sizeable pay reductions in going from the extremely well paid positions in those two sectors into their new employments.

Shifts within Economic Sectors

While high-paying occupations were accounting for an increasing share of employment in the services sector, shifts of a different kind were taking place through most of the eighties in both the manufacturing and agricultural sectors. In the so-called "basic" industries—steel, textiles, and automobiles—capacity outstripped demand, and newer materials were substituted for old. Supplies of copper and other metals likewise outpaced demand. Productivity gains, quite steady in manufacturing and poor in services, hastened supply-demand imbalances.

Likewise in agriculture, U.S. grain farming ran consistent surpluses over several decades, usually mitigated by commodity loans, price supports, export subsidies, or all three. More specialized forms of agriculture—vegetable, nursery, fish farms and others—fared much better, with little or no need for governmental intervention. Livestock growers also did without price supports, but grain economics caused considerable price and profit fluctuation. Technological advances in the Third World brought grain self-sufficiency to many countries and often enabled them to go from import to export status in particular crops.

The Productivity Problem

There is general agreement that one of the major problems confronting the U.S. economy through the rest of the century is lagging productivity in the services sector. *Business Week* magazine called productivity the nation's "No. 1 Underachiever"[13] and identified the United States as having the second-worst services productivity record of the leading industrialized and industrializing countries for the 1981–85 period. (However, manufacturing productivity was improving encouragingly in the late eighties.)

The poor performance has been attributed partially to the aging capital plant

Figure 4.1
Productivity Growth in Manufacturing and Nonfarm Businesses, 1965–85

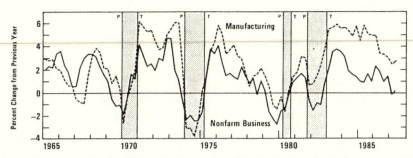

Source: Congressional Budget Office, *The Economic and Budget Outlook: An Update*, August 1987, 12.

Note: Peaks and troughs of recession periods reflected by P and T.

(caused largely in turn by the energy crisis, a low national savings rate, and timidity of corporate management in the light of economic uncertainty), but mostly to extremely low improvement rates in the services sector. This in turn has been attributed to difficulties in productivity measurement in many office-type services, inadequate education and other skills in parts of the labor force, inadequate allocation of private and public resources to research and development, and the failure to carry through to implementation in offices and factories many basic research findings and product inventions.

It should be emphasized that within the services sector state and local government employment comprises a substantial portion, nearly 12 million, including teachers and health workers employed by those governments. Consequently, these governments by their actions as employers exercise considerable influence, and thus bear considerable responsibility, with regard to salaries and wages, productivity, and other economic factors within the services sector.

As figure 4.1 illustrates, annual nonagricultural business productivity improvement tracked quite well with manufacturing until the seventies, after which service productivity grew at an average rate considerably below that for manufacturing. The Congressional Budget Office pointed out that "in the service-producing sector . . . productivity growth—as currently measured—virtually ceased in the early 1970s."[14]

Changing Composition of the U.S. Labor Force

In addition to the already-mentioned factors of integrated world markets and manufacturing overcapacity, two others are affecting and will continue to affect the U.S. labor force in the years ahead—deregulation of business and industry and the declining power of labor unions in wage setting. Another factor, associated with deregulation, is the spread of "privatization" of state-owned and operated industries in Europe and of public services delivered by local and state governments in the United States.[15]

Changes in labor-force composition may well be the most marked since the end of World War I, exceeding even the great changes brought about over the past two decades through the entry of millions of women into part- or full-time employment. The major ones are the following:

- The population from which the labor force is drawn will become older, with working-age workers in greater scarcity. The baby-boom generation is aging, with the oldest members of that generation reaching retirement age in about 2010.[16]
- Barring an epidemic or other health or environmental disaster, people will live to increasingly older ages.[17]
- As the baby-boom generation passes through the 30–40 age bracket, the labor force will grow more slowly than in the preceding two decades.
- Economic trends call for an increasingly better-educated population, making for a tight labor market in many occupational categories.
- The proportion of white males will decrease drastically, and the proportion of new foreign immigrants, legal and illegal, and of Hispanic and other ethnic minorities will increase sharply.[18] Of the new entrants to the labor force in the 1985–2000 period, nearly half, 42 percent, are estimated to be native white females, followed by native white males, 15 percent; native nonwhite females and immigrant males, 13 percent each; immigrant females, 9 percent; and native nonwhite males, 7 percent.[19] Under these estimates 43 percent of the new entrants would be nonwhite or immigrant.
- Despite the dominant position of female occupants of new jobs in the seventies and eighties, the rate of increase in the proportion of women in the labor force will level off as the number begins to approach a practical maximum.

It has been estimated that of all the new jobs to be created during the forthcoming period, more than half will require some education beyond high school, with a third being filled by college graduates and only 4 percent by persons at the low skill or education level (less than eighth grade).[20]

Obviously, formidable problems will continue to confront state and local governments in adjusting to the new economic and labor-force realities. Future workers must be educated adequately, many at high levels of competence and adaptability; dislocated manufacturing and agricultural workers will need assistance in preparing for new careers and new locations; and perhaps most difficult, working-age persons outside the labor force will need to be encouraged, helped, and—in many cases of prior welfare dependency—required to join or rejoin the working population.

LABOR-FORCE PREPARATION, RETRAINING, AND ADJUSTMENT

Economic and labor-force trends and projections obviously demand intense efforts by state and local governments, school districts and the private sector to

- provide education of such rigor and content as is needed to equip a new generation of Americans to enter, and participate successfully in, a labor force that will be in a continuing process of change;

- provide retraining, relocation, and other adjustment assistance to those displaced from employment by technological, cyclical, and other external factors; and

- ensure to the maximum extent possible an equality of job opportunity and progress, and make special efforts to bring into labor-force participation those now and in the future who may have dropped out.

In this section several aspects of education for economic growth will be discussed, including various reform proposals for public K–12 education and for public and private higher education, needs for increased scientific rigor, and better-qualified teachers, and the shortage of high school, college, and graduate-level students interested or majoring in science, mathematics, and engineering. Education of the urban disadvantaged youth and the associated problems of school dropout prevention and retrieval will be reviewed in chapter 5.

Education for Economic Survival and Growth

Technological change and global competition make it imperative to equip students in public schools with skills that go beyond the "basics." For productive participation in a society that depends ever more heavily on technology, students will need more than minimal competence in reading, writing, mathematics, science, reasoning, the use of computers, and other areas. Mobilizing the education system to teach new skills, so that new generations reach the high general level of education on which sustained economic growth depends, will require new partnerships among all those who have a stake in education and economic growth. The challenge is not simply to better educate our elite, but to raise both the floor and ceiling of educational achievement in America.[21]

Strengthening of K–12 public education has been a major and urgent concern of the nation's governors since the early eighties, when a national commission described the public elementary and secondary education scene as a "rising tide of mediocrity."[22] Since the state government is primarily responsible for assuring free K–12 public education and providing a system of public higher education, policy leadership begins at the state capitol, shared by the governor and the legislature. As at the national level, policy leadership initiative usually rests with the executive in the first instance, with the decision-making responsibility resting with the legislative body. The governors began to focus upon education reform as a top-priority issue in the early eighties and later intensified their concern. In early 1987, through the National Governors' Association (NGA), they enunciated a set of goals in "Education for Economic Growth":

1. Development and implementation of state plans for K–12 public education improvement

2. Creation of broad and effective partnerships among business, labor, and the education professions, including business partnerships with individual schools

3. Increasing financial, human, and institutional resources for education, with enriched academic content and improved management by school systems

4. Public expression of a new and higher regard for teachers, with states, communities, media, and the business community devising new ways to honor teachers

5. Making the academic experience more intense and productive, with firm, explicit, and demanding requirements of discipline, attendance, homework, grades, and other essentials of effective schooling and with an increase in the duration and intensity of academic learning

6. Providing quality assurance in education, including (a) systems for measuring teacher effectiveness and rewarding outstanding performance; (b) action by state governments, cooperating with teachers, to improve the teacher certification process and make it possible for qualified outsiders to serve in the schools; (c) tightened procedures for deciding which teachers to retain or dismiss; (d) measurement of student progress through periodic tests of skills and achievement, with promotion based on mastery and not age; (e) identification by schools and communities of skills they expect the schools to impart; and (f) stricter college and university entrance requirements

7. Improved leadership and management in the schools, including (a) pinning responsibility on principals for attainment and maintenance of academic quality; (b) principals' pay tied to effectiveness; (c) higher standards for recruiting principals and monitoring their performance; and (d) more effective management techniques in the schools

8. Paying more attention to unserved and underserved students, including (a) increasing female and minority participation; (b) more equitable state education finance measures; (c) identifying and challenging academically gifted students; (d) strenuous efforts among school personnel and parents to reduce absences and dropouts; and (e) inclusion of handicapped students in economic growth programs[23]

Resolutions of the NGA require a three-fourths majority for adoption. Consequently, these goals constituted a significant nonpartisan policy position carrying a commitment by state governments to move determinedly to improve the quality of public elementary and secondary education in the United States. Policy positions along the same lines had emanated from the National Conference of State Legislatures (NCSL), assuring state legislative support of the objectives. Specifically, the NCSL resolution emphasized that "education is a policy function reserved to the states. . . . State constitutions most often charge the legislature with the overall responsibility of providing for educational opportunity and excellence."[24]

Two points should be noted regarding items 1 and 3 in the list of NGA goals— development of state plans and increased financial resources for education. State plans are much harder to implement than to formulate, and in their formulation generalities are much easier to come by than are specific, controversial policy positions. Due to resource scarcity and to manageability problems, states are faced with painful choices, such as whether to emphasize basic education or to

try to expand the curriculum generally; whether to concentrate on college prep-
aratory programs or vocational education; and whether to increase resources for
all schools or to target them to disadvantaged schools or courses for the gifted,
and if targeted to either, how to deal politically with the perceived resulting
neglect of the vast majority of students and schools that fall into neither category.[25]

Despite the growing consensus as to the direction and content of needed
education reforms, and the fact that between 1983 and 1987 spending for K–12
public education increased by $40 billion or so, some researchers claim that
most of the increases went into higher salaries for teachers and the capital and
administrative costs of running schools, with education reform the last to get a
share. On the other hand, experts in education finance such as Allan Odden at
the University of Southern California say that reform goals have received substantially increased financing. Mary Futrell, president of the National Education
Association, was quoted in 1987 as saying that despite increases in education
budgets, "I don't see these increases going directly into the classroom."[26]

The subjects being studied by state legislative interim committees are an
important data source on relative priorities of state legislatures in any given year.
Legislative sessions in all but a handful of states stay in session for periods of
about six months for those meeting annually; however, during the interim between each session, regular legislative committees or special study committees
continue their work. In 1987, for example, more states (forty) were reporting
interim study activity in education than in any other field (thirty-six in environmental and natural resources). More individual issues were being studied in
health and medical care and education than in any other field.[27]

Of the forty states reporting interim committee activity, the average list of
issues per state was around a half dozen. Aside from finance, which is always
an issue, some of the more significant, unusual, or difficult issues being studied
in 1987 included teacher certification in Arkansas; goals for educational excellence in Arizona; economic demands of the Pacific Rim on educational and social
institutions in California; analysis of vocational program outcomes in Florida;
state minimum competency assessment programs in Kansas; alternatives available to school districts with large numbers of high-risk students in Michigan;
year-round schools in Nebraska; and identification of all state worker-training
programs and the relationship between these programs and educational institutions and agencies in Ohio. Thirty-eight separate educational issues were under
study in Utah and thirty-four in Washington.

How to stimulate local school districts to make increased efforts toward educational excellence has long been a frustrating issue for state governments. The
state is legally responsible for public education, but school operation and internal
curriculum emphasis rest with local districts. Nationally and in a number of
states sporadic attention has been directed to "education vouchers" to enable
greater parental choice between public and private schools and among individual
public schools. Such proposals are viewed by many as drawing resources from

public education. Choice among schools within a system or among districts is limited by transportation cost and school desegregation considerations. Minnesota in the 1985–87 period began experimental efforts toward more attendance-area flexibility by permitting and encouraging interdistrict (usually in adjoining districts) and intradistrict transfers, while protecting racial-balance desegregation orders. The intention of such experimentation was to place poorly performing schools under parent opinion and financial pressure to improve.[28]

Teacher competence in subject matter, the need for substantive as well as instructional methodology, has been a simmering policy issue in K–12 education, especially in the public schools, since the early fifties. The Carnegie Forum on Education and the Economy in 1986 issued through its Task Force on Teaching as a Profession a report on *A Nation Prepared*. The report called for voluntary national certification of teachers through a nongovernmental certification organization.[29] The NGA policy statement supported the objectives of the report and commended it to all levels of government for cooperation in achieving the report's objectives.[30]

As a direct result of the Carnegie task force's recommendation, the National Board for Professional Teaching Standards came into being in late 1987 and began addressing a crucial part of the teacher qualification problem—certification. The certification process had become routine over several preceding decades; anyone with an undergraduate degree from a school of education was certified almost automatically. The activation of the new board and a proposal by a City University of New York panel to require a subject-matter major combined with practice teaching were viewed by many as signals of a new day in teacher training and certification.[31]

The teacher competence issue has been particularly sensitive in the fields of science and mathematics and grows more so with the realization that these skills are required in increasing numbers of people through the rest of the century. Shortcomings in mathematical skills in all but a fraction of the nation's youth were highlighted in a 1988 report of the National Assessment of Educational Progress, based on tests given to 150,000 pupils over the 1972–86 time period. The report's assessment of U.S. high school math performance in 1986 was "dismal." Among the findings of the report were that (1) the average Japanese high schooler does better at math than the top 5 percent of U.S. students; (2) over a fourth of middle-school students cannot handle elementary school math; and (3) many math teachers are unsure of their own math knowledge and skills.[32]

The principal mission assigned to the National Science Foundation (NSF) in its 1950 enabling legislation was improving "research and education in the sciences." NSF initiated an aggressive program in the mid-fifties involving summer institutes for high school teachers of science and mathematics. State legislatures and state boards of education began to increase gradually the number of college hours of subject-matter courses required for teaching a particular subject, but resistance by teachers' colleges and university schools of education was very strong.

Numerous factors were inherent in the problem, including the difficulty of predicting teacher shortage areas in particular fields, the need of local school districts for certified teachers in any field during the progress of the baby-boom generation through the elementary and secondary grades, and the inability of school districts to match private-sector pay for majors in the natural sciences and mathematics (coupled with the unwillingness of state and local boards of education and teacher organizations to authorize differential levels of pay based on labor market demand for particular specialties). Another factor has been the disinclination of women, who comprise a near majority of elementary and a sizeable proportion of high school teachers, to major in the natural sciences or mathematics.

In 1983 a commission established by the National Science Board (the NSF policy-setting body) submitted "a plan of action for improving mathematics, science and technology education for all American elementary and secondary education students so that their achievement is the best in the world by 1995."[33] Among its recommendations were the following:

• Action by the national government to identify national education goals, by state governors to stimulate change, and by local school boards to foster partnerships with business, government, and academia in solving academic and financial problems of the public schools

• Top priority on retraining, obtaining, and retaining high-quality math, science, and technology teachers and providing them with a work environment conducive to effectiveness

• More time devoted to math, science, and technology throughout elementary and secondary grades and substantial lengthening of the school day, week, and/or year.[34]

The report went on to recommend (1) rigorous state certification standards and avoidance of artificial barriers to entry of qualified individuals into teaching (that is, relaxation of requirements for special teachers especially qualified in the subject matter, such as retired civilian or military scientists and engineers, but lacking certain education credits); (2) requiring high school science and math teachers to have a full college major in the subject, a limited number of effective education courses, and practice teaching under a qualified teacher; (3) requiring teachers to be "computer literate"; (4) a larger teacher-training role by liberal arts colleges and academic departments, with basic education courses revised to incorporate new findings as they arise in the behavioral and social sciences; and (5) adjustment of teacher compensation to attract highly qualified teachers in shortage areas.[35]

Arthur Wise and colleagues at the Rand Corporation Center for the Study of the Teaching Profession in early 1987 issued a report dealing with effective teacher recruitment and selection processes.[36] Some of the recommendations in that report were relevant to the NSF call for better-qualified teachers and a good

Figure 4.2

Average Annual Growth in Science and Engineering Employment, 1976–86

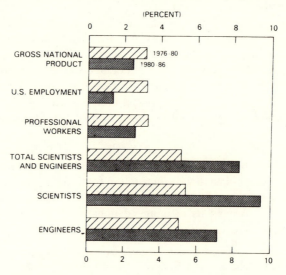

Source: National Science Foundation, *Human Talent for Competitiveness*, NSF–87–24, 1987, 2.

working environment; others related to problems of ''difficult schools'' (reviewed in chapter 5).

Too few high-tech education and career choices is a condition that seems to threaten U.S. leadership in science and technology in the nineties. Data compiled by the NSF from its own and other sources highlight the difficulties in quality and quantity.[37]

In the 1976–86 decade the employment of scientists and engineers increased three times faster than total U.S. employment and twice as fast as total professional employment, as shown in figure 4.2. In the period 1965–84 West Germany and Japan increased greatly the deployment of scientific and engineering personnel to research and development. In the early to mid-sixties nearly 70 such personnel were so engaged in the U.S. for each 10,000 members of the labor force, compared to 20–25 for Japan, West Germany, and Britain. In 1984 the U.S. number had dropped somewhat to 65, while Japan had increased its deployment to nearly 60 and West Germany to over 40. Science and engineering degrees as a percentage of all degrees were slightly lower in 1984 than in 1960; in U.S. universities nearly 60 percent of doctoral degrees in 1985 were awarded to foreign students—over 40 percent in math and over 30 percent in physics. One of the most striking factors in these discouraging data is the decline, shown in figure 4.3, in the proportion of first university degree awardees in science and engineering that go ahead to earn doctorates in the ensuing seven-year period.

To reverse these trends, it is estimated that for the United States to maintain

Figure 4.3
Science and Engineering Baccalaureates Attaining Ph.D. Degrees Seven Years Later

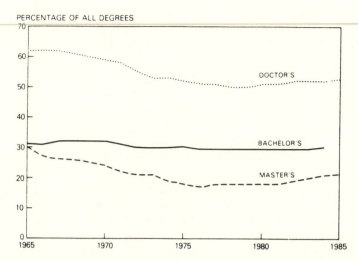

Source: National Science Foundation, *Human Talent for Competitiveness*, NSF–87–24, 1987, 6.

the existing number of science and engineering degree awards into the next century, it will be necessary that the proportion of degree awards in these fields increase by as much as 50 percent. This is because the twenty-two-year-old population peaked in 1983 and will decline by one-fourth before leveling off around the year 2000.

The numbers problem is exacerbated by the fact that (1) women enrolled for undergraduate study outnumber men, but they earn only 16, 15, and 6 percent, respectively, of doctorates in the physical sciences, mathematics, and engineering; and (2) blacks and Hispanics represent about 20 percent of the population (one-third by 2020) but in the mid-eighties were accounting for less than 2 percent of physical science and engineering doctorates.[38]

The NSF, in outlining these skill shortages in science and engineering higher education and career choices, expressed the following concerns about the reward system in academia and business:

Finally, our ability to attract people to the sciences and engineering is a function of the reward system. Today, there is a perception that law and business students are better off in their future careers than science and engineering majors. We must act to change this perception, and the reality behind it, if we want to compete successfully against other countries. With respect to attracting doctoral candidates to university research careers in particular, that means not only better faculty salaries, but also first class research opportunities and high quality instrumentation and facilities.

**Labor-Force Retraining, Relocation, and Adjustment
Assistance**

Given estimates of population and labor-force composition and the prospect
of continuing economic volatility and structural change, the shocks of job displacement in the nineties probably will be similar in many respects to those of
the late eighties. It also is likely that the problems of retraining and other
employee adjustment will be at least as severe as heretofore.

Retraining needs in the labor force are difficult to estimate, but some orders
of magnitude can be established. The civilian labor force is estimated to grow
from 115.5 million in 1985 to 122.7 million in 1990 and to 129.2 million in
1995, with a 1990–95 growth rate of 5.3 percent for the period or 1.1 percent
annually, compared to an annual increase of 2.8 percent for 1975–80 and 1.6
percent for 1980–85.[40] Economic projections by the CBO, running through the
early nineties, indicate an unemployment rate of between 5.7 and 6.0 percent,
which would produce at any one time 7 to 8 million unemployed.[41]

However, it is likely that the proportion of "frictional" unemployment (periods accompanying voluntary job change) will grow as the pace of economic
and technological change quickens somewhat in the next decade. Based on a
profile of unemployment in mid–1987 and the proportion of the unemployed
pool without work for six months or more (14.6 percent),[42] it is prudent to
assume a level of potential need for employee retraining, relocation, or other
adjustment assistance of 1 million or more nationwide at any one time.

An analysis of a Bureau of Labor Statistics (BLS) survey of 318 manufacturing
workers in a sample to represent 607,378 workers displaced by plant closings,
shift phaseouts, or a failure of a self-owned business was conducted by Marie
Howland and George Peterson in 1984. They found that (1) a plurality of displaced workers returned to work in the same industry; (2) workers displaced
from locally declining industries had the longest unemployment periods and the
greatest decline in living standards; (3) the reemployment success of displaced
workers was determined, in addition to local market conditions, by the worker's
age, education, race, and sex; and (4) most displaced workers suffered large
financial losses. It was also found that poorly educated and minority workers
needed readjustment assistance more than others. Those fifty and over were able
to engage in preclosing bargaining with employers for early retirement, severance
pay, and continuance of health insurance.[43]

A significant portion of retraining and relocation assistance is provided by
private employers, often involving transfer to another facility at a different
location or to a different line of work at the same location as before layoff.
However, state governments, local education and social service agencies, and
various parts of local governments bear a considerable share of both financial
and operational responsibility for any public programs designed to help absorb
layoff shocks and to assist workers in obtaining reemployment.

In a policy statement adopted in early 1987 the NGA noted several key features of worker adjustment assistance. (1) Workers should be assisted regardless of the technical or economic cause of unemployment—technological change, international competition, or market forces in general. This would include dislocated farmers, unemployment insurance recipients and exhaustees, potentially dislocated workers, and other structurally unemployed individuals. (2) Early intervention strategies operate most effectively in a cooperative environment where information is shared among labor, management, and government (for example, possible, likely, or definite plant closings or reductions in work force). (3) A variety of services is involved, such as adult educational literacy or other basic education, training alternatives, job-search assistance, income support, and other support services.[44]

The Howland-Peterson study and surveys in individual states stimulated increased state experimentation with new approaches to worker retraining and adjustment. These include (1) use of a specified portion of unemployment compensation funds for retraining of those laid off or likely to be laid off; (2) intervention at an earlier, prelayoff stage; (3) bonuses and other incentives for finding and taking new jobs instead of remaining on unemployment compensation through the entire benefit period; and (4) willingness to consider and implement a relocation assistance option. Early intervention was a basic ingredient of most state and local strategies; respective programs in California and New Jersey in modifying traditional uses of unemployment insurance monies for retraining and bonuses for early reemployment, as well as various other state programs, were publicized actively by the NGA.[45]

As another facet of the early intervention approach, several states in the early eighties considered, and at least three enacted, legislation requiring advance notification of plant closures (California, Maine, and Wisconsin). In the ACIR draft economic growth and development policy bill that resulted from its report on *States and Distressed Communities*, provisions drawn from those three states included (1) sixty days advance notice to the state economic development agency; (2) an optional provision drawn from the Maine law requiring severance pay liability of one week's pay for each year of employment unless a severance plan already existed for the employer or if the closure was forced by a physical calamity; (3) from California, the establishment of a state Economic Adjustment Team to work with the business community and local governments in developing mitigating measures in the event of closures and to assist communities upon request in dealing with effects of closures; and (4) identification and simplification of regulatory requirements found to inhibit establishment, conduct, or operation of business activity in the state.[46] Experience in the states having notification requirements provided useful pro and con evidence in congressional consideration and adoption in 1987–88 of federal legislation under the interstate commerce clause to mandate such advance notification nationwide.

A continuing shift of economic activity from the agricultural sector confronts all levels of government with a serious economic and human problem. Similar to job shifts in industry, but usually more wrenching, are the shifts from agriculture to nonagricultural work, especially for owners losing their farms. The shift of economic activity and employment activity out of agriculture into other sectors had been occurring for over half a century. It reaccelerated in the early eighties when a decline in exports and excellent harvests brought farm income below the break-even point for many small and moderate-sized farms, the owners of which had borrowed heavily to expand their holdings of land and equipment in the late seventies.

In 1960 there were 4.0 million farms in the United States, averaging 297 acres, a farm population of about 15 million (8.7 percent of the nation's population), and farm employment of 7.1 million persons (5.2 million family members and 1.9 million hired workers). By 1970 this had dropped to 2.9 million farms, averaging 374 acres, a farm population of 9.7 million (4.8 percent), and 4.5 million employed; in 1985 the number of farms was 2.2 million, averaging 455 acres; the farm population was 5.4 million (2.2 percent), and farm employment was 3.1 million (2.0 million family members and 1.1 million hired workers). Of the more than 2 million farms, three-fourths had sales below $40,000 per year.[47]

The following summary in early 1986 from the congressional Office of Technology Assessment (OTA) frames the economic facts and public policy options in stark terms. "Approximately 1 million farms will disappear between now and the year 2000, mostly moderate-size and small farms. About 50,000 large farms (above $250,000 in annual sales) will then account for 75 percent of U.S. agricultural production."[48] Those projections, if accurate, mean that the number of farms will drop by half from the 1985 level and leave approximately 1 million farms at the end of the century.

The OTA report makes the following points, each related to federal farm price or income support policy:

• Large-scale farms do not need direct government payments and/or subsidies to survive.

• Moderate-sized farms ($100,000 to $250,000 in sales) require farm programs to survive and be successful. Targeting of income support to moderate-sized farms could prolong their survival. To aid this group, the risk of operating in an open market environment could be reduced, and opportunities for employment outside agriculture could be created for those who are unable to compete. The (federal-state) Extension Service could play a significant role in providing this aid.

• With few exceptions, small and part-time farms—having less than $100,000 in sales— are not viable economic entities in the mainstream of commercial agriculture, nor can they be.

• Small subsistence farmers, who have limited resources and often limited abilities, represent a genuine problem for which public concern is warranted. These indeed are the rural people left behind. Price and income support programs can do little to solve their problems.

The report also notes that the disappearance of farm operations from small towns will have repercussions on other businesses in rural communities and on the labor pool in general, which must absorb those workers whose livelihood once depended on agricultural production.[49]

Federal government policy generally lies outside the purview of this book; it must be observed, however, that it has been a political fact of life for decades that a large part of federal support payments goes to farms that need them least. Given (1) the makeup of the agriculture committees of the Congress, the members of which come mostly from agricultural states, and (2) the wide economic ramifications for small-town businesses, the fertilizer industry, country banks, and a host of other interests, any prompt rationalization of federal policy in this area is highly unlikely. Meanwhile, economic forces gradually are bringing about the liquidation of most of the family farms. Western European countries are in a similar policy bind.[50]

Much of the fallout from continuing out-migration from agriculture will land on state governments, especially their extension services, employment agencies, and special worker adjustment programs. The NGA policy statement on agricultural adjustment, initially adopted in August 1983 and revised in 1985 and 1987, sets forth objectives of agricultural adjustment policy as follows:

1. Targeting economic assistance based on need and farm characteristics and not production levels, for the purpose of diversifying the rural economic base

2. Easing the transition for farm families seeking technical assistance, training, and retraining to link economic opportunities and people

3. Linking scientific discovery to low-cost, efficient technology

4. Disseminating national and international marketing opportunities to put people to work

The policy statement points out that "in a turbulent international economy, there is a premium on diversification and flexibility. . . . For individual farmers, this may mean new crops, or a more flexible, entrepreneurial approach to marketing and financial management, or reliance on off-farm income."[51] For crop diversification, some shifts have been occurring from traditional crops highly vulnerable to foreign competition into such localized crops as berries, grapes, Christmas trees and other nursery items, ornamental shrubbery, and aquaculture. The Council of State Planning Agencies reported that at least twenty states are promoting entrepreneurial market development for farmers wishing to diversify.[52]

Among types of state agricultural financial assistance, the NGA has suggested the exploration of (1) state guarantee programs or state-private loan loss reserve funds to help in preserving fundamentally sound yet currently stressed farmers; (2) tandem federal-state financial assistance programs; and (3) creation of secondary markets for long-term agricultural real estate credit mortgages. For those farmers unable to continue farming, the NGA policy statement recommends the targeting of employment training and counseling services to assist in the transition into other occupations.[53]

Specific measures for retraining, adjustment, and relocation for laid-off or otherwise displaced workers were addressed by the ACIR in its report on state aid to distressed communities. The report listed optional measures that might be considered by states. These included (1) reconciling entry-level and other job requirements of private employers with the curriculum offerings of public and private secondary, vocational, technical, community college, and higher-education institutions, including the appropriate reprogramming of existing state vocational and other education funds and employment-training monies; (2) authorizing, with appropriate limitations and safeguards, the use of unemployment insurance trust funds for training and retraining unemployment compensation recipients to hasten reemployment and for sustaining work sharing, work-week reductions, and similar measures as alternatives to employee layoffs; (3) authorizing private employee stock-ownership plans and state technical assistance and information provided to employers and employee organizations concerning such plans; and (4) reexamining state laws and regulations concerning labor work rules and related provisions affecting employment and employee productivity.[54] The report noted that legislation once designed to achieve job security for some may have been rendered counterproductive by the basic industrial changes taking place.

Relocation assistance is a controversial and difficult aspect of coping with structural change and recessionary impacts upon the labor force. Changes in skill requirements, the formation of new occupations, and the decline of others will necessitate a higher degree of occupational movement and job location in the future, with lessened certainty of following a single line of work between entry to and retirement from the labor force.

Not surprisingly, in the absence of structural or cyclical influences, the mobility of labor-force members has tended to vary directly with education and inversely with age. For example, in 1982–83, 5.9 and 4.9 percent, respectively, of persons aged 55 to 64 and 65 and over moved during a twelve-month period; during the same period, of those in the 20–24 and 25–29 age brackets, 34.5 and 30.6 percent were movers. Similarly, only 10.1 percent of persons with less than 8 years of schooling moved, while 17.7 percent of those with 1 to 4 years of college moved during the same period.[55]

A continuing public policy issue from 1960 to 1980 was whether geographical mobility should be influenced or accommodated by governmental action. In a 1968 report dealing with urban and rural growth, the ACIR suggested several components of a national policy to influence population movement, including (1) establishment of a federal-state matching program of resettlement allowances for low-income persons migrating from labor surplus areas and (2) enactment of federal legislation to eliminate or reduce the migrational influences of interstate variations in public assistance standards and benefits.[56]

Any such recommendation for relocation assistance in moving to new job opportunities was considered politically off-limits for most of the seventies; the policy preference in state capitals and Washington was for place-oriented rather than people-oriented approaches to structural displacement in the labor market— helping bring jobs to the places where the people were (for example, model-

Table 4.1

Employment Status of Noninstitutional Population (NIP), Resident Armed Forces (RAF), Civilian Labor Force (CLF), and Persons Not in Labor Force (NLF), Selected Years, 1955–88 (Numbers in Millions)

```
                          (Numbers in Millions)
===============================================================
                   Employed                 Unemployed      NLF
        Tot.   No.   %   No.   %   No.   %    No.   %    No.   %
Year    NIP    LF   NIP  RAF  NIP  CLF  NIP    LF        NIP
---------------------------------------------------------------
1955   111.7  67.1 60.0 2.1  1.9  62.1 55.6  2.9  4.3  44.7 40.0
1960   119.1  71.5 60.0 1.9  1.6  65.8 55.2  3.9  5.4  47.6 40.0
1970   139.2  84.9 61.0 2.1  1.5  78.7 56.5  4.1  4.8  54.3 39.0
1975   154.8  95.5 61.6 1.7  1.1  85.8 55.4  7.9  8.3  59.4 38.4

1980   169.3 108.5 64.1 1.6   .9  99.3 58.7  7.6  7.0  60.8 35.9
1982   173.9 111.9 64.3 1.7  1.0  99.5 57.2 10.7  9.5  62.1 35.7
1985   179.9 117.2 65.1 1.7   .9 107.2 59.6  8.3  7.1  62.7 34.9
1987   184.5 121.6 65.9 1.7   .9 112.4 60.9  7.4  6.1  62.9 34.0
1988*  186.0 123.1 66.2 1.7   .9 114.7 61.7  6.6  5.4  62.9 33.8
---------------------------------------------------------------
```

Source: Bureau of Labor Statistics, *Employment and Earnings*, July 1987, tables A1, A4, pp. 8, 11.

* April 1988 from *Employment and Earnings*, May 1988, table A–4, p. 7.

cities and community development programs), rather than helping people to get to the places where the jobs were. This policy orientation was criticized by President Carter's Commission for a National Agenda for the Eighties.[57]

However, realities of the 1980–83 recession caused action at national, state, and local levels of government to provide financial aid to individuals displaced from manufacturing and to others unemployed because of plant closures and other structural changes in the economy. Title III of the Job Partnership Training Act of 1982 provided for adjustment assistance, including relocation, to unemployed persons for whom jobs elsewhere were located.

Utilization of "discouraged workers" and other persons of working age not in the labor force is yet another challenge to a private sector that will be extremely anxious for workers in the nineties and to state and local governments. Table 4.1 shows for selected years the size and nature of a pool combining nonutilized workers not participating in the labor force and underutilized workers working only parts of the calendar year or working on a part-time rather than a full-time basis because of precluding economic factors rather than personal preference. Figures 4.4 and 4.5 show the composition of this pool by reason of not looking for or desiring a job. A detailed breakdown by age, race, and sex of those not participating in the labor force and the reasons for nonparticipation is shown in appendix 4.A.

In addition to those persons not in the labor force for the reasons shown in figure 4.4, a significant portion of the employed labor force works part-time (22.1 million in April 1988, of which 1.7 million were in full-time jobs but a

Figure 4.4
Persons Wanting But Not Seeking Work, by Reason, 1987

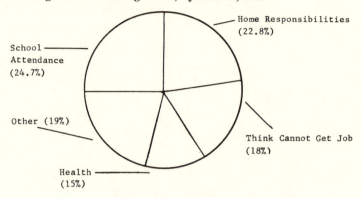

Source: Bureau of Labor Statistics, *Employment and Earnings*, January 1988, table 36, p. 200.

Figure 4.5
Status of Underutilized Members, Civilian Labor Force, Annual Average, 1987

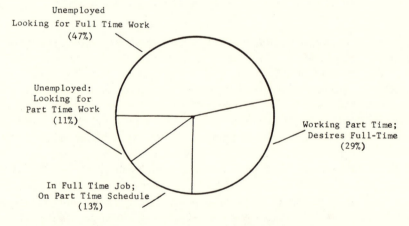

Source: Bureau of Labor Statistics, *Employment and Earnings*, January 1988, tables 3, 7, pp. 160–162, 167.

part-time schedule and 20.4 million were on a regular part-time basis). Of the 20.4 million, 17.2 million were on that basis voluntarily and 3.2 million for mostly economic reasons. Combined (1.7 and 3.2), there were nearly 5 million persons working part-time who preferred to be full-time. This was 4.2 percent of the civilian labor force (CLF) at the time. A detailed breakdown of employed and unemployed persons looking for full- and part-time work in 1987 is shown in appendix 4.B. (It should be emphasized that numbers of discouraged and other persons not participating full-time in the labor force can only be estimated, especially those in part-time status and desiring a better situation. There are a great many ifs involved.)[58]

Briefly, in 1987, 7.7 million persons were unemployed, 5 million were working part-time but desiring full-time, and 5.9 million were "discouraged workers," not counted in the labor force but wanting a job, making a total of 18.6 million nonutilized and underutilized persons desiring work or fuller work. This approaches one out of nine persons of the noninstitutional population (NIP), aged sixteen or over, not counting members of the urban underclass who for behavioral and other reasons are not participating in the work force.

A considerable number of the discouraged workers (and of those working part-time or for less than six months out of the year in successive years for reasons other than childbirth or illness) go on and off the welfare rolls as dictated by economic necessity. These persons are not part of the urban or rural underclass; they are threatened with becoming "welfare dependent" but do not succumb. Many of them are in the "working poor" category. They represent a vital potential for the work force of the nineties but are hampered by lack of access to day care, transportation, medical care, necessary employment training, job-search assistance, and other social services. State governments and especially private-sector employers and local governments working together will need to address these needs vigorously in the nineties.

JOB BARRIERS: DAY CARE, TRANSPORTATION, AND HEALTH SERVICES

This section reviews the various state and local steps that might be taken to enable discouraged workers and part-time workers desiring to work full-time to gain or increase CLF participation. Most of the steps would require increased investment; several are controversial; and nearly all fail to be cost-effective in some situations.

Major impediments severely limit job search and opportunity for (1) the working poor in full-time employment; (2) persons not in the labor market; and (3) part-time workers desiring full-time work. These barriers include (1) difficulty in arranging for child care; (2) transportation from residence to workplace; and (3) lack of access to health care, especially by mothers with young children.

These difficulties are most acute in large metropolitan areas. Many new job opportunities are centered in suburbia, and increasingly in exurbia, thereby confronting job seekers with a choice between perhaps-unaffordable auto commuting or tortuous public transportation routes fashioned for an earlier era. The cost and insufficient supply of day-care facilities too often are exacerbated by excessive state and/or local regulations. The availability of health care for those on welfare and its unavailability during most probationary entry-level employment raise an agonizing choice for the female single-parent householder.

In this section day-care provision and regulation and transportation issues will be reviewed. Health care will be examined in a broader context as it relates to

(1) members and potential members of the labor force; (2) the lack of health insurance coverage for many persons below age sixty-five; and (3) retired and disabled people who require long-term care (LTC) in nursing homes or other facilities. Health issues related to Medicaid, drug abuse, AIDS, and maternal and child health care are reviewed in chapter 5.

Day Care

Delivery of day-care services is primarily a private profit or nonprofit function, although local government may choose to deliver some of the service directly. For regulation—a public responsibility—the state government sets the parameters for local government regulation, although for larger day-care centers, state regulators may play a direct role. The state government may also provide financial incentives to private providers and/or users of day-care services, particularly for those persons on or coming off welfare rolls or for members of the "working poor."

The female portion of the nation's work force has been projected to be 47 percent by 2000, and 60 percent of the new entrants to the work force during the period 1985–2000 are estimated to be female. Most of the increase in the female portion will continue to comprise women with young children.[59] Furthermore, the proportion of all children under six whose mothers worked grew from 19 percent in 1960 to 37.6 percent in 1977 and 53.1 percent in 1987.[60] This was despite the claims of some that mothers on welfare with children under six could not be expected to participate in the labor force. During this period, others contended that a combination of part-time work, with the mother taking care of the children, and care by relatives or a neighbor would solve most of the problem, with a consequent limited concern necessary at any level of government.

The proportion of working mothers with minor (under eighteen) children grew from four out of ten in 1970 to over half in 1982; it stood at three-fifths (60.2 percent) in 1987. A breakdown by type of family for 1977 and 1987 is shown in table 4.2

Kinds of arrangements for child care. Child care arrangements fall into five general census categories: (1) care in child's home, with subcategories of care by father, other relative, and nonrelative; (2) care in another home, either by a relative or nonrelative; (3) care in a group-care center; (4) care by the mother herself while working; and (5) other arrangements, including child taking care of self. Table 4.3 summarizes the use of these arrangements by working mothers having children under five years of age.

In 1984–85 care by father or relative in own or other home (39.2 percent) was the predominant mode, followed by care by a nonrelative, either in the child's home or in another home (27.6 percent), and care in an organized facility such as a group-care center or a nursery school or other preschool facility (24.8 percent), while 8.3 percent of the mothers cared for the child at home. These

Table 4.2
Labor Force (LF) Participation by Mothers of Children under 18 by Family Type, 1977 and 1987

(Numbers in Thousands)

Age of Children & Family Type	1977			1987		
	Total Children	Mother in LF Number	Per Cent	Total Children	Mother in LF Number	Per Cent
Total Children	60,584	28,892	47.7	58,438	35,170	60.2
Age 6 to 17	43,467	22,462	51.7	38,637	24,657	63.8
Under 6	17,117	6,431	37.6	19,801	10,513	53.1
Married Couple Families	50,279	23,341	46.4	45,464	27,870	61.3
Age 6 to 17	35,499	17,930	50.5	29,355	19,113	65.1
Under 6	14,780	5,411	36.6	16.109	8,756	54.4
Female-Maintained Families	9,499	5,551	58.4	11,492	7,301	63.5
Age 6 to 17	7,266	4,532	62.4	8,180	5,543	67.8
Under 6	2,223	1,020	45.7	3,312	1,757	53.0
Male-Maintained Families	807			1,483		

Source: Bureau of Labor Statistics, Press Release USDL 87-345, August 12, 1987, table 2.

Totals do not always add precisely due to rounding.

Table 4.3

Principal Types of Child Care Arrangements Used by Working Mothers 18 to 44 Years Old for Youngest Child under Age 5, by Full-Time and Part-Time Employment, June 1977 and Winter 1984–85

(Numbers in thousands)*

Arrangement	Winter, 1984-85			June, 1977		
	Total	F. T.	P. T.	Total	F. T.	P. T.
No. of Children	6,666	4,263	2,403	3,987	2,645	1,342
Percent	100.0	100.0	100.0	100.0	100.0	100.0
Care in Own Home	28.8	23.2	39.2	31.9	27.6	40.3
Father or Relative	23.5	18.5	32.7	25.6	21.7	33.2
Non-relative	5.3	4.7	6.5	6.3	5.9	7.1
Care in Another Home	38.0	42.7	29.9	40.4	46.1	29.4
Relative	15.7	15.9	15.5	18.0	20.3	13.6
Non-relative	22.3	26.8	14.4	22.4	25.8	15.8
Organized Facility**	24.8	29.8	16.6	12.5	14.3	8.9
Care by Mother While Working	8.3	5.0	14.2	10.7	7.3	17.3
Other***				4.4	4.6	4.0

Source: Excerpted from Bureau of the Census, *Child Care Arrangements of Working Mothers, June 1982*, Current Population Reports, P–23, no. 129, table A, p. 4, for 1977; same title, Series P–70, no. 9, table 3, p. 15, for Winter 1984–85.

* Data for 1977 based on number of mothers; data for 1984–85 based on number of children.
** E.g., group centers.
*** "Other" includes child taking care of self. 1977 Census Survey also included non-responses and "don't knows."
Percentages do not always total 100 due to rounding.

data were for all working mothers, employed either full- or part-time, regardless of marital status. It will be noted also from the table that for mothers working part-time, the option of the mother caring for the child while at work (14.2 percent) ran fairly close to the proportion being cared for at a group center (16.6 percent). Not shown in the table, but drawn from the same data set, the modes for full-time workers with husband, if any, absent were (1) care by a relative in the child's home or elsewhere (31.6 percent); (2) organized facility (32.2 percent); (3) in another home by a nonrelative (29.5 percent); and (4) mother taking care of child at work (3.1 percent).[61]

Moving from young, preschool children to those of school age—the "latch-key" phenomenon—who are left alone after their release from school, hopefully at home or in the care of older siblings, the available data are less precise. A Census Bureau survey of after-school care of school-age youth in the mid-eighties (December 1984) showed that 28.9 million children five to thirteen years of age were enrolled in school. Eight million, between a third and a fourth, spent time during nonschool hours "alone or in the care of someone other than a parent." Stated another way, 72 percent of these students were regularly supervised by a parent during all nonschool hours, and the vast majority of those who were not cared for by their parents were cared for by a sibling or another person fourteen or older. Only 1 percent were not supervised at night.[62] A statistical breakdown of these caretaker arrangements by age of child, type of household, labor-force status of mother, and race appears in appendix 4.C.

Data on the proportion of nonworking mothers who would work if child care services were available tend to be inconclusive because of the subjective nature of the question and the impossibility of separating hope or wishful thinking from probability. Census data in 1982 showed relatively higher affirmative response rates among single mothers, blacks, and those of low income (likely to have been affected by income and racial disparities).[63]

Employer participation in child care. According to a Bureau of Labor Statistics survey, about 2 percent, or 25,000, of the nation's establishments with ten or more employees were sponsoring day-care centers for their workers' children in the summer of 1987. An additional 3 percent, or 35,000 establishments, were providing financial assistance to be used specifically for day care. Another 6 percent assisted with day-care referrals or counseling. Thus a total of 11 percent of this employer group of predominantly small firms were involved in one way or another in the provision of day care for employees. Of firms with 250 or more employees, 14 percent were providing financial assistance or sponsored centers, and another 18 percent helped with referrals and counseling.[64] In summary, while still limited, employer participation in day care has been expanding quite rapidly. As more private-sector fringe benefit plans are converted to a "cafeteria" type, it can be expected that an increasing number of large and moderate-sized companies will include child care assistance as one of the fringe options.

An experiment was conducted in the mid-eighties in the Twin Cities area by the Control Data Corporation, in which absenteeism, turnover, and other employee-satisfaction measures were applied to employees of another firm in the metropolitan area. The personnel records of ninety employees over a twenty-month period were reviewed in three groups of thirty each: (*a*) with children in a day-care center for which the company was assisting; (*b*) using other day-care modes; and (*c*) with no minor children. It was found that the rate of absenteeism for those participating in the company-assisted plan was 4.4 percent, compared to 6.0 percent for nonparticipants, and the rates for turnover were 1.77 and 6.3 percent. Those in and outside of industry advocating employer-assisted child care plans argue that increasingly, child care is a competitive issue. It will help attract and hold workers and reduce turnover, absenteeism, error, and accidents. Those doubting the wisdom of such assistance gave as reasons for not getting involved such factors as lack of economic justification, cost, insurance problems, assumption of implied obligation even through referral assistance, quality control, equity issues, and danger of getting sued for one reason or another.[65]

Policy options for state-local governments. Criteria for choosing policy approaches fall into two parts. First, how, if at all, should the local government provide encouragement or financial assistance through subsidy or otherwise to private proprietary or nonprofit providers to deliver child care services to (*a*) working mothers needing such service at any income level or (*b*) low-income users? Second, what framework should states establish for themselves or for local governments to initiate on their own for regulating day-care service delivery, particularly by the organized day-care centers and the home-based, small group-care deliverers? Policy approaches in financial and other assistance issues include the following possibilities, among others:

- No assistance involvement of any kind; services left to the market and to the initiatives of the individuals concerned

- Information, referral, and other placement services to low-income families or to all families, including information as to the nature of available federal or state tax or other public or private assistance; no direct financial assistance involvement

- No financial involvement, except to include day-care financial assistance as an option in state-local employee fringe benefit packages

- No additional financial involvement other than use of part of federal social services block grant for services to those families meeting the income standards

- Operating subsidies to private deliverers to cover part or all of the cost to (*a*) welfare recipients entering or returning to labor force or (*b*) low-income families; or inclusion of indirect subsidy to all users, such as free or reduced rent of government-owned space to delivering entity

Approaches to regulatory issues include the following:

- No regulations other than those applicable to proprietary or nonprofit entities delivering other human services

- Special health and safety regulations to organized centers; registration only for home-based delivery

- Special health, safety, professional staffing, and other regulations applicable to child care; licensing of centers and registration or licensing of home-based delivery

Day-care regulation. Regulation is a difficult economic, fiscal, and social issue that lies squarely with state and local governments. With the growing private-sector role and the small percentage of public subsidy to day care that originates with the federal government, there would appear to be limited leverage for a federal regulatory role. However, through future amendments to 1988 federal welfare reform legislation that provided federal participation in transitional day-care assistance, the Congress conceivably could endeavor to micromanage day-care provision, as it has with substantial justification, imposed nursing home standards under Medicaid assistance, as discussed later in this chapter.

The case for some regulation of day-care providers by local governments within the parameters of any governing state legislation is clear. The principal issues are (*a*) where to draw the line between licensing and registration and (b) how strict and comprehensive licensing standards should be for the larger, organized day-care centers. As shown in table 4.3, a sizeable share of day-care service is provided either in the child's home or in the home of a relative. Licensing probably will remain the prevailing regulatory mode for centers; child abuse and other problems provide an argument for tighter inspections under a registration system, as well as raising other questions of insurance coverage and tort liability.

But each notch of increased regulation may bring an increase in service cost. With each increase comes conflicting fiscal pressures and higher barriers for the working poor and welfare clients to surmount in trying to move into, or stay in, the labor force. On the other hand, the health and safety of children is of high public social concern. Consequently, state and local governments must balance these concerns as they make the necessary regulatory decisions.

Transportation to Jobs

For a jobholder or seeker in the lower wage or income quartile, getting from home to work in most of the nation's metropolitan areas is a major concern. Most of the new jobs will continue to accrue in urban areas, but of these, an increasingly dominant proportion are being created in "outer cities." These cover the range from inner or middle suburbs to exurbia. All are relatively far from the central business district of the central city. On the other hand, for most metropolitan areas, most of the unemployed and discouraged workers, as well as members of the urban underclass, are found in the central city.

The locational gap separating jobs and job seekers is clear in table 4.4. The relatively low unemployment rate for black and Hispanic workers in the suburbs is encouraging. Although higher than for whites, it is lower than in the central city and suggests that for minority members, as well as whites, if they live closer to employment places, fewer will be unemployed. However, as a rule, higher-cost housing in the suburbs tilts the black and Hispanic residence there toward those of higher income—and very likely, higher-paid jobs. Housing costs, as well as transportation, deter movement of minorities to the suburbs.

The data in table 4.4. become more discouraging when placed on a trend line. Table 2.5 shows the continuing shift over the past two decades of industrial employment from the central city to outer areas. Within the industrial employment category, the outward shift has been most severe for manufacturing and wholesale/retail, while for services, it has been smaller and in some cases has represented some improvement in the central-city position. However, John Kasarda has pointed out that many of the new service jobs require skills not possessed by central-city minority residents.

Kasarda showed that for nine U.S. cities over the 1970–80 period, entry-level

Table 4.4

Civilian Work Force Locations and Employment/Unemployment in Metropolitan Areas, June 1987 (Numbers in Thousands)

	Total	Central City	Suburbs
Civ. Non-Inst. Pop.	142,030	58,863	85,167
Civ. Labor Force	94,546	36,554	57,992
Per cent of CNIP	66.6	64.3	68.1
Unemployed	5,677	2,764	2,913
Rate	6.0	7.6	5.0
Unemployment, White	4,070	1,593	2,477
Rate	5.0	5.8	4.7
Unemployment, Black	1,424	1,066	358
Rate	13.2	14.6	10.3
Unemployment, Hispanic	652	402	250
Rate	8.3	9.1	7.2
Not in Labor Force	47,484	20,308	27,175
Per Cent, NILF	33.4	35.7	31.9
NILF, White	37,996	14,910	25,086
Per Cent NILF, White	33.2	35.0	32.1
NILF, Black	5,957	4,538	1,419
Per Cent NILF, Black	35.6	38.3	29.1
NILF, Hispanic	4,020	2,491	1,529
Per Cent NILF, Hisp.	33.8	36.0	30.1

Source: Bureau of Labor Statistics, *Employment and Earnings*, July 1987, 74.

Data for races other than black and white not shown.

jobs (average education level below high school completion) declined for New York, Philadelphia, Baltimore, Boston, St. Louis, and Atlanta, while increasing greatly in Houston and slightly in Denver and San Francisco. The data indicated also that all of the cities except St. Louis showed gains in the numbers of knowledge-intensive jobs (average level of two-plus years of college), with large increases in Houston, Denver, and San Francisco and modest increases for the other five.[66]

By 1983, in terms of total employment, the proportion of total metropolitan-area employment located in the suburbs had approached or far exceeded 50 percent in New Orleans (47), Denver and New York (55), Baltimore (60), Philadelphia and San Francisco (nearly 65), and St. Louis and Washington, D.C. (70). Notable examples of the outer-city critical mass, including high-density office buildings, regional and national headquarters of corporations, and hotels and restaurants, have been the South Coast Metro Center and Irvine in Orange County, California, Tyson's Corner, Virginia, Buckhead, Georgia, and the area northwest of Philadelphia.[67]

However, the historical development of expressway and other road networks in metropolitan areas makes transportation from suburb to suburb and from inner city to suburb very costly and time-consuming, and in a great many cases wholly impracticable if the trip is to be via public transportation. Not only were the expressways built on a hub-and-spoke pattern when the central business district was Rome, with all roads leading to it, but the bus and rail routes were placed similarly. This left the need for concentric circular transportation routes to be met in the eighties and nineties.

Consequently, the geography and economics of most urban transportation systems in the nineties place severe limitations on travel from central-city residential neighborhoods to outer-city employment centers by bus and rail transportation—usually requiring a combination of the two. As a *New York Times* editorial pointedly commented: "By public transportation, it can take two hours and several transfers to get from Chicago's South Side to the O'Hare Airport area. . . . For an employed Atlantan without a car, jobs in Cobb and Gwinnett counties might as well be in China."[68] Traffic decongestion measures, including employer-provided van, bus, and other transportation directly from residential neighborhoods in both the central city and inner suburbs to outer-city employment centers, appear to be a major option for consideration by local and state governments and by both private and public employers. Removing or mitigating the transportation deterrent to unemployed or discouraged central-city workers should be a major public policy and employer economic objective in those areas and occupations where labor shortages exist or threaten to arise.

For workers or potential workers at lower pay or income scales who live in the central city and desire to work in a suburban employment center or elsewhere in suburbia, direct travel from home or home neighborhood to the workplace is limited to those situations where an express bus or subway stop is within walking distance from home and where the place of employment is within walking distance from one of the bus or subway stops. If the employer happens to run shuttle vans or other transportation to the one or two major public transportation discharge points nearest to the workplace, part of the potential employee's problem is solved, but intra-central-city travel to the public transit stop remains.

Employer-provided vans picking up workers at collection points in the central city can make the job opportunity a viable one. For example, in the Washington, D.C., metropolitan area, severe labor shortages exist in and around several suburban centers of employment, while unemployment continues higher than the national average in the central city. Suburban employers have begun to attract District of Columbia residents to employment by paying travel expenses, offering bonuses, and picking up workers in the city in vans or through employer-subsidized car-pool arrangements. Through these and other private and public actions, District residents, over a one-year period, obtained 25 percent of the new jobs in the metropolitan area, although they comprised only 17 percent of the area labor force.[69]

The object of any and all of these options is to lower the transportation barriers and/or to lessen fiscal requirements for more freeway lanes. They tend to center on reducing the proportion of single-occupant automobiles in the daily flow of workers from home to work, while at the same time providing some opportunities for lower-income people to get from residence to work. Several earlier policies that seemed well justified at the time tended to worsen congestion, especially in suburban areas:

• Provision of cheap or free parking by employers
• Requirement in local government growth management plans and building codes for generous amounts of off-street parking within new buildings
• Discriminatory tax treatment of private cars and public transportation (for example, a provision in the federal tax code allowing free parking as a business-deductible fringe benefit, tax-free to the employee, but limiting employer subsidization of public transportation to $15 per employee per month)

Newer options for state and local governments include the following:

• Deregulation of paratransit (jitneys, fixed-route taxicabs, and so on) to permit service to low-density areas not justifying bus or other public transportation
• Subsidization of employer-provided van pooling, especially from the central city, with incentives related to degree of employee participation
• Negotiations with private employers, involving financial incentives and regulatory actions, to favor group riding among employees
• Shuttles from major rail or bus stops to the work site or to a location within walking distance of two or more work sites
• Imposition of parking fees for public employees, with a reduced or no fee for car pooling
• Offer of discounted public transportation to employees working in traffic-congested areas
• Differential fees in parking lots and on-street meters to car occupancy, time of day, and parking duration
• Requiring developers to charge for parking in new buildings as a condition of local approval of a building plan

Most of these types of measures are both complex and controversial; any policy action that tends to inhibit the enjoyment of a single-occupancy vehicle as the preferred means of travel to work arouses intense opposition. Nevertheless, auto traffic gridlock in congested metropolitan areas is hardly likely to be solved by construction alone; more lanes tend to fill quickly as drivers move to more convenient peak periods for journeys to work.[70]

Health Care

Health care in the United States is a critical, contentious, and pervasive issue of public policy, confronting not only national, state, and local governments, but corporate management, labor unions, and other segments of the political economy. It is a serious and omnipresent personal issue facing most Americans (excepting only healthy adolescents and young adults without children). The range of issues is wide, with most being interdependent with others. Because of this interdependence among health, welfare, drugs, AIDS, and similar societal concerns, it is necessary to separate our examination of the health spectrum into two parts. The aspects just mentioned are linked inextricably to the federal-state Medicaid program and consequently to welfare and poverty, and are examined in chapter 5. The other major issues of the present and foreseeable future concern rising costs, affordable insurance, and long-term care (LTC) for the disabled and elderly. They will be reviewed at this point, since the delivery of public health services and the regulation of health insurance are intertwined with the overall economy, yet comprise a major responsibility of state government and larger local governments.

It should be emphasized, however, before leaving for later the problem of health care for the poor, that health care, like day care, transportation, and housing, is a key element in attaining and maintaining a qualified and mobile work force and a stable economy. A significant deterrent to discouraged workers in seeking or accepting employment is the absence of access to health care; this is especially the case with mothers of younger children. Many discouraged workers go on and off welfare, depending on the periods of employment and unemployment. For a discouraged worker, an unemployed worker on welfare, or a person on welfare with no work experience, to seek or accept a private- or public-sector position is to give up, at least for a time, health protection being provided under Medicaid.

In this section three broad issue areas will be reviewed: (1) rising medical costs because of new technology and other factors, and the state-local regulatory role in health costs; (2) the health-uninsured population and the roles of state and local governments in facilitating broader coverage; and (3) long-term health care of the disabled and elderly and how it can best be delivered and regulated.

Rising costs of medical facilities and services. In 1986 national health care expenditures totaled $458 billion, averaging $1,837 per capita and comprising 10.9 percent of the GNP, up from 10.6 percent in 1985, 9.1 percent in 1980, 8.5 percent in 1976, and 6.0 percent in 1966.[71] (One consumer organization, Public Citizen Health Research Group in Washington, D.C., contended that up to a third of this national expenditure is wasted, due to a variety of unnecessary medical procedures and other causes.)[72] In 1980 the United States stood approximately in the middle of the major European countries and Canada in health care expenditures; the high was 9.6 percent for West Germany and the low was 5.8 percent for the United Kingdom. For other countries in the group, Sweden and the Netherlands were above the U.S. level, and France and Canada somewhat below.[73] Medical costs have risen considerably faster than the general price level. From 1967 at 100, the consumer price index stood at 345.3 in October 1987, while the medical component of the CPI stood at 461.3. Within the medical component, prescription drugs had increased the least (299.6) and hospital room costs the most (799.4).[74]

In the late eighties national, state, and local governments and the private sector were making concerted efforts to stem the increase in health costs. These efforts had begun in state and federal governments several years earlier and intensified subsequently. Concerns in the private sector arose with the onset of double-digit inflation, which saw health costs for retirees escalating rapidly. Efforts to restrain costs and/or to render health insurance plans more equitable and affordable included the following:

- Replacement of retrospective fee-for-service reimbursement systems of payment to providers with a prospective system based on a list of nearly 500 hospital-associated procedures, called "diagnosis related groups" (DRGs), with a maximum allowable reimbursement amount for each (initiated by the Congress for Medicare and picked up in varying degrees by private and public employers and health insurance carriers).

- Other measures to reduce hospital stays and costs—admission approval by two doctros; confinement of some procedures to outpatient handling, or insurance payment of a higher proportion of the cost if these procedures were on an outpatient rather than inpatient basis; second opinions on surgery; and association of length of stay with nature of ailment or injury.

- Shift from fee-for-service to prepaid health maintenance organizations (HMOs) or preferred providers (PPOs); by 1983 the populations covered under the two systems had about equaled those covered by fee-for-service.[75]

- Shift in private-sector retiree health coverage from a defined benefit to a defined contribution basis (Digital Equipment Corporation, a relatively new company in 1987, had 110,000 employees and 1,000 retirees; Bethlehem Steel had 38,000 employees and 70,000 retirees. The ratio of employees to retirees was 3 to 1 for Fortune 500 companies).[76]

- Shift of part of insurance cost from government or employer to individual through increase in copayment requirements, thereby providing an incentive to the consumer toward greater selectivity and economy in elective procedures.

- Enactment of state laws mandating a public utility-type regulation of new hospitals and other medical facilities through a "certificate of need" (CON) procedure, designed to minimize duplication of facilities and equipment and to avoid hospital overbuilding; this was pioneered by some states in the early seventies and picked up and later dropped by the federal government in health planning legislation; it was still in place in about forty states in 1987.

- Enactment in some states of hospital rate control legislation and creation of regulatory commissions, again similar to public utility rate regulation.

The health insurance problem. An estimated 35 million persons were not covered or protected under the combined governmental and private health plans in existence toward the close of the eighties (32.4 million in 1986, as estimated by the Public Health Service).[77] Practically all of these were under sixty-five years of age. Upon reaching sixty-five, persons covered by Social Security automatically become eligible for Medicare A (hospital) and may voluntarily participate in Medicare B (physicians, tests, other medical) through a combination of a monthly premium and a matching contribution from the federal Medicare fund. Furthermore, in 1988 the Congress expanded Medicare to encompass catastrophic illness. For persons below sixty-five, the health insurance picture had the following aspects in early 1988:

- Persons below the poverty line were eligible for coverage under Medicaid, a federal-state matching program, with considerable participation by local governments in some states via county or city hospitals.
- Practically all public and larger private employers were providing some kind of health care protection for employees and retirees.
- Many states had elected to expand Medicaid to cover pregnant women and children below the age of five to a considerable distance above the poverty line, with costs for this being matched by the federal government.[78] State Medicaid coverage of such women with infants one year of age and below and at or below seventy-five percent of the poverty line was mandated by the federal Medicare Catastrophic Coverage Act of 1988.

The uninsured population—an estimated two-thirds of whom worked or were dependents of workers—comprised the following groups, among others:

- Self-employed persons of low income
- Students
- Low-paid workers (for example, 150 to 200 percent of federal poverty level) who could not afford insurance premiums, even if their employer paid part
- An estimated one-third (about 4 million) of poverty households, many of whom could qualify for Medicaid (a) if they knew about it, (b) took the trouble to apply, and (c) surmounted the difficulties—many of them procedural—in establishing eligibility

During 1987, about half the states were considering expansions in Medicaid eligibility. Some were beginning to reimburse hospitals for care of the medically indigent. Others were creating revenue pools and reimbursing on the basis of indigent caseloads; still others were using direct state appropriations and mandating counties to share in medically indigent costs. In addition, more than a dozen states considered plans designed to make substantial inroads upon the size of the uninsured population. The state insurance plans were directed toward ultimate coverage of all or most of the uninsured.

Hawaii had become the first state to require health coverage by private employers, the plan becoming effective in 1982. The state health department estimated in 1987 that only 5 percent of the population remained uninsured; these were persons working less than twenty hours a week, seasonal workers, immigrants not qualifying, full-time students over twenty-one, or nonworking spouses or children of low-wage earners.

Three 1987–88 plans were enacted that gained wide attention—in Wisconsin, Washington, and Massachusetts. The Wisconsin objective was ultimately to cover 450,000 uninsured residents, but at the outset was confined to pilot projects limited to uninsured persons below 175 percent of poverty level, with costs shared between the state and the individual.

The Washington plan was based on case-managed use of prepaid care; it subsidized premiums from state general revenues for those with incomes at or below 200 percent of poverty level. It was estimated that up to 40 percent of the state's uninsured residents would be covered. The most comprehensive approach was in Massachusetts, which—after much controversy—enacted the legislation in early 1988. Under it, responsibility for meeting most of the uninsured problem was placed on the private sector. The legislation required Massachusetts employers of five or more persons to provide all of their employees working more than a specified number of hours a week with health insurance coverage. It paralleled a similar proposal advanced in Congress in 1987 by Democratic Senator Edward Kennedy of Massachusetts and others.[79]

As individual states get comprehensive health insurance plans in place, congressional action to mandate employer provision of such insurance might be delayed indefinitely, forestalled, or speeded up, depending upon results. State activity in this area is another example of the role of state governments as political laboratories of the nation.

Long-term care and nursing homes. Advances in medical technology have been producing an increasing life span. The number of persons sixty-five and over is projected to grow from about 25 million (11.3 percent of total population) in 1983 to 65 million (about 21 percent) by 2030. The very old (eighty-five and over) have been projected to reach 8.6 million, or about 3 percent of the population in 2030.[80]

While elderly mortality rates are decreasing, morbidity rates are rising—a longer life and poorer health. At any one time in the mid-eighties, between 5 and 6 percent of the elderly were in nursing homes and similar facilities, and about two-thirds of these were senile. An estimated 1.2 million persons were in nursing homes in 1986, with an average stay for those for whom it was the last residence of about two years. The 1986–87 average annual cost was $22,000.[81] In 1985 the proportion of total population in each age group that was institutionalized in nursing homes was 1 percent for those 65 to 74, but 22 percent for those 85 and over (25 percent for women and 15 percent for men, and 23 percent for white persons and 14 percent for black.)[82] Table 4.5 shows that over 40 percent of Medicaid outlays were for nursing home care in 1986.

The incidence of the long-term care (LTC) problem in proportions of population (not necessarily in relative costs) varied considerably geographically. The projected percentage by 2000 of state population of persons 85 and over is highest for Alaska (18 percent), followed by other states in the top quartile of 16 to 18 percent (New Hampshire, Vermont, Massachusetts, Connecticut, West Virginia, Ohio, Iowa, North Dakota, Nebraska, New Mexico, and New York). The lowest quartile states (10.9 to 14.2 percent) are Utah (11 percent), followed by Hawaii, Idaho, Wyoming, Colorado, Arizona,

Table 4.5

Medicaid Population and Payments by Eligibility Category and Medical Service Type, Selected Years, 1972–86

(Numbers in Thousands; Payments in Millions of Dollars)

A. Recipients By Eligibility Category:

Year	Total No.	65 and Over No.	65 and Over % MP	Blind & Disabl. No.	Blind & Disabl. %MP	AFDC Chil.	AFDC Adults	Other No.	Other
1972	17,606	3,318	18.8	1,733	9.8	7,841 44.5	3,137 17.8	1,576	9.0
1980	21,605	3,440	15.9	2,911	13.5	9,333 43.2	4,877 22.6	1,499	6.9
1986	22,405	3,140	14.0	3,172	14.2	9,954 44.4	5,618 25.1	1,368	6.1

B. Recipients and Payments (combined federal, state, local), By Service Type:

Type of Service	1972 No.	1972 % Used	1972 Payments Amt.	1972 Payments % for Type	1980 No.	1980 % Used	1980 Payments Amt.	1980 Payments % for Type	1986 No.	1986 % Used	1986 Payments Amt.	1986 Payments % for Type
Total	17,606	100.0	$6,300	100.0	21,605	100.0	$23,311	100.0	22,405	100.0	$40,878	100.0
Hospital (IP)*	2,872	16.3	2,670	42.4	3,746	17.3	7,187	30.8	3,570	15.9	11,406	27.9
Hospital (OP)*	5,215	29.6	365	5.8	9,705	44.9	1,101	4.7	10,711	47.8	1,983	4.9
Intermed.-Skilled Nursing Facil.	552	3.1	1,471	23.3	1,516	7.0	9,876	42.4	1,544	6.9	17,449	42.7
Clinic	501	2.8	41	.7	1,531	7.1	320	1.4	2,033	9.1	810	2.0
Laboratory	3,523	20.0	81	1.3	3,212	14.9	121	.5	7,122	31.8	424	1.0
Physician Servcs.	12,282	69.8	794	12.6	13,765	63.7	1,875	8.0	14,808	66.1	2,545	6.2
Dental Services	2,397	13.6	170	2.7	4,652	21.5	462	2.0	5,143	23.0	529	1.3
Home Health Care	105	.6	24	.4	392	1.8	332	1.4	593	2.6	1,352	3.3
Other**	4,131	23.5	683	10.8	6,926	32.1	2,037	8.7	8,500	37.9	4,268	10.4

Source: Department of Health and Human Services, *Social Security Bulletin, Annual Statistical Supplement, 1987*, 40–41, 75, 252–254.

* Includes mental hospital in- and out-patients.
** Excludes recipients of prescription drugs; includes drug payments; includes "family planning," "other practitioner," and "other care."
Beginning in fiscal year 1980, recipients' categories do not add to unduplicated total because of small number that are in more than one category during year.

Texas, Arkansas, Mississippi, Alabama, Florida, South Carolina, and Virginia.[83]

The House Select Committee on the Aging estimated that 67 percent of single elderly nursing home patients "spend down" (combination of income and assets) to the state Medicaid eligibility level in one year.[84] However, the extent of asset transfer to children prior to entering a nursing home is difficult to estimate and even harder to regulate. The federal estate and gift tax law permits a couple of any age to give $20,000 a year, free of gift tax, to an unlimited number of individuals. Thus a couple with a net worth of $100,000 living off Social Security and any other pension or income can dispose of all assets to two children over a three-year period, leaving Medicaid to pick up the tab for whatever time, if any, they may need to spend in a nursing home, which at average rates of duration and cost in 1986–87 would have resulted in a Medicaid outlay of $88,000. From the standpoint of the elderly person, a very distressing aspect of the nursing home situation is that the cost of care may very well consume the entirety of what had been saved for over a lifetime to pass on to one's children.

However, from the standpoint of national and state governments, many children, working poor, and others of low income originally intended to be helped by Medicaid go without full protection because Medicaid pays one-half or more of all nursing home costs. In budgetary competition at both national and state levels, due to the political power of the elderly, the younger groups often lose out. (1988 federal catastrophic medical care legislation raised the level of permissable assets that could be retained by certain nursing home patients when establishing Medicaid eligibility.)

The NGA conducted a study of six states' efforts directed toward more efficient and equitable resource allocation approaches to the LTC problem. The states were Maine, Maryland, Illinois, Arkansas, Oregon, and Wisconsin. Several common denominators were noted:

• A set of policies maximizing home, family, and neighbor help (community-based care) and reserving nursing home and similar facilities for acute or serious cases, thus giving the elderly more options

• A standard set of components in client (elderly person no longer able to care for oneself without some help) assistance procedure—screening as to needed care level, and helping to arrange it

• Strict eligibility criteria for nursing home admission

• Use of multiple funding sources—state general revenue, Medicaid, and federal grants for social services and those eligible under the Older Americans Act

• Use of family care providers (Medicaid reimbursement at specified rates to family member caring for client)

• Coordination of these activities at a focal point in the state government[85]

In 1983 the national government contracted with the National Institute of Medicine of the National Academy of Sciences to study the problem of quality-of-care assurance in the nation's nursing homes. It reported in early 1986 and proposed a structure and process by which care quality should be improved and maintained, centering around more consultation with the patient as to regimen and maintaining a sanitary and decent environment for patients.[86] In late 1987 Congress enacted into law several of the recommendations in the institute's report.[87]

How to meet the present and future fiscal problem associated with LTC, especially for nursing home patients, is extremely complex and controversial.

As of early 1988 **a growing share of LTC** costs was being met from Medicaid, which in turn is **financed for the most part** from state and federal general revenues. (First five months, **up from 100 days,** covered by Medicare under federal legislation enacted in 1988.) Alternatives are numerous, but can be described in four general groups:

- Increase copayments with more rigorous rules on preadmission asset transfers, especially for persons with above-median incomes and/or net worth in the upper third or upper quartile of the total population.

- Tax incentives and public subsidies toward purchase of LTC insurance.

- Increase Medicare premiums and taxability of Social Security benefits, with proceeds going to a Medicare LTC fund, and the freed-up Medicaid funds going to assure fuller protection of the poverty and medically indigent population below age sixty-five, particularly young children.

- Increase the Social Security payroll tax on the working (and still-working retired) population, or the higher-income portion thereof, with the proceeds going into the Medicare LTC fund.

There appears to be widespread agreement about the desirability of maximizing (a) in-home assistance; (b) community-based services—adult day care, transportation, telephone reassurance, friendly visiting, respite care; and (c) specialized housing such as board and care homes before resort to institutional care at a nursing home. There also is apparent agreement about state risk pooling and encouragement to the insurance industry to come up with LTC policies. However, there is a wide disagreement about the desirability of expanded federal financing for any further programs for the elderly, resource allocation already being skewed heavily in that direction. There also is disagreement about copayment requirements, asset transfer rules, and the financial base for any public subsidies for insurance coverage (that is, whether the cost should be shared among the Medicare population or across the entire nonpoverty spectrum of state or federal taxpayers).

The American Association of Retired Persons (AARP), in its legislative program, supports (1) further private-sector approaches that include acceleration of efforts to develop LTC insurance policies, including LTC benefits under employer-based insurance plans, and (2) continued testing of social health maintenance organizations (SHMOs) to provide a full range of acute care, LTC, and social services at reduced cost.

In addition to risk pools, the association leans toward favoring "expanding Medicare coverage to include long-term care benefits. Possible financing mechanisms include increased premiums under Medicare and increased excise taxes, such as on alcohol and cigarettes." Finally, the AARP recommends eliminating the stringent spend-down requirements of a number of states and relating the cost of LTC services to the patient's ability to pay.[88] This is a key point; does ability to pay relate only to income? Does net worth have any relationship to "ability to pay"?

At the other end of the spectrum of the LTC debate, former Colorado governor Richard Lamm, after observing that the nation spends "10 times more capita of the federal budget on the elderly than on our children . . . the elderly have the highest disposable income . . . we have 265,000 millionaires on, or eligible for Medicare," concludes, "I think we should base new federal programs on *need* rather than *age*."[89]

It is obvious that LTC for the elderly is an enormous problem fiscally, equitably, generationally, and emotionally. From the numerous state initiatives described here could come definitive successful and unsuccessful results that would form the basis for a new state-federal policy for the intermediate future. On a longer-term basis, it is likely that American society will need to review its social as well as economic policies in the light of new medical, technological, and ethical realities.[90]

THE HOUSING/HOMELESS PROBLEM

Several economic and fiscal changes began occurring in the mid- to late eighties that tended to exacerbate the housing problem in both urban and rural areas, particularly for low- and moderate-income people. These included (1) continuing rise in the price of housing, augmented by skyrocketing prices for building lots in many urban areas; (2) the expiration of the contract period for federally assisted housing under Section 8 programs for new and existing housing, whereunder developers and subsequent building owners of multifamily dwellings agreed to reserve a proportion of the units for rental to low- and moderate-income persons for a period of twenty years; (3) restrictions placed upon the issuance of housing tax-exempt revenue bonds in the federal tax reform legislation of 1986 (often it is necessary to have a generous mix of moderate-income, in contrast to low-income, units for a project to be economically viable, due to tenant nervousness about socioeconomic "tipping points"); (4) an economic turnaround in a considerable number of urban areas brought about through downtown redevelopment, "gentrification" of residential neighborhoods, demolition of existing single-family housing, and closing of mobile home parks and single-room occupancy hotels (SROS), all of which tended to displace or otherwise reduce the number of housing units available for persons of low income; and (5) continued conversion of multifamily rental housing into condominium or cooperative ownership.

Likewise, housing displacements resulting from these changes, coupled with two other phenomena, brought about a substantial increase in the number, visibility, and public consciousness of the homeless or "street people." These were (1) the earlier deinstitutionalization of many persons from state mental health facilities and the inability to replace state institutional care with community mental health facilities (attributable to neighborhood opposition, lack of state legislative support, and a variety of other causes); and (2) spread of alcohol and other drug addiction among the urban poor and not-so-poor. Demand for emergency shelter facilities and services grew, especially during each winter season in the northern states. The refusal of many of the homeless to go to shelters after they became available raised serious new legal and ethical questions in dealing with the problem.

Endeavoring to cope with the combined housing/homeless problems among low-income persons and others physically or mentally impaired, especially in the large cities, has evolved into one of the priority issues confronting state and local governments in the nineties. By the late eighties the situation had spurred countless new public policy and private enterprise initiatives, as well as increased emphasis upon, and resource allocation to, those state and local programs and policies that had been producing effective results. Before examining this collection of older and newer ideas and program initiatives, it is well to note some general economic and fiscal issues often overlooked in several decades of federal, state, and local policies and efforts to stimulate housing investment for virtually all income levels through the combined use of federal subsidies and state-local tax-exempt financing.

Economic and Fiscal Issues

Whether the nation has been and is investing too little or too much in housing construction has been debated by economists and housing finance experts over a long period. Anthony Downs and others have argued that the broad band of housing investment has been favored more than necessary in national and subnational policy, while the tendency has been to underinvest in housing in an economically efficient way at the low-income end of the spectrum.[91] Edwin Mills found a discrepancy between social returns to housing and nonhousing capital, indicating that the "social return to housing is only about 55 percent of that to nonhousing and that, based on an efficiency criterion, we have accumulated about 25 percent too much housing."[92]

Set against these economic efficiency arguments are the widely claimed advantages of homeownership as a cohesive force in the societal structure and a crucial part of the American dream. Also, it is argued that homeownership increases the civic responsibility of the individual and is a strong stabilizing force in the political economy. The congressionally stated objective in the Housing Act of 1954, echoed by successive administrations that had begun with Truman and Eisenhower, of "a decent home for every American" has continued to strike an affirmative note across the political spectrum.

However, the distributional effects upon the principal actors in housing transactions—homebuyers, builders, sellers of existing dwellings, and lenders—may require closer analysis than heretofore.[93] The limitation on state-local housing revenue bonds by the 1986 tax reform legislation has often been cited as a factor exacerbating the low-income housing shortages. For present purposes it is as-

sumed that if tax exemption of any kind of state-local revenue bonds is economically and fiscally justified as a matter of intergovernmental policy, low-cost
and low-income housing carries a high priority within the tax-exempt category.

Housing Demand and Low-Income Housing Shortages

The Census Bureau, the Joint Harvard-MIT Center for Housing Studies, the
National Association of Realtors (NAR), and the Rutgers University Center for
Urban Policy Research each made estimates in the late eighties on household
numbers, homeownership, and the composition of households. The number of
households in 1995 was projected at 100.3 million in the middle of the three
Census Bureau projections, 98.4 million by Rutgers researchers, and 100.6
million by the Joint Center. The census and the Joint Center projected the number
of households in 2000 at 105.9 and 106 million, respectively, and this figure
was supported by the NAR.[94]

The shortage of available housing units for low-income occupants, becoming
more critical in the late eighties, appears to be an indisputable fact, not a theory,
insofar as the rental market is concerned, and in all likelihood for low-income
home purchasers as well. A decline in the federal housing-support level from
over $30 billion in 1981 to less than $10 billion in 1986 was brought about by
a combination of (1) uncertainty about the efficacy of the conventional housing
programs; (2) a growing federal deficit; and (3) a policy shift by the Reagan
administration away from a construction/developer-oriented approach to housing
support to a consumer-choice approach through housing vouchers. This last
approach met vigorous opposition from supporters of the conventional programs.

However, time, rather than policy or politics, caused a significant change in
low-income unit availability. Section 8 of the Housing Act of 1969 required, as
a condition of federal construction or rental assistance subsidies, the reservation
of a designated proportion of units in a building or development for low-income
occupancy for a period of twenty years. For mortgage interest subsidy programs,
a prepayment option at the end of twenty- and forty-year mortgages was provided.
Thus the obligation upon the owner to maintain such a reservation expires at the
end of the twenty-year period if the owner opts to prepay the balance due on
the mortgage. Given a fairly tight housing rental market in most urban areas, a
shift of rental units to a higher-income classification would be a natural outcome.
An early 1987 survey by the National League of Cities (NLC), to which 444
cities responded, produced reports of existing or looming housing shortages of
''severe proportions'' in more than half the cities (53.4 percent); this proportion
of severity was exceeded only by that for the homeless (58.0 percent).[95] The
NLC and the General Accounting Office estimate that 448,000 of these mortgage
subsidy units may be lost by 2005, as well as a range of 880,000 to 1.1 million
rental subsidy subsistence units expiring between 1985 and 2000 unless renewed.[96]

Earlier State-Local Housing Initiatives

Prior to the seventies most states were "viewed by those concerned with housing and urban revitalization at best as 'sleeping giants' and at worst as potential barriers between local communities and federal government assistance. . . . Clearly some state governments have contributed to local problems. For this reason alone, they should become part of the solution."[97]

By the late sixties, no doubt hastened by the reapportionment of legislatures, state governments began to come alive regarding urban problems. In 1968 the National Commission on Urban Problems (chaired by former senator Paul Douglas of Illinois), recommended a series of actions by state governments on housing. These included (1) establishment of a state agency for development planning and review to adjudicate and supervise decisions by state and local agencies regarding land use (among other duties); (2) expansion of personal choice of persons of all income levels in their selection of housing location; (3) requiring the assurance by local governments of housing variety; (4) enactment of legislation requiring multicounty or other regional agencies to adopt regional housing plans; (5) enactment of a state policy encouraging the provision of housing for employees of all income levels in areas reasonably close to employment areas; and (6) adoption of statewide mandatory housing codes by all states.[98]

The ACIR had preceded the Douglas Commission by a year or two in making several of these recommendations and in drafting suggested state legislation for carrying them out; in other cases, recommendations of both commissions found their way into similar model state legislation promulgated by the Council of State Governments in its annual volumes of *Suggested State Legislation*. A 1975 update of ACIR draft legislation, reflecting its recommendations to that point, contained a volume on housing and community development, including draft bills on (1) state agencies for community affairs, urban development financing, and housing finance; (2) housing rehabilitation assistance; (3) uniform relocation assistance; (4) "new community" districts; (5) fair housing; (6) regional fair-share housing allocations; (7) a state building code; (8) mobile and manufactured housing; and (9) assistance to local governments for building inspection and state registration of building code enforcement officers.[99]

With two exceptions, these propositions had found their way into many state statutes by 1980, a substantial number before 1975. "New communities," a popular concept among urban planners and a variety of elected state and local officials in the early seventies, after several failed developments and an occasional success, fell into relative disuse in a few years. Except in New Jersey and two or three other states, the concept of regional fair-share housing allocations was considered excessively strong medicine for housing discrimination. (Use in New Jersey was triggered by a state supreme court edict—the "Mount Laurel" decision of 1975.)

The state role in housing finance had assumed great importance by 1980. This involved subsidizing (via tax-exempt securities) low- and moderate-income housing, both single- and multifamily, benefiting buyers, renters, builders, and lenders, the last through state housing agency guarantees of loans. The state role in land use regulation strengthened greatly over the same period and had some beneficial effects on housing. State building code activity lessened unnecessary variations among local building codes and thereby reduced the cost of housing at all income levels. The state override of local government objections to mobile homes on fixed foundations and meeting other aesthetic and safety requirements increased somewhat the supply of affordable housing; state legislation to protect tenant rights and equities in condominium conversions helped stem to some extent the decreases in affordable housing arising from conversions and other impacts of gentrification.

Many local governments moved quickly to take advantage of these kinds of state legislation; some led the way by enacting local ordinances, which then formed the basis of even broader state legislation. In some cases, more progressive local governments found themselves constrained by new state legislation because of pressures in the legislatures from more conservative suburban and rural members.

Other initiatives and developments that were important in the eighties in dealing with housing affordability for low- and moderate-income purchasers and renters included the following:

- Experimentation with housing vouchers and housing allowances[100]

- Increased emphasis on rehabilitation in contrast to new construction (in 1986 rehab expenditures accounted for nearly 43 percent of all housing investment)[101]

- Mandated set-aside of a minimum percentage of building or development units for low- and moderate-income purchase or rent[102]

- Linkage of affordable housing to local government approval of commercial development (beginning with the Community Development Block Grant Act of 1974, requiring that local development plans include a housing assistance plan)[103]

- Urban homesteading and other creative uses of residential property taken over by local governments for tax delinquency or other reasons (for example, property is taken over at low or nominal cost by low-income family who rehabilitates it at own time and expense and then takes title)

In addition to building code reform, some other deregulatory proposals bore fruit, such as state and local legislation on mobile and other types of factory-built homes, which had the effect of requiring that local zoning and other land use regulations treat factory-built housing no differently from conventional site-built housing, other than in width and square-foot requirements generally applicable in the home manufacturing industry.[104] Since factory-built housing comprises between 15 and 30 percent (depending on the year) of all detached housing starts, it represents a major remaining source of moderately low-cost housing. (In perhaps a replay of consumer desires for compact cars a decade earlier, foreign manufacturers might point the way for bringing affordable housing back into reach of U.S. lower-income home seekers.)[105]

Trends toward tenant management associations in subsidized housing arose from a major drawback to "conventional public housing," wherein local housing agencies had constructed and managed large-scale multifamily developments— often high-rise—reserved for low-income occupancy. These buildings, because of their homogeneous nature, often became notorious urban ghettos, such as Pruitt-Igoe in St. Louis and the Cabrini-Green and Henry Horner developments in Chicago. Management often was characterized by what columnist Neal Peirce termed "foot-dragging public housing authorities with a plantation mentality toward their housing 'clients' " in describing how a tenant management corporation had transformed a public housing disaster into an economically viable situation.[106]

A number of states and localities enacted laws or ordinances in the seventies and eighties to redress economic leverage imbalances between landlords and tenants. Two of the most troublesome aspects of these relationships had been failures of landlords to make necessary repairs and retaliation through eviction, rent increases, or general harassment against tenants making complaints to code enforcement or other public agencies. A number of states made a tenant's obligation to pay dependent on the landlord's covenant to make repairs; some enacted "repair and deduct" legislation enabling tenants after proper notice to the landlord to make such repairs as necessary to correct code violations and deduct the amount of receipted bills from their rent obligations.[107]

Later Housing Policy Positions of State-Local Governments

The position of the NGA regarding housing needs and issues adopted in 1980 and modified in succeeding years proposed the following kinds of state actions, in addition to continuance of past programs of state housing finance agencies:

1. Consideration by states of using their pension funds to provide mortgages to public employees, shared-equity programs to lower initial down payments in return for a share of eventual capital gains, and direct provision of loans for single-family housing

2. Working with lending institutions, real estate developers, and local governments to encourage new housing production and reclamation of abandoned buildings

3. Examination of land development and housing policies and regulations to amend those that unnecessarily add to the production costs and, in collaboration with local governments, to reduce the building regulatory portion of the cost of new housing through model codes and supporting the introduction of new technologies[108]

Although these steps had been taken by a number of states, beginning in the seventies, the breadth of state programs reflected in the adoption of the policy statement seemed to show an approaching consensus among most of the states as to their roles and responsibilities in housing.

The policy position of the National Association of Counties (NACO), updated to 1986–87, in addition to endorsing linkage of community development and housing, a state building code, and housing assistance financing roles, included the following additional policy proposals for state, other local government, and county action: (1) by all governmental levels, to analyze the potential impact on housing costs of land use regulations considered for adoption; (2) to ensure opportunity for using manufactured housing; (3) dislocation assistance to ease gentrification impacts, and right of first refusal of tenants in rehabilitation and conversion actions; and (4) inclusion of a housing element in all county comprehensive plans.[109]

The fiscal, economic, and social costs of gentrification, in contrast to corresponding benefits, often are not given sufficient consideration in the formulation of community redevelopment plans. In addition to the human and economic costs of gentrification mentioned in the NACO platform, other negative aspects from the standpoint of the local budget include increased demands for services, infrastructure, and other amenities, other impacts on public services, and the problem of speculative increases in surrounding blighted property values that might be unsupportable in the long run. (Positive aspects are more obvious—decreasing vacancy rates, rising property values, better public safety and other stabilizing features, and visible examples of the central city as a good place to move into.)[110]

Key elements in the policy platform of the NLC relating to housing were the following:

1. In general, it supported the traditional federal housing assistance programs, but at a sharply increased level (400,000 units annually in the housing assistance categories plus 200,000 units annually in mortgage interest subsidization) and with a heavier emphasis on conservation and rehabilitation than in the past.

2. It agreed that vouchers might be a useful addition to existing programs, but argued that such vouchers do not add to housing stock that would be accessible to low-income people, and proposed instead an expanded Section 8 program serving all eligible households and conditioned on the highest of either local or federal standards, on the handling of all assistance payments through the local housing agency to the landlord involved, and on the allowance (presumably out of federal funds) of adequate administrative fees to the local agency.

3. It opposed "cashing out" housing assistance as a part of any reformed welfare program because of the unlikelihood that sufficiently large new infusions of money into the welfare system would be fiscally or politically tolerable.

4. It favored a limited role of state government in housing, except to the extent that the involvement brings a commensurate increase in state outlays for housing, and recommended that any such increase in involvement should come through consultation with the state municipal league (the organization of municipal officials within the state).

5. It proposed the possible eventual absorption of some or much federal housing assistance within an enlarged community development block grant, with the housing assistance plan element of the CDBG being the focus for such a transition.

6. It believed that as middle- and upper-class reinvestment in urban neighborhoods occurs, provision must be made through housing programs for low- and moderate-income and aged persons potentially displaced by such gentrification.[111]

The policy positions of the National Association of Housing and Redevelopment Officials (NAHRO), as they related to state and local responsibilities, urged that local government initiate or recommit itself to an ongoing and comprehensive planning process, and collaborate with private business, neighborhoods, and nonprofit citizens' groups to achieve community development goals.[112]

In draft state legislation prepared in 1984 as a part of its report on distressed communities, the ACIR included provisions on financial and other state housing activity drawn from the most comprehensive of the state laws then on the books, not limited to the specific steps proposed in the recommendations described earlier. Other less common provisions (with states from which they were primarily drawn shown in parentheses) included the following:

1. Energy utilization and basic repair loans and repayable grants (Minnesota) and loans for migratory labor facility rehabilitation (Maryland)

2. Rental assistance, both through state or local housing leasing initiatives and renter discovery of suitable units (Massachusetts)

3. Homeownership assistance in condominium and mobile home park conversions (California)

4. Issuance of taxable bonds for housing purposes (especially relevant after 1986 tax reform legislation) and state-local pension fund investment in such issues (Massachusetts)

5. Authorization for investment of state funds in real estate mortgages (Wyoming)

6. State-local relations in housing, including allocation of loan commitment ceilings by state housing finance agency (HFA), prior notification to local governments of state housing projects, and delegation of certain state housing decisions to local governments or authorities (for example, local management of a state-owned or financed project) (Minnesota and Maryland)

7. Reserving a portion of the tax increment in renewal projects for the provision of replacement housing (California)[113]

State-created Housing Trusts with Dedicated Revenue Sources

State-created housing trusts financed from taxes or fees imposed on real estate–related transactions or other revenue sources were a new development in the late eighties that seemed to have potential. Such housing trust funds provide a fiscal base for state and local support of low-income housing through construction subsidies, rental allowances, or other methods. The concept was based on the Interest on Lawyers' Trust Accounts (IOLTA) program that finances legal services to the poor. It was estimated that nationwide income from tenant security deposit, sale, and mortgage escrow interest could total $1.7 billion annually.

In 1985 and 1986 eight states enacted trust fund laws with revenue sources; they included California, using off-shore oil revenues; Florida and Maine, using taxes on real estate transactions or aspects thereof; and Connecticut, Kentucky, North Carolina, New York, and Rhode Island, using other sources. Local governments creating trust funds were Atlantic City, Dade County, Florida, Denver, Duluth, and Montgomery County, Maryland.[114]

New and Future State-Local-Private Initiatives and Options

The various statements of policy by organizations of state and local government, although marking a fairly active and creative role of these governments regarding low-income housing assistance as of the late eighties, obviously were not adequate for the future. For one thing, little was being said about public-private partnerships in housing, although the private-sector role in housing was dominant in many aspects. Second, the replacement of low-cost or otherwise affordable low-income housing that is demolished in the process of gentrification, urban redevelopment, or general economic growth is a problem cutting across the local government processes and agencies concerned with land use regulation, landlord-tenant affairs, housing, and economic development. Two crucial considerations often are neglected when low-income housing units are abolished or upgraded, or when residential land is up-zoned to higher density or to commercial use: (1) the replacement of a comparable number of affordable units for the low-income level and (2) the relocation of the people occupying the low-income units being demolished. The latter factor often involves litigation.[115] The cost of protecting the displaced persons from homelessness during the development process is likely to be much lower than the social and financial costs of trying to cope with the resulting homelessness at a later time.

Third, the emerging problem of the homeless and other negative spinoffs from gentrification—counterbalancing some of its very positive aspects in neighborhood revitalization and appearance—coupled with rapidly escalating housing costs in the late eighties, called for new ideas, including what columnist Neal Peirce termed "an alternative low-income housing supply system" that contrasted with programs that "in the name of helping the poor, provide windfalls for speculators, financiers, developers, and the construction industry and in the process, touch only a fraction of the problem."[116]

If a future federal financial support for low-income housing assistance, or its cash equivalent, at a level somewhat above that of the mid-eighties is assumed, state and local government and nonprofit organizations will need to bear a substantially larger fiscal share of this public policy area than was the case in the seventies and early eighties. The term "cash equivalent" is thrown into the assumption because of the apparently lower cost nationwide of federally assisting low-income housing by other than construction-oriented approaches. A switch to assisting poor people more directly than via the housing industry through new construction is not a foregone conclusion, however. The political constituency of the "housing coalition" (building trades, developers, architects, home build-ers, realtors, building supply manufacturers and distributors, mortgage bankers, savings and loan associations, and many other groups associated with housing and/or construction) is formidable, and only budgetary considerations and op-position to substantial increases in federal income taxes would be likely to provide counterbalances that would lead the Congress to consider low-cost alternatives.

There are strong economic arguments in favor of each of the two approaches: (1) via rental assistance to the renter through a voucher, housing allowance, or inclusion in an "income maintenance" replacement for the federal-state welfare system and (2) via subsidized mortgage financing of new and rehabilitated hous-ing with appropriate reservations for low-income owners or tenants. Two major arguments, among others—one economic and one political—support the con-struction-oriented approach, represented by earlier and more recent federal pro-grams such as conventional public housing, Section 236 rental assistance, Section 235 homeownership assistance, and Section 8 new construction and substantial rehabilitation. All of these were initiated on the basic principle of federal sub-sidization of the construction of new units or rehabbing of existing units, with the combination of the subsidy and what the low-income occupants could afford adding up to a fair rate of return to the builder or developer. This approach has a multiplier effect through the developer, builder, supplier, and wage-earner chain; it helps level out the ups and downs of the construction industry and exercises a somewhat stabilizing effect on the national economy. Second, it adds to total housing stock, an important consideration if there is a real shortage of adequate housing units as a totality—with much controversy over the "if."

On the political side, finding a majority at national, state, or most local levels in support of more public expenditure to help the poor is very difficult, as in the case of a housing voucher or rental allowance program; a construction ap-proach welds the housing coalition necessary to provide the necessary majority.[117] In the 1987 NLC poll cities were asked to indicate the most cost-effective federal housing vehicle. Seventy-three percent selected the housing elements in the community development block grant program; second was Section 8 existing housing, a direct renter-assistance program, with 47 percent. In the 20 percent range were rental rehabilitation and public housing modernization/operating sub-sidy programs. Low-income public housing (construction) and Section 8 newly constructed housing trailed with 12 and 10 percent, respectively. (The 444 re-spondents seemed fairly well distributed by size and geography; New York, San Diego, San Francisco, Detroit, Dallas, Philadelphia, Pittsburgh, Cleveland, St. Louis, and Denver were among the respondents.)[118]

As early as 1968 the Douglas Commission was arguing for a housing policy that would be targeted partially toward the use of community groups such as churches, charities, and other nonprofit organizations as bases for helping to house the poor. The potential role of these and other private-sector organizations reemerged as the severity of the low-income housing shortages and associated homeless populations became more apparent. Columnist Peirce, developer James Rouse, Ford and other foundations, and city and state officials began to explore less costly ways to help make low-income housing more available. Roles of public-private partnerships in community redevelopment and revitalization will be examined in the concluding section of this chapter. The housing element of these endeavors is summarized here.

- Considerable reductions in costs can be made by community groups in such ways as eliminating use of architects and general contractors, using used fixtures and furnishings in rehabilitation work, and making heavy use of community volunteers.

- Greater use can be made of many state, local, nonprofit, and private plans and programs, rather than unitary, masterminded, all-inclusive initiatives from the housing subcommittees of the U.S. House and Senate. (State housing programs in Virginia and Maryland depend on nonprofit groups to find eligible families and oversee newly renovated housing.)

- The Enterprise Foundation, founded in 1981 by James Rouse, whose firm developed the city of Columbia, Maryland, and major renewal projects in Boston, Norfolk, and elsewhere, raised $19 million and helped initiate large housing rehabilitation and related projects in the District of Columbia, Pittsburgh, Baltimore, Philadelphia, and Oakland.

- City governments, by imposing requirements upon new developments for housing linkage, reduced rents to low-income tenants, and other measures, are able to increase considerably the supply of available units. These requirements have a cost, of course, usually dissipated throughout the local real estate market.

- A real estate transfer or other special tax, imposed by local government, can help fund substantial additions to low-income housing; such was the plan initiated by the city of Chattanooga to build 500 new homes and refurbish over 13,000 through the period ending in 1996, with a nonprofit organization coordinating the effort and the city levying an earmarked tax.[119]

Neal Peirce noted that the key question in much of this is "How can you encourage home ownership or alternatives that give residents a real stake in their neighborhood?"[120] Many states, with Massachusetts, California, New York, Maryland, and Colorado leading, were endeavoring to find new approaches to the old and expensive issue of low-income housing. In addition to the cities mentioned earlier, Boston, Chicago, New York, Miami, Philadelphia, Minneapolis, Pittsburgh, Denver, Indianapolis, Oakland, and Cleveland were very active on the local government side.

Additional legislative or other initiatives that might be considered by state and local governments, some of which have been illustrated by examples in this section, include the following:

- Amendment of state-local surplus property legislation to require, as an additional step prior to selling at open auction any residential building or other structure potentially convertible into single- or multifamily occupancy for low-income tenants or purchasers via homesteading or some other route, examination by state and local housing agencies to ascertain its possible suitability for low-income housing purposes. (Squatters in fifty-eight abandoned city-owned buildings in New York transformed themselves into a mutual housing association and obtained loans to renovate the buildings for living space.)[121]

- Reappraising design, construction, and amenity standards with a view to lowering cost (middle-income standards for low-income housing raise costs and reduce the number of units obtainable from a given amount of dollars).

- Aggressive action by state and local governments to rehabilitate quickly and bring back into use an estimated 70,000 public housing units vacant due to disrepair.[122]

- Reassessment of rent control and its effects and appropriate amendatory or repeal action. Studies of rent control effects show that less abandonment occurs if rents are permitted to rise in relation to that charged when a vacancy occurs in a controlled unit, since rent control costs are shared between landlord and tenants recently moving in. They also show that strict controls provide short-run protection to tenants but entail the risk of harming the housing stock, while less restrictive controls shift part of the burden from landlords to more mobile tenants.[123]

- Encouraging better code enforcement and improving landlord-tenant equities through "repair and deduct" laws.

- Enlarging the role of nonprofit organizations in housing assistance programs and reassessing degrees of governmental control exercised over their participation (for example, should a local government have a veto power over a federal or state housing agency relationship with a nonprofit organization in the local community, or should local control be exercised through standards for general application?).

- Assessing possible trade-offs between elderly owners of large houses and the housing needs of low-income families with children in terms of property transactions, zoning changes, and potential housing-use economies.

- Possible use of community land trusts by nonprofit organizations to acquire and retain land and then effect long-term leases to private or public parties for re-lease to low- or moderate-income tenants.[124]

The Homeless

During the mid- to late eighties, the numbers of visible and identifiable homeless persons increased greatly. These were individuals without shelter, of all ages and ethnic groups, many of whom were sleeping in the open in the nonwinter months, some sleeping over grates, in building vestibules, and any other available sheltered place during the winter season. That the homeless had become a permanent problem was apparent as the recession of the early eighties ended, and as national unemployment rates dropped to 6 percent and below and to 3 percent in some urban areas, but without corresponding drops in the numbers of homeless men, women, and children. The number of homeless persons was estimated to be within a wide range of 250,000–350,000 (within a span of 192,000 to 586,000 in a report by the U.S. Department of Housing and Urban Development [HUD])[125] all the way to 3 million.[126]

The composition of the homeless population has been hard to pin down beyond certain points. It has generally been agreed that the largest single category of the homeless are the unemployed, followed by the mentally ill and persons afflicted with alcohol and other drug abuse, no category being exclusive of another. Two distinct governmental actions—one state and the other local—are agreed as highly contributory to the homeless population: (1) discharge of patients from state mental institutions prior to the availability of adequate community mental health facilities, with the latter hampered by lack of federal, state, and local funding and by strong neighborhood opposition, particularly in urban areas, to the opening of such facilities in their community; and (2) the disappearance of single-room occupancy hotels in central cities, sometimes for code violations and often for economic reasons, and the failure to provide for alternate facilities.

The *National Municipal Policy* of the NLC described the nature and causes of the problem along the following lines. The homeless problem exists in both urban and rural areas (although it is much more noticeable and acute in the cities) and increasingly involves families, largely families headed by women. The homeless group has a disproportionate number of minorities, people with physical and mental disabilities, and others who have failed economically. The homeless condition is an assortment of personal, social, economic, and political problems, often present in combinations. The causes noted by NLC, in addition to the three mentioned at the outset—unemployment, mental handicaps, and substance/alcohol abuse—include lack of affordable housing for families and individuals, income support, and job training and employment assistance. NACO and NGA policy statements have expressed concerns and descriptions similar to these, though in more general terms.

However, among all the state and local government organizations, the U.S. Conference of Mayors (USCM) addressed the homeless problem in the most specific terms. That was understandable, because the problem has been concentrated in the large central cities, and the mayor must lead efforts to meet, and hopefully improve, the situation. In 1987 the twenty-six cities led by the mayors making up the USCM'S Task Force on Hunger and Homelessness were surveyed as to the conditions of hunger, homelessness, housing availability, and general economic conditions. On homelessness, the responses, in brief, were the following:

- In all cities but one, the demand for shelter increased in 1987.
- The twenty-six-city average for unmet shelter demand was 23 percent.
- The condition was expected to increase in nearly all the surveyed cities.
- The causes most identified were (1) lack of affordable housing; (2) mental illness and lack of services for the mentally ill; and (3) employment-related problems.
- The average percentages of elements of the homeless population were as follows for

family status: single men (49), families with children (33), single women (14), and unaccompanied youth (4); for personal condition: substance abuse (35), severely mentally ill (23), employed full- or part-time (22).

• Twenty-two of the cities were using locally generated revenues for shelters and related services; seventeen were using state grants; and all but one were using federal grants.

The highest percentage of employed shelter occupants was in San Antonio (54), with Detroit, Norfolk, New York, Portland, and Portsmouth reporting none. Substance abusers were proportionately highest in Philadelphia and Portland (60). Some cities reported none. Mentally ill percentages were 40 or more in Louisville, Minneapolis, San Juan, and Seattle.[127]

In contrast to the general surveys by HUD and the large city survey by the USCM, the Institute for Research on Poverty undertook a longitudinal study of a sample of homeless people in Minneapolis over a four-month period in 1985–86 and compared the results with other sample studies in Chicago and urban Ohio. The three studies found the homeless to be predominantly male (75–80 percent); age in the thirties (average 32, 33, and 39); education, three years of high school; marital status, never married or separated-divorced, with presently marrieds averaging only 6 to 9 percent; prior crime conviction, 54 percent in the Minneapolis group; psychiatric hospitalization, 18.5, 30.6, and 23.0 percent, respectively; and employment any time in prior month from 22 to 39 percent, and full-time employed, only 4 to 9 percent. The Minneapolis sample showed less direct relation with mental illness than in other reports.[128]

One factor possibly accounting for some of the statistical disparities as to marital status of homeless persons (largely single men in some surveys, many families with children in others) is that of "welfare hotel" occupants. Housing of public assistance recipients with children in welfare hotels has been an established but questionable and controversial feature of the welfare system in a number of states and cities for decades. If only "street people," homeless shelter occupants, and applicants for shelter spaces were counted, smaller numbers and a substantially different marital composition would result.

Possible state and local government policy, fiscal, and other actions needed to help deal with the homeless problem are numerous and often controversial. The NGA policy position recognized that states that bore responsibility for deinstitutionalization actions had exacerbated the problems of the poor and had increased the homeless population of individuals with no identifiable, permanent residence.[129] The organizations of both state and local governments believe strongly that the federal role in support of community mental health facilities as initially outlined in the Mental Health Systems Act of 1980 but repealed in 1981 should be reinstated, and that the Emergency Food and Shelter program should be continued.

Most but not all the items listed here for state and local government policy consideration are drawn from the NLC *National Municipal Policy, 1987*. The state agenda includes consideration of the following, not in any specific order of priority:

1. Revision where appropriate of legislation dealing with commitment of mentally ill persons to hospital care or enrollment for supervised care (that is, community mental health facilities, personal care boarding home, and so on). At the end of 1986, six states had enacted legislation to make it possible to commit persons for reasons in addition to the current criterion of danger to self or to others; persons unable to provide for basic needs, such as shelter, or who would suffer severe and abnormal mental, emotional, or physical distress if not hospitalized could also be committed. These are the criteria in a model law devised in 1983 by the American Psychiatric Association. Following the enactment of the broader legislation in the state of Washington, the number of people involuntarily committed nearly doubled, and half of those desiring voluntary treatment were turned away. (Thus an apparent prerequisite for legislative changes in commitment bases would be the availability of adequate facilities.)

2. Ensuring the provision of adequate "general assistance" payments to homeless persons if they qualify on income grounds.

3. Financial and technical assistance to local governments in dealing with their homeless populations.

4. Participation in the federal-state emergency assistance component of the AFDC categorical welfare program.

5. Making available surplus state supplies and quarters such as National Guard armories, bedding, blankets, and so on.

6. Cessation of state restrictions on length of stays in state-funded shelters for battered women and children, and requirement of transition assistance including job training, health care, and mental health care services upon departure.

7. Helping finance construction of low-income housing through the various housing finance mechanisms described earlier.

8. Reviewing and revising procedures for patient discharge from state hospitals and after-care services to ensure the transition to adequate housing.

9. Reviewing and revising foster care termination arrangements to ensure successful transition into independent living.

10. Coordinating state vocational training, employment, mental health, and homeless institutions and services.

11. Precluding neighborhood or local government absolute veto of state-financed community mental health facility sites; if the selected site were vetoed, the local unit would be required to provide an alternative site. (The "not in my neighborhood" syndrome applies also to other public facility siting and subsidized housing.)

For local governments, the NLC proposed the following actions:

1. Needs assessment and integration of housing needs into overall human services and facilities planning.

2. Establishing and operating emergency shelters and outreach facilities.

3. Making available surplus school and other public spaces for use in emergencies.

4. Use of city- or county-owned tax foreclosure properties for housing homeless families.

5. Working with school boards to waive residency requirements in providing vocational training and transportation to homeless children.

6. Adopting zoning practices that ensure the availability of necessary sites for shelters and transitional facilities.

7. Decriminalizing vagrancy-specific laws and repealing ordinances prohibiting public sleeping.

8. Preventing unnecessary evictions and providing emergency rental assistance.

9. Fostering public-private partnerships for homeless care.

10. Establishing inclusionary zoning and linkage programs to mitigate the loss of low-income housing and to add new units to the housing stock.

11. Public and/or private acquisition of lodging facilities and single-room occupancy hotels for shelters and permanent housing.

12. Coordinating local Private Industry Council efforts to provide employment and training opportunities to homeless individuals.

Among the many problems confronting state-local governments in the nineties, coping with the tragedy of the homeless may well be the most difficult because it comprises so many elements. To change directions, laws, and procedures for treating the mentally ill is a tremendous task in itself.

THE PUBLIC INFRASTRUCTURE PROBLEM

An adequate network of physical facilities over, by, and through which products and information are transferred from generators and producers to users and consumers has been an essential for economic progress since the Industrial Revolution. Roads, ships, railroads, mail service, and the telegraph were sufficient through the 1880s. As the pace of scientific advance quickened throughout the ensuing century, the demand for newer, faster, stronger, and better facilities to support the extractive, manufacturing, and service sectors increased commensurately. This network of physical facilities has come to be described by the word 'infrastructure.''

Much of the nation's physical infrastructure is publicly owned; a greater proportion is public in most of the other industrialized countries, although the proportion is decreasing gradually both abroad and here. Public physical infrastructure in the United States represents a modest share of total government spending, as shown in figure 4.6 (declining from 14 to 7 percent over the quarter century 1960–85). However, state-local spending for hospital and highway infrastructure is outpaced only by education and welfare.

The U.S. Postal Service, augmented by private delivery services, comprises an important part of the nation's public infrastructure; the same is true of the

Figure 4.6
Public Works Spending as a Percentage of Total Public Expenditures, 1960–84

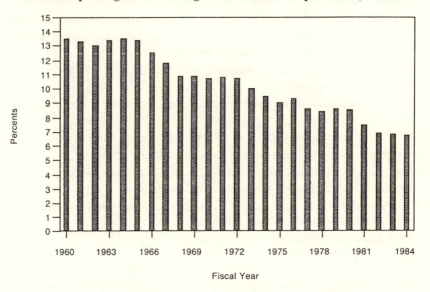

Source: National Council on Public Works Improvement, *The Nation's Public Works: Defining the Issues*, September 1986, 49

telecommunications industry, which is privately owned. However, primary attention here will be devoted to the categories that loom largest in intergovernmental expenditure and where the physical facilities are ends in themselves, in contrast to public buildings.

A Public Works Improvement Act was passed by the Congress and became law in 1984 (Public Law 98–501), establishing a National Council on Public Works Improvement (NCPWI) and directing it to submit interim reports and a final report in early 1988 on the state of the nation's public physical infrastructure, with recommendations as to alternative methods of meeting national infrastructure needs to effectuate balanced growth and economic development. The council carried out a substantial research program, and due to its depth, diversity, and recency, much of the analysis presented here is drawn from NCPWI-sponsored studies, as well as from data and findings from the CBO, the GAO, the Joint Economic Committee of the Congress, and other sources. Eight major categories of public works will be reviewed here, with three issue areas of each being covered—governmental roles, financing, and regulation. The eight categories fall into three groups: (1) transportation: highways, streets, and bridges; mass transit; and aviation; (2) water: water resources (ports, inland navigation, flood control, urban drainage, dam safety, and shoreline protection); water supply; and wastewater treatment; (3) waste: solid waste and hazardous waste. How to provide and finance the development and maintenance of these infrastructure modes in the nineties is the first major issue; second is the harmonization, through a combination of public regulation and incentives to the private sector, of infrastructure availability and, in growing areas, the staging of physical development so that congestion is minimized and fiscal equity between private developers and the general public is maintained.

Background and Present Governmental Roles

As shown in Table 4.6, expenditures for these eight categories of infrastructure grew in constant dollars from $60.4 billion in 1960 to over $100 billion in 1985. Highways increased only modestly, from $36 billion to $45 billion, while mass transit grew by nearly six times. However, in 1960 most expenditures in the transit category were private, but by 1975 most were public. Figure 4.7 shows the relative proportion of public infrastructure expenditure going to each of the major categories.

The issue of governmental roles will be explored by (1) an examination of existing roles; (2) a review of contrasting proposals for changes in roles and financing, followed by a set of proposals generated by studies in 1986 and 1987 under the aegis of the NCPWI; and (3) criteria that might be used at national, state, and local levels in clarifying functional and fiscal responsibilities. Use will be made of the research done by the NCPWI and of reports from the CBO and the Joint Economic Committee of the Congress, as well as other contrasting views on the issues.

Roles of federal, state, local, and private sectors in 1987. Relative roles and the emphasis given to capital expenditures in contrast to those for operation and maintenance (O&M) were in a period of substantial change in the late eighties for most of the eight major infrastructure categories. This was especially the case for water resources, wastewater treatment, and hazardous waste. A major aspect of these changes was reflected in the fact of decreasing growth rates in public spending for infrastructure (from 3.6 percent of GNP in 1960 to 2.6 percent in 1985), with sharp decreases in capital outlay and sharp increases for operation and maintenance.

Some principal recent and emerging changes in public infrastructure and associated causal factors were the following:

- O&M outlays were exceeding those for capital. (Highways, large airports, inland waterways, ports, and, to a large extent, wastewater treatment systems were mostly in place, while repair, maintenance, and rehabilitation costs for these large systems had been increasing sharply.)
- Private-sector roles in O&M were growing moderately in solid waste, hazardous waste, and local bus transit and somewhat in a few other areas, and were likely to increase for capital financing in water. (The growing attractiveness of contracting out in such areas as solid waste collection and treatment and wastewater treatment plant operation and the impact of water resource cost sharing seemed to be more than enough to offset declines attributable to tax reform.)

Table 4.6
Public Works Spending by Major Mode and Level of Government, 1960 and 1985

(Amounts in billions of 1984 dollars)

	1960						1985					
	Fed.		State		Local		Fed.		State		Local	
	Amt.	%	Amt.	%	Amt.	%	Amt.	%	Amt.	%	Amt.	%
Highways	$12.19	34	$15.50	43	$8.57	24	$13.23	29	$19.22	43	$12.63	28
Airports	1.65	60	.08	3	1.00	37	4.15	58	.37	5	2.58	36
M. Transit	0	0	.58	24	1.86	76	3.37	26	2.29	18	7.34	56
W. Resrces	4.26	69	1.05	17	.84	14	3.69	51	2.15	30	1.40	19
Wastewater	.17	4	.12	3	3.96	93	3.28	26	.25	2	9.11	72
W. Supply	.37	6	0	0	6.17	94	.74	5	.35	2	13.75	93
Solid Waste	0	0	0	0	2.16	100	0	0	0	0	5.04	100
Total	$18.64	31	$17.33	29	$24.49	40	$28.46	27	$24.64	23	$51.85	50

Source: National Council on Public Works Improvement (NCPWI), *The Nation's Public Works: Defining the Issues*, September 1986 Report to the President and the Congress (Washington D.C.: NCPWI c/o ACIR), for 1960–84 data; 1985 data from estimates provided to NCPWI by Apogee Research, Inc., September 29, 1987. Council's final report, *Fragile Foundations: A Report on America's Public Works*, February 1988, available from U.S. Government Printing Office.

Figure 4.7
Proportionate Public Spending for Major Infrastructure Categories, 1985

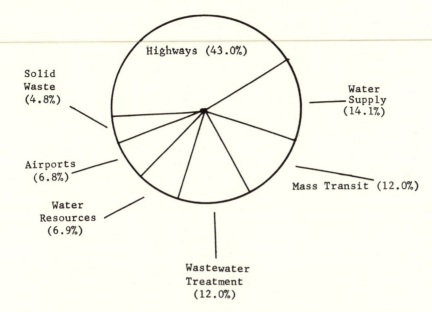

Source: National Council on Public Works Improvement (NCPWI), *The Nation's Public Works: Defining the Issues*, Report to the President and the Congress, 1986, 2; unpublished table by Apogee Research, Inc., September 1987.

• State and local governmental roles were increasing in relation to the federal role in most categories due to federal deficit problems, water resource cost sharing, and weaker justification for federal O&M assistance where large systems are completed or nearly so.

Federal roles in three principal role measures (policy and standard setting, capital financing, and facility ownership/operations) in 1987 were reported as follows:

• In policy and standard setting, the federal role appeared leading or dominant in (*a*) interstate highways; (*b*) deep-port dredging; (*c*) waterways and water resource dams; (*d*) air traffic control; (*e*) wastewater treatment; and (*f*) hazardous waste.

• In capital financing for infrastructure, as in all other federal aid to state and local governments, the role was decreasing. However, the federal role remained leading or dominant in (*a*) nonlocal highways and bridges; (*b*) mass transit; (*c*) water resources; (*d*) small airports; (*e*) air traffic control; and (*f*) wastewater treatment.

• In ownership/operations and O&M financing, the federal interest was leading or dom-inant only in (*a*) port dredging, (*b*) inland waterway locks and navigational aids, (*c*) major dams, and (*d*) air traffic control; it was nonexistent or negligible in all of the other categories, except that it was moderate in operational assistance to mass transit.

State-local and private-sector roles appeared to be as follows:

- Although federal financing was significant in all of the infrastructure areas except solid waste and water supply, state-local governments were providing 95 percent of O&M public financing.
- The state-local role was dominant in the policy, priority-setting, construction/ownership, and operations areas except for air traffic control, port dredging, inland waterway locks, and federally owned dams.
- Generally, the private-sector role was strongest in programs having sharper goals, where recapture of service costs through charges is feasible, such as the benefits to users of hazardous waste, water supply, and solid waste services. (Almost all hazardous waste management facilities were privately owned and operated; the private role in solid waste was growing; 16 percent of the population was being served by privately owned and operated water systems.)
- The private financial role was highest in water supply and port landside facilities; although small, the private role was growing rapidly in major airport expansion and toll highways and in contract operation of facilities, except for water resource facilities. Even contracting for air traffic control was being considered as an option.

Regulatory aspects of infrastructure are of two major types in the eight modes being examined here. (1) Most of the ''environmental'' infrastructure programs came into being because of the perceived need for federal regulation of the subject area—wastewater treatment, hazardous waste, and water supply (and the potential additional subcategory of underground aquifer conservation, protection, and enhancement). (2) The other federally aided programs, undertaken primarily for economic development purposes, have had attached to them a variety of federal conditions. Some of these have been tied to the specific category, such as beautification, speed limits and control of drunk driving in the highway program, and discount fares for senior citizens and a union veto on use of aid funds in the mass transit program. Other requirements are governmentwide, extending across the entire direct federal expenditure and grant-aid spectrum; all programs involving direct or assisted construction must provide for relocation of displaced people or businesses, environmental assessments or impact statements, and payment of prevailing (usually union-scale) wage rates pursuant to the Davis-Bacon Act.

The program-specific regulatory needs and objectives must be matched against the extent of financial participation if economies and diseconomies of federal and other governmental roles are to be properly assessed from an economic and fiscal point of view. Data for this purpose are not available; some estimates have been made, with state highway administrators concluding that something like a 20 percent additional cost accompanies federal aid involvement in a highway or highway facility.

Infrastructure revenue sources. In most of the categories except water resources, the principal revenue sources consisted of general-obligation or revenue bonds for capital outlay, with interest and retirement of principal being part of the annual operating budget. For O&M costs, revenues comprised a combination of charges to users and other categories of UBF, plus a subsidy from governmental budgets to cover the difference between UBF and expenditure requirements, as described in chapter 3. On occasion, special charges upon polluters and other "responsible parties" may be a part of income.

Research, technology, and experimentation is an essential part of the infrastructure equation. Aside from federally conducted or sponsored research in highways and in some of the environmental regulatory programs, a great deal of research and experimentation with new approaches and technologies has been going on in state-local governments and the private sector. Unfortunately, the rigidity of much federal enabling legislation has provided little incentive for these governments or private enterprise to strive for more cost-effective approaches.

Needed Role Changes

Contrasting views on needed rate changes cover a broad spectrum. Following are summaries from various sources, other than the organized set of studies commissioned by the NCPWI.

An expanded federal role. A report of an infrastructure advisory committee to the Joint Economic Committee of the Congress in 1984 recommended four basic changes in governmental roles: (1) creation of a National Infrastructure Fund to bring about the establishment of a national capital pool from which interest-free loans to state and local governments could be made; (2) development of a coordinated national infrastructure needs assessment program; (3) congressional review of infrastructure standards; and (4) an early evaluation of statutory and administrative rules governing federally aided infrastructure projects.[130] The national pool would be added to then-current programs, with the latter subject to restructuring after the proposed reviews.

The Committee on National Urban Policy of the National Research Council in 1983 argued for the development of a "national system of infrastructure" and also for a national infrastructure bank. It also urged an active federal role in connection with "the need to assess need."[131]

Not surprisingly, given the magnitude of federal aid in the various infrastructure categories, several of the organizations of state and local governments have maintained strong policy positions in favor of continued federal aid in these fields, but also have urged greater flexibility in the aid-program structures.[132]

A reduced or nonexpanded federal role. In a 1983 report the CBO set forth three strategies for "correcting inefficiencies stemming from current federal policies": (1) adjusting federal user fees both to produce a reliable measure of national needs and to correct present misalignments among users; (2) limiting the federal role to infrastructure investments with clear national importance; (3)

redirecting existing federal aid to alter the bias toward capital-intensive investment decisions.[133]

The CBO made recommendations on three of the major infrastructure categories—highways, wastewater treatment, and dams/waterways. In the second
chapter of its 1983 report the CBO observed that though federal, state, and local
highway interests often overlap, the extent of national interest varied considerably
among the various highway programs. "If existing federal highway resources
were concentrated on roads of greatest national importance, aid for all but the
Interstate and Primary systems, along with their related bridge projects, could
be dropped." The report further pointed out that "such a shift would place the
full burden of financing Secondary and Urban roads on state and local governments. . . . This burden could be eased by reducing the federal tax on motor fuel
by 3 cents per gallon, permitting the states to raise their tax revenues by $3.4
billion a year—enough to replace fully the reduced federal aid."

On dams and waterways, the 1983 report again set forth options for change
in pointing out that "financial accountability for water projects could be spread
among all levels of government by increasing the nonfederal share . . . and implementing user fees. . . . Such changes would result in higher prices for water
resource services for direct beneficiaries and for nonfederal governments. In
turn, water resources officials would be more likely to promote only the most
efficient water projects. . . . Three alternatives to current policy—a federal loan
program, a redirection of the federal role, and institution of block grants—could
be effective in furthering this goal."

On wastewater treatment, a 1985 CBO report examined four options: (a)
continuing current policy; (b) the (Reagan) administration's four-year phaseout
proposal; (c) replacing project grants with state revolving loan funds; and (d)
continuing current policy with regulatory reforms. On the fourth option, the
report noted that "the Congress could instead view secondary treatment plants
as only one of a number of investments to achieve cleaner water. Hence, efficiency would no longer be defined as achieving secondary treatment at the lowest
cost, but instead, achieving clean water by any means at the lowest national
cost."[134]

T. G. Palmer in a 1983 report recommended maximum privatization of public
physical infrastructure, especially the yet-to-be-constructed portions. He cited
two major adverse characteristics in a public approach to infrastructure: (1)
exaggerated needs emanating from bureaucrats and engineers (if a facility isn't
perfect, it isn't good enough); and (2) the distorting effect of public programs
toward new construction and the attractiveness of consultant fees, cost overruns,
and the naming of facilities after prominent political figures.[135]

The ACIR in a 1984 report found that although some of the nation's infrastructure was suffering serious problems, "most infrastructure problems are
manageable with existing financing mechanisms. Coordinated federal, state, and
local action, however, is required in many instances to make existing programs
more efficient in physical infrastructure renewal." There were five dissents from

another recommendation that implied opposition to increases in federal financing—by two congressmen, one senator, one governor, and one state legislator.[136]

Findings and Recommendations from the NCPWI Studies

With the exception of solid waste, each of the other seven modal reports[137] mentioned the desirability of some shift in current governmental roles.[137] In general, most changes called for shifts in responsibility away from federal agencies and toward state and local bodies—that is, giving the responsibilities to the levels of government that directly operate and maintain most infrastructure services. Only in certain aspects of environmental regulation and hazardous waste management were proposals made to expand the federal role.[138]

The reports noted both general and specific shortcomings in present intergovernmental and public-private-sector roles in public infrastructure. In terms of current and prospective "states of condition," highways, water resources (as improved by 1986 to require very substantial nonfederal matching [50 percent or more] on each project), solid waste, and wastewater treatment seemed to be performing at or close to the adequacy level; aviation and water supply quite well; and mass transit and hazardous waste badly needing improvement.

On the financial side, two major recommendations dominated the reports: (1) pricing proposals, including marginal or incremental pricing, such as for peak use; and (2) low-capital approaches, such as conservation and other measures that could substitute for or stretch out the need for new facilities. These two thrusts related closely to public-private-sector roles because they formed a basis for considerably greater private participation, along with UBF approaches examined earlier.

Two other common threads ran through the recommendations: (1) an expanded role for research, especially at the federal level in hazardous waste, in product modification to lessen generation of solid waste and in several other areas, and in relaxation of federal barriers to state, local, and private experimentation with more cost-effective means of achieving program objectives; and (2) a sharpened and clarified federal role in the regulatory area.

On the private-sector role, the reports found the potential to be high in wastewater treatment plant operation and in providing hazardous waste, water supply, and solid waste services. The reports found that despite present legal barriers, opportunities exist for a considerably increased role in highways (toll roads), mass transit (reincarnation of private ownership, especially buses), and paratransit. The shift from 100 percent federal financing in water resources might automatically push the private sector into a larger role, especially in port landside facilities.

In assembling the often-conflicting views summarized here, it would be well to examine each of them in the light of criteria listed in the "Sorting Out National and State-Local Responsibilities" section of chapter 2, especially the one in which national action is warranted if the fiscal magnitudes are beyond the capacity of state and local governments and are not susceptible to user-based financing. This criterion argues against some but not all of the federal aid elements in the infrastructure area.

However, the magnitude criterion, along with special legal and regulatory circumstances, argues for considerably increased federal financial involvement in the hazardous waste area, which is discussed at some length in chapter 6. Under the various criteria in chapter 2, the national interest is highest in the interstate highway system and its bridges, high-volume deep-water ports, high-volume inland waterways, and some water resource projects where full cost recovery on all parts of the project is not feasible or fair. Turning back the noninterstate portions of the highway program to the states would necessitate the coincident transfer of part of the federal gasoline tax, which would allow state discretion as to the highway-transit mix. In general, the thrust of the NCPWI modal report recommendations comports well with the various sorting-out criteria in chapter 2.

The State Government Role in Helping Infrastructure Problems

States have an important responsibility in assisting local governments financially and providing technical assistance to the smaller local units on engineering and other operating problems. Although most physical infrastructure can be financed out of user charges and earmarked gasoline taxes, there are always up-front costs in capacity expansion and in new construction. In its report on distressed communities, adopted in 1983 and published in 1985, the ACIR developed draft state legislation for state assistance to local units with lesser fiscal capacity in infrastructure repair and reconstruction. Major optional provisions of the draft bill were (1) creation of an interagency council for state and local physical infrastructure for the purpose of state-local consultation, planning, and coordination; (2) creation of a state Community Facilities Financing Corporation to issue revenue bonds and provide loan assistance to local units through purchase of local bonds or guarantee of such bonds; (3) creation of a Community Facilities Revolving Loan Fund from which self-liquidating loans would be made; and (4) creation of a grant and loan fund to be financed from state general-obligation bonds and legislative appropriations, plus repayments from local units. Priority for grant and loan assistance would be limited to distressed local communities, defined as those in which the median family income fell into the bottom quartile for all local governmental units in the state.[139]

Growth Management and Infrastructure Availability

Beginning in the seventies, some state governments and more local governments became increasingly concerned about the pace of commercial and residential development and its impact upon urban and rural environments and the amenities associated therewith. As time passed, state legislatures began to set up ground rules under which growth limitation controls could be imposed at the local level.[140] Florida enacted a series of growth management laws, the most comprehensive being in 1985. Previous and potential legal challenges have made it necessary that state and local governments proceed carefully in imposing land use controls. However, one area not tested in the higher courts as of 1988 might provide a strong base of defense for these governments—limitations on commercial and residential development based on the availability of the necessary public physical infrastructure to accommodate the increased population, traffic, and other impacts to be created by the proposed development.

In growing localities and multicounty regions a serious lag often develops between governmental approval of a development and the provision of the necessary public facilities to service it. The consequences are especially acute in the case of surface transportation, water supply, and wastewater treatment. Legislation may be needed in a number of states, along with implementing ordinances at the local level, to require local governing bodies in the exercise of land use regulatory powers to ascertain, prior to approval of sizeable industrial, commercial, or residential projects, that the necessary infrastructure is already available, or if not, will come on line by the time it is needed to serve the new development. Similar action on the part of substate regional bodies, or in their absence by the state itself, could also be required.

For example, in 1972 Montgomery County, Maryland, enacted an Adequate Public Facility Ordinance providing that no preliminary plan of subdivision could be approved unless the county planning body had determined that "public facilities are adequate to support and service the area of the proposed subdivision." In addition to road access and capacity, necessary public facilities were defined to include those "such as police stations, firehouses, health clinics and schools."[141] Key provisions of the ordinance appear in appendix 4.D. Legislation along the same lines was adopted at the state level in Florida in 1985.[142]

PUBLIC-PRIVATE PARTNERSHIPS FOR COMMUNITY REVITALIZATION

Of the thousands of neighborhood- or community-based civic and other non-profit organizations involved in partnerships with local governments, a great majority exist for the pursuit of community economic development and/or socioeconomic stabilization. Public-private-sector relationships of several types were examined in chapter 3; here partnerships for community development and revitalization will be reviewed.

Number and Types of Community Development Partnerships

Public-private partnerships operating for purposes of community development number in the many thousands, so many that only the major objectives, approaches, and organizational forms can be summarized here. There are no census-type or other organized data available that would permit description through tables or charts. They are increasing both in numbers and varieties; as new ventures are undertaken, an occasional new approach worth replicating elsewhere appears. The Committee for Economic Development (CED),[143] the National Association of Housing and Redevelopment Officials (NAHRO),[144] the U.S. Department of Housing and Urban Development (HUD),[145] and the Ford Foundation[146] have published highly useful information and examples. Also useful have been the proceedings of three conferences on public-private partnerships in 1982–83, cosponsored by the U.S. Conference of Mayors (USCM) and the Atlantic Richfield Company (ARCO), involving many state and local organizations, business, government, and community leaders, and other public- and private-sector executives.[149]

Sectoral Context for Community Development Organizations

The 1982 CED report on urban public-private partnerships provides a useful sectoral context within which community development populations can be viewed, beginning with public- and private-sector roles.[148] The public-sector financial and operating roles in this field were described in the preceding sections dealing with infrastructure and housing/homeless issues. The private-sector role comprises direct activities by business firms that contribute money, expertise, and facilities to community foundations, civic organizations, and other groups, including public-sector endeavors. The not-for-profit part of the private sector and the structure of the nonprofit corporation provide the bases for most public-private partnerships for community development.

The community development activity of nonprofit organizations is concentrated in three categories—foundations, intermediary organizations, and community/neighborhood-based self-help organizations. Foundation support and other activity may rest in the general-purpose foundations such as Ford, MacArthur, Dayton-Hudson, and countless others, or in foundations with objectives and activity concentrated in the community development area such as the Enterprise Foundation, which grew out of the for-profit activities of the Rouse companies.

Intermediary organizations provide financial, technical assistance, informational, and other backstopping services to assist foundations, corporations, and other donor organizations in formulating and channeling the housing and community development part of their contributions budget. On the financial assistance side, the Local Initiatives Support Corporation (LISC) is the major national supporter of local community development partnerships.

LISC was founded in 1979 as a national nonprofit enterprise, organized as a joint effort of the Ford Foundation, with a $4.75 million contribution, and of six major private firms, collectively contributing $4.6 million. By 1986 LISC was reported to have assets of over $100 million and was assisting 375 organizations in 35 states, with projects in 118 towns and cities. A 1983 outside evaluation of LISC-supported activities showed that its "speculative demand" category of projects (the other two being "assured demand" and "non-marketable socially valued") scored 43 percent in production of expected output, 23 percent in expected financial return to sponsor, and 84 percent in expected financial return to LISC.[149]

In addition to foundations, other major financial support for community development has come from local, regional, and national banks, religious groups, charities, and individual corporations. National backstopping organizations have included the National Development Council (organization help), Center for Community Change (technical assistance and publications), Development Training Institute (training of local partnership organizers and managers), and the National Cooperative Bank, federally initiated, later "privatized" (loans to cooperatives).[150]

Financial support comes also from local, state, and federal governments. The local operating or delivery agents for state programs for housing, community development, and aid for distressed communities frequently are nonprofit partnership organizations. Significant help comes also from local government shares of the federal Community Development Block Grant (CDBG) program. In 1987 a panel formed under the aegis of HUD's National Program for Community Development Excellence selected eighty-nine local partnership projects for recognition, of which ten received awards for "national excellence." Seven of these were to local public-private partnerships of the community development corporation type (such as one formed in 1976 at Chinle, Arizona, by the Navajo Nation for a successful shopping center, and the York Road Planning Area Committee in Baltimore for the rehabilitation of a deteriorating commercial strip).[151]

Community development corporations (CDCs) comprise the most numerous and important of the community development partnership categories. Other types of these "self-help organizations" identified in the CED report are (1) cooperatives, owned and controlled by their members, such as Jubilee Housing in Washington, D.C.; (2) community development credit unions, which are financial cooperatives, extending credit to residents and investing community resources for improvement purposes; and (3) community investment trusts established by concerned individuals.[152]

Community Development Corporations: Characteristics

CDCs in 1987 were estimated to number between three and five thousand. Neal Peirce and Carol Steinbach note three basic characteristics of CDCs: community initiation and control, economic development objectives, and targeted attention.

Legal control of the organization through a board composed largely of community residents is an essential for public cohesion in support of the organization.

Also, in contrast to corporate boards and many public-sector advisory or governing boards, the time and talent commitments of individual board members to an active, working role has been the rule with few exceptions. Most CDCs have been directed predominantly toward economic development objectives, although many embrace human services objectives as well; the latter are essential because community revitalization depends on achieving social as well as economic vitality. Unless organized specifically for commercial or industrial objectives, most other CDCs embrace housing—usually housing rehabilitation—as a major objective.

Practically all CDCs have been organized around a defined geographic area of an overlying unit of government. This often is legally as well as substantively necessary, because if all or some board members are elected by members of the corporation, eligibility must include a legal residence. An election from a whole city would be highly unmanageable. However, the type of area varies; some comprise the most depressed neighborhoods; others are formed in working-class neighborhoods as a stabilizing and arresting rather than a resurrecting force. CDCs exist in rural as well as urban areas, often rural depressed regions such as Appalachia, the Ozarks, or the Mississippi Delta.[153]

CDCs are most prevalent in the older northeastern and midwestern cities and in some western cities. The Chicago and Boston areas tend to lead in the most and strongest CDCs, with New York, Philadelphia, Pittsburgh, Cleveland, Denver, Washington, Hartford, Miami, Indianapolis, St. Louis, Los Angeles, Baltimore, and others also prominent. With some exceptions, these include the most troubled cities of the seventies, many of which were seeing better times by the late eighties. Financial overhead is austere. "Lucky is the CDC with more assets than a couple of typewriters, a computer, copier and coffee machine. And lots of folding chairs."[154]

CDCs: Activities, Legal Structure, Partnership Barriers, and Issues of Future Scale

CDC activities cover the entire spectrum of community development objectives. The project activity groupings used by HUD in its 1987 awards program for local partnerships and the number falling into each group were commercial, 50; housing, 40; public facilities, 33; public services, 23; industrial, 22; and other, 16. The ten national awards embraced the following elements: commercial, 7; housing and public facilities, 5 each; industrial, 3; and public services, 1. The approaches and techniques used by the national awardees were local development corporation organizational form, 6; tax credits, 5; bond issues, 4; job training, 2; and loan pools, enterprise zones, and deregulation, 1 each. Various other techniques were used by all ten.[155]

Peirce and Steinbach described the three-decade history of CDCs as follows. The first generation was pioneering and expansive; though abuse was a rarity and many projects were successful, there were enough economic failures to raise a yellow flag and a misuse of federal funds to raise a red one for some overly expansive or aggressive leaders. The second generation was leaner and widely diverse, with some new CDCs growing out of low-income housing groups, others from the community action agencies, and some from immigrant populations, all with a variety of federal support sources, both on the development and human services sides. The third generation, in the eighties, was reassessing the marketplace, with a premium on entrepreneurship. There was growing business acumen and a shift from starting own (CDC-owned) businesses to equity, loan, and technical assistance support of home-grown businesses in their midst. However, "core support" of a nonproject nature became increasingly competitive as the number of viable CDCs increased. Foundations and a handful of local and state governments picked up some of the drop-off in general federal and foundation support of earlier years.[156]

For many of the CDCs, creation comes via state or local legislation, either of a general nature governing the chartering of nonprofit corporations or from a specific law dealing with community development activities. A draft state legislative bill accompanying the ACIR report on distressed communities and drawing upon CDC provisions from state statutes on the books in early 1984 provided for the following types of internal governance of a CDC:

1. Authorization for establishment by local unit of government of a unit within the government to carry on the activities of a CDC, including power to issue revenue bonds for community development purposes

2. All or some board members appointed by local government

3. All or some board members elected (a) by residents of the geographic area specified in the organization's articles of incorporation; (b) at a special election from time to time called by the CDC board or the overlying local government; (c) by the initial members of the board; or (d) at an initial election convened by the overlying government unit and subsequently at annual meetings of the corporation members

4. All board members elected or selected as set forth in the petition for incorporation.[157]

The powers of CDCs are spelled out in some statutes. The rationale for such statutory or ordinance specification has been state restrictions upon commingling private and public funds; consequently, the specification of public purpose may be desirable. Also, one power of CDCs is to receive and spend state or local government funds, either directly or through such indirect means as state income tax credits for private contributions to CDCs.

As of 1984, when the ACIR draft bill was prepared, all of the following traits had been specified in one or more state statutes: (1) one or more target areas (variously defined as in bottom portion of resident income or area economic activity levels); (2) a paid-up membership of not less than a specified percentage of the total households of the area; (3) membership open to all target-area residents, with a specified minimum percentage of membership limited to the area; (4) an annual membership fee (for example, $1 to $10); (5) a specified minimum percentage or fraction of board members to be area residents; (6) nonoverlapping of territorial scope of CDCs; (7) creation of subsidiary neighborhood or other corporations; (8) dissolution by board or vote of corporation members and continuation of corporation open to referendum at any time by specified number of petitioners; (9) tax credits for contributions to community-based organizations, including CDCs; amount of credit equal to specified percentage of contribution or specified percentage of amount by which such contribution exceeded those of a base period preceding effective date of credit provision; and automatic repeal of credit after a specified number of years from date of enactment.

The following barriers to partnership development were identified by participants in the ARCO-USCM conferences in 1982–83:

• Inadequate expertise. Not all members will bring to the partnership all the tools and knowledge necessary.

• Unrealistic expectations and public-sector overestimation of private-sector financial ability. Often the resources simply are not available to the private sector, even when the development makes good economic sense. Also, the private sector may underestimate the time required in the public development process.

• Resource inadequacies. Either financial or physical resources may be lacking. Sometimes there are not adequate public or private funds. There may be a lack of sites, adequate utilities, or public works.

• Development priorities. The local government's agenda may not be the same as the private sector's. Even when the ultimate objective is the same, there may be disagreement on the order in which certain activities should take place.[158]

The issue of the future scale of CDC activity was confronting state and local governments, foundations, federal agencies, and the Congress as the decade of the eighties was drawing to a close. Despite the impressive record being made by these partnerships, questions were being raised as to whether or not it was possible to meet community development needs without a large infusion of federal funds on a multiyear basis. The issue was intermeshed with future financing mechanisms through which HUD and state housing finance agencies would give support to the low-income housing segment of community development needs.

Some argue that a conversion of some or most federal housing programs into a separate block grant or an enlarged CDBG is the best alternative, regardless of the level of federal support, in light of the demonstrated need for local and state flexibility in dealing with low-income housing and emergency shelter needs. Others contend that before federalizing, and possibly ruining, the CDC type of activity with national standards ad infinitum, the formation of state and multistate regional associations and other groupings of public-private partnerships, as is occurring in Massachusetts and the rest of New England, is the next appropriate step, with additional state government financial help and with further state action in creating housing trust funds.[159]

A related question is the extent to which the national Congress would be willing to go the partnership route on any kind of block grant support basis, because under block grants, "project pushing" in the congressional appropriation process is curbed if not entirely eliminated. A matching grant with local partnerships on a fifty-fifty basis might comport with political realities in Washington, but it might leave states and their housing trust funds stranded, especially if the program were financed by a national tax on real estate transfers, a revenue source federally abandoned in the late sixties and currently the source of revenue for many of the local and state housing trusts.

Additional Partnership Roles of State Government

In mid-1987 twenty-six states had authorized enterprise zones, whereby "pockets of poverty" in urban and rural areas were identified geographically and designated legally for preferential regulatory, tax, and other public policy treatment in order that economic dislocation might be countered and public and private development resources be targeted to the zones.[160] Most of the state incentives provided in state enterprise zone legislation have been on the tax rather than the regulatory side; most of the deregulatory legislation and implementing actions have been local in nature and have involved land use regulation, building permit, and housing code requirements. Tax incentives have included abatements on various state and local taxes—real estate, sales, corporate income, and franchise and utility taxes and motor vehicle licensing fees. Some states have extended tax relief to persons working in the zone as well as zone employers.[161]

Findings from ten case studies of state-designated enterprise zones conducted by the HUD Office of Program Analysis and Evaluation included the following, among others:

- For some small and medium-sized cities starting economic development programs, the enterprise zone designation has become an organizing mechanism for the community to assess its needs, weigh its resources, and put together a package of programs that, in addition to the enterprise zone incentives, becomes the city's principal economic development strategy.

- In large cities that have developed economic development strategies and made use of all available federal and state programs, the advent of enterprise zones was viewed by local officials as another tool in the city's overall program.

- Zone designation induces business investment in the zones because it is seen by investors as evidence of a long-term commitment to, and interest in, the zone by local government.

- The rate and pattern of new investment activity varied greatly from zone to zone. Some of the communities studied had experienced a slow but steady increase in investment.

Other communities still awaited significant economic results. Still others had experienced an initial flurry of investment followed by a marked slowdown in the rate of new investment.[162]

Establishing linkages among state and private universities, their institutional and faculty research programs, and the business community is another major role of state government in fostering public-private partnerships for economic development. Virginia, Texas, and many other states have been active in this role for several years. The crucial importance to the nation's economy of bridging the gap among academic basic research, applied research, and the commercialization of research results was noted at the outset of this chapter. The long and successful experience of the states, through their experiment stations attached to the land-grant universities, in bringing science and technology to practical application on the nation's farms has been emulated in many countries. Similar cooperation among the national and state governments and the private sector might be able to achieve comparable results in nonagricultural fields.

The review in this chapter of economic, fiscal, and other problems, beginning with the new global economy and moving through the issues of employment dislocation, transportation, day care, infrastructure, housing, and public-private partnerships for community development and revitalization, underscores the increasingly economic nature of problems confronting state and local government in the nineties. When individual state governments have more employees in Tokyo and other foreign capitals hustling for foreign trade than in Washington hustling for federal grants, one knows that times have changed drastically from the period when states were viewed as the "fallen arches" of the American federal system, failing to connect effectively between national and local levels of government. Further illustrations of the changed domestic environment have been 1) the growing orientation of local governments to the private sector; (2) the leadership by the states in reforms in public education and welfare; and (3) the extent of state-local agreement on the necessity for an overhaul of federal housing assistance programs and greater flexibility to local and state governments in their implementation.

NOTES

1. Fosler, R. S., *The New Economic Role of American States* (New York: Oxford University Press, 1988). See also Fosler, R. S., "The Future Economic Role of Local Governments," *Public Management (PM)*, April 1988, 3–9.

2. "Can America Compete? Its Options Are a Surge in Productivity or a Lasting Decline," *Business Week*, April 20, 1987, 44–69.

3. Ibid., 46.

4. Johnston, W., *Workforce 2000: Work and Workers for the 21st Century* (Indianapolis: Hudson Institute, June 1987), 5–6. See also Belous, R., and Wycoff, A., "Trade Has Job Winners, Too," *Across-the-Board*, September 1987, 53–55.

5. "Reduction of Trade and Budget Deficits: Key to Reviving Manufacturing,"

Policy and Research Report 17, no. 1 (Washington, D.C.: Urban Institute, April 1987): 9 (a summary based on Stone, C., and Sawhill, I., "Labor Market Implications of the Growing Internationalization of the U.S. Economy," an Urban Institute Changing Domestic Priorities paper prepared for the National Commission for Employment Policy).

6. National Governors' Association (NGA), "Committee on International Trade and Foreign Relations," *National Governors' Association Policy Positions, 1986–87* (Washington, D.C.: National Governors' Association, January 1987), 335–336.

7. Ibid.

8. Ibid. See also Clarke, M., *Revitalizing State Economies* (Washington, D.C.: National Governors' Association, 1985).

9. Bureau of Labor Statistics (BLS), *Employment and Earnings*, December 1987, table B–2, pp. 53–54.

10. Bluestone, B., and Harrison, B., *The Great American Job Machine: The Proliferation of Low Wage Employment in the U.S. Economy* (A study prepared for the Joint Economic Committee of the Congress, December 1986) 19. See also Levy, F., *Dollars and Dreams* (New York: Russell Sage Foundation, 1987); and Thurow, L., "The Disappearance of the Middle Class: It's Not Just Demographics," *New York Times*, February 5, 1984, F–3.

11. McMahon, P., and Tschetter, J., "The Declining Middle Class: A Further Analysis," *Monthly Labor Review*, September 1986, 23, 25. For further contrasting views, see Rosenthal, N., "The Shrinking Middle Class," *Monthly Labor Review*, August 1985, 9–22; and Lawrence, R., "Sectoral Shifts and the Size of the Middle Class," *Brookings Review*, Fall 1985, 3–10.

12. Congressional Budget Office (CBO), *Trends in Family Income, 1970–86*, 1988, xiii.

13. "Productivity: Why It's the No. 1 Underachiever," *Business Week*, April 20, 1987, 54–55. See also Swoboda, F., "GE's Automation Forces Changes in Labor Relations," *Washington Post*, October 18, 1987, H–1, H–14 (quality circles, output-based compensation, and piecework).

14. CBO, *The Economic and Budget Outlook: An Update*, August 1987, 12.

15. Johnston, *Workforce 2000*, 49–50.

16. Ibid., 79–80.

17. U.S. Congress, House of Representatives, Committee on Ways and Means, *Retirement Income for an Aging Population*, Committee Print WMCP: 100–22, 100th Cong., 1st sess., August 25, 1987, vii.

18. Bureau of the Census, *Projecting the Hispanic Population, 1983 to 2080*, P–25, no. 995, 16–17.

19. Johnston, *Workforce 2000*, 95.

20. Ibid., 97–98.

21. NGA, "Education for Economic Growth," *National Governors' Association Policy Positions, 1986–87, Winter Meeting Supplement*, April 1987, 8 (the education statement was initially adopted in February 1982, and amended in August 1983, February 1985, August 1986, and February 1987).

22. National Commission on Excellence in Education, *A Nation at Risk* (Washington, D.C.: U.S. Department of Education, 1983) 5.

23. NGA, "Education for Economic Growth," 8–10.

24. National Conference of State Legislatures (NCSL), "Elementary and Secondary Education," *Goals for State-Federal Action, 1987–88*, 1987, 62–63.

25. Robbins, J., "Strategic Plan Directs Education's Success," supplement on "Education Business," *City and State*, October 1987, 10.

26. Fiordalisi, G., "School Reform Efforts Lag, Despite Increased Spending," ibid., 1; see also Reich, R., *Education and the Economy* (Washington, D.C.: National Education Association [NEA], 1988), 17–20; and Reinhold, R., "School Reform: 4 Years of Tumult, Mixed Results," *New York Times*, August 10, 1987, A–1, A–14.

27. Brewer, L., "State Legislative Interim Study Activities, 1987," *Information from CSG* (Council of State Governments), September 1987, 3, 12–17.

28. Materials from Minnesota Department of Education, St. Paul, and the Public Services Redesign Project, Hubert H. Humphrey Institute of Public Affairs, University of Minnesota, Minneapolis. See also Putka, G., "Parents in Minnesota Getting to Send Kids Where They Like," *Wall Street Journal*, May 13, 1988, 1.

29. Task Force on Teaching as a Profession, *A Nation Prepared* (Washington, D.C.: Carnegie Forum on Education and the Economy, May 1986).

30. NGA, "Education for Economic Growth," 10–11.

31. Fiske, E., "Main Issue in Improving Schools: Teachers," *New York Times*, August 19, 1987, B–1.

32. Dossey, J., Mullis, I., Lindquist, M., and Chambers, D., *The Mathematics Report Card: Are We Measuring Up?* (Princeton, N.J.: Educational Testing Service, National Assessment of Educational Progress, 1988). See also "Flunking Grade in Math—U.S. Students Are Barely Beyond the Basics," *Time*, June 20, 1988, 79.

33. National Science Board Commission on Precollege Education in Mathematics, Science, and Technology, *Educating Americans for the 21st Century* (Washington, D.C.: National Science Foundation [NSF], September 1983), cover page.

34. Ibid., vii, viii.

35. Ibid., pp. viii, ix, 27–37.

36. Wise, A., Darling-Hammond, L., Berry, B., et al., *Effective Teacher Selection from Recruitment to Retention* (Santa Monica, Calif.: Rand Corporation, January 1987).

37. NSF, *Human Talent for Competitiveness*, NSF 87–24. (Washington, D.C.: National Science Foundation, 1987) 2–10.

38. Ibid., 9.

39. Ibid., 11.

40. Bureau of the Census, *Statistical Abstract of the United States, 1987*, table 639, p. 376.

41. CBO, *The Economic and Budget Outlook: An Update*, August 1987, xix.

42. Bureau of the Census, *Statistical Abstract of the United States, 1987*, tables 1093, 1097, 1098, pp. 619, 621.

43. Howland, M., and Peterson, G., "Labor Market Conditions and the Reemployment of Displaced Workers" Working Paper no. 6 (Institute of Urban Studies, University of Maryland; Urban Institute, February, 1986), 3.

44. NGA, "Worker Adjustment," *National Governors' Association Policy Positions, 1986–87, Winter Meeting Supplement*, sec. C–17, pp. 27–28 (adopted February 1987). See also MacManus, S., "Linking State Employment and Training and Economic Development Programs," *Public Administration Review*, November 1986, 640–650.

45. NGA, *Making America Work: Jobs, Growth, and Competitiveness* (Washington, D.C.: NGA, July 1987), 10–30. Also Voisin, E., "Reagan Finds a Model: New Jersey Reaches Skilled Unemployed," *City and State*, March 1987, 13. Also: *Making America Work: A Followup Report*, August 1988.

46. U.S. Advisory Commission on Intergovernmental Relations (ACIR), "5.108, Economic Growth and Development Policy Act," (draft state legislation) sect. 11 (Washington, D.C.: ACIR), 18–26.

47. U.S. Congress, Office of Technology Assessment (OTA), "Technology, Public Policy, and the Changing Structure of American Agriculture," *OTA Brief*, March 1986, 1. See also General Accounting Office (GAO), *Targeting Farm Payments* (RCED–87–99), June 10, 1987; and Halicki, T., "Farming against the Grain: The Family Farm Cannot Keep Up with Trends in U.S. Agriculture," *National Voter* 37, no. 5 (January 1988): 4–11.

48. OTA, "Techonology," 1.

49. Ibid., 1. See also Kilman, S., and Brown, J. M., "Blighted Bounty: Rich Harvest Masks Long-Term Erosion of Farm Economy," *Wall Street Journal*, November 9, 1987, 1.

50. "Beyond Mountains and Lakes: Imagine—European Agriculture without Surpluses. It's Not Impossible," *Economist* 305, no. 7518 (October 3, 1987): 18–19.

51. NGA, *National Governors' Association Policy Positions, 1986–87, Winter Meeting Supplement*, 77–80.

52. Nothdurft, W., Vaughan, R., and Popovich, M., *Creating an Entrepreneurial Farm Economy: A New State Policy Approach* (Washington, D.C.: Council of State Planning Agencies, 1986) 13–15.

53. NGA, *National Governors' Association Policy Positions, 1986–87, Winter Meeting Supplement*, 80.

54. ACIR, *The States and Distressed Communities: The Final Report* Report A–101, November 1985, 246–248.

55. Bureau of the Census, *Geographic Mobility, March 1982–March 1984*, Series P–20, no. 393, October 1984, tables E and I, pp. 3–4. See also National Research Council, "The Mobility of People and Jobs: Forces Shaping the Urban Future," in *Critical Issues for National Urban Policy: A Reconnaissance and Agenda for Further Study* (Washington, D.C.: National Academy Press, 1982), 13–32.

56. ACIR, *Urban and Rural America: Policies for Future Growth*, A–32, April 1968, 145–149.

57. President's Commission for a National Agenda for the Eighties, "Local Economic and Fiscal Distress," chap. 4 in *Urban America in the Eighties* (Washington, D.C.: Government Printing Office, 1980), 41–52.

58. See Uchitelle, L., "America's Army of Non-Workers," *New York Times*, September 27, 1987, 3–1, 3–6; and McCarthy, M., "In Increasing Numbers, White-Collar Workers Leave Steady Positions," *Wall Street Journal*, October 13, 1987, 1, 20.

59. Johnston, *Workforce 2000*, 85.

60. BLS, "Over Half of Mothers with Children One Year Old or Under in Labor Force in March 1987," Press release USDL 87–345, August 12, 1987, table 3.

61. Bureau of the Census, *Who's Minding the Kids? Child Care Arrangements, Winter 1984–85*, Household Economic Studies, P–70, no. 9, May 1987, table 3, p. 15.

62. Bureau of the Census, *After-School Care of School-Age Children, December 1984*, Current Population Reports, P–23, no. 149, January 1987, 1–2. See also U.S. Department of Health and Human Services (HHS), *School-Age Day Care Study: Final Report*, March 15, 1983, 6; CBO, *Reducing Poverty among Children*, May 1985, 136–148; and Reinhold, R., "California Tries Caring for Its Growing Ranks of Latchkey Children," *New York Times*, October 4, 1987, E–4.

63. Bureau of the Census, *Child Care Arrangements for Working Mothers, June 1982*, Series P–23, no. 129, November 1983, table H, p. 18.

64. BLS, "BLS Reports on Employer Child Care Practices" (for Summer 1987), Press release USDL 88–7, January 15, 1988.

65. Friedman, D., "Child Care for Employees' Kids," *Harvard Business Review*, March/April 1986, 28–34. See also Peirce, N., "Day Care Is Gaining Acceptance (In Corporate America)," *Philadelphia Inquirer*, January 6, 1986, 9A; Evans, J., "State-subsidized Child Care Services," *State Government*, Spring 1975, 93–98; "Day Care," in *"Report of the Task Force on Local Government Response to Fiscal Pressure* (Washington, D.C.: Greater Washington Research Center, December 1982), pp. 9–35–9–54; and "California Makes Business a Partner in Day Care," *Business Week*, June 8, 1987, 2.

66. Kasarda, J., "Urban Change and Minority Opportunities," in Peterson, P., ed., *The New Urban Reality* (Washington, D.C.: Brookings Institution, 1985), 49–51.

67. Hartshorn, T., and Muller, P., *Suburban Business Centers: Employment Implications* (Prepared for Economic Development Administration, U.S. Department of Commerce, 1987). See also Stevens, W., "Defining the Outer City: For Now Call It Hybrid," *New York Times*, October 12, 1987, A–14; idem, "Beyond the Mall: Suburbs Evolving into 'Outer Cities,' " *New York Times*, November 8, 1987, E5.

68. "Who Will Speak for the Inner Cities?" *New York Times*, January 7, 1988, (editorial).

69. "D.C. Labor Pool Making a Splash in Suburbs," *Washington Post*, October 4, 1987, A–1.

70. Transportation Research Board, *Transportation System Management in 1980: State of the Art and Future Directions*, TRB Special Report 190 (Washington, D.C.: National Research Council [NRC], National Academy of Sciences [NAS] 1980). See also TRB, *Transportation System Management for Major Highway Reconstruction*, Special Report 212 (Washington, D.C.: National Research Council, National Academy of Sciences, 1987) and Montgomery County, Maryland, County Council, *Report of Consensus Committee on Growth Management Issues* (Rockville, Md.: County Council, January 1986).

71. HHS, U.S. Public Health Service (USPHS), *Health, United States, 1987*, March 1988. 3.

72. "Waste Not, Want Not," *Wall Street Journal*, April 22, 1988, 30R (medicine and health dialogue).

73. "American Survey—Health Care: The Battle to Contain Costs," *Economist*, October 3, 1987, 34, 36.

74. HHS, *Social Security Bulletin* 50, no. 10 (October 1987): 21, 58.

75. "American Survey—Health Care," 34, 36. See also Manning, W., et al., *A Controlled Trial of the Effect of Prepaid Group Practice in the Utilization of Medical Services*, R 3029-HHS (Santa Monica, Calif.: Rand Corporation, September 1985).

76. Foulkes F., and Paul R., "Containing Retiree Health Care Expenses: Company Liabilities Are Soaring," and Duggan, T. P., "Pass Along the Costs to the Consumer," *New York Times*, November 29, 1987, F–2.

77. HHS, USPHS, *Health, United States 1987*, 794.

78. This collection of actions is drawn from *State Health Notes* (monthly newsletter) (Washington, D.C.: Intergovernmental Health Policy Project, George Washington University), April, June, and October 1987 issues; *Economist*, "American Survey—Health

Care,'' October 3, 1987; ''Legislating Quality Health Care at a Reasonable Cost,'' *Rand Checklist*, no. 336, March 1985; and Colman, W., *Cities, Suburbs, and States* (New York: Free Press, 1975), 215–225.

79. *State Health Notes*, April, June, and November 1987, 1–4, 1–3, and 1–3, respectively; Pear, R., ''States Act to Provide Health Care Benefits to Uninsured People,'' *New York Times*, November 22, 1987, 1, 44; and Peirce, N., ''States Are Trying Universal Health Insurance,'' *National Journal*, November 7, 1987, 2812.

80. Bureau of the Census, *Projections of the Population of the United States by Age, Race, and Sex*, Series P–25, no. 952, May 1984, table 6, p. 86.

81. NGA, *Building Affordable Long Term Care Alternatives: Integrating State Policy*, April 1987. See also ''Long Term Care: A Political Time Bomb,'' *Business Week*, November 30, 1987, 40; and National Institute of Medicine, *Toward a National Strategy for Long Term Care of the Elderly* (Report of a planning study by a committee of the institute), April 1986.

82. *Health, United States, 1987*, 3.

83. NGA, *Building Affordable Alternatives*, B–14. See also Otten, A., ''States Alarmed by Outlays on Long Term Care, Seek Ways to Encourage More Private Coverage,'' *Wall Street Journal*, February 11, 1988, 58; Rice, D., and Wick, A., ''Impact on an Aging Population: State Proportions'' (Prepared for Administration on Aging, HHS) (Institute for Health and Aging, University of California at San Francisco, 1985).

84. U.S. Congress, House Select Committee on the Aging, *Long Term Care and Personal Impoverishment: Seven in Ten*, 100–630 (Washington, D.C.: Government Printing Office, 1987), 9.

85. NGA, *Building Affordable Long Term Care Alternatives*, 48–51.

86. National Institute of Medicine, *Improving Quality of Care in Nursing Homes* (Report of a study by a committee of the institute), March 1986.

87. P. L. 100–203, Committee Print. See also Pear, R., ''New Law Protects Rights of Patients in Nursing Homes,'' *New York Times*, January 17, 1988, 1, 17.

88. AARP, *Summary of the 1987 National Legislative Policy* (Washington, D.C.: American Association of Retired Persons, 1987), 39.

89. Lamm, R., ''We Can't Afford the Health Plan,'' *New York Times*, February 19, 1987, op-ed. For contrasting views, see Crikmer, B., ''How to Handle Long Term Health Care,'' *New York Times*, January 1, 1988, op-ed; and Morrison, P., *Changing Family Structure: Who Cares for America's Dependents?* Report N–2518-NICHD (Santa Monica, Calif.: Rand Corporation, 1986).

90. Callahan, D., *Setting Limits: Medical Goals in an Aging Society* (New York: Simon and Schuster, 1987). See also Otten, A., ''Ethicist Draws Fire with Proposal for Limiting Health Care to Aged,'' *Wall Street Journal*, January 22, 1988, 29; idem, ''Local Groups Attempt to Shape Policy on Ethics and Economics of Health Issues,'' *Wall Street Journal*, May 25, 1988, p. A–27.

91. Downs, A., *Public Policy and the Rising Cost of Housing*, Brookings General Series Reprint 344 (Washington, D.C.: The Brookings Institution, 1978). See also Hughes, J., and Sternlieb, G., *The Dynamics of America's Housing* (New Brunswick, N.J.: Center for Urban Policy Research, Rutgers University, 1987).

92. Mills, E., ''Dividing Up the Investment Pie: Have We Overinvested in Housing?'' *Business Review* (Federal Reserve Bank of Philadelphia), March/April 1987, 13–23.

93. Durning, D., and Quigley, J., ''On the Distributional Implications of Mortgage

Revenue Bonds and Creative Finance," *National Tax Journal* 38, no. 4 (December 1985): 513–523.

94. National Association of Realtors, *The Demand for Housing and Home Financing into the 21st Century* (Washington, D.C.: National Association of Realtors, 1987), 1, 3, 5, 7. The individual reports documenting the projections were Bureau of the Census, "Projections of the Number of Households and Families, 1986 to 2000," *Current Population Reports*, Series P–25, no. 986, 1986; Sternlieb, G., and Hughes, J., "Demographics and Housing in America," *Population Bulletin* 41, no. 1 (January 1986): 26–27; Pitkin, J., and Masnick, G., "Households and Housing Consumption in the United States, 1985 to 2000: Projections by a Cohort Method," RJ86–1 (Cambridge, Mass.: Joint Center for Housing Studies of MIT and Harvard University, 1986) see also "Home Ownership and Housing Affordability in the United States, 1963–1985" (Joint Center, 1986; CBO, *Federal Subsidies for Public Housing: Issues and Options*, June 1983; CBO, *The Housing Finance System and Federal Policy: Recent Changes and Options for the Future*, October 1983; CBO, *Rural Housing Programs: Long-Term Costs and Their Treatment in the Federal Budget*, June 1982; Mariano A., "House Prices Seen Tripling by 2000," *Washington Post*, September 26, 1987, E1, E4; Zolkos, R., "Housing Crisis Looms in Expiring Federal Funds," *City and State*, October 1987, 3, 25; and Peirce, N., "Waves of Homeless Just a Start: It Can Get a Lot Worse,"*Nation's Cities Weekly* [and other newspapers]), April 27, 1987.

95. National League of Cities (NLC), "A Time to Build Up: A Survey of Cities about Housing Policy," *Special Research Report*, February 23, 1987, 7.

96. Ibid. See also CBO, *The Potential Loss of Assisted Housing Units as Certain Mortgage Interest Subsidy Programs Mature*, March 1987.

97. Keefe, F., and Barker, M., "Housing and the States," in Nenno, M., and Brophy, P., eds., *Housing and Local Government* (Washington, D.C.: ICMA, 1982), 163–164.

98. National Commission on Urban Problems (Douglas Commission), *Building the American City* (Washington, D.C.: Government Printing Office, 1968), 236–252, 269–270, 295.

99. ACIR, Bill nos. 6.101 through 6.110; 6.201, 6.202; 6.301 through 6.305. (Draft state legislation). (Washington, D.C.: ACIR, 1975).

100. Bradbury, K., and Downs, A., *Do Housing Allowances Work?* (Washington, D.C.: Brookings Institution, 1981); also Herbers, J., "Mobility for the Poor Sought in Housing Plan," *New York Times*, June 1, 1985, 1.

101. "Housing Rehab Expenditures Continue Upward Trend," *Joint Center Review* (Cambridge, Mass.: Joint Center for Housing Studies of MIT and Harvard University), June 1987, 1.

102. Witte, W., Nenno, M., and Brophy, P., "Profiles of Innovative Local Housing Administration," in Nenno and Brophy, *Housing and Local Government*, 198.

103. Ibid., Nenno, M., and Brophy, P., "Housing and Local Government," 181–182. See also "D.C. Panel Inches Forward on Housing Linkage Rules," *Washington Post*, October 7, 1987, E1, E12, E13, E23–E24.

104. "6.302, ACIR, "Factory-Built Homes and Structures Act" (draft state legislation), sec. 8. 1984, 15–17.

105. "Builders Brace for Foreign Competitors: Overseas Firms Have Advanced Manufactured Home Technology," *Washington Post*, November 7, 1987, F–1.

106. Peirce, N., "From a Jungle, to a Neighborhood," *Philadelphia Inquirer* (and other newspapers), September 10, 1984, op-ed.

107. Rybeck, R., *Meeting America's Housing Needs: A Progressive Agenda* (Washington, D.C.: Conference on Alternative State and Local Policies, 1982), 47–48.

108. *National Governors' Association Policy Positions, 1986–87*, 144–247. See also NGA, *Decent and Affordable Housing: A Challenge to the States*, 1986, 19–26; and Council of State Community Affairs Agencies (COSCAA), *State Housing Initiatives: A Compendium*, 1986.

109. National Association of Counties (NACO), *American County Platform, 1986–87*, 13–18.

110. Berry, B., "Islands of Renewal in a Sea of Decay," in Peterson, *New Urban Reality*, 81–82. See also National Urban Coalition, *Displacement: City Neighborhoods in Transition* (Washington, D.C.: National Urban Coalition, 1978).

111. NLC, *National Municipal Policy, 1987*, December 3, 1986, 44–49. For recommendations of other organizations regarding low-income housing, see U.S. Congress, Senate Committee on Banking, Housing, and Urban Affairs and House Committee on Banking, Finance, and Urban Affairs, *A New National Housing Policy*, 100th Cong., 1st sess., Joint Committee Print (S. Prt. 100–58), October 1987, 1,097 pages; and National Housing Task Force (Rouse Committee), *A Decent Place to Live*, March 1988, 68 pages.

112. National Association of Housing and Redevelopment Officials (NAHRO), *Better Places to Live: The Future of the Public Role in Housing and Urban Development* (Washington, D.C.: National Association of Housing and Redevelopment Officials, 1984), 17.

113. ACIR, "6.103. State Housing Finance and Rehabilitation Agency Act," 1984 (draft state legislation).

114. Nenno, M., *New Money and New Methods: A Catalog of State and Local Initiatives in Housing and Community Development*. Washington, D.C.: (NAHRO, September, 1986), 11–14. (Volume carrying same title, updated in 1988.)

115. "Housing: A New American Dilemma—How Lawyers' Committees Are Coping Coast to Coast," *Committee Report* (Lawyers' Committee for Civil Rights Under Law) 2 no. 2 (Spring 1988): 1.

116. Peirce, N., "New Ideas Help Low-Income Housing," in "Perspective," *Richmond Times Dispatch*, May 3, 1987.

117. Aaron, H., "Housing Allowances versus Construction-linked Subsidies," in Bradbury and Downs, *Do Housing Allowances Work?* 87–96.

118. NLC, "Survey of Cities," 10.

119. Peirce, "New Ideas," and Jordan, M., "Help from Closer to Home: Local, Nonprofit Groups Expand Role," *Washington Post*, March 30, 1987, A–1.

120. Peirce, N., "State's New Role: The Funding and Building of Public Housing," *Nation's Cities Weekly*, May 4, 1987, 4. See also Stegman, M., and Holden, J. D., "States, Localities Respond to Federal Housing Cutbacks," *Public Management* (November 1987): 2–7; Solem, J., "Housing Provisions of the 1986 Tax Reform Act: Can the States Make Them Work?" *National Tax Journal* 40, no. 3 (September 1987): 419–429; and Van Bruane, M., "Tax Exempt Multi-Family Housing Bonds: Creating the Future after Tax Reform," *Public Management* 69, no. 11 (November 1987): 11–14.

121. Erlanger, S., "New York Turns Squatters into Homeowners," *New York Times*, October 12, 1987, A–1, D–11.

122. Klotowitz, A., and Johnson, R., "A Housing Paradox: Many Are Homeless, Public Units Empty," *Wall Street Journal*, February 10, 1988, 1.

123. Schnare, A., Turner, M., and K. Heintz, *Rental Housing Study, 1984: Executive Summary* (Washington, D.C.: Urban Institute, April 1985).

124. Voisin, E., "Communities Own Land to Control Housing Prices," *City and State*, October 1987, 25.

125. Office of Policy Development and Research, U.S. Department of Housing and Urban Development, *A Report to the Secretary on the Homeless and Emergency Shelters*, May 1984, 8–19. See also Bingham, R., Green R., and White, S., *The Homeless in Contemporary Society* (Newbury Park, Calif.: Sage Publications, 1987).

126. NLC, *National Municipal Policy, 1987*, 68.

127. U.S. Conference of Mayors (USCM), *The Continuing Growth of Hunger, Homelessness, and Poverty in America's Cities, 1987*. (Washington, D.C.: USCM, 1987), 1, 2.

128. Piliavian, I., and Sosin, M., "Tracking the Homeless," *Focus* (Madison, WI: Institute for Research on Poverty: University of Wisconsin Winter 1987–88) 20–24.

129. NGA, "The Homeless," *National Governors' Association Policy Positions, 1986–87*, 117–118. See also USCM, *Continuing Growth of Hunger*, 36–37; NACO, *American County Platform, 1986–87*, 73–74; NLC, *National Municipal Policy, 1987*, 67–70; Nenno, M. (ed.), *Assistance for Homeless Persons*. A NAHRO Resource Book for Housing and Community Development (Washington, D.C.: NAHRO, 1988). Goleman, D., "States Move to Ease Law Committing Mentally Ill," *New York Times*, December 9, 1986, C–1; Ansberry, C., "Forgotten Cause? Community Facilities for the Mentally Ill Are Few and Overburdened," *Wall Street Journal*, September 25, 1987, 1, 10; Brady, J., "Society's Failure Bared by Chill Winds," *City and State*, October 1987, 10; Peirce, N., "A Few Glimmers of Hope for America's Street People," *Kansas City Star*, September 19, 1982; and idem, "The City-Church Partnership in Sheltering the Homeless," *Nation's Cities Weekly*, January 21, 1985.

130. U.S. Congress, Joint Economic Committee (JEC), *Hard Choices: A Report on the Increasing Gap between America's Infrastructure Needs and Our Ability to Pay for Them* (Report of an infrastructure advisory committee to the JEC), February 1984.

131. National Research Council, Committee on National Urban Policy, "Investing Private and Public Capital in the Urban Future," chap. 5 in Hanson, R. (ed.), *Rethinking Urban Policy: Urban Development in an Advanced Economy* (Washington, D.C.: National Academy Press, 1983).

132. NACO, *American County Platform, 1986–87*, 136–141; NGA, *National Governors' Association Policy Positions, 1986–87*, 25; and NLC, *National Municipal Policy, 1987*, 35.

133. CBO, *Public Works Infrastructure: Policy Considerations for the 1980's*, April 1983 (quotations on: three strategies, 14–15; improving highway investment, 31–35; and water resources, 81).

134. CBO, *Efficient Investments in Wastewater Treatment Plants*, June 1985, xiv.

135. Palmer, T., "Infrastructure: Public or Private?" *Policy Report* (Cato Institute), May 1983.

136. ACIR, *Financing Public Infrastructure*, A–96, June 1984.

137. National Council on Public Works Improvement (NCPWI), *Fragile Foundations: A Report on America's Public Works* (Washington, D.C.: Government Printing Office, 1988); *The Nation's Public Works: Executive Summaries of Nine Studies* (Washington, D.C.: NCPWI, May 1987). The eight modal studies and one intermodal study done for and published by the NCPWI, May 1987 were Pisarski, A., *A Study of Policy Issues in*

Highways, Streets, and Bridges; Kirby, R., and Reno, A. (Urban Institute), *A Study of Policy Issues in the Public Works Category of Mass Transit*; Mudge, R. (Apogee Research, Inc.), *U.S. Aviation: Making a Good System Better*; Revis, J., and Tarnoff, C., *Intermodal Transportation and Public Works Programs*; Schilling, K., et al., *Water Resources: The State of the Infrastructure*; Wade Miller Associates, Inc., *Infrastructure Policy Issues in Water Supply*; Olinger, L. (Apogee Research, Inc.), *Wastewater Management: Current Policies and Future Options*; Clunie, J., and Beck, R., *Report to the National Council on Public Works Improvement on Solid Waste*; and Rubin, K. (Apogee Research, Inc.), *U.S. Hazardous Waste Management Control Programs: Current Policies and Options for Improvement*. Also see NCPWI, *Defining the Issues*, Appendix B, pp. 79–80, for a list of commissioned background papers. McDowell, B., "Federalism and America's Public Works," *Publius*, Summer 1988, 97–113.

138. Apogee Research, Inc., "A Synthesis of Policy Recommendations of Eight Public Works Reports," prepared for the NCPWI, June 11, 1987, 18–22.

139. ACIR, "6.111, Community Facilities Reconstruction Financing Act" (draft state legislation), 1984.

140. De Grove, J., *Land, Growth, and Politics* (Chicago: American Planning Association Planner's Press, 1984).

141. *Montgomery County* (Maryland) *Code, Annotated*, chap. 50 (Subdivision of Land), sec. 35(k).

142. *Florida Statutes*, 163.3177 (3)(a); 163.3202 (2)(g).

143. Committee for Economic Development (CED), *Public-Private Partnership: An Opportunity for Urban Communities* (New York: Committee for Economic Development, 1982).

144. Nenno, *New Money and New Methods*.

145. Office of Community Development, U.S. Department of Housing and Urban Development (HUD), *Outstanding Local Partnerships in Community Development*, 1987.

146. Peirce, N., and Steinbach, C., *Corrective Capitalism: The Rise of America's Community Development Corporations* (New York: Ford Foundation, July 1987). See also: Osborne, D., *Laboratories of Democracy* (state-sponsored partnerships for community and other economic development. (Boston: Harvard Business School Press, 1988).

147. Atlantic Richfield Co. (ARCO) and U. S. Conference of Mayors, *Partnerships, Public and Private*, Conference Report, March 29–31, 1982, and *Partnerships III*, April 26–28, 1983. See also Ayers, H. B., "The 'Long Arm' Meets the 'Invisible Hand,' " *New York Times*, February 2, 1987, A–17.

148. CED, *Public-Private Partnership*, 43–49.

149. Nenno, *New Money and New Methods*, 6, 8.

150. Peirce and Steinbach, *Corrective Capitalism*, 81, 85.

151. HUD, *Outstanding Local Partnerships*, 1–10.

152. CED, *Public-Private Partnership*, 48–49.

153. Peirce and Steinbach, *Corrective Capitalism*, 12–17.

154. Ibid., 17.

155. HUD, *Outstanding Local Partnerships*, HUD, 51–56.

156. Peirce and Steinbach, *Corrective Capitalism*, 19–35.

157. ACIR, "6.112, "Neighborhood Improvement, Assistance, and Organization Act" (draft state legislation), secs. 3, 8–11, pp. 6–17, 33–40, 1984. The bill is drawn from an Iowa law; rest from Michigan (Act no. 338, Public Acts of 1974, as amended through January 22, 1981); Florida (*Florida Statutes*, sec. 288.601; Wisconsin (*Wisconsin

Statutes 233.02); Minnesota (*Minnesota State Agency Rules*, Department of Economic Development, ED 104, April 1976); and New York (S. 9409, A. 12735).

158. ARCO-USCM, *Partnerships III: Public/Private*, Conference Report, April 26–28, 1983, 22–23. See also Davis, P., ''Why Partnerships Now?'' *National Civic Review*, January–February 1987, 32–33.

159. For an elaboration of these issues, see Peirce and Steinbach, *Corrective Capitalism*, 37–43.

160. NGA, ''Emerging Issues, Alternative Strategies in Economic Development,'' *Governors' Bulletin*, January 2, 1987, 2–3; Nenno, *Housing and Community Development: Maturing Functions of State and Local Government* (Washington, D.C.: NAHRO, 1989).

161. Office of Policy Development and Research and Office of Community Planning and Development, HUD, *Enterprise Zones in America: A Selected Resource Guide* (including bibliography), August 1986, 2.

162. Office of Community Planning and Development, HUD, *State-Designated Enterprise Zones: Ten Case Studies*, August 1986, iii, iv.

Chapter 5 ⸻

Poverty and the Urban Underclass

From the sixties on, urban researchers and public officials were speaking out with increased urgency about a deadly cancer eating at the hearts of many of the nation's largest cities. Robert Weaver asked in 1966: "Will the metropolitan areas of tomorrow have a core of low-income, colored families surrounded by middle- and upper-income whites in the suburbs? . . . Will downtown business and cultural institutions wither away from lack of support?"[1] Edward Banfield was saying in 1970: "So long as the city contains a sizable lower class, nothing basic can be done about its most serious problems. Good jobs may be offered to all, but some will remain chronically unemployed. . . . The streets may be filled with armies of policemen, but violent crime and civil disorder will decrease very little."[2]

Fortunately, the seventies and early eighties saw some of the worst aspects of Weaver's questions and Banfield's hypothesis becoming somewhat moot; unfortunately, other aspects became even more impervious to the then-existing policies and programs for mitigating the conditions of the central-city poor.[3] The invisible wall between suburb and central city was to become increasingly economic rather than racial as many upper- and middle-income blacks followed their white counterparts to the suburbs.[4] The economic recovery in much of the New England and mid-Atlantic areas, combined with a "gentrification" trend, saw Boston, Baltimore, and various other central cities in the Northeast and elsewhere improving their economic and fiscal bases.

However, the persistence of poverty, poor schools, and social alienation in the older large cities led the National Research Council's Committee on National Urban Policy to identify "the urban underclass" as one of five critical major urban issues.[5] The other four were job mobility and the separation of job opportunity and residence; New Federalism and the management of scarcity; new relationships between public and private sectors; and urban infrastructure. As we examine the underclass problem, the first of these four issues comes back into prominence, because the absence of that ''first real job'' is one of the major characteristics of the class; transportation and other difficulties discussed earlier that deter unemployed persons from grasping relatively profuse job opportunities within the same metropolitan area comprise critical barriers to surmount. The alternative is continued geographic entrapment of disadvantaged youth in an environment virtually without hope for job seekers with limited skills.

In the National Urban Policy Committee's 1982 review of the underclass phenomenon, several questions were posed and areas of research suggested. Is the size of the underclass growing or declining? What is the degree of permanency? What is the extent of concentration among blacks and Hispanics, and what is the proportionate incidence in central cities and inner suburbs? It was suggested that research on these questions combine analyses of statistical data on urban neighborhoods with field observations, develop a carefully selected sample of central-city and inner-suburban census tracts and component blocks, and give careful study to such identified areas, both in the field and with census and other data for different years, so that trends in concentration and other aspects might be ascertained.[6]

Earlier research by Kenneth B. Clark[7] and Patrick Moynihan,[8] and subsequent studies by William Julius Wilson,[9] Urban Institute researchers Isabel Sawhill, Erol Ricketts, and colleagues,[10] Rockefeller Foundation official Jim Gibson, Harvard researcher Mary Jo Bane, and a number of others have shed considerable light on the committee's questions. There appears to be an emerging conclusion that the underclass, if it is to be studied and diagnosed in a manageable way, must be defined as a group for whose members a combination of socioeconomic and behavioral characteristics exist. For example, if the underclass were defined primarily in terms of poverty, the numbers could range up to 20 million or higher, scattered geographically across the country and embracing many rural as well as metropolitan areas.[11] It would be both inaccurate and inexcusable to brand all of those in a poverty status, many transitionally so, as members of a lower class or underclass. Even if a test of ''permanent welfare dependency'' were applied (for example, on welfare continuously for eight or more years), with numbers up to 2 million at any one time, a satisfactory criterion would not result.

William Wilson defined the underclass as ''that heterogeneous grouping of inner-city families and individuals who are outside the mainstream of the American occupational system. Included in this population are persons who lack training and skills and either experience long-term unemployment or have dropped out of the labor force altogether; who are long-term public assistance recipients; and who are engaged in street criminal activity and other forms of aberrant behavior.''[12]

William Boyd, president of the Johnson Foundation, used these words: ''This distressed population differs from the poor of past generations in its youthfulness, its ignorance, its alienation, its self-destructive behavior and its threat to society. Unemployed and unemployable, the group is fed by a steady flow of dropouts from schools which are ill-equipped to teach youth who are ill-equipped to learn."[13]

Richard Nathan defined the underclass similarly, but with an additional political aspect: it "consists of such groups as long-term welfare recipients, street criminals, and delinquent youth—on the whole, people who are hard to love, and thus politically hard to assist. Programs to rehabilitate these groups are tremendously difficult to design and implement." Nathan's words "street criminals and delinquent youth" to help typify the behavioral component of the underclass were expanded and made somewhat more specific by Robert Reischauer: "Such behavior includes participation in the underground economy, substance abuse, criminal activity, [and] fathering or bearing a child out of wedlock."[14]

For present purposes, a combination of individual attributes usually, but not always, found in each and every underclass member will be used to examine the various dimensions of the problem and the several often, but not always, interrelated public policy options that confront all state governments and local governments in many areas. Several policy issues lying, or which might lie, in the federal sphere will be noted insofar as they strongly affect state-local capabilities. The principal personal and environmental attributes of the underclass include the following:

1. Economic: (a) low to nonexistent legitimate wage/salary income; (b) income below poverty threshold; (c) little or no work experience; (d) no entry-level job opportunity in immediate area; (e) on welfare or illegal livelihood

2. Family structure: (a) for children, one-parent or older-sibling household, or foster home; (b) for single-parent household, usually female, not married, often never married

3. Medical/health: (a) teenage motherhood; (b) inadequate or no prenatal care; (c) low birth weight of child; (d) limited access to adequate medical care; (e) high rate of drug/alcohol addiction; (f) if IV drug user, moderate rate of AIDS infection

4. Education: (a) usually below twelve, often below eight school years completed; (b) neighborhood served by poor school with high dropout rates

5. Behavioral: (a) antisocial and/or illegal behavior; (b) if male, irresponsible attitude toward fatherhood; (c) scorn of work ethic and school achievement

6. Environmental: (a) sizeable proportion, often majority, of neighborhood residents in underclass, with most or all of foregoing conditions, traits, and tendencies; (b) strong peer pressure against education and legal, entry-level work and toward drug use or distribution and other illegal activity

The specific state and local governmental actions to alleviate these conditions often are uncertain, contradictory, and controversial. They range from sex education for children and teenagers and creation of an orderly, motivating, and productive learning environment in the schoolroom to workfare requirements for welfare recipients. Poverty incidence, family structure, health problems, welfare reform options, how far government can and should go, how much it should

Table 5.1
Percentage of Civilian Noninstitutional Population Not in the Labor Force, by Location and Race, 1987

Race	Total	Central City	Suburb	Non-Metropolitan
All races	33.5	35.7	31.9	37.8
White	33.2	35.0	32.1	37.3
Black	35.6	38.3	29.1	41.4
Hispanic	33.8	36.0	30.7	32.2

Source: Bureau of Labor Statistics, *Employment and Earnings*, July 1987, table A–76, p. 74.

spend, which levels might finance and execute particular policies and programs, and how public and private efforts may be most effectively related comprise the focus of this chapter.

THE ECONOMIC DIMENSION

Several factors tend to converge in placing central-city residents with limited education at a serious disadvantage in a struggle for economic survival.

Nonparticipation in the Labor Force

In 1987 the nation's civilian unemployment rate averaged 6.2 percent (white, 5.0 percent; black, 13.2 percent; and Hispanic, 8.3 percent). It was 7.6 percent in central cities, 5.0 percent in the suburbs, and 6.9 percent in nonmetropolitan areas (2.3 percent for farm and 7.4 percent for nonfarm). Central-city unemployment rates for whites, blacks, and Hispanics were, respectively, 5.8, 14.6, and 9.1 percent; in the suburbs the respective rates were 4.7, 10.3 and 7.2 percent. These data, combined with those in table 5.1, underscore the relatively disadvantaged position of central-city residents of all races and of blacks and Hispanics in all areas. Table 5.1 summarizes the distribution by residence and race of persons not in the civilian labor force in mid-1987.

William Wilson pointed out that examination of a long-term trend in unemployment rates showed that for three-year intervals during the period 1948 to 1980, with the exception of 1972, 1975, and 1980, the black-white unemployment ratio had worsened (1.7 in 1948 to 2.1 in 1980, with black and other races at 5.9 percent and white at 3.5 percent in 1948, compared to 12.3 and 5.9 percent in 1980).[15] Data in Appendix 4.B show the black-to-white 1987 ratio growing to 2.4 for men and 2.5 for women.

Family Incomes and Poverty Measurement

The economic status and confidence level of American families and individuals were receiving increased attention in 1987 and 1988, not only because of an approaching national election, but also because of growing public concern with the future of national and world economies, budget deficits, and a variety of social problems (family structure, value systems, drugs, crime, and a perception among some of a "new permanence of poverty"). Factual data on several of these areas of concern were themselves becoming a new focus of controversy. Were real incomes rising or falling, were people saving less and living beyond their means, was poverty, especially outside the "underclass population," becoming more permanent, and was drug use growing or receding?

Controversy over measurement of these phenomena was intensifying because of its direct effect upon public policy and spending, especially in the public welfare and other poverty-related areas, but also in drug and other health and criminal justice areas, where ascertained or perceived severity of the problem dictated the level and direction of public policy responses. In summarizing family income trends in the 1970–86 period, a 1988 CBO report found the perception of little if any improvement in family economic well-being to be inaccurate because it ignored four important factors:

- It fails to account for reduced living costs resulting from declining average family size.
- It uses an inflation index that has overstated the increase in living costs.
- It understates income by omitting items received in kind, such as health insurance and food stamps.
- It overstates income available for consumption by using a pretax measure.[16]

To these measurement and analytical deficiencies the following could be added, with regard to current measures and perceptions of economic well-being or despair:

- The cost of living varies tremendously across the country; a given amount of cash can provide comfort in one area, while affording little better than bare subsistence in another.
- Vestment in pension, health care, and a variety of other employer-provided fringe benefits, both during employment and in retirement, removes or reduces the need to save further for these purposes, thus increasing both sense of economic security and disposable income for consumption.
- New products and quality change over time may produce a rise in living standards that is immeasurable, or nearly so.
- Tilting in the opposite direction from the other three factors are increased carrying costs of owner-occupied housing and tax burdens (included in some measures of income), but excluded from others.[17]

The CBO study of family incomes, after adjusting for family composition and price-level changes, but excluding effects of taxes and in-kind income, found a 20 percent increase in real family income over the 1970–86 period, but with some groups faring much better than others. The elderly income rose "from about twice the poverty thresholds to over three times for those in families, and from just above the poverty level to more than one and one half times for unrelated individuals. At the other extreme, single mothers with children experienced only a slight growth [and were] just above the poverty thresholds over the period as a whole."[18] Going into the nineties, the single mother with children obviously has been, and continues to be, in the most severe economic straits of any group in American society.

Poverty in the Central Cities and in Underclass Areas

The apparent improvement in economic conditions in central cities of the Northeast in the late eighties had not been reflected or foretold in the 1980 census. That census showed the fifty largest U.S. cities to have a higher proportion of poverty and racial minorities in 1980 than in 1970. About 4.4 million persons (up from 3.4 million in 1970, despite a drop of about 1 million in total population from 1970) were below the poverty line and living in a "poverty area" (a census tract where 20 percent or more of the population were below the poverty level in income). Of the approximately 6.7 million persons below the poverty line in those cities in 1980, 2.6 million were white and 3.1 million black.[19]

Ricketts and Sawhill of the Urban Institute undertook to define underclass members on an area rather than an individual basis. They defined underclass areas as those having a high proportion of persons with defined nonmainstream behaviors—high school dropouts, men not regularly attached to the labor force, nonworking welfare recipients, and households headed by single mothers with children. They identified 880 census tracts in which there was an above-average prevalence of all four conditions.

These underclass areas had a 1980 population of 2.6 million (about 1 percent of the nation's population). Of the 880 areas, 40 percent were not extreme poverty areas, and 72 percent of poverty areas (those areas in which 40 percent of the people were poor) were not underclass areas. Nationally, only 5 percent of the poor lived in underclass areas. Thus poverty and underclass areas overlapped but were by no means coterminous. Of the 2.6 million persons living in "underclass areas," only about 40 percent, or 500,000, of the areas' adult population had no regular attachment to the labor force, either directly through a job or indirectly through marriage. These individuals lay clearly outside Wilson's "American occupational mainstream" and comprised the chronically unemployed segment of the urban underclass.[20]

Ricketts and Sawhill found that relative population characteristics present in underclass areas and in the United States as a whole varied in most but not all respects. Subsequent Urban Institute research showed that the urban percentage was 99 in underclass areas and 77 in the United States as a whole. Other relative presences in underclass and the United States, respectively, were Northeast, 36 and 25; North Central, 27 and 24; South, 26 and 30; West, 11 and 21; unemployed adult men, 56 and 3; white, 28 and 82; black, 59 and 12; Hispanic, 10 and 3;

high school dropouts aged 16–19, 36 and 13; ratio of adult females in 18–64 age bracket to males, 1.20 and 1.05; and families headed by women, 60 and 19.[21]

The highest numbers of underclass areas were found in the following metropolitan areas, in descending order: New York–Northeastern New Jersey (155); Chicago (66); Detroit (59); Newark (30); Philadelphia (29); Baltimore (27); and Los Angeles–Long Beach (26). Several other metropolitan areas followed with lower numbers. In the percentage of metropolitan-area census tracts falling into underclass areas, Paterson, New Jersey, had 13.8 percent. Others in descending order on the high side were Louisville, 7.2; Newark, 6.4; New York–Northeastern New Jersey, 5.9; and Detroit, 5.3. On the low side, St. Louis had 2.5 percent; Philadelphia, 2.4; and Cleveland, 2.0. Falling in between were Atlanta, Baltimore, Chicago, Columbus, Rochester, Milwaukee, and Cincinnati. It should be emphasized that to interpret these figures properly, the configuration of each metropolitan area must be taken into account. Another table showed that the population living in underclass areas numbered 2.5 million, approaching 1 percent of the population (of which about 500,000 met the definition of an underclass member). Excluding women with preschool children, 500,000 of the 2.5 million were able-bodied and not in the labor force (NILF); 260,000 of the NILF group were prime-age males not working, and 300,000 of the group were on welfare. Other estimates embrace a possible range from .8 to 2.4 percent of the population.[22]

The numbers may seem relatively small, but the seriousness and breadth of the problem are frightening, and the size, however estimated, seems to be growing gradually. Three numbers—2.5 million, the 500,000, and 260,000—are crucial. We have noted the barriers dividing central-city unemployed, discouraged, or minimally qualified potential workers from job opportunities—transport, day-care, and medical services. A key question is this: If, with some public subsidy, employer-provided transport, day-care, and medical services were made available, how large a proportion of the quarter million males and of the total 500,000 able-bodied and not working would become and remain fully employed? And conversely, how many still would not be working?

Children in Poverty

For children, the geographic and employment incidence of poverty is similar. Even more serious for the underclass—since children both in poverty and living in an underclass area are doubly at risk—is the combination of economic disadvantage and a neighborhood cultural home-school-peer environment that discourages work, schooling, and mainstream social behavior.

Table 5.2 shows the extent of poverty concentration in central cities and among female-headed families and minority groups. Some improvement in poverty rates occurred between 1983 and 1987. A CBO report in 1985, using 1983 data, showed poverty rates among children to be 22 percent and among those in female-

Table 5.2

Numbers and Percentages of Persons, Families, and Children below Poverty Level by Age, Race, Residence, and Family Type, 1986

(Numbers in Millions)

Category	All Races			White			Black			Hispanic		
	Total No.	No. BPL	Per Cent	Total No.	No. BPL	Per Cent	Total No.	No. BPL	Per Cent	Total No.	No. BPL	Per Cent
Age, Persons												
All Ages	238.55	32.37	13.6	202.28	22.18	11.0	28.87	8.98	31.1	18.76	5.12	27.3
Under 18	62.95	12.88	20.5	51.11	8.21	16.1	9.63	4.15	43.1	6.65	2.51	37.7
Under 18, Related, in Families	61.92	12.26	19.8	50.39	7.71	15.3	9.46	4.04	42.7	6.50	2.41	37.1
Residence												
In Metro Areas	184.85	22.66	12.3	154.93	15.05	9.7	23.56	6.74	28.6	17.31	4.57	26.4
In Central Cities	73.76	13.30	18.0	53.97	7.54	14.0	16.47	5.13	31.2	10.03	3.13	31.1
In Poverty Areas	20.41	7.40	36.2	10.06	3.25	32.3	9.55	3.84	40.2	4.99	2.07	41.4
Out of Cent. Cities	111.09	9.36	8.4	100.96	7.51	7.4	7.09	1.61	22.6	7.28	1.44	19.8
In Poverty Areas	5.69	1.76	30.9	4.02	1.04	25.9	1.56	.70	44.6	1.51	.57	37.7
Out of Metro Areas	53.71	9.71	18.1	47.35	7.14	15.1	5.31	2.25	42.3	1.45	.55	38.2
In Poverty Areas	12.43	3.74	30.1	8.66	1.95	22.5	3.30	1.62	49.2	.59	.27	45.8
Families & Persons												
All Families	64.49	7.02	10.9	55.68	4.81	8.6	7.10	1.99	28.0	4.40	1.09	24.7
Female Headed Fams.	10.45	3.61	34.6	7.23	2.04	28.2	2.97	1.49	50.1	1.03	.53	51.2
Children Below 18	12.76	6.94	54.4	7.60	3.52	46.3	4.84	3.25	67.1	1.78	1.19	66.7
All Other Families**	54.05	3.41	6.3	48.45	2.77	5.7	4.13	.50	12.1	3.37	.56	16.5
Children Below 18	49.19	5.31	10.8	42.76	4.19	9.8	4.65	.79	17.0	4.73	1.22	25.8
Unrelated Individuals	31.68	6.85	21.6	27.14	5.20	19.2	3.71	1.43	38.5	1.69	.55	32.8

Source: Bureau of the Census, *Money Income and Poverty Status of Families and Persons in the United States, 1986*, Current Population Reports, P–60, no. 157, July 1987, Tables 16, 18, 20, pp. 1–7, 26–27, 30, 34.

Note: Poverty level is based on cash income; excludes noncash benefits. Poverty-level estimates for 1986 that include such benefits appear in Census Bureau Technical Paper 57, *Estimates of Poverty Including the Value of Noncash Benefits, 1986*.
[a] Percents occasionally off by one or more tenths due to rounding. All percents coincide with those in the Census tables.
[b] Includes male-maintained families.

headed minority households to be 70 percent. However, when the budget share instead of cash measure of income was used, the poverty rate for single-parent households of all races dropped from 51.1 to 43.5 percent.[23] In 1983 and 1986 poverty thresholds for a family of three were $8,000 and $8,737, respectively (cash, pretax family income). For single persons they were $5,000 and $5,572, and $20,000 and $22,497 for nine persons or more.

Two groups of children and their families are in poverty or are threatened by it. The first group, among the "working poor," are those families, containing about 3 million children, who receive no welfare payments or food stamps. The family heads work substantial amounts but end up at about the poverty line. The second group comprises up to 15 million children, many receiving welfare benefits. The family heads work little, and many are in the urban underclass.[24]

Using 1985 census surveys, Sheldon Danziger and Peter Gottschalk found, regarding "low-earning" family heads (those earning below $204 per week in 1984 dollars, such persons not being able to earn the poverty line income for a family of four, even if working fifty-two weeks at the current wage), that 29.9 percent of all families with children had "low earnings"—25.5 percent for whites, 51.5 percent for blacks, and 44.0 percent for Hispanics. For female-headed families with children, 65.5 percent were low earners—61.4 percent for whites, 72.7 percent for blacks, and 79.8 percent for Hispanics.[25]

Policy Options for Mitigating Underclass Poverty

In the consideration of state-local policy options concerning members of the urban underclass and the class as a group, it is necessary, but difficult, to distinguish between those measures directed primarily toward the underclass and those applicable to the general population. Furthermore, it also is necessary to distinguish throughout between children and adult members of the underclass. Many inner-city poor children, though not in underclass families, are nevertheless at high risk of being drawn into that class.

For adult members of the underclass, measures discussed earlier to broaden labor-force participation through lowering barriers in transport, day care, housing, and other factors also are applicable here. Two additional policy options have received increased attention.

Approximately half the states had failed to extend AFDC eligibility to include two-parent families with children. (These states had about one-third of the AFDC national caseload in the mid-eighties.) Such action was mandated in federal welfare reform legislation in 1988. This change should remove the necessity of a marital split-up in order for the mother and dependent children to qualify for assistance and conversely would remove a marriage or "man-in-the-house" penalty for a single mother hoping to establish a two-parent family. The CBO estimated in 1985 that if all states acted to include two-parent families, about 100,000 additional families would become eligible to join the then 3.7 million recipient families. The additional costs to the states would total $200 million.[26]

The issues involved here are (1) fiscal priorities among competing claims within and from outside the social programs area; (2) a possible disincentive for one or both parents to rejoin or continue in the labor force; and (3) various possible effects on family structure and stability. Some states undoubtedly view intact families as better able to help themselves and thus be less in need of aid than a single-parent family. A variant among states not now covering families with an unemployed worker is the extent of general assistance (GA) provided to the unemployed parent. In states such as New York, where local governments bear a large part of general assistance costs, an increase in the state share, permitting an increase in total GA to the unemployed person, has been an alternate way to lessen the disparity in treatment of one- and two-parent families with dependent children.

States could legislate to require AFDC recipients to participate in work or work-related activities. (This was also included in the 1988 federal legislation, but with much flexibility left to the states.) This could have the effect of edging some long-term welfare dependents into or back into the labor force, producing a dual benefit of enlarging a work force projected to be tight in the nineties, while reducing the welfare caseload. This might be especially marked if transport, day-care, and medical eligibility deterrents were substantially mitigated during the transitional or probationary period following successful job placement.

The question of resource allocation between efforts to move underclass parents into the labor force and eventually into the "occupational mainstream" and efforts to reduce the risk to poor children of being drawn into the underclass pervades state-local policy considerations. Relative costs and benefits between adults and children and within the adult category between the young and the mature are inevitably crucial in a period of public revenue scarcity.

Before leaving the economic/poverty discussion, it should be emphasized that rural poverty in a number of states is as pervasive as in urban areas, if not more so. Economic development, along with the adjuncts of job training and health care availability discussed earlier, appears to be the primary policy arena within which resource allocations are made, in contrast to the welfare reform arena for urban poverty in general and the underclass problems in particular.

FAMILY STRUCTURE

Large-scale and long-term departures from traditional family structure have been a major social phenomenon in the United States over the last half century.

- Divorce moved from a status of exception to the ordinary; unmarried-couple households multiplied from tiny population fractions into the millions.
- Despite dramatic advances in the reliability of contraceptive practices and the nationwide legalization of abortion, out-of-wedlock births and teenage pregnancies in the United States have been the highest in the Western world.
- Responsibilities of fatherhood are absent from the consciences of many young males.
- The household headed by a single, never-married mother has become the norm in many poor inner-city areas and among some minority groups. All of these departures are elements of a major behavioral characteristic of the urban underclass—absence of stable family structures and relationships.

Number and Economic Status of Families Headed by Single Mothers

In March 1986, 15.7 percent of white children and 50.6 percent of black children were living in a female-headed household. Children under the age of eighteen numbered 62.8 million and accounted for 26 percent of the U.S. population. There were 50.9 million white, 9.5 million black, and 6.4 million Hispanic children, and 2.3 million children of other races; 46.4 million lived in married-couple households, 13.1 million in female-maintained households, 1.6 million in father-maintained households, and 1.6 million in other household situations. The mean household annual income was $35,521 for the married-couple households, but only $11,352 for female-maintained ones; in the latter, $10,929 was the mean annual income for white women, $8,691 for blacks, and $8,762 for Hispanics.[27]

Data at one point in time may distort the picture of family condition over a lifetime, or even over a child-rearing period. The duration of single motherhood for white women is considerably less than for black women. The lifetime prevalence rate for single motherhood has been estimated at 42 percent for whites and 86 percent for blacks.[28] Low-income housing shortages discussed earlier, especially of housing available for families with several children, may well influence future numbers of female-headed households as young mothers move in with parents or other relatives. Also, the neighborhood in which the relatives live, as well as the nature of the new home environment, can be crucial for the growing children.

The national aggregates just noted understate greatly the extent of single motherhood and female-headed households in underclass and other areas of concentrated poverty. William Wilson noted that in 1980, 27,000 families lived in public or assisted housing projects managed by the Chicago Housing Authority; of these families, only 11 percent were married-couple families.[29]

Some Causes for Increased Numbers of Households Headed by Single Females

Researchers at the Institute for Research on Poverty (IRP), the Urban Institute, the Rand Corporation, the Census Bureau, and other organizations have conducted intensive research on the personal motivations and external influences affecting the decisions or circumstances necessitating single women to become mothers or causing the breakup of families, leaving the mother to rear the children. Married women with children may find themselves the head of household through divorce, separation, or death of husband, with the initiative in the first two resting with the woman, man, or both. The never-married woman may become a mother intentionally or unintentionally, as a result of various motivations:

- To show independence from, or rebellion against, parental control or other home conditions

- A combination of low grades in school, few educational expectations, and early physical maturity

- An unwillingness to enter into marriage with the available male, coupled with a desire to have children

- A desire for children strong enough to choose birth over abortion and keeping the child over adoption

- Especially in deciding to have additional children, the availability of increased welfare benefits

- Unavailability of contraceptive information

- Disinclination to use contraceptives or the unwillingness of the male to use them or to cooperate with, or acquiesce in, her use of them

- Peer pressure toward sexual activity and nonuse of contraceptives

- Increasing employment opportunities for women, providing a basis for an independent life style and nondependence upon husband or other male for economic support

- Work and work-related stress as a separation or divorce factor[30]

The Rand Corporation analyzed National Center for Educational Statistics data and tracked 13,000 sophomore women for two years, comparing those who became single mothers and those who did not. To dissociate interconnections among factors contributing to the decision to want or to have a child, multivariate analyses were used, producing findings that low family socioeconomic status was significant for blacks, less so for Hispanics, and not at all for whites; coming from a female-headed or other "nontraditional" family increased chances of motherhood for blacks and Hispanics, but not for whites; parent-child communication was most important for whites, parental supervision for blacks, and religiosity for Hispanics; and peer attitudes toward single parenthood mattered for whites and Hispanics but not significantly for blacks.[31]

Inadequate Child Support from Absent Parent

Table 5.3 summarizes the extent to which female-headed families with children received child support payments (CSPs) from absent fathers or other parent. Most of the contrasts in the table are not surprising. The highest proportion awarded CSPs were the better-educated, white, married, or divorced women; only 18.4 percent of the never-married women were awarded help. A much lower proportion of women below the poverty level were awarded support, presumably because of lack of income or assets of the absent father. Once women were awarded support, however, the proportion of delinquencies did not vary greatly among the categories of mothers.

Data for fiscal year 1987 showed that the three states with the highest overall percentages of child support cases in which collections were made were Mas-

Table 5.3

Child Support Payments (CSPs) Awarded and Received by Women with Own Children under 21, 1985

(Numbers in thousands)

Category	No.	% Awarded CSP's	No. Due CSP's	% Rec. CSP's	Mean Amt.
All women	8,808	61.3	4,381	74.0	$2,215
Married*	2,322	82.0	1,416	68.5	1,966
Divorced**	3,045	81.8	2.179	75.1	2,538
Separated	1,363	43.1	453	84.3	2,082
Never Married	2,009	18.4	303	76.2	1,147
School Yr. Comp.					
Below 12	2,230	45.2	750	67.1	1,835
H. S. Grad.	4,176	63.3	2,152	74.3	2,040
1-3 Yrs. Coll.	1,653	70.7	1,003	74.6	2,447
4 + Yrs. Coll.	748	76.6	476	82.1	2,978
Race					
White	6,341	70.6	3,651	74.6	2,294
Black	2,310	36.3	657	72.0	1,754
Hispanic	813	42.1	282	68.1	2,011
Below Pov. Level	2,797	40.4	905	65.7	1,383

Source: Bureau of the Census, *Child Support and Alimony, 1985*, Series P–23, no. 152, August 1987, 5.

* Remarried women, post-divorce.

** Previous marriage ended in divorce.

"All women" includes approximately 69,000 widowed women who are excluded from remaining numbers due to inadequate data base for statistical comparison purposes.

"Race" does not include breakdown for other races (Asians, Native Americans, etc.).

sachusetts, 41.3; Delaware, 35.7; and South Dakota, 35.4. The highest for AFDC and foster care cases were Delaware, 46.9; Massachusetts, 31; and Vermont, 30.2. The three lowest jurisdictions for all cases were Montana, 5.6; Oklahoma, 6.0; and New Mexico, 6.2. For AFDC and foster care cases, they were Arizona, 2.0; Oklahoma, 2.8; and New Mexico, 3.2.[32] The full state-by-state listing appears in Appendix 5.A.

Wisconsin adopted child support legislation in 1983 providing three key features: (1) a formula to determine the amount of the CSP; (2) collection through withholding; and (3) an assured benefit. The legislation was preceded by a long period of research and drafting, beginning in 1978, and followed by legislatively sanctioned demonstration trials in several counties. The formula, legislatively set, was based on a percentage of the absent parent's gross income: 17 percent for one child and 25, 29, 31, and 34 percent, respectively, for two, three, four, and five or more children. The amounts due were to be withheld from paychecks and transferred to the custodial parent. Judges could vary awards from the presumptive standard, but only after a written finding.[33]

The assured benefit under the Wisconsin plan was lower than the AFDC benefit, but unlike AFDC benefits was not reduced dollar for dollar from earnings. By supplying benefits outside the welfare system, such a plan provides a supplement to earnings and reduces dependence on AFDC. Congressional legislation in 1984 made the first $50 in CSPs exempt from family budget calculations upon which AFDC benefits had been based.[34] Some viewed as a weakness the failure of the 1984 federal legislation to set a payment standard, leaving the individual states to do so. Others argued that uniform national dollar standards would be a mistake because of large variations in area living costs. (1988 federal welfare reform legislation mandated a formula approach, but with a great deal of flexibility left to the states.)

State-Local Policy Options to Strengthen Family Structure

Those state options for strengthening family structure that relate to AFDC benefits always must be considered within the context of federal ground rules for that intergovernmental welfare program. Obviously, states can expand eligibilities through use of their own funds. The effect upon family structure of state AFDC eligibility was noted earlier. For the household headed by a single female and for young women deciding whether or not to risk childbirth through premarital sexual activity, state and local governments can undertake various steps. In framing measures such as the following, policymakers need to keep in mind that mother-only families are the most economically depressed in American society, and no other group remains in poverty so long:

- Assuring through public libraries, public health clinics, and other outlets the availability of contraceptive information (sex education in the schools and school-associated health clinics that include sexual counseling are discussed later)
- Enacting state legislation such as the Wisconsin plan for child support to assure that absent parents meet financial responsibilities to their children
- Ensuring that economic realities and moral responsibilities to children are given appropriate weight in legislation pertaining to separation and divorce

MEDICAL/HEALTH SERVICES FOR THE URBAN POOR

Health conditions in underclass and inner-city poverty areas are appalling, despite the scope and cost of programs to improve access to medical and other health care by public and private agencies over several decades. Most disconcerting from a public policy standpoint are the physical and environmental health conditions of young children. Parental neglect is widespread, raising serious ethical, legal, and other questions for state and local health and law enforcement officials and for the medical and health professions as to the kinds and degrees of intervention that could or should be undertaken. These problems grew more serious in the eighties and could very well become even worse in the nineties unless vigorous corrective steps are taken by public and private agencies and, most important, by parents.

Four major intergovernmental programs involving the federal government are basic to the availability of health services to poor people. One of these—food stamps—is federally financed in its entirety as to benefits and is state and county administered, one-half the costs being borne by the national government. The other three programs are financed jointly by the national government and the states, with local governments in some states participating in benefit costs. Medicaid, the largest, bears all or most hospital and other medical costs of persons eligible and participating. A supplemental food program for women, infants, and children (WIC) provides benefits for low-income women, infants, and children up to age five, covering prenatal, postpartum, and breastfeeding periods. Alcohol, drug abuse, and mental health (ADAMH) programs provide counseling and rehabilitative services, with many state programs administered on a sliding-fee basis relative to income.

Another program should be noted here. Aid to families with dependent children (AFDC), the principal "welfare" program in the country, provides cash assistance to mothers and dependent children, with families having an unemployed father also being eligible in about half the states, as of mid-1988, but with such eligibility extended for all states under 1988 welfare reform legislation. Health care and food costs, like other necessities, are included in the family budget, upon which AFDC and other public assistance benefits are calculated.

Also federally aided, but in smaller magnitudes and federal proportions, is the broad category of public health services. These services vary widely among states and localities because of varying choices in resource allocation. The services are delivered by state, county, and/or city health departments. Nonprofit social organizations deliver some of the services, with or without state or local subsidy. This group of services is crucial to underclass and poverty areas, especially for inoculations, examinations, and maternal and child health care.

Food stamps, Medicaid, WIC, ADAMH, and public health services are central to the health aspects of the urban underclass problem. In stage-of-life order, these health aspects are the following:

1. Availability of accurate information, presented in stages, beginning at an early age, and in candid and balanced terms, regarding human sexual behavior and moral responsibility values associated therewith, the reproductive process, contraception, abortion pros and cons, and venereal diseases, including their recognition and prevention

2. Information, counseling, and medical services relating to personal, social, and economic consequences of teenage pregnancy and family-planning counseling before and after pregnancy and before and after birth of children

3. Prenatal, postpartum, and infant care and nutrition, including nurse home-visitor programs for high-risk mothers

4. Newborn screening and other procedures for identification and treatment of mental retardation and mental health problems that can begin to appear at an early age and are often associated with low-weight births

5. Child safety restraints in automobiles

6. Alcohol and drug addiction and rehabilitation

7. Special problems associated with acquired immune deficiency syndrome (AIDS) and its interrelationship with intravenous (IV) drug use, prostitution, and poverty

The principal state and local medical and health services available to the poverty population, with most of them available also to the general population, include emergency medical and ambulance services; emergency room hospital service; community or neighborhood public health services delivered through health clinics or centers; and similar centers or clinics for mental health, drug and alcohol rehabilitation, and related problems. Additional services to the poor, supported from public funds, include nursing home care and maternal and child health services. Most of these services are delivered by private practitioners and facilities, with state and local support drawn from federal-state Medicaid funds, supplemented by federal and state grants, either in block or categorical form. By far the largest single financial source of health assistance to the poor is the Medicaid program.

The Medicaid Population

About three-fifths of Medicaid financing comes from the national government ($23 billion federal to $18 billion state-local in 1986).[35] Various matching ratios apply, ranging upward from 50 percent federal (eleven states and the District of Columbia) to 78.42 percent federal (Mississippi). State governments have significant latitude in extending eligibility to include the "medically needy" and wide discretion in the extent to which information about the availability of benefits is brought to the attention of poor people through outreach programs. Conversely, health care providers keep rather fully informed about federal, state, and other Medicaid regulations.

For various reasons, many poor families and poor children do not receive Medicaid benefits in any given year. This can be because they (1) did not need to visit a doctor or hospital (understandable for many adolescents, especially where school health services are provided); (2) did not realize that Medicaid would cover the full cost if the family were truly needy and had no financial reserves to draw upon; (3) knew about Medicaid but did not feel seeking eligibility to be worth the hassle with public officialdom; or (4) failed to act out of sheer neglect.[36] Regarding bureaucratic barriers, a study of 1985–86 data in seventeen Southern states showed that of 1 million people denied Medicaid assistance, 23 percent were denied for income reasons and 62.7 percent for failure to comply with paperwork and other procedural requirements.[37] As noted earlier, 1988

Table 5.4

Poverty Population, by Households and Persons in Households, by Number below Poverty Level (BPL), and Medicaid Coverage, 1986

Category	Number in Poverty			Medicaid Coverage			
	NIP[a]	Poverty Pop.				Percent of	
		No.	%NIP	Total	No. BPL	BPL	PP[b]
All Househlds	89,479	11,901	13.3	8,521	4,893	57.4	41.1
Hshlds. 65 +	18,998	2,877	15.1	2,314	1,003	43.3	34.9
Female Head	10,445	3,613	34.6	3,422	2,418	70.7	66.9
With Chldren	7,094	3,264	46.0	2,826	2,273	80.4	69.6
Persons							
All Persons	238,534	32,370	13.6	19,739	12,805	64.9	39.6
White	202,282	22,183	11.0	12,725	7,653	60.1	34.5
Black	28,871	8,993	31.1	6,180	4,638	75.0	51.6
Other	7,401	1,194	16.1	834	514	61.6	43.0

Sources: Bureau of the Census, *Poverty in the United States 1986*, P–60–157, tables 1, 4, 7, and 14, June 1988; *Receipt of Selected Noncash Benefits 1986*, Technical Paper 57, table 1, July 1987 and associated unpublished data, tables 2, 8; *Social Security Bulletin, Annual Statistical Supplement, 1987*, p. 84.

[a] NIP = noninstitutional population.
[b] PP = poverty population.

federal welfare reform legislation mandated fuller inclusion of women and young children at or close to the poverty line.

Table 5.4 summarizes the composition of the noninstitutionalized Medicaid population (poor people in nursing homes and other facilities are not included, although the full cost of care is often borne by Medicaid). In 1986, on a national aggregate basis, Medicaid covered 8.5 million households, made up of 19.7 million persons; this was 9.5 percent of all households (89.5 million). Of those households covered, 57.4 percent were below the poverty level; conversely, 42.6 percent were not. Many of the latter group were "medically needy" under individual state laws or regulations. Some patients were eligible temporarily due to catastrophic health costs in the given year. If the "recipient value share" or other measure of poverty that includes noncash benefits were used, the proportion of Medicaid recipients below the poverty line would be smaller than shown in the table. However, under all measures, several million poverty households were without Medicaid protection.

If it is the policy of state and local governments to assure access to medical and health services by those mothers and children of greatest future risk, then outreach efforts to advertise Medicaid eligibility might be concentrated upon single mothers with children in poverty households, or more tightly targeted to those in such households in underclass areas, to make sure that Medicaid eligibility and the availability of family-planning and child health services is made known to all such mothers. Outreach involves much more than television and radio spots and information placed in newspapers and on bulletin boards. Some city health bureaucracies require advance appointments for a visit to a clinic or to the city health department, and this may require travel to another part of the city. On the other hand, public health vans may visit poor areas on a regular basis, amounting to "quasi house calls."[38] Neglect of family-planning, prenatal, and young-child health care can have irreversible consequences for both women and children, with social and fiscal ripple effects enduring for many years and extending far beyond the perimeters of the medical/health care area. (In any event, a careful review of paperwork requirements and a more helpful attitude on the part of state, county, and other public officials and employees seems called for in light of the study of Medicaid procedures cited earlier.)

Managing Medicaid reimbursements to private providers is a major fiscal and management problem for local governments. Although numerous federal rules apply, much flexibility exists. State and local governments need to ensure that the care provided is nondiscriminatory to patients in quality and to governments in efficiency and economy (for example, no "gold-plating" of services through unnecessary tests). A major and controversial question is how government can monitor and regulate reimbursed services without impairing efficiency, quality of care, and professional-patient relationships.

For example, research conducted by the Rand Corporation, HHS, and others has shown that often, but not always, public purchase of Medicaid services on a prepaid basis from health maintenance organizations (HMOs) can result in (a) greater attention to preventive health care, with resultant long-term savings, and (b) lesser short-term costs, especially in hospitalization, due to the built-in incentive to the organization to deliver care in as cost-effective a manner as possible. A 1984 Rand research report contended that future Medicare and Medicaid costs would become unbearable in the absence of substantial reform in the reimbursement and standard-setting process. For Medicaid, these included facilitation of the movement toward a prepaid, capitated basis; modifying eligibility and eliminating marginal benefits; expanding patient cost sharing; and giving states yet more flexibility in setting hospital rates and purchasing goods and services in high volume.[39] Conversely, medical associations, hospital administrators, and others point to two dangers in the HMO route, especially where strong governmental fiscal pressure is applied: (a) care is delivered in an increasingly assembly-line, time-clock mode, undermining patient-physician relationships; and (b) unduly early hospital discharges can impede orderly and adequate recovery from illness or surgery.

Teenage Motherhood

An estimate of teenage pregnancy outcomes in 1980 showed, in descending order, 38 percent abortions; 27 percent marriage; 18 percent single motherhood;

13 percent miscarriage; and 4 percent adoption.[40] Of about 560,000 teenage mothers in 1985, nearly a third (32 percent) were at or below the poverty line, and three out of ten were receiving public assistance.[41]

In addition to poverty, one or more of several adverse health factors may face many pregnant teenagers. If the prospective mother is a user of drugs other than, or in addition to, marijuana (cocaine, "crack," heroin, LSD, and so on), the prospects are high, in the absence of withdrawal, that the baby will be inherently addicted when born. If the mother is an IV drug user, unless she is tested and found negative, she may be infected with the AIDS virus. Preliminary research has indicated that from 30 to 65 percent of babies born to infected mothers will already be infected.[42] Heavy smoking can also adversely affect the developing fetus. All of these are factors for the prospective mother and her counselor(s) to take into account in arriving at a decision whether or not to terminate the pregnancy, if this is an option being considered.

Closely connected with those decisions is the willingness or ability, or lack thereof, of the prospective mother to go onto an adequate prenatal diet and to obtain prenatal medical examinations and guidelines during the pregnancy. Data from the 1980 national natality survey showed a strong relationship between the "wantedness" of pregnancy and the decision to seek proper prenatal care.[43] Thirty percent of the more than 1 million pregnant teenagers yield second and third babies, and U.S. girls under fifteen are five times more likely to give birth than their counterparts in any other developed country.[44] The Institute of Medicine study of low-weight births, citing research by the Alan Guttmacher Institute, stated that "about 9.5 million low-income and 5 million sexually active teenagers needed subsidized (i.e. supported at least in part by public funds) family planning care, but over 40 percent of both groups did not obtain medically supervised contraceptive care."[45] Continuance of drug or alcohol abuse and heavy smoking, coupled with improper diet and the failure to receive adequate prenatal care, leads inevitably to a high level of infant mortality, accompanied or preceded by low weight of the baby at birth.

Table 5.5 shows lowest and highest incidence, by state, of low-birth-weight babies and infant mortality. Three facts stand out in the table: (1) a very close— practically direct—correlation between low weight at birth and the infant mortality rate for those states having high rates in both categories; (2) a clustering of both high categories around the District of Columbia and states in the deep South; (3) in both categories, and in both high and low state groups, a shocking disparity between whites and blacks.

The first of these facts is a medical relationship, with low and very low (1,500 grams or below) birth weight a major survival factor, both at birth and during the first year. Reports from various sources underscore the close relationship among malnutrition, low birth weight, and mental retardation. Twice as many low-weight births occur in low-income families; these same families account for a majority of all mentally defective children in the country.

The second fact is reflective of high poverty rates in the high state group. The

Table 5.5
Rates for Low-Birth-Weight Babies, Infant Mortality, and Births to Single Mothers by Race in Selected States, 1985, and Initial Prenatal Care by Age and Race, 1970–85

State	Low Birth Weight (Under 2,500 gr.)			Infant Mortality (Death in 12 Mos.)			Live Births to Unmarried Mothers		
	All	Wh.	Blk.	All	Wh.	Blk	All	Wh.	Blk.
U.S. 1985	6.8	5.6	12.4	10.6	9.3	18.2	22.0	14.5	60.1
U.S. 1970	7.9	6.8	13.9	20.0	17.8	32.6	10.7	5.7	37.4
Minnesota	4.8	4.6	9.8	9.2	9.1	16.6	15.1	12.4	64.1
North Dakota	4.9	4.8	6.9	8.5	8.2	*	11.5	8.5	6.9
Alaska	4.9	4.5	10.6	11.5	9.8	19.1*	18.3	11.3	26.7
Iowa	5.1	5.0	10.2	9.1	8.9	16.3*	13.6	12.2	61.8
New Hampshire	5.0	5.0	8.2	9.4	9.4	*	13.4	13.3	24.6
California	6.0	5.3	11.9	9.6	9.2	16.2	24.6	22.3	56.2
Texas	6.8	5.9	12.2	10.4	9.7	15.9	16.4	11.6	48.2
New York	7.0	5.6	11.9	11.1	9.7	16.8	28.1	18.7	62.2
Florida	7.5	6.0	12.4	11.4	9.2	18.5	25.8	13.9	63.3
Illinois	7.2	5.4	13.5	12.1	9.5	22.2	25.7	13.3	71.8
Mississippi	8.8	5.9	12.2	14.4	10.0	19.5	32.9	8.5	61.0
S. Carolina	8.6	5.9	13.0	14.6	10.6	21.1	26.4	9.4	54.0
Louisiana	8.7	5.9	13.1	12.5	9.1	18.1	28.6	10.0	58.1
Dist. Col.	13.3	5.2	15.3	20.4	9.9	23.1	56.7	16.3	67.1

Initial Pre-Natal Care, By Per Cent of Live Births, Race, and Age

	First Trimester			Third Trimstr. or None			Below 20		
	All	Wh.	Bl.	All	Wh.	Bl.	All	Wh.	Bl.
1970	68.0	72.4	44.4	7.9	6.2	16.6	17.6	15.2	31.3
1980	76.3	79.3	62.7	5.1	4.3	8.8	15.6	13.5	26.5
1985	76.2	79.4	61.8	5.7	4.7	10.0	12.7	10.8	23.0

Source: U.S. Public Health Service, *Health, United States, 1987*, March 1988, 38–39, 46–47; National Center for Health Statistics (NCHS), *Monthly Vital Statistics Report*, July 17, 1987, 29.

Note: State data: infant mortality, 1983–85; otherwise 1985.
* Rate is of doubtful reliability where number of births is below 5,000 and not shown where births number below 1,000.

third—great differences in rates between births to blacks and whites—undoubtedly has a highly poverty-related cause, perhaps coupled with a high incidence of adverse health practices (smoking and drug or alcohol use) among black mothers; drug/alcohol use also is somewhat associated with poverty.

As would be expected, infant mortality rates tend to be much higher in the inner city than elsewhere because of poverty factors and the higher incidence of drug addiction among young mothers. About a quarter million dangerously underweight babies are born in the United States each year, and their chance of survival to the first birthday is approximately one in ten. Each year about 300,000 women give birth after little or no prenatal care, and their babies comprise two-thirds of infant deaths.[46]

In the 1985–88 period the U.S. House Select Committee on Children, Youth, and Families conducted a series of hearings interspersed with reviews of research and evaluation reports drawn from a wide range of governmental, academic, medical, and other professional reports and journals as to the relative effectiveness of program expenditures in several areas. The ratios of savings (future expenses avoided or reduced by use of the program) to expenditure and 1986–87 proportion of eligible children and youth being served or not served were as follows: supplemental food program (WIC), 3/1, 44 percent being served; prenatal care, first trimester, 3.38/1, 24 percent not being served; Medicaid-financed comprehensive prenatal care, 2/1, 3 million of 12.95 million children below poverty line not served; childhood immunization, 10/1, 15 to 25 percent not served, depending on the disease; preschool education, 6/1, half of 10.7 million children enrolled in public or private preschool programs; and compensatory education, 3,700/750, 50 percent being served.[47]

Drug and Alcohol Abuse

In 1986 the National Institute on Drug Abuse (NIDA) (one of the National Institutes of Health) issued a report on the use of drugs in 1985 by age group and by four drug categories—marijuana/hashish, the hallucinogens (LSD, PCP, and others), inhalants, and cocaine, along with several others including heroin, stimulants, sedatives, tranquilizers, analgesics, alcohol, and cigarettes. The highlights of incidence in the total population of age twelve and over (190.7 million) of having tried (once or more in lifetime) and current use (within month preceding survey) included the following:

- For marijuana/hashish, 33 percent of total population had tried and 10 percent were current users (a decline from 11 percent in 1982), with heaviest use in the 18–25 age group (22 percent).

- For cocaine, 12 percent had tried and 3 percent (5.75 million) were users, an increase from 2 percent, with heaviest use in the 18–25 age group (8 percent).

- Heroin use had declined to below .5 percent of any age group; 1 percent of the population had tried it (1.9 million).

- Hallucinogen use was at a 1 percent level, with heaviest (2 percent) in the 18–25 age group.

- Alcohol had the highest current use in the total population (59 percent), with 86 percent having tried it; current use was at a 72 percent level for the 18–25 age group and 61 percent for the group 26 and over.

• Current cigarette use was at 32 percent for the population, with the 18–25 age group at 37 percent.

For the 12–17 age group, heaviest current use of all drugs was alcohol (32 percent), cigarettes (16 percent), marijuana (12 percent), inhalants (4 percent) and cocaine, stimulants, and analgesics (2 percent each).

A NIDA survey of the high school graduating class of 1987 showed, as did the 1982 survey, a significant regional difference in use; for cocaine, with similar differentials in the other drug categories, the "annual prevalence of current use," was: Northeast, 13.3 percent; North Central, 7.5 percent; South, 7.0 percent; and West, 16.4 percent. Additionally, the NIDA 1987 study covered a representative sample of private and public high school graduates of the classes of 1975 through 1986, essentially representing all high school graduates aged 19–29, including those attending college. Drug-use trends for this group comprised a rise in the early seventies, with peaking at different times: Nonmedical use of tranquilizers and barbiturates occurring in the mid-seventies; marijuana in 1978; PCP, 1979; LSD, 1980 and amphetemines, 1982. Cocaine did not peak until 1986, with "reported use in the prior year" dropping from 20 percent to 16 percent in 1987. For eight years prior to 1986, there had been relatively no change in the rate of cocaine experimentation.[48] However encouraging the 1987 survey results may appear, it should be emphasized that the 19–29 age group studied included no high school dropouts. Within underclass areas in the same time period, usage intensified to several times that of the total population in the age group.

Public policy issues as to how to stem the supply of, and curb the demand for, hard drugs in the late eighties were similar to those of the mid-seventies, with the exception of random and mandatory testing. They included (1) the diffusion among agencies at both national and state levels of responsibility for apprehending distributors and rehabilitating users; (2) the efficacy of methadone maintenance as a rehabilitation measure for heroin addicts; (3) the search for more effective drug education programs in the schools and elsewhere; (4) more recently, mandatory random drug testing of sensitive categories of public and private employees (law enforcement, truck, plane, and train operators, air traffic controllers, and so on). Mandatory testing had moved to the front burner of federal, state, and large private-employer policy.

The issue of methadone maintenance assumed an additional dimension; it had been found effective in keeping persons off heroin and in enabling them to resume regular employment in the labor force, thereby yielding dividends in crime reduction, enhancement of personal confidence, and a saving in public expenditure for repeated rehabilitation attempts. However, it was argued that one form of addiction was being replaced by another, and that only if substantial resources of money and talent in counseling, follow-up, and related rehabilitative activities were available could permanent cures be effected. Consequently, in national legislation and in some states expenditure for maintenance alone was

Table 5.6
Percentage Distribution of AIDS Deaths among Adults (over 15) by Race and Transmission Category, 1987

		Percentage			
Category	No.	White*	Black*	Hisp.	Other*
Homosexual					
/bisexual	5,050	72.7	17.0	9.2	1.1
IV Drug Users	1,386	23.2	54.0	22.5	.3
IV DU's					
/homosexual	582	62.2	28.2	9.1	.5
Heterosexual**	338	17.5	73.1	9.2	.3
Hemopheliacs/other					
clotting disorder	87	88.5	5.7	4.6	1.1
Blood transfusion	252	74.6	17.1	5.6	2.8
Undetermined	302	45.0	36.8	16.9	1.3
Total	7,997	60.2	27.2	11.6	.9

Source: U.S. Public Health Service, *Health United States, 1987*, 1988, table 39, pp. 84–85.

* Non-Hispanic.
** Heterosexual contact with person having AIDS or at risk of AIDS, and persons without other identified risks born in countries where heterosexual transmission is believed prevalent.

not permitted without the other ancillary services. This caused a rising backlog of persons desiring methadone treatment, with inadequate public funds available for the required array of associated services.

AIDS and the Underclass

Some say it is only a matter of time before the most important occupations at 8th and M [in Washington, D.C.]—prostitution and drug dealing—are supplanted by the work of undertakers.[49]

The AIDS epidemic has tended to center in urban areas. For 1987, U.S. diagnosed cases totaled 20,940 (13,095 in 1986), with deaths numbering 8,146 (down from 8,959 in 1986). Over 60 percent of the national 1986 caseload existing was concentrated within ten metropolitan areas, according to the USPHS National Centers for Disease Control in Atlanta: New York, San Francisco, Los Angeles, Houston, Washington, D.C., Miami, Newark, Chicago, Philadelphia, and Dallas. For the years 1982–87 and including scattered pre-1982 reports, the cumulative diagnosed cases totaled 49,975. Of these, nearly 70 percent had come from five states: New York (13,174), California (11,141), Florida (3,624), Texas (3,465), and New Jersey (3,240).[50] Table 5.6 shows the 1987 distribution of AIDS deaths by transmission category and race. Heterosexual cases were tending to be concentrated in the black and Hispanic populations, as well as in the drug-associated transmissions.

The Intergovernmental Health Policy Project at George Washington University estimated fiscal year 1988 state fund expenditures for AIDS programs at around $155 million, with proportionate purposes of education/information, 21 percent; support services, 19 percent; research, 17 percent; patient care, 16 percent; testing/counseling, 12 percent; and the remainder for administration and miscellaneous activities.[51]

Major issues confronting state legislatures in 1989 included such actions and questions as (1) mounting education campaigns directly through state health agencies and indirectly through and assistance to local governments and private organizations to inform the public about risks of AIDS and precautions to be taken to avoid infection; (2) provision of free needles to IV drug users;[52] (3) incidence reporting by health officials and whether or not to provide confidential information to sexual partners; (4) penalties against carriers of the virus who knowingly infect others; (5) prohibiting discrimination against persons with AIDS; and (6) voluntary or mandatory testing of various categories of people (such as food handlers, health service personnel, and applicants for marriage licenses) for presence of the virus. Congress debated similar measures nationally in 1988.

CONTINUED FAILING GRADES FOR INNER-CITY PUBLIC SCHOOLS

When you see dropout rates of 60 percent, when you look at the disaster that is the New York City school system, you have to be concerned for the city, the state, the nation and yourself.[53]

In the late eighties Governor Mario Cuomo and Donna Shalala (former Hunter College president) were calling the New York City school system a ''disaster'' and a ''rotten barrel,'' respectively. Secretary of Education William Bennett was saying to the Chicago school system, ''You've got close to educational meltdown here.''[54] In St. Louis one in four girls were becoming pregnant before reaching the twelfth grade. In Detroit dropout rates were reported at 80 percent in the worst areas, with a citywide rate of 41 percent. In Boston fifty-five students were expelled during 1987 for carrying guns. In Texas, with a three-to-one disparity range in per pupil expenditures, in some inner-city districts where need was greatest, spending was the lowest.[55]

These conditions and the officials and reporters describing them were echoing a decade-old public frustration with the state of public education in the nation's central cities. Because of the continually increasing concentration of poor people in these cities, with the accompanying health and behavioral problems, public school systems and especially the principals and teachers in individual schools serving underclass areas were facing seemingly insurmountable problems.

In a 1988 report entitled *An Imperiled Generation,* the Carnegie Foundation for the Advancement of Teaching found the condition of urban schools to be

Table 5.7

K–12 Public School Enrollment by Race 1986–87, per Pupil Revenue, and External Aid 1985–86 for Selected City Districts

City	Enroll-ment	Per Pupil Revenue*	Ext. Aid* Amt.	%	White	Black	Hisp.	Other
New York	939,142	$5,406	$2,487	46.0	21.3	38.1	33.9	6.7
Los Angeles	584,883	4,184	3,552	84.9	17.7	18.2	55.7	6.3
Chicago	412,661	3,957	2,517	63.6	14.1	62.9	24.4	3.1
Philadelphia	195,552	4,578	2,576	60.2	24.1	63.6	9.0	3.2
Houston	193,855	3,304	1,372	41.5	37.4	42.6	17.0	3.0
Detroit	190,679	3,777	2,565	67.9	9.2	88.1	1.9	.8
Dallas	132,388	3,506	1,180	33.7	20.5	48.9	28.2	2.4
San Diego	108,254	4,018	2,531	63.0	44.3	18.5	19.4	17.8
Memphis	105,091	2,767	2,299	83.1	22.2	77.8	neg.	neg.
Milwaukee	93,731	4,698	3,033	64.6	34.0	53.9	7.5	4.6
San Francisco	66,978	3,988	3,297	82.7	15.2	18.4	21.4	45.0
Indianapolis	50,628	4,099	2,629	64.1	51.6	47.0	.6	.8
St. Louis	46,636	4,964	3,531	71.1	24.0	76.0	neg.	neg.

Source: Council of the Greater City Schools for 1986–87 enrollment; Bureau of the Census, *Finances of Public School Systems in 1985–86*, GF 86, no. 10, 1988, table 9, for 1985–86 per pupil district revenue and per pupil external aid.

* External aid: includes state and federal aid, 1985–86. For portions by state, see appendix 1.E.

desperate and stated that "bold, aggressive action is needed now to avoid leaving a huge and growing segment of the nation's youth civically unprepared and economically unempowered." The report cited numerous examples from the six city schools visited (New York, Los Angeles, Chicago, Houston, Boston, and Cleveland). From Boston came one appraisal stating that in addition to a 44 percent dropout rate, "over 40 percent of those who do reach 12th grade score below the 30th percentile on a standardized reading test. They may graduate, but they are functionally illiterate."[56]

It is apparent from data already presented that young children emerging from infancy in the underclass areas at age three face heavy odds in mortal, economic, and societal survival. It was against these kinds of darkening prospects that the Committee for Economic Development (CED) in 1987 issued a "call on the nation to embark upon a third wave of reform that gives the highest priority to early and sustained intervention in the lives of disadvantaged children."[57]

Pertinent Data on Inner-City Public and Private Education

Table 5.7 shows 1986–87 K–12 enrollment and racial composition and 1985–86 per capita expenditures and external federal and state aid for the nation's thirteen largest city public school systems. Appendix 5.B presents similar data for an additional number of the largest systems. The disparity in fiscal capacity between central-city and suburban areas is nowhere so evident and critical as in resources and expenditures for public education, even in those states where state funds comprise 70 percent or more of state-local expenditures for K–12 education. As the CED report points out, "Wealthier school districts routinely spend more per pupil than do schools that serve the inner city. But schools serving the disadvantaged need more resources, not less, because [their children require greater effort and therefore] . . . are in greater need."[58]

About $150 billion annually, or 5.3 percent of the GNP, was required to keep public schools in operation in the fiscal year 1985–86.[59] To this must be added amounts in the magnitude of $50 billion for private education (the 1984–85 estimate was $47 billion), comprised of tuition payments by parents (estimated at $15 billion in 1987) and support from a variety of religious, philanthropic, and other nonprofit and for-profit sources. Corporations in 1987 were spending millions of dollars annually on over 46,000 partnership arrangements with local public school districts, according to the National School Boards Association (NSBA).[60] Employer-provided formalized learning programs were estimated at $30 billion for 1984.[61]

Preschool: What Happens at Age Three?

Beginning with the Head Start program—a part of the War on Poverty initiative of the Johnson administration in the mid-sixties—a belief grew among local social agencies, foundations, educators, and others in the child welfare services field that for a young child living in a stressful home environment, an early transfer for at least part of most days from such an environment into a more orderly and happy surrounding was necessary if the child were to enter school with anywhere close to an even chance of progressing satisfactorily through the early school years. Later research results, although somewhat mixed and controversial, tended to show that Head Start and other preschool pupils benefited from that early experience. As the plight of young children in poverty and underclass homes worsened in the seventies and eighties, convictions about the desirability of preschool opportunities for poor children aged three to five strengthened and were translated into policies and programs in some states.

By 1987 the desirability—and indeed the necessity—of preschool orientation for poor children was being voiced in several quarters:

- The National Governors' Association (NGA) stated that "states should work with four- and five-year olds from poor families to help them get ready for school and to decrease the chances that they will drop out later."[62]
- The CED *Children in Need* report called for "quality pre-school programs for all disadvantaged three and four year olds," observing that such programs "have been shown to improve school readiness, enhance later academic and social performance, and reduce the need for remedial education during the school years."[63]
- A *Business Week* editorial endorsed the CED report recommendations and specifically "quality pre-school enrichment programs for all disadvantaged three- and four-year olds."[64]

- A *New York Times* editorial underscored a finding of a House Select Committee that "$1 spent on pre-school education can save $4.75 in later social costs."[65]

- Kentucky Governor Martha Layne Collins stated: "Early childhood programs cost money and sometimes a lot of it. But crime costs more, overcrowded prisons cost more, welfare costs more, and undereducation costs more."[66]

In the fall of 1985, .84 million children were enrolled in public nursery schools and 1.63 million in similar private schools. This 2.47 million nursery school enrollment represented a 42 percent increase from 1975.[67] In 1984 over 70 percent of white nursery school students were in private schools, but only a third of black nursery schoolers were.[68] Despite the interest and support being voiced in 1987, it was still apparent that many of the children needing this kind of preschool preparation the most were receiving the least.

Typically, nursery and other preschool activities combine day-care, play, health, and early education components. For children from underclass homes, play-socializing in a pleasant environment, along with overdue health attention, may be the most important. Educational experts differ strongly as to the wisdom of encouraging trying to recognize letters or numbers at the age level of three to four, or even in kindergarten. David Elkind has blamed ambitious parents for getting children into teacher-directed and other learning situations too soon.[69] However, for children from underclass homes, the "ambitious parent pressure" may be much less a risk than a disturbing home and neighborhood environment, characterized all too often by brawling and physical violence in the home and gunfire in the halls and streets.

The thrust of programs for preschool child care is toward giving the young child a break from a disquieting home environment. Some argue that this kind of policy, carried onward through day care during the early school years, amounts to a preemption by state authority, removing child custody from the mother and home. (This line of argument dissuaded President Nixon from approving a congressionally passed, comprehensive bill for a federally aided day-care program in the early seventies, when conservative objections on religious and family-structure grounds were augmented by claims that the mother's place was in the home with children and not at work and that the government should not tilt the balance toward going to work.)

A difficult legal and ethical issue can arise when a mother declines to permit her child to be enrolled in a preschool activity even though the daily life of the child at home is one of parental neglect. Consequently, state legislation authorizing and financing preschool programs needs to be drafted carefully to deal with this and other issues.

For example, it was pointed out in a 1987 CSG report that "pressure for preschool places will be driven by working mothers' need for reliable child care and by the struggle for educational advantage for their children among middle class parents. . . . The states' interest may be in ensuring the quality and safety of all pre-school programs and concentrating on serving those who can benefit most."[70]

This kind of targeting to the neediest may make sense fiscally and socially; however, it is symptomatic of countless similar issues facing state legislatures in authorizing programs needed most by the poor but being forced by political considerations to widen eligibility to the point that only a few of both groups, the needy and nonneedy, are served. A political middle ground often sought is to follow a user-charge pattern, with no charge to the needy and a charge of less than the full cost to the nonneedy.

Attendance Areas, School Building Use, and Physical Security

The elementary school years are critical for a child from, or living in, an underclass household or area, and such a child needs all possible support. Several educational, social, environmental, and other factors come into consideration and conflict:

- To the extent that parental interest warrants or permits, parent-teacher involvement is imperative, so that urging, encouraging, cautioning, and other communication with the child, at school and home, may be mutually supportive.

- Interaction among the school, parents and their PTA, and the community, including participation of the principal, teachers, and other school personnel in general community affairs and reciprocal support by the community and its organizations, is helpful in many ways; it shows the kids that the school, as an organization, is both deserving and receiving respect from the adult community.

- Maintenance of discipline and physical security in the classroom, in the building, and on school grounds is absolutely necessary for an adequate learning environment.

- Use of the school building after hours, on weekends, and in vacation periods for school, child and day-care, and community activities benefits the pupil from a disagreeable household; it allows time for reading, homework, or recreation and is helpful to working mothers, while at the same time strengthening school-community linkages and neighborhood cohesion and stability.

All of these factors assume a neighborhood school at the elementary level and a somewhat enlarged area for middle and high school; they may run counter to court orders or to state and/or local policies for interschool transport for racial balance, fiscal, or other administrative reasons. Conversely, if the neighborhood is crime-infested and physical security tenuous or impossible, these children-at-risk may be much better off attending a school in a better neighborhood. This may mean closing, temporarily or permanently, some neighborhood schools; at the least it means a thorough review of attendance-area policies and the assets and liabilities of the options available.[71]

Regardless of attendance-area decisions, the underutilization of school buildings appears unconscionable from educational, community, fiscal, and all other viewpoints except that from middle- and higher-income parents who absolutely insist on a summerlong vacation in the schools. (This issue was dividing the Los Angeles Unified School District in 1987.) The needs of these families clash with those of lesser means whose concerns may embrace day-care spaces for working mothers, community recreation availabilities, and most important, availability of classes for remedial and regular purposes. The long vacation in most public schools is a serious deterrent to adequate subject-matter coverage in an increasingly rigorous curriculum. The NGA report on educational results summed it up thus: "It makes no sense to keep closed half a year [the other 180 days] the school buildings in which America has invested a quarter of a trillion dollars while we are undereducated and overcrowded."[72]

The concept of the neighborhood school as a center for community activity and a meeting place for discussing problems and working to get children off to a good start educationally and socially is weakened considerably if its attendees are from another area; the school-community linkage has been severed. Table 5.7 shows distressingly small white enrollments in most of the large city districts. To the extent that busing for racial balance has caused "white flight" from public schools, it would indicate that for inner-city districts, shifting pupils out of their neighborhoods, except for purposes of getting them away from unusually dangerous conditions, probably has become educationally and sociologically counterproductive.

Pregnancy Prevention and the Role of Sex Education

As noted already, U.S. teenagers now experience one of the highest pregnancy rates in the Western world, totalling 1.1 million, resulting in nearly half a million abortions and 400,000 births annually; and lack of access to accurate reproductive and contraceptive information appears to have been one of the leading reasons for teenage pregnancy. Pregnancy is by far the leading cause of school dropout for females. Sex education is included in many if not most state and/or locally prescribed high school curricula, but two controversies nearly always surround these courses.

First, contraceptive information often is omitted or is presented in such nonspecific terms as to be inadequate for the purpose. Second, of equal if not greater importance, many schools do not include sex education as a requirement before senior high school. The AIDS problem—recognized in 1987 by a majority of the public as the nation's most serious health problem—will make it necessary to introduce some basic sex information in the schools at an earlier stage, but with contraceptive information presented later. Pregnancy, abortion, and birth data show that heterosexual activity has been beginning as early as age twelve and is fairly widespread by fifteen or sixteen. Therefore, if either value-oriented or sex education or both are to be effective, their introduction would need to come several grades earlier than has traditionally been the case.

The sex education recommendations of the CED report were as follows:

In-school health services are an appropriate mechanism through which to provide sex education, pregnancy prevention programs and follow-up services, and substance abuse programs. In the area of birth control information and services, each school should work with parents and others in the community to design a health services program that conforms to specific community needs, values, and standards.[73]

A 1985 report by the House Select Committee on Children, Youth, and Families dealing with what was being done in the states about the teen pregnancy problem found (1) inadequate information on the extent of teen pregnancies and their outcomes; (2) prevention programs given less emphasis than programs for already pregnant or parenting teens; and (3) few efforts toward teen fathers.[74]

As of April 1985 seventy-one school-based clinics were in operation in twenty-seven states, according to the Support Center for School-Based Clinics in Houston, supported by the Center for Population Options. Common characteristics of these clinics included (1) comprehensive medical services as part of the school day, including prescription and dispensation of medication; (2) operation by established medical providers; and (3) staffing by nurse practitioners aided by a mix of paraprofessionals from social work, mental health, and nursing. Many adolescents were being seen who had had no prior medical exposures, and 10 to 20 percent had previously undetected health problems.[75]

The NGA Task Force on Teenage Pregnancy reviewed results from such school-based clinics and reported the following: (1) from the St. Paul clinic, a 40 percent reduction in teenage pregnancy rates over a ten-year period; a decline in school dropout rate from 45 percent to 10 percent in three years; and a repeat pregnancy rate among mothers who stayed in school of 2 percent; (2) from West Dallas, a reduction in hospitalizations and school absenteeism; (3) and from an evaluation of the Johns Hopkins Self-Help Center Clinic, a finding of an average delay of seven months in the initiation of sexual activity among teenagers with three years' exposure to the clinic.

The task force listed possible state and local initiatives: (1) counseling postponement of teenage sexual activity through family life and sex education courses; (2) making available and urging contraceptive use where activity has begun; (3) impressing upon male teenagers the fact that creating a baby also creates an eighteen-year financial and moral obligation; and (4) enhancing basic skills, self-esteem, and the perception of positive life options.[76]

The NGA, CED, various health and education authorities, and state legislative bodies have concurred generally in the desirability of (1) encouraging pregnant teenagers and those with babies, as well as their fathers, to stay in school and (2) requiring that access to prenatal and postnatal care be assured by school and health authorities. Where part of the school building also serves as a facility for day care, the babies of mothers still in school can be tended in a pleasant surrounding.

Three important shifts in public opinion appear to have occurred by 1988. First, the need for reintroduction of societal values (concepts of right and wrong, the individual's responsibility to fellow humans, tolerance, compassion, and honesty to one's self and to others) into the educational curriculum was increasingly recognized. Second, there was agreement that teenage pregnancy was indeed a serious problem for children, schools, parents, communities, the economy, and society in general and that continuing efforts should be made to keep pregnant teenagers in school or get them back into school as promptly as possible, with careful attention to health care in the interim. Third, the need to impress upon young males the seriousness of fatherhood and the moral and legal responsibility for financially supporting any fathered child was emphasized.

Thus the key public policy issues facing public schools in the inner city seem to be the following: (1) Should school-based or neighborhood health clinics offering health services to students include contraceptive counseling and/or referrals, prescriptions, or issuance of contraceptives to students? (2) Should such clinics include discussion of abortion as an option with pregnant female students?

The NGA task force urged states to activate research on alternate approaches, comparing incidence of sexual activity, pregnancy, births, and abortions as among (a) schools that stressed abstinence and omitted contraception from sex education courses; (b) schools that included contraception in sex education courses; (c) schools that included in health clinic functions counseling, referral, prescriptions, and other assistance in birth control information and obtaining the necessary medication or devices; (d) schools that combined values education and sex education and clinics with unrestricted counseling and assistance; and (e) schools with no sex education courses or sexual counseling in clinics but with a strong emphasis on moral values and responsibilities in one or more other courses. The task force contended that the more tangible information available as to outcomes from these various approaches, the better position parents, school personnel, and state legislators and other officials would be in to make decisions on these difficult issues.[77]

Dropout Frequency, Prevention, and Retrieval

States and their constituent school districts count, or fail to count, students dropping out of school in many different ways. One of the simplest and most consistent definitions is that used by the U.S. Bureau of the Census in its Current Population Survey reports, in which the numbers of persons in the 16–24 age bracket not enrolled in school and not high school graduates are counted as dropouts. High school completion can include attainment of the general education development (GED) equivalency diploma certification.

Census data for 1985 showed 4.3 million dropouts in the 16–24 age bracket (3.5 million white, 700,000 black, and 100,000 of other races). Fourteen percent of youths aged 18–19 were dropouts (16 percent men and 12 percent women). Data for 1985 and the ten years preceding showed the dropout rate holding steady at about 13 to 14 percent, with a slow decline in the rates for blacks.[78] However, for schools in underclass areas, rates were much higher (40 to 50 percent and

Table 5.8

Principal School-related, Family-related, and Other Reasons for Leaving School Cited by Dropouts from 1980 Sophomore Cohorts by Sex

```
=================================================================
Reasons                                             Per Cent
                                               Male      Female
-----------------------------------------------------------------

School-Related

  Expelled or suspended                        13          5
  Poor grades                                  36         30
  "School not for me"                          35         31
  Could not get along with teachers            21         10

Family-Related

  Married or planning to marry                  7         31
  Pregnant                                    ---         23
  Had to support family                        14          8

Work-Related

  Offered job                                  27         11
  To enter military                             7          1
-----------------------------------------------------------------
```

Source: U.S. General Accounting Office, *School Dropouts*, 1986, 14, derived in turn from National Center for School Statistics, U.S. Department of Education, *High School and Beyond*, NCES 930221b, March 1985.

Note: Universe was 2,289 dropouts from more than 30,000 10th graders in 1980 from 1,015 high schools. (Some gave more than one reason for dropping out; thus percentages do not add up to 100.)

even higher, especially for minority youth).[79] Students from families of low-income, low-skill wage earners and limited educational backgrounds had dropout rates about three times those from the top end of the socioeconomic scale (22 versus 7 percent).[80]

Another study found that in schools where over one-half the students lived in poverty, the dropout rate was 30 percent. It also was found that southwestern states were suffering the highest rates (21 percent) and the Pacific Northwest the lowest (9 percent).[81] Several studies of dropouts noted the interdistrict fiscal resource disparity problem.

Reasons and danger signals for dropping out require two vantage points of reference: (*a*) reasons given by the individual students dropping out and (*b*) the leading indicators of dropout risks as identified in the various studies of the problem. Table 5.8 shows major reasons given by the students.

Studies of the dropout population have found the following characteristics most frequently present:

• From family low on socioeconomic scale (for example, income, school years completed by parents, low skills)

- Single-parent, welfare family in the South or a large city
- From a minority ethnic group
- In the vocational, as contrasted to the academic, school track
- Low achievement scores, low grades, dissatisfaction with school, lower self-esteem
- Record of delinquency and/or truancy
- Pregnancy
- Substantial number of employment hours while in high school
- Two or more years behind grade level
- Having relatively little knowledge of the labor market[82]

Dropout prevention measures being proposed in the mid- and late eighties rested on a variety of bases, including (a) a caring and committed school staff; (b) parental involvement; (c) motivational stimuli in the curricula; (d) other school system changes; and (e) local government and business community involvement and support.[83] Several proposed measures touch two or more of these bases.

From many sources came an urgent recommendation for smaller schools (for example, 300 to 400 students), with a lower student-teacher ratio (below twenty to one); it is extremely difficult to create a "caring environment" with a mass-production, assembly-line process. The smaller schools would permit more individualized attention and lower the risk of individual students getting lost in the shuffle.

Gaining the interest, support, and active participation of parents (termed the "home curriculum" in the CED report) is crucial because of the typically low initial interest and feeling for educational values in many disadvantaged homes. A strong rise in parent involvement was a major factor in a number of turnarounds from worst to better or best schools in inner cities. "Schools need to adhere to a code of discipline that requires consultation with parents before punishment is imposed."[84]

Identification of "dropout risk" students at the elementary level should be stressed, with special teacher and counselor attention from that point on throughout subsequent grades until the student is adjudged no longer at risk; this should be tied in closely with grade promotions or retentions.

Incentives to stay in school need to be improved. Possible approaches include pairing potential dropouts with caring adults; privately supported college scholarship assistance programs; involvement of at-risk students in extracurricular programs; alternative schools within the high school structure; and work and community service exposure.[85]

Year-round schools and the use of school buildings as an alternative to the street in spare time after school hours should be considered.

There is an urgent need to counter peer disdain for academic achievement. "Born into poor, often fatherless homes, many of these children grow up in gang-ridden neighborhoods where the arbiters of street culture disdain academic achievement. For many of these students there is tremendous social pressure against achievement in school. Blacks are often accused of 'acting white' if they study."[86]

Teams of teachers, counselors, and city health and social workers could work with at-risk students and parents on academic, discipline, health, and other problems. "Educators are understandably reluctant to assume the responsibility of social workers and health care providers. However . . . where environmental problems sabotage a child's development and progress, the schools have no choice but to provide leadership . . . [and to serve as] catalytic institutions to resolve them."[87]

Conversely, the traditional "arms-length" relationship between city halls and boards of education should be terminated. "You [mayors] pay for the schools' failures—to the tune of $4,600 per dropout per year in higher social spending and law enforcement costs . . . and you pay politically too. Most of your constituents don't know who's on the school board, . . . but they know their mayor, and when they're unhappy about the schools, a bit of that unhappiness rubs off on City Hall."[88]

Business-school partnerships can learn of skill shortcomings noted by local private employers in employment of high school graduates; provide work exposure and potential future employment to dropout risks; and provide financial and other support to the school. "[Business] . . . has demonstrated its commitment to educational excellence through a broad spectrum of partnerships with the schools. It is now incumbent upon business to focus its collaborative activities more sharply on disadvantaged children. . . . We urge business to become a driving force . . . and a prime advocate of educational initiatives for disadvantaged youngsters. . . . The business community should take the lead in encouraging and supporting higher funding levels where they are needed both for early prevention programs and for the public education system."[89]

In 1985 the National Education Association (NEA) expanded the scope of its National Foundation for the Improvement of Education (NFIE). It established a new and major base of financial and programmatic support from the nearly 2 million teachers and other members of NEA. A portion of annual NEA dues was pledged to support the foundation's new activities. It obtained initial and continuing public support also from a broad range of business, civic, and other community-type organizations, as well as from the NGA, the NCSL, the Education Commission of the States, and other governmental bodies. Its initial and major project under the expanded mission—Operation Rescue—was aimed at reducing the number of public school dropouts. Through 1986–87 NFIE was making grants to local NEA chapters for the establishment or expansion of promising dropout-prevention approaches. Of the twenty-one NFIE grants in 1986–87, three went to major central-city districts with a number of underclass areas—Los Angeles Unified (after-school tutoring at a 96 percent Hispanic school); San Antonio Independent (expansion of high school literacy programs in three schools) and Memphis (child care services for teen parents).[90]

Dropout retrieval measures comprise a highly important part of coping with the overall dropout problem. Those that return to school and graduate and those who pursue outside study and achieve an equal level of basic cognitive skills required for a high school diploma can then proceed to higher education or go directly into the work force on an approximately even competitive basis. In terms of numbers, effective retrieval measures, with a significant qualitative caveat discussed later, are as important on a long-term basis as the prevention measures. The Congressional Research Service (CRS) in 1986 estimated that close to 50 percent of teenage dropouts later completed their secondary education.[91]

The test for the general equivalency diploma (successful completion of the general educational development program) has become known and widely accepted as a rough equivalent of a high school diploma. Passing rates on the test vary from state to state. In 1985, 414,000 persons passed the test and received the diploma, which was 15 percent of the number graduating from high school that year (2.7 million). High school seniors that year totalled 73.3 percent of the country's seventeen-year-old population; however, only 32 percent of the GEDs awarded that year were to seventeen-year-olds or less, or 3.6 percent of the total population of that age, raising the percentage of seventeen-year-olds graduating or completing the GED to about 77 percent.[92] However, some studies have shown that many pass the GED test with only a sixth-grade reading level, and only about 8 percent of GED holders who go on to college complete as much as two years of college study.[93]

Employer perceptions may not be fully negative toward the GED holder, however, in comparison with the high school graduate. There may be a recognition that cognitively, the GED represents a lesser degree of achievement, perhaps equating to a need for two additional years of training or relevant experience in order to equal the high school graduate. In contrast, especially to employers interested in employing qualified disadvantaged youth for less difficult positions, the fact that the individual has pursued the GED after dropping out of school indicates a degree of ambition, perseverance and diligence that results in worker potential equal to, or perhaps exceeding, that of a high school graduate with average or below-average grades.[94]

Structural Changes in Large-City School Systems

Beset as they are with the educational, health, poverty, discipline, dropout, and other problems associated with urban underclass areas, some of the largest school systems appeared in the late eighties to be in policy, administrative, and competency chaos. It was obvious that the system had become too top-heavy, unresponsive, and in critical need of immediate and drastic change. Many changes, such as the community use of school facilities, revision in tenure and other personnel aspects (for example, tenure for principals in New York City was a contentious issue for state officials in 1987–88), and other basic structural changes required action on the part of local boards of education, local governments, and state governments.

Some of these weaknesses were addressed by teachers, principals, parents, and others at the local level. Schools in the Miami-Dade system in Florida (the country's fourth-largest) were beginning to confront the "rigidity" problem, one that is bred by size and nurtured through inertia—a major difference between urban public and private schools. "The biggest difference . . . is not the students. . . . It is, rather who controls the educational process . . . private schools . . . are autonomous units, answerable directly to the people who pay for them. Bureaucratic trivia is at a minimum. Parental involvement is usually high."[95] (Of course, the socioeconomic fact of direct correlation among parent income, parental support, and student achievement accounted for most of the point being made, but it did not explain or justify the public bureaucracy problem.) The base for change in Florida was in a school board–teacher union agreement for joint superintendent-union waiver of any rule or procedure—subject to board ratification—that seemed to be impeding the efficient, equitable, and competent delivery of educational services. This allows teachers to come up with changes for fund reallocation, curricula, working conditions, and other needed alterations as seen through their eyes.

Fortunately, the two major national teacher organizations—NEA and the American Federation of Teachers (AFT)—were beginning to show increasing responsiveness in the late eighties to the problems that had been festering in the public school systems for two decades (for example, NEA's concern with the dropout problem). On the structural problems such as bureaucratic inertia, the AFT gave unqualified support to the concept of a testing and certifying system for the nation's teachers. AFT president Albert Shanker, in comparing the problems of public education with those of the auto industry, was quoted as saying, "We can't just put new tail fins on. We've got to build a new car!"[96]

The structure and size of the two teacher unions (a nearly three-to-one NEA advantage in membership size and a more complex NEA governance and organizational structure) permits comparatively greater flexibility in the AFT in forcing change upon locals. Many state NEA affiliates play a strong but complicating role in NEA policy formulation. Arthur Wise of the Rand Corporation commented that "[the AFT] is out in front right now on the professionalism agenda, at least as it pertains to changing the way school districts do business."[97]

Summary Comments

In addition to the measures for dropout prevention and retrieval and for general improvement in inner-city schools serving underclass and other poverty areas, there are some less widely supported and more controversial policy options which may warrant attention.

Targeting of most of new money for education to the worst schools. The widely supported proposal for a move to smaller schools in city systems and to lower student-teacher ratios in schools serving disadvantaged pupils should be implemented on a staged and targeted basis, rather than across the board. Since in most city areas more than half the large increase in expenditures needed will come from state governments, and a large part of the remainder from local taxpayers, pressures will be strong to spread the increased funds around the state to include every district with any "countable" proportion of students from low-income households (which in turn are defined quite liberally in some federal and state program legislation; for example, those below 70 to 80 percent of median family income). The resulting help to the most seriously distressed schools within city districts would be modest indeed.

The business community should consider carefully the targeting question in the light of the political forces operating in a disequalizing direction in the distribution of public funds when the conditions of central-city schools border on the indescribable. The combined public and private objective here is to move the highest possible number of otherwise hopelessly unqualified youth into the labor force within the context of a given resource input.

Getting the best teachers into the worst schools. The reward system in most districts, both union and nonunion, operates in such a way as to place the most experienced teachers in the highest-achieving and most orderly schools and let those with the lowest seniority "cut their teeth" in very difficult and least desirable assignments. The schools with the highest proportion of underclass enrollment cannot appreciably improve their performance without highly competent and knowledgeable as well as sincere and dedicated personnel. The U.S. foreign service, the military, and most large private employers provide additional compensation for hardship, hazardous, and other highly demanding duty posts; any school system that operates in the opposite direction is acting adversely to the objectives so widely supported for improving the educational lot of the disadvantaged.

Increasing the accountability of school, principal, teacher, and other personnel for improved cognitive and affective student outputs, with state intervention where deterioration persists. Most public schools and many city schools have come a substantial distance from the sixties and the disdain by the education establishment in those days for comparative analyses of school performance as measured by the cognitive abilities of students and for the inclusion of any value-oriented courses in the curriculum. However, the economic and social costs of inadequate cognitive and behavioral preparation in underclass areas have become much more apparent, and the improved school performance has not kept up with the deteriorating environment in those areas. Accountability needs to progress beyond tests; many believe that the student population is being overtested, at least in conventional standardized achievement tests.[98] State government receivership, as enacted in New Jersey and half a dozen other states and endorsed by the NGA, seems warranted but dangerous. It needs to be evaluated rigorously as experience is gained through practice, and modified or tightened accordingly.

Giving a helping hand to parochial and other private schools in underclass areas. In some poverty-impacted urban school districts, Catholic, Lutheran, and other private schools have for two or more decades been islands of relative stability in a sea of chaos.[99] Many of them are striving mightily to serve the disadvantaged youth in their areas. Because of smaller size, tighter discipline, and other factors less hindering to adequate performance than in their public counterparts, they often have performed in exemplary fashion.

Several of the proposals of the CED, the NGA, and others for restructuring large-city school systems into a "bottom-up" mode have incorporated some of the features that have enabled the private schools to continue persevering and often prevailing against the overwhelming problems confronting educational efforts in underclass areas. The business community and city governments, to the extent permitted by state law and court decisions, should not exclude the private schools in their supportive and collaborative arrangements for improved education of the urban underclass.

Providing employment placement assistance to both graduating and dropout students. For many years most high schools have given considerably more counselor time to college placement than to employment placement. Inner-city schools have an equal obligation to help a student not bound for college, whether graduating or dropping out, to get that first "real job"—a vital juncture in his or her future prospects for economic survival.

Collaboration among public school boards, local governments, and civic and social agencies in providing community service instruction and experience. In underclass areas civic education and civic responsibilities are subjects and values given relatively little attention in most curricula. Civics instruction, coupled with work in a local government or private community agency, might well be a useful bridge to postgraduation employment as well as preparation for useful citizenship.

In relation to school employment and welfare, the Wisconsin legislature enacted a "learnfare" program effective in 1987, aimed at students from thirteen to nineteen. It precluded their being counted for AFDC benefit purposes if they were not attending school regularly. This was expected to bring several thousand young adults back to school as well as preventing several thousand others from dropping out.[100] Similarly, school attendance as a prerequisite for obtaining and retaining a driver's license by teenagers was being discussed in some states.

ANTISOCIAL BEHAVIOR IN THE URBAN UNDERCLASS

A former executive at the Chicago Housing Authority, the landlord for the city's approximately 40,000 public housing units, concedes that "after 4:30 the gangs run these developments." . . . Some compare Henry Horner [a public housing project] with war zones like Beirut and Northern Ireland. . . . In Belfast, . . . the IRA "kneecaps" people who have disobeyed its laws. In the projects people are shot in the legs for disobeying gangs' rules.[101]

Thus life, crime, and punishment go on in the nation's underclass areas. As Edward Banfield said in 1970, "The streets may be filled with armies of policemen, but violent crime and civil disorder will decrease very little.'' Hopeless? Possibly, but not beyond hope if public policy so wills.

Neal Peirce reported from New York City in 1986 about a visit to Spofford, ''a children's jail infamous for inmate abuse, staff disorder and high escape rates.'' To this institution were committed children charged with, and awaiting trial for, more serious crimes, such as alleged ''car thieves, pickpockets, crack pushers, robbers, muggers and sometimes rapists and murderers—all aged 10 to 16.'' (The incarceration rate for this age group for such crimes was 4,000 a year in New York City.) They were described by New York City's commissioner of juvenile justice as ''Both a risk and at risk, victims and victimizers, bad and sad.''

The good news in the Peirce report was the just-completed overhaul of the jail. ''Security was rapidly tightened, food made edible, children organized into carefully supervised learning and living units.'' Shortly after admission, all were being given physicals, often the first in their young lives; after medical attention they were being placed under their own caseworker, with associated staff helping as needed. Many but not all were being turned around, back into school or at work.[102]

Central-City Crime

Various aspects of the criminal justice system are reviewed in the next chapter. Here summary data on central-city crime are presented. Table 5.9 shows crime rates for the largest metropolitan areas, with rates broken down between central cities and suburban areas. Aggregated reported city arrests by crime type, age, and ethnic group appear in Appendix 5.C. In interpreting the data, care must be taken to differentiate among various metropolitan area configurations, especially whether one or more than one central city is included, and the number and relative populations and population concentrations of the suburban counties included in the metro area.

In 1986, 1.744 million persons were arrested in cities of 10,000 and over for ''index crimes'' (murder and negligent manslaughter; forcible rape; robbery; aggravated assault; burglary; larceny-theft; motor vehicle theft, and arson). Of the arrests, 362,700 were for violent crime (first four of the index crimes)[103] and the remainder for property crime, as shown in figure 5.1.

Among the policies and practices of general applicability in the criminal justice area, some of the more difficult of which are discussed in chapter 6, one of special relevance to inner cities is that of police-community relations and the role of citizen volunteers in helping keep neighborhoods safe. Much literature and data are available on this subject, as the same techniques have been applied successfully in many jurisdictions, including underclass areas.[104]

Table 5.9

Index and Violent Crimes per 100,000 Population in Selected Large Metropolitan Areas, Inside and Outside Central Cities (ICC, OCC), 1987

Metro Area*	Population (000)			Index Crime Rate			Violent Crime Rate		
	MSA	ICC	OCC	MSA	ICC	OCC	MSA	ICC	OCC
New York	8,499	7,284	1,215	8,310	9,018	4,108	1,793	2,037	339
Los Angeles	8,506	3,342	4,758	6,784	8,638	5,402	1,352	1,911	977
-Long Beach	8,506	406	4,660	6,784	7,650	5,402	1,352	1,137	977
Chicago	6,144	3,018	3,126	NA	NA	NA	NA	NA	NA
Philadelphia	4,848	1,649	3,199	4,427	5,732	3,751	616	1,054	390
Detroit	4,369	1,092	3,277	7,680	12,698	6,011	1,024	2,548	517
Washington	3,612	622	2,990	5,263	8,471	4,600	617	1,615	410
Houston	3,252	1,738	1,514	7,645	9,392	5,643	765	1,090	390
Boston	2,847	576	2,271	5,133	11,624	3,469	677	2,061	323
Atlanta	2,609	430	2,179	7,869	15,577	6,351	816	2,998	386
St. Louis	2,465	429	2,036	5,301	12,653	3,739	690	2,274	355
Baltimore	2,317	765	1,549	6,263	8,513	5,131	993	1,856	561
Minneapolis -	2,311	359	1,686	6,004	12,599	4,261	436	1,538	133
St. Paul	2,311	266	1,686	6,004	7,911	4,261	436	847	133
Dallas	2,354	1,010	1,344	11,133	16,282	7,282	1,049	1,989	343
San Diego	2,257	1,041	1,216	6,990	8,483	5,700	722	876	588

Pittsburgh	2,130	389	1,741	3,131	7,907	2,060	356	1,107	187
Tampa et. al.	1,971	286	1,698	8,449	17,017	5,335	1,056	3,069	482
St. Ptrsbrg	1,971	247	1,698	8,449	10,600	5,335	1,056	1,492	482
Newark	1,902	318	1,584	6,128	12,558	4,833	878	2,789	491
Cleveland	1,873	548	1,325	4,729	8,256	3,244	501	1,266	182
Phoenix	1,968	933	1,035	7,590	9,028	6,288	648	880	440
Miami	1,822	385	1,437	12,387	15,075	11,592	1,814	2,900	1,510
Seattle	1,780	494	1,437	8,421	14,885	5,968	562	1,448	225
Denver	1,648	510	1,138	7,222	9,056	6,386	576	683	496
San Francisco	1,628	768	860	6,116	7,511	4,853	892	1,208	607
Kan. Cy MO -	1,528	444	921	7,079	11,995	4,210	871	1,914	273
K.C., KS	1,528	163	921	7,079	10,420	4,210	871	1,486	273
Milwaukee	1,386	608	778	5,489	8,262	3,292	505	985	128
New Orleans	1,323	550	773	7,620	9,273	6,464	937	1,396	613
San Antonio	1,284	920	364	10,874	12,929	5,733	577	662	364
Indianapolis	1,219	479	740	5,125	6,325	4,342	507	946	222
Buffalo	968	326	642	4,742	7,592	3,255	549	1,077	275

Source: U.S. Department of Justice, Federal Bureau of Investigation, *Crime in the United States, 1987*, July 1988, appendix IV, "Index of Crimes, Metropolitan Statistical Areas, 1987," 319–346.

[a] Metropolitan areas are single metropolitan statistical areas (MSAs); in addition to Los Angeles–Long Beach, certain others may contain relatively small cities of 50,000 or more, such as Alexandria, Virginia, and Frederick, Maryland, in the Washington MSA.

[b] NA: Data not available due to definitional differences between state of Illinois and the FBI.

Figure 5.1
Arrests for Index Crimes in Cities by Crime Category, 1987

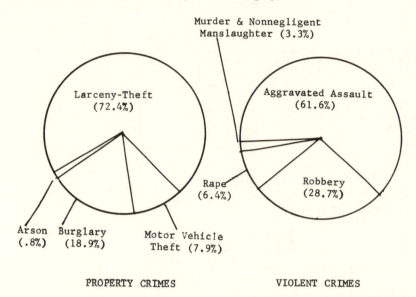

Murder & Nonnegligent
Manslaughter (3.3%)

Larceny-Theft
(72.4%)

Aggravated Assault
(61.6%)

Rape
(6.4%)

Robbery
(28.7%)

Arson   Burglary
(.8%)   (18.9%)

Motor Vehicle
Theft (7.9%)

PROPERTY CRIMES   VIOLENT CRIMES

Source: U.S. Department of Justice, Federal Bureau of Investigation, *Crime in the United States*,
July 1988, tables 42, 43, 44, 45, p. 190.

Behavioral Problems among Inner-City Minority Youth

Central-city rates for school dropouts, juvenile delinquency, drug use and dealing, and arrests and convictions for both violent and property crimes are universally higher for minority than for white youth, and the relative rates for black males are especially high. Wide differences of opinion exist as to causes for this disparity; there is general agreement about the objective to be pursued— a drastic reduction in all the rates mentioned.

Economic and urban demographic change and prior and existing racial discrimination are nearly always cited as the principal culprits in the evolution and growth of the underclass, but with strong disagreement as to which of the two has been and is the dominant one. Likewise, in the consideration of public policies for mediation of the multitude of educational, behavioral, and economic difficulties being examined here, wide and deep differences arise as to where the initiative and the onus of responsibility rest for future action, and as to the relative emphases, including public resource allocation, through which new efforts would be implemented.

Black, Hispanic, and other racial and ethnic minority members "who have made it" in entering middle- and upper-income classes, and those prominent in business, politics, sports, the arts, and other walks of life are looked to often for initiative in the increasingly serious underclass problem. Roger Wilkins has commented:

A few blacks have attained previously unheard of positions in politics, entertainment, business, the professions and . . . athletics. . . . Many other blacks have filled in behind these super-achievers. . . . The black middle class has grown from 15 percent of the black population in 1960 to about 37 percent today. But the problems of the black poor will not be addressed effectively . . . until that 37 percent of us begin to lead the way. . . . Let's be honest: Just as cross-race contacts are fraught with anxiety and fear, so are cross-class contacts. Probably the best place to start . . . is in the inner city schools. Volunteers can . . . serve as successful role models for children sorely in need of them. . . . From such beginnings . . . new energies and political strategies would surely develop and new moral guidance would be given to the rest of America.[105]

Bart Landry is more cautious about the middle-class role: "Relatively fewer blacks are making it into the middle class and those already there are experiencing an erosion of their already tenuous economic position. . . . Some of the blame can be attributed to a sluggish economy [but] scarcity has led to an intensification of employment discrimination. . . . Educated blacks are not getting their fair share of available white-collar jobs."[106]

Jane Gibbs places primary responsibility on government: "Billions for defense weapons that do not work, millions for farm subsidies to grow crops that are destroyed, yet, this government cannot find the funds to raise 2 million black families above the poverty line . . . feed 4 million poor black children . . . and provide jobs for one million young black men. . . . As this 'underclass' grows . . . more frustrated and alienated, no ghetto walls will be strong enough to contain their hostility and rage. . . . The only real protection is prevention and that message has not yet fully penetrated the . . . powerful groups in our society." Gibbs goes on to urge stable black families in underclass areas to mobilize "to form support networks for single parent families, to set up child care and food co-operatives, to establish crime watch committees . . . and to volunteer as aides in the schools, [so that] the community would gradually be transformed from a disorganized ghetto to a liveable urban neighborhood."[107]

As discussed earlier in connection with public-private partnerships for community revitalization, there seems to be a consensus that strengthening and "empowerment" of neighborhood and other "intermediary structures" (churches, clubs, private social agencies, and others) are essential so that these formerly strong stabilizing influences may be brought to bear in reestablishing "liveable urban neighborhoods" in the nation's inner cities.

STATE AND LOCAL ROLES IN WELFARE REFORM

"Welfare," as a government program aiding needy or "deserving" people (in contrast to the term "general welfare" as used in the U.S. Constitution), can be defined broadly or narrowly. Its broadest definition would encompass public policies and programs, the inclusion or eligibility for which is limited to persons or other entities with incomes or assets below a specified level, described programmatically as "means-tested." The GAO in 1986 identified 95 such federal programs and classified them in seven groups:

1. Cash assistance (14): aid to families with dependent children (AFDC); pensions to needy veterans; general assistance to Indians; weatherization assistance; and supplemental security income (SSI) for needy blind, aged, and disabled

2. Education (23): bilingual education; migrant education; Head Start; student loans and grants; and handicapped education

3. Food (13): food stamps; special supplemental food program for women, infants, and children (WIC); national school lunches; child care food; and nutrition for the elderly

4. Medical (5): Medicaid; migrant health centers; and community health centers

5. Housing (22): low-rent public housing; rural-housing repair loans and grants; Section 8 low-income housing assistance; and rehabilitation loans

6. Service programs (10): legal services; child welfare services; and senior-citizen service centers

7. Jobs and employment programs (8): Job Corps; dislocated worker assistance; and U.S. employment service.[108]

The needs-based programs of greatest relevance to the urban underclass and falling within the rubric of "welfare reform" are (1) AFDC; (2) SSI (aid to needy blind, aged, and disabled); (3) GA (general assistance), which aids needy adult persons below sixty-five and without children—a solely state and local program, with no federal funds involved; and (4) FS (food stamps), a federally financed program (except for shared administrative costs) giving food aid to low-income persons. In this concluding section on the urban underclass, the nature and financing of the three cash-assistance welfare programs and the food stamp program will be summarized, major state-local approaches to welfare reform will be discussed, and several fiscal and other policy options in such reform will be reviewed.

The Welfare Population and State-Local Welfare Costs

It is through the three programs of AFDC, SSI, and GA that most cash assistance is rendered to needy persons (about $32 billion in federal, state, and local funds; $41 billion in Medicaid and $11 billion in food stamps comprised the other major segments of 1986 public assistance expenditures of about $100 billion). Because of the political clout and resulting veneration accorded the elderly under many public policies in the U.S. and the general public sympathy for blind and disabled persons, the SSI category, since its federalization in the mid-seventies, is sometimes considered an entitlement rather than a welfare program. Table 5.10 shows the relative percentages of employment payrolls, other income, social insurance, and welfare payments for selected years.

Table 5.10
Gross National Product and Personal Income by Income Category, Selected Years, 1960–87

(Dollar amounts in billions)

Year	(1)	(2)	(3)	(4)	(5)	(6)	(7)	(8)	(9)
1960	402.3	79.4	271.9	67.6	23.9	5.9	3.3	.8	9.3
1965	540.7	78.2	362.0	67.0	34.2	6.3	4.1	.8	13.3
1970	811.7	81.7	548.7	67.6	65.2	8.0	9.5	1.2	27.9
1975	1,265.0	79.1	806.4	63.7	143.2	11.3	21.0	1.7	50.4
1980	2,165.3	79.3	1,356.7	62.7	252.7	11.7	30.1	1.2	88.7
1985	3,327.0	83.0	1,974.8	59.4	384.8	11.6	81.0	2.4	148.9
6-87	3,731.0	83.9	2,200.6	59.0	425.4	11.4	91.8	2.5	168.8

Source: *Social Security Bulletin* 50, no. 10 (October 1987): 54.

Key: (1) Personal Income, Amt.; (2) % of GNP; (3) Wages and Salaries, including payments in kind, but excluding private pension income, Amt.; (4) % of GNP; (5) Social Insurance (nonwelfare government transfers such as OASDHI [Old Age-Survivors-Disability-Hospital Insurance], workers compensation, and so on), Amt.; (6) % of GNP; (7) Public Assistance (AFDC, SSI, Emergency Assistance to AFDC and GA), Amt.; (8) % of GNP; (9) Social Insurance Contributions, Amt.

In 1986 public assistance recipients totaled about 16 million persons: SSI, 4.3 million; AFDC, 11.1 million (7.4 million children, 3.7 million adults); and GA, 1.3 million.[109] There were 19.4 million FS recipients, many but not all of whom were receiving assistance under one of the three cash programs; the same was true of 22.4 million Medicaid recipients. The 16 million were between 6 and 7 percent of the population and took 2.5 percent of GNP, compared to 1 percent in 1950 and 1.2 percent in 1970. Estimates of poverty in the mid-eighties ranged from the high teens to 30 million, depending on the measure, between 9 and 14 percent of the population. Table 5.11 shows the composition, cost, and growth of the public assistance population over the 1964–86 period.

Supplemental security income (SSI) is financed primarily by the national government ($9.5 billion federal and $2.5 billion state in 1986), covering needy aged, blind, and totally or partially disabled persons, with all states except Texas and West Virginia supplementing the federal benefits to some extent as of mid-1987.[110] The supplemental payments are encouraged under a federal matching arrangement. Some states administer the supplements directly; in other states the supplements are handled by federal administrators. In July 1987, SSI recipients comprised 1.5 million needy persons sixty-five or over, 2.8 million were totally or partially disabled, and 83,000 blind.[111]

AFDC is financed jointly from federal and state-local funds, with the federal matching percentage ranging from 50 (as in Washington and New Jersey) to 74.84 (as in West Virginia) for fiscal year 1988, and administrative costs shared equally. As of 1987, forty states were bearing all state-local benefit costs; ten states required local financial participation, with six requiring local provision of

Table 5.11
Recipients and Payments under Major Public Assistance Programs, 1964–86

(Recipients in Millions; Payments in Billions of Dollars)

Program	1964 Rec.	1964 Pymts.	1974 Rec.	1974 Pymts.	1984 Rec.	1984 Pymts.	1986 Rec.	1986 Pymts.
Supp. Sec. Inc.		(1)	4.0	$5.2	4.0	$10.1	4.3	$12.0
Aged			2.3	2.5	1.5	2.8	1.5	3.1
Blind; Disabled			1.7	2.7	2.5	7.2	2.9	9.0
AFDC	4.1	$1.5	10.9	7.9	10.8	14.6	11.1	18.0
Children	1.0	---	7.8	---	7.1	---	7.4	---
Adults	3.1	---	3.0	---	3.7	---	3.7	---
Food Stamps	.4	NA	12.9	2.7	20.9	10.7	19.4	11.0
Medicaid	Neg.	Neg.	21.5	10.0	21.6	33.9	22.4	41.0
Gen. Asstnce.	.8	.3	.8	.8	1.4	1.4	1.3	2.0
Other Pub. Asst. (2)		2.2		3.5		16.2		16.0
Total		$4.4		$20.1		86.9		100.0

Source: Bureau of the Census, *Federal Expenditures by State for Fiscal Year 1986*, table 2; *Social Security Bulletin, Statistical Supplement, 1987*, tables 191, 217–219, 222, 224; NASBO, *State Expenditure Report, 1988*; *Government Finances 85–86*, table 1.

(1) Preconsolidation.
(2) Includes variety of smaller programs (such as energy assistance, social services and community services block grants, refugee assistance, women-infant-children nutrition, Head Start, and work incentive [WIN]).

25 percent or more of the nonfederal share (New York and North Carolina, 50 percent; Colorado, 42.7 percent; Indiana, 40 percent; and New Jersey and North Dakota, 25 percent). The program gives aid to needy families with dependent children under eighteen. Twenty-six states and the District of Columbia were providing aid to two-parent families where the principal earner was unemployed. In 1986 most families had been on the rolls for fewer than three years, but 26 percent had been on the rolls for five years or more, up from 23 to 24 percent in 1983–85. For 49 percent, parents were not married to each other. Black families comprised 41 percent of the caseload, with 40 percent white and about 14 percent Hispanic. The average monthly payment to an AFDC family of three averaged $360; the payment represented 93 percent of the available cash income.[112]

General assistance (GA) is entirely state-financed in a number of states; in others it is shared between state and local governments; and in a few states the entire financial burden falls upon local governments. GA aids those persons below sixty-five not covered by AFDC. In early 1988 over thirty states had GA programs, with fiscal year 1988 general fund outlays of over $2 billion. The 1985 GA caseload covered over 1 million cases.[113]

During the 1974–84 period of high inflation, the purchasing power of public assistance benefits eroded, with the erosion tempered by greatly increased participation in the food stamp program. Table 1.4 and appendix 1.D show state-by-state expenditures for welfare and the distribution of welfare costs in each state among federal, state, and local fiscal sources. For state-local governments, welfare expenditures comprised, in order of magnitude, AFDC, GA, and SSI supplements, although this differs in some states especially in those without a GA program.

Among the factors not apparent from table 5.11 are the following: (1) Medicaid costs rose despite little change in its population, primarily because medical costs outpaced CPI increases throughout the high-inflation period and thereafter; and (2) food stamp participation and cost increases reflected a congressional objective of supporting demand for agricultural products as well as helping feed the hungry. Obvious from the table is the relative stability of AFDC and Medicaid clientele in the 1974–84 decade, despite a modest increase in total population during that period. (In the 1974–84 period food stamp expenditures doubled, while the number of stamp recipients increased only 62 percent.)

A paper prepared by the ACIR staff in 1986–87 listed five major developments in the effects of changes in the economy, public assistance payment flows, and demographic and social changes over the two-decade period:

1. Economic stagnation reduced job opportunities for the poor and reduced real wages for workers overall.

2. Growth in public assistance payments, in real dollar terms, slowed by 1976 and then nearly flattened out after 1977.

3. The composition of the poverty population changed. Senior citizens, a historically poor group, became a smaller proportion of the poverty population, while women and households headed by women became a larger proportion of the poor.

4. Public assistance payments themselves may have slowed the decline in poverty insofar as certain poor persons became dependent on those payments and experienced reduced incentives to seek employment.

5. The transfer effect of income support programs on reducing poverty (without curbing dependency) waxed between 1966 and 1973 and waned thereafter, following closely the level of spending for the relevant cash welfare programs. Antidependency programs for welfare recipients, however, were never funded above miniscule levels.[114]

Major Avenues in Welfare Reform

Several policy alternatives in revising the intergovernmental responsibilities and financing of the AFDC and GA systems have been advanced over the past two decades, with little progress toward resolution prior to the mid-eighties. Earlier proposals for nationalizing welfare policy and financing gained wide support in the early seventies from state and local officials, the CED, the ACIR, and the Nixon administration.[115] Legislation to accomplish this was proposed by the Nixon White House, passed the House of Representatives, and failed by one vote to get a favorable motion by the Senate Finance Committee (blocked by Republican Senator John Williams of Delaware), with the result that a compromise act was passed that federalized three of the existing four categories of public assistance (the needy aged, the blind, and the partially or totally disabled). AFDC, the most contentious category, remained intergovernmental, and GA, which would have been folded into the federalized system, was left untouched as a state-local program.

Somewhat preceding the debate over nationalization of the welfare system, the concept of a "negative income tax" or "guaranteed minimum income" had been attracting growing attention in economic and political circles. Under this concept, a minimum level of income support would be provided to poor people or families to bring them up to and sustain them at the subsistence level until they could better themselves on their own. The direct payments from the Treasury to people falling below the tax-filing level would have been administered in a fashion similar to the more recent low-income earned tax credit. Initial federally financed experiments of such an approach to test the effects upon work incentive and family stability were optimistic. Later results were inconclusive in some respects but did show a drop-off in labor-force participation, especially in married-couple families.[116] The political support for a guaranteed minimum income faded in the late seventies.

Substantial subsequent opinion began to turn away from federalizing and toward the view that the program should remain a shared national-state one. Two factors have supported this position: (1) many social services (education, training, job placement, health, and day care) necessary to achieve a transitory, in contrast to a permanent, welfare dependency status for recipients are state-local in character, but also intertwined with AFDC; and (2) the Congress is likely to be unable to resist pressures to equalize benefits upward to the highest common denominator, with disastrous results for the federal budget.

Other opinion, keeping the intergovernmental character, but with federal absorption of a higher share of the costs and with a national uniform minimum benefit level, gained considerable political support, including that of the Evans-Robb Committee. The American Public Welfare Association (APWA) supported a federally mandated process for maintaining a minimum level, but one set in each state in relation to its own cost-of-living levels and applied in accordance with the federal criteria, avoiding a single national dollar poverty percentage level that might be unduly high in some states or regions.[117]

It was much easier for those of diverse philosophies and vantage points to agree about the weaknesses of the system in the early eighties than to reach a consensus about precisely what should be done. Eight former secretaries of the Department of Health, Education, and Welfare (HEW) (Anthony Celebrezze, Kennedy administration; Wilbur Cohen, Johnson; Robert Finch, Nixon; Arthur Flemming, Eisenhower; Patricia Harris, Carter; David Mathews, Ford; Elliot Richardson, Nixon; and Abraham Ribicoff, Kennedy) were convened and consulted by the Johnson Foundation, Inc., of Racine, Wisconsin, with Ribicoff not present but reviewing the resulting papers. Former secretaries not participating included Oveta Culp Hobby and Caspar Weinberger, from the Eisenhower and Nixon periods. Weaknesses identified in the system were stated as follows: "It (1) is replete with inequities; (2) encourages family break-up; (3) encourages teenage pregnancies; (4) serves as a disincentive to work; (5) discourages thrift and savings; (6) is costly; (7) is too bureaucratic; (8) is a poor fit with our federal system of government." The group tended to favor a minimum national benefit level funded fully by the national government, with one-fourth of state supplements matched by Washington, and including incentives for work and saving.[118]

Most critical public attention was focused upon the AFDC and GA programs and especially upon able-bodied adults in those programs. The feeling is most pointed toward unemployed mothers in the AFDC program, because such a high proportion of mothers with small children are in the work force already, many of them being in the "working poor" category. Consequently, the need to encourage, enable, or require able-bodied AFDC mothers to enter or reenter the workforce was central to welfare policy debates in the eighties.

By the end of 1987 a somewhat broader consensus had emerged to the effect that a renewed focus should be placed on the concepts of self-sufficiency, social obligation, family, and community. An ACIR staff paper summarized the social obligation of recipients as including completion of high school, preparation for work, active search for a job, and, failing the latter, performance of available or designated work. The reciprocal obligation assumed by taxpayers is to provide temporary income support and, beyond that, to facilitate (presumably with cash) the transition to work and self-sufficiency. More specifically, there seemed to be agreement that work incentives and/or requirements, as well as child support and flexibility for state experimentation with work requirements should be strengthened, including transitional aid for child and medical care and, in some cases, transportation.[119]

But significant issues remained: (1) a national minimum benefit standard; (2) whether the national share of welfare financing should be increased; and (3) whether states not now including unemployed parents in AFDC should be required to do so.[120] In addition to these three intergovernmental legislative issues, basic philosophical differences, although narrowed considerably from earlier years, persisted: (1) whether all able-bodied welfare recipients should be required to register for work and training and accept employment in the private sector if it was offered, and whether the requirement should include welfare mothers with young children; and (2) whether welfare recipients should be expected to accept any work offered or only those jobs meeting some kind of middle-class standard of pay and benefits.

Until the eighties, states were largely precluded by national rules from requiring recipients to work (''workfare''). Following the lifting of the prohibition, well over half the states began active experimentation with programs to move recipients into private or public employment. Evaluations of these programs concluded that modest and encouraging, but not dramatic, progress was being made.

A GAO study found that ''work programs can have modest success in getting participants into jobs, increasing their earnings, and decreasing their welfare dependency. The programs seem to make the biggest difference to participants without work experience.''[121] A CBO report stated: ''Perhaps the most important finding is that work-related programs such as job search assistance and training have repeatedly been shown to be effective in increasing the average earnings of economically disadvantaged female participants, especially those who lack recent work experience. . . . Whether work-related programs for welfare recipients save taxpayers money in the long run by reducing expenditures for transfer programs by more than their costs [transitional day care, Medicaid, and so on] is not known.''[122]

On the basic political and fiscal issues of whether work requirements are justified and/or effective, some further research began to bear fruit. The most extensive research on the costs and benefits of work-related programs for welfare recipients prior to 1988 had been through studies conducted by the Manpower Demonstration Research Corporation (MDRC) covering a number of states and localities. Among the MDRC findings in individual studies were the following:

- There were significant reductions in the amounts of AFDC received by the work incentive groups compared with control groups.

- A majority of participants in workfare activities appeared to accept the requirement as a legitimate objective of the welfare system.

- Workfare participants will have reduced their reliance on welfare and increased their tax payments to offset transitional assistance and other costs by the end of five years.
- In terms of overall societal benefits, MDRC estimated that over a five-year period societal benefits exceeded their costs, the excess ranging from $300 to $2,000 per participant for the 5-year period.[123]

Richard Nathan, chairman of the MDRC and a leading architect of welfare reform in the Nixon administration, commented on welfare and workfare in general: "The states' new-style workfare reforms are very promising. The states are on a roll and are making important changes that, in a quiet way, really count for something."[124]

A second major issue concerned the "acceptability" of proffered work under workfare programs; this has both economic and racial aspects and involves disagreements as to what job availabilities really are at any given time and distance from the proffered work place, as well as the recipient's qualifications in relation to the job proffered. One view holds that the substantial reductions in jobs in the goods-producing sector of the economy have in fact removed employment availability from inadequately educated youth in the inner cities; since jobs being created in the service sector call for higher qualifications and are located mainly in the suburbs, entry-level, lower-skilled positions in construction and related occupations have removed employment accessibility from inner-city youth. (As pointed out in an earlier chapter, the factor of transportation between inner-city residence and suburban job opportunities has been increasingly critical in many metropolitan areas.) It is held further that because access to jobs is increasingly based on educational criteria, "the consignment to inner city schools guarantees the future economic subordinacy" of inner-city, largely minority youth.

Another view has held that part of the cause of high unemployment rates and proportions of persons not looking for work among the minority youth in inner cities is that available jobs have become less attractive and that "many would rather live off benefit programs . . . than accept work that is 'dirty' or low-paid." This view contends further that offering welfare recipients new benefits along with jobs continues to encourage welfare dependency because the job, with the sweeteners, becomes esstentially a benefit rather than an obligation on the part of the individual to secure minimum competencies as the price of economic and societal self-sufficiency and parity.[125]

Welfare reform legislation adopted by the 100th Congress in the fall of 1988 struck a middle ground in confronting several of the foregoing questions. A national minimum benefit level was rejected, and "workfare," with some conditions attached, received explicit legislative approval. On the other hand, those states not including married-couple families with dependent children that otherwise met economic-need standards were required to encompass such families within the AFDC program. Also, federal financial participation was approved for transitional assistance in day care and Medicaid for persons and families leaving the welfare rolls for employment, and such assistance was related to state workfare programs.[126]

Flexibility was provided for continued experimentation by states in devising new approaches to welfare-employment-family relationships issues. Thus, the pro-and-con arguments about coverage of two-parent families, workfare, and transitional maintenance of day care and Medicaid still confront the states in deciding whether to meet only the federal minima or to go beyond them. Despite the new ground broken in the new legislation, many viewed the law as still another incremental step—albeit a substantial one—in fashioning effective public policy on this complex of major socioeconomic issues that has occupied continuously a prominent place in domestic governance in the United States for the past half-century.

State-Local Administrative Issues

How to administer welfare programs, especially those to which workfare requirements and/or transitional welfare-to-work benefits are being added, involves three major issues, among others: (1) state or local delivery responsibility; (2) case management; and (3) responsibility for handling work requirements and/ or transitional benefits. The first is an old question with new dimensions; the other two arise when a decision is made to shift from an income-support to a welfare-to-work policy orientation.[127]

Division of responsibility for public assistance administration between state and local governments (the latter comprising counties in most states outside New England) follows two general patterns: (*a*) state administration, with state agency personnel deployed throughout the state, usually in an office in each county seat, and multicounty district offices in large-area states with numerous counties; and (*b*) local administration under close state supervision, including merit-system personnel provisions. For a simple system of reviewing eligibility, placing the person on AFDC or GA if eligible, and monitoring the disbursement of benefits, the latter form has been adequate, as well as intergovernmentally equitable if the local governments are required to share in the costs, especially where GA is totally a local responsibility. As workfare requirements and transition assistance are added, the complexity exceeds the managerial capacity of nearly all but the large urban counties with a wide variety of professional staff upon which to draw.

Due to literacy and motivational shortcomings in the case of substantial numbers of recipients, especially in the inner cities, a strong brokerage or "case management" role falls to the welfare agency if job search and placement assistance and/or other responsibilities are assumed. To send a client to a public employment office with no preparation except a referral slip is practically useless. (The employment office refers to potential employers on a most highly qualified basis; otherwise its placement record and credibility goes down within the bureaucratic hierarchy and the business community respectively.) The handling of recipients on an individualized, case-by-case basis, although costly, becomes nearly essential, involving coaching, tutoring, cajoling, and otherwise helping recipients through the welfare-to-work cycle required to reach the policy objective.

Finally, if the welfare-to-work cycle is to be traversed at a satisfactory cost/successful-placement ratio, the welfare, employment, or other agency made responsible for ensuring the accomplishment of the whole task must assemble on its own staff or have otherwise at its beck and call the necessary specialty skills involved. These include employment counseling and placement, psychological counseling, arranging for day care and medical care, and other competencies. If these specialized tasks are to be carried out by other agencies, a performance-based contract or comparably strong fiscal arrangement is necessary. Physical location of the related services is important; referral from one building to another blocks away often is disastrous.

Choices between state and local administration, whether to go to a case management approach, and between centering responsibility in a single agency with one-stop handling of clients or a more decentralized approach all depend greatly on relative costs and the priority given to welfare prevention versus attempted rescue of long-term dependents. The last is one of the key decisions in resource allocation to the numerous alternative components of the urban underclass problem.

SUMMARY COMMENTS ON THE UNDERCLASS DILEMMA

The urban underclass problem is interlaced with many different aspects and public functions, nearly all of which (except for an overall financial one—the size of the federal contribution) lie within the legal responsibilities of state-local governments. It is clear that some parts of the underclass problem are nearly hopeless for at least one generation. This is the dropout–drug use–drug selling–robbery–execution-style-murder cycle in which a large number of young people twelve and up in underclass areas are involved. Unless drastic change in the inner-city public education systems occurs fairly quickly, large numbers of youth will continue to be lost to the streets, and many teenage females will join the ranks of welfare mothers. The first orders of business for city political, school, business, and black and other minority leadership, along with many others, would appear to be (1) getting drugs off the street and out of the schools; (2) bringing order to classroom and school buildings and grounds; and (3) instilling in minority youth, especially black males, a restored feeling of responsibility, hope, and self-confidence.

Of equal urgency is a concerted effort among local officials and private employers to match up unemployed inner-city youth and entry-level jobs in outlying areas and to make the necessary transport arrangements. Transitional day-care and Medicaid access for single mothers requires cooperative and painstaking case managing and difficult financial decisions among local, state, and private employers as to the order of priorities. Adequate drug treatment funds and facilities, both in the city underclass areas and in the prisons, represent a double or triple opportunity on health and AIDS, employment, and crime fronts, while mitigating a major problem in the inner-city schools.

The bottom line to the desperation of the underclass crisis was perhaps best expressed by Anthony Downs: "I believe in continuing to try to improve conditions, no matter what the odds. . . . Hope is a virtue when it goes beyond a purely rational response to the visible facts. Realism in assessing the situation, but hope surpassing realism when trying to influence policy and launch remedial actions: that is where the best future for America's large cities lies."[128]

NOTES

1. Weaver, R., *The Urban Complex: Human Values in Urban Life* (Garden City, N.Y.: Anchor Books, 1966), 228.

2. Banfield, E., *The Unheavenly City* (Boston: Little, Brown, 1970), 210–211.

3. Wilkerson, I., "Growth of the Very Poor Is Focus of New Studies," *New York Times*, December 20, 1987, 26; Hornblower, M., "New York, New York: South Bronx, 10 Years after Fame; In Ghetto, Ideas for Urban Redemption Seem to Have Run Out," *Washington Post*, August 25, 1987, 1.

4. Garreau, J., "Black Elites Transcending Race Barriers," *Washington Post*, November 29, 1987, A–1, A–16–A17 (part of article series, "The Emerging Cities. Blacks: Success in the Suburbs," covering Washington, D.C., Los Angeles, Long Island, Atlanta, Chicago, and Detroit).

5. National Research Council, Committee on National Urban Policy, *Critical Issues for National Urban Policy: A Reconnaissance and Agenda for Further Study* (Washington, D.C.: National Academy Press, 1982), ix, 33–53.

6. Ibid., 50–51.

7. Clark, K., *Dark Ghetto: Dilemmas of Social Power* (New York: Harper and Row, 1965).

8. U.S. Department of Labor, Office of Policy Planning and Research, *The Negro Family: The Case for National Action* (Commonly known as the "Moynihan Report") (Washington, D.C.: U.S. Department of Labor, 1965).

9. Wilson, W., *The Truly Disadvantaged: The Inner City, the Underclass, and Public Policy* (Chicago: University of Chicago Press, 1987); idem, "The Urban Underclass in Advanced Industrial Society," in Peterson, P., ed., *The New Urban Reality* (Washington, D.C.: Brookings Institution, 1985); idem, *The Hidden Agenda: Race, Social Dislocations, and Public Policy in America* (Chicago: University of Chicago Press, 1980); idem, "The Black Community in the 1980's: Questions of Race, Class, and Public Policy," *Annals of the American Academy of Political and Social Science* 454, 1981, 26–41; *The Declining Significance of Race: Blacks and Changing American Institutions*, 2nd ed. (Chicago: University of Chicago Press, 1980). For contrasting views on relative causal factors of economics, job location, and prior and existing racial discrimination, see Landry, B., *The New Black Middle Class* (Berkeley: University of California Press, 1987), introductory chapter. For other views, see Butler, S., and Kondratas, A., *Out of the Poverty Trap: A Conservative Strategy for Welfare Reform* (New York: Free Press, 1987); and Reischauer, R., "America's Underclass: Even a Small Proportion Can Un-

dermine the Promise and Strength of the Nation," *Public Welfare* 45, no. 4 (Fall 1987): 26–31 (this issue contained comments of Brookings scholar Robert Reischauer and articles by San Antonio mayor Henry Cisneros, Connecticut social welfare commissioner Stephen Heintz, University of Connecticut school of social work dean Nancy Humphreys and Pennsylvania state senator Roxanne Jones).

10. Sawhill, I., "Poverty and the Underclass," in Sawhill, I., ed., *Challenge to Leadership: Economic and Social Issues for the Next Decade* (Washington, D.C.: Urban Institute Press, 1988), 215–252. See also Ricketts, E., and Sawhill, I., "Defining and Measuring the Underclass"; Ruggles, P., and Marton, W., "Measuring the Size and Characteristics of the Underclass: How Much Do We Know?"; and Ruggles, P., and Williams, R., "Transitions in and out of Poverty: New Data from the Survey of Income and Program Participation" (published research papers) (Washington, D.C.: Urban Institute, 1986).

11. Ross, C., and Danziger, Sheldon, "Poverty Rates by State, 1979 and 1985: A Research Note," *Focus* (Madison, Wis.: University of Wisconsin, Madison, Institute for Research on Poverty (IRP)) 10 no. 3 (Fall 1987): 1–5. The lowest poverty rate in 1979 was in Connecticut, with 5.9 percent of the population; the lowest rate (estimated by the authors) for 1985 was in New Hampshire with 6.0 percent, and the highest were 22.9 and 22.3 percent for Mississippi, Arkansas, and West Virginia, respectively.

12. Wilson, "The Urban Underclass," 133.

13. "Program Summary 1986: President's Report," *Wingspread Journal* (9:1), 1987, special insert, p. 4.

14. Nathan, R., "The Underclass Challenges the Social Sciences," *Wall Street Journal*, July 8, 1983, op-ed, and Reischauer, R., "America's Underclass," 28.

15. Wilson, "The Urban Underclass," 143.

16. Congressional Budget Office (CBO), *Trends in Family Income, 1970–1986*, 1988, xiii–xv.

17. Minarik, J., "Family Incomes," in Sawhill, *Challenge to Leadership*, 33–66. See also O'Hare, W., "Is America Poorer Than We Think?" *Washington Post*, June 19, 1988, C–3; Danziger, Sheldon, "Anti-Poverty Policy and Welfare Reform" (Paper prepared for Rockefeller Foundation Conference on Welfare Reform, Williamsburg, Virginia, February 16–18, 1988); and Berlin, G., "The New Permanence of Poverty," *Ford Foundation Letter* 19, no. 2 (June 1988): 1–8.

18. CBO, *Trends in Family Income*, xiii–xiv.

19. Herbers, J., "Poverty of Blacks Spreads in Cities," *New York Times*, January 26, 1987, A–1, A–27. See also "American Survey—Helping the Poor: Town and Country," *Economist*, August 29, 1987, 20–22.

20. Ricketts and Sawhill, "Defining and Measuring the Underclass," 8–9.

21. Sawhill, "Poverty and The Underclass," 230.

22. Ricketts and Sawhill, "Defining and Measuring the Underclass," tables 5 and 6, and Reischauer, "America's Underclass," 29.

23. CBO, *Reducing Poverty among Children*, May 1985, xi–xii.

24. Estimates from Danziger, "Anti-Poverty Policy."

25. "The Changing Economic Circumstances of Children: Families Losing Ground," *Focus* 9, no. 1 (Spring 1986): 6–10, based on summary of Danziger, Sheldon, and Gottschalk, P., "How Have Families with Children Been Faring?" Institute for Research on Poverty (IRP) Paper no. 801–85 in *Focus* (Spring 1986), 6–10.

26. CBO, *Reducing Poverty among Children*, 40.

27. Bureau of the Census, *Household and Family Characteristics, March 1986,* Current Population Reports, Series P–20, no. 148, tables 4, 9, pp. 33, 36.

28. Garfinkel, I., and McLanahan, S., *Single Mothers and Their Children: A New American Dilemma* (Washington, D.C.: Urban Institute Press, 1986), 46–47.

29. Wilson, "The Urban Underclass," 138.

30. Garfinkel and McLanahan, *Single Mothers,* 55–85, and Danziger, Sandra, "Teenaged Childbearing and Welfare Policy," *Focus* 10, no. 1 (Spring 1987): 16–20 (based on Danziger, Sandra, "Breaking the Chains: From Teen-Age Girls to Welfare Mothers; or, Can Social Policy Increase Options?" in Meyer, J., ed., *Ladders out of Poverty* (Washington, D.C.: American Horizons Foundation, 1986). See also Peirce, N., "Pregnancy and the Black Teenager," *Philadelphia Inquirer,* June 28, 1982, op-ed; and idem, "Black Leaders Tackle the Issue of Fatherless Families," *Philadelphia Inquirer,* April 18, 1983.

31. Abrahamse, A., Morrison, P., and Waite, L., *Beyond Stereotypes: Who Becomes a Single Teenage Mother?* R–3489–HHS/NICHD (Santa Monica, Calif.: Rand Corporation, 1988), 62.

32. U.S. Department of Health and Human Services (HHS), Office of Child Support Enforcement, *Twelfth Annual Report to the Congress, 1988,* tables 24 and 29.

33. Corbett, T., "Child Support Assurance: Wisconsin Demonstration," *Focus* 9, no. 1 (Spring 1986): 1–5.

34. Garfinkel and McLanahan, *Single Mothers,* 136–137.

35. HHS, *Social Security Bulletin, Annual Statistical Supplement, 1987,* 40–41; Office of Policy Development, Executive Office of the President, *Up from Dependency: A New National Public Assistance Strategy, Supplement 1,* December 1986.

36. Wilkerson, K., "Infant Mortality: Frightful Odds in the Inner Cities," *New York Times,* June 26, 1987, A–1, A–20.

37. Southern Governors' Association and Southern Legislative Conference, *Study of the AFDC-Medicaid Eligibility Process in the Southern States* (Washington, D.C.: Southern Regional Infant Mortality Project, April 1988).

38. Gross, J., "Healing on Wheels: Vans for Welfare Children," *New York Times,* January 27, 1988, A–1, B–24.

39. Lohr, K., and Marquis, S., *Medicare and Medicaid: Past, Present, and Future,* N–2088–HHS/RC (Santa Monica, Calif.: Rand Corporation, May 1984), summarized in *Rand Checklist,* no. 336, March 1985, 7.

40. Danziger, Sandra, "Teenaged Childbearing," 17.

41. Ibid., using data from Moore, K., Simms, M., and Betsey, C., *Choice and Circumstance: Racial Differences in Adolescent Sexuality and Fertility* (New Brunswick, N.J.: Transaction Books, 1986), table 2.3, p. 12.

42. "AIDS Virus in Pregnancy Studied," *New York Times,* November 21, 1987, 32.

43. Committee to Study the Prevention of Low Birthweight, National Institute of Medicine, *Preventing Low Birthweight: Summary* (Washington, D.C.: National Academy Press, 1985), 18.

44. Children's Defense Fund, *The Health of America's Children: Maternal and Child Health Data Book* (Washington, D.C.: Children's Defense Fund, 1988).

45. Committee to Study the Prevention of Low Birthweight, *Preventing Low Birthweight,* 18.

46. Hayes, C., *Risking the Future: Adolescent Sexuality, Pregnancy, and Child-*

bearing, National Research Council, Commission on Behavioral, Social Science, and Education, Committee on Child Development Research and Public Policy. (Washington, D.C.: National Academy Press, 1987).

47. U.S. Congress, House Select Committee on Children, Youth, and Families, "Opportunities for Success: Cost Effective Programs for Children, Update 1988," Committee press release, April 4, 1988, 6–8.

48. HHS, U.S. Public Health Service (USPHS), National Institute on Drug Abuse (NIDA), "Highlights of the 1985 National Household Survey on Drug Abuse," *NIDA Capsules*, C–86–13 (Rockville, Md.: NIDA, November 1986) 1–4; and University of Michigan News and Information Service, news release January 12, 1988 (attached to *HHS NEWS* RPO 689 news release, January 13, 1988), p. 3. See also NIDA, *National Survey on Drug Abuse: Main Findings, 1982*, 83–1263, pp. 43–44; Peirce, N., "Thinking Out a Drug Program," *Boston Globe*, September 8, 1986; Colman, W., *Cities, Suburbs, and States* (New York: Free Press, 1975), 225–233. New York State Legislative Commission on Expenditure Review, *Alcohol and Substance Abuse Prevention Programs*, September 1986, 25–39; and idem, *Methadone Program*, December 1981, S1–S7.

49. Wartzman, R., "AIDS Heaps Hardship on Washington Slum Called the Graveyard," *Wall Street Journal*, November 4, 1987, 1, 20.

50. HHS, USPHS, *Health, United States, 1987*, 1988, table 40, p. 86.

51. As reported by Ahern, C., "States Pressured to Battle AIDS," *City and State*, April 25, 1988, 3, 34.

52. "Beyond Needles: The AIDS War," *New York Times*, February 11, 1988 (editorial).

53. "Cuomo Says Sympathy Can Aid Minority Youth," *New York Times*, November 10, 1987, B–3; "For Shalala, 'Rotten' Reality of School System," *New York Times*, November 5, 1987, B–3.

54. Johnson, D., "Chicago Leads Way in City School Woe," *New York Times*, December 9, 1987, B–8.

55. Bowen, E., et al., "Education: Getting Tough," *Time*, February 1, 1988, 52–58 (cover story).

56. Carnegie Foundation for the Advancement of Teaching, *An Imperiled Generation: Saving Urban Schools* (Princeton, N.J.: Princeton University Press, 1988), xiii–xv. See also: The William T. Grant Foundation Commission on Work, Family and Citizenship, *The Forgotten Half: Pathways to Success for America's Youth and Families*. (Washington, D.C.: Youth and America's Future: The William T. Grant Foundation, 1988).

57. Committee for Economic Development (CED), *Children in Need: Investment Strategies for the Educationally Disadvantaged* (New York: Committee for Economic Development, 1987), 3. For a contrasting view on singling out children for priority attention, see Danziger, Sheldon, and Smolensky, E. Institute for Research on Poverty (IPR), "The Welfare of All the Poor," *New York Times*, October 1, 1987, op-ed.

58. CED, *Children in Need*, 10.

59. Bureau of the Census, *Government Finances in 1985–86*, November 1987, table 1, p. 1; U.S. Department of Education, Office of Educational Research and Improvement, Center for Education Statistics, *Digest of Education Statistics, 1987*, May 1987, table 23, p. 26; and estimate by Feistritzer, E., Director of the National Center for Education Information, Washington, D.C., in "Public vs Private: Biggest Difference Is Not the Students," *Wall Street Journal*, December 1, 1987, 36.

60. National School Boards Association (NSBA), "Partners in Education," *The American School Board Journal,* April 1987, special insert.

61. Carnevale, A., "The Learning Enterprise," *Training and Development Journal* (Alexandria, Va.: American Society for Training and Development), January 1986, 1.

62. National Governors' Association (NGA), *Time for Results: The Governors' 1991 Report on Education,* 1986, 3.

63. CED, *Children in Need,* 11.

64. "Poor Children Need Special Help," *Business Week,* September 21, 1987, 130 (editorial).

65. "For Children: A Fair Chance," *New York Times,* September 6, 1987 (editorial).

66. As reported by Peirce, N., "The States Focus on Children," *Philadelphia Inquirer,* November 24, 1986, 15A.

67. U.S. Department of Education, *Digest of Education Statistics, 1987,* table 37, p. 48.

68. Census Bureau, *Current Population Reports,* Series P–20, no. 394, October 1984.

69. Elkind, D., *Miseducation: Preschoolers at Risk* (New York: Knopf, 1987); idem, *The Hurried Child: Growing Up Too Fast Too Soon* (Reading, Mass.: Addison-Wesley, 1981).

70. O'Rourke, J., "Education for the Future," in *States' Summit '87: Issues and Choices for the 1990's* (Lexington, Ky.: Council of State Governments, 1987), 20.

71. For additional points and varying views, see Carmody, D., "Schools to Be Year-Round in Experiment; Officials Plan Program for Poor New York Areas," *New York Times,* October 26, 1987, B–11; Raspberry, W., "Who Will Educate These Kids?" *Washington Post,* November 14, 1987, A–27 (district boundary issues in Milwaukee); and articles by Clotfelter, C., Colman, W., Orfield, G., and Taylor, W., in *School Desegregation in Metropolitan Areas* (U.S. Department of Health, Education, and Welfare, National Institute of Education, October 1987), 27–62, 115–121.

72. NGA, *Time for Results,* 3.

73. CED, *Children in Need,* 52.

74. U.S. Congress, House of Representatives, *Teen Pregnancy: What Is Being Done? A State-by-State Look,* 1985, xiii–xiv.

75. From Lovick, S., "School-Based Clinic Shows Promise," *Wingspread Journal* (9:1) A Conference on "Private Grantmakers and Adolescent Pregnancy," Racine, Wisconsin, 1987, p. 1 of Special Section insert "Teen Pregnancy: A National Tragedy."

76. NGA, Task Force on School Dropouts, *Bringing Down the Barriers,* Report no. 3082, 1987, 64–65.

77. Ibid., 64.

78. U.S. General Accounting Office (GAO), *School Dropouts: The Extent and Nature of the Problem,* GAO/HRD–86–106BR, July 1986, 5–6.

79. *Ford Foundation Letter* 15, no. 3 (1984): 1.

80. GAO, *School Dropouts,* 15, citing Borus, M., and Carpenter, S., "Choices in Education," chap. 4 in *Youth and the Labor Market: Analyses of the National Longitudinal Survey* (Kalamazoo, Mi: W. E. Upjohn Institute for Employment Research, 1984). See also Ekstrom R., Goertz, M., Pollock, J., and Rock, D., "Who Drops Out of High School and Why? Findings from A National Study," in Natriello, G., ed., *School Dropouts: Patterns and Policies* (New York and London: Teachers College Press 1986, 1987. © Teachers College, Columbia University), 52–69; Earle, J., Reaser, K., and Roach,

V., *Female Dropouts: A New Perspective* (Alexandria, Va.: National School Boards Association, 1987), 9; Hahn, A., and Danzberger, J., with Lefkowitz, B., *Dropouts in America: Enough Is Known for Action* (Washington, D.C.: Institute for Educational Leadership, 1987), 9–26; Hodgkinson, H., *All One System: Demographics of Education, Kindergarten through Grade School* (Washington, D.C.: Institute for Educational Leadership, 1985); Johnson, C., and Ullman, H., "The Third World in America's Cities: City Schools That Shape America's Future or Failure. A Look at Urban School Finance and Funding" (Draft, NSBA, September 1987); and NGA, Task Force on School Dropouts, *Bringing Down the Barriers*, 36–56.

81. Hahn and Danzberger, *Dropouts in America*, 13.

82. Ibid., 16–26.

83. GAO, *School Dropouts: Survey of Local Programs*, HRD/87–108, July 1987, 3, 20 ("Caring and committed staff; non-threatening learning environment; low student-teacher ratio; individualized instruction; program flexibility; links with social service agencies; involvement of parents in student's development; links with employers"). See also Natriello, *School Dropouts*, 125; and CED, *Children in Need*, 55 ("Smaller schools, smaller classes, and more individualized instruction").

84. Hahn and Danzberger, *Dropouts in America*, 36–37.

85. CED, *Children in Need*, 57–59; Berger, J., "Keeping Likely Dropouts in School," *New York Times*, November 25, 1987, B–10 (on Atlanta's "Cities in Schools" program); and Peirce, N., "Using Summer School for New Challenges," *Philadelphia Inquirer*, July 4, 1987, 7a.

86. Johnson, "Chicago Leads Way in City School Woe" (Comment by Gary Orfield, University of Chicago).

87. Hahn and Danzberger, *Dropouts in America*, 29.

88. Kearns, David T., Xerox chairman and CEO, address at the annual meeting of the U.S. Conference of Mayors, Nashville, June 16, 1987 (Mimeo) (Washington, D.C.: U.S. Conference of Mayors).

89. CED, *Children in Need*, 15–16.

90. National Foundation for the Improvement of Education (NFIE), *A Blueprint for Success: Community Mobilization for Dropout Prevention* (Washington, D.C.: NFIE, 1987); idem, *1985–86 Annual Report*, 1987.

91. GAO, *School Dropouts: The Extent and Nature of the Problem*, 20. (The CRS study referenced was Library of Congress, Congressional Research Service, "High School Dropouts," Issue Brief IB 86003, updated to April 1986.)

92. U.S. Department of Education, *Digest of Education Statistics, 1987*, tables 69 and 70, pp. 83–84.

93. Hahn and Danzberger, *Dropouts In America*, 47. See also NGA, Task Force on School Dropouts, *Bringing Down the Barriers*, 48–49.

94. Informal assessment by an official of the American Society for Training and Development, December 1987.

95. Feistritzer, "Public vs. Private," December 1987. See also Fiske, E., "Miami Schools: Laboratory for Major Changes—Area Schools' Experiment Makes Managers of Teachers," *New York Times*, January 10, 1988, A–1.

96. Trost, C., "Shanker, Once-Militant Head of Teachers' Union, Now Is Called an Original Thinker in Education," *Wall Street Journal*, November 24, 1987, 66.

97. Olson, L., and Rodman, B., "Seeking Profession's 'Soul': Pressured to Lead, Unions Take Divergent Path," *Education Week* 7, no. 9 (November 4, 1987): 1.

98. Putka, G., "Fervor for Tests May Raise Just Too Many Questions," *Wall Street Journal,* December 2, 1987, 32.

99. Stout, H., "More Non-Catholics Using Catholic Schools: Parents Are Seeking Better Education and Stricter Discipline," *New York Times,* November 28, 1987, B–1.

100. Malozzi, V., "Tying Welfare to School Attendance," *New York Times,* January 3, 1988, Education section, 7–8.

101. Klotowitz, A., "Back at the Henry Horner Homes," *Wall Street Journal,* December 10, 1987, 28.

102. Peirce, N., "How Bad Kids Can Be Reclaimed," *Philadelphia Inquirer,* October 13, 1986, 15–A.

103. U.S. Department of Justice, Federal Bureau of Investigation (FBI), *Crime in the United States,* July 1987, table 45, p. 194.

104. International City Management Association (ICMA), *Local Government Police Management,* 2nd ed. (Washington, D.C.: 1982), National Crime Prevention Council (NCPC), *Success of Community Crime Prevention* (Washington, D.C.: NCPC, 1987), idem, *Preventing Crime in Urban Communities* (Washington, D.C.: NCPC, 1986); and National Sheriff's Association, Neighborhood Watch Packet (Alexandria, Va., 1987).

105. Wilkins, R., "Dr. King's Unfinished Business: Middle-Class Blacks Need to Carry On His Crusade for the Poor," *Washington Post,* January 17, 1988, op-ed.

106. Landry, *New Black Middle Class,* 231, 232.

107. Gibbs, J., ed., *Young, Black, and Male in America: An Endangered Species* (Dover, Mass.: Auburn Books, 1988), 355, 358–359. See also Berger, P., and Neuhaus, R., *To Empower People: The Role of Mediating Structures in Public Policy* (Washington, D.C.: American Enterprise Institute, 1977).

108. GAO, *Needs-based Programs: Eligibility and Benefit Factors,* GAO/HRD–86–107FS, July 1986, 3–8.

109. *Social Security Bulletin* 50, no. 10 (October 1987): tables M–20, M–21.

110. Ibid., table M–30, p. 50.

111. Ibid.

112. HHS, Office of Family Assistance, Family Support Administration, *Characteristics of State Plans for Aid to Families with Dependent Children, 1987 Edition,* 359; idem, *AFDC, Characteristics and Financial Circumstances of Recipients, 1986,* 1, 2.

113. *Social Security Bulletin* 50, no. 10 (October 1987): table M–30, p. 50; and NASBO, *State Expenditure Report, 1988.*

114. U.S. Advisory Commission on Intergovernmental Relations (ACIR), "Public Assistance in the Federal System" (Docket book memorandum), May 15, 1987, 12.

115. CED, *Improving the Public Welfare System,* April 1970, 58–63; ACIR, *State Aid to Local Government,* Report A–34, April 1968, 16–19, and on repeated occasions thereafter, the last being in ACIR, *An Agenda for American Federalism: Restoring Confidence and Competence,* A–86, June 1981, formally reversed in June 1987.

116. Federal Reserve Bank of Boston and Brookings Institution, Munnell, A., ed., *Lessons from the Income Maintenance Experiments: Proceedings of a Conference Held at Melvin Village, New Hamsphire, September, 1986* (Boston: Federal Reserve Bank of Boston, 1987), 1–9.

117. American Public Welfare Association (APWA) and National Council of State Administrators of Human Services, *One Child in Four: Investing in Poor Families and Their Children—A Matter of Commitment* (Washington, D.C.: APWA, 1986), 7; 22–24.

118. Johnson Foundation, *Welfare Policy in the United States: A Critique and Some*

Proposals Derived from the Experiences of Former Secretaries of Health, Education, and Welfare (Racine, Wis.: Johnson Foundation, 1982), 5–10.

119. ACIR, "Public Assistance in the Federal System" August 21, 1987, 4–5 (Docket book memorandum), expressed in NGA *Policy Positions, 1986–87*, p. 104 and *Policy Positions, 1987–88, Amended*, pp. 63–67.

120. Positions of NGA and provisions of legislative proposal by Senator Moynihan of New York, et al. For contrasting views, see APWA, *One Child in Four*, 7.

121. GAO, *Work and Welfare: Current AFDC Work Programs and Implications for Federal Policy*, GAO/HRD–87–34, January 1987, 115.

122. CBO, *Work-related Programs for Welfare Recipients*, April 1987, 43.

123. Five final reports (New York: Manpower Demonstration Research Corporation): Friedlander, D., et al., *Arkansas: Final Report on the WORK Program in Two Counties*, September 1985; idem, *Maryland: Final Report on the Employment Initiatives Evaluation*, December 1985; Goldman, B., et al., *California: Final Report on the San Diego Job Search and Work Experience Demonstration*, February 1986; Ricco, J., et al., *Virginia: Final Report on the Virginia Employment Services Program*, August 1986; and Friedlander, D., et al., *West Virginia: Final Report on the Community Work Experience Demonstrations*, September 1986. For a summary of the five reports, see Gueron, J., *Reforming Welfare with Work* (New York: Ford Foundation, 1987) 13–32.

124. Nathan, R., "A Step-by-Step Approach," in editorial review "Why It's So Tough to get Welfare Reform," *New York Times*, March 30, 1987, A–14. See also "Welfare Reform May Finally Be in the Works: Liberals and Conservatives Are Inching toward Agreement on a National 'Workfare' Program," *Business Week*, November 2, 1987, 108–110; and "Off to Work: Too Many of Britain's Single Parents Don't Have a Job. A Carrot Could Help Them Get One," *Economist*, October 24, 1987, 17–18.

125. From comments by Wilson, W., and Mead, L., in "The Obligation to Work and the Availability of Jobs: A Dialogue between Lawrence M. Mead and William Julius Wilson," *Focus* 10, no. 2 (Summer 1987): 11–19. On the job location factor, see also Kasarda, J., "The Regional and Urban Redistribution of People and Jobs in the U.S." (Paper prepared for the National Research Council Committee on National Urban Policy Workshop, Washington, D.C., July 1986). For further contrasting views on workfare and welfare reform, see Butler, S., and Kondratas, A., *Out of the Poverty Trap* (New York: Free Press, 1987); Raspberry, W., "All in the Community," *Washington Post*, March 25, 1988, op-ed; Ellwood, D., *Divide and Conquer: Responsible Security for America's Poor* (New York: Ford Foundation, 1987); Freeman, R., and Holzer, H., eds., *The Black Youth Employment Crisis* (Chicago: University of Chicago Press, 1986); Gibbs, *Young, Black, and Male*; Mead, L., *Beyond Entitlement: The Social Obligations of Citizenship* (New York: Free Press, 1986); Murray, C., *Losing Ground* (New York: Basic Books, 1984); McLanahan, S., et al., "Charles Murray and the Family," in *Losing Ground: A Critique*, SR 38 (Madison, Wis.: Institute for Research on Poverty, August 1985): NGA, *Bringing Down the Barriers*, 1987.

126. Family Support Act of 1988 (PL100–485).

127. Chadwin, M., Mitchell, J., Nightingale, D., "Reforming Welfare: Lessons from the WIN Experience," *Public Administration Review*, May–June 1981, 372–380; and National Academy of Public Administration, *Welfare Reform Dialogue* (Washington, D.C.: National Academy of Public Administration, 1988).

128. Downs, A., "The Future of Industrial Cities," in Peterson, *New Urban Reality*, 294.

Chapter 6 _____

State-Local Issues in Regulatory and Legal Systems

This chapter will examine those aspects of public regulatory and legal systems in the United States that appear likely to be of major concern to state and local governments over the coming decade. On the regulatory side, this will include (1) a summary review of constitutional, statutory, and other legal bases for the exercise of public regulatory power; and (2) economic and social bases of regulation and the political environment within which regulation occurs. Problem areas of overlap in federal and state-local regulation, especially in environmental, public health, and safety areas will be identified, as will issues in state and local growth management policies and land use regulation. Finally, some illustrative alternative approaches to direct regulation will be discussed and options for regulatory change presented.

The regulatory system operates within a larger legal framework in which public and private business is conducted and from which, in the administration of criminal justice, come the laws and rules providing for an ordered society. Particular aspects of the U.S. legal system to be reviewed are product and tort liability, the civil litigation explosion, and the correctional segment of criminal criminal justice. Some policy options for change will be presented.

EXISTING REGULATORY FRAMEWORK

In this section, the legal bases for public regulation of private activity are discussed, followed by an examination of regulatory objectives and types. The principal economic concepts, including alternative approaches and criteria for public intervention to correct market failures or imperfections will be reviewed. Relating and balancing regulatory costs and benefits are examined in some detail. Finally, issues of intergovernmental relations in the regulatory area, and especially state and local roles in the management of urban growth and development are reviewed in the light of fiscal equities and evolving judicial postures on the "taking clause" of the U.S. Constitution. The key question repeatedly coming before the courts is the extent to which environmental or other regulation that prevents any use of real or personal property purchased in good faith constitutes a taking of such property for public use without compensation as prohibited in the Fifth Amendment.[1]

Legal and Typological Bases

Legal bases of public regulatory power comprise two major constitutional sources. (1) Police power is exercised by state and local governments within the framework of respective state constitutions, statutes, and judicial interpretations thereunder to safeguard the health, safety, and general well-being of their respective citizens. (Most definitions of the police power involve the principle of regulating the conduct of one person so that another person will not be unreasonably endangered or restricted in the use and enjoyment of public and private property.)[2] (2) Specific regulatory powers of the national government are placed with the national Congress under express provisions of the Constitution. Aside from provisions protecting personal and property rights, the provisions most relevant to regulation are (1) the interstate commerce clause empowering and directing Congress to regulate commerce among the states; and (2) the power of Congress to tax and spend for the "general welfare," constituting the legal base for most grant-in-aid legislation and its accompanying requirements and conditions. Additionally, past and potential interpretations by the federal judiciary of these and other constitutional provisions must always be taken into account.

Various economic and social concerns for public regulation emerge from increasing societal complexity, and these are translated and merged into pressures for political action. Scientific and technological progress, coupled with urbanization, inevitably generates new socioeconomic problems. On the economic side, advances in communications and transportation technology have produced regional, national, and world markets in many products and services. This leads to increased mobility of population and jobs and calls for broadened exercise of congressional power to regulate interstate commerce in order to flatten out the shock waves of national and international economic change.

On the social side, advances in such areas as pesticide development, nuclear power generation, and gene splicing have aroused concerns about health and safety, aesthetic and other environmental values, and risk reduction both in personal and economic security. In the sixties and seventies these concerns brought a broadened political perception of the role of the public sector—in contrast to market forces—in helping assure not only an economically robust nation, but a healthy, safe, and pleasant one as well. Most of the resulting political pressure for public environmental, economic, and other regulation was directed toward national rather than state and local governments because of (1) lack of faith in state-local capacity, will, compassion, and integrity to deal adequately and fairly with the issues raised and (2) susceptibility of individual state-local governments to economic competition from adjoining jurisdictions that might impose less strict regulatory controls.

Regulatory typology can be based upon the objects, purposes, or methods of regulation. The objects or addressees of public regulatory action in economic and environmental areas comprise principally (1) Private firms, individuals, and state-local governments per se (for example, as employers, polluters, antitrust violators, and so on); and (2) state-local governments in their role of regulators under state police and other powers.

Public regulatory activities can, of course, be categorized by purpose or field, such as (1) human rights and personal liberty guarantees; (2) economic security and enhancement; (3) crime deterrence; (4) occupational health and safety; (5) facilitation of flow of commerce; and (5) natural resource/environmnental protection, especially in the areas of air, water, and soil pollution.

Regulatory activity can be classified also in terms of regulatory method. Broadly, there are two ways to regulate: (1) directly, through laws prohibiting or requiring certain actions and implementation of those laws through the issuance of specific orders to perform or cease performing a particular act, or (2) indirectly, through economic and other incentives or penalties designed to direct or influence behavior of the regulatees along lines deemed to be in the public interest.

Some Economic and Administrative Aspects of Regulation

From about 1955 through 1975, public regulatory activity grew from trickle to flood dimensions in many states and in the Congress. This was a period of problem recognition and the legislating, often with inadequate scientific, engineering, and economic bases and with insufficient attention to administrative, enforcement, and intergovernmental aspects, of specific quantitative goals and standards. Health, aesthetic, and other social objectives were paramount; economic and administrative considerations took a back seat in legislative halls. During the Carter administration, a lessening of economic regulatory activity began in transportation and oil and gas pricing; concurrently, reviews of the overall federal regulatory framework and process were initiated. Public opinion was shifting, and the Reagan call in 1980 for ''getting government off the backs of the American people'' evoked a strong positive political response.

The ensuing deregulatory agenda at the national level rested primarily on the need for a better balance among the economic, administrative, and social aspects of the regulatory process, both in Washington and in the states. This included a review of the role of government in the market system; clarification of regulatory laws; comparing economic and other regulatory costs against estimated benefits; and balancing the relative roles of federal, state, and local governments and of legislators, administrators, and judges in public regulation.

The principle of interdependence of government and the marketplace in a capitalistic system was enunciated thus by the late Arthur Okun:

Most Americans know that our government and our private economy depend on each other. . . . Strikingly, the government needs the marketplace in two distinct ways—one as a support and one as a counterweight. As a support for government in a capitalistic system, the private economy is the goose that lays the golden eggs. The marketplace finances the public efforts to educate our youth, protect our shores, and aid our poor. As a counterweight, the decentralization of power inherent in a private enterprise economy supplies the limitation of government that is essential to the survival of democracy.

On the other side, the marketplace depends critically on the government and on the exercise of its legal power to make and enforce the rules of economic activity. The value of contracts, promises to pay and money itself stems from the power of politicians and bureaucrats to penalize the violators of the rules of the market game. Without the government as referee, there would be no game.[3]

Within this context the historic economic relationship between government and the market system generally has placed primary reliance on the latter, with public regulatory action being used to compensate for market imperfections. Swings in public opinion and policy have shifted the balance from time to time.

Criteria for governmental regulatory intervention to correct market limitations have been articulated from an economic standpoint, with varying points of view, by James McKie,[4] Charles Schultze,[5] the Committee for Economic Development (CED),[6] and other economists and groups. Generally, the goals of regulation cluster around the values of efficiency and equity, and the balance between the two. Additional values, such as progress (research and development and technological advance) and stability (prices, wages, and employment levels), have been proposed also. We are concerned here with the first three because of general concurrence that any public policies directed toward economic stabilization rest at the national level. Regarding when to intervene, the American Bar Association (ABA) Commission on Law and the Economy listed seven "asserted conditions" frequently cited as requirements for public intervention: (1) to control monopoly power; (2) to control windfall profits; (3) to compensate for inadequate information to consumers; (4) to eliminate "excessive" competition; (5) to avoid distortions when third parties pay the bill (for example, Medicare); (6) to restructure an industry to promote economy of scale (for example, railroad reorganization); and (7) to protect individuals from their own irresponsibility (for example, seat belts and motorcycle helmets).[7]

The economic effects of proposed intervention often are an important part of the debate as to when to intervene. The late eighties saw movement on the part of both the Congress and the states toward shifting part of the cost of social programs to individual firms throughout the economy in the areas of health insurance, day care, and parental leave.[8]

On how, as well as when, the CED and others have urged careful and selective approaches: (1) setting criteria for intervention, including those of feasibility and cost-effectiveness; (2) establishing goals and selecting the best method, including specific goals legislatively enacted, with maximal reliance on the market system; and (3) evaluating results of the intervention. The CED report recommended further that "if action by government is necessary, it should first try to achieve its goal by using incentives and penalties rather than dictating one path that industry must follow. If it is absolutely necessary to set detailed goals, government should avoid specifying how the goals must be met and instead let the market determine the most cost-effective means."[9] The CED concluded that excessive public regulatory activity had imposed enormous costs on the economy, contributing to inflation, reducing productivity, and retarding economic growth.

Regarding productivity, Robert Crandall[10] and others noted that despite serious difficulties in measuring causal relationships, some negative economic and equity impacts seemed apparent in worker safety and pollution control programs due to the diversion of capital away from production enhancement and toward environmental protection (economic), especially where emission and other performance standards were applied to new but not to existing facilities (equity). "Environmentalists" and others favoring stricter regulation contended that if benefits of regulation, together with all output, including pollution control equipment manufacture, were counted, along with costs of existing pollution, productivity might be shown to be actually increasing.

Public use of the private interest expresses the economic and philosophical case for use of the market wherever possible in the pursuit of social objectives. It was stated persuasively by Charles Schultze in 1977:

> For a society that traditionally has boasted about the economic and social advantages of Adam Smith's invisible hand, ours has been strangely loath to employ the same techniques for collective intervention. Instead of creating incentives so that public goals become private interests, private interests are left unchanged and obedience to the public goals is commanded.
>
> Collective intervention is not the same thing as collective coercion. While some element of coercion is implicit in any social intervention, the use of market-like incentives to achieve public purposes minimizes that element. . . . Because the legitimate occasions for social intervention will continue to multiply as society becomes more complex, . . . the collective coercion component of intervention should be treated as a scarce resource . . . and reserved for times when it promises large benefits.[11]

However, there are formidable barriers to general use of market devices (such as taxes, charges, and other penalties, and subsidies, tax credits, and other rewards) to achieve regulatory objectives. For the public regulatory area in general, these include (1) difficulty in measuring relative costs and benefits in achieving a particular regulatory objective—such costs and benefits being indispensable components in calculating a possible incentive or penalty; (2) a perceived need in the political arena to place a stigma on pollution or other actions perceived as contrary to the public interest—"pricing it out" connotes semirespectability; (3) inevitability of winners and losers in any pricing system, while legislators prefer to create only winners; and (4) shorter-run and more visible results, as least in public perception, through a "thou shalt not" regulation than through a financial incentive system that requires time to work through the market system, but which in the long run might very well be far more efficient and equitable.

Issues in Cost-Benefit Ratios as Regulatory Tools

Frequently, those pressing for direct regulation prefer to defer or ignore comparative factors of economic cost and social benefit. Paul Johnson refers to the "George Custer syndrome"—take action at any cost, do it as quickly as possible, and leave the figuring (and thinking) till later. Much of the national environmental regulation of the seventies is alleged by Johnson and others to fit the Custer syndrome.[12] Ralph Nader and many other environmental and consumer protection advocates argue vigorously that health, safety, beauty, and other attributes of a satisfactory quality of life cannot be measured in dollar terms, that action was long overdue, and that any adjustments necessitated by economic, administrative, or other factors can be made sometime in the future.

The ideal of a risk-free society represents one of the key points of division in the conceptual conflict between risk elimination and risk mitigation through the establishment of acceptable thresholds of risk. In its 1979 report the CED observed that "the extra costs [research, development, compliance] of achieving zero risk, rather than an acceptable threshold of risk, are often enormous. The pursuit of zero risk forces the government and private sector to allocate a disproportionate share of their limited resources to eliminating risk in a very small segment of total economic activity. The pursuit of reduced risk generally, according to benefits achieved per unit of investment, would reap much greater reward."[13]

Along the same line, Aaron Wildavsky reviewed two theories and strategies in dealing with risk. One, traditional in a free enterprise system, is the trial-and-error approach, with its attributes of flexibility, speed in introducing new products and methods, and continuing corrections for mistakes. The second approach is one of strict regulation, especially in food, medicine, and other categories of product safety, and essentially is one of no trial without prior ironclad insurance against error, typified by years of delay in introducing new drugs and medical procedures and opposition even to the testing of new products or processes. Wildavsky argues that the first approach produces more "net safety" than the second.[14]

Difficulties in cost and benefit measurement and analysis are numerous and pervasive. Cost-benefit analysis (CBA), involving the measurement of relative costs and benefits arising from regulatory action and the assessment of risks, brings a confrontation between economic and social (including moral) values. The technical and emotional issues are extremely complex; the task of balancing and resolving these conflicts is placed upon the political and legal processes.

Prior to the late seventies and the beginnings of economic deregulation, the debate about public environmental regulation was conducted primarily in benefit terms; the costs by nature were unknown, neglected, or hidden—the administrative ones being submerged in national or state-local budget arithmetic and the compliance ones being passed on to consumers or stockholders. With growing public unease about the intrusiveness and complexity of particular regulations, increasing attention began to be directed to the cost side of the equation.

Regulatory cost measurement comprises a number of elements and differing approaches. Elements receiving more attention in recent years include effects of particular kinds of regulation on intraindustry resource allocation and on research and development initiatives. Initially, studies of regulatory cost were confined to a particular existing or proposed regulation and its cost impact on one or more producers or on a branch of a particular industry. Subsequent cost studies became more comprehensive, such as the one conducted by Arthur Anderson and Co. for the Business Roundtable and covering several industries and regulatory areas.[15]

Approaches to cost measurement have included (1) cost comparisons given the absence or presence of a particular regulation; (2) calculation of direct and indirect operating costs and annualized capital costs, minus any offsets attributable to resultant production or other efficiencies arising from facility or process change; (3) estimated incremental costs over and above an estimated level of environmental or other mandated improvement that "would have occurred" from competition, social pressure, media attention, or other nonregulatory sources; and (4) administrative and compliance costs. Obviously, measuring regulatory benefits is considerably more difficult because of (1) diffusion or nonexistence of information sources; (2) nonmarketability of many benefits; (3) spillover aspect of many benefits from the primary foci of the regulatory action; and (4) the highly subjective nature of many regulatory benefits, especially in the environmental area.

In contrast to the economic and fiscal logic of CBA preceding public regulatory action, strong emotional and moral considerations have been advanced by those concerned with environmental or health/safety protection. Ralph Nader, Joan Claybrook, Edmund Muskie, Mark Green, Henry Waxman, and a host of others have questioned the effectiveness, appropriateness, and even the morality of applying CBA to some or many regulatory issues in the health, safety, and environmental fields.

Steven Kelman summarized the moral/ethical case thusly: "(1) In areas of environmental, safety, and health regulation there may be many instances where a certain decision might be right even though its benefits do not outweigh its costs. (2) There are good reasons to oppose efforts to put dollar values on non-marketed benefits and costs. (3) . . . it is not justifiable to devote major resources to the generation of data for cost-benefit calculations." Kelman went on to observe: "It is amazing that economists can proceed in unanimous endorsement of [cost-benefit analyses] unaware that [such a] conceptual framework is highly controversial in the discipline from which it arose—moral philosophy."[16]

Some have contended that CBA might have prevented Salk vaccine development and that the abolition of slavery might not have survived such an analysis.

Others have argued that railroads probably would never have spanned the continent had environmental impact statements been required in the late 1800s.

Regulatory Administration and Intergovernmental Overlap

Numerous public administration scholars have dealt with the diverse aspects of environmental and other regulatory policy analysis and administration. Three important factors, among others, affect greatly the degree to which environmental laws and regulations thereunder can be executed effectively, economically, and equitably: (1) Respective federal, state, and local responsibilities; (2) organizational structure and coordinative power at the three governmental levels; and (3) the "environmental litigation explosion" in federal and state court systems.

Overlapping jurisdiction of the national and state governments became apparent following the enactment of a wide range of federal regulatory legislation in the seventies. National supersession of state regulatory power via the interstate commerce clause occurred intermittently in the nation's early history and remained in a fairly stable pattern during most of this century (food and drugs, air traffic control, and so on). In such total preemption states are required to vacate the interstate regulatory field, and federal officials assume full legal, administrative, and financial responsibility.

The ACIR, in a 1984 report, categorized additional regulatory forms as (1) partial preemption, placing final decisions and control with the national government, but leaving much of the actual regulatory responsibility—and costs—with the states; (2) direct federal orders to state-local governments to protect (or cease countenancing violations of) civil and other constitutional rights; and (3) conditional sanctions attached to federal aid in the form of (*a*) "program-specific," (*b*) "cross-cutting," or (*c*) "cross-over" varieties.[17]

Partial preemption rests on supersession power that is national, but applied partially, with federal law setting policy and regulatory standards, leaving enforcement to the states, though under continual federal surveillance and second-guessing. Partial preemption has two forms: (*a*) voluntary state participation, whereunder the state may decide to return to the superseded field and share enforcement responsibility; and (*b*) unilateral legal conscription of state enforcement machinery.

The Clean Air Act of 1970 and its 1977 amendments probably represented the most intrusive forms of national regulation from a state-local viewpoint. The legislation made no pretense that state participation was to be voluntary, and full national authority coerced the states into administering a federalized function. Each state had to submit a plan equal to or surpassing federal standards. The Environmental Protection Agency (EPA) was empowered to compel state enforcement of federally drafted revisions to state plans. (Also, section 303 of the clean water legislation, in mandating state development of intrastate water quality standards, subject to EPA review, approval, and revision, implied "legal conscription.")

Some substantial economic, fiscal, and administrative impacts of these types of regulation are the following:

1. Judicial legislation arising from statutory ambiguity and remedy prescription (sometimes involving judicial receivers for activities not complying with federal requirements, such as the 1984 appointment of a court master by a Boston judge to assume control of a water pollution agency pending state legislative action to comply with a court order finding that federal water pollution standards were being violated by the agency.)

2. Rigid uniformity, such as the application under the Clean Water Act of the same treatment level for relatively clean, rural intrastate waters as for industrially polluted rivers in urban areas.

3. Exorbitant incremental costs resulting from unduly utopian legislative goals, as further refined judicially. Advanced wastewater treatment standards, applied nationwide, with no differentiation among individual situations, can entail scores of billions of dollars over the long run. The cost of the top 5 percent increment of improvement often equals or exceeds the cost of the first 80 percent.[18]

4. Ineffective performance through lack of flexibility and selectivity in targeting the situations most in need of correction. This is accentuated by distortion of priorities resulting from availabilities and conditions of federal or state aid and can cause uneconomic design decisions (for example, "gold-plating" sewage treatment plants) if someone else's money is being spent.

5. Blurred political accountability, arising from all of these factors and occurring inevitably when more than one governmental level finances a function, increasing when private-sector regulation is involved, and exacerbated when federal and state courts become enmeshed in clarifying ambiguous legislation.

Two additional aspects of the intergovernmental system should be noted in connection with using economic measures in environmental protection activities. First, state government experimentation with these measures is highly desirable, not only to further test their efficacy in practice, but to provide resulting information to national political leadership as to the pros and cons of expanding a particular successfully tested measure to nationwide application. Second, an important characteristic of a federal, in contrast to a unitary, governmental system constrains somewhat the application of economic incentives, especially where the initiating or administering authorities are state or local governments. If pollution-abatement measures are to be initiated at that level, the spectre of interstate or interlocal economic competition arises. Furthermore, where agencies or facilities of the national government are themselves significant polluters, the levying of charges or fines by a subnational government is constrained by the legal principle of intergovernmental tax immunity ("power to tax is power to destroy").

The organizational framework for environmental policy resolution is a key administrative consideration, both nationally and in the states. At the national level, the resolution of policy differences in executing environmental regulatory legislation involves primarily EPA on the one hand and the Office of Management and Budget (OMB) on the other. Before 1977 or thereabouts, EPA and other regulatory agencies such as the Occupational Safety and Health Administration (OSHA) and the Food and Drug Administration (FDA) were each practically on their own in formulating, publishing, and enforcing those regulations necessary to carry out legislative mandates. Subsequently, the Executive Office of the President, through cabinet committees and OMB, became much more involved as public concern about overregulation sharpened.[19]

At the state level, organizational structure varies from state to state. Increasingly, machinery is being established in governors' offices for the review and reconciliation of policy differences. Often strong conflicts in state policy objectives between environmental and economic/employment values develop regarding new industrial and commercial development. In 1984 the ACIR published draft state legislation providing for interagency coordination, under the governor, of state regulatory activity.[20]

Special Federal-State Problems in Water and Waste Pollution

In pollution abatement and the handling of both general and hazardous waste, overlap between state and federal responsibilities, uneconomic allocation of resources, and complex legal issues have retarded progress. These areas present both serious problems and challenging opportunities for formulating and implementing improved policy approaches.

Undue rigidity of national water pollution abatement standards became a more serious issue. Public reporting of a decade's experience under the clean water legislation of the seventies had been mostly positive. Not given as much attention in the Congress and the media had been reports by the General Accounting Office, the Congressional Budget Office, and others: (1) observed changes in water quality following advanced wastewater treatment levels not always commensurate with the associated incremental costs; (2) serious inflation impact upon capital costs of treatment facilities; (3) sludge disposal problems increased by higher treatment levels; and (4) emergence of agricultural and urban runoff directly into streams as a pollution source that reached or exceeded treatment plant discharges in many areas. These problems pointed to a need for exploring new approaches to water pollution abatement, especially in resource allocation and in conservation pricing of water use.[21] They included the following:

1. Selective modifications of zero discharge goal and advanced treatment requirement might be worthwhile. As in air pollution abatement, the cost per treated unit increases steeply as "purity" or "zero discharge" is approached.

2. Given high incremental costs and growing fiscal constraints in the public sector, it might be highly desirable for clean water legislation to be amended to allow flexibility in standard setting by river basin in the light of basin water quality history and other appropriate factors. This would change the 1965 basic policy for national uniformity, which in hindsight appears to some to have been inordinately costly.

3. In some areas agricultural and urban runoff at particular seasons even pollutes the effluent from sewage treatment plants at advanced secondary levels. To try to regulate such runoff by direct federal control methods would be difficult and unduly costly at best. This nonpoint-source aspect of water pollution abatement, though included in federal legislation in 1987, does not appear to have great significance in the absence of substantial federal money. Furthermore, although state experimentation has been proceeding, much more perhaps can be learned from this step-by-step process than through uniform promulgation of untried standards by EPA.

   Examples of state-local measures that might influence behavior in an appropriate direction include (a) building-code provisions for sediment control associated with new construction; (b) storm sewer improvement and impoundment basins financed through geographic-specific taxing districts; (c) economic incentives for farmers and suburban homeowners to schedule fertilizer application during low-rainfall periods, and for farmers to utilize terracing, no-till cropping, and other means of reducing soil, nutrient, and pesticide discharges into streams.

4. Experience in various local jurisdictions has shown that water conservation practiced on a year-round basis can substantially reduce the need for expanded water and wastewater treatment facilities. Various pricing methods developed by private and public water and sewer utilities to encourage conservation have included (a) uniform commodity rate (no decrease for high volume); (b) seasonal rates (higher during peak seasons); (c) peak-demand rates (facility expansion costs to meet peak demands are allocated to peak-demand users); and (d) inclining commodity rates (unit charge increases with total volume used).

Obscure accountability in solid waste regulation is one of the most recent and complex areas of environmental and regulatory concern and is a major potential area of opportunity for state and local experimentation with economic alternatives and/or supplements to direct regulation. However, it also is one of the areas of physical infrastructure in which studies conducted for the National Council on Public Works Improvement (NCPWI) recommended a substantially expanded national government role.

Most responsibility for nonhazardous solid waste has been borne by local governments under overall policies laid down in state law. There appears to be a national regulatory role, however, for one segment of the activity—a reduction at the manufacturing stage of products and materials that are not biodegradable. While state governments can, do, and should regulate the use of products and materials, regulation of manufacturing standards for products moving in interstate commerce clearly falls within the national regulatory power for the Congress to exercise if it sees fit. Variations in manufacturing standards from state to state may tend to fragment the market and vitiate the economies of mass production. On the other hand, some changes in manufacturing processes that reduce the amount of waste that would otherwise be generated might be effected through state or local action. (A two-year in-plant technical assistance program in Ventura County, California, accomplished a drop of 70 percent in wastes sent for disposal, as reported by the congressional Office of Technology Assessment.)[22]

For hazardous wastes, the cleanup and tort liability problems are incredibly complex.[23] Insurance carriers and the chemical industry in the late eighties were into a confrontation over the issue, which was tied in closely with the tort liability situation in our civil legal system, largely under the purview of state legislatures. There was also an increasing tendency for juries to award punitive damages to persons suffering from a product thoroughly tested at its origination, but encountering newly discovered hazards unknown in the scientific world at the earlier time. New substances that are, or may be, hazardous are being identified constantly. This situation bodes ill for U.S. competitiveness in the absence of international agreements on environmental risks. An individual company in the chemical and related fields may be increasingly hesitant to innovate with new products in the absence of some means of dealing with a future unknown hazard that might develop.

Consequently, two major issues confront the national and state governments, respectively. Nationally, the question is whether to extend an umbrella of liability limitation over the hazardous waste and substances area of the kind accorded to the nuclear power industry under the Price-Anderson Act, and if so, how. For the states, the issue is how to deal with tort liability and the search by plaintiffs and juries for "deep pockets" against which to impose punitive damages.

Safety in the work place is another area of interstate commerce where state regulatory powers prevail in the absence of national preemptive law or in the absence of federal administrative reach in the implementation of such a law. A case in point is federal occupational safety and health legislation and its execution by the same-named agency (OSHA). Due to administration policy in the eighties, the reach of OSHA was restrained in order to better target its resources, although it was contended that hostility toward the legislative intent also was a factor. In any case a number of states continued to inspect and prosecute vigorously those employers found in violation of either federal or state standards. This also occurred in the areas of consumer protection and financial takeovers of one company by another; in the latter area the Congress threatened from time to time to enact preemptive legislation in order to achieve nationwide uniformity of treatment.

Both in workplace safety and other regulatory areas ostensibly covered by federal legislation, states can move in to fill the void. Offenders can be prosecuted under the state criminal code; states can enact laws conferring civil penalties upon violators of either state or federal law; and states can finance special units in the offices of state attorneys general and local prosecutors to go after offenses in any area that has been ostensibly preempted under federal law but not fully implemented for whatever reason.[24]

LAND USE REGULATION AND GROWTH MANAGEMENT

In contrast to environmental concerns, natural resources, workplace safety, and other regulatory areas, all of which involve the exercise of a mixture of national, state, and local regulatory powers, land use, both urban and rural, has remained a nearly exclusively state-local power. It is exercised under the state police power, usually through the processes of planning, zoning, subdivision regulation, and farmland preservation. Prior to the seventies land use planning and zoning powers, although resting with the state government, had been delegated constitutionally or statutorily to local governments, mostly municipalities, which in turn exercised the power through local charter provisions and ordinances, rules, and procedures thereunder. The major legal check upon the local regulatory power rested in any limitations or reservations expressed in the state delegation, and in the "taking clause" of the Fifth Amendment to the U.S. Constitution, which provides that no persons shall "be deprived of life, liberty, or property, without due process of law; nor shall private property be taken for public use without just compensation."

The Many Faces of Land Use Regulation and Growth Management

After World War II the principal, and often the only, public regulation of the land settlement pattern as population spread from city to countryside was through the process of planning, zoning, and subdivision approval. Land was classified for appropriate use under master plans, and building permits were not issued unless the building or subdivision plan met all of the detailed requirements of the local government, including conformity with the zoning criteria and associated provisions. Without a framework of this kind, suburban-area land use today would be incredibly more chaotic than it is already.

Land use regulation has several objectives and uses, which in their implementation can have strong positive or negative economic, fiscal, social and environmental effects:

- Residential, industrial, and commercial development can proceed in an orderly and equitable way, or the opposite.

- If accompanied by an "adequate public facility" requirement in connection with public infrastructure, the construction of necessary roads, schools, and other public facilities can be harmonized with the pace of development and vice versa.[25]

- Through land use planning and zoning, "clean industry," such as research and development (R&D), shopping centers, luxury apartments, and other developments of a high tax-yielding nature can be zoned in, and housing for people to be employed in the new developments, especially the low-income ones, can be zoned out. This is called exclusionary zoning.[26]

- Construction of needed but not necessarily scenic facilities such as a power, water filtration, or sewage treatment plant or a community mental health facility, though attractive on the outside, can sometimes be delayed endlessly in lawsuits contesting zoning decisions of the local government. This is called the "not in my back yard" (NIMBY) syndrome.

- Up to a point, the pace of development can be stretched out so as to avoid extreme peaks and valleys in employment and other economic activity in the construction and related trades in the community.

- Open space and other environmental or aesthetic objectives or features can be furthered or protected.

State-Local Responsibilities in Land Use Regulation

Over the past two decades California, Florida, New Hampshire, New Jersey, Oregon, and a few other states have been reasserting state authority over local regulatory actions in the land use field.[27] Their actions have included the following:

- Requiring that those land use decisions at the municipal level having an impact upon neighboring jurisdictions be subject to one or more levels of review—the overlying county; a multicounty regional planning body if one exists; or the state planning agency[28]

- Identifying specific geographical areas, such as coastal, wetland, and other environmentally fragile locations, in which land use regulation is vested in a state agency or for which any local land use decisions must receive state approval (for example, the California State Coastal Commission)

- Requiring all counties or counties of certain population characteristics to assume land use regulatory responsibilities for certain types of development and to prepare, adopt, and maintain county comprehensive land use plans (Florida and others)

- Requiring that local land use plans and zoning ordinances and regulations allow for certain types of housing and for other uses specified in the statute—inclusionary zoning (New Jersey)[29]

- Requiring that developments over a certain acreage, dwelling units, or other measures of substantial economic or geographic impact be reviewed and approved by the state (New Hampshire, Maine)

- Imposing land use controls as a part of protecting coastal or other environmentally threatened areas (Delaware in the seventies; Chesapeake Bay interstate agreement among Virginia, Maryland, District of Columbia, and Pennsylvania in 1986–87)

In brief, the recapture by state governments of land use regulatory powers previously delegated in toto to local governments was exceptional in the seventies and, except for Florida and a handful of other instances, continued to be so in the eighties. For the most part, the earlier initiatives were environmentally oriented. There appeared some indication in 1987 of a rekindling of interest on the part of state governments, driven by concern about housing availability and urban land costs. At the 1987 annual meeting of the Council of State Community Affairs Agencies, thirteen states identified housing/growth management as a top-priority concern. It also is possible that new legal issues will force state governments in the nineties into a more active growth management role in some aspects and a more restrained role in others.

Although citizen movements to achieve more strict growth management controls enjoy substantial support in politically conservative jurisdictions (for example, Orange County, California), such controls and the motivation behind them can be called into question. Columnist George Will contends that the California slow-growth movement "represents the growing desire of the possessing classes . . . for laws to protect the value of the positional good of life in a choice location."[30]

From a far different philosophical perspective, urban economist Anthony Downs also raises strong questions. "This situation [traffic congestion] threatens to worsen if rapid growth continues. Hence suburban and even some city residents have started to demand limits on the size and speed of future growth . . . this whole controversy about . . . growth limits is mostly between two relatively well-off groups: Current residents and real estate developers. Both tend to ignore a much deeper issue connected with metropolitan growth: continued exclusion of the poor from the suburbs . . . over 25 percent of all U.S. children are black or Hispanic. Most go to school in big-city school systems that provide very low-quality educations. Suburban growth-slowing policies would worsen this situation by increasing suburban housing costs even more. . . . However, suburbs themselves cannot effectively open their borders . . . without major housing subsidies. . . . Only the federal government can tax its non-poor residents to aid the poor without driving many of those non-poor residents beyond its boundaries to escape such taxation."[31]

Public Actions to Preserve Farmland and Other Open Space

Aesthetic values for many citizens represent a key part of environmental protection; urbanization and other natural resource development bring "visual pollution" to the countryside and forest. To slow down or cushion this process, national and state governments, respectively, have acted to set aside wilderness and other park areas and to encourage the preservation of farmland. Acquisition is the usual method for the former; for the latter, many states have established a system of preferential farmland assessment for property tax purposes, so that higher taxes on farmland lying in the path of urban development may be avoided by assessing the land at its agricultural rather than its market value. Many economists and tax administrators view this method as far more costly and inequitable than (a) the acquisition of agricultural or scenic easements or (b) sale by the landowner to the local government or a developer of development rights commensurate with the area of the farm and the governmental transfer of those rights from low- to higher-density areas within the local jurisdiction. This allows keeping the land in agricultural use indefinitely without financial penalty to the landowner.[32]

If, as frequently suggested, environmental standards were set on the basis of individual river or stream basins rather than by a single, uniform statewide or national standard, the encompassing boundary would become a special-authority or district form of local or substate regional governmental structure. Stream drainage, erodable land conservation, and urban runoff control nearly always are noncoterminous with the boundaries of general governments (cities, counties, and states). Usually it is necessary to tie such "environmental district" programs and activities to appropriate state and local governments for coordinative and financial administration purposes.[33]

The Taking Clause in Growth Management

In 1987 the U.S. Supreme Court handed down three important substantive decisions concerning the taking clause of the Constitution. In the first case, coming from Pennsylvania, a land use regulation prevented coal companies from mining more than half of any of their coal located under or near specified structures, in order to minimize danger of a sinking of the land and consequent destruction or damage to structures. The Court ruled that this regulation came under the general police power of the state as it relates to public safety and welfare and consequently was not a taking.[34]

The second case concerned development exactions in California, where, as noted earlier, they came into widespread use after passage of Proposition 13. Under the state environmental protection laws, state or local governments could mitigate the impact of new development on the environment by requiring the provision of public facilities or other amenities. Later legislation legitimized such "bargained agreements" between developers and state or local governments. In this case the public amenity required was access to a beach across privately owned land. This exaction was found by the court to constitute a taking, but one that could be defended if it "substantially advances a legitimate state interest." The Court stated also that while governmental actions in general can be sustained if they meet the rational basis test, a challenge based on a taking requires substantial or additional justification.[35]

A third case involved the imposition by a local government of a development moratorium on land in a flood plain. Subsequently, a suit was filed by the owners claiming damages. The Court remanded the case to the state court for a determination as to whether the moratorium constituted a taking, but held that a temporary taking entitled a property owner to compensation if the effect of the taking was to deny a landowner all use of a piece of property.[36]

Possibly as important as the decisions themselves was language in the majority and minority opinions. The historical principle on taking had been laid down in an opinion by Justice Oliver Wendell Holmes in a 1922 case.[37] Until 1987 that opinion had been the last word on the substance of the taking issue: "The general rule at least is, that while property may be regulated to a certain extent, if regulation goes too far it will be recognized as a taking."

The majority in its opinion on the First Lutheran Church case stated that "a strong public desire to improve the public condition is not enough to warrant achieving the desire by a shorter cut than the constitutional way of paying for the change.'' Justice John Paul Stevens in his dissent expressed the fear that the Court's decision would have a ''chilling'' impact on land use regulation because of the possibility of having to pay damages.[38]

John DeGrove, former Florida secretary of community affairs and a national authority on state roles in growth management, expressed a cautionary but not fearful note regarding the impact of the decisions rendered so far: ''The Court is beginning to take a more critical look at the land use regulatory activity of state and local government. . . . This means that careful and detailed studies should be done as a basis for comprehensive planning and land use regulation.''[39]

THE CIVIL LITIGATION EXPLOSION: ARE WE SUING TOO MUCH?

During the eighties, it became more and more apparent that the nation's legal systems, both national and state, were becoming seriously clogged. Not only were the systems themselves in trouble, but on the civil side, the overload plus the new kinds of litigation outcomes were having serious economic, health care, and other negative ramifications throughout American society. This did not mean that the civil legal system and the participants in it—plaintiffs, trial attorneys, judges, and juries—were necessarily at fault. But it did mean that state governments—legislatures, courts, and executive branches—needed to study, evaluate, and chart some courses of action, because the great bulk of civil litigation in the country takes place in state, not federal, courts. It is the purpose here to identify the major concerns in this area, ascertain the underlying causes of the problems, and examine the currently discussed remedial measures, noting the principal contrasting views on each.

Major Aspects of the Increase in Civil Litigation

The following developments and trends have contributed to an increase in adversarial proceedings in the civil justice system. Some of these have been inevitable; others arise from both intended and overlooked provisions of national and state legislation and interpretations thereof.

- Growing complexity of society in general, and especially in scientific, technological, economic, health, and environmental aspects
- A consequent and great increase in public regulation of private-sector activities and in national regulation of various actions of state and local governments, accompanied by prescriptive processes, the absence of, or deviation from, being susceptible to court challenge, and resulting widespread delay in the dispensing of civil justice
- The ambiguity of legislation, which in its implementation leads to recourse to the judiciary for resolution of legislative intent
- Judicial ascertainment of additional rights, especially in recent years, including those flowing from state constitutions[40]

- A public view of courts, especially federal courts, as instruments of remediation for legislative inaction or unwillingness to enact legislation desired by particular groups
- Elevation of "public participation" in public policy decisions to a due process right[41]
- Governmental subsidies to plaintiffs (for example, attorney fees in successful challenges to official acts)
- Judicial tendency to substitute own remedies for legislative shortcomings and to maintain jurisdiction over an issue for extended periods
- Slow rate of evolution of alternative processes for conflict resolution
- Expansion in judicial standing, both by legislative act and by judicial decision
- Extension of tort liability in commercial and industrial areas to product quality and performance, and in the public sector to both corporate and personal capacities of officials, employees, and community service volunteers
- A trend toward ever higher and more generous jury awards for punitive as well as actual damages

State-Local Government Measures Taken or under Consideration

Beginning in the seventies and at a more rapid pace thereafter, state legislatures and courts took measures to reduce the volume of litigation and/or to mitigate some of the perceived excesses growing out of these developments and trends. These included the following:

1. Establishing special courts or other conflict resolution procedures to handle small or specialized claims
2. Similar actions regarding landlord-tenant relations in the housing area
3. Reorganizing state and local court systems to provide simpler, unified state systems
4. Assuming part or all of court costs previously borne by local governments, sometimes excluding in this assumption costs of judicial resolution of civil and criminal matters arising under local ordinance rather than state law, with the assumption formula adjusted downward from 100 percent to account for the then-prevailing relative incidence of the locally based proceedings
5. Authorizing judges to refer cases to conclusive arbitration procedures
6. Authorizing voluntary use of neighborhood panels or other conflict resolution procedures as "courts of first resort"
7. Initial appointment, rather than election, of judges, with later election, if any, limited to the question of whether or not the judge is to be retained in office
8. Establishment of court administrators to be responsible for administrative and management aspects of the respective judicial systems
9. Procedures for judicial discipline and removal of judges and for mandatory retirement

The eventual outcomes of these measures were generally positive; however, alternative conflict resolution procedures require continuing evaluation because of the tendency to overproceduralize, among other reasons. (Such an analysis of arbitration machinery in California by Rand rendered a "modest success" verdict.)[42] In the early eighties urban neighborhoods began to experiment with community boards to hear grievances and endeavor to settle them without getting into legal processes, such boards being supported by nonprofit organizations and contributions from users.[43]

Tort Liability Reform

The various changes and experiments, although curbing the rate of increase in litigation, did not stem the rising tide. Other steps have been proposed, all of which are quite controversial. Any restriction upon standing of parties or justiciability of issues usually is opposed by trial lawyers for obvious reasons and by consumer, environmental, or other groups that are experiencing more success in achieving policy objectives through the judicial branch than through the legislative branch of the governmental system.

Product liability and its extension. As pointed out earlier in connection with hazardous waste liability, changing legal concepts, moving away from a showing of fault or negligence, were having wide economic ramifications, extending to the country's competitiveness in international trade. In its policy position the NGA has pointed out that "affordable liability coverage has become increasingly more difficult to obtain . . . resulting in a severely adverse effect . . . throughout the nation." The NGA proceeded in 1986 to declare that "governors [should] urge Congress to adopt a federal uniform product liability code."[44]

NGA supported even further federal action by suggesting that in addition to a uniform product liability code, Congress should assess the impact of a uniform code on "public safety and consumer protection and, if deemed appropriate, enhance federal safety and consumer protection standards." The NGA policy statement concluded that "there must also be effective oversight of the insurance industry so as to guarantee that the needs of both American business and American consumers are met and protected." Areas of the insurance industry needing special policing in the view of the NGA were rate increases, insurance availability, practices on cancellation and nonrenewal of policies, coverage restriction, and reinsurance. In effect, the governors were saying that unless the states were able to tighten up substantially their oversight of the insurance industry, the national government should be prepared to move into still another area presently occupied by state government.[45]

However, as of the end of 1987 the governors apparently were not speaking for all of state government; the Council of State Governments (CSG) at its annual meeting voted to oppose legislation pending in the Congress that would involve the national government in insurance regulation, and the National Conference of State Legislatures (NCSL) was continuing to oppose a national product liability code on federalism grounds. The NCSL principles on national preemption include a clear showing that "[1] . . . exercise of authority in a particular area by individual states has resulted in "widespread and serious conflicts imposing a severe burden on national economic activity or other national goals. [2] . . . preemption of state law is the only reasonable means of dealing with the problem; [and 3] solving the problem is not merely desirable, but necessary to achieve a compelling national objective."[46]

On product liability, the NCSL policy statement claims that the proposed federal legislation "fails to meet the standards necessary for preemption." It states further that the proposed legislation would dictate a "single set of rules controlling the timeliness of claims and the admissibility of evidence . . . [and] would place state legislatures and state courts in an intolerable legal strait-jacket."[47]

It may well be that federal regulation will be extended into two new areas—product liability and insurance regulation—and that federal regulatory jurisdiction will be further expanded in areas it already partially occupies—workplace safety and consumer protection. If (and it is a very large if) such extension were accomplished via an unambiguous statute, a large dent would have been made in plaintiff opportunity, at least in state courts, and given proper drafting and content, the area of potential litigation in the federal courts would be kept to a modest level. Moves in these directions, of course, would be expected to meet the strong objections of trial lawyers and perhaps of some specialized consumer groups that have particularly strong bases of support in individual states.

Caps on punitive damage awards had been considered in some states by the end of 1987, with a scattering of enactments, most of which attacked the problem tangentially. However, in this area, as in product liability, pressure from manufacturers and other industrial and commercial groups had been growing for partial or total national preemption of this aspect of tort liability. Large companies such as the Manville Corporation (asbestos claims), A. H. Robins Company (injuries and unwanted pregnancies from a contraceptive device), and Texaco were forced into bankruptcy because of overhanging damage awards, a considerable portion of each being punitive rather than actual damages. Punitive damages are supposed to punish for negligence or illegal acts, but when they take away most of the assets of large companies, they can wreak economic havoc. Some attorneys are beginning to argue that such damages can violate the prohibition of excessive fines contained in the Eighth Amendment to the U.S. Constitution. Plaintiff attorneys argue, on the other hand, that if it takes the bankruptcy of a company to end the threat of asbestos to human life, so be it.[48]

In the mid-eighties the Reagan administration, despite its strong tilt toward devolutionary federalism, concluded that national intervention was becoming necessary for economic reasons that it considered predominant, including the chilling effect of these awards on private enterprise innovation in new technology and new products, but also because it threatened the economic survival of otherwise-strong business firms. As a former Reagan White House official commented to this writer, "It finally came down to a choice between ambulance chasers and robber barons,'' and economics and international competitiveness took priority over principles of federalism.

Policy reports from the federal executive branch proposed eight major principles for tort law reform, some being preemptive of existing state law: (1) retention of fault as the basis for liability; (2) basing causation findings on credible scientific and medical evidence; (3) elimination of joint and several liability; (4) limitation of noneconomic damages to a fair and reasonable amount (for example, $100,000); (5) installment payments of economic damages; (6) reduction of awards by collateral compensation sources for same injury; (7) declining percentage of award for attorney fees (for example, 25 percent on first $100,000, 15 percent on the next, and so on); and (8) provision of alternative dispute resolution mechanisms. No caps, other than under state law, following certain criteria, were proposed on awards for economic injury.

Other limitations on tort liability would apply to federal contractors and the federal government itself. Criteria for exclusion from liability applying to federal contractors (including state and local governments when acting in such a contractual capacity) would constitute suggested criteria for states to include in amendments to their own tort liability laws.[49]

In the case of product liability and caps on punitive damages, the national government would be moving into regulatory areas previously the domain of the states. As in the earlier de facto repeal of the McFadden Act (reserving regulation of branch banking to the states), technological change and the nationalization and globalization of economies comprise forces much stronger than federalism principles and the spirit of the Tenth Amendment in the gravitation of economic regulation to the central government.

Tort liability of public officials and governmental entities increased considerably during the late seventies and throughout the eighties, largely through judicial decisions. Key initial decisions in the U.S. Supreme Court opened the "window of vulnerability" for state and local officials by holding that local governmental bodies no longer had "sovereign immunity" from civil litigation initiated by an injured party under the Civil Rights Act of 1871 (United States Code, Section 1983). The first decision ending sovereign immunity occurred in 1978 in *Monell v. New York City Department of Social Services*.[50] Subsequently, in two 1980 cases the Court contracted the immunity area further by holding local governments responsible in statutory as well as constitutional violations and ruling further that if the injured party prevailed in court, attorney fees could be recovered from the defending government.[51]

The number of suits filed in federal courts subsequent to, and based upon, these decisions did not increase as drastically as had been feared. However, tort liability suits against local governments increased greatly in state courts. These were not primarily based on the federal decisions, but upon the general tendency at both state and federal levels in those years to legislate and adjudicate in favor of lesser immunity, to provide more grounds to sue, and to impose upon elected

and appointed officials personal as well as corporate liability for errors of judgment or other transgressions.

During the same period that immunities were being reduced or eliminated and
bases for tort litigation broadened, drastic swings in interest rates caused insurance carriers to raise their premiums or to refuse to renew policies in functions
or activities that were becoming more vulnerable to damage awards. Consequently, local governments faced painful dilemmas in the early to mid-eighties,
with choices ranging from ceasing functions that were lawsuit prone (for example,
playgrounds and pools) to dropping their liability policies and going to self-
insurance, either alone or through risk pooling with other governmental units.
Some public officials, particularly those serving in unpaid, decision-making
positions, resigned rather than be exposed to suits, which, even though unsuccessful, would produce legal costs for the defendants. Juries tended to view local
government as having "deep pockets" and were sympathetic to injured parties.
Personal as well as corporate liability of officials arose from state court decisions
or statutory provisions of "joint and several liability" under which a party in a
suit can be responsible for all damages, no matter how small the degree of
negligence.[52]

Fortunately, by 1988 state legislatures were amending statutes so as to confer
personal immunity on elected and appointed officials and employees for actions
taken in an official capacity and to facilitate the forming of risk pools for self-
insurance purposes. At one point in 1986 it was estimated that two-thirds of the
local governments were operating without liability insurance. Some counties
took their police cars off the road because they could not afford insurance. In
1986 over 1,400 bills on the liability problem were introduced in forty-four
states. Michigan and Massachusetts overhauled their liability statutes, and twelve
states changed their provisions on joint and several liability.[53]

Employment, employee negligence, and employee references. Suits were filed
and won in which an employer was found liable for negligent or illegal acts
committed by an employee because of insufficient preemployment reference
checking. Other suits were filed by ex-employees, accusing former employers
of giving unjustified unfavorable references and thereby defaming the plaintiff.
These developments began to cause employers to decline to respond to reference
checks in order to avoid the choice between making false statements on the one
hand ("very satisfactory employee") or running the risk of being sued. Consequently, other employers seeking to learn more about prospective employees
in order to minimize future liability found themselves "cut off at the pass."[54]

Reform of tort liability statutes has been, and continues to be, under consideration in many states. The Rand Corporation's Institute for Civil Justice has
conducted research on a number of tort liability issues, with mixed conclusions.

On the impact of fee arrangement of lawyer effort (contingency or hourly
basis), one study found no significant difference on smaller cases. On the severity
and frequency of medical malpractice claims, caps on awards significantly reduced severity and shorter statutes of limitation reduced frequency, but research-

ers cautioned that the tort reform goal should not be to reduce claims costs but to deter medical negligence and assure timely compensation of victims. On the general need for tort reform, ''The underlying problem is the inability to decide whether we in the United States want to have a pure compensatory system, in which everyone is compensated for every injury . . . , or a fault-based liability system in which compensation is limited in a strict, comparative, or contributory way to those who have caused the injury.''[55]

Getting at Other Roots of the Litigation Explosion

In addition to the shift away from fault as the basis of tort liability, several other developments in the U.S. legislative, legal, and judicial systems have spurred increases in civil litigation. Some of these involve lawmaking, others the judicial review process.

Reducing ambiguity in national and state regulatory and other statutes obviously must rest with the Congress and the state legislatures. Corrective action in most aspects necessarily begins with the judiciary committees of the legislative body. Urgently needing correction has been the tendency of legislators, as part of the struggle to get bills passed, to fashion ambiguously worded compromise provisions on sensitive issues, leaving future clarification to the judiciary.

Worth consideration may be a legislative rule setting forth standards of ''legal adequacy'' (for example, clarity, enforceability, avoidance of overly prescriptive or unmeetable statutory goals, and specification of conflict resolution procedures) for proposed legislation being reported to the floor and making absence of legal adequacy clearance by the counsel or other legislative officer subject to point of order.

The long life of ''judicial receiverships'' tends to distort the concept of checks and balances at both national and state levels. Not infrequently, in such areas as school desegregation, unsatisfactory prison conditions, breakup of the AT&T system, and water pollution violations, judges, in deciding constitutional and other cases brought before them, issue orders designed to correct the unconstitutional or illegal condition and maintain jurisdiction until it is determined judicially that the matter has been substantially resolved. The continuance of the court's jurisdiction often, but not always, is exercised through a court-appointed master. The master, as an officer of the court, becomes essentially a receiver or administrator of that portion of the activity that has been found unsatisfactory. Sometimes, as in school desegregation, court jurisdiction may continue for a decade or more, or a court master may be running a sewage treatment system for several years.

Judicial prescription and/or administration of remedies, especially in instances of an unconstitutional statute, may tend to preempt the constitutional role of the legislative branch, and also that of the executive on occasion. If the legislative body fails to amend the statute within a reasonable time, a further judicial order or other appropriate judicial action could follow. Worth consideration might be statutory specification by the legislative body (empowered in the U.S. and many state constitutions to provide by law for the conduct of the judicial process) of procedures to be followed by the judiciary in cases where federal or state laws are found unconstitutional, including judicial referral to the appropriate legislative body for correction within a specified time. This would give the legislative branch, which initiated the legislation in the first place, the first crack at correcting its mistake, without the need for judicial assumption of the lawmaking function.

Streamlining the judicial review process would reduce greatly the time needed to finalize a governmental action. In environmental and other areas of litigation where failure to follow proper procedure to the very last letter and beyond is actionable, with no statutory deadline for challenging administrative action, great costs in money and time can be incurred. If building a particular facility is subject to challenge on more than one ground, it often is possible for plaintiffs to play out each basis sequentially rather than in parallel. Some projects, such as the Seabrook nuclear power plant in New Hampshire, can be kept in court for a decade or longer.

By the late eighties the failure of a number of states and localities to enact legislation and establish processes for assuring that necessary infrastructure is in place by the time new development is built out, as described in chapter 4, was resulting in serious traffic and other congestion. More often than not, the public facilities were not built because of neighborhood objection. In the enactment of enabling legislation for comprehensive land use planning and regulation, care needs to be taken to assure that reasonable limits are placed upon the susceptibility of administrative decisions to prolonged legal challenge.

Is the United States in a state of legal slavery? This question is raised occasionally in assessing the adversarial system of civil justice; often comparisons are made with other countries. Data from the Ministry of Justice of Japan show the United States leading the other four major democracies. In 1986 lawyers per 100,000 people ranged from 279 in the United States to 11 in Japan, with Britain at 114, West Germany at 77, and France at 29. On the same measure, the United States had 12 judges, Japan 2, Britain 50, West Germany 28, and France 8.[56] Comparisons with Great Britain are most appropriate, of course, since the American legal system was inherited from England. The disparity in the number of lawyers is striking. Companies in Japan hardly ever sue one another, because in such cases trade between litigants must cease. The number of lawyers is limited stringently, and there are not enough to go around. Some argue that although the British legal system has served America well, the volume of civil litigation has approached the unmanageable.

MAJOR CRIMINAL JUSTICE ISSUES

In the late sixties and early seventies numerous studies were made of law enforcement and the criminal justice system. Public concern had been rising about law and order, especially in metropolitan areas and most particularly in the central cities. On the police function, "common denominator" recommendations in many of the resulting reports included (1) consolidation of small municipal police departments; (2) increased use of civilian personnel; (3) increased specialization of certain functions on a metropolitan basis (for example, communications and laboratory work); (4) higher entrance requirements for employment of police officers; (5) active crime prevention efforts by the police in cooperation with the community, and otherwise improving police-community relations; (6) enactment of state legislation establishing a system of mandatory crime reporting; and (7) clarifying the legal authority and liability of police officers in the conduct of their duties.[57] With the exception of the consolidation of small departments, which subsequently took the direction of shifting specialized functions and overall police jurisdiction to county or higher levels, and the maintenance of supplemental police patrol functions at the small-city or village level, these measures no longer arouse much controversy.

On the correction front, major attention was being given to depopulating large institutions and moving toward community-based programs and facilities, alternatives to incarceration, emphasis on rehabilitation, and giving greater priority to probation and parole. Several new issues surfaced subsequently, including overcrowding, raising the money for new construction, differential treatment of "career criminals" and those with no or fewer previous offenses, and greater equity and uniformity in sentencing.

Attention here will be given to statistical data on the criminal and correctional populations; equity and efficiency values in arrests, detention, and judicial sentencing; acute problems on the correctional front; and a summary of the major policy issues facing state and local governments in this field.

Crime and Correctional Categories and Incidence

Table 6.1 shows the high and low states in violent crime rates, ranked in order of aggregate index for violent crime. Appendix 6.A shows similar and additional data for all the states. It should be emphasized that the rates are adjusted for population, but not for population density. Similar data for cities were shown in table 5.9.

For corrections, table 6.2 shows prison population for regions and selected states at the end of 1987 by number, rate per 100,000 state population, and percentage by race. A state-by-state breakdown appears in appendix 6.B.

Equity and Efficiency Values in the Criminal Justice System

The data in these tables and those in chapter 5 show repeatedly a highly disproportionate number of blacks involved in the criminal justice system in the arrest, conviction, and incarceration stages. The same is true of persons given death sentences and those executed for crimes. It is also true that among crime victims, blacks suffer in a far higher number than their percentage of the total

Table 6.1

Crimes per 100,000 Population: Aggregate Violent Crimes, Murder, Robbery, and Property Crimes for Selected States,* 1987

	Violent Crime	Murder**	Robbery	Property Crime
U. S.	610	8.3	213	4,940
Florida	1,024	11.4	357	7,497
New York	1,008	11.3	503	4,944
California	918	10.6	301	5,588
Illinois	796	8.3	314	4,620
Michigan	780	12.2	277	5,677
North Dakota	57	1.5	8	2,776
South Dakota	120	1.8	12	2,558
Vermont	137	2.7	17	4,135
West Virginia	137	4.8	31	2,053
New Hampshire	150	3.0	26	3,222
Montana	151	4.1	24	4,448

Source: U.S. Department of Justice, Federal Bureau of Investigation, *Crime in the United States, 1987*, July 10, 1988, table 4, pp. 44–51.

* Does not include District of Columbia; shown as Washington, D.C. in table 5.9.
** Includes nonnegligent manslaughter.

population. This is especially the case in central-city crimes. Professor William Wilson has noted that in the seventies 80 percent of those committing murder in Chicago were black, as were 70 percent of those murdered. By 1983 murder victims numbered 513 blacks, 108 Hispanics, and 95 whites, with the perpetrators in similar proportions (515, 102, and 58, respectively.)[58]

These data and many others raise persistent questions about the extent of racial discrimination in the criminal justice system, as well as the extent to which external forces—economic, social, fiscal, and others—are at the root of the disproportion of blacks and Hispanics arrested, convicted, or otherwise involved in crime, particularly violent crime. Health and criminal justice data show a strong connection between drug abuse and crime, and there are many other highly negative economic and social outcomes relating to drugs.

Since the late sixties the Rand Corporation has been conducting research in criminal justice and has completed several studies of equity in the system. Using 1980 data from California, Michigan, and Texas, Rand researchers studied the crime cycle from commission through sentencing and on to parole or release, controlling for a variety of external factors. The study "found no evidence of discrimination against minorities in arrests . . . , or in felony convictions. However, once convicted, blacks and Hispanics were more likely than their white counterparts to get prison sentences . . . , get longer sentences and to serve more time."[59] (A racial profile of the U.S. prison population appears in figure 6.1.)

Table 6.2

Inmates in Federal and State Prisons per 100,000 General Population and by Race, for Selected States, December 1987

Region or State	Total No.	Ratio to Pop.	White	Black	Percents Other (1)	Other (2)	Unknown
U.S.	581,020	239	50.2	45.3	0.9	0.3	3.3
Federal	48,300	20	67.3	30.3	1.7	0.7	0.0
State	532,720	219	48.6	46.6	0.9	0.3	3.6
State Inmates:							
Northeast	88,932	177	47.4	49.9	0.1	0.2	2.4
Midwest	110,279	185	50.7	45.6	0.9	0.1	2.4
South	221,813	264	39.6	55.4	0.5	0.0	4.5
West	111,696	227	65.7	27.2	2.2	1.2	3.7
Minnesota	2,546	60	64.4	24.1	8.2	0.1	3.2
North Dakota	430	64	84.9	0.9	14.0	0.2	0.0
West Virginia	1,461	77	84.7	15.1	0.0	0.1	0.0
New Hampshire	867	82	97.1	2.8	0.1	0.0	0.0
Alaska	2,528	482	56.0	9.0	34.0	1.0	0.0
Delaware	2,939	456	42.1	57.6	0.1	0.1	0.0
Nevada	4,434	440	60.6	30.4	0.9	0.9	7.1
Illinois	19,850	171	32.1	59.9	0.1	0.0	7.8
Florida	32,445	270	45.1	52.4	0.0	0.1	2.5

Source: Bureau of the Census, *State Population and Household Estimates with Age, Sex, and Components of Change 1981–87*. Current Population Reports, P–25, no. 1024, table 1, December 1987, p. 11.

U.S. Department of Justice, Bureau of Justice Statistics, *Correctional Populations in the United States 1987*, table 5.6 (forthcoming 1989).

Notes: Other (1): American Indian or Alaskan Native. Other (2): Asian or Pacific Islander. Percents do not always add to exactly 100 due to rounding.

A subsequent report in 1985 on the effect of sentencing guidelines on minorities found that "the use of guidelines does not overcome racial disparities in sentencing, supervision and parole decisions. Paradoxically, it may widen them, for reasons that are complex and probably intractable."[60]

Economic efficiency is one of the key factors to be considered by state and local governments in the allocation of fiscal resources. But in corrections, in contrast to the crime prevention, investigation/apprehension, and judicial stages of the criminal justice system, economic efficiency, although very important, is a more difficult measure to apply, because research and practice have not yet produced conclusive answers to a key aspect of the corrections process: who are the "violent predators" among the hundreds of thousands of prison inmates at

Figure 6.1
U.S. Prison Population by Race, 1987

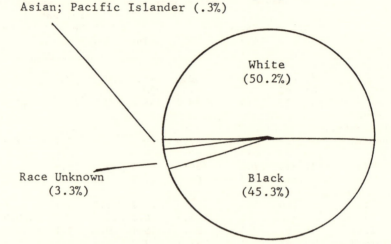

American Indian; Alaskan Native (.9%)
Asian; Pacific Islander (.3%)

White
(50.2%)

Race Unknown
(3.3%)

Black
(45.3%)

Source: U.S. Department of Justice, Bureau of Justice Statistics, *Correctional Populations in the United States, 1987.* table 5.6 (forthcoming 1989).

any one time? What are the indicators that would identify those persons who should be incarcerated over long, fixed periods?

Two constant indicators of "career criminal" tendencies emerge in a review of profiles of correctional inmates and earlier arrestees. First, for many years, rates of recidivism continued high. (In 1986 over 80 percent of state prison inmates had been previously sentenced to probation or incarceration as a juvenile or adult.) Second, drug use during or in days or weeks preceding the commission of a crime emerged as a continuing high statistic (found in 1974 and 1979 surveys). 1986 sample surveys of inmates, comprising inmate record reviews and personal interviews, were conducted by the Census Bureau for the Bureau of Justice Statistics of the U.S. Department of Justice. These surveys showed percentages of inmates using illegal drugs to be (1) 35 percent at time of offense; (2) 62 percent regular use at some previous period; and (3) 43 percent use on a daily basis in the month before the last offense. Use at the time of offense was 33 percent for murder, 32 percent for rape, and 42 percent for robbery. Thirty-five percent of inmates reported regular past use of a major drug (heroin, methadone, cocaine, LSD, or PCP).[61] Cited earlier was the strong relationship between drug use and (1) dropping out of school, (2) chronic inability to hold a job, and (3) AIDS infection. From 53 to 79 percent of the men arrested for serious offenses in twelve major U.S. cities between June and November of 1987 tested positive for illegal drugs.[62]

As the seriousness of drug use and awareness of its association with criminal behavior escalated, increased attention was directed to drug testing, raising a variety of law enforcement and civil rights issues, the latter including illegal search and seizure, due process rights, and confidentiality.[63] Several cities, in cooperation with the Department of Justice, began testing arrestees (mostly for street crimes such as burglary, assault, and grand larceny) on a routine but voluntary basis, with the rate of declination in 1987 averaging about 10 percent for interviews on drug use and 20 percent for urine testing. The percentages of arrestees testing positive for any illegal drug, including marijuana, and for cocaine, respectively, were as follows: New York, 79 and 63; Los Angeles, 69 and 47; Chicago, 73 and 50; San Diego, 75 and 44; Washington, D.C., 77 and 52; New Orleans, 72 and 45; Indianapolis, 40 and 11; Phoenix, 62 and 43; Detroit, 66 and 53; and Portland, Oregon, 70 and 31. The rate for heroin in New York was 25 percent.[64]

Many state prisons have been found to be overcrowded, unsanitary, and afflicted by abusive and dehumanizing discipline and housing. A considerable number of prisons have come under court order at one time or another. Governors and state legislatures have faced extremely difficult, frustrating, and conflicting considerations: public safety; high cost of prison construction and prisoner incarceration; public demand for less lenient treatment of felons convicted of violent crimes; and opposition of county and city governments and affected neighborhoods to siting a prison in or near them. This opposition is almost universal in urban areas, but in low-income, rural areas state institutions such as prisons often bring employment and trade to a fading community. Several planks of correctional reform platforms of a decade ago have been weighed in practice and found wanting. Rand researcher Joan Petersilia stated: "What options do states have [for prison population overcrowding]? History offers only two: build more prisons . . . or put offenders back into the community through probation or early parole release. Unfortunately, history also demonstrates the shortcomings of both options."[65]

Occasional findings from practice or research have shown the following:

- Granting probation to felons constitutes a serious threat to the public; many commit further crimes while on probation or while awaiting trial.[66]

- Locating state prisons in rural areas in states with a high urban and/or minority population exacerbates social and racial tensions because of the fiscal necessity of hiring prison personnel from the surrounding rural territory.[67]

- Mandatory, long-term incarceration for specified types of crimes, unless limited to a restricted potential group, causes prohibitive costs in prison construction and expansion.[68]

- Progress has been made in identifying indicators of continued violent predatory behavior, but implementation of such indicators would produce substantial omissions and commissions and would not even be possible on the basis of prison records alone.[69]

• Considerable potential exists for community service, restitution, and other alternatives to incarceration, but public opinion thereon is often adverse.

Researchers at Rand and elsewhere have found that a small fraction of arrestees account in the long run for over half of total offenses in the nonproperty category. An offender's record, especially as a juvenile, is a much better predictor of a criminal career than type of offense. Among the best predictors of repeat offenses have been a consistently criminal attitude, repeated probation violations, and regular use of or addiction to, drugs. Social and psychological information about these kinds of things are usually not available from official records.[70]

Obviously, experimentation with community service, part-time detention (being tried in at least one county in forty states), and "house arrest" through electronic surveillance (California, Florida, Kentucky, Missouri, Oregon and Utah) may already have produced some economically efficient alternatives to incarceration. These appear to be socially (though not necessarily politically) safe alternatives if applied only to misdemeanants or white-collar felons, for example. (Victims' rights groups tend to oppose community service for drunk driving, embezzlement, or other crime that resulted in personal injury or property loss to the affected group.)[71] They may at the same time exacerbate some racial and other equity issues discussed earlier.[72]

A few additional issues, some of which have been alluded to earlier, confront state and local governments, especially the former, in deploying fiscal resources most effectively and marshalling the requisite public support in order to deal with public safety and correctional problems:

• Considering safety to the community as a factor in whether or not to allow bail pending trial.

• Conversely, assuring expeditious trials—justice delayed is justice denied.

• Tightening regulation of the private security industry. It is as large as the public safety forces, has as much money spent on it, and is often unlicensed or otherwise unregulated.

• Authorizing, guiding, and assisting neighborhood crime prevention efforts.

SUMMARY COMMENTS ON REGULATORY AND LEGAL SYSTEMS

It seems clear that both regulatory and legal systems in the United States have become overloaded, particularly in the environmental and tort liability areas, and are threatened with an even greater overload in the decade ahead. This is especially the case for state governments, which not only have wide latitude in which to operate, but which on occasion see a pressing need to attend to nationally preempted areas that are going wholly or largely unattended. Sole reliance on direct regulation and on adversarial legal processes can bring considerable unnecessary economic cost and far less than optimally equitable results in advancing and protecting the public interest.

More Economical and Effective Public Regulation

The public regulatory field may need, first, a more careful differentiation among ends, means, and methods, and second, the identification of some viable alternatives to existing goals, policy approaches, and administrative and legal processes. Some optional means could include the use of (1) the marketplace to effect desirable changes in behavior on the part of businesses and individuals, such as through research dissemination and public service advertising (for example, seat-belt use); (2) tax incentives and disincentives; (3) subsidies or other rewards for the desired changes in behavior; (4) user fees, exactions, or fines in connection with economic or other development projects; and (5) bargained agreements among government, potential regulatees, and citizen groups (often most effective when both sides are afraid of losing if carried to court).

If, after alternatives are examined, the conclusion is reached that direct governmental regulation is the only or best means of achieving the environmental objective, ascendingly rigorous alternative arrangements might include use of (1) state-local government fiscal or administrative mechanisms; (2) a performance standard, but with regulatees free to select the method by which the standard is achieved; and (3) specification of a level of technology, with or without precise specification of the content of such technology.

Public opinion and consequent legislative, administrative, and judicial activity over the past two decades unquestionably has produced a cleaner, healthier, and more attractive physical environment, both in the great outdoors and in the workplace; action was necessary and overdue, and the country obviously is much better off as a result. However, if public health and safety regulation in the United States is to be rationalized in economic as well as in social and political terms, amending legislation will be necessary; improved regulatory management and innovative enforcement attitudes and procedures will not suffice. The Reagan administration was moderately successful in the latter but not in the former. Significant regulatory relief occurred, but substantive reform did not.

One of the better avenues to economic rationality in the regulatory field may lie in authorizing economic measure experimentation by state governments. Some current major areas of such experimental opportunity include (1) abatement of nonpoint-source water pollution; (2) conservation-oriented water pricing; (3) financial and technological alternatives for hazardous and other solid waste management and disposal; and (4) container deposits and refunds or other waste recycling programs. Given the two-decade preference by the Congress for the direct order method and the strong misgivings by affected groups about economic alternatives, conclusive successful experience in some states and localities probably will be essential to persuade the Congress to effect nationwide changes to a new approach.

Finally, regarding the current overall U.S. regulatory framework, some general points should be kept in mind:

1. A compelling need will arise in the future for still further federal regulatory initiatives to meet economic, social, environmental, and other pervasive and urgent nationwide problems.

2. A procedural framework of legislatively established principles and criteria should be in place so that such future calls for action can be assessed in terms of needs, costs, and alternative modes.

3. Economic, intergovernmental, fiscal, and enforceability issues should be addressed as part of the initial legislation.

4. Intergovernmental deregulation will have to proceed on a variety of fronts; given moderate success in some further grant consolidation, many of the aid-associated problems mentioned earlier could be further eased to a substantial degree.

5. Selective enforcement or general ignoring of regulatory requirements is a temporary expedient; legislative cleanup must follow.

6. Last, there seems to be a need to get away from the "worst possible case" mind-set in formulating and administering regulatory laws and to give priority to the normal case and the bulk of the potential caseload, while taking into account both the best and worst situations.

Streamlining the Legal System

The challenge of streamlining the legal system rests primarily with state legislatures; the extension of standing in federal regulatory statutes will need to be addressed by the Congress and the federal judiciary. During the expansion of litigation, there have been only limited attempts in individual states to develop new forms of conflict resolution within our adversarial legal system, such as bargaining, mediation, and arbitration. It has seemed that "virtually all regulatory processes cluster near the adjudicatory end of the spectrum. . . . Even informal rulemaking has been relentlessly judicialized, formalized, and rationalized."[73]

In civil litigation it may well be that a combination of national and state action will be required in product liability, mergers and takeovers, and some other areas where litigation and liability questions begin to seriously threaten the free flow of interstate commerce. But the initiative in developing alternative dispute resolution approaches, effecting tort liability reform, and dealing with the other areas of civil and criminal justice will, by and large, depend upon the states, with local governments in the forefront in such aspects as police-community relations and restoring law and order to troubled neighborhoods.

Perhaps the most crucial link in the criminal justice chain is drug control and addiction treatment. Research cited earlier indicates that drug addiction by first offenders is a key indicator for future criminal behavior as long as the addiction remains.[74] Supervised drug treatment for first and successive offenders, including mandatory commitment for treatment, as in mental health, may be an approach to which states will wish to allocate increased resources.

Three conclusions that seemed compelling to a growing number of observers emerged during the eighties: the public regulatory system and its innumerable parts will need to receive more attention on both economic and equity sides than heretofore; the civil justice system must be reduced in scope and complexity, lest it threaten the nation's economic position; and ways and means must be found to bring the drug/crime/correction/recidivism cycle under better control.

NOTES

1. This section draws considerably from Colman, W., "Overview of Governmental Regulation in the United States: Legal, Economic, and Social Aspects," in Stocker, F., ed., *The Role of Exactions in Controlling Pollution*, Tax Policy Roundtable, Property Tax Series TPR–15 (Cambridge, Mass.: Lincoln Institute of Land Policy, 1987), 7–33.

2. Michelman, F. I., and Sandalow, T., *Materials on Government in Urban Areas: Cases, Comments, Questions* (St. Paul: West Publishing Co., 1970), 3.

3. Okun, A. M., *Our Blend of Democracy and Capitalism: It Works But Is in Danger*, Reprint 351 (Washington, D.C.: Brookings Institution, 1979), 1.

4. McKie, J. W., "The Ends and Means of Regulation," Reprint 287 (Washington, D.C.: Brookings Institution, 1974).

5. Schultze, C. L., *The Public Use of the Private Interest* (Washington, D.C.: Brookings Institution, 1977).

6. Committee for Economic Development (CED), *Redefining Government's Role in the Market System* (New York: CED, July 1979).

7. American Bar Association, Commission on Law and the Economy, *Federal Regulation: Roads to Reform*, Washington, D.C.: American Bar Association, November 1979.

8. "Mandated Uncompetitiveness," *Wall Street Journal*, April 9, 1987 (editorial).

9. CED, *Redefining Government's Role*, 98–99.

10. Crandall, R. W., "Environmental Protection Agency," *Regulation*, November–December 1980, 20; Crandall, R. W., and Portney, P., "Environmental Policy," in *Natural Resources and the Environment: The Reagan Approach* (Washington, D.C.: Urban Institute Press, 1984), 47–81.

11. Schultze, *Public Use of the Private Interest*, 6.

12. Johnson, P., "The Perils of Risk Avoidance," *Regulation*, May-June 1980, 15–19.

13. CED, *Redefining Government's Role*, 98–99.

14. Wildavsky, A., *Searching for Safety* (New Brunswick, N.J.: Transaction, 1988).

15. Simon, M., "The Business Roundtable Study: What We Did," *Regulation*, July–August 1979, 20–25.

16. Kelman, S., "Cost-Benefit Analysis: An Ethical Critique," *Regulation*, January–February 1981, 34. See also Acton, J. P., "Measuring the Monetary Value of Lifesaving Programs," *Law and Contemporary Problems* (Duke University Law School) 40 (1976): 46–72, 1976, also published by Rand Corporation as P–5675.

17. U.S. Advisory Commission on Intergovernmental Relations (ACIR), *Regulatory*

Federalism: Policy, Process, Impact, and Reform, Report A–95, February 1984. See also Beam, D. R., "From Law to Rule: Exploring the Maze of Intergovernmental Regulation," *Intergovernmental Perspective* (ACIR), Spring 1983, 7–22; Madden, T. J., and Remes, D. H., "The Courts and the Administration: Marching to Different Drummers," *Intergovernmental Perspective,* Spring 1983, 23–29; Muller, T., and Fix, M., "Federal Solicitude, Local Costs: Impact of Federal Regulation on Municipal Finances," *Regulation,* July–August 1980, 29–36; and Rosener, J. B., "Making Bureaucrats Responsive: A Study of the Impact of Citizen Participation on Staff Recommendations in Regulatory Decision Making," *Public Administration Review,* July–August 1982, 339–345.

18. Congressional Budget Office (CBO), *Efficient Investment in Wastewater Treatment,* 1985, 25–42, 60–65. See also General Accounting Office, *Billions Could Be Saved through Waivers for Coastal Wastewater Treatment Plants,* May 22, 1981.

19. National Academy of Public Administration (NAPA), *Presidential Management of Rulemaking in Regulatory Agencies,* January 1987; White House, "Regulatory Planning Process," Executive Order 12498 and Memorandum from the President for the Heads of Executive Departments and Agencies, *Presidential Documents,* vol. 21, no. 7, 11–14.

20. ACIR, 5.108, "Economic Growth and Development Policy Act" (draft state legislation), 1984.

21. GAO, *Billions Could Be Saved;* CBO, *Efficient Investment in Wastewater Treatment;* Greater Washington Research Center (GWRC), "Water and Sewage," chap. 4 in *Report of the Task Force on Local Government Response to Fiscal Pressure,* December 1982, 4–1–4–38; and Miranowski, J., et al, "Productivity and Resource Use Impacts of Environmental Regulations on the Agricultural Economy," in Stocker, *Role of Exactions,* 1987, 107–122.

22. "From Pollution to Prevention: A Progress Report on Waste Production," *OTA Report Brief,* June 1987. Full OTA report with same title: U.S. Government Printing Office, stock no. 052–003–01071–2.

23. Apogee Research, Inc., *The Nation's Public Works: Report on Hazardous Waste Management* (Washington, D.C.: National Council on Public Works Improvement, May 1987), 6; Walsh, M. W., "Risky Business: Insurers Are Shunning Coverage of Chemical and Other Pollution," *Wall Street Journal,* March 19, 1985, 1; Naj, A., "Can $100 Billion Have 'No Material Effect' on Balance Sheets?" *Wall Street Journal,* May 11, 1988, 1; Scanlon, R., ed., *Hazardous Materials and Hazardous Wastes: Local Management Options* (Washington, D.C.: International City Management Association [ICMA], 1987); Coy, J., "Waste Disposal and the Environmnent," *States' Summit '87* (Lexington, Ky.: Council of State Governments, 1987), 49–56; and General Accounting Office, *State Experiences with Taxes on Generators or Disposers of Hazardous Waste,* GAO/RCED–84–146, May 4, 1984.

24. Holtzman, E., "States Step In Where OSHA Fails to Tread," *Wall Street Journal,* March 31, 1987, op-ed; Barrett, P., "Attorneys General Flex Their Muscles: States Join Forces to Press Consumer and Antitrust Concerns," *Wall Street Journal,* July 13, 1988, 25.

25. Rose, F., "California Towns Vote to Restrict Expansion As Services Lag Behind," *Wall Street Journal,* November 27, 1987, 1.

26. Frieden, B., "The Exclusionary Effect of Growth Controls," in Schnidman, F., and Silverman, J., eds., *Housing Supply and Affordability* (Washington, D.C.: Urban

Land Institute, 1983), 103–110; Schmidt, W., "Chicago Plan Aims to Curb Factory Loss," *New York Times,* December 10, 1987, A–1.

27. De Grove, J., *Land, Growth, and Politics* (Washington, D.C.: American Planning Association, 1984). See also Liner, B., ed., *Intergovernmental Land Management Innovations* (Cambridge, Mass.: Lincoln Institute of Land Policy, 1986); and deHaven-Smith, L., "Regulatory Theory and State Land Use Regulation: Implications from Florida's Experience with Growth Management," *Public Administration Review,* September–October 1984, 413–420.

28. ACIR, "5.202, Local Planning, Zoning, and Subdivision Regulation" (draft state legislation), secs. 12, 13, 1975.

29. *South Burlington County NAACP v. Township of Mount Laurel,* New Jersey Supreme Court, 1975. See also Fleming, A., "Mandatory Inclusionary Housing as a Local Option in Florida," *Environmental and Urban Issues* 30, no. 3 (April 1988): 8–11.

30. Will, G., "Fending Off the Future in Orange County," *Washington Post,* August 30, 1987.

31. Downs, A., "Traffic Congestion and Growth Limitation Policies," *Urban Land,* September 1987, 38–39.

32. *Montgomery County* (Maryland) *Code, Annotated,* sec. 59-A–6.1, "Transfer of Development for Agricultural Preservation"; also, secs. 2-B–1 through 2-B–19.

33. Smith, R., "Reorganization of Rural Transportation Authorities to Maintain Urban-Suburban Constituency Balance," *Public Administration Review,* March–April 1987, 171–179.

34. *Keystone Bituminous Coal Association v. De Benedictus,* 107 S. Ct. 1232 (U.S. March 10, 1987).

35. *Nollan v. California Coastal Commission,* 107 S. Ct. 3141 (U.S. June 9, 1987).

36. *First English Evangelical Lutheran Church of Glendale v. County of Los Angeles,* 107 S. Ct. 2378 (U.S. June 9, 1987).

37. *Pennsylvania Coal v. Mahon,* 260 U.S. 393 (1922).

38. Taub, T., "The Current Status of the Taking Issue," *Florida Environmental and Urban Issues* 14, no. 4 (July 1987): 10–11.

39. Ibid., 4. For contrasting views, see also Epstein, R., "Private Property Makes a Comeback," *Wall Street Journal,* July 23, 1987, op-ed; Haar, C., and Kayden, J., "Private Property vs. Public Use," *New York Times,* July 29, 1987, op-ed; Peirce, N., "Property Rights versus Public Rights: Black Tuesday at the Supreme Court," *County News,* June 29, 1987; and Bosselman, F., and Stroud, N., "The Current Status of Development Exactions," *Florida Environmental and Urban Issues* 14, no. 4 (July 1987): 8–9.

40. Mosk, S., "The Emerging Agenda in State Constitutional Law," *Intergovernmental Perspective,* Spring 1987, 19–22. In the same issue, see also Friedman, L., "An Historical Perspective on State Constitutions," 9–13; Lutz, D., "The United States Constitution as an Incomplete Text," 14–17; and Maltz, E., "Federalism and State Court Activism," 23–26.

41. Rosener, "Making Bureaucrats Responsive," 339–345.

42. Hensler, D., Lipson, A., and Rolph, E., *Judicial Arbitration in California: The First Year,* R–2733-ICJ (Santa Monica, Calif.: Rand Corporation, 1981). Executive Summary in "Civil Justice," *A Bibliography of Selected Rand Publications,* August 1986, 22–23.

43. Peirce, N., "A Path to Neighborhood Justice," *Miami Herald,* June 10, 1982;

Davis, I. R., "Magistrates and Arbitrators Unclog Connecticut Courts," *National Civic Review,* September 1983, 430–434; and Gold, P., "Soothing Skills for Troubled Times," *Insight,* November 16, 1987, 48–50 (use of negotiating skills in arbitration).

44. National Governors' Association (NGA), *National Governors' Association Positions, 1986–87,* January 1987, 268.

45. Ibid.

46. National Conference of State Legislatures (NCSL),"Preemption," Law and Justice, *Official Policy,* 1987.

47. Ibid., "Preemption of Product Liability," *Law and Justice,* 1987.

48. Labaton, S., "Business and the Law: Cut in Punitive Awards Sought," *New York Times,* October 12, 1987, D–2. See also Barrett, P., "Courts Lend Sympathetic Ear to Claims for Compensation Based on Cancer Fears," *Wall Street Journal,* December 14, 1988, B1.

49. White House, Tort Policy Working Group, *Report of the Tort Policy Working Group on the Causes, Extent, and Policy Implications of the Current Crisis in Insurance Availability and Affordability,* February 1986; idem, *An Update on the Liability Crisis,* March 1987.

50. 436 U.S. 658 (1978).

51. Lee, Y., "Civil Liabilities of State and Local Governments: Myth and Reality," *Public Administration Review,* March–April 1987, 160–170. The two cases were *Owen v. City of Independence, Missouri,* 445 U.S. 622 (1980), and *Maine v. Thibeaut,* 448 U.S. 1 (1980).

52. Muzychenko, J., "Local Governments at Risk: The Crisis in Liability Insurance," *Municipal Yearbook, 1987* (Washington, D.C.: ICMA, 1987), 3–7; ACIR, *Governments at Risk: Liability Insurance and Tort Reform,* SR–7, 1988.

53. Roberts, J., "State Actions Affecting Local Governments," *Municipal Yearbook, 1987,* 55–56.

54. Reibstein, L., "Firms Face Lawsuits for Hiring People Who Then Commit Crimes," *Wall Street Journal,* April 30, 1987, sec. 2, p. 1.; Lewin, T., "Boss Can Be Sued for Saying Too Much," *New York Times,* November 27, 1987, B–26 (employers "no longer provide references but will only confirm a worker's dates of employment and job title").

55. See the following Rand Corporation reports: Kritzer, H., et al., *The Impact of Fee Arrangement on Lawyer Effort,* P–7180-ICJ, January 1986; Danzon, P., et al., *The Effects of Tort Reforms on the Frequency and Severity of Medical Malpractice Claims,* P–7211-ICJ, March 1986; and Shubert, G., *Some Observations on the Need for Tort Reform,* P–7189-ICJ, January 1986. These are listed in *Civil Justice: A Bibliography of Selected Rand Publications,* SB–1064, August 1986, 42–43. See also Director, Institute for Civil Justice, Rand Corporation, *Report on the First Six Program Years: April, 1980– March, 1986.*

56. Tokyo correspondent, "A Law unto Itself," *Economist,* August 22, 1987, 32.

57. Colman, W., *Cities, Suburbs, and States* (New York: Free Press, 1975), 148– 149.

58. Wilson, W., *The Truly Disadvantaged: The Inner City, the Underclass, and Public Policy* (Chicago: University of Chicago Press, 1987), table 2.1, 23.

59. Rand Corporation, *Criminal Justice Research at Rand,* January 1985, 21. Specific projects and reports on equity in the criminal justice system included Petersilia, J., *Racial Disparities in the Criminal Justice System,* RO2947-NIC, June 1983; idem, *Reexamining*

the Effects of Race on Imprisonment Decisions R3226-NIC, forthcoming; Greenwood, P., et al., *Prosecution of Adult Felony Defendants: A Policy Perspective* (Lexington, Mass.: D. C. Heath and Co., 1976); Wildhorn, S., et al., *Indicators of Justice: Measuring the Performance of Prosecution, Defense, and Court Agencies Involved in Felony Proceedings* (Lexington, Mass.: D. C. Heath and Co., 1977); Greenwood, P., "The Felony Disposition Process," in Kadish, S., ed., *Encyclopedia of Crime and Justice* (New York: Free Press, 1983); and Petersilia, J., "Racial Disparities in the Criminal Justice System: A Summary," *Crime and Delinquency*, January 1985, 15–34.

60. Rand Corporation, *Criminality, Justice, and Public Safety: A Bibliography of Selected Rand Publications*, SB 1059; October 1986, 45 (Abstract). The complete report was Petersilia, J., and Turner, S., *Guideline-based Justice: The Implications for Racial Minorities*, R–3306-NIC, January 1985. See also Applebome, P., "With Inmates at Record High, Sentence Policy Is Reassessed," *New York Times*, April 25, 1988, A–1.

61. Innis, C., "Profile of State Prison Inmates 1986," *Special Report*, Tables A, 10, 11, 12 (Washington, D.C.: U.S. Department of Justice, Bureau of Justice Statistics January 1988) 2, 6–8.

62. National Institute of Justice, Department of Justice (DOJ) press release, January 21, 1988, p. 1.

63. Wish, E., "Drug Testing," *Crime File Study Guide*, U.S. DOJ, National Institute of Justice, NCJ 104556, 1988.

64. National Institute of Justice, *Drug Use Forecasting*, and DOJ press release. January 21, 1988, pp. 3–4. See also Wish, E., and Johnson, B., "The Impact of Substance Abuse on Criminal Careers," in Blumstein, A., et al., eds., *Criminal Careers and Career Criminals*, vol. 2 (Washington, D.C.: National Academy Press, 1986), 52–88.

65. Petersilia, J., *Expanding Options for Sentencing* (Santa Monica, Calif.: Rand Corporation, 1987) p. v.

66. Petersilia, J., Turner, S., Kahan, J. and Peterson, J., Executive Summary, *Granting Felons Probation: Public Risks and Alternatives*, R3186-NIS. *Criminality, Justice and Public Safety*, Rand 1986, p. 44.

67. Feeley, M., and Olin, L., *Criminal Justice and Corrections* (Washington, D.C.: National Governors' Association, 1982) 49–77.

68. Rand Corporation, *Criminal Justice, Research at Rand*, 8.

69. Feeley and Olin, *Criminal Justice and Corrections*, 5–43, Rand Corporation, 3–7.

70. Ibid.

71. Petersilia, *Expanding Options*, vi–ix.

72. Rand Corporation, *Criminal Justice Research at Rand*, and Feeley and Olin, *Criminal Justice and Corrections*, are relevant to the listed issues. See also Barrett, P., " 'Rocket Docket': Federal Courts in Virginia Dispense Speedy Justice," *Wall Street Journal*, December 3, 1987, 33; idem, "Harried Judges Rely on 'Special Masters' to Settle Tough Suits; Is It Assembly-Line Justice?" *Wall Street Journal*, November 5, 1987, 1; Kaufman, I., "The Public's Right to Speedier Justice," *New York Times*, October 16, 1987, op-ed; Kerr, P., "War on Drugs Puts Strain on Prisons, U.S. Officials Say," *New York Times*, September 25, 1987, B–5; and Crawford, B., "Law Enforcement Volunteers Stretch Tax Dollars," *AARP News Bulletin* 25, no. 10 (February 1988): 1.

73. Schuck, P. H., "Litigation, Bargaining, and Regulation," *Regulation*, July–August 1979, 26–34.

74. U.S. Department of Justice, Bureau of Justice Statistics, Innis, C., "Profile of State Prison Inmates, 1986," January 1988, 6–7.

Conclusions

The pendulum has swung back to states and localities.... Five kinds of actions are necessary in response to the changing government setting. First, we see the rebirth of states as the laboratories of democracy. Second, we find a resurgence of public-private partnerships. Third, the participation of philanthropic institutions has taken on new significance. Fourth, interest in structural change has been renewed. Finally, we see increased attention to government corruption and mismanagement because dollars are scarce (*National Civic Review*, November–December, 1987, p. 470).

Thus, in late 1987, spoke Richard Thornburgh, former Pennsylvania governor and subsequently director of Harvard's Institute of Politics, in addressing the annual conference of the National Civic League. The 1978–87 decade witnessed widespread evidence of each of the five changes in American government and its relationship with the private sector, and of the heightening of community spirit in many places. How long-lasting these new directions may be, only time will tell; one fact is indisputable. The nation is in a period of substantial economic, political, and social change, and the decade ahead will challenge the best of political and civic leadership in ability, courage, and perseverance.

THE ECONOMIC AND FISCAL CHALLENGE

As the nation seeks, within the context of international economic forces, feasible policy approaches to its numerous and serious problems of domestic governance, fiscal considerations restrain primary reliance upon new governmental programs. Instead, an increased premium is placed upon (1) augmenting particular governmental resources with existing public or new private monies; and (2) squeezing more results out of a given outlay of public funds.

One path of expediency utilizing the first approach has always been open to national and state governments in endeavors to initiate new programs without facing up to cost considerations. That is to mandate the new activity upon a subordinate or junior fiscal partner in the governmental system (national to state or state to local). However, during the 1977–87 period, nearly one-third of the states adopted constitutional or statutory provisions requiring reimbursement of all or part of the additional costs to local governments resulting from state mandates. The existence of these provisions has necessitated extra measures of preenactment soul-searching in the legislative bodies; in most states both foes and supporters of the process agree that a slowdown in mandated expenditures has occurred (offsetting to some degree the built-in tilt toward the expenditure side of national, state, and local budgeting).

Another example of resource augmentation used from time to time without direct governmental taxation and expenditure has been the establishment of an economic or social goal and mandating implementation of measures toward its achievement, including its complete or partial financing, by the private sector. Social insurance, occupational health and safety, and environmental protection standards illustrate this approach.

State-local policy initiatives described earlier involve both the private-sector mandate-incentive approach and that of improving effectiveness of the public-sector dollar in dealing with economic, structural, and demographic change—underemployment, health and day care, housing, and physical infrastructure. These are the most urgent and critical economic and fiscal issues that face state and local governments. In most of these clusters, government must work hand in hand with the nonprofit and for-profit segments of the private sector. In such cooperation one partner usually must take the initiative for legal, capacity, or other reasons.

Among the most serious responsibilities facing state government are (1) to continue the overhaul of the public education system so that the knowledge and interpersonal abilities of coming generations can provide the skills and other qualities that our economy and society require; (2) to reshape the state role in mental health so that the goal of community-based mental health facilities and treatment may be realized and those homeless persons with mental health histories or problems may be given adequate attention; (3) to review, revise, and strengthen legal and regulatory systems so as to lessen their complexity and cost and bring more equity and economic efficiency to the tort liability system; to explore the alternatives to direct governmental regulation whenever appropriate, while not hesitating to enter new or unattended regulatory areas; and to move with special dispatch in the judicial and correctional aspects of the criminal justice system, particularly as they relate to the identification of, and response to, career criminal behavior; (4) to reexamine state revenue systems to improve equity, reduce or eliminate preferences no longer justified, and provide local governments with needed revenue-raising flexibility; and (5) to continue to explore various approaches toward long-term health care for the disabled and reducing long-term welfare dependency of those able to be, but not in, the labor force.

Among the crucial responsibilities facing local governments, especially cities, urban counties, and city school systems is that of marshalling the intervention strategies needed to deal with mounting poverty and despair in underclass and other areas. These include (1) outreach activities by county and city health departments to bring maternal and child health care to all who need it and are legally eligible for assistance; (2) early childhood exposure to organized play and education, including working directly with parents of children seemingly at risk; (3) intensified work with children and parents during early grades; and (4) getting drugs off the streets and out of the schools. Also facing local governments are the continual needs (1) to root out waste and corruption wherever they exist; (2) to create effective partnerships with local business, labor, and other private groups, and (3) to improve the effectiveness with which local services are provided to the public, wherever feasible allowing some room for choice on the part of the service user.

THE SOCIOECONOMIC EQUITY CHALLENGE

As the domestic role of the national government began to recede during the 1978–88 period, concern increased about the economic and social equity of many public policies as they had evolved over preceding years. These uneasy questions have included the following:

- What is happening to middle-class values? Has "soaking the rich and neglecting the poor" become a comfortable political stance of middle-class self-interest?
- Has the distribution of income and wealth become more distorted? This issue is debated endlessly.
- Has an entire "imperiled generation" of poor people—mostly minority, female-headed families with children, and adults living in underclass areas in the inner cities—been condemned to poor or no education, early unwed motherhood for teenaged females, and for adults, perpetual unemployment and illiteracy in an environment of crime, violence, and drug addiction, and an unhealthy and often shortened life?

As discussed earlier, the distribution of income is hard to assess because income is hard to define and measure, and because living costs vary widely from one geographic area to another. Consequently, little consensus has emerged among public policy analysts about what is happening to income distribution, although its concentration within the top income quintile appears to have increased, due in part to the upward movement out of the middle class. Likewise, but more apparent, has been an increased concentration in the bottom quintile, due partly to a sizeable increase in numbers of single mothers with children. Income distribution is a research as well as a public policy issue.

Some states are much more active than others in mounting outreach programs to establish Medicaid eligibility for underclass and other poverty families with young children. Fiscal pressures, bureaucratic procedures, and outright discrimination—both economic and racial—seem to be at work in this problem area. The high percentage of denials of Medicaid eligibility for procedural, as opposed to factual, reasons in Southern and other states emphasizes the need for strong state action. Most Medicaid-eligible but nonparticipating mothers have inadequate education and transportation to fill out the necessary forms and make the necessary trips. Moreover, the long-range costs to state and local governments of health service neglect in family planning and prenatal and young-child health care outweigh considerably the added costs to those governments of what the shorter-range Medicaid outlays would be. Also, the wide racial disparity in state rates on low birth weight and infant mortality shown earlier is a cause for deep concern on both discrimination and fiscal grounds.

Of particular concern and sensitivity has been the increasingly minority racial composition of the urban underclass, of school dropouts, of convicted felons, of drug addicts, of single-parent families, and of discouraged workers no longer seeking work. Considerable differences exist among black and Hispanic leaders as to whether upper- and middle-income members of those groups have a personal responsibility to provide role-model counsel, encouragement, prodding, and other stimuli to central-city and other youth at risk.

Some believe that movement on the economic front by the federal government is a prerequisite, and that if public service employment is opened up to all who need it, the educational and social problems will ease over time. Others point to another minority—the Asians—who are setting records in academic achievement, hard work, family structure, and community values that whites and most other ethnic groups find very hard to match. In any case, striking an appropriate balance of responsibility among public, private, and individual responsibilities in this area probably is the most sensitive equity, financial, and behavioral issue that faces central-city civic and political leadership and many state governments in the decade ahead.

THE CIVIC CHALLENGE

The extent and depth of "civic spirit" has been a key factor affecting the economic progress and social stability of urban communities. Economically depressed and socially unstable conditions often are accompanied by a lack of such spirit, with weak or nonexistent citizen associations and apathetic citizen participation in government or other community affairs. Many communities, both affluent and depressed, have seen a substantial increase in "neighborhood negativism" and a subordination of the public interest to self-interest on almost any occasion when the state or local government is trying to deal with difficult problems.

The kinds of experiences gleaned from and described in reports of the CED, the National Civic League, and others comprise a message of advice to leaders in business, labor, government, and public education in communities that sense a need to seek "civic renewal." (1) In philanthropic undertakings, stop trying to pick only "winners"; begin nurturing and supporting less certain endeavors with long-range potential. (2) Install or expand programs of civic education and community service as parts of both educational and correctional programs. (3) Provide avenues of dispute resolution short of the courtroom. (4) Prevent long-range urban planning from becoming an exclusive responsibility of the public sector. (5) Empower and assist neighborhoods to do more on their own and to have a direct voice in governmental decisions affecting them. (6) Initiate or strengthen communication among diverse neighborhood populations.

On occasion it becomes necessary for civic leadership to challenge government—even oppose it—especially when public action on a sensitive political or other difficult problem is required and none is forthcoming. For most of the time, however, civic and governmental interests coincide and are mutually supportive.

THE PUBLIC POLICY RESEARCH AND ANALYSIS CHALLENGE

For some of the most difficult and expensive problems facing state-local government (long-term health care, housing affordability and increasing homelessness, drugs, and the correctional and legal systems), none of the policy approaches taken or under consideration seem to inspire widespread confidence because of continuing uncertainty as to what the odds are, or whether all the right questions have yet been posed. This points to the need for further information gathering or, in most cases, further research and analysis before the enactment of universal legislation (not necessarily before demonstration projects). These needs embrace (1) additional data, both of a trend and intermittent nature; (2) case studies, including the use of control groups for some and the following of a particular group or sample over a substantial time period in others; and (3) evaluative studies of the outcomes of a particular policy or program, covering a single or multiple jurisdictions or geographical areas. There are several questions discussed in this book upon which more information, or analysis, or both, appears to be badly needed and would be of much assistance toward informed policy decisions.

The first concerns the measurement of income, asset wealth, and other factors. To know what is happening to the middle class and to income distribution among quintiles, and to be able to establish meaningful measures of poverty, it is necessary to assign values to vested pension, health, and other benefits in the case of the working population and to in-kind and other transfers and benefits in the case of both the poor and elderly populations. Activities of the Census Bureau and various organizations regarding measurement of in-kind transfers and methods by which they might be used to adjust cash income measures were described earlier.

Related to poverty threshold definition, expanded data on cost-of-living differences among states and geographic regions and within states between urban and rural areas and new insights on the methodological handling of such data are needed to enable states to make sustainable adjustments to national measures of poverty and of economic status generally. Accounting for intrastate cost-of-living and other price-level differences would enable economic and equity improvements in a variety of state programs of fiscal transfers to local units and to individuals.

Improvement in measurement of local government fiscal capacity and tax effort is essential in those cases where it is thought desirable to take fiscal capacity into account in state aid programs.

State and local governments collectively presently extend billions of dollars of tax and other financial incentives designed to attract and retain business establishment and to encourage its expansion. Knowledge of the relative cost-effectiveness of types and levels of such incentives would be highly useful to state and local governments and to private businesses as each party negotiates about and considers such incentives when locational decisions are being made.

Evaluative studies of various kinds of public-private partnerships, both of the civic- and development-based types are needed as state-local governments move into ever closer and more complex relations with private business. These studies would help identify replicable strengths and avoidable weaknesses in such undertakings.

The NGA has recommended careful research follow-up of school-based clinics and other approaches to preventing teenage pregnancy.

In the correctional field, the Rand Corporation studies of inmate profiles and the search for reliable indicators of future recidivism seem to be clarifying some new possibilities. Rand and other research sponsored by the Institute of Justice seems to indicate that drug addiction, after one or two convictions, especially if the person were under the influence of drugs when committing the crime, is a strong indicator of career criminal behavior as long as the addiction continues or reemerges.

The five-year experiment in several states under the Manpower Demonstration Research Corporation on the efficacy of work-related requirements for welfare recipients may be a pattern that could be followed in other aspects of welfare reform and in some of the other substantive areas of needed research being considered here.

The one policy issue area seemingly the most urgent for the country and for state-local government is that of drug use and treatment. Various research projects have been undertaken regarding prevention measures, such as drug education in the schools and the "just say no" and "zero tolerance" approaches. However, state and local governments and the many nonprofit organizations engaged in operating drug treatment and rehabilitation centers apparently can provide information about course completion rates, but limited or no information about permanent cures or lengths of subsequent abstinence.

The National Institute of Justice has generalized its research on drugs to the extent that it can conclude (a) that drug use is a major factor in the onset and repetition of criminal behavior and (*b*) that treatment saves at least as much in prevented or deferred crime as it costs. Given the strong logical appeal of a policy of drug treatment "on demand" in the light of long waiting lists, further conclusive or strong evidentiary data on treatment outcomes would appear extremely urgent.

In brief, if the states are to fulfill their role as the nation's political laboratories, the application of research methodology followed by pilot undertakings in these areas of high uncertainty seems indicated. In the meantime, within the context of limited resources, legislative attention will necessarily be directed to actions that can be taken promptly, without costly long-term experimentation. Especially attractive may be those efforts that do not involve large amounts of money. A considerable number of these were described in earlier chapters.

THE POLITICAL AND PUBLIC MANAGERIAL CHALLENGE

Following the decline—or cessation of expansion—of the national government's domestic role in 1978, the tasks confronting many public managers in federal departments and agencies tended to become less exciting than in earlier days. There were important exceptions, as in the science- or technology-oriented agencies or parts of agencies—the National Science Foundation, the National Aeronautics and Space Administration, the National Institutes of Health, and parts of the Defense and Agriculture departments. Managing the status quo, "don't rock the boat," and "wait until the dust settles" were part of the psychological environment for much of the federal bureaucracy, exacerbated by the fact that White House officials used anti–civil service rhetoric with little or no provocation.

Conversely, new problems were crowding in upon state and local governments, a great many of which necessitated a new or relatively untried public initiative. New methods of service delivery, mobilizing neighborhoods to combat crime, mitigating community economic distress or natural disaster, regulating medical costs, and many other very difficult problems were clamoring for attention. New ideas, imagination, improvisation, entrepreneurship, and similar risk-taking qualities were at a premium. Therefore it was not surprising that an increasing proportion of university graduates in public administration began to shun the federal service and to enter state-local government, nonprofit interest groups pursuing public policy causes of one kind or another, or nonprofit think tanks doing public policy research. Hopefully, 1989 and the nineties will see the federal service regaining some of its attractiveness. On the higher education side, some new and old questions about preparation for the public service clearly require reexamination.

Barring a complete turnaround in the international economic situation and in U.S. public opinion, the new generation of public managers will continue to face a much wider spectrum of subject matter than in earlier years. Many will work in an "enterprise fund accounting" environment, in contrast to earlier, nearly exclusive reliance on appropriated funds. Consequently, economics, public finance, managerial accounting, marketing, economics, and other business-school types of subjects will become necessary major accretions to the public administration curriculum. University bureaus of governmental research likewise will need to become more widely knowledgeable in the new approaches and environments in order to do justice to their technical assistance roles vis-à-vis local governments in the state.

The old question of the place of community and other public service in the university reward system may take on new urgency as the midcareer training and technical assistance functions assume new dimensions. Finally, the old question reemerges as to the most appropriate university "home" for public administration (separate school or department; connected to a department of political science or government; associated with the business school; or other location). Some argue that the convergence of required private- and public-sector management skills might make the business association more appropriate under certain circumstances, dependent on the history, breadth, and general thrust of the business curriculum.

Throughout this book the extreme difficulty of many emerging policy issues and the dangers of bureaucratic inertia and unresponsiveness to the citizenry have been constant themes; they may have made uneasy reading for public administration scholars and practitioners. The emphasis upon business-government partnerships may have sounded like a plea for limited government. To the contrary, the coming decade will see a larger public policy universe in the nation than ever before, and political and managerial leadership in all areas of government will face greater challenges than ever before in peacetime. The three great changes from the past are relative stringency in resources, seeming intractability of problems, and a much wider array of participants in the pursuit of public purposes and the implementation of public policies.

For those who favor a strong activist role for government and for those concerned about social and fiscal equity in the formulation of public policy, the management challenge has another dimension. Undoubtedly, in the years ahead many conditions unforeseen in the eighties will arise and plead for governmental attention. If sufficient elbowroom is to be preserved for state and local government to meet the truly crucial issues of the late twentieth century and to move into the next, care must be taken that public resources are continually husbanded and used toward those activities representing the optimum between economic efficiency and fiscal/social equity. Examples have been presented here of subsidies and other public policies that are needlessly squandering scarce resources. It would be a rather ironic outcome for those favoring an active, responsible, and responsive government role, through present neglect or opposition to assuring the most economical use of existing resources, to thereby foreclose the availability of resources in future years for purposes considerably more crucial than those being protected today.

Appendices

Appendix 1.A
Neighborhood Subunits of Government

1. Legal status: A legal entity of a city or urban county government.
2. Establishment: (a) At initiative of (1) city or county governing body, or (2) petition signed by specified percent of qualified voters of a geographic area described in the petition, to perform functions and carry on activities described.
    (b) Form: A charter amendment or ordinance.
    (c) Process: However initiated, public hearing convened by city/county governing body, followed by formal establishment, or submission to voters of described area. If approved, creation must occur within time period specified in statute.
3. Governing body of sub-units: Neighborhood council, with members serving staggered terms. Variable size (e.g., 5 to 50). Council members elected by block areas, at large or combination. Vacancies filled by county/city governing body, appointee to serve until next election.
4. Activities and powers: Any powers delegated by city/county governing body, or included in charter. Might include: Review and comment on contemplated city/county action affecting service area; recommendations to city/county on any matter council wishes; conduct of neighborhood self-help projects; can receive funds from city/county or other source; levy poll tax on residents not to exceed (e.g., $5 or $10 per year); all meetings open.
5. Dissolution: By city/county governing body or in response to request of council or a petition signed by specified percent of service area residents. If sub-unit created at initiative of a petition, city/county proposal to dissolve subject to referendum of voters of service area.

Source: Extracted from sec. 6, ACIR draft bill 6.112, "Neighborhood Improvement, Assistance, and Organization Act," 1984.

Appendix 1.B
States Ranked by Degree of Local Discretionary Authority, 1980

A Composite (all types of local units)	B Cities Only	C Counties Only	Degree of State Dominance of Fiscal Partnership*
1 Oregon	Texas	Oregon	2
2 Maine	Maine	Alaska	2
3 North Carolina	Michigan	North Carolina	1
4 Connecticut	Connecticut	Pennsylvania	2
5 Alaska	North Carolina	Delaware	1
6 Maryland	Oregon	Arkansas	2
7 Pennsylvania	Maryland	South Carolina	2
8 Virginia	Missouri	Louisiana	2
9 Delaware	Virginia	Maryland	1
10 Louisiana	Illinois	Utah	1
11 Texas	Ohio	Kansas	2
12 Illinois	Oklahoma	Minnesota	2
13 Oklahoma	Alaska	Virginia	1
14 Kansas	Arizona	Florida	2
15 South Carolina	Kansas	Wisconsin	1
16 Michigan	Louisiana	Kentucky	2
17 Minnesota	California	California	2
18 California	Georgia	Montana	3
19 Missouri	Minnesota	Illinois	2
20 Utah	Pennsylvania	Maine	2
21 Arkansas	South Carolina	North Dakota	1
22 New Hampshire	Wisconsin	Hawaii	3
23 Wisconsin	Alabama	New Mexico	2
24 North Dakota	Nebraska	Indiana	2
25 Arizona	North Dakota	New York	2
26 Florida	Delaware	Wyoming	2
27 Ohio	New Hampshire	Oklahoma	3
28 Alabama	Utah	Michigan	1
29 Kentucky	Wyoming	Washington	1
30 Georgia	Florida	Iowa	2
31 Montana	Mississippi	New Jersey	3
32 Washington	Tennessee	Georgia	2

Appendix 1.B (continued)

A	B	C	
Composite (all types of local units)	Cities Only	Counties Only	Degree of State Dominance of Fiscal Partnership*
33 Wyoming	Washington	Nevada	2
34 Tennessee	Arkansas	Tennessee	2
35 New York	New Jersey	Mississippi	3
36 New Jersey	Kentucky	New Hampshire	3
37 Indiana	Colorado	Alabama	2
38 Rhode Island	Montana	Arizona	2
39 Vermont	Iowa	South Dakota	2
40 Hawaii	Indiana	West Virginia	1
41 Nebraska	Massachusetts	Nebraska	3
42 Colorado	Rhode Island	Ohio	2
43 Massachusetts	South Dakota	Texas	3
44 Iowa	New York	Idaho	2
45 Mississippi	Nevada	Colorado	1
46 Nevada	West Virginia	Vermont	2
47 South Dakota	Idaho	Missouri	3
48 New Mexico	Vermont	Massachusetts	1
49 West Virginia	New Mexico	-	1
50 Idaho	-	-	2

Source: Reproduced from ACIR, *Measuring Local Discretionary Authority*, M-131, 1981, table 20, p. 59.

[a] Fiscal partnership applies to column A: 1—Dominant state sector (65% or more of total state-local tax revenue); 2—strong (50–65%); 3—junior (below 50%).

Appendix 1.C
State-Local Direct General Expenditures, by Federal, State, and Local Shares;
Percent of State Personal Income (SPI) and State Percents Related to U.S.
Average (100.0), 1986

Region and State	Total (Millions)	Percentage Shares Fed.	St.	Loc.	% of SPI	% US Avg.
United States	$604,455.4	19	46	35	18.3	100.0
New England	32,819.8	20	53	27	16.3	89.2
Connecticut	8,235.5	17	51	32	14.4	78.6
Maine	2,703.5	26	48	26	19.5	107.0
Massachusetts	15,811.4	20	56	23	16.6	90.8
New Hampshire	2,078.9	19	38	43	13.9	76.3
Rhode Island	2,604.6	23	53	24	19.3	105.9
Vermont	1,385.9	24	51	25	21.4	117.1
Mid-East	127,762.4	20	41	40	19.2	105.3
Delaware	1,783.4	19	58	23	20.1	110.0
Dist. of Columbia	2,938.2	46	NA	54	25.9	141.6
Maryland	11,514.4	18	47	35	16.5	90.5
New Jersey	21,313.7	16	49	34	16.4	89.7
New York	64,256.5	19	36	45	22.5	123.3
Pennsylvania	25,956.2	22	45	33	16.3	89.3
Great Lakes	101,126.9	19	46	35	17.8	97.7
Illinois	27,155.0	19	44	37	16.0	87.5
Indiana	10,984.2	20	48	32	16.1	87.9
Michigan	25,360.0	19	44	37	20.5	112.3
Ohio	24,616.2	19	46	34	17.3	94.9
Wisconsin	13,011.6	18	48	33	20.7	113.4
Plains	42,618.2	18	46	36	18.3	100.1
Iowa	6,951.4	17	49	34	19.1	104.8
Kansas	5,862.4	16	41	43	17.4	95.1
Minnesota	12,846.6	17	46	37	21.8	119.1
Missouri	9,698.3	20	47	34	14.6	79.7
Nebraska	3,826.0	18	40	42	17.9	98.3
North Dakota	1,838.0	22	58	20	22.3	121.9
South Dakota	1,595.5	26	43	32	20.2	110.6
Southeast	119,325.0	20	47	33	17.6	96.4
Alabama	8,614.6	21	51	29	20.1	109.9
Arkansas	4,371.0	24	50	26	17.7	96.9
Florida	24,790.1	14	41	45	15.9	86.9
Georgia	13,424.9	20	43	37	17.9	98.1
Kentucky	7,162.1	24	54	22	17.8	97.3
Louisiana	10,907.8	19	49	32	21.6	118.3
Mississippi	5,135.9	26	45	29	21.4	117.2
North Carolina	12,099.3	20	54	26	16.7	91.2
South Carolina	6,661.6	20	54	26	18.8	103.0

Appendix 1.C (continued)

==

Region and State	Total (Millions)	Percentage Shares Fed.	St.	Loc.	% of SPI	% US Avg.
Tennessee	9,213.7	24	41	35	17.2	94.3
Virginia	12,803.2	18	48	34	15.4	84.5
West Virginia	4,140.8	24	52	24	21.0	114.9
Southwest	56,541.3	15	43	42	17.8	97.5
Arizona	8,428.9	12	46	42	20.7	113.2
New Mexico	3,987.7	19	62	19	25.2	138.0
Oklahoma	7,364.4	17	51	32	18.2	99.9
Texas	36,760.2	15	39	46	16.7	91.2
Rocky Mountain	19,052.4	20	42	38	20.7	113.3
Colorado	8,387.8	17	38	45	17.5	96.0
Idaho	1,984.2	23	46	31	17.8	97.3
Montana	2,280.1	24	41	35	25.2	137.7
Utah	4,132.9	22	47	30	24.0	131.2
Wyoming	2,267.4	22	45	33	33.7	184.4
Far West*	97,304.2	18	50	31	18.3	100.1
California	76,082.3	18	50	31	18.0	98.4
Nevada	2,564.3	17	46	37	18.9	103.6
Oregon	7,210.4	20	43	37	21.3	116.4
Washington	11,447.1	18	55	27	18.7	102.5
Alaska**	5,039.4	10	69	22	53.2	291.3
Hawaii	2,865.9	19	64	18	19.7	107.8

Source: ACIR, *Significant Features of Fiscal Federalism, 1988 Edition* M-155-II, 1988, tables 47.1, 48.

[a] NA = not applicable.

[b] Excludes Alaska and Hawaii.

[c] High revenue yield from mineral extraction and high cost of living and service delivery help account for high percentage of personal income.

Appendix 1.D
Federal, State, and Local Shares of State-Local Direct Expenditures for Highways and Public Welfare, Fiscal Year 1986
(Amounts in Millions of Dollars)

Region and State	Highways Amount	Share Fed	St	Loc	Welfare Amount	Share Fed	St	Loc
U.S.	$49,368.2[a]	29	45	26	$74,645.9	57	36	7
New England	2,380.4	27	44	29	5,232.7	50	47	3
Connecticut	696.0	31	43	26	1,101.3	47	46	7
Maine	283.4	26	45	29	474.0	64	34	1
Massachusetts	828.5	19	48	33	2,784.4	47	52	1
New Hampshire	239.5	28	42	30	239.1	53	26	22
Rhode Island	172.0	46	30	24	458.3	55	45	0
Vermont	161.1	31	44	25	175.6	72	27	0
Mideast	9,050.7	27	41	32	19,596.5	59	27	14
Delaware	163.3	29	54	17	122.2	55	45	0
Dist. of Col.	91.6	61	NA[b]	39	526.6	49	NA[b]	51
Maryland	1,071.9	35	60	4	1,299.8	49	50	1
New Jersey	1,780.5	24	46	30	2,466.8	53	41	6
New York	3,589.0	19	29	52	11,107.4	62	17	21
Pennsylvania	2,354.4	35	48	17	4,073.6	56	44	0
Great Lakes	7,918.7	27	48	25	15,230.9	51	42	7
Illinois	2,403.1	28	48	24	3,810.6	45	50	4
Indiana	891.9	31	65	4	1,275.5	63	24	13
Michigan	1,581.4	29	45	26	4,092.5	54	41	5
Ohio	1,905.2	28	49	23	3,954.9	46	44	9
Wisconsin	1,137.0	17	36	47	2,097.5	54	36	10
Plains	4,998.7	27	43	30	4,986.0	54	34	12
Iowa	899.6	24	52	24	837.7	52	40	9
Kansas	774.5	26	38	36	495.3	53	45	2
Minnesota	1,312.1	21	38	40	1,935.0	46	31	23
Missouri	1,022.5	32	50	18	1,013.3	65	33	1
Nebraska	485.8	27	44	29	375.2	58	35	8
North Dakota	240.6	40	35	25	181.0	59	34	8
South Dakota	263.5	36	30	33	148.4	71	21	8
Southeast	11,122.6	31	50	19	10,955.4	70	28	3
Alabama	825.5	37	43	21	749.3	57	33	10
Arkansas	514.4	31	60	9	507.3	84	15	1
Florida	1,898.7	23	51	27	1,830.5	53	41	6
Georgia	1,177.9	35	39	26	1,167.7	71	29	0
Kentucky	820.9	33	54	12	944.6	69	29	2
Louisiana	1,084.9	25	47	27	983.6	77	23	0
Mississippi	593.6	30	44	26	519.2	79	19	2
North Carolina	981.3	34	57	10	1,140.4	74	14	13
South Carolina	439.2	33	53	14	605.2	82	15	3
Tennessee	926.4	37	47	16	1,050.0	70	27	4

Appendix 1.D (continued)

==

Region and State	Highways Amount	Share Fed	St	Loc	Welfare Amount	Share Fed	St	Loc
Virginia	$ 1,353.9	28	58	14	$ 1,009.5	66	30	4
W. Virginia	505.7	45	49	6	448.0	66	34	0
Southwest	5,873.2	25	46	29	4,027.4	57	36	7
Arizona	912.4	23	58	19	604.9	22	47	31
New Mexico	428.5	27	50	24	291.6	67	29	3
Oklahoma	702.2	25	57	18	786.2	57	43	0
Texas	3,830.1	25	41	34	2,344.7	64	32	4
Mountain	2,169.5	35	41	24	1,638.6	63	32	6
Colorado	803.9	28	37	34	815.8	58	36	7
Idaho	255.4	40	47	14	155.7	72	19	9
Montana	340.5	41	41	18	208.1	68	20	12
Utah	414.0	48	31	22	355.9	68	32	0
Wyoming	355.7	28	55	17	103.2	57	41	2
Far West [c]	5,223.4	34	37	29	12,420.7	52	44	4
California	3,423.6	33	35	32	10,454.6	52	43	4
Nevada	278.6	44	35	22	146.5	49	35	16
Oregon	551.6	31	57	13	577.0	65	30	5
Washington	969.6	34	36	31	1,242.6	41	59	0
Alaska	483.7	22	68	10	274.9	39	56	6
Hawaii	147.4	29	36	35	282.7	58	40	1

Source: ACIR, *Significant Features of Fiscal Federalism 1988 Edition*, M-155-II, 1988, tables 51 and 53.

[a] Does not include expenditures financed directly by the federal government. For FY 1986, these totaled $568 million and $25,790 million for highways and welfare, respectively.

[b] NA = not applicable.

[c] Excludes Alaska and Hawaii.

Appendix 1.E
Federal, State, and Local Shares of State-Local Expenditures for Health and Hospitals and for K–12 Public Education, Fiscal Year 1986

Region and State	Health and Hospitals Amount	Share Fed	Share St	Share Loc	K-12 Public Education Amount	Share Fed	Share St	Share Loc
U. S.	$53,612.9[a]	7	48	45	$151,332.8	6	50	44[b]
New England	2,552.0	9	73	18	8,233.7	5	40	55
Connecticut	581.8	15	79	6	2,355.0	5	39	56
Maine	130.2	16	59	26	693.2	8	51	41
Massachusetts	1,481.0	5	70	26	3,715.1	5	44	51
New Hampshire	115.3	13	84	3	572.1	4	6	90
Rhode Island	186.4	12	88	0	546.6	5	38	57
Vermont	57.2	28	68	4	351.8	6	36	58
Mideast	10,027.9	6	57	37	31,796.0	5	43	52
Delaware	92.5	17	82	0	427.2	9	68	23
Dist. of Col.	282.0	6	NA[c]	94	404.9	11	NA	89
Maryland[d]	471.4	9	88	4	2,873.0	6	40	54
New Jersey	1,272.6	8	61	31	6,250.6	4	43	53
New York	6,438.5	4	49	47	14,076.7	5	42	53
Pennsylvania	1,470.9	10	80	11	7,763.6	4	46	50
Great Lakes	8,386.8	7	49	44	26,140.1	5	42	53
Illinois	1,751.5	7	51	42	7,018.7	8	39	53
Indiana	1,098.4	8	38	54	3,397.9	4	58	38
Michigan	2,541.5	6	53	41	6,208.7	4	34	62
Ohio	2,004.6	9	47	43	6,334.3	5	46	49
Wisconsin	990.8	6	52	42	3,180.6	5	36	59
Plains	3,833.9	7	45	48	10,509.5	6	44	50
Iowa	680.9	5	39	57	1,721.8	6	43	51
Kansas	470.6	10	48	42	1,662.3	5	44	51
Minnesota	1,030.8	6	46	49	2,904.0	4	56	40
Missouri	1,064.7	8	46	47	2,572.6	6	39	55
Nebraska	402.6	6	40	54	866.1	5	28	67
North Dakota	98.5	12	84	4	393.5	8	53	38
South Dakota	85.9	30	47	23	389.2	11	28	61
Southeast	14,135.4	8	40	52	30,046.7	9	55	36
Alabama	1,360.5	4	41	55	1,928.4	12	72	16
Arkansas	377.7	10	48	41	1,172.6	10	61	28
Florida	2,673.9	7	32	61	6,134.1	7	53	40
Georgia	2,514.9	8	22	70	3,146.4	8	56	36
Kentucky	472.0	13	52	35	1,756.9	11	68	20
Louisiana	1,294.4	8	51	42	2,520.8	11	54	36
Mississippi	784.0	8	29	63	1,211.0	16	54	30

Appendix 1.E (continued)

Region and State	Health and Hospitals Amount	Share Fed	St	Loc	K-12 Public Education Amount	Share Fed	St	Loc
N. Carolina	$1,161.5	8	56	36	3,439.6	8	64	28
S. Carolina	905.0	8	51	41	1,876.5	10	58	32
Tennessee	1,155.7	7	33	59	2,168.3	11	49	40
Virginia	1,145.1	8	69	23	$3,539.5	6	34	60
W. Virginia	290.7	11	42	48	1,152.5	10	64	26
Southwest	4,613.3	8	41	50	15,866.7	8	51	41
Arizona	410.3	9	37	53	1,500.0	8	65	27
New Mexico	302.5	11	67	22	968.3	13	75	12
Oklahoma	723.2	7	47	47	1,621.8	8	65	29
Texas	3,177.3	8	38	54	11,776.6	7	46	47
Mountain	1,489.4	14	44	43	5,350.1	5	46	49
Colorado	661.2	13	45	42	2,381.9	5	39	56
Idaho	184.2	10	21	69	539.1	8	62	30
Montana	118.5	15	55	30	658.4	8	50	42
Utah	290.5	18	67	15	1,114.7	6	56	39
Wyoming	235.0	12	22	66	656.0	2	38	60
Far West[e]	8,235.4	6	46	48	23,390.0	7	67	26
California	6,780.2	4	47	49	16,745.1	8	69	23
Nevada	177.0	9	26	65	481.9	4	36	60
Oregon	417.1	7	66	26	1,783.5	5	29	66
Washington	861.1	16	38	46	2,902.0	6	76	19
Alaska	142.6	4	70	26	828.8	5	78	17[f]
Hawaii	196.2	9	88	3	648.7	9	91	Neg[f]

Source: ACIR, *Significant Features of Fiscal Federalism, 1988 Education*, M-155-II, 1988, tables 55 and 57.

[a] Does not include health and hospital expenditures of the federal government; these totaled $15,093 million in FY 1986.

[b] Local and other revenue.

[c] NA = not applicable.

[d] Because of irregularities in the FY 85 and 86 data, percentage figures for Maryland are for FY 84.

[e] Excludes Alaska and Hawaii for health and hospitals; includes them for education.

[f] Neg. = negligible (about $200,000).

Appendix 1.F
State Restrictions on Local Government Tax and Expenditure Powers, October 1985

States	Overall Property Tax Rate Limit	Specific Property Tax Rate Limit	Property Tax Levy Limit	General Revenue Limit	General Expenditure Limit	Limits on Assessment Increases	Full Disclosure
Total Number	12	31	22	6	6	7	14
Alabama	CMSA						
Alaska	CMSD	CMSB					
Arizona			CMD		CMSA	CMSA	
Arkansas		CMSB	CMA		CMSA	CMSA	
California	CMSA		CMSA[1]				
Colorado		CSB	CMB		SD		CMSA
Connecticut							
Delaware		SD					
Washington, DC	CMA		CA[1]				C
Florida		CMSB					CMSD
Georgia							CD
Hawaii		SB					
Idaho		CMSB	CMSA				
Illinois		CMSB	CMSA				CMSA
Indiana			CMSA				
Iowa		CMB[3]					
Kansas			CMD		SD	CMSA	
Kentucky	CMSB	CMSA					
Louisiana		CMSD					CMSA
Maine			CMSA[1]				
Maryland				CMA		CMD	CMD
Massachusetts			CMSA				
Michigan	CSB	MB	CMSD				
Minnesota		CMSB	CMSA	MB	SD		
Mississippi		CMSB	CMSA	CMSA			CMSA

State						
Missouri		CMSB		CMSA		CMSD
Montana		CMSB				
Nebraska		CMSB		CMSA[5]		
Nevada	CMSB	SB	CMD			
New Hampshire						
New Jersey		CMSB			MSD	
New Mexico	CMSB	CMSB	CD		CMSA	
New York		CMD	CMSA		CMSA, CMA[2]	
North Carolina		CMSA				
North Dakota		CMSD[1]				
Ohio	CMSB	CMSB				
Oklahoma	CMSB	CMSB				
Oregon		CMSB	CMSB		CMSA	
Pennsylvania		CMSB[4]				
Rhode Island			M			M
South Carolina						CMSA
South Dakota		CMSB				CMSA
Tennessee						
Texas		CMSD				
Utah		CMSB				
Vermont						CMD
Virginia	CMSD	CMSD	CMSD	SD		
Washington	CMSB	CMSD				
West Virginia		CMSB				
Wisconsin		CMSB				
Wyoming		CMSA				

C—County   M—Municipal   S—School District
B—Enacted before 1970   D—1970 to 1977   A—1978 and after
Const.—Constitutional   Stat.—Statutory

[1]Limits follow reassessment.
[2]Applicable to only New York City and Nassau County.
[3]Only for selected districts (Fire, Library, Cemetery, etc.)
[4]Jurisdictions with home rule charters are not subject to limits.
[5]Expires December 31, 1984.

Source: Reproduced from ACIR, *Significant Features of Fiscal Federalism, 1987 Edition*, M-151, table 78, p. 116.

Appendix 1.G

Percentage Distribution of Local Government only General Revenue, by Source, State, and Region, Fiscal Year 1986

Region and State	LOCAL General Revenue	Federal Aid	State Aid	Property Taxes	General Sales Tax	Individual Income Tax	Corporate Income Tax	Other Taxes	All User Charges	Miscellaneous General Revenue
United States	$380,662.6	5.4%	33.3%	28.2%	4.2%	1.8%	0.4%	3.5%	13.2%	10.0%
New England	16,731.0	7.6	30.5	48.0	0.0	0.0	0.0	1.1	8.6	4.3
Connecticut	4,000.8	4.5	24.6	58.3	0.0	0.0	0.0	1.1	7.1	4.5
Maine	1,208.7	7.0	31.5	45.8	0.0	0.0	0.0	0.4	10.5	4.8
Massachusetts	8,847.0	9.3	36.0	39.6	0.0	0.0	0.0	1.2	9.7	4.2
New Hampshire	1,092.4	6.3	12.5	68.5	0.0	0.0	0.0	1.5	7.5	3.7
Rhode Island	1,062.2	7.5	26.8	56.6	0.0	0.0	0.0	0.7	4.6	3.8
Vermont	520.0	6.7	24.1	57.8	0.0	0.0	0.0	0.6	6.4	4.5
Mideast	87,324.2	6.3	30.9	29.7	5.0	5.4	1.8	3.7	9.5	7.6
Delaware	707.7	7.9	43.4	19.9	0.0	2.6	0.0	1.4	15.9	9.0
Washington, DC	3,449.8	39.0	0.0	14.0	10.5	12.9	4.4	8.0	5.1	6.1
Maryland	6,593.3	6.4	27.8	27.9	0.0	13.6	0.0	5.6	9.1	9.5
New Jersey	12,582.0	4.2	34.9	45.6	0.0	0.0	0.0	1.1	8.6	5.7
New York	47,681.3	4.4	32.4	27.9	8.5	3.9	3.0	3.7	10.0	6.2
Pennsylvania	16,310.1	6.3	30.7	27.4	0.0	9.2	0.0	4.2	9.7	12.5
Great Lakes	61,948.8	5.5	32.6	33.7	2.4	3.0	0.0	2.2	12.7	8.0
Illinois	16,933.1	6.7	26.8	35.5	6.7	0.0	0.0	5.4	10.7	8.2
Indiana	6,932.3	4.9	37.5	30.9	0.0	1.6	0.0	0.6	15.0	9.6
Michigan	14,774.8	4.9	30.9	39.0	0.0	2.4	0.0	1.1	14.1	7.6
Ohio	15,346.1	6.0	33.7	27.5	2.2	8.9	0.0	1.3	12.1	8.4
Wisconsin	7,962.5	3.8	41.7	34.4	0.0	0.0	0.0	0.6	13.1	6.4
Plains	25,762.6	4.9	30.8	30.2	3.0	0.6	0.0	2.4	15.0	13.1
Iowa	4,178.8	4.1	33.5	37.1	0.0	0.0	0.0	0.7	16.2	8.4
Kansas	3,739.6	3.4	23.8	34.3	4.0	0.0	0.0	2.3	12.3	19.8
Minnesota	8,510.5	4.3	38.1	26.1	0.1	0.0	0.0	1.1	14.2	16.1
Missouri	5,373.5	6.6	26.7	22.8	9.1	3.1	0.0	6.5	16.8	8.5
Nebraska	2,308.6	5.2	19.4	39.9	2.5	0.0	0.0	1.7	20.3	10.9
North Dakota	858.5	6.9	40.2	28.6	0.2	0.0	0.0	1.0	8.8	14.3
South Dakota	793.2	8.4	22.0	42.6	6.3	0.0	0.0	2.1	9.3	9.2

Southeast	70,671.6	5.4	32.8	22.1	4.9	0.4	0.0	4.7	18.0	11.8
Alabama	4,396.6	6.0	34.7	9.5	9.7	1.0	0.0	5.8	22.8	10.5
Arkansas	2,217.3	5.6	40.5	19.2	3.6	0.0	0.0	2.9	15.5	12.6
Florida	17,735.7	4.9	29.5	25.9	0.3	0.0	0.0	6.3	19.4	13.8
Georgia	8,854.2	5.6	26.7	22.5	6.0	0.0	0.0	4.2	25.0	10.0
Kentucky	3,512.7	6.1	37.8	13.4	0.0	6.1	0.0	6.0	11.7	18.9
Louisiana	5,856.4	4.8	30.7	14.5	17.0	0.0	0.0	2.9	16.6	13.5
Mississippi	3,002.1	5.3	41.5	19.3	0.0	0.0	0.0	1.2	22.5	13.2
North Carolina	7,240.1	6.0	41.1	22.2	6.6	0.0	0.0	1.0	11.1	12.0
South Carolina	3,304.0	5.4	35.7	26.4	0.0	0.0	0.0	2.5	20.2	9.9
Tennessee	5,231.9	6.8	26.6	21.6	10.8	0.0	0.0	3.9	21.2	9.1
Virginia	7,304.1	4.5	32.5	31.1	4.8	0.0	0.0	9.0	10.8	7.4
West Virginia	2,016.6	4.7	42.8	19.2	0.0	0.0	0.0	4.6	13.7	14.8
Southwest	36,560.9	4.5	29.5	29.8	5.2	0.0	0.0	2.7	13.7	14.6
Arizona	5,741.8	5.2	34.7	22.4	5.1	0.0	0.0	2.2	10.4	20.0
New Mexico	2,137.1	8.0	49.2	9.8	5.5	0.0	0.0	2.3	9.4	16.0
Oklahoma	4,031.3	5.1	34.6	19.2	10.8	0.0	0.0	1.8	16.1	12.3
Texas	24,650.7	3.9	25.7	35.0	4.3	0.0	0.0	3.0	14.5	13.6
Rocky Mountain	11,785.5	4.7	28.7	30.4	7.0	0.0	0.0	2.1	12.6	14.5
Colorado	5,697.9	4.1	25.7	29.7	11.6	0.0	0.0	2.7	12.5	13.7
Idaho	1,064.1	5.9	38.6	28.2	0.0	0.0	0.0	1.1	19.6	6.5
Montana	1,194.1	7.7	23.8	40.8	0.0	0.0	0.0	1.8	10.6	15.2
Utah	2,353.5	4.9	32.4	25.9	5.1	0.0	0.0	2.3	9.1	20.2
Wyoming	1,476.0	3.4	31.5	33.1	2.8	0.0	0.0	0.5	14.9	13.8
Far West[1]	67,131.4	4.2	42.3	20.6	4.5	0.0	0.0	4.7	14.0	9.7
California	54,414.0	3.6	44.3	19.5	4.8	0.0	0.0	4.5	13.6	9.7
Nevada	1,643.4	4.8	37.9	17.9	0.3	0.0	0.0	9.4	20.0	9.7
Oregon	4,253.0	8.5	23.7	41.3	0.0	0.0	0.0	4.4	13.2	8.9
Washington	6,821.0	6.2	39.6	16.9	5.6	0.0	0.0	5.0	16.5	10.2
Alaska	2,065.4	3.2	41.0	22.5	2.7	0.0	0.0	1.0	12.8	16.8
Hawaii	681.2	17.1	7.1	49.0	0.0	0.0	0.0	10.5	8.9	7.4

[1]Excluding Alaska and Hawaii.

Source: Reproduced from ACIR, *Significant Features of Fiscal Federalism, 1988 Edition,* M-155-II, table 35.

389

Appendix 1.H
State Income Taxes: Number of Brackets, Top Marginal Rate, and Dollar
Threshold above Which Rate Applies, October 1987

State	No. Brks.	Top Rate*	Thresh-old	State	No. Brks.	Top Rate*	Thresh-old
AL	3	5.0%	$3,000	MS	3	5.0%	$10,000
AZ	7	8.0	6,930	MT	10	11.0	46,400
AR	6	7.0	25,000	MO	10	6.0	9,000
CA	6	9.3	23,950	NE	4	5.9	27,000
CO	FTI	5.0		NH**	1	5.0	1,200
CT**	11	12.0	100,000	NJ	3	3.5	50,000
DE	14	8.8	40,000	NM	7	8.5	41,600
DC	3	10.0	20,000	NY	8	8.5	14,000
GA	6	6.0	7,000	NC	5	7.0	10,000
HI	8	10.0	20,000	ND	8	12.0	50,000
ID	8	8.2	20,000	OH	8	6.9	100,000
IL	1	2.5	TNI	OK	7	6.0	7,500
IN	1	3.2	AGI	OR	3	9.0	5,000
IA	9	9.98	45,000	PA	Var.	2.1	Var.
KS	8	9.0	25,000	RI	FTL	23.46	Fed.
KY	5	6.0	8,000	SC	5	7.0	10,000
LA	3	6.0	50,000	TN**	1	6.0	
ME	8	10.0	25,000	UT	6	7.75	3,750
MD	4	5.0	3,000	VT	FTL	25.8	Fed.
MA	1	5.0***	TNI	VA	4	5.75	14,000
MI	1	4.6	TNI	WV	5	6.5	60,000
MN	4	9.0	16,000	WI	4	7.9	30,000

Source: ACIR, *Significant Features of Fiscal Federalism, 1988 Edition,* December 1987, M-155-I, table 16, pp. 28–32.

Abbreviations: AGI: adjusted gross income; Fed.: tied to federal brackets and rates; FTI: federal taxable income; FTL: federal tax liability; TNI: taxable net income; var.: various.

* Rates for single taxpayers or married, filing separately. Rates apply to taxable income.

** Only on interest, dividends, etc. ("unearned income").

*** 10.0 percent rate on interest, dividends, etc.

Appendix 2.A
State Fiscal Discipline Management Tools, 1984

	Balanced Budget Requirement	Gubernatorial Line Item Veto	Constitutional Debt Restrict.	Tax and Expenditure Limits	Require Super-Majority Vote to Pass Tax	Index Income Tax	Fiscal Note Review Procedure	Program Evaluation & Sunset	"Rainy Day" Funds
TOTAL	49	43	30	18	7	10	41	29	24
New England									
Connecticut	X	X					X	X	X
Maine	X	X	X			X		X	
Massachusetts	X								
New Hampshire	X						X	X	
Rhode Island	X		X	X			X	X	X
Vermont								X	
Mideast									
Delaware	X	X			X			X	X
Maryland	X	X					X	X	
New Jersey	X	X	X				X		
New York	X	X					X		
Pennsylvania	X	X					X	X	X
Great Lakes									
Illinois	X	X	X				X	X	X
Indiana	X		X	X			X	X	X
Michigan	X	X	X				X		X
Ohio	X	X	X				X		
Wisconsin	X	X	X			X	X		
Plains									
Iowa	X	X	X			X	X		X
Kansas	X	X	X			X	X		X
Minnesota	X	X	X					X	X
Missouri	X	X	X	X			X		
Nebraska	X	X	X				X		
North Dakota	X	X	X				X		X
South Dakota	X	X	X		X				

Appendix 2.A (continued)

	Balanced Budget Requirement	Gubernatorial Line Item Veto	Constitutional Debt Restrict.	Tax and Expenditure Limits	Require Super-Majority Vote to Pass Tax	Index Income Tax	Fiscal Note Review Procedure	Program Evaluation & Sunset	"Rainy Day" Funds
TOTAL	49	43	30	18	7	10	41	29	24
Southeast									
Alabama	X	X	X				X	X	
Arkansas	X	X			X		X		
Florida	X	X			X		X		X
Georgia	X	X	X				X	X	X
Kentucky	X	X	X				X		X
Louisiana	X	X	X	X	X		X	X	X
Mississippi	X				X		X		
North Carolina	X						X		
South Carolina	X					X	X		
Tennessee	X	X	X	X			X	X	X
Virginia	X	X	X	X			X	X	X
West Virginia	X	X	X				X	X	X
Southwest									
Arizona	X	X	X	X		X	X	X	
New Mexico	X	X	X				X	X	X
Oklahoma	X	X						X	
Texas	X	X	X	X			X	X	
Rocky Mountain									
Colorado	X	X	X	X		X	X	X	X
Idaho	X	X	X	X			X		X
Montana	X	X		X		X	X	X	
Utah	X	X	X				X	X	
Wyoming	X	X	X				X	X	X
Far West									
California	X	X	X	X		X	X		X
Nevada	X			X	X	X	X		
Oregon	X	X	X	X		X	X	X	
Washington	X	X	X	X			X	X	
Alaska	X	X	X	X			X	X	X
Hawaii	X	X	X	X			X	X	X

Source: ACIR, *Fiscal Discipline in the Federal System: National Reform and the Experience of the States,* A-107, July 1987, table 2, p. 38.

Appendix 2.B
State Income Tax Exclusion/Exemption of Pension Income from Social Security, State, Local, Federal, or General Pension Income, Tax Year 1988

(Amounts in Thousands of Dollars)

State	SS	GPI	ST	LO	Fed	State	SS	GPI	ST	LO	Fed
Alabama	Ex	---	Ex	8^a	Ex	Minnesota	50%	5 ea			
Arizona	Ex	---	Ex		2.5	Mississippi	Ex	5 ea	Ex	Ex	
Arkansas	Ex	6	6^b			Missouri	50%	---	Ex	Ex	
California	Ex	---				Montana	50%	3.6	Ex	Ex	3.6
Colorado	50%	20 ea				Nebraska	50%	---			
Delaware	Ex	2-3				New Jersey	Ex	7.5-10			
Dist. of Col.	Ex	---	3	3	3	New Mexico	Ex	---	Ex	Ex	3
Georgia	Ex	4 ea	Ex			New York	Ex	20	Ex		
Hawaii	Ex	Ex	Ex	Ex	Ex	North Carolina	Ex	---	Ex	Ex	3
Idaho	Ex	---	$10\text{-}15^c$			North Dakota	50%	---	5^d		
Illinois	Ex	Ex	Ex	Ex	Ex	Ohio	Ex	---			
Indiana	Ex	---	2^d			Oklahoma	Ex	---	Ex		4
Iowa	50%	---	Ex	Ex	5^d	Oregon	Ex	---	Ex		5
Kansas	50%	---	Ex	Ex	Ex	Pennsylvania	Ex	Ex	Ex	Ex	Ex
Kentucky	Ex	---	Ex	Ex	4	South Carolina	50%	3	Ex	3	3
Louisiana	Ex	6 ea	Ex			Utah	50%	3.6			
Maine	Ex	---				Virginia	Ex	---	Ex	2^d Ex	
Maryland	Ex	9.1 ea (less SS)				West Virginia	50%	---			
Massachusetts	Ex	---				Wisconsin	50%	---	Ex^d		
Michigan	Ex	7.5-10	Ex	Ex							

Source: ACIR, *Significant Features of Fiscal Federalism 1989 Edition* Vol I. M-163, Table 20, pp. 38–42, Derived in turn from survey of state departments of revenue, Fall 1988, and Commerce Clearing House, *State Tax Reporter*.

Notes: States without income tax on earned income and those basing tax entirely on federal taxable income or federal tax liability not shown.

Abbreviations: Ex = All pension income from column source excluded or exempt.

GPI = General pension income; exclusion/exemption irrespective of source.

Amount of exclusion/exemption often has an age differential and may be subject to Social Security offsets, total income, or other limitation. May be for each (ea) person in joint return or for any one return. 50%. Same as federal.

[a] Public safety retirement exclusion of $8,000. [b] Limited to $6,000 for post-1989 retirees. [c] Up to $9,789 each and $14,682, joint, on civil service, military, and Idaho public safety pension benefits. [d] Indiana, up to $2,000 less SS on civil service and $2,000 military. Iowa, civil service up to $5,627/ $8,184, less SS. North Dakota, city public safety, federal civil service and military benefits. West Virginia, public safety benefits fully exempt and up to $2,000 military or state retirement benefits. Wisconsin, limited to teacher retirement benefits and benefits from certain Milwaukee city and county retirement systems.

Appendix 2.C
List and Coverage of Selected Draft State Legislative Bills of the Advisory Commission on Intergovernmental Relations in the Fields of Revenue, Budget, and Fiscal Management

1.304: *State Technical Assistance to Local Governments*

(a) Authorizes and encourages all state agencies to make technical assistance available to local governments on either reimbursable or nonreimbursable basis, depending on essentiality to state agency mission.

(b) State agencies authorized to perform continuing services for local units on contractual basis.

(c) Authorizes local use of state procurement, communications, data processing, and other state facilities or services on actual cost basis. (4 pp.)

2.205: *Transfer of Functions Between Municipalities and Counties*

A general authorization for transfers of functions by mutual action of each governing body. (2 pp.)

3.103: *Property Tax Organization and Administration*

(a) Qualifications of assessors.

(b) Value appraisal of tax-exempt properties and publication of properties and values on annual basis.

(c) Other provisions regarding assessment appeals, hearings, etc. (9 pp.)

3.110: *Full Disclosure of Property Tax Increases*

(a) Prescribes local budget procedure for determining portion of revenue needs to be met from property taxation.

(b) Calculation of a "constant rate"—the rate necessary to be applied against the tax base, optionally of new construction completed in past 12 months, to obtain the same dollar amount as preceding year's tax levy.

(c) Publication and public hearings if constant rate is proposed to be increased for forthcoming fiscal year. (7 pp.)

3.203: *Authorization for a Local Income Tax*

(a) Authorization, including specification of local unit type(s) eligible to use.

(b) Process for imposing, including maximum permitted rate.

(c) Mandatory piggy-backing on state tax (if state has one). (4 pp.)

3.204: *Authorization for a Local Sales Tax*

(Similar structure to 3.203.)

3.207: *State Revenue Sharing*

(a) Eligible units.

(b) Composition of allocation formula.

(c) Local hearings on contemplated use of year's allocation.

(d) Disbursement process. (7 pp.)

4.101 and 4.102: *State Regulation of Local Financial Accounting, Reporting, and Auditing and Prevention of and Controlling Local Government Financial Emergencies*

(a) Mandates uniform fiscal year for all local governments.

(b) Requires filing annual financial report in standard format laid down by state financial agency.

(c) Failure to file within specified time followed by visit of state personnel to complete the report.

(d) Defines local financial emergency (e.g., unable to meet bond payments).

(e) Establishes state financial control board with broad powers to act until financial affairs of local unit stabilized.

(f) Provides legal authority to local units to file petitions with federal bankruptcy court. (3 and 7 pp.)

4.108: *Indexation of the Individual State Income Tax*

(a) Gives optional bases for inflation factor, centering on Consumer Price Index.

(b) After determination of inflation factor for preceding year, adjustment of each dollar amount in statutory tax bracket amounts by amount of inflation factor. (4 pp.)

4.111: *Pooled Insurance*

(a) Creates statewide insurance pool for voluntary participation by local governments.

(b) Provides for premium setting.

(c) Claims processing and other administrative provisions. (4 pp.)

Appendix 3.A
Service Delivery Approaches of Cities and Counties (ICMA 1982 Survey)

Service	No of cities and counties reporting	Local government employees In part (%)	Local government employees Exclusively (%)	Intergovernmental agreements (%)	Contracting Profit (%)	Contracting Neighborhood (%)	Contracting Non-profit (%)	Contracting Franchises (%)	Contracting Subsidies (%)	Contracting Vouchers (%)	Volunteers (%)	Self-help (%)	Incentives¹ (%)
Public works and transportation													
Residential solid waste collection	1,376	12	49	8	35	0	0	15	1	0	0	1	1
Commercial solid waste collection	1,106	25	29	7	44	0	0	19	1	0	0	1	0
Solid waste disposal	1,223	15	38	31	28	0	2	5	0	0	0	0	0
Street repair	1,643	34	65	5	27	0	1	0	0	0	0	0	0
Street/parking lot cleaning	1,483	11	84	3	9	0	0	0	0	0	0	1	0
Snow plowing/sanding	1,287	19	79	4	14	0	0	0	0	0	0	0	0
Traffic signal installation/maintenance	1,569	37	54	14	26	0	2	1	0	0	0	0	0
Meter maintenance/collection	640	8	88	4	7	0	0	0	0	0	0	3	0
Tree trimming/planting	1,451	39	54	5	31	1	1	1	0	0	3	3	0
Cemetery administration/maintenance	703	17	69	4	11	1	8	1	1	0	3	1	0
Inspection/code enforcement	1,588	14	82	7	7	0	1	0	0	0	0	0	0
Parking lot/garage operation	780	17	75	7	12	0	2	2	1	0	0	0	1
Bus system operation/maintenance	508	21	26	42	24	1	9	5	9	0	1	4	0
Paratransit system operation/maintenance	560	29	19	29	23	2	21	4	14	3	8	0	0
Airport operation	530	27	39	26	24	0	4	9	2	0	1	0	0
Utility meter reading	1,200	23	64	9	10	0	1	10	0	0	0	0	0
Utility billing	1,243	25	62	10	13	0	1	9	0	0	0	0	0
Street light operation	1,284	21	30	21	39	0	2	14	0	0	0	0	0
Public safety													
Crime prevention/patrol	1,660	22	74	5	3	5	2	0	0	0	10	5	0
Police/fire communication	1,684	16	75	14	1	0	3	0	0	0	3	0	0
Fire prevention/suppression	1,516	18	69	9	1	1	3	0	1	1	18	1	0
Emergency medical service	1,333	28	40	17	14	1	10	3	5	0	16	0	0
Ambulance service	1,214	20	31	17	25	1	10	4	8	0	15	0	1
Traffic control/parking enforcement	1,505	7	90	5	1	0	1	0	8	0	1	0	0
Vehicle towing and storage	1,285	14	7	2	80	0	0	7	0	0	0	0	0

396

Health and human services

Service	Number										[1]
Sanitary inspection	939	14	53	36	1	0	6	0	1	0	0
Insect/rodent control	1,037	23	45	29	14	0	5	0	1	0	1
Animal control	1,482	16	63	13	6	1	9	1	1	0	0
Animal shelter operation	1,225	14	37	30	13	6	18	1	3	2	0
Day care facility operation	436	20	7	16	35	2	37	2	15	1	2
Child welfare programs	558	39	27	28	5	4	24	1	8	1	0
Programs for elderly	1,189	58	19	21	4	4	29	1	13	3	1
Operation/management of public/elderly housing	602	22	21	43	13	1	18	0	5	0	2
Operation/management of hospitals	361	10	18	25	30	1	27	1	4	1	1
Public health programs	721	37	26	30	8	2	27	1	9	2	0
Drug/alcohol treatment programs	626	31	10	30	6	4	41	1	13	1	1
Operation of mental health/retardation programs/facilities	512	26	13	34	7	3	40	1	15	1	1

Parks and recreation

Service	Number										[1]
Recreation services	1,444	39	52	9	4	5	13	2	4	1	0
Operation/maintenance of recreation facilities	1,535	35	58	9	8	3	9	9	2	0	0
Parks landscaping/maintenance	1,573	20	76	5	9	1	2	1	1	0	0
Operation of convention center/auditoriums	448	16	70	10	5	1	6	3	2	0	1
Operation of cultural/arts programs	702	47	11	11	7	8	39	2	18	2	0
Operation of libraries	1,153	21	50	28	1	1	10	0	6	0	0
Operation of museums	498	26	21	16	4	3	32	1	17	0	0

Support functions

Service	Number										[1]
Building/grounds maintenance	1,672	25	73	4	20	0	1	0	0	0	0
Building security	1,497	11	86	3	8	0	1	0	0	0	0
Fleet management/vehicle maintenance											
Heavy equipment	1,643	37	59	2	32	0	0	0	0	0	0
Emergency vehicles	1,558	34	59	3	31	0	0	0	0	0	0
All other vehicles	1,631	32	63	2	29	0	0	0	0	0	0
Data processing	1,466	23	64	11	23	0	2	0	2	0	0
Legal services	1,608	29	42	6	49	0	2	0	2	0	0
Payroll	1,720	11	86	3	10	0	1	0	1	0	0
Tax bill processing	1,241	21	65	9	11	0	6	0	6	1	0
Tax assessing	1,038	14	57	29	7	0	4	0	4	0	0
Delinquent tax collection	1,213	17	62	20	10	0	3	0	3	1	0
Secretarial services	1,657	5	94	1	4	0	0	0	0	0	0
Personnel services	1,663	8	90	2	5	0	1	0	1	0	0
Labor relations	1,513	25	70	3	23	0	1	0	1	0	0
Public relations/information	1,545	12	87	1	7	0	2	0	1	0	0

1. Regulatory and Tax Incentives

Source: Reproduced from Valente, C. F. and Manchester, L. D. *Rethinking Local Services: Examining Alternative Delivery Approaches,* (Washington, D.C.: International City Management Association, 1984), xv.

Appendix 4.A
Discouraged Workers: Persons Not in Labor Force Wanting, But Not Seeking,
Work, by Reason, Sex, Age, and Ethnic Group, Annual Average, 1987

Reason, race, and Hispanic origin	Total	Age 16-24	Age 25-59	60 +	Men	Women
White						
Total not in CLF	53,669	8,089	17,669	27,910	17,410	36,258
Do not want job now	49,455	6,636	15,422	27,399	15,931	33,524
Want, not looking	4,213	1,451	2,248	511	1,479	2,734
Reason not looking:						
School attendance	1,016	805	206	5	518	498
Health; disability	649	53	450	145	340	309
Home duties	932	207	682	43	0	932
Other reasons*	923	224	521	178	342	581
Think can't get job	693	162	389	140	279	414
Black						
Total not in CLF	7,359	2,025	2,643	2,691	2,641	4,717
Do not want job now	6,075	1,491	1,987	2,597	2,210	3,865
Want, not looking	1,284	535	657	94	431	852
Reason not looking:						
School attendance	333	277	56	0	159	174
Health; disability	188	18	132	37	72	116
Home duties	295	99	192	5	0	295
Other reasons*	174	51	104	20	73	100
Think can't get job	294	90	173	32	127	167
Hispanic Origin						
Total not in CLF	4,327	1,207	2,029	1,090	1,208	3,119
Do not want job now	3,749	971	1,723	1,055	1,012	2,734
Want, not looking	578	237	307	34	195	384
Reason not looking:						
School attendance	150	119	31	0	75	76
Health; disability	72	5	53	15	40	32
Home duties	160	46	110	3	0	160
Other reasons*	90	25	58	7	32	58
Think can't get job	106	42	55	10	48	58
Reasons: All Races						
Age	132	20	30	82	54	78
Lack educ. or exp.	136	52	86	3	45	91
Other handicap	86	24	49	13	32	54
No use looking	366	107	230	30	163	203
No jobs available	306	66	191	50	132	174

Source: Bureau of Labor Statistics, *Employment and Earnings*, January 1988, tables 36 and 37, pp. 200–201.

* Includes small number of men not looking for work because of "home duties."

Appendix 4.B
Unemployed and Underutilized Workers in Civilian Labor Force by Sex, Age, and Race, Annual Average, 1987

(Numbers in Thousands)

Category	In CLF	PT Invol.	Short Sched.	Total	% CLF	UR	Total U/U
Total, Age 16+	119,865	3,695	1,706	5,401	4.5	6.2	10.7
Age 16-19	7,988	574	133	707	8.9	16.9	25.8
20 and Over	111,877	3,121	1,573	4,694	4.2	5.4	9.6
Men, Age 16+	66,207	1,502	1,011	2,513	3.8	6.2	10.0
Age 16-19	4,112	273	73	346	8.4	17.8	26.2
20 and Over	62,095	1,229	938	2,167	3.5	5.4	8.9
Women, Age 16+	53,658	2,194	695	2,889	5.4	6.2	11.6
Age 16-19	3,875	301	60	361	9.3	15.9	25.2
20 and Over	49,783	1,893	634	2,527	5.1	5.4	10.5
White							
Men, Age 16+	57,779	1,192	853	2,045	3.5	5.4	8.9
Age 16-19	3,547	225	62	287	8.1	15.5	23.6
20 and Over	54,232	966	791	1,757	3.2	4.8	8.0
Women, Age 16+	45,510	1,766	567	2,333	5.1	5.2	10.3
Age 16-19	3,347	255	52	307	9.2	13.4	22.6
20 and Over	42,163	1,511	515	2,026	4.8	4.6	9.4
Black							
Men, Age 16+	6,486	260	132	392	6.0	12.7	18.7
Age 16-19	463	40	10	50	10.8	34.7	45.5
20 and Over	6,023	220	122	342	5.7	11.1	16.8
Women, Age 16+	6,507	366	103	469	7.2	13.2	20.4
Age 16-19	435	40	7	47	10.8	34.9	45.7
20 and Over	6,072	326	97	423	7.0	11.6	18.6

Source: Bureau of Labor Statistics, *Employment and Earnings*, January 1988, tables 3 and 7, pp. 160–162, 167.

Abbreviations: CLF: civilian labor force; PT Invol.: working part-time rather than full-time for nonvoluntary reasons; Short Sched.: on a full-time job, but shift or hours cut back at employer initiative for economic or other reasons; UR: rate of unemployment for sex/age category; Total U/U: combined total of unemployed and underutilized persons as a percentage of the civilian labor force.

Appendix 4.C
Caretaker Arrangements for Children Age 5 to 13 in School by Household Type and Race, December 1984

(Numbers of Children in Millions)

	Total No.	Parent No.	Parent %	Sibling Relative* No.	Sibling Relative* %	Non-Relative No.	Non-Relative %	No Adult No.	No Adult %
All Households and Children									
All Races	28.9	21.8	75.5	2.7	9.3	2.3	7.8	2.1	7.2
White	23.3	17.6	75.4	1.9	8.3	1.9	8.3	1.8	7.8
Black	4.3	3.2	75.9	.6	13.7	.2	5.6	.2	4.3
All Households Mother Employed Full Time (F.T.)									
All Races	10.6	5.7	54.3	1.8	16.9	1.6	14.8	1.4	13.5
White	8.3	4.4	52.8	1.3	15.8	1.3	15.9	1.3	15.0
Black	1.8	1.1	60.9	.3	20.7	.2	10.3	.1	7.4
Married Couple Mother Emp. F.T.									
All Races	7.9	4.6	58.0	1.2	14.7	1.1	13.8	1.0	13.0
White	6.6	3.7	56.6	.9	13.9	1.0	14.6	.9	14.3
Black	1.0	.7	67.3	.1	15.8	.1	9.4	.1	6.7
Household Maintained by Woman Emp. F.T.									
All Races	2.5	1.1	42.8	.6	24.0	.4	17.8	.4	14.9
White	1.6	.6	37.3	.4	23.5	.3	21.3	.3	17.7
Black	.8	.4	54.3	.2	25.5	.1	11.5	.1	8.0

Source: Bureau of the Census, *After-School Care of School-Age Children: December 1984*, P-23, no. 149, January 1987, table 1, pp. 7–10.

* Age 14 or over

Appendix 4.D
Key Provisions of Adequate Public Facilities Ordinance, Sec. 50–35,
Montgomery County **(Maryland)** *Code Annotated*

(k) Adequate public facilities. No preliminary plan of subdivision shall be approved unless the planning board determines that public facilities are adequate to support and service the area of the proposed subdivision. The applicant shall, at the request of the planning board, submit sufficient information and data on the proposed subdivision to demonstrate the expected impact on and use of public facilities by possible uses of said subdivision.

(1) Public facilities may be determined to be adequate to service a tract of land or an affected area when the following conditions are found to exist.

   a. The tract or area is adequately accessible by means of roads and public transportation facilities. Said area or tract to be subdivided shall be deemed adequately accessible via roads and public transportation facilities if any of the following conditions are present:

   (i) Existing roads are adequate to accommodate the traffic that would be generated by the subject subdivision in addition to the existing traffic, and are publicly maintained, all-weather roads; or

   (ii) Such additional roads, necessary in combination with existing roads to accommodate the additional traffic that would be generated by the subject subdivision, are proposed on an adopted master plan and are programmed in the current adopted capital improvements program or the State Highway Administration's five-year program for construction with public or private financing; or

   (iii) Public bus, rail, or other form of mass transportation sufficient to serve the proposed subdivision, in combination with (i) or (ii) or both, is available or programmed within the area affected or within one-third mile of the subdivision under consideration.

   (iv) In its determination of the adequacy of a road to accommodate traffic, the planning board shall consider recommendations of the State Highway Administration or county department of transportation, the applicable levels of traffic service, peak hour use and average use, and any other information presented.

   b. The tract or area has adequate sewerage and water service.

   (i) For a subdivision dependent upon public sewerage and water systems:

   1. Said area or tract to be subdivided shall be deemed to have adequate sewerage and water service if located within an area in which water and sewer service is presently available, under construction, or designated by the county council for extension of water and sewer service within the first two (2) years of a current approved ten-year water and sewerage plan.

   2. If said area or tract to be subdivided is not situated within an area designated for service within the first two (2) years of a current

approved ten-year water and sewerage plan, but is within the last eight (8) years of such plan, it shall be deemed to have adequate water and sewerage service if the applicant provides community sewerage and/or water systems as set forth in subtitle 5 of article Health-Environmental of the Annotated Code of Maryland approved by the state department of health and mental hygiene, the Washington Suburban Sanitary Commission, the county health department and the Montgomery County council.

Appendix 5.A
Child Support Collections as a Percentage of AFDC–Foster Care and Total Cases by State, Fiscal Year 1987

```
===============================================================
```

State	Caseload*		Collections		Per Ct.	
	All	AFDC-F	All	AFDC-F	All	AFDC-F
U. S	8,740 K	5,765 K	1,535 K	604 K	17.6	10.5
Alabama	152,565	94,445	23,155	11,572	15.2	12.3
Alaska	18,564	10,130	4,222	1,038	22.7	10.2
Arizona	90,349	58,306	6,138	1,470	6.8	2.5
Arkansas	66,931	48,173	10,580	5,506	15.8	11.4
California	806,487	522,277	154,565	76,170	19.2	14.6
Colorado	100,414	70,431	8,629	4,092	8.6	5.8
Connecticut	94,311	73,070	23,221	13,337	24.6	18.3
Delaware	22,188	6,097	7,931	2,858	35.7	46.9
Dist. of Col.	54,462	32,672	3,402	2,138	6.2	6.5
Florida	414,177	289,762	29,497	16,489	7.1	5.7
Georgia	244,225	191,287	25,593	10,710	10.5	5.6
Hawaii	44,347	29,494	5,979	3,175	13.5	10.8
Idaho	15,615	10,247	3,774	1,245	24.2	12.1
Illinois	467,115	406,876	28,831	14,352	6.2	3.5
Indiana	120,577	83,878	28,947	16,188	24.0	19.3
Iowa	60,704	37,877	10,456	7,015	17.2	18.5
Kansas	87,485	67,898	9,058	3,798	10.4	5.6
Kentucky	143,488	78,618	22,402	6,853	15.6	8.7
Louisiana	199,891	170,599	21,611	9,916	10.8	5.8
Maine	31,445	20,682	8,596	4,734	27.3	22.9
Maryland	155,367	75,160	21,758	9,073	14.0	12.1
Massachusetts	106,066	55,500	43,760	17,211	41.3	31.0
Michigan	733,774	493,758	184,551	58,364	25.2	11.8
Minnesota	92,686	58,488	28,579	12,442	30.8	21.3
Mississippi	132,009	103,844	8,892	4,544	6.7	4.4
Missouri	116,447	72,767	21,159	6,483	18.2	8.9
Montana	29,432	26,098	1,649	849	5.6	3.3
Nebraska	41,995	19,224	13,095	2,555	31.2	13.3
Nevada	20,660	8,781	4,857	1,645	23.5	18.7
New Hampshire	21,963	16,069	6,455	981	29.4	6.1
New Jersey	296,881	179,329	76,888	25,182	25.9	14.0
New Mexico	74,788	67,902	4,637	2,175	6.2	3.2
New York	469,784	281,296	114,826	38,196	24.4	13.6
North Carolina	176,120	118,132	32,412	17,089	18.4	14.5
North Dakota	10,188	6,272	1,995	1,130	19.6	18.0
Ohio	560,137	437,368	74,387	35,273	13.3	8.1
Oklahoma	104,738	52,558	6,335	1,468	6.0	2.8
Oregon	90,799	44,232	26,555	5,935	29.2	13.4
Pennsylvania	682,900	307,021	170,890	48,817	25.0	15.9
Rhode Island	39,741	19,287	5,842	3,092	14.7	16.0

Appendix 5.A (continued)

```
============================================================
```

State	Caseload*		Collections		Per Ct.	
	All	AFDC-F	All	AFDC-F	All	AFDC-F
South Carolina	124,992	103,317	13,660	10,495	10.9	10.2
South Dakota	11,473	8,194	4,062	1,887	35.4	23.0
Tennessee	233,596	127,106	24,387	9,430	10.4	7.4
Texas	273,047	120,386	24,246	9,167	8.9	7.6
Utah	27,314	15,233	7,635	3,627	28.0	23.8
Vermont	9,042	6,578	2,951	1,984	32.6	30.2
Virginia	285,044	239,519	30,086	10,813	10.6	4.5
Washington	165,245	111,135	31,766	18,110	19.2	16.3
West Virginia	49,785	49,180	4,060	2,107	8.2	4.3
Wisconsin	209,921	144,834	68,800	26,847	32.8	18.5
Wyoming	13,133	11,661	1,301	738	9.9	6.3

Source: U.S. Department of Health and Human Services, Office of Child Support Enforcement, tabulations for *Twelfth Annual Report to the Congress, 1988*, for period ending September 30, 1987.

* Annual average.

Appendix 5.B

K-12 Public School Enrollment by Race and per Pupil Revenue for Selected Additional Districts, 1986–87

District	Enroll-ment	Per Pupil Revenue	Exter-nal Aid	Percentages by Race				
				A.In.	As.	Blk.	Hisp.	Wh.
Atlanta	66,649	$4,588	$2,080	N	1	92	1	7
Baltimore	118,081	3,353	2,078	N	N	80	N	19
Boston	60,166	6,437	2,654	N	8	47	18	26
Buffalo	46,035	5,238	3,586	1	1	48	6	43
Cincinnati	52,077	4,417	2,421	N	1	60	N	39
Columbus	65,570	4,264	2,188	N	2	45	1	52
Dayton	29,609	4,971	2,794	N	N	61	N	38
Dade Co. FL	254,235	4,350	2,557	N	1	33	43	23
Denver	60,282	4,764	1,423	1	4	22	36	37
Dist. Col.	84,630	5,034	511	N	1	91	4	4
Fresno	59,112	3,824	3,186	1	14	11	33	42
Long Beach	65,010	3,626	3,069	N	18	18	25	38
Nashville	65,084	3,284	1,295	2	N	36	N	61
New Orleans	84,415	3,302	1,917	N	3	87	1	8
Omaha	41,638	3,825	1,423	1	1	27	3	68

Appendix 5.B (continued)

District	Enroll-ment	Per Pupil Revenue	Exter-nal Aid	Percentages by Race A.In.	As.	Blk.	Hisp.	Wh.
Pittsburgh	39,901	6,276	2,546	N	1	52	N	46
Portland OR	51,880	5,131	1,354	2	8	15	2	73
Richmond VA	28,659	5,191	2,157	N	1	87	N	12
Rochester NY	32,018	5,728	2,937	N	3	54	13	30
St. Paul	32,392	5,098	2,462	2	14	15	6	63
San Antonio	60,820	3,188	2,550	N	N	13	79	8
Seattle	43,564	4,382	3,169	3	20	24	5	48
Tucson	55,421	3,370	2,058	3	2	6	33	57
Tulsa	44,282	3,156	1,851	5	1	27	1	66

Source: Tabulations of the Council of the Great City Schools; U.S. Department of Education, Office of Civil Rights, *1986 Elementary and Secondary School Civil Rights Survey: District Summary*, December 1987, various pages, alphabetical by state and within state; per pupil revenues and external aid from preliminary data in Bureau of the Census, *Finances of Public School Systems in 1985–86*, 1988, table 9.

A. In. = American Indian, including Alaskan Natives.

As. = Asian or Pacific Islander.

N = less than .5 percent.

Appendix 5.C
City Arrests by Crime Category, Age, and Race, 1987

Offense Charged	Total	Sex		Percentages Age					Race		
		M	F	Un. 18	19–24	25–29	30–34	35+	Wh.	Bl.	Oth.
Index, Violent	378.2	88.7	11.3	16.5	31.4	19.6	13.8	18.7	46.9	51.6	1.5
Aggr. Assault	233.0	86.2	13.8	13.6	28.4	19.9	14.1	22.9	53.9	44.5	1.6
Robbery	108.5	91.9	8.1	23.4	37.6	18.3	10.3	9.3	33.5	65.4	1.1
Forcible Rape	24.1	98.8	1.2	16.6	29.5	20.4	13.6	19.4	44.6	54.0	1.4
Murder*	12.6	87.6	12.4	10.5	35.5	20.3	13.5	22.1	37.5	60.7	1.7
Index, Property	1,476.2	74.7	25.3	34.2	29.1	14.4	9.9	14.7	63.4	34.5	2.2
Larceny-Theft	1,068.7	68.4	31.6	32.8	27.5	13.0	9.7	17.2	64.5	33.3	2.3
Burglary	278.7	91.9	8.1	36.5	34.0	13.6	8.1	8.3	62.7	35.7	1.6
Motor Veh. Theft	117.4	90.5	9.5	40.1	34.1	12.1	6.8	6.9	55.0	43.1	1.9
Arson	11.4	86.1	13.9	43.0	21.2	11.9	8.7	15.4	69.2	29.0	1.7
Other Crimes											
Driving Und. Inf.	871.7	87.7	12.3	1.7	29.6	22.2	15.6	31.7	87.0	11.2	1.8
Drunkenness	589.4	90.8	9.2	3.5	24.5	18.6	14.9	39.6	77.1	20.1	2.7
Drug Violations	643.6	85.3	14.7	10.4	38.6	22.7	14.1	14.7	59.7	39.5	.8
Disorderly	541.8	81.0	19.0	15.0	37.2	16.5	10.4	18.2	61.4	37.0	1.7
Other assaults	539.9	84.9	15.1	15.5	30.4	20.4	13.8	20.3	58.2	39.9	2.0

Appendix 5.C (continued)

Offense Charged	Total	Sex		Percentages Age					Race		
		M	F	Un. 18	19-24	25-29	30-34	35+	Wh.	Bl.	Oth.
Liquor law viol.	398.7	82.4	17.6	27.0	48.8	8.4	5.3	9.8	86.2	10.6	3.1
Vandalism	186.9	89.3	10.7	43.4	28.6	12.1	7.1	9.5	72.6	25.6	1.8
Fraud	154.9	60.6	39.4	10.8	27.8	20.8	16.3	24.4	62.2	36.8	1.0
Weapon possess.	135.0	92.1	7.9	16.8	34.4	18.1	11.7	19.6	56.8	41.8	1.4
Runaways	106.0	42.2	57.8	100.0	NA	NA	NA	NA	81.5	16.1	2.4
Stolen property**	95.2	88.3	11.7	27.1	36.9	14.5	9.7	11.9	55.7	43.3	1.0
Prostitution/vice	95.0	35.2	64.8	2.3	41.8	28.0	14.5	14.7	57.3	41.3	1.4
Curfew/loitering	75.0	75.2	24.8	100.0	NA	NA	NA	NA	71.7	26.3	2.0
Sex offenses***	65.1	91.3	8.7	16.7	24.1	17.4	13.2	28.9	74.3	24.1	.9
Forgery****	58.4	65.4	34.6	10.1	36.7	21.4	15.2	17.1	63.0	35.9	1.2
Vagrancy	30.2	89.0	11.0	6.9	28.9	16.6	14.7	34.8	58.7	38.4	2.9
Family abuse	24.8	74.6	25.4	9.6	26.5	20.6	17.0	26.5	62.1	34.4	3.5
Gambling	19.9	86.8	13.2	2.5	15.6	15.3	13.5	56.2	36.7	57.4	5.8
Suspicion	10.3	84.9	15.1	35.5	29.8	14.5	8.4	17.1	46.1	53.1	.8
Embezzlement	7.0	58.8	41.2	8.6	40.2	18.9	12.2	17.8	66.7	32.2	1.1
All other*****	1,881.9	84.3	15.7	13.3	35.2	18.9	12.9	20.4	57.7	40.4	2.0

Source: U.S. Department of Justice, Federal Bureau of Investigation, *Crime in the United States*, July 10, 1988, tables 42, 43, 44, 45, pp. 190–193.

* Includes nonnegligent manslaughter.

** Includes buying, receiving, or possessing.

*** Excluding prostitution/vice.

**** Includes counterfeiting.

***** Excluding traffic offenses.

Percentages do not always total exactly 100 due to rounding.

Appendix 6.A

Index Crimes and Crime Rates by State, 1987 (Numbers Reported in Thousands)

```
==================================================================
```

Region/State	Total	Rate Per 100,000 Population Viol.	Property	Mur.	Rob.	MVT
U.S.	5,550	610	4,863	8.3	213	529
New England	4,599	422	4,177	3.4	139	656
Connecticut	4,996	419	4,577	4.9	178	529
Maine	3,532	152	3,380	2.5	26	173
Massachusetts	4,734	565	4,169	3.0	177	924
New Hampshire	3,372	150	3,222	3.0	26	217
Rhode Island	5,286	360	4,926	3.5	108	784
Vermont	4,271	137	4,135	2.7	17	199
Mid-Atlantic	4,916	709	4,213	8.0	334	619
New Jersey	5,262	541	4,721	4.6	233	845
New York	5,952	1,008	4,944	11.3	503	703
Pennsylvania	3,163	369	2,794	5.4	144	349
South Atlantic	5,916	673	5,243	10.0	217	453
Delaware	4,939	431	4,508	5.1	123	312
Dist. of Colum.	8,452	1,610	6,841	36.2	717	1,012
Florida	8,503	1,024	7,479	11.4	357	677
Georgia	5,792	577	5,216	11.8	209	492
Maryland	5,478	768	4,710	9.6	290	582
North Carolina	4,650	484	4,166	8.1	94	224
South Carolina	5,162	665	4,497	9.3	101	281
Virginia	3,960	295	3,665	7.4	106	254
West Virginia	2,191	137	2,053	4.8	31	162
E. South Cent.	4,058	447	3,610	9.0	123	325
Alabama	44518	559	3,892	9.3	112	263
Kentucky	27092	338	2,932	7.5	90	193
Mississippi	3,439	270	3,169	10.2	57	161
Tennessee	4,666	534	4,132	9.1	194	567
W. South Cent.	6,901	596	6,305	10.7	191	619
Arkansas	4,245	412	3,833	7.6	79	207
Louisiana	5,873	693	5,180	11.1	179	413
Oklahoma	6,026	418	5,608	7.5	110	605
Texas	7,722	631	7,091	11.7	227	735
E. North-Cent.	5,114	572	4,542	7.6	206	486
Illinois	5,417	796	4,620	8.3	314	540
Indiana	4,120	329	3,791	5.6	89	355
Michigan	6,457	780	5,677	12.2	277	752
Ohio	4,575	421	4,154	5.8	153	383
Wisconsin	4,169	250	3,920	3.5	66	247
W. North-Cent.	4,417	344	4,073	4.4	95	279
Iowa	4,140	231	3,909	2.1	36	151
Kansas	4,904	361	4,543	4.4	82	253
Minnesota	4,616	285	4,330	2.6	103	301
Missouri	4,708	545	4,163	8.3	164	426

Appendix 6.A (continued)

| Region/State | Rate Per 100,000 Population | | | | | |
	Total	Viol.	Property	Mur.	Rob.	MVT
Nebraska	4,132	251	3,880	3.5	47	166
North Dakota	2,833	57	2,776	1.5	8	123
South Dakota	2,678	120	2,558	1.8	12	96
Mountain	6,161	465	5,696	6.2	109	359
Arizona	7,182	613	6,576	7.5	138	423
Colorado	6,451	468	5,984	5.8	119	436
Idaho	4,156	214	3,942	3.1	24	167
Montana	4,599	151	4,488	4.1	24	238
Nevada	6,371	696	5,676	8.4	273	555
New Mexico	6,547	629	5,918	10.1	108	346
Utah	5,619	230	5,389	3.3	53	210
Wyoming	4,031	283	3,748	2.0	20	139
Pacific	6,568	804	5,763	9.4	264	730
Alaska	5,378	455	4,922	10.1	73	486
California	6,506	918	5,588	10.6	301	830
Hawaii	5,818	263	5,555	4.8	98	366
Oregon	6,979	540	6,429	5.6	196	465
Washington	7,017	440	6,578	5.6	141	395

Source: U.S. Department of Justice, Federal Bureau of Investigation, *Crime in the United States*, July 10, 1988, table 4, pp. 44–51.

Note: Index crimes: murder and nonnegligent manslaughter, forcible rape, robbery, aggravated assault, burglary, larceny-theft, motor vehicle theft (MVT), and arson, the first four being violent crimes and the latter four, property crimes.

Appendix 6.B
General and Prison Populations, by State, Incarceration Rate (IR), and Racial Distribution Percentages, December 31, 1987

| Region or State | General Pop. (000) | Prison Pop. (Total) | IR[a] | Race of Inmates (Percents) | | | | |
				White	Black	Other (1)	(2)	Un-known
U.S. Total	243,400	581,020	239	50.2	45.3	0.9	0.3	3.3
Federal		48,300	20	67.3	30.3	1.7	0.7	0.0
State		532,720	219	48.6	46.6	0.9	0.3	3.6
Northeast	50,217	88,932	177	47.4	49.9	0.1	0.2	2.4
Connecticut	3,211	7,511	234	32.8	43.7	0.1	0.1	23.3
Maine	1,172	1,328	113	97.1	1.1	1.5	0.2	0.0
Massachusetts	5,855	6,268	107	59.4	33.4	0.2	0.3	6.7
New Hampshire	1,057	867	82	97.1	2.8	0.1	0.0	0.0
New Jersey	7,627	13,662	179	34.0	66.0	0.0	0.0	0.0
New York	17,825	40,842	229	49.9	49.7	0.2	0.3	0.0
Pennsylvania	11,936	16,267	136	43.3	56.6	0.1	0.1	0.0
Rhode Island	986	1,428	145	70.2	29.4	0.2	0.2	0.0
Vermont	548	759	139	100.0	NR	NR	NR	NR
Midwest	59,538	110,279	185	50.7	45.6	0.9	0.1	2.4
Illinois	11,582	19,850	171	32.1	59.9	0.1	0.0	7.8
Indiana	5,531	10,827	196	68.4	31.5	0.1	0.0	0.0
Iowa	2,834	2,851	101	76.7	21.0	0.1	1.5	0.7
Kansas	2,476	5,781	233	60.4	33.7	1.2	0.4	4.4
Michigan	9,200	23,879	260	41.4	56.4	0.4	NR	1.7
Minnesota	4,246	2,546	60	64.4	24.1	8.2	0.1	3.2
Missouri	5,103	11,146	218	60.0	40.0	0.0	0.0	0.0
Nebraska	1,594	2,086	131	68.2	27.9	3.5	0.5	0.0
North Dakota	672	430	64	84.9	0.9	14.0	0.2	0.0
Ohio	10,784	23,653	219	51.0	47.9	0.0	0.0	1.1
South Dakota	709	1,133	160	74.3	2.3	23.4	0.0	0.0
Wisconsin	4,807	6,097	127	58.1	38.9	2.4	0.1	0.6
South	83,885	221,813	264	39.6	55.4	0.5	0.0	4.5
Alabama	4,083	12,827	314	39.7	60.2	0.1	0.0	0.0
Arkansas	2,388	5,441	228	51.2	48.6	0.0	0.1	0.1
Delaware	644	2,939	456	42.1	57.6	0.1	0.1	0.0
Dist. of Columbia	622	7,645	1,229	2.6	97.4	0.0	0.0	0.0
Florida	12,023	32,445	270	45.1	52.4	0.0	0.1	2.5
Georgia	6,222	18,575	299	38.3	61.7	NR	NR	NR
Kentucky	3,727	5,471	147	67.2	32.8	0.0	0.0	0.0
Louisiana	4,461	15,375	345	27.8	72.2	0.0	0.0	0.0
Maryland	4,535	13,467	297	27.7	72.1	0.1	0.0	0.2
Mississippi	2,625	6,880	262	29.8	69.2	0.1	0.1	0.8
North Carolina	6,413	17,218	268	42.0	54.7	2.5	0.1	0.7

Appendix 6.B (continued)

Region or State	General Pop. (000)	Prison Pop. (Total)	IR[a]	Race of Inmates (Percents)				
				White	Black	Other (1)	(2)	Un-known
Oklahoma	3,272	9,639	295	61.6	30.5	5.7	0.1	2.1
South Carolina	3,425	12,664	370	39.5	60.2	0.1	0.0	0.2
Tennessee	4,855	7,624	157	56.5	41.4	NR	NR	2.1
Texas	16,789	38,821	231	35.5	42.3	0.0	0.0	22.2
Virginia	5,904	13,321	226	41.2	58.4	NR	NR	0.4
West Virginia	1,897	1,461	77	84.7	15.1	0.0	0.1	0.0
West	49,209	111,696	227	65.7	27.2	2.2	1.2	3.7
Alaska	525	2,528	482	56.0	9.0	34.0	1.0	0.0
Arizona	3,386	10,948	323	79.8	16.3	3.7	0.1	0.1
California	27,663	66,975	242	60.5	34.9	0.5	0.1	3.9
Colorado	3,296	4,808	146	75.3	21.5	0.8	0.2	2.2
Hawaii	1,083	2,268	209	24.9	5.1	0.0	48.5	21.6
Idaho	998	1,435	144	94.5	1.7	2.9	0.8	0.1
Montana	809	1,187	147	80.5	1.9	17.4	0.2	0.2
Nevada	1,007	4,434	440	60.6	30.4	0.9	0.9	7.1
New Mexico	1,500	2,710	181	86.6	10.0	3.2	0.2	0.0
Oregon	2,724	5,482	201	83.8	13.3	2.4	0.1	0.3
Utah	1,680	1,874	112	87.7	9.0	2.0	0.6	0.7
Washington	4,538	6,131	135	67.5	19.2	4.1	1.1	8.1
Wyoming	490	916	187	80.9	4.1	4.3	0.2	10.5

Source: Bureau of the Census, *State Population and Household Estimates With Age, Sex, and Components of Change 1981–87*. Current Population Reports, P-25, no. 1024, table 1, December 1987, p. 11.

U.S. Department of Justice, Bureau of Justice Statistics, *Correctional Populations in the United States 1987*, table 5.6 (forthcoming 1989).

Notes: a: Number of inmates per 100,000 of the total general population.

Other: (1) American Indian or Alaska Native. (2) Asian or Pacific Islander.

NR: Not reported.

Figures include both jail and prison inmates for Connecticut, New Hampshire, Delaware, District of Columbia, Alaska and Hawaii. In those states jails and prisons are combined in one system.

Percentages do not always total exactly 100 due to rounding.

Bibliographical Essay

The primary focus of this reference work is a collection of major policy issues that throughout the nineties will be confronting state and local governments and the array of private organizations collaborating with those governments in dealing with such issues. Except for the areas of fiscal policy and methods of delivering public services, attention is concentrated on policy substance rather than administrative processes. These substantive components lie in the ten functional and program areas of community development, corrections, day care, education, environmental and other regulation, health, housing, law enforcement, transportation, and welfare. Policy options—not prescriptions or recommendations—are presented, along with contrasting views on each side (or several sides) of the respective issues.

Given the purpose and emphasis of the book, the materials used in its preparation comprise the following categories: (1) aggregated data, from the Bureau of the Census and other governmental and nonpublic agencies and organizations; (2) functionally oriented issue analyses based on individual and institutional research; and (3) conceptual underpinnings for particular policy approaches and evaluative studies of particular policy outcomes. For those in government or in academia concerned with public policy formulation and execution at state and local levels, a summary of some major sources in the three categories may be helpful, both to users of this book and those working on issues not treated, or treated insufficiently for their particular purposes.

In the category of nationally aggregated data, the Bureau of the Census of the U.S. Department of Commerce publishes two series devoted primarily to state and local governments. The Census of Governments, taken every five years, includes volumes on organization, taxable property values and assessment-sales price ratios, public employment, government finances, local government in major urban areas, and some additional topical reports such as pension systems and state aid to local government. The Government Finance series has seven parts, each published annually: government finances in general, and a volume each on state, county, city, and public school system finances; state government tax collections, state and local retirement systems, and local government finances in major county areas.

In addition to financial information, the Census Bureau publishes nationally aggregated data on business establishments, especially the quinquennial censuses of manufactures, wholesale and retail trade, and selected services. These provide information on numbers of establishments, employees, payroll, and other categories, all broken down by state, metropolitan area, county, and city. Finally, through its *Current Population Reports* and other surveys, the Census Bureau publishes data at varying intervals on household income, poverty, population mobility, and numerous other demographic and economic elements in such specialized areas as transportation and housing.

The Bureau of Labor Statistics of the U.S. Department of Labor publishes monthly, yearly, and other periodic data on employment and earnings, including unemployment, part- and full-time employment, cost-of-living and price-level changes, and fringe benefits such as health care, pensions, and day-care referral and other employer-provided counseling and assistance.

The U.S. General Accounting Office (GAO) and the Congressional Budget Office (CBO) collect and publish nationally aggregated state and local government data from time to time in special studies of federal programs of grants-in-aid to state and local governments. Periodic data broken down by state, and sometimes by local or metropolitan area, are published by other federal agencies.

Aggregated fiscal data on state and local governments are published also on an annual basis by the U.S. Advisory Commission on Intergovernmental Relations (ACIR) in its *Significant Features of Fiscal Federalism* and by the National Association of State Budget Officers (NASBO), in collaboration with the National Governors' Association (NGA).

The International City Management Association (ICMA) publishes a *Municipal Yearbook,* providing a directory of city governments and a variety of financial, functional, and other information on cities and urban counties. The Council of State Governments (CSG) publishes a biennial *Book of the States,* which includes legal, organizational, and personnel data by state, as well as major developments in state governments for the preceding two years.

Quantitative and qualitative information and analyses in particular policy areas and issues are originated and published under the sponsorship of numerous governmental agencies, academic institutes, foundations, or special-interest groups. Many are associated with a particular function, such as the Transportation Research Board and the Institute of Medicine of the National Academy of Sciences–National Research Council, the MIT-Harvard Joint Center for Housing Studies, the University of Wisconsin's Institute for Research on Poverty, and countless individual scholars ranging from Henry Aaron at Brookings to Aaron Wildavsky and William Julius Wilson at Berkeley and Chicago.

Conceptual underpinnings for particular policy approaches and evaluative studies of particular policy outcomes have been drawn from research by individual scholars, from policy reports by, or under the aegis of, research institutions and organizations (for example, the American Enterprise Institute, the Brookings Institution, the Rand Corporation and the Urban Institute), and from scholarly monographs and articles in professional journals (for example, *Public Administration Review, National Tax Journal, Social Science Quarterly,* and regional and other journals in economics, government, and sociology). The evaluation studies are especially important because they comprise the link between experimental policy initiatives and a firming-up of long-range policy. Individual researchers exploring policy outcomes in one or more states or localities often are in the best position to examine the effectiveness of localized policy experimentation. The larger institutions often are in a position to undertake case studies involving more numerous units or larger areas. Finally, evaluations by the CBO and GAO of intergovernmental programs often provide useful information and insights to state and local officials.

Following is a summary listing of monthly or other periodic publications of state and local governments, community and neighborhood associations, and of other organizations closely involved in the policy areas covered in this work.

Academy for State and Local Government (ASLG), The State and Local Legal Center: *Court Report* (monthly).

American Association of Retired Persons (AARP): *News Bulletin* (monthly).

American Enterprise Institute (AEI): *Regulation* (bimonthly).

American Planning Association (APA): *Planning Magazine* (monthly); *Journal of the American Planning Association* (quarterly).

American Public Welfare Association (APWA): *Public Welfare* (quarterly).

American Public Works Association (APWA): *APWA Reporter* (monthly); *Proviews (quarterly).*

Americans for Generational Equity (AGE): *Generational Journal* (quarterly).

Center for Community Change (CCC): *Community Change* (quarterly).

Council of State Community Affairs Agencies (COSCAA): *The States in Housing* (monthly).

Council of State Governments (CSG): In addition to the biennial *Book of the States,* CSG publishes an annual volume of *Suggested State Legislation;* also, *Journal of State Government* and "State Government Research Check List" (bimonthly), and *State Government News* (monthly).

Council of State Housing Agencies (CSHA): *HFA Update* (monthly).

Council of State Planning Agencies (CSPA): *Report to the Governor* (quarterly).

Education Commission of the States (ECS): *Education Leader* (quarterly).

Government Finance Officers Association (GFOA); *Government Finance Review* (bimonthly); *GFOA Newsletter* (monthly).

International City Management Association (ICMA): In addition to the *Municipal Yearbook,* ICMA publishes *Baseline Data Reports* (bimonthly) and *Management Information Service* and *Public Management* (monthly).

National Association of Attorneys General (NAAG): *A-G Report, Court Report,* and *State Constitutional Law Bulletin* (all monthly).

National Association of Counties (NACO): *County News* (biweekly).

National Association of Housing and Redevelopment Officials (NAHRO): *Journal of Housing* (bimonthly); *NAHRO Monitor* (monthly).

National Association of Neighborhoods (NAN): *NAN Bulletin* (monthly).

National Association of State Budget Officers (NASBO): *Fiscal Survey of the States* (annually, in collaboration with National Governors' Association).

National Association of Towns and Townships (NATaT): *Reporter* (monthly).

National Center for Neighborhood Enterprise (NCNE): *In the News* (bimonthly).

National Center for State Courts (NCSC): *State Court Journal* (quarterly).

National Civic League: *National Civic Review* (bimonthly).

National Conference of State Legislatures (NCSL): *State Legislatures* (monthly).

National Downtown Association (NDA): *Center City Report* (bimonthly).

National Governors' Association (NGA): *Governors' Weekly Bulletin* (weekly).

National Institute of Municipal Law Officers (NIMLO): *Municipal Law Court Decisions* (bimonthly).

National League of Cities (NLC): *Nation's Cities Weekly* (weekly).

National School Boards Association (NSBA): *National School Board Journal* (monthly).

U.S. Conference of Mayors (USCM): *Mayor* (biweekly).

Urban Land Institute (ULI): *Urban Land* and *Land Use Digest* (both monthly).

Index

Aaron, Henry, 102

Accountability, political: budgetary and, 79; federal aid to state and local government and, 112; federalism and, 69, 70; income tax indexation and, 105; local government and, 25–26, 55–56; public service delivery and, 19, 150–51; regulatory systems and, 339; responsibilities of, 71; special districts and, 30

Accounting and auditing, 108–9, 111, 113–14

Agriculture, 63, 187, 191–92; economic shifts and farm subsidies, 204–5

AIDS, 65, 210, 219, 287, 291–92, 297. *See also individual cities and states*

Aid to Families with Dependent Children (AFDC), 96–97, 108, 240, 277, 281–83, 306, 312–22. *See also individual cities and states;* Urban underclass; Welfare

Air pollution control, 18, 36, 70, 338

Airports and air traffic control, 243, 245–49; contracts for services, 159; franchising, 155

Alabama: education finance in, 41; health care, 223; human resources, 64; local discretionary authority, 32; local income tax, 107; property tax, 51, 55; state mandates, 45; tax competition, 101

Alaska: boroughs in, 20; county discretionary authority, 35; county governments, 21; education finance, 41; health care, 222; incarceration rate, 357; infant mortality, 288; school districts, 22; state constitution, 19; state income tax, 50, 54; state-local expenditures, 37; welfare, 39

Ambulance and emergency medical service, 140, 155, 164

American Association of Retired Persons, 82, 85–86, 225

American Bar Association, 334

American Business Conference, 177

American Federation of State, County, and Municipal Employees, 162

American Federation of Teachers, 304

American Public Welfare Association, 317

Americans for Generational Equity, 85

Anaheim, CA, employment in, 92

Antitrust issues, 171

Arizona: health care in, 222; human resources in, 64; income tax indexation, 105; legislative committees in, 197; mental health in, 160; population of, 91; tax and spending limits, 73; welfare in, 39

Arkansas: health care in, 223; legislative committees in, 197; local discretionary authority in, 32; welfare in, 39

cial review in, 354; land use regulation in, 344; local general revenue in, 52; "locations," 20; no line-item veto in, 73; no tax and spending limits in, 73; sales tax in, 102; state constitutions of, 19; state income tax in, 50; no state sales tax in, 54; state-local expenditures in, 38; state mandates in, 45; welfare in, 39

New Jersey: AFDC in, 315; AIDS in, 291; annexation of, 27; fair share housing in, 229; hazardous waste in, 160; local general revenue in, 52; local government studies of, 37; property tax in, 55; tax exemptions in, 88; tax and spending limits in, 73, 76; townships in, 21; urban underclass in, 275; zoning in, 344

New Mexico: child support in, 281; education finance in, 41; health care in, 222; jails in, 160; local general revenue in, 52; sales tax in, 105; state-local expenditures in, 37; state mandates in, 45

New Orleans, LA: arrestee drug use in, 359; crime in, 308; employment in, 216

New York City: AIDS in, 291; arrestee drug use in, 359; case management for at-risk children, 11; City University of New York, 198; civic associations in, 178; community development corporations in, 254; corrections, 307; crime rate in, 308; education in, 292–93, 303; employment in, 92, 94, 216; the homeless in, 239; housing in, 235–36; government corruption in, 111; income loss in, 90; local income tax in, 107; neighborhood governance in, 23; population of, 90; probationers in small business program, 11; state financial supervision of, 109; urban underclass in, 275

New York State: AFDC in, 315; AIDS in, 291; annexation of, 27; crime rate in, 356; debt restrictions in, 44; the environment and, 64; hazardous waste and, 37; health care in, 222; housing

in, 148, 236; housing trust funds in, 234; human resources in, 64; infant mortality in, 288; local general revenue in, 52; property tax in, 55; property tax exemptions in, 88; state-local expenditures in, 37; state mandates in, 45; tax preferences in, 106; townships in, 20; welfare in, 39

Niskanen, William A., 102

Noncash benefits, 83

Nonprofit corporations and organizations, 23, 37, 44, 83, 108, 128–30, 138, 148, 150–51, 164–66, 176–77, 210, 214, 234–37, 251–57

Nonservice alternatives, 67, 109–10

Nontax revenues, 67, 104–5. *See also* User-based financing

Norfolk, VA: commercial development in, 149; the homeless in, 239; housing in, 236

North Carolina: AFDC, 315; annexation of, 27; county discretionary authority in, 34; county governments in, 21; housing trust funds in, 234; local discretionary authority in, 32; no line-item veto in, 73; population of, 91; school districts in, 22; special legislation in, 34; state constitutions of, 19; welfare in, 39

North Central states: townships in, 21; urban underclass in, 274

North Dakota: AFDC, 315; county home rule in, 37; crime rate in, 356; health care in, 222; incarceration rate in, 357; infant mortality in, 288; state-local expenditures in, 37

Northeast states: community development corporations in, 254; urban underclass in, 274

Northwest states, school dropouts in, 300

Oakland, CA: housing in, 236; local fiscal capacity in, 96

Occupational health and safety, 332–33, 342, 350

Occupational licensing, 18

Odden, Allan, 197

Off-track betting, 67

About the Author

WILLIAM G. COLMAN is a private consultant and is a long-time elected member of the National Academy of Public Administration. He has held a number of policy and managerial posts in federal, state, and local governments, serving in both elective and appointive local office, and on state and national policy advisory bodies. He was executive director of the U.S. Advisory Commission on Intergovernmental Relations during its first ten years. Subsequent to retirement from federal service, he has been a visiting professor and consultant and has written frequently on public finance and urban problems.